Canine and Feline Nutrition

A Resource for Companion Animal Professionals

Canine and Feline Nutrition

A Resource for Companion Animal Professionals

Linda P. Case, M.S.

Department of Animal Sciences,
College of Agriculture,
University of Illinois,
Urbana, Illinois

Daniel P. Carey, D.V.M.

Director,
Technical Communications Department,
The Iams Company,
Lewisburg, Ohio

Diane A. Hirakawa, Ph.D.

Vice President,
Research and Development,
The Iams Company,
Lewisburg, Ohio

 Mosby

St. Louis Baltimore Berlin Boston Carlsbad Chicago London Madrid
Naples New York Philadelphia Sydney Tokyo Toronto

Mosby

Dedicated to Publishing Excellence

Editor: Linda L. Duncan
Developmental Editor: Jo Salway
Project Manager: Gayle Morris
Manufacturing Supervisor: Linda Ierardi
Design Manager: Susan Lane
Book and Cover Designer: Paul Uhl Associates

Printed in the United States of America

Composition by Shepherd, Inc.
Printing/binding by R.R. Donnelley and Sons, Co.

Mosby-Year Book, Inc.
11830 Westline Industrial Drive
St. Louis, Missouri 63146

International Standard Book Number 0-8151-1536-9

95 96 97 98 99 / 9 8 7 6 5 4 3 2 1

Dedicated To

Clay Mathile . . .
a leader and visionary
whose integrity and commitment to enhancing
the health and well-being of companion animals
is only surpassed
by his unique ability to inspire
and encourage others to develop talents,
stretch imaginations, and
believe that the impossible can become reality

DPC and DAH

And

My husband, Mike, my best friend always; and to
my parents, Jean and Bob Palas,
who taught me about the good things in life

LPC

Preface

Man has a long and very complex history of association with dogs and cats. This relationship has its roots in the early domestication of companion animals and has evolved to exist in today's society in a vast variety of forms. Both the dog and the cat were originally domesticated to serve a number of utilitarian functions. Although some dogs and cats still fulfill these roles, the primary reason that most people in our society keep pets today is for companionship. In recent years, scientific study of human-animal interactions have revealed that these relationships are very strong and enduring components of the lives of many pet owners. Pet ownership has also been shown to provide numerous physiological and psychological benefits. Keeping companion animals has become a national pastime, and taking proper care of dogs and cats is of great interest to the many pet owners and professionals who work with these animals.

Along with proper health care and medical attention, nutrition is an important component of the care of all dogs and cats. An understanding of basic nutrition and of the nutrient requirements of healthy dogs and cats is integral to the understanding of practical feeding practices. Such knowledge enables pet professionals to provide optimal nutritional care throughout life, which contributes to lasting health and longevity. *Canine and Feline Nutrition: A Resource for Companion Animal Professionals* provides the reader with an understanding of the science of companion animal nutrition and with practical feeding management information for dogs and cats. Information provided in this book is of value to veterinarians, animal scientists, nutritionists, breeders, exhibitors, judges, trainers, and hobbyists. The book may also serve as a resource for companion animal management and nutrition courses in the fields of animal science and veterinary medicine.

Canine and Feline Nutrition: A Resource for Companion Animal Professionals is organized into six sections. These sections address basic principles of nutrition; nutrient requirements of dogs and cats; pet food production and selection; feeding management throughout all stages of life; feeding problems, fads, and fallacies; and the dietary management of nutritionally responsive diseases. Current research is reviewed, and balanced discussions of controversial issues of dietary management are presented. Differences between the nutrient requirements and feeding practices of dogs and cats are addressed throughout the book. To facilitate use by readers with a wide range of backgrounds and interests, illustrative tables and summary boxes are included that present technical material at a level that can be of practical use.

Section 1 is written as a basic introduction to the science of nutrition, without application to specific species. Chapters within the section are arranged according to each of the basic nutrients and the processes of digestion and absorption. These chapters will be of value to students and professionals who require introductory information about the science of nutrition. Section 2 addresses the specific nutrient requirements of dogs and cats and includes chapters that examine energy balance in companion animals, comparative nutrient requirements, and the metabolic idiosyncracies of the cat. Major differences between the nutritional needs of dogs and cats are examined. Section 3 provides a detailed overview of the formulation, production, and use of commercial and homemade pet foods. Chapters include information about the history, regulation, and marketing of commercial foods; nutrient content and types of foods; and procedures for evaluating the diets of dogs and cats. Practical information about the selection of appropriate pet foods is included for pet owners. Section 4 includes feeding and diet recommendations for nutritional care throughout various stages of life. Information in the chapters within this section will be useful to breeders and veterinarians who seek practical information for their animals and clients. Section 5 addresses nutritional and dietary misconceptions that are commonly reported by pet owners and professionals. The chapters examine the problems of overfeeding and obesity, supplementation with specific nutrients, nutrient imbalances that occur as a result of improper feeding practices, and a variety of currently popular nutritional fads and fallacies. Section 6 deals with a number of health problems in dogs and cats that can be managed or treated with diet. Chapters address inherited disorders of metabolism, diabetes mellitus, feline lower urinary tract disease, certain types of dermatoses, chronic kidney disease, and feline hepatic lipidosis. The chapters in this section provide a resource for veterinarians, nutritionists, and breeders who are involved in the treatment or study of these diseases.

ACKNOWLEDGMENTS

Several individuals were instrumental in the preparation of the completed manuscript for this book. The authors would like to thank Jill Cline, M.S. (Ph.D. candidate in canine nutrition, University of Illinois), who created the tables and diagrams for each chapter; Pat Norris, M.S., who provided editing support and was instrumental in developing the book's final format; and Jan Tremaine, certified Editor in the Life Sciences, who wrote the glossary and key point summaries.

Linda P. Case

Contents

SECTION 5

Feeding Practices: Problems, Fads, and Fallacies

SECTION 5

SECTION 6

Nutritionally Responsive Disorders

Basics of Nutrition

I n recent years researchers have been able to explain why humans bond so strongly to their pets, and they have also discovered that the relationship between humans and animals is often beneficial to human health. It is not surprising that the strong emotional attachment that people feel for their pets is coupled with a concern for providing them with the best in health care and nutrition. Advances in veterinary medicine have resulted in vaccination programs that protect dogs and cats from many life-threatening diseases and in medical procedures that contribute to lengthened life-spans. Likewise, progress in the field of nutrition has generated an improved understanding of canine and feline dietetics and the development of well-balanced pet foods that contribute to long-term health, and aid in the prevention of chronic disease.

Today's competitive market contains a vast array of foods, snacks, and nutritional supplements for dogs and cats. These products are sold in grocery stores, feed stores, pet shops, and veterinary hospitals. Products vary significantly in nutrient composition, in availability, digestibility, and palatability, and in physical form, flavor, and texture. Some foods are formulated to provide adequate nutrition throughout the pet's life-span, and other foods have been marketed specifically for a particular stage of life or for a specific disease state. This large selection of commercial products, combined with the periodic propagation of popular nutritional fads and fallacies, has resulted in much confusion among pet owners and companion animal professionals regarding the nutritional care of dogs and cats.

A basic understanding of the fundamentals of nutrition is a necessary prerequisite for evaluating pet foods and making decisions about a pet's nutritional status. The term *nutrition* refers to the study of food and the nutrients and other components that it contains. This includes an examination of the actions of specific nutrients, their interactions with each other, and their balance within a diet. In addition, the science of nutrition includes an examination of the way in which an animal ingests, digests, absorbs, and uses nutrients. This section provides an overview of each of the essential nutrients. Energy, water, carbohydrate, fat, protein, vitamins, and minerals are examined in detail. An examination of the normal digestive and absorptive processes in dogs and cats is also provided. Subsequent sections address the specific nutrient

requirements of dogs and cats, the types and compositions of pet foods, feeding management throughout the life cycle, feeding problems, and the management of nutritionally-responsive diseases. Information contained in this book will enable pet owners, students, and companion animal professionals to make informed decisions about the diets and nutritional health of dogs and cats throughout all stages of life.

Like all living animals, dogs and cats require a balanced diet to grow normally and to maintain health once they are mature. *Nutrients* are components in the diet that have specific functions within the body and that contribute to growth, body-tissue maintenance, and optimal health. *Essential nutrients* are those components that cannot be synthesized by the body at a rate that is adequate to meet the body's needs. Therefore essential nutrients must be supplied in the diet. *Nonessential nutrients* can be synthesized by the body and can be obtained either through de novo synthesis or from the diet. Along with a requirement for energy, all animals require six major categories of nutrients. These categories are water, carbohydrates, proteins, fats, minerals, and vitamins. Energy, although not a nutrient per se, is required by the body for normal growth, maintenance, reproductive performance, and physical work. Approximately 50% to 80% of the dry matter of a dog's or cat's diet is used for energy.

CHAPTER 1

Energy

W ith the exception of water, energy is the most critical component that must be considered in a diet. Like all animals, companion animals require a constant source of dietary energy in order to survive. Plants obtain energy from solar radiation and convert it to energy-containing nutrients. Other animals consume plants and either use them directly for energy or convert plant nutrients into other energy-containing molecules. The primary form of stored energy in plants is carbohydrate; the main form of stored energy in animals is fat. Energy is necessary for the performance of the body's metabolic work, which includes maintaining and synthesizing body tissues, engaging in physical work, and regulating normal body temperature. Given its importance, it is not surprising that energy is always the first requirement that is met by an animal's diet. Regardless of a dog's or cat's needs for essential amino acids from dietary protein or essential fatty acids from dietary fat, the energy-yielding nutrients of the diet will first be used to satisfy energy needs. Once energy needs are met, nutrients are available for other metabolic functions.

Animals are capable of regulating their energy intake to accurately meet their daily caloric requirements. When allowed free access to a balanced, moderately palatable diet, most dogs and cats will consume enough food to meet, but not to exceed, their daily energy needs.[1,2,3] *Energy density* or *caloric density* refers to the concentration of energy in a given quantity of food (see p. 10). When the energy density of a diet is decreased, animals respond by increasing the quantity of food that they consume, which results in a relatively constant energy intake.[3,4] If an animal's food intake is regulated by total energy intake, the composition of all other nutrients in the diet must be

balanced with respect to the diet's energy density. This balance should be calculated to ensure that when a dog or cat consumes a quantity of food adequate to meet its caloric needs, all other nutrient requirements will be met at the same time.

Contrary to popular belief, dogs and cats are unable to self-regulate their intake of most other essential nutrients. Although there is some evidence that adult dogs will select a diet that is moderately high in protein, this effect has been observed only when neither energy nor protein were limited in the experimental diets.[5] Factors such as palatability and the ratio of dietary fat to carbohydrate may have significantly affected the dogs' dietary selections in this study. Moreover, there is no evidence indicating that dogs or cats will overconsume on a diet that is high in energy but low in protein in an attempt to meet their protein needs. Companion animals that are deficient in a particular vitamin, mineral, or essential amino acid will not seek foods that contain the nutrient or preferentially select a diet that is abundant in the deficient nutrient. In contrast, dogs and cats that are deficient in energy will spontaneously increase their caloric intake until energy balance is achieved.[1,2]

Although all dogs and cats have the ability to properly regulate their energy intake, this natural tendency can be overridden by environmental factors. A diet of pet foods that are both highly palatable and energy-dense leads to chronic overconsumption in some companion animals. Today's competitive pet food market includes many foods that are high in both palatability and caloric density. Coupled with this fact is a decline in physical activity among many pets in today's society. In recent years many cats have moved from the barnyard into the house, where their working role as mousers and pest-controllers has been effectively eliminated. Many companion animals now lead happy but relatively sedentary lives exclusively as house pets. Likewise, dogs have evolved from working companions to unemployed house dogs, lacking adequate daily exercise. These two changes have led to an epidemic of overeating and obesity among dogs and cats in the United States. Surveys have shown that obesity is the most common nutritional problem that is seen by practicing veterinarians today.[6] These changes indicate that it may no longer be wise to rely on the dog's and cat's inherent abilities to regulate energy intake. Although companion animals certainly have this ability, many do not self-regulate because of the nature of the food they eat and the type of life-style they lead. In most cases, portion-controlled feeding is the best way to control a pet's energy balance, growth rate, and weight status (see Section 4, pp. 213–214).

MEASUREMENT OF ENERGY IN THE DIET

Energy has no measurable mass or dimension, but the chemical energy contained in foods is ultimately transformed by the body into heat, which can be measured. Nutrients that provide energy in an animal's diet include carbohydrate, fat, and protein. The chemical energy of foods is most often expressed in units of calories or kilocalories (kcal). A *calorie* refers to the amount of heat energy necessary to raise the temperature of 1 gram of water from 14.5°C to 15.5°C. Because a calorie is a very small unit, it is not of practical use in the science of animal nutrition. The kilocalorie, which is equal to 1000 calories, is the most commonly used unit of measure. A second unit of measurement for energy

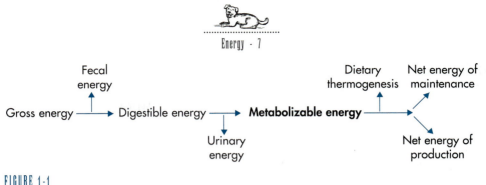

FIGURE 1-1
Partitioning of dietary energy.

is the kilojoule (kJ), which is a metric unit. A *kilojoule* is defined as the amount of mechanical energy that is required for a force of 1 newton to move a weight of 1 kilogram by a distance of 1 meter. To convert kilocalories to kilojoules, the number of kilocalories is multiplied by 4.18.

The caloric value of foods can be measured using direct calorimetry. This process involves the complete combustion (oxidation) of a premeasured amount of food in a bomb calorimeter, resulting in release and measurement of the food's total chemical energy. This energy is called the food's *gross energy* (GE). Animals cannot use all of a food's GE because energy losses occur during digestion and assimilation. *Digestible energy* (DE) signifies the amount of energy available for absorption across the intestinal mucosa. Apparent DE can be calculated by subtracting the indigestible energy that is excreted in the feces from the GE of the food. Additional energy losses occur as a result of the production of combustible gases and the excretion of urea in the urine. The incomplete oxidation of absorbed dietary protein by the body results in the production of urea. Because the production of combustible gases in dogs and cats is minimal, only urinary losses are typically accounted for. *Metabolizable energy* (ME) is the amount of energy ultimately available to the tissues of the body after losses in the feces and urine have been subtracted from the GE of the food. ME is the value that is most often used to express the energy content of pet food ingredients and commercial diets. Similarly, the energy requirements of dogs and cats are usually expressed as kilocalories of ME. ME can be subdivided to yield net energy and the energy lost to dietary thermogenesis. *Dietary thermogenesis*, also called the specific dynamic action of food, refers to energy needed by the body to digest, absorb and assimilate nutrients. *Net energy* is that energy available to the animal for the maintenance of body tissues and for production needs such as physical work, growth, gestation, and lactation (Figure 1-1).

The ME of a diet or feed ingredient depends on both the nutrient composition of the food and the animal that is consuming it. For example, because of the length and structure of its gastrointestinal tract, a nonruminant herbivore such as the horse can derive a greater amount of energy from grass than can a dog or cat. Therefore the ME value of grass for a horse will be higher than the ME value of grass for a companion animal. Three possible methods can be used to estimate the ME values of a feed ingredient or diet for a given species. These methods are direct determination using feeding trials and total collection procedures, calculation from analyzed levels of protein, carbohydrate, and fat in the diet, and extrapolation of data collected in other species.

Calculation
Metabolizable energy = $(GE_{food}) - (GE_{feces} + GE_{urine})$

Example
1100 kcal = 3600 (food) − 2500 (feces + urine)

FIGURE 1-2
Calculation and example of metabolizable energy.

Direct Determination in Feeding Trials

Data collected in actual feeding trials with the species in question is the most accurate method for determining a food's ME content. The diet or feed ingredient is fed to a number of test animals, and feces and urine are collected throughout a predesignated time period. Determination of the energy content of the feed, feces, and urine allows direct calculation of ME (Figure 1-2). However, direct measurement of ME values in dogs and cats can be extremely time-consuming and costly and requires access to large numbers of test animals. To date, many of the ME values for commonly used pet food ingredients have not been directly measured. However, the manufacturers of some of the premium pet foods routinely measure the ME of their formulated pet foods and ingredients through the use of controlled feeding trials.

Calculation Method

ME values can also be determined using mathematical formulas that estimate a food's ME from its analyzed carbohydrate, protein, and fat content. The formulas that have been derived for dog and cat diets include constants that account for fecal and urinary losses of energy. The GE values, which represent total energy content, for mixed carbohydrate, fat, and protein are 4.15, 9.40, and 5.65 kcal/g, respectively.[7] However, as mentioned earlier, animals are incapable of using all of the energy present in food nutrients. The inefficiency of digestion, absorption, and assimilation result in energy losses. In human foods, the Atwater factors of 4-9-4 kcal/g are commonly used to estimate ME values for carbohydrate, fat, and protein. These factors were calculated using estimated digestibility coefficients of 96% for fat and carbohydrate and 91% for protein.[8] A *digestibility coefficient* is the proportion of the consumed nutrient that is actually available for absorption and use by the body. The ME value of protein was further reduced to account for urinary losses of urea.

Although it appears reasonable to use Atwater factors to determine the ME content of dog and cat foods, digestibility data collected in these two species indicate that the Atwater factors tend to overestimate ME values of most pet foods. This miscalculation occurs because the digestibility of many pet food ingredients is lower than the digestibility of most foods consumed by humans. Digestibility data collected in dogs from 106 samples of dry, semimoist, and canned commercial dog foods showed that the average digestibility coefficients for crude protein, acid-ether extract (a measure of fat content), and nitrogen-free extract (a measure of soluble carbohydrate content) were 81%, 85%, and 79%, respectively.[9] The fact that pet food ingredients are generally lower in

TABLE 1-1
Digestibility Coefficients and Factors

NUTRIENT	HUMAN FOOD DIGESTIBILITY COEFFICIENT	ATWATER FACTOR	PET FOOD DIGESTIBILITY COEFFICIENT	MODIFIED ATWATER FACTOR
Carbohydrate	96%	4 kcal/g	85%	3.5 kcal/g
Protein	91%	4 kcal/g	80%	3.5 kcal/g
Fat	96%	9 kcal/g	90%	8.5 kcal/g

digestibility than the foods consumed by humans causes the Atwater factors to be inaccurate for use in estimating the ME of pet foods. The National Research Council's 1985 recommendations for dogs suggested that digestibility coefficients of 80%, 90%, and 85% be used for the protein, fat, and carbohydrate in commercial dog foods.[6] When GE values are readjusted for digestibility and urinary losses, ME values of 3.5, 8.5, and 3.5 kcal/g are assigned to protein, fat, and carbohydrate, respectively (Table 1-1). These values are referred to as *modified Atwater factors*. Although these values provide a better estimate of ME values for pet foods than do the Atwater factors, they may still underestimate the ME values of high-quality dog foods that contain highly digestible protein sources and low levels of indigestible fiber. Conversely, the ME value of those foods that contain high amounts of plant fiber and/or poor quality meat sources will be slightly overestimated by these factors.[7]

Several formulas for estimation of the ME in cat foods have been derived from digestibility data collected in direct feeding trials and from studies of the correlations between analyzed values and values of ME measured in vivo.[9,10] However, little data are available on the DE of specific cat foods or cat food ingredients. Moreover, this information is usually not readily available. In general, calculation of ME from analyzed levels of carbohydrate, fat, and protein in the diet using modified Atwater factors provides a reasonably accurate estimate of the ME for cat foods, as long as crude fiber is used to estimate the total fiber in the food.[10] A recent study of 14 commercial cat foods produced in the United States found that the minimum percentage of fat reported on the guaranteed analysis panel of the pet food label can also be used to estimate the food's ME. The equation ME = 3.075 + 0.066 (fat) provides a quick and simple method of estimating ME from information that is readily available on all pet food labels.[10]

Data from Other Species

The lack of direct data measuring DE and ME in cat food ingredients and the inadequacy of mathematical formulas for use with many types of foods have resulted in the use of data from other species. The National Research Council assigned ME values from swine data to ingredients commonly used in cat foods whenever direct data on the cat were not available.[11] This information was included in the 1986 edition of the publication *NRC Nutrient Requirements of Cats*. Although this third method of estimating ME values of a food is not as accurate as direct measurement, data collected in swine experiments have been reported to correlate well with values from other simple-stomached animals.[11]

Energy Density

The *energy density* of a pet food refers to the number of calories provided by the food in a given weight or volume. In the United States, energy density is expressed as kilocalories of ME per kilogram (kg) or pound (lb) of diet. In most European countries, the unit kJ/kg is used. The importance of energy density in companion animal nutrition cannot be overemphasized. It is the principle factor that determines the quantity of food that is eaten each day and therefore directly affects the amount of all other essential nutrients that an animal ingests. A diet's energy density must be high enough to allow the pet to consume a sufficient amount of food to meet its energy needs. If the energy density is too low, food intake will be restricted by the physical limitations of the gastrointestinal tract, resulting in an energy deficit. In other words, the animal would not be physically able to consume enough of the low-energy diet to meet its caloric requirements. Such a diet is said to be "bulk limited." If levels of the essential nutrients in such a diet were not balanced relative to energy density, multiple nutrient deficiencies could also occur.

When the caloric density of a pet food is high enough for an animal to consume a sufficient quantity to meet its daily energy needs, energy density will be the primary factor that determines the quantity of food that is consumed each day. As a food's energy density increases, the total volume of food that is consumed decreases. However, feeding a highly palatable pet food can override a pet's tendency to correctly regulate intake. The sale of pet foods that are energy dense and highly palatable has led many owners to the use of portion-controlled feeding to manage their pet's daily food intake. Maintenance of normal body weight and growth rate are the criteria most often used to determine the appropriate quantity of food. Therefore, even when under the pet owner's control, a pet's level of energy intake is *still* the primary factor that affects the quantity of food that is fed.

Because energy intake determines total food intake, it is important that diets are properly balanced so that requirements for all other nutrients are met at the same time that energy needs are satisfied. For this reason, it is more appropriate to express levels of energy-containing nutrients in the food in terms of ME concentration rather than in terms of percentage of the food's weight. Using this unit, values can be compared in any type of food or diet, regardless of water, nutrient, or energy content. For example, a complete and balanced dry dog food contains 27% protein as a percentage of weight and supplies 3800 kcal of ME/kg. Adjusted Atwater factors can be used to estimate the proportion of energy that protein contributes to the food. The calculations in Table 1-2 show that 24.8% of the food's energy is contributed by protein. These figures can be compared to a canned dog food that contains 7.0% protein on a weight basis and supplies 980 kcal of ME/kg. When expressed as a percentage of calories, the protein in the canned food also supplies approximately 25% of the food's calories (Table 1-2).

Two foods that appear enormously different when compared in terms of percentage of protein on a weight basis actually contain the same amount of protein when expressed as a percentage of total calories. Differences in the water content and energy density of the two foods account for the drastic differences in nutrient content when

TABLE 1-2

Sample Calculation to Convert Percentage of Weight to Percentage of Energy in the Diet

FOOD TYPE	PROTEIN (%)	×	MODIFIED ATWATER FACTOR	÷	KCAL/100G OF FOOD	× 100%
Dry 27	×	3.5	÷	380	24.8	
Canned	7	×	3.5	÷	98	25.0

expressed as a percentage of weight. Attempting to compare the two foods when protein is expressed as a percentage of weight can be very confusing. Conversion to units of energy allows an accurate comparison of levels of the energy-containing nutrients in different pet foods. Because dogs and cats are fed to meet their caloric requirements, these two foods will supply an equal quantity of protein when fed at the correct level.

The energy density of a food must be known in order to estimate the quantity of food necessary to meet a pet's energy requirement. The Association of American Feed Control Officials (AAFCO), a regulating group responsible for the standards governing commercially prepared pet foods, requires that the energy value of a pet food be expressed in kilocalories of ME. If ME information is not included on a pet food label, it can be calculated using the proximate analysis of the food. If the proximate analysis is not available, the guaranteed analysis provided on the label of all pet foods can be used as a rough estimate of nutrient content. The modified Atwater factors provided earlier are used to calculate the amount of energy contributed by carbohydrate, protein, and fat. For example, the guaranteed analysis on a bag of a dry dog food reads as follows:

- Crude protein: Not less than 26%
- Crude fat: Not less than 15%
- Crude fiber: Not more than 5%

An estimate of the mineral content of the food, commonly called ash, must then be made. High-quality dry pet foods generally contain between 5% and 8% ash. The food's carbohydrate content can then be estimated by subtraction:

- 100% − % Protein − % Fat − % Ash = % Carbohydrate
- 100 − 26 − 15 − 5 − 7 = 47%

Calories provided by each nutrient in 100 g of food can then be estimated (Table 1-3). The total calories in 100 g of food is 383, or 3830 kcal/kg of food. This figure can also be divided by 2.2 to convert to energy density per pound of food. The quantity of food to feed can be estimated by dividing the pet's daily energy requirement by the energy density of the diet. For example, if an adult dog requires 1100 kcal/day and is fed a diet containing 1740 kcal/lb, approximately 10 ounces of food should be fed each day. An 8-ounce cup of dry pet food might weight 3 ounces. Therefore, this dog would require approximately 3⅓ cups of this food per day (see the box on the following page). It is important to be aware that each dog and cat is an individual and that these calculations

TABLE 1-3
Determination of Energy Density from Guaranteed Analysis

NUTRIENT	PERCENTAGE IN DIET	×	MODIFIED ATWATER FACTOR	=	KCAL/100 G OF FOOD
Protein	26	×	3.5	=	91
Carbohydrate	47	×	3.5	=	164.5
Fat	15	×	8.5	=	127.5
			Total calories	=	382

Total 382 kcal/100 g × 1000 g/kg = 3820 kcal/kg (energy density)
3820 kcal/kg × 1 kg/ 2.2 lb = 1736.4 kcal/lb food (energy density)

Sample Calculation to Estimate Amount of Food Required Daily

Energy requirement of an adult dog: 1100 kcal/day
Energy density of the diet: 1736 kcal/lb

Step 1

1100 kcal/day ÷ 1736 kcal/lb = 0.63 lb of food

Step 2

0.63 lb × 16 ounces/lb = 10.13 ounces

If an 8-ounce cup of dry dog food weighs 3 ounces, then:

Step 3
10 ounces of dry pet food ÷ 3 ounces/cup ≈ 3.3 or 3⅓ cups of dry pet food per day.

---

provide only a guideline or starting point when determining a pet's daily needs. The amount of food should be adjusted to attain optimal growth in young animals and optimal body weight and condition in adult animals. Adult pets in optimal condition are well-muscled and lean. Although their ribs cannot be readily seen, they should easily be felt when palpated.

Energy Imbalance

Energy imbalance occurs when an animal's daily energy consumption is either greater or less than its daily requirement, leading to changes in growth rate, body weight, and body composition. Excess energy intake is much more common in dogs and cats than is energy deficiency. During growth, overconsumption of energy has been shown to have several detrimental effects on dogs, especially those of the large and giant breeds. When an excess amount of a balanced, high-energy pet food is fed to growing puppies, maximal growth rate and weight gain can be achieved. However, studies with growing dogs have indicated that maximal growth rate is not compatible with healthy bone growth and development.[12] Feeding growing puppies to attain maximal growth rate appears to be a significant contributing factor in the development of skeletal disorders such as osteochondrosis and hip dysplasia[12-15] (see Section 5, pp. 293–296).

A second problem associated with an energy surplus during growth involves fat cell hyperplasia. Studies with laboratory animals have shown that the generation of an excessive number of fat cells in the body as a result of overfeeding at a young age can predispose an animal to obesity later in life.[16,17] Although research on fat cell hyperplasia during growth has not been conducted in the dog or cat, it is possible that these species are affected in a similar manner. In adult dogs and cats, surplus energy intake leads to obesity and its medical complications (see Section 5, pp. 271–272). Inadequate energy intake results in reduced growth rate and compromised development in young dogs and cats and in weight loss and muscle wasting in adult pets. In healthy animals this condition is most commonly seen in hard working dogs or in pregnant or lactating females that are being fed a diet that is too low in energy density.

WATER

In terms of survivability, water is the single most important nutrient for the body. Although animals can live after losing almost all of their body fat and more than half of their protein, a loss of only 10% of body water results in death.[18] Approximately 70% of lean adult body weight is water, and many tissues in the body are composed of between 70% and 90% water. Intracellular fluid is approximately 40% to 45% of the body's weight, and extracellular fluid accounts for 20% to 25%. The presence of an aqueous medium within cells and in many tissues is essential for the occurrence of most metabolic processes and chemical reactions.

Within the body, water functions as a solvent that facilitates cellular reactions and as a transport medium for nutrients and the end products of cellular metabolism. Because of its high specific heat, water is able to absorb the heat generated by metabolic reactions with a minimal increase in temperature. This property allows the many heat-generating reactions within the body to continue with a minimal change in body temperature. Water further contributes to temperature regulation by transporting heat away from the working organs through the blood and by evaporating in the form of sweat on the outer surface of the body. Water is an essential component in normal digestion because it is necessary for hydrolysis, the splitting of large molecules into smaller molecules by the addition of water. The digestive enzymes of the gastrointestinal tract are secreted in solution. The aqueous medium facilitates the interaction of food components with the digestive enzymes. Elimination of waste products from the kidneys also requires a large amount of water, which acts as both a solvent for toxic metabolites and a carrier medium.

All animals experience daily water losses. Urinary excretion accounts for the greatest volume of loss in most animals. Obligatory fluid loss from the kidney is the minimum that is required for the body to rid itself of the daily load of urinary waste products. A certain quantity of water is necessary to act as a solvent for these end products. The remaining portion of urinary water loss, called *facultative loss*, is excreted in response to the normal water reabsorption rate of the kidney and to mechanisms responsible for maintaining proper water balance in the body. Fecal water accounts for a much smaller portion of water excretion. The amount of water that actually appears in the feces is very low compared to the amount that is absorbed across the gastrointestinal tract and returned to the body during digestion. Fecal water loss becomes substantial only when aberrations in intestinal capacity to absorb water occur. A third route of water loss is evaporation from the lungs during respiration. In dogs and cats this water loss is very important for the regulation of normal body temperature during hot weather. Panting substantially increases respiratory water loss and thus heat loss. Because of these mechanisms of temperature regulation, water losses from respiration and evaporation during hot weather can be very high in both dogs and cats.

Daily water consumption must compensate for these continual fluid losses. A pet's total water intake comes from three possible sources: water present in food, metabolic water, and drinking water. The quantity of water present in the food depends on the type of diet. Commercial, dry pet food may contain as little as 7% water, but some canned rations contain up to 80% water.[19,20] Within limits, increasing the water content of pet foods increases the diet's acceptability. Many owners are able to increase their pet's consumption of a dry food by adding a small amount of water to it immediately before feeding. Studies have shown that both dogs and cats are able to maintain water balance with no source of drinking water when fed diets containing more than 67% moisture.[21-23] Dogs appear to be able to readily compensate for changes in the amount of water present in food by increasing or decreasing voluntary water intake. Cats also have this ability, but they seem to be less precise in their adjustment.[19,24,25]

Metabolic water is the water that is produced during oxidation of the energy-containing nutrients in the body. Oxygen combines with the hydrogen atoms contained in carbohydrate, protein, and fat to produce water molecules. The metabolism of fat produces the greatest amount of metabolic water on a weight basis, and protein catabolism produces the least amount.[18] For every 100 g of fat, carbohydrate, and protein oxidized by the body, 107, 55, and 41 ml of metabolic water are produced, respectively. The rate of metabolic water production depends on an animal's metabolic rate and on the type of diet. Regardless of these factors, metabolic water is fairly insignificant because it accounts for only 5% to 10% of the total daily water intake of most animals.

The last source of water intake is voluntary drinking. Factors affecting a pet's voluntary water consumption include the ambient temperature, type of diet that is fed, level of exercise, physiological state, and health. Water intake increases with both increasing environmental temperature and increasing exercise because more evaporative water is lost as a result of the body's cooling mechanisms. The amount of calories that are consumed also affects voluntary water consumption. As energy intake increases, more metabolic waste products are produced and the heat produced by nutrient metabolism increases. In these circumstances, the body requires more water to excrete waste products in the urine and to contribute to thermoregulation.

Diet type and composition can also dramatically affect voluntary water intake. A study with dogs found that when test animals were fed a diet containing 73% moisture, they obtained only 38% of their daily water needs from drinking water. When they were abruptly switched to a diet containing only 7% water, voluntary water intake immediately increased to 95% or more of the total daily intake.[19] In both dogs and cats, increasing the salt content of the diet caused an increased drinking response. When the level of salt in the diet of a group of cats was increased from 1.3% to 4.6%, voluntary water intake nearly doubled.[19] This effect may have practical significance given the high level of salt that is present in some commercial pet foods. Generally, if fresh, palatable water is available and proper amounts of a well-balanced diet are fed, most pets are able to accurately regulate water balance through voluntary intake of water.

CHAPTER 2

Carbohydrates

arbohydrates are the major energy-containing constituents of plants, making up between 60% and 90% of dry-matter weight. This class of nutrients is comprised of the elements carbon, hydrogen, and oxygen and can be classified as monosaccharides, disaccharides, or polysaccharides. *Monosaccharides*, often referred to as the simple sugars, are the simplest form of carbohydrate. A monosaccharide is comprised of a single unit containing between three and seven carbon atoms. The three hexoses (6-carbon monosaccharides) that are most important nutritionally and metabolically are glucose, fructose, and galactose (Figure 2-1).

Glucose is a moderately sweet, simple sugar that is found in commercially-prepared corn syrup and in sweet fruits such as grapes and berries. It is also the chief end product of starch digestion and glycogen hydrolysis in the body. Glucose is the form of carbohydrate that is found circulating in the bloodstream and is the primary form of carbohydrate used by the body's cells for energy. Fructose, commonly referred to as "fruit sugar," is a very sweet sugar that is found in honey, ripe fruits, and some vegetables. It is also formed from the digestion or acid hydrolysis of the disaccharide sucrose. Galactose is not found free form in foods. However, it makes up 50% of the disaccharide lactose, which is present in the milk of all species. Like fructose, galactose is released during digestion. Within the body, galactose is converted to glucose by the liver and eventually enters the circulation in the form of glucose.

Disaccharides are made up of two monosaccharide units linked together. Lactose, the sugar found in the milk of all mammals, contains a molecule of glucose and a molecule of galactose. It is the only carbohydrate of animal origin that is of any significance

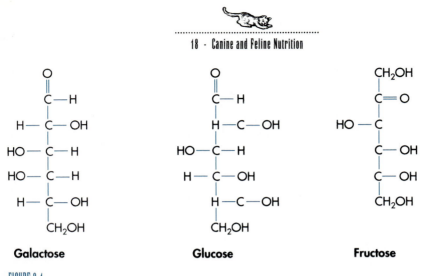

Galactose

Glucose

Fructose

FIGURE 2-1
Basic carbohydrate structure

in the diet. Sucrose, commonly recognized as table sugar, contains a molecule of glucose linked to a molecule of fructose. It is found in cane, beets, and maple syrup. Maltose is made up of two glucose molecules linked together. This disaccharide is not commonly found in most foods, but it is formed as an intermediate product in the body during the digestion of starch.

Polysaccharides are composed of many single monosaccharide units, linked together in long and complex chains. Starch, glycogen, dextrins, and dietary fiber are all polysaccharides. Starch is the chief carbohydrate source present in most commercial pet foods. Cereal grains such as corn, wheat, and rice are the major ingredients that provide this starch. Glycogen is the storage form of carbohydrate in the body. It is found in the liver and in muscle, and it functions to help maintain normal glucose homeostasis in the body. Dextrins are polysaccharide compounds that are formed as intermediate products in the breakdown of starch. They are created during normal digestive processes in the body and through the commercial processing of some foods. The monosaccharide units found in starch, glycogen, and dextrin molecules have alpha-configuration and are linked together by alpha-bonds. This type of bond can be readily hydrolyzed by the endogenous enzymes of the gastrointestinal tract and yields monosaccharide units upon either digestion or chemical hydrolysis.

Dietary fiber is plant material that consists primarily of several forms of carbohydrate. The major carbohydrate components of dietary fiber include cellulose, hemicellulose, pectin, and the plant gums and mucilages. Lignin, a large phenylpropane polymer, is the only noncarbohydrate component of fiber. Plant fiber differs from starch and glycogen in that its monosaccharide units have beta-configuration and are linked together by beta-bonds. These bonds resist digestion by the endogenous enzymes of the gastrointestinal tract. As a result, dietary fiber cannot be broken down to monosaccharide units for absorption in the small intestine.

Although dogs and cats do not directly digest dietary fiber, certain microbes found in the large intestine (colon) are able to break down fiber to varying degrees. This bac-

TABLE 2-1
Dietary Fiber Fermentation in Dogs

FIBER TYPE	SOLUBILITY	FERMENTABILITY
Beet fiber	Low	Moderate
Cellulose	Low	Low
Rice bran	Low	Moderate
Gum arabic	High	Moderate
Pectin	Low	High
CM-cellulose	High	Low
Methylcellulose	High	Low
Cabbage fiber	Low	High
Guar gum	High	High
Locust bean gum	High	Low
Xanthan gum	High	Moderate

From Iams Technical Center Data, 1994, Lewisburg, Ohio.

terial fermentation produces short-chain fatty acids (SCFA) and other end products. The SCFAs that are produced in greatest abundance are acetate, propionate, and butyrate. The magnitude of bacterial digestion depends on factors such as the type of fiber that is present in the diet, gastrointestinal transit time, and the intake of other dietary constituents.[26] For example, in dogs and cats, pectin and other soluble fibers are highly fermentable, beet pulp is moderately fermentable, and cellulose is nonfermentable (Table 2-1). Ruminants and herbivorous animals are able to derive a significant amount of energy from the SCFAs produced by the bacterial fermentation of fiber. However, non-herbivores, such as the dog and the cat, cannot do this because of the relatively short and simple structure of their large intestine. Although SCFAs are produced in these species, there is no mechanism for the absorption of large amounts of SCFAs in the large intestine. Therefore total energy balance of dogs and cats is not significantly affected by the production of SCFAs from dietary fiber.

In dogs and cats however, the SCFAs that are produced from fiber are an important energy source for the epithelial cells lining the gastrointestinal tract. The enterocytes and colonocytes of the large intestine are active cells that have a high turnover rate and rely on SCFAs as a significant energy source. Recent research has shown that dogs that are fed diets containing moderately fermentable fiber have increased colon weights, mucosal surface area, and mucosal hypertrophy compared to dogs fed a diet containing a nonfermentable fiber source (Table 2-2).[27] These changes provide a measure of the absorptive capacity of the colon and indicate increased cellular activity and health. Although a highly fermentable fiber source has similar effects on colon weight and morphology, diets containing this type of fiber result in poor stool quality. It appears that the best fiber sources for companion animals are those that are moderately fermentable and provide adequate levels of SCFAs for the intestinal mucosa.[27,28] Fiber in the diets of dogs and cats also functions as an aid in the proper functioning of the gastrointestinal tract and as a dietary diluent that decreases the total energy density of the diet (see Section 2, p. 94; see also Section 5, pp. 287–289).

TABLE 2-2
Effects of Fiber Source on the Canine Colon

	CELLULOSE	BEET PULP	PECTIN/GUM ARABIC	INTERPRETATION
Colon weight (g/kg body weight)	6.09	6.52	6.62	More is better
Surface area ratio	0.146	0.156	0.154	More is better
Cryptitis, (# per 5 dogs)	4	1	3	Less is better
DNA content (μg/mg)	47.4	40.4	38.4	Less is better

Data from Reinhart GA, Moxley RA, Clemens ET: *Dietary fibre source and its effects on colonic microstructure and histopathology of beagle dogs*, Waltham Symposium on the Nutrition of Companion Animals, 1993.

In the body, carbohydrate has several functions. The monosaccharide glucose is an important energy source for many tissues. A constant supply of glucose is necessary for the proper functioning of the central nervous system, and the glycogen present in the heart muscle is an important emergency source of energy for the heart. Glycogen in the liver and muscle can be hydrolyzed when circulating glucose is low to supply additional carbohydrate fuel to cells. Carbohydrate also supplies carbon skeletons for the formation of nonessential amino acids and is needed for the synthesis of other essential body compounds such as glucuronic acid, heparin, chondroitin sulfate, the immunopolysaccharides, and deoxyribonucleic acid (DNA) and ribonucleic acid (RNA). When conjugated with proteins or lipids, some carbohydrates also become important structural components in the body's tissues.

Dietary carbohydrate provides animals with a source of energy and assists in proper gastrointestinal tract functioning. Only a limited amount of carbohydrate can be stored in the body as glycogen, so when dietary carbohydrate is consumed in excess of the body's energy needs, most is metabolized to body fat for energy storage. Therefore consumption of dietary carbohydrate in excess of an animal's energy needs can lead to increased body fat and obesity. In addition to its function in supplying energy to the body, digestible carbohydrate also has a protein-sparing effect. Just as animals eat to meet their energy needs, the body satisfies its energy requirement before using energy-containing nutrients in the diet for other purposes. If adequate carbohydrate is supplied in the diet, protein will be spared from being used for energy and can then be used for tissue repair and growth. Although dietary fiber does not contribute appreciably to energy balance in dogs and cats, a moderate level in the diet is beneficial. Plant fiber provides SCFAs to cells lining the intestine, helps to stimulate normal peristalsis, provides bulk to intestinal contents, and reduces gastrointestinal transit time (see Section 2, p. 94).

CHAPTER 3

Fats

D ietary fat is part of a heterogeneous group of compounds known as the *lipids*. These compounds are classified together because of their solubility in organic solvents and their insolubility in water. They can be further categorized into simple lipids, compound lipids, and derived lipids. The *simple lipids* include the triglycerides, which are the most common form of fat present in the diet, and the waxes. Triglycerides are made up of three fatty acids linked to one molecule of glycerol (Figure 3-1), and waxes contain a greater number of fatty acids linked to a long-chain alcohol molecule. *Compound lipids* are composed of a lipid, such as a fatty acid, linked to a nonlipid molecule. Lipoproteins, which function to carry fat in the bloodstream, are a type of compound lipid. The *derived lipids* include sterol compounds, such as cholesterol, and the fat-soluble vitamins.

Triglyceride is the type of fat that is most important in the diet and that can be differentiated in foods according to the type of fatty acids that each triglyceride contains. Fatty acids vary in carbon chain length and may be saturated, monounsaturated, or polyunsaturated. Most food triglycerides contain predominantly long-chain fatty acids (with even number of carbon atoms between 16 and 26). Two exceptions are butter and coconut oil, which contain appreciable amounts of short-chain fatty acids. Saturated fatty acids contain no double bonds between carbon atoms and thus are "saturated" with hydrogen atoms. Monounsaturated fatty acids have one double bond, and polyunsaturated fatty acids contain two or more double bonds (Figure 3-2). In general, the triglycerides in animal fats contain a higher percentage of saturated fatty acids than do those in vegetable fats. Most plant oils, with the exception of palm, olive, and coconut oils, contain between 80% and 90% unsaturated fat; animal fats contain between 50% and 60% unsaturated fat.[7]

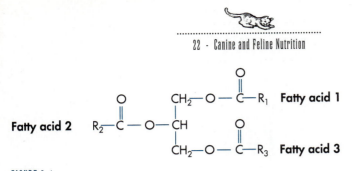

FIGURE 3-1
Triglyceride structure

Fat has numerous functions within the body. Triglycerides are the body's primary form of stored energy. Major depots of fat accumulation are present under the skin as subcutaneous fat, around the vital organs, and in the membranes surrounding the intestines. Some of these depots can be readily observed in obese dogs and cats. Fat depots have an extensive blood and nerve supply and are in a constant state of flux, providing energy in times of need and storage in times of energy surplus. They also serve as insulators protecting the body from heat loss, and as a protective layer that guards against physical injury to the vital organs. Although animals have a very limited capacity to store carbohydrate in the form of glycogen, they have an almost limitless capacity to store surplus energy in the form of fat.

In addition to providing energy, fat has numerous metabolic and structural functions. Fat insulation surrounds myelinated nerve fibers and aids in the transmission of nerve impulses. Phospholipids and glycolipids serve as structural components for cell membranes and participate in the transport of nutrients and metabolites across these membranes. Lipoproteins provide the transport of fats through the bloodstream. Cholesterol is used by the body to form the bile salts that are necessary for proper fat digestion and absorption, and it is also a precursor for the steroid hormones. Along with other lipids, cholesterol forms a protective layer in the skin that prevents excessive water loss and the invasion of foreign substances. The essential fatty acid arachidonic acid is the precursor of a group of physiologically and pharmacologically active compounds called prostacyclins, prostaglandins, leukotrienes, and thromboxanes. These compounds have extensive hormonelike actions in the body and are involved in processes such as vasodilation and vasoconstriction, muscle contraction, blood pressure homeostasis, gastric acid secretion, regulation of body temperature, regulation of blood clotting mechanisms, and control of inflammation.

In the diet, fat provides the most concentrated form of energy of all the nutrients. Although the gross energy (GE) of protein and carbohydrate is approximately 5.65 and 4.15 kilocalories per gram (kcal/g), the GE of fat is 9.4 kcal/g. In addition to containing more energy, the digestibility of fat is also usually higher than that of protein and carbohydrate. When mixtures of plant and animal fat were fed to adult dogs, estimates of apparent fat digestibility ranged between 80% and 95%.[29,30] A second study reported that the apparent digestibility of the fat in several commercially prepared dry-type dog foods varied between 70% and 90%. Within each brand of food, the apparent fat digestibility was consistently higher than either protein or carbohydrate digestibility.[31] Therefore

Saturated

Lauric acid

$$CH_3-CH_2-CH_2-CH_2-CH_2-CH_2-CH_2-CH_2-CH_2-CH_2-CH_2-COOH$$

Monounsaturated

Palmitoleic acid

$$CH_3-CH_2-CH_2-CH_2-CH_2-CH_2-CH=CH-CH_2-CH_2-CH_2-CH_2-CH_2-CH_2-CH_2-COOH$$

Polyunsaturated

Linoleic acid

$$CH_3-CH_2-CH_2-CH_2-CH_2-CH=CH-CH_2-CH=CH-CH_2-CH_2-CH_2-CH_2-CH_2-CH_2-CH_2-COOH$$

Alpha-linolenic acid

$$CH_3-CH_2-CH=CH-CH_2-CH=CH-CH_2-CH=CH-CH_2-CH_2-CH_2-CH_2-CH_2-CH_2-CH_2-COOH$$

Arachidonic acid

$$CH_3-CH_2-CH_2-CH_2-CH_2-CH=CH-CH_2-CH=CH-CH_2-CH=CH-CH_2-CH=CH-CH_2-CH_2-CH_2-COOH$$

FIGURE 3-2
Types of fatty acids

increasing the percentage of fat in a pet's diet provides a very concentrated, readily digested source of energy that substantially increases the caloric density of the food.

Dietary fat also provides a source of essential fatty acids and acts as a carrier that allows the absorption of the fat-soluble vitamins. The body has a physiological requirement for two distinct families of essential fatty acids, the n-6 and the n-3 series.[32] This terminology denotes the position of the first double bond in the molecule counting from the terminal (methyl) end of the chain. The most important fatty acid of the n-6 series is linoleic acid (Figure 3-2). In most animals, gamma-linolenic acid and arachidonic acid can be synthesized from linoleic acid by alternating desaturation and elongation reactions. Therefore, if adequate linoleic acid is provided in the diet, there is not a dietary requirement for gamma-linolenic acid or arachidonic acid. Although the dog is able to synthesize these fatty acids, the cat is one of the few species that requires a dietary source of arachidonic acid, even when adequate linoleic acid is present in the diet (see Section 2, pp. 96–97). In the n-3 family, alpha-linolenic acid also appears to have essential fatty acid properties.[33] However, it is difficult to induce a deficiency of this fatty acid, so its exact role in the nutrition of dogs and cats is still unknown.

All of the essential fatty acids are polyunsaturated. Linoleic acid and the linolenic acids contain 18 carbon atoms and 2 and 3 double bonds, respectively. Arachidonic acid contains 20 carbon atoms and 4 double bonds (Figure 3-2). In most animals the best

sources of linoleic acid are vegetable oils such as corn, soybean, and safflower oils. Poultry fat and pork fat also contain appreciable amounts of linoleic acid, but beef tallow and butter fats contain very little. Arachidonic acid, on the other hand, is found only in animal fats. Some fish oils are rich in this essential fatty acid, and pork fat and poultry fat also supply a small amount.[7]

Fat in the diets of companion animals also plays a role in contributing palatability and acceptable texture to food. This is obviously a critical function because no pet food, regardless of how well-formulated it is, can be nutritious if it is not eaten. A study conducted with cats found that diets containing 25% to 40% fat were preferred to low-fat diets, but increasing the fat content further tended to decrease the diet's acceptability.[34] This effect of dietary fat is complicated by the fact that as the fat content in the diet increases, so does energy density. Animals require decreased quantities of calorie-dense foods to satisfy their energy requirements. However, the increased palatability of foods high in fat can encourage some pets to overconsume. Therefore, although fat does lend increased palatability to a diet, this effect can rapidly lead to overeating as the energy density of the diet rises. For this reason, well-balanced pet foods that are energy-dense and contain moderate to high levels of fat must often be fed on a portion-controlled basis.

CHAPTER 4

Protein and Amino Acids

P roteins are complex molecules that, like carbohydrate and fat, contain carbon, hydrogen, and oxygen. In addition, all proteins contain the element nitrogen, and the majority contain sulfur. All proteins contain approximately 16% nitrogen. This consistency has resulted in the development of the nitrogen balance test, which is used to estimate an animal's body protein status. Nitrogen balance tests measure intake and excretion of nitrogen in animals that are fed a test diet. Net loss or gain of nitrogen then indicates increases or decreases in total body protein reserves (see Section 2, pp. 101–102). Amino acids are the basic units of proteins and are held together by peptide linkages to form long protein chains (Figures 4-1 and 4-2). Proteins can range in size from several amino acids to large, complex molecules that consist of several intricately folded peptide chains, and they can be classified as either simple or complex forms. Once hydrolysis begins, simple proteins yield only amino acids or their derivatives. Examples include albumin in blood plasma, lactalbumin in milk, zein in corn, and the structural proteins keratin, collagen, and elastin. Complex or conjugated proteins are made up of a simple protein combined with a non protein molecule. Some types of complex proteins include the nucleoproteins, glycoproteins, and phosphoproteins.

Proteins in the body have numerous functions. They are the major structural components of hair, feathers, skin, nails, tendons, ligaments, and cartilage. The fibrous protein collagen is the basic material that forms most of the connective tissue throughout the body. Contractile proteins such as myosin and actin are involved in regulating muscle action. All of the enzymes that catalyze the body's essential metabolic reactions and are essential for nutrient digestion and assimilation are also protein molecules. Many hormones that control the homeostatic mechanisms of various systems in the body are

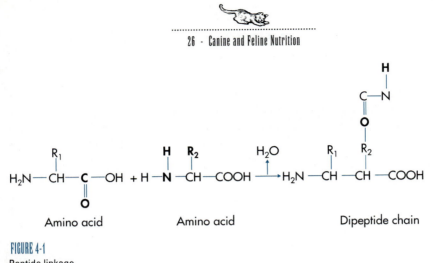

Amino acid   **Amino acid**   **Dipeptide chain**

FIGURE 4-1
Peptide linkage

Alanine

Glutamine

Glycine

Lysine

FIGURE 4-2
Simple protein chain

composed of protein. For example, insulin and glucagon are two hormones involved in the control of normal blood glucose levels. Proteins found in the blood act as important carrier substances. These include hemoglobin, which carries oxygen to tissues; transferrin, which transports iron; and retinol-binding protein, which carries vitamin A. In addition to their transport functions, plasma proteins also contribute to the regulation of acid-base balance. Lastly, the body's immune system relies on protein substances. The antibodies that maintain the body's resistance to disease are all composed of large protein molecules.

The protein present in the body is not static, but rather it is in a constant state of flux involving degradation and synthesis. Although tissues vary greatly in their rate of turnover, all protein molecules in the body are eventually catabolized and replaced. During growth and reproduction, additional protein is needed for the accretion of new tissue. A regular influx of protein and nitrogen, supplied by the diet, is necessary to maintain normal metabolic processes and to provide for tissue maintenance and growth. The body has the ability to synthesize new proteins from amino acids, provided that all of the necessary amino acids are available to the tissue cells. At the tissue and cellular level it is inconsequential whether the amino acids that are present were synthesized by the body, supplied from the diet as single amino acid units, or supplied from the diet in the form of intact protein. Therefore it is correct to state that the body does not really have a protein requirement per se but rather has a requirement for certain amino acids and for a level of nitrogen. This requirement is still addressed as a protein requirement in the diet because most practical diets contain intact protein sources, not individual amino acids.

There are 22 alpha-amino acids found in protein chains. The term "alpha" denotes the attachment of the amino group (NH_2) to the first (alpha-) carbon in the molecule. Of these 22 alpha-amino acids, if an adequate source of nitrogen is supplied in the diet, dogs and cats are able to synthesize 12 at a sufficient rate to meet the body's needs for growth, performance, and maintenance. These are called the *nonessential*, or dispensable, amino acids, and they may either be supplied in the diet or synthesized by the body. The remaining 10 amino acids cannot be synthesized at a rate that is sufficient to meet the body's needs. These are the *essential* amino acids, and they must be supplied in the pet's diet. In addition to these 10, the cat has an additional requirement for taurine, a beta-sulfonic acid (see Section 2, pp.110–113). The essential and nonessential amino acids are listed in the accompanying box.

Dietary protein serves several important functions. It provides the essential amino acids, which are used for protein synthesis in the growth and repair of tissue, and it is the body's principal source of nitrogen. Nitrogen is essential for the synthesis of the nonessential amino acids and of other nitrogen-containing molecules, such as nucleic acids, purines, pyrimidines, and certain neurotransmitter substances. Amino acids supplied by dietary protein can also be metabolized for energy. The gross energy of amino acids is 5.65 kilocalories per gram (kcal/g). When fecal and urinary losses are accounted for, the metabolizable energy of protein in dog and cat diets is approximately 3.5 kcal/g, approximately the same amount of energy that is supplied by dietary carbohydrate. Animals are unable to store excess amino acids. Surplus amino acids are used either directly for energy or are converted to glycogen or fat for energy storage. An ancillary function of the protein in dog and cat diets is to provide a source of flavor. Different flavors are created when food proteins are cooked in the presence of carbohydrate and fat.[35] In general, as the protein content of a diet increases, so does its palatability and acceptability.

The degree to which a dog or cat is able to use dietary protein as a source of amino acids and nitrogen is affected by both the digestibility and the quality of the protein included in the diet. Proteins that are highly digestible and contain all of the essential amino acids in their proper proportions relative to the animal's needs are considered

Essential and Nonessential Amino Acids for Dogs and Cats

Essential Amino Acids	Nonessential Amino Acids
Arginine	Alanine
Histidine	Asparagine
Isoleucine	Aspartate
Leucine	Cysteine
Lysine	Glutamate
Methionine	Glutamine
Phenylalanine	Glycine
Tryptophan	Hydroxylysine
Threonine	Hydroxyproline
Valine	Proline
Taurine (cats only)	Serine
	Tyrosine

high-quality proteins. In contrast, those that are either low in digestibility or limiting in one or more of the essential amino acids are of lower quality. The higher the quality of a protein in a diet, the less quantity that is needed by the animal to meet all of its essential amino acid needs. Various methods for evaluating the protein quality in foods have been developed (see the box on the following page). Each of these methods has specific advantages and disadvantages with respect to efficacy of evaluating the overall quality of protein sources that are included in foods formulated for companion animals.

Several analytical tests predict protein quality based entirely on the protein's essential amino acid composition. *Chemical score* is an index that involves comparing the amino acid composition of a given protein source with the amino acid pattern of a reference protein of very high quality. Egg protein is typically used as the reference protein and is given a chemical score of 100. The essential amino acid that is in greatest deficit in the test protein is called the limiting amino acid because it will limit the body's ability to use that protein. The percentage of that amino acid present in the protein relative to the corresponding value in the reference protein determines the chemical score of the test protein. The three amino acids in food proteins that are most often limiting are methionine, tryptophan, and lysine. In some pet foods, arginine and isoleucine have also been reported to be limiting, according to analysis by chemical score.[36] Although chemical score provides useful information concerning the amino acid deficits of a protein source, its value is based entirely on the level of the most limiting amino acid in the protein and does not take into account the proportions of all of the remaining essential amino acids.

A modified version of chemical score, called the essential amino acid index (EAAI), measures the contribution that a protein makes to all of the essential amino acids, rather than only to the one in greatest deficit. A protein's EAAI is calculated as the geometric mean of the ratios of each of the essential amino acids in the test protein to their corresponding values in the reference protein.[37] Lastly, the total essential amino acid content (E/T) is calculated as the proportion of the total nitrogen in a protein source that is contributed by essential amino acids. Although chemical score and EAAI both indicate

Methods to Determine Protein Quality

Chemical Score

$$\frac{\text{Limiting amino acid in the test protein (\%)}}{\text{Particular amino acid in the reference protein (\%)}}$$

Essential Amino Acid Index (EAAI)

$$\frac{\text{Amino acid in the test protein (\%)}}{\text{Same amino acid in the reference protein (\%)}} \Bigg\} \begin{array}{l}\text{Summed for all}\\\text{essential amino acids}\end{array}$$

Total Essential Amino Acid Content (E/T)

$$\frac{\text{Amount of nitrogen from essential amino acids in the protein source}}{\text{Amount of total nitrogen in the protein source}}$$

Protein Efficiency Ratio (PER)

$$\frac{\text{Weight gained by animals (g)}}{\text{Protein consumed by animals (total g)}}$$

Biological Value (BV)

$$\frac{\text{Food nitrogen} - (\text{Fecal nitrogen} + \text{Urinary nitrogen})}{\text{Food nitrogen} - \text{Fecal nitrogen}}$$

Net Protein Utilization (NPU)

BV of protein × Digestibility of protein

the quality of a protein's amino acid profile, the E/T measures the total quantity of essential amino acids within a particular protein source.

Estimations of protein quality from amino acid composition are helpful in assessing protein quality when combinations of different proteins are used in a food and for assessing protein sources that have been supplemented with purified amino acids. However, these tests are limited by the fact that they provide no information regarding the digestibility of a protein or the availability of its amino acids. For example, the heat used in processing can damage food protein, resulting in a decreased availability of certain amino acids. Simply using an analytical analysis based on amino acid composition would not reveal this change. Therefore the thorough assessment of a protein source ultimately requires that feeding trials are conducted in which the protein in question is fed to a predetermined number of test animals.

Protein efficiency ratio (PER) is one of the simplest and most commonly used feeding tests for measuring protein quality. Weanling male rats or growing chicks are fed an adequate diet containing the test protein for up to 28 days. Weight changes are mea-

sured and PER is calculated as the grams in weight gained divided by the total grams of protein consumed. The PER value indicates the ability of a protein source to be converted into tissue in a growing animal. One criticism of using PER as a measure of protein quality in dog and cat foods is that this test assumes that weight gain in growing animals is directly related to nitrogen retention. Although this has been proven to be true in rats, some investigators believe that this may not be a consistent relationship in the growing dog.[34] In addition, any factor that influences the test animals' rate of growth during the study, regardless of whether it is related to protein quality, will affect the calculated PER value. One method of accounting for these problems is to include a positive and negative control group in the PER study. The positive control group is fed a diet containing a reference protein (egg), and the negative group is fed a protein-free diet. The effects of the nonprotein group are subtracted from the effects in the test protein group when the study is completed.

Biological value and net protein utilization provide accurate measures of protein quality, but they are more time consuming and labor intensive to conduct than are PER tests. Biological value (BV) is defined as the percentage of absorbed protein that is retained by the body. It is a measure of the ability of the body to convert absorbed amino acids into body tissue. Nitrogen balance studies must be conducted in which food, fecal, and urinary nitrogen is collected and measured. Animals must be in a state of physiological maintenance, and the diet must contain adequate carbohydrate and fat to ensure that the protein in the diet is not metabolized for energy. True BV can be determined by first accounting for fecal and urinary losses of endogenous nitrogen when the animal is consuming a protein-free diet. One problem with using BV as a measurement of protein quality is that it does not account for protein digestibility. Theoretically, if the small portion of a very indigestible protein that is absorbed is used efficiently by the body, it could still have a very high BV value.

Net protein utilization (NPU) is calculated as the product of a protein's BV and its digestibility. NPU therefore measures the proportion of consumed protein that is retained by the body. A protein that is 100% digestible would have BV and NPU values that were the same. On the other hand, a poorly digested protein would have a much lower NPU value than BV value. Although BV and NPU are considered very important indicators of protein quality, data collected in nitrogen balance experiments can be affected by the level of protein in the diet, energy intake, and the physiological state of the animal. Overall, in addition to one or more of the tests described earlier, the quality of protein in a pet food should always be assessed through trials in which the food is fed to the animals for which it was developed. Long-term effects on health and vitality must also be evaluated to fully determine the quality of a particular protein or mixture of proteins in a food.

CHAPTER 5

Vitamins

Vitamins are organic molecules that are needed in minute amounts to function as essential enzymes, enzyme precursors, or coenzymes in many of the body's metabolic processes. Although they are organic molecules, vitamins are not classified as carbohydrate, fat, or protein; they are not used as energy sources or structural compounds. With a few exceptions, most vitamins cannot be synthesized by the body and must be supplied in the food.

A general classification scheme for vitamins divides them into two groups: the *fat-soluble vitamins* and the *water-soluble vitamins*. The fat-soluble vitamins are A, D, E, and K; the water-soluble group includes members of the B-complex vitamins and vitamin C. Fat-soluble vitamins are digested and absorbed using the same mechanisms as dietary fat, and their metabolites are excreted primarily in the feces through the bile. In contrast, most of the water-soluble vitamins are absorbed passively in the small intestine and are excreted in the urine. Excesses of fat-soluble vitamins are stored primarily in the liver. With the exception of cobalamin, the body is unable to store significant levels of the water-soluble vitamins. As a result, the fat-soluble vitamins, specifically vitamins A and D, have much higher potential for toxicity than do the water-soluble vitamins. Similarly, because they can be stored, deficiencies of fat-soluble vitamins develop much more slowly in animals than do deficiencies of the water-soluble vitamins. A summary of food sources, and signs of deficiency and excess of the vitamins is shown in Table 5-1.

TABLE 5-1
Vitamin Deficiencies, Excesses, and Major Dietary Sources

VITAMIN	DEFICIENCY	EXCESS	SOURCES
A	Impaired growth, reproductive failure, loss of epithelial integrity, dermatoses	Skeletal abnormalities, hyperesthesia	Fish liver oils, milk, liver, egg yolk
D	Rickets, osteomalacia, nutritional secondary hyperparathyroidism	Hypercalcemia, bone resorption, soft-tissue calcification	Liver, some fish, egg yolk, sunlight
E	Reproductive failure pansteatitis in cats	Non-toxic, may increase vitamins A and D requirements	Wheat germ, corn and soybean oils
K	Increased clotting time, hemorrhage	None recorded	Green leafy plants, liver, some fish meals
Thiamin	CNS* dysfunction, anorexia, weight loss	Non-toxic	Meat, wheat germ
Riboflavin	CNS dysfunction, dermatitis	Non-toxic	Milk, organ meats, vegetables
Niacin	Black tongue disease	Non-toxic	Meat, legumes, grains
Pyridoxine	Microcytic, hypochromic anemia	None recorded	Organ meats, fish, wheat germ
Pantothenic acid	Anorexia, weight loss	None recorded	Liver, kidney, dairy products, legumes
Biotin	Dermatitis	Non-toxic	Eggs, liver, milk, legumes
Folic acid	Anemia, leukopenia	Non-toxic	Liver, kidney, green leafy vegetables
Cobalamin	Anemia	Non-toxic	Meat, fish, poultry
Choline	Neurological dysfunction, fatty liver	Diarrhea	Egg yolk, organ meats, legumes, dairy products
C	Not required by dogs/cats	Non-toxic	Citrus fruit, dark green vegetables

*CNS, Central nervous system.

VITAMIN A

The general term *vitamin A* actually includes several related chemical compounds called retinol, retinal, and retinoic acid. Of these molecules, retinol is the most biologically active form. In the body, vitamin A has functions involving vision, bone growth, reproduction, and maintenance of epithelial tissue. This vitamin's role in vision is well established. In the rods of the retina, retinal combines with a protein called opsin to form rhodopsin, also known as visual purple. Rhodopsin is a light-sensitive pigment that enables the eye to adapt to changes in light intensity. When exposed to light, rhodopsin splits into retinal and opsin, and the energy that is released produces nerve transmissions to the optic nerve. In the dark, rhodopsin can then be regenerated by the combination of new retinal and opsin molecules. During vitamin A deficiencies, less retinal is available to regenerate rhodopsin; thus the rods of the eye become increasingly sensitive to light changes, eventually resulting in night blindness.

Vitamin A is also essential for the formation and maintenance of healthy epithelial tissue. This tissue includes the skin and the mucous membranes lining the respiratory and gastrointestinal tracts. Vitamin A is believed to be necessary for both the proliferation and differentiation of cells and for the production of the mucoproteins found in the mucus produced by some types of epithelial cells.[38,39] Mucus secretions of epithelial tissue maintain the integrity of the epithelium and provide a barrier against bacterial invasion. In the absence of vitamin A, the differentiation of new epithelial cells beyond the squamous type to mature mucus-secreting cells fails to occur and normal epithelial cells are replaced by dysfunctional, stratified, keratinized cells.[39] Epithelial tissue that does not function properly leads to lesions in the epithelium and to increased susceptibility to infection.

Normal skeletal and tooth development and reproductive performance also depend on vitamin A. The vitamin's role in bone growth appears to involve the activity of the osteoclasts and osteoblasts of the epithelial cartilage and may be related to cellular division and maintenance of cell membranes through glycoprotein synthesis. Experiments with laboratory animals have shown that vitamin A is also essential for spermatogenesis in males and for normal estrous cycles in females.[38]

The origin of all vitamin A is the carotenoids, which are synthesized by plant cells. Carotenoids are dark red pigments that provide the deep yellow/orange color to many plants. Vegetables such as carrots and sweet potatoes contain high amounts of these compounds. Deep green vegetables also contain these pigments, but their color is masked by the deep green color of chlorophyll. When animals consume the carotenoids in plants, an enzyme located in the intestinal mucosa converts these compounds (which are commonly called provitamin A) to active vitamin A (Figure 5-1). The active vitamin is then absorbed and stored in the liver.

Although several different carotenoids are capable of providing vitamin A, beta-carotene is the most plentiful in foods and has the highest biological activity. Animal products do not contain carotenoids but can provide active vitamin A when included in the diet. Fish-liver oils contain the highest amounts, and more common foods such as milk, liver, and egg yolk also contain vitamin A.

Like most animals, dogs are capable of converting carotenoids to active vitamin A; therefore they do not require an animal source of this vitamin in the diet. However, the enzyme that is essential for splitting the beta-carotene molecule is either absent or grossly deficient in the domestic cat. As a result, the cat is unable to convert carotenoid pigments to vitamin A and must receive a source of preformed vitamin A in the diet (see Section 2, p. 119).

VITAMIN D

Vitamin D consists of a group of sterol compounds that regulates calcium and phosphorus metabolism in the body. As with vitamin A, there are provitamin forms of this vitamin. These are vitamin D_2 (ergocalciferol) and vitamin D_3 (cholecalciferol). Vitamin D_2 is formed when the compound ergosterol, which is found in many plants, is exposed to ultraviolet (UV) radiation. This conversion occurs only in harvested or injured plants,

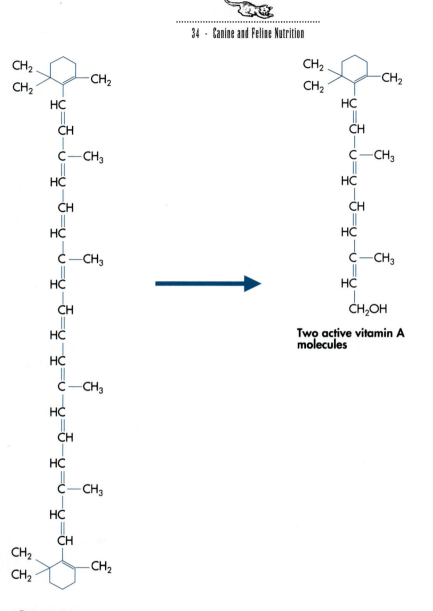

Beta-carotene

Two active vitamin A
molecules

FIGURE 5-1
Conversion of beta-carotene to vitamin A

not in living plant tissue. Therefore this form of vitamin D is only of significance to ruminants and nonruminant herbivores that are consuming sun-dried or irradiated plant materials. The second form of provitamin D, vitamin D_3, is the form that is of greatest nutritional importance to omnivores and carnivores, such as the dog and cat. It is synthesized by the body when 7-dehydrocholesterol, a compound found in the skin of ani-

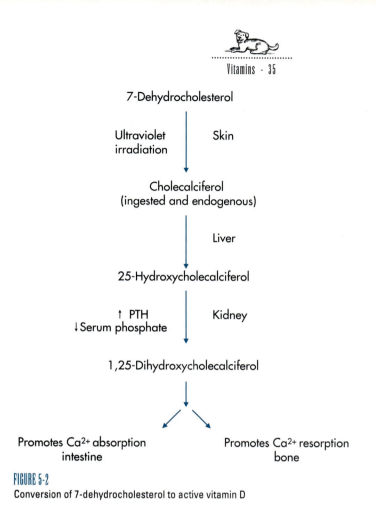

7-Dehydrocholesterol

Ultraviolet irradiation — Skin

Cholecalciferol
(ingested and endogenous)

Liver

25-Hydroxycholecalciferol

↑ PTH
↓ Serum phosphate — Kidney

1,25-Dihydroxycholecalciferol

Promotes Ca²⁺ absorption intestine

Promotes Ca²⁺ resorption bone

FIGURE 5-2
Conversion of 7-dehydrocholesterol to active vitamin D

mals, is exposed to UV light from the sun. This form of vitamin D can be obtained either through synthesis in the skin or from the consumption of animal products that contain cholecalciferol. Because active vitamin D is synthesized by the body and because of the regulatory functions that it has within the body, some controversy exists regarding its classification. Although some scientists believe that vitamin D should be considered a hormone, others continue to classify it as a vitamin. Regardless of its categorization, precursors of vitamin D are obtained through the diet, and its functions are intricately involved with normal calcium and phosphorus homeostasis in the body.

Both ingested and endogenous vitamin D_3 (cholecalciferol) are stored in liver, muscle, and adipose tissue. Cholecalciferol is an inactive, storage form of vitamin D. To become active, it must first be transported from the skin or intestines to the liver; there it is hydroxylated to 25-hydroxycholecalciferol. This compound is then transported through the bloodstream to the kidney, where it is further converted to one of several possible metabolites. Metabolites include 1,25-dihydroxycholecalciferol, also called calcitriol, which is the most active form of vitamin D (Figure 5-2). The conversion of 25-hydroxycholecalciferol to calcitriol in the kidneys occurs in response to elevated parathyroid hormone (PTH), which is released from the parathyroid gland in response

to decreasing serum calcium. A decrease in serum phosphorus also stimulates the formation of active vitamin D in the kidney. Although inactive vitamin D is considered a vitamin, calcitriol is often classified as a hormone because it is produced in the body and because of its mechanism of action in the body.

Active vitamin D functions in normal bone tissue development and maintenance and is an important component involved in the homeostasis of the body's calcium and phosphorus pools. These effects are mediated through the influence of vitamin D on calcium and phosphorus absorption from the gastrointestinal tract and deposition in bone tissue. At the site of the intestine, vitamin D stimulates the synthesis of calcium-binding protein, which is necessary for the efficient absorption of dietary calcium and phosphorus. Vitamin D also affects normal bone growth and calcification by acting with PTH to mobilize calcium from bone and by causing an increase in phosphate reabsorption in the kidney. The net effect of vitamin D's actions in intestine, bone, and kidney is an increase in plasma calcium and phosphorus to the level that is necessary to allow for the normal mineralization and remodeling of bone. A deficiency of vitamin D causes impaired bone mineralization and results in osteomalacia in adult animals and rickets in growing animals (see Section 2, pp. 121–122).

Sources of vitamin D for dogs and cats are varied. Endogenous vitamin D is produced when exposure to sunlight results in the conversion of the precursor 7-dehydrocholesterol in the skin to cholecalciferol. Irradiation is most effective in animals that have light-colored skin and sparse hair coats. Dark-pigmented skin and heavy coats can substantially decrease an animal's ability to produce endogenous vitamin D. The effectiveness of sunlight also depends on the intensity and wavelength of the light that is absorbed and the amount of time that the animal spends outside. Sunlight during the summer months and at high altitudes is most effective as a stimulus for vitamin D production. In general, most natural food substances contain very little vitamin D, although egg yolks, liver, and certain types of fish contain moderate amounts. Among the few concentrated food sources of vitamin D are the fish liver oils, particularly cod liver oil. Because natural foods are low in this vitamin, most commercially prepared pet foods are enriched with vitamin D to ensure that dogs and cats receive adequate amounts of this vitamin, regardless of the amount of daily sunlight that they receive.

Vitamin E

Vitamin E is made up of a group of chemically related compounds called the tocopherols and tocotrienols. Alpha-tocopherol is the most active form of vitamin E and is the compound most commonly found in pet foods. Several active synthetic forms of vitamin E have also been produced and are commonly included in processed foods. Within the body, vitamin E is found in at least small amounts in almost all tissues; the liver is able to store appreciable amounts.

Vitamin E's chief function in the diet and in the body is as a potent antioxidant. Unsaturated fatty acids that are present in foods and in the lipid membranes of the body's cells are very vulnerable to oxidative damage. Vitamin E interrupts the oxidation of these fats by donating electrons to the free radicals that induce lipid peroxidation (see

Section 3, Fig. 16-2). Peroxidation of the body's lipids can destroy the structural integrity of cell membranes, resulting in impairment of normal cellular functioning. Peroxidation of fats in foods causes rancidity and a loss of the nutritional value of the food's essential fatty acids. In addition to its action on polyunsaturated fatty acids, vitamin E also protects vitamin A and the sulfur-containing amino acids from oxidative damage. As a direct result of these functions, an animal's requirement for dietary vitamin E depends on the level of polyunsaturated fatty acids in its diet. Increasing polyunsaturated fatty acid levels in pet foods causes a concomitant increase in a dog's or cat's vitamin E requirement.

A second important interrelationship exists between the trace mineral selenium and vitamin E. Selenium is a cofactor for the enzyme glutathione peroxidase, which functions to reduce the peroxides that are formed during the process of fatty acid oxidation. The inactivation of these peroxides by glutathione peroxidase protects the cell membranes from further oxidative damage. By preventing the oxidation of cell-membrane fatty acids and the formation of peroxides, vitamin E spares selenium. Likewise, selenium has a similar effect and is able to reduce an animal's vitamin E requirement.

In nature, vitamin E is synthesized by a variety of different plants. Food sources that are rich in the tocopherols include wheat germ and the oils of corn, cottonseed, soybean, and sunflower. In general, the vitamin E content of an oil increases along with its linoleic acid concentration. Most animal food sources supply only limited amounts of vitamin E. Egg yolk can contain a moderate amount of vitamin E depending on the diet of the hen, but milk and dairy products are very poor sources. The vitamin E in commercially prepared foods is susceptible to oxidation and destruction, along with the fat in the diet. Therefore proper storage of foods is necessary to both prevent oxidative changes to fat and to maintain proper vitamin E levels.

VITAMIN K

Vitamin K is comprised of a group of compounds called the quinones. Vitamin K_1 (phylloquinone) occurs naturally in green plants, and vitamin K_2 (menaquinone) is synthesized by bacteria in the large intestine. Several synthetic analogues have also been prepared. Menadione (vitamin K_3), the most common form of synthetic vitamin K, has vitamin activity that is two to three times higher than that of natural K_1. Like all animals, dogs and cats have a metabolic need for vitamin K. However, at least a proportion of this requirement can be obtained from bacterial synthesis of the vitamin in the intestine.

The best-known function of vitamin K is its role in the blood clotting mechanism. Specifically, it is required for the liver's synthesis of prothrombin (factor II) and three other clotting factors, factors VII, IX, and X, in the liver. Vitamin K acts as a cofactor for the enzyme that carboxylates glutamic acid residues in a prothrombin-precursor protein to form gamma-carboxyglutamic acid. The conversion of these amino acids facilitates the binding of prothrombin to calcium and phospholipids, a process that is necessary for the occurrence of normal blood clotting. It appears that vitamin K has a similar role in the activation of other proteins that contain glutamic acid residues in bone and kidney tissue.[40]

Vitamin K is found in green, leafy plants such as spinach, kale, cabbage, and cauliflower. In general, animal sources contain lower amounts of vitamin K; liver, egg, and certain fish meals are fairly good sources. The synthesis of vitamin K by bacteria in the large intestine of dogs and cats can contribute at least a portion, if not all, of the daily requirement in these species. Therefore a dietary supply of this vitamin only becomes significant when bacterial populations in the large intestine are reduced, such as during medical treatment with certain types of antibiotics, or when there is interference with absorption or use of vitamin K from bacterial sources.

B-COMPLEX VITAMINS

The B-complex vitamins are water-soluble vitamins that were originally grouped together because of similar metabolic functions and occurrence in foods. These nine vitamins act as coenzymes for specific cellular enzymes that are involved in energy metabolism and tissue synthesis. *Coenzymes* are small organic molecules that must be present with an enzyme for a specific reaction to occur. The vitamins thiamin, riboflavin, niacin, pyridoxine, pantothenic acid, and biotin are all involved in the use of food energy. Folic acid, cobalamin, and choline are important for cell maintenance and growth and/or blood cell synthesis.

Thiamin

Thiamin, also referred to as vitamin B_1, is a component of the coenzyme thiamin pyrophosphate, which plays an important role in carbohydrate metabolism. Thiamin pyrophosphate is necessary for the decarboxylation and transketolation reactions that are involved in the use of carbohydrate for energy and conversion to fat and the metabolism of fatty acids, nucleic acids, steroids and certain amino acids. Because of its importance in carbohydrate metabolism, an animal's thiamin requirement depends upon the level of carbohydrate that is present in the diet. A deficiency of thiamin can significantly affect the functioning of the central nervous system because of its dependency on a constant source of carbohydrate for energy. Natural food sources of thiamin include lean pork, beef, liver, wheat germ, whole grains, and legumes. Although it is present in a large variety of foods, thiamin is a heat-labile vitamin and thus is readily destroyed by the high heat involved in the processing of many pet foods. To assure adequate levels in pet foods, most companies supplement with an excess quantity of this vitamin before processing to ensure that the amount in the finished product is still sufficient. Naturally occurring thiamin deficiency is very rare in dogs and cats and is usually the result of the presence of anti-thiamin factors in the food rather than to an absolute vitamin deficiency (see Section 5, p. 307).

Riboflavin

Riboflavin (vitamin B_2) is named for its yellow color (flavin) and because it contains the simple sugar D-ribose. It is relatively stable to heat-processing, but it is easily destroyed by exposure to light and irradiation. Riboflavin functions in the body as a component of two different coenzymes, flavin mononucleotide and flavin adenine dinucleotide. Both of these coenzymes are required in oxidative enzyme systems that function in the release of energy from carbohydrates, fats, and proteins, as well as in several biosynthetic pathways. Food sources of riboflavin include milk, organ meats, whole grains, and vegetables. In addition, microbial synthesis of riboflavin occurs in the large intestine of most species. The quantity that is synthesized appears to depend on both the species of animal and the level of carbohydrate that is fed.[7] However, the extent to which this source contributes to the daily riboflavin requirement of the dog and cat is unknown.

Niacin

The third B vitamin, niacin (nicotinic acid), is closely associated with riboflavin in cellular oxidation-reduction enzyme systems. After absorption, niacin is rapidly converted by the body to nicotinamide, the metabolically active form of the vitamin. Nicotinamide is then incorporated into two different coenzymes, nicotinamide adenine dinucleotide and nicotinamide adenine dinucleotide phosphate. These coenzymes function as hydrogen-transfer agents in several enzymatic pathways that are involved in the use of fat, carbohydrate, and protein. Meat, legumes, and grains all contain high amounts of niacin. However, a large proportion of the niacin present in many plant sources is in a bound form and is unavailable for absorption.[41] The niacin in animal sources is found primarily in an unbound, available form. In addition to consuming niacin in the diet, most animals also synthesize this vitamin as an end product of the metabolism of tryptophan, an essential amino acid. As a result, the level of tryptophan in the diet directly affects an animal's dietary requirement for niacin. Dogs are capable of synthesizing niacin from tryptophan; because cats cannot synthesize niacin from tryptophan, they must receive all of their niacin requirement from the diet (see Section 2, pp. 114–116).

Pyridoxine

Pyridoxine, vitamin B_6, is comprised of three different compounds: pyridoxine, pyridoxal, and pyridoxamine. Pyridoxal, which is a component of the coenzyme pyridoxal 5´-phosphate, is the biologically active form. This coenzyme is necessary for many of the transamination, deamination and decarboxylation reactions of amino acid metabolism and is active to a lesser extent in the metabolism of glucose and fatty acids. Pyridoxal 5´-phosphate is also required for the synthesis of hemoglobin and the conversion of tryptophan to niacin. In the same manner that thiamin requirement varies with the carbohydrate level in the diet, the pyridoxine requirement of animals depends on the level of protein in the diet. Pyridoxine is widespread in foods, with organ meats, fish, wheat germ, and whole grains providing adequate amounts. Dietary deficiencies of this vitamin in dogs and cats have not been reported.

Pantothenic Acid

Pantothenic acid was named from the Greek term *pan*, meaning *all*, because this vitamin occurs in all body tissues and in all forms of living tissue. Once absorbed, pantothenic acid is phosphorylated by adenosine triphosphate (ATP) to form coenzyme A. This coenzyme is essential for the process of acetylation, a universal reaction involved in many aspects of carbohydrate, fat, and protein metabolism within the citric acid cycle. Pantothenic acid is found in virtually all foods. As a result, deficiencies of this vitamin are extremely rare. Rich sources of pantothenic acid include organ meats such as liver and kidney, egg yolk, dairy products, and legumes.

Biotin

The vitamin biotin is a coenzyme required in several carboxylation reactions. It acts as a carbon dioxide carrier in reactions in which carbon chains are lengthened. Specifically, biotin is involved in certain steps of fatty acid, nonessential amino acid, and purine synthesis. Biotin is found in many different foods, but its bioavailability varies greatly. Eggs provide a very rich source of this biotin, but egg white contains a compound called avidin, which binds biotin and makes it unavailable for absorption. Thoroughly cooking eggs destroys avidin and allows the biotin in the yolk to be used. Other food sources of biotin include liver, milk, legumes, and nuts. Intestinal bacteria also synthesize biotin; it is believed that a large proportion, if not all, of an animal's requirement can be met from this source.[7,11] Deficiencies are not generally a problem; however, the treatment of dogs and cats with antibiotics that decrease the bacterial population of the large intestine can cause an increase in the dietary requirement for biotin.

Folic Acid

Folic acid (folacin) is active in the body as tetrahydrofolic acid. This compound functions as a methyl-transfer agent, transporting single-carbon units in a number of metabolic reactions. An important role of folic acid is its involvement in the synthesis of thymidine, a component of deoxyribonucleic acid (DNA). When folic acid is deficient in the body, the inability to produce adequate DNA leads to decreased cellular growth and maturation. This is manifested clinically as anemia and leukopenia in deficient animals. Food sources of folic acid include green, leafy vegetables and organ meats such as liver and kidney. Like several of the other B vitamins, folic acid is synthesized by the bacteria of the large intestine in dogs and cats. It appears that most, if not all, of the daily requirement of dogs and cats can be met from this source.

Cobalamin

Cobalamin (vitamin B_{12}) contains the mineral cobalt and is unique in that it is the only vitamin that contains a trace element. Similar to folic acid, cobalamin is involved in the transfer of single-carbon units during various biochemical reactions. It is also involved in fat and carbohydrate metabolism and is necessary for the synthesis of myelin. As a result, a deficiency of vitamin B_{12} leads to both anemia and impairment of neurological functioning. In most animals, absorption of cobalamin from the diet is facilitated by a protein that is produced in the intestine, called *intrinsic factor*. The absence of this factor can lead to vitamin B_{12} deficiency. Although the presence of intrinsic factor has not been demonstrated in dogs or cats, it is likely that absorption occurs through the same mechanism in these species.

Cobalamin is only found in foods of animal origin. Rich sources of cobalamin include meat, poultry, fish, and dairy products. This vitamin is also unique for a B vitamin because, once absorbed from the diet, excesses can be stored by the body. The liver is the primary storage tissue; muscle, bone, and skin also contain small amounts of cobalamin. Deficiencies of cobalamin are extremely rare as a result of the very small amounts that are needed by the body and the body's ability to store appreciable amounts of the vitamin.

Choline

The last B vitamin, choline, acts as a donor of methyl units for various metabolic reactions in the body. Choline is a precursor for the neurotransmitter substance acetylcholine and is necessary for normal fatty-acid transport within cells. Unlike other vitamins, choline is also an integral part of cellular membranes. Choline is a component of two important phospholipids, phosphatidylcholine (lecithin) and sphingomyelin. Lecithin is essential for normal cell-membrane structure and function, and sphingomyelin is found in high concentrations in nervous tissue.

The body is capable of synthesizing choline from the amino acid serine. In this reaction, methionine acts as a methyl donor, and folacin and vitamin B_{12} are also necessary. It is not known if sufficient choline is produced by dogs and cats to maintain health without a dietary source of this compound. Because choline and methionine both function as methyl donors in the body, diets that are high in methionine can replace some of an animal's choline requirement. Choline is also widespread in food sources. Egg yolk, organ meats, legumes, dairy products, and whole grains all supply high amounts of choline. Because of its synthesis in the body, its presence in many foods, and the ability of methionine to spare choline, dietary deficiencies of choline have not been reported in dogs and cats.

Vitamin C (Ascorbic Acid)

Ascorbic acid, commonly known as vitamin C, has a chemical structure that is closely related to the monosaccharide sugars. It is synthesized from glucose by plants and most animal species, including dogs and cats. When present in foods, ascorbic acid is easily destroyed by oxidative processes. Exposure to heat, light, alkalies, oxidative enzymes, and the minerals copper and iron all contribute to losses of vitamin C activity. Oxidative loss of vitamin C is inhibited to some extent by an acid environment and by the storage of foods at low temperatures.

The body requires ascorbic acid for the hydroxylation of the amino acids proline and lysine in the formation of collagen. Collagen is the primary constituent of osteoid, dentine, and connective tissue. It is produced in quantity by osteoblasts during skeletal growth; therefore it is important for normal bone formation. When ascorbic acid is not available, the synthesis of several types of connective tissue within the body is impaired. In animal species that have a dietary requirement for vitamin C, such as humans, this results in a condition called *scurvy*. Clinical signs of scurvy include impaired wound healing, capillary bleeding, anemia, and faulty bone formation. Bone abnormalities that are associated with scurvy are the result of impaired cartilage synthesis.

With the exception of humans and a few other animal species, all animals are capable of producing adequate levels of endogenous vitamin C and therefore do not have a dietary requirement for this vitamin. Ascorbic acid is produced in the liver from either glucose or galactose through the glucuronate pathway. The adult dog produces approximately 40 milligrams per kilogram (mg/kg) body weight of ascorbate each day.[42] This is a relatively low amount compared to other mammalian species. However, controlled research studies in the dog have shown that this species does not require an exogenous source of vitamin C for normal development and maintenance.[43-45] Similarly, no requirement for dietary ascorbic acid has been demonstrated to exist in the cat.[11,46]

In recent years a number of breeders, dog show enthusiasts, and pet owners have been routinely administering high levels of supplemental vitamin C to their dogs' diets in the hopes of preventing or curing certain developmental skeletal disorders. To date, no controlled research studies have been published that show any efficacy of supplemental ascorbic acid in this role. On the other hand, a substantial amount of evidence exists that directly refutes this claim.[47,48] Currently the use of high amounts of supplemental vitamin C in the diets of healthy dogs and cats is not recommended and may even be contraindicated (see Section 5, pp. 300–301).

CHAPTER 6

Minerals

M inerals are inorganic elements that are essential for the body's metabolic processes. Only about 4% of an animal's total body weight is comprised of mineral matter; however, like the vitamins, the presence of these elements is essential for life. A general classification scheme divides minerals into two groups, macrominerals and microminerals. *Macrominerals* are those minerals that occur in appreciable amounts in the body and account for most of the body's mineral content. They include calcium, phosphorus, magnesium, sulfur, and the electrolytes sodium, potassium, and chloride. *Microminerals*, often referred to as the trace elements, include a larger number of minerals that are present in the body in very small amounts. These minerals are required in very small quantities in the diet.

Minerals have a variety of functions in the body. They activate enzymatically catalyzed reactions, provide skeletal support, aid in nerve transmission and muscle contractions, serve as components of certain transport proteins and hormones, and function in water and electrolyte balance. Significant interrelationships exist between many of the mineral elements that can affect mineral absorption, metabolism, and functioning. Specifically, the presence of excesses or deficiencies of some minerals can significantly affect the body's ability to use other minerals in the diet. As a result, the level of most minerals in the diet should be considered in relation to other components of the diet with a goal of achieving an optimal overall dietary balance. Although most of the minerals will be discussed separately in this section, the importance of these interrelationships will be addressed when they are of practical significance to the nutrition of dogs and cats. A summary of food sources and signs of mineral deficiency and excess are shown in Table 6-1.

TABLE 6-1
Mineral Deficiencies, Excesses, and Major Dietary Sources

MINERAL	DEFICIENCY	EXCESS	SOURCES
Calcium	Rickets, osteomalacia, nutritional secondary hyperparathyroidism	Impaired skeletal development, contributes to other mineral deficiencies	Dairy products, poultry and meat meals, bone
Phosphorus	Same as calcium deficiency	Causes calcium deficiency	Meat, poultry, fish
Magnesium	Soft-tissue calcification, enlargement of long bone metaphysis, neuromuscular irritability	Dietary excess unlikely, absorption is regulated according to needs	Soybeans, corn, cereal grains, bone meals
Sulfur	Not reported	Not reported	Meat, poultry, fish
Iron	Hypochromic microcytic anemia	Dietary excess unlikely, absorption is regulated according to needs	Organ meats
Copper	Hypochromic microcytic anemia, impaired skeletal growth	Inherited disorder of copper metabolism causes liver disease	Organ meats
Zinc	Dermatoses, hair depigmentation, growth retardation, reproductive failure	Causes calcium and copper deficiency	Beef liver, dark poultry meat, milk, egg yolks, legumes
Manganese	Dietary deficiency unlikely, impaired skeletal growth, reproductive failure	Dietary excess unlikely	Meat, poultry, fish
Iodine	Dietary deficiency unlikely, goiter, growth retardation, reproductive failure	Dietary excess unlikely, goiter	Fish, beef, liver
Selenium	Dietary deficiency unlikely, skeletal and cardiac myopathies	Dietary excess unlikely, necrotizing myocarditis, toxic hepatitis and nephritis	Grains, meat, poultry
Cobalt	Dietary deficiency unlikely, vitamin B_{12} deficiency, anemia	Not reported	Fish, dairy products

CALCIUM AND PHOSPHORUS

Calcium and phosphorus are usually discussed together because their metabolism and the homeostatic mechanisms that control their levels within the body are closely interrelated. Calcium is a principal inorganic component of bone. As much as 99% of the body's calcium is found in the skeleton; the remaining 1% is distributed throughout the extracellular and intracellular fluids. Phosphorus is also an important component of bone. Approximately 85% of the body's phosphorus is found in inorganic combination with calcium as hydroxyapatite in bones and teeth. Most of the remaining portion of this mineral is found in the soft tissues in combination with organic substances.

The calcium in bone provides structural integrity to the skeleton and also contributes to the maintenance of proper blood calcium levels through ongoing resorption and deposition. The calcium in bone tissue is not in a static state but is constantly being mobilized and deposited as bone growth and maintenance take place and as the body's needs for plasma calcium fluctuate. The level of circulating plasma calcium is strictly controlled through homeostatic mechanisms and is independent of an animal's dietary intake of calcium. Circulating calcium has essential roles in nerve impulse transmission, muscle contraction, blood coagulation, the activation of certain enzyme systems, the maintenance of normal cell-membrane permeability and transport, and cardiac function.

Phosphorus that is present in bone is found primarily in combination with calcium in the compound called hydroxyapatite. Like calcium, this phosphorus lends structural support to the skeleton and is also released into the bloodstream in response to homeostatic mechanisms. The phosphorus that is found in the soft tissues of the body has a wide number of functions and is involved in almost all of the body's metabolic processes. It is a constituent of cellular deoxyribonucleic acid (DNA) and ribonucleic acid (RNA), of several B-vitamin coenzymes, and of the cell membrane's phospholipids, which are important for regulating the transport of solutes into and out of cells. Phosphorus is also necessary for the phosphorylation reactions that are part of many oxidative pathways of the metabolism of the energy-containing nutrients. Phosphorus is a component of the high-energy phosphate bonds of adenosine triphosphate (ATP), adenosine diphosphate, and cyclic adenosine monophosphate.

As mentioned previously, the body has several strictly controlled homeostatic mechanisms that are designed to maintain a constant level of circulating plasma calcium. These mechanisms involve the parathyroid hormone (PTH) and calcitonin and active vitamin D, or calcitriol. PTH is released into the bloodstream in response to a slight decrease in plasma calcium. This hormone stimulates the synthesis of active vitamin D in the kidney and increases the resorption of calcium and phosphorus from bone. It also works on the kidney tubules to increase calcium resorption and decrease phosphorus resorption, resulting in increased retention of calcium in the body and increased losses of urinary phosphate. In turn, the active vitamin D produced by the kidney in response to PTH acts at the site of the intestine to increase the absorption of dietary cal-

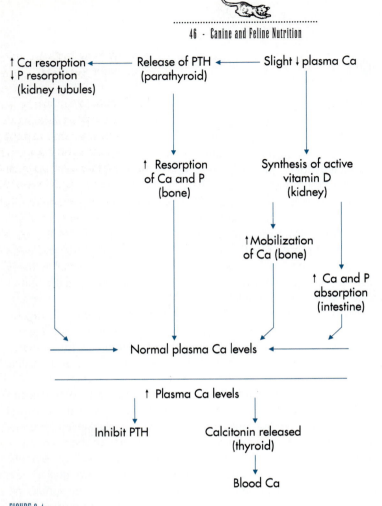

↑ Ca resorption ◄——— Release of PTH ◄——— Slight ↓ plasma Ca
↓ P resorption   (parathyroid)
(kidney tubules)

↑ Resorption   Synthesis of active
of Ca and P   vitamin D
(bone)   (kidney)

↑ Mobilization
of Ca (bone)

↑ Ca and P
absorption
(intestine)

————————► Normal plasma Ca levels ◄————

↑ Plasma Ca levels

Inhibit PTH   Calcitonin released
(thyroid)

Blood Ca

FIGURE 6-1
Regulation of calcium and phosphorus balance

cium and phosphorus. In conjunction with PTH, vitamin D also enhances the mobilization of calcium from bone by increasing the activity of osteoclasts. Overall, the net action of PTH is to increase serum concentration of calcium and decrease the serum concentration of phosphorus. The net effect of active vitamin D is to increase levels of both serum calcium and phosphorus (Figure 6-1).

When the blood calcium level is normal, PTH secretion is inhibited through a negative feedback mechanism, and calcitonin, a hormone produced by the parafollicular cells (C cells) of the thyroid gland, is released. Calcitonin functions to reduce blood calcium levels by acting primarily to increase osteoblastic activity and decrease osteoclastic activity in bone tissue. The end result is a decrease in calcium mobilization from the skeleton. Calcitonin is also released in response to hypercalcemia and the release of certain hormones, such as gastrin. Under normal physiological circumstances, PTH and active vitamin D are the most important regulators of calcium homeostasis, with calcitonin playing a more minor role. However, calcitonin may be of increased importance in the normal homeostatic mechanisms of calcium regulation during growth, pregnancy, and lactation.

In addition to having common homeostatic mechanisms in the body, calcium and phosphorus also have an important relationship to each other within the diet. Once adequate levels of calcium and phosphorus have been included in the diet, it is important to consider the ratio of the amount of calcium to phosphorus. Excess dietary calcium forms an insoluble complex with phosphorus, resulting in decreased phosphorus absorption. Similarly, high levels of phosphorus or phytate in the diet can inhibit calcium absorption. Phytate is a phosphorus-containing compound found in the outer husks of cereal grains. Although this compound is high in phosphorus, the mineral is poorly available to the body. The recommended ratio of calcium to phosphorus in pet foods is between 1.2:1 to 1.4:1 in dogs and 0.9:1 to 1.1:1 in cats.[7,11,49] Feeding animals foods that have an improper calcium/phosphorus ratio or supplementing balanced foods with high amounts of either one of these minerals can lead to calcium or phosphorus imbalance. Such problems are usually manifested as skeletal disease in growing and adult animals (see Section 5, pp. 296–300).

Foods vary greatly in their calcium content. Dairy products and legumes contain high amounts, but cereal grains, meat, and organ tissues contain very little calcium. Phosphorus, on the other hand, is widely distributed in foods. Foods that contain both phosphorus and calcium include dairy products and legumes. Fish, meats, poultry, and organ meats are also very rich sources of phosphorus. However, these foods are very deficient in calcium, and so their inclusion in the diets of dogs and cats must be balanced by a dietary source of calcium to ensure that an adequate calcium/phosphorus ratio is still maintained.

MAGNESIUM

Although magnesium is a macromineral, its amount in the body is much lower than that of calcium and phosphorus. Approximately 60% to 70% of the magnesium found in the body exists in the form of phosphates and carbonates in bone. Most of the remaining magnesium is found within cells, and a very small portion of the body's magnesium is present in the extracellular fluid. In addition to its role in providing structure to the skeleton, magnesium functions in a number of metabolic reactions. A magnesium-ATP complex is often the form of ATP that is used as a substrate in many of these processes. As a cation in the intracellular fluid, magnesium is essential for the cellular metabolism of both carbohydrate and protein. Protein synthesis also requires the presence of ionized magnesium. Balanced in the extracellular fluids with calcium, sodium, and potassium, magnesium allows proper transmission of nerve impulses and muscle contraction.

Magnesium is widespread in food sources and is abundant in whole grains, legumes, and dairy products. A deficiency of this mineral is not common in dogs and cats. However, excess magnesium in the diets of cats has been implicated as having a possible causal role in the occurrence of feline lower urinary tract disease (see Section 6, pp. 361–363).

SULFUR

Sulfur is required by the body for the synthesis of a number of sulfur-containing compounds. These include chondroitin sulfate, a mucopolysaccharide found in cartilage, the hormone insulin, and the anticoagulant heparin. As part of the amino acid cysteine, sulfur is found in the regulatory tripeptide glutathione. Glutathione is present in all cells and functions with the enzyme glutathione peroxidase to protect cells against the destructive effects of peroxides. It may also have a role in the transport of amino acids across cell membranes. In addition, sulfur is a constituent of the two B vitamins biotin and thiamin. Within the body, sulfur exists almost entirely as a component of organic compounds. The largest proportion of the body's sulfur is found within proteins as a component of the sulfur-containing amino acids cystine and methionine.

Most dietary sulfur is provided by methionine and cystine. Inorganic sulfates present in the diet are very poorly absorbed by the body and do not contribute an appreciable amount of sulfur. Sulfur deficiency has not been demonstrated in either dogs or cats, and it is believed that diets containing adequate amounts of the sulfur-containing amino acids will provide adequate amounts of sulfur.

IRON

Iron is present in all body cells, but the largest proportion of the body's iron is found as a component of the protein molecules hemoglobin and myoglobin. Hemoglobin is found in red blood cells and transports oxygen from the lungs to the tissues; myoglobin binds oxygen for immediate use by muscle cells. Iron is also a cofactor for several other enzymes and is a component of the cytochrome enzymes, which function in hydrogen ion transport during cellular respiration.

Dietary iron is poorly absorbed by most animals. Approximately 5% to 10% of the iron that is present in the diet is absorbed by the body.[50,51] The amount of iron that is absorbed is effected by several factors, including the body's need for the mineral, the environment of the intestinal lumen, and the type of foods that are fed. Iron that is in the ferrous state ($+2$) is more readily absorbed than iron that is in the ferric ($+3$) state. Therefore an acidic (reducing) environment in the intestine generally enhances iron absorption. Similarly, heme iron, which originates from the hemoglobin and myoglobin in animal food sources, is better absorbed than nonheme iron, which is found in plant sources and some animal foods. Low stores of iron in the body and increased metabolic need, such as during growth and gestation, result in increased efficiency of iron absorption. Dietary factors that can inhibit iron absorption include the presence of phytate, phosphates, and oxalates in the diet and the intake of excess dietary zinc.[52,53]

Iron is transported in the bloodstream bound to a transport protein called transferrin and is stored in tissues bound to two other proteins, ferritin and hemosiderin. Ferritin and transferrin are also involved in the regulation of iron absorption and transport. Chief storage sites for iron in the body are the liver, spleen, and bone marrow. Most animals are very efficient at conserving iron, so losses of this mineral from the body are minimal. The iron of hemoglobin is recycled and reused when red blood cells are catabolized and only minute amounts are lost by renal excretion. As a result, the requirement for iron only increases drastically during periods of unusual blood loss, such as parturition, major surgery, injury, or in severe parasitic infections or gastrointestinal disease. Iron deficiency results in a hypochromic, microcytic anemia, which is often manifested clinically by fatigue and depression. Conversely, iron, like most trace elements, is toxic if ingested in excessive amounts.

Organ meats such as liver and kidney are the richest sources of iron; meat, egg yolk, fish, legumes, and whole grains also provide adequate amounts. All of the iron in plants and approximately 60% of the iron in animal foods is in the form of nonheme iron, which is not absorbed as efficiently as heme iron. Anemia as a result of a dietary deficiency of iron is extremely rare in dogs and cats. Chronic blood loss that occurs during severe parasitic infections or hemorrhage is more likely to be the cause of iron deficiency in these species.

COPPER

The metabolism and functions of copper are closely tied to those of iron. Copper is necessary for normal absorption and transport of dietary iron. Along with iron, copper is essential for the normal formation of hemoglobin. Most of the copper that is found in blood is bound to the plasma protein ceruloplasmin. This protein is a copper-dependent ferroxidase that functions as a carrier of copper and in the oxidation of plasma iron, which is necessary for binding to transferrin. Ceruloplasmin may also be involved in the mobilization of iron from storage sites in the liver. As a component of several different metalloenzymes, copper is required for the conversion of the amino acid tyrosine to the pigment melanin, for the synthesis of the connective tissues collagen and elastin, and for the production of ATP in the cytochrome oxidase system. Another copper metalloenzyme, superoxide dismutase, functions to protect cells from damage by superoxide radicals. Copper is also necessary for normal osteoblast activity during skeletal development.

The highest concentration of copper in the body is found in the liver. After absorption from the intestine, copper is transported through the portal vein to the liver complexed with the plasma protein albumin. Metallothioneins, small–molecular-weight cytoplasmic proteins, bind copper and are involved in regulating its transport into the liver. Copper is stored in the liver, where it is incorporated into ceruloplasmin and other proteins for use by the body. Excess copper is excreted in the bile.

Not surprisingly, copper deficiency results in a hypochromic, microcytic anemia that is similar to that seen with iron deficiency. Other signs of deficiency include depigmentation of colored hair coat and impaired skeletal growth in young animals. Although copper deficiency is not common in dogs and cats, an inherited disorder of copper metabolism that results in copper toxicosis occurs in several different breeds of dogs (see Section 6, pp. 339–340).

Zinc

The trace mineral zinc is widely distributed in many tissues of the body, and its actions influence carbohydrate, lipid, protein, and nucleic acid metabolism. Zinc is a component of many of the metalloenzymes, which include carbonic anhydrase, lactic dehydrogenase, alkaline phosphatase, carboxypeptidase, and aminopeptidase. Zinc also functions as a cofactor in the synthesis of DNA, RNA, and protein; it is essential for normal cellular immunity and reproductive functioning. Like iron, the absorption of zinc from the diet is effected by several factors. The body's efficiency of zinc absorption increases with increasing need for this mineral. Animal sources of zinc, such as meat and eggs, are generally more readily absorbed than are plant sources. Dietary compounds that act to decrease zinc absorption include excess levels of calcium, iron, copper, fiber, and the presence of phytates.[54] Metallothioneins have a high affinity for binding to zinc and are involved in the regulation of zinc absorption and metabolism.

Because of its role in protein synthesis, zinc deficiency is usually associated with growth retardation in young animals. Other clinical signs include anorexia, hypogeusia in humans (diminished taste acuity), testicular atrophy, impaired reproductive performance, immune system dysfunction, conjunctivitis, and the development of skin lesions. In dogs and cats, skin and hair coat changes are usually the first clinical signs of zinc deficiency. These have been described as dull, coarse hair coat and skin lesions that show parakeratosis and hyperkeratinization.[55] Although not common, naturally occurring zinc-responsive dermatoses have been identified in companion animals.[56–58] In addition, a genetically influenced abnormality in zinc absorption and metabolism may exist in some breeds, resulting in an increased zinc requirement in effected animals (see Section 6, pp. 340–341).

Manganese

Like most of the other microminerals, manganese functions as a component of several cell enzymes that catalyze metabolic reactions. A large portion of manganese is located in the mitochondrion of cells where it activates a number of metal-enzyme complexes that regulate nutrient metabolism. These complexes include pyruvate carboxylase and superoxide dismutase. Manganese is also necessary for normal bone development and reproduction. Foods that are good sources of manganese include legumes and whole-grain cereals. Animal-based ingredients are generally poor sources of manganese. Naturally occurring manganese deficiency has not been reported in either dogs or cats. However, manganese deficiency is characterized in other species by decreased growth, impaired reproduction, and disturbances in lipid metabolism.

Iodine

Iodine is required by the body for the synthesis of the hormones thyroxine and tri-iodothyronine by the thyroid gland. Thyroxine stimulates cellular oxidative processes and regulates basal metabolic rate. The principal sign of iodine deficiency is goiter, an enlargement of the thyroid gland. Cretinism, a syndrome characterized by failure to grow, skin lesions, central nervous system dysfunction, and multiple skeletal deformities, can occur in young animals that are fed a severely deficient diet. However, naturally occurring iodine deficiency does not commonly occur in dogs or cats.

Selenium

As an essential component of the enzyme glutathione peroxidase, selenium protects cell membranes from oxidative damage. Glutathione peroxidase deactivates lipid peroxides that are formed during oxidation of cell-membrane lipids. In this role, selenium has a close relationship with vitamin E and the sulfur-containing amino acids methionine and cystine. Vitamin E protects the polyunsaturated fatty acids in cell membranes from oxidative damage, and thus it prevents the release of lipid peroxides. By reducing the number of peroxides that are formed, vitamin E spares the cellular use of selenium. The sulfur-containing amino acids are important in selenium metabolism because they are necessary for the formation of glutathione peroxidase. Sources of selenium include cereal grains, meat, and fish. Because selenium is abundant in foods, naturally occurring deficiencies are not a problem in dogs and cats. However, like other trace elements, the ingestion of excess selenium is toxic.

Cobalt

Cobalt is a constituent of vitamin B_{12}. Currently no function for cobalt in the body has been identified. Additional cobalt does not appear to be required by dogs and cats when their diet contains adequate amounts of vitamin B_{12}.

Other Microminerals

There are several trace elements that have been shown to be required by other species of mammals, but they have not yet been demonstrated to be essential for dogs and cats. These include molybdenum, tin, fluorine, nickel, silicon, vanadium, and arsenic. It is highly likely that dogs and cats also require these elements, even though minimum requirements have not yet been established. These minerals are widespread in food ingredients and are required by the body in very minute amounts. Conversely, all have been shown to be highly toxic when fed in large doses.

Electrolytes: Potassium, Sodium, and Chloride

Potassium is the main cation that is found in the intracellular fluid. Approximately one third of the cell's potassium is bound to protein and the rest is found in the ionized form. Ionized potassium within cells provides the osmotic force that maintains proper fluid volume. Cellular potassium is also required for numerous enzymatic reactions. The small concentration of potassium present in the extracellular fluid aids in the transmission of nerve impulses and the contraction of muscle fibers. The maintenance of potassium balance is especially important for the normal functioning of heart muscle. Many foods contain potassium. Meats, poultry, and fish are all rich sources, and whole-grain cereals and most vegetables also contain high amounts. Because of the abundance of potassium in most foods, potassium deficiency that is of dietary origin is highly unusual in dogs and cats.

Ionized sodium is the major cation found in the extracellular fluid. Sodium in this compartment provides the primary osmotic force that maintains the aqueous environment of the extracellular fluid. It functions in conjunction with other ions to maintain the normal irritability of nerve cells and the contractibility of muscle fibers. Sodium is also necessary for the maintenance of the permeability of cell membranes. The sodium "pump" controls electrolyte balance between the intracellular and extracellular fluid compartments. The chief source of sodium in the diet is in the form of table salt, sodium chloride, which is used for food preservation in most commercially prepared foods. In addition to processed products, foods that have a naturally high sodium content include dairy products, meat, poultry, fish, and egg white. Because of its abundance in foods, sodium deficiency is not a problem in dogs and cats. Conversely, excess sodium intake has been implicated as a possible causal factor in hypertension in some human populations.[59,60] These observations, coupled with the high sodium content of some commercial pet foods, has led investigators to examine the effects of high sodium intake in dogs. Results indicate that hypertension is not a common problem in this species. Moreover, dogs appear to be physiologically resistant to excess salt intake.[61,62]

Chloride ion accounts for about two thirds of the total anions present in the extracellular fluid. It is necessary for the regulation of normal osmotic pressure, water balance, and acid-base balance in the body. It is also necessary for the formation of hydrochloric acid (HCl) in the stomach. HCl is required for the activation of several gastric enzymes and for the initiation of digestion in the stomach. Because most of the chloride that animals consume is associated with sodium, the amount consumed daily generally parallels sodium intake. Like potassium and sodium, dietary chloride deficiency has not been found to be a common problem in dogs and cats.

CHAPTER 7

Digestion and Absorption

The process of digestion breaks down the large, complex molecules of many nutrients into their simplest, most soluble forms so that absorption and use by the body can take place (Table 7-1). The two basic types of action that are involved in this process are mechanical digestion and chemical, or enzymatic, digestion. Mechanical digestion involves the physical mastication, mixing, and movement of food through the gastrointestinal tract. Chemical digestion involves splitting the chemical bonds of the complex nutrients through enzymatically catalyzed hydrolysis. The three major types of foods that require digestion are fats, carbohydrates, and proteins. Most of the fat in food is hydrolyzed to glycerol, free fatty acids, and some monoglycerides and diglycerides before absorption takes place. Complex carbohydrates are broken down to the simple sugars, glucose, galactose, and fructose. Protein molecules are hydrolyzed to single amino acid units and some dipeptides. As dietary nutrients are digested, they are transported down the digestive tract by a series of contractions of the muscular walls of the gastrointestinal tract. The process of digestion and absorption begins when food first enters the mouth and ends with the excretion of waste products and undigested food particles in the feces.

MOUTH

In all species, the mouth functions to bring food into the body, initiate physical mastication, and mix the food with saliva. Saliva is secreted in response to the sight and smell of food. It acts as a lubricant to facilitate both chewing and swallowing and also serves

TABLE 7-1
Digestive End Products of Carbohydrate, Protein, and Fat

NUTRIENT	ENZYMES	END PRODUCTS
Carbohydrates	Amylase Lactase Sucrase Maltase	Glucose Galactose Fructose
Proteins	Dipeptidase Amino peptidase Pepsinogen Pepsin Nucleotidase Nucleosidase Trypsin Chymotrypsin Carboxypeptidase Nuclease	Dipeptides Single amino acids
Fats	Intestinal lipase Pancreatic lipase	Glycerol Free fatty acids Monoglycerides, diglycerides

to solubilize the dietary components that stimulate the taste buds and impart flavor to food. Compared to many ruminant and herbivorous species that thoroughly masticate their food, dogs and cats often swallow large boluses of food with little or no chewing. An examination of the teeth of dogs and cats presents important distinctions between these two species. Although domesticated dogs and cats have the same number of incisor and canine teeth (six incisors and two canines on the top and bottom jaws), the mouth of the dog contains more premolars and molars than does the cat's mouth. These teeth are associated with an increased capacity to chew and crush food, which is indicative of a diet containing a larger proportion of plant material. Thus the dentition of dogs is suggestive of a more omnivorous diet than is the dentition of cats, which is more typical of the pattern seen in most obligate carnivores.[63] Although both dogs and cats are "meat-eaters," the dog has evolved to consume a diet that is slightly more omnivorous in nature than that of the cat.

ESOPHAGUS

Food passes from the mouth to the stomach through the esophagus. The cells of the mucosal lining of the esophagus secrete mucus, which further aids in lubricating food as it passes to the stomach. As the food reaches the end of the esophagus, the cardiac sphincter, a ring of muscle at the junction between the esophagus and stomach, relaxes to allow food to enter the stomach. This ring relaxes in response to the peristaltic movements of the esophagus. It then immediately constricts after food has passed to prevent reflux of the stomach contents back into the lower esophagus.

STOMACH

The stomach acts as a reservoir for the body, allowing food to be ingested as a meal rather than continuously throughout the day. In addition to its storage function, the stomach also initiates the chemical digestion of protein, mixes food with gastric secretions, and regulates the entry of food into the small intestine. Gastric glands, which are located in the mucosal lining of the corpus portion of the stomach, secrete mucus, HCl, and the proteolytic enzyme pepsinogen. Mucous secretions protect the gastric mucosa and also lubricate the ingested food. HCl is necessary to maintain a proper pH for the occurrence of enzymatic action. It functions to slightly alter the composition of ingested fat and protein in preparation for further action by digestive enzymes in the small intestine. Along with previously formed pepsin, HCl also converts pepsinogen to the enzyme pepsin. This enzyme initiates hydrolysis of protein molecules to smaller polypeptide units.

Both neurological and hormonal stimuli are important for the secretion of HCl and mucus by the stomach. Neurological stimuli are produced in response to the anticipation of eating, the sight and smell of food, and the presence of food in the stomach. In addition, psychological stimuli such as fear, stress, and anxiety can effect gastric secretions and gastrointestinal functioning in animals. The hormone gastrin is released in response to the presence of food and distention of the stomach. It is produced by mucosal glands in the antrum portion of the stomach. Gastrin stimulates the secretion of HCl and mucus and also increases gastric motility. Another local hormone, enterogastrone, is produced by glands located in the duodenal mucosa. Enterogastrone is secreted in response to the presence of fat entering the duodenum and counteracts gastrin's activity by inhibiting acid production and gastric motility.

Peristaltic movements of the stomach slowly mix the ingested food with gastric secretions, preparing it for entry into the small intestine. The mucosal cells located in the antral portion of the stomach secrete a mucus that has a more alkaline pH and is low in digestive enzymes. Thorough mixing in this portion results in the production of a semifluid mass of food called chyme. Chyme must pass through the pyloric sphincter to enter the small intestine for further digestion. Like the cardiac sphincter, the pyloric sphincter is a ring of muscle that is usually in a constricted state. This ring relaxes in response to the strong peristaltic contractions that originate in the stomach and travel toward the intestine. While open, this sphincter allows small amounts of chyme to enter the duodenum. The pyloric sphincter serves to control the rate of passage of food from the stomach into the small intestine. The rate of gastric emptying is affected by the osmotic pressure, particle size, and viscosity of the chyme, as well as the degree of gastric acidity and volume. In general, large meals have a slower rate of emptying than small meals, liquids leave the stomach faster than solids, and high-fat meals cause a decrease in stomach-emptying rate. Diets that contain soluble fiber as a fiber source cause a decreased rate of stomach emptying compared to diets that contain insoluble dietary fiber.

SMALL INTESTINE

Before reaching the small intestine, most of the digestive processes that have occurred in dogs and cats have been mechanical in nature. The chyme that is delivered through the pyloric sphincter to the duodenum is a semifluid mass made up of food particles mixed with gastric secretions. Carbohydrates and fats are almost unchanged in composition, but the protein in the food has been partially hydrolyzed to smaller polypeptides. Even this digestion is not crucial, however, because the enzymes of the small intestine are capable of completely digesting intact dietary protein. Therefore the major task of chemical digestion and the subsequent absorption of nutrients occurs in the small intestine.

Further mechanical digestion also occurs in the small intestine through the coordinated contractions of its muscle layers. These movements thoroughly mix the food mass with intestinal secretions, increase the exposure of digested food particles to the mucosal surface, and slowly propel the food mass through the intestinal tract. Constant sweeping motions of the intestinal villi, which line the surface of the mucosa, mix the chyme that is in contact with the intestinal wall and increases the efficiency of absorption of digested particles. After food has entered the small intestine, large quantities of mucus are secreted by the Brunner's glands, which are located immediately inside the duodenum. This mucus protects the intestinal mucosa from irritation and erosion by the gastric acids that are entering from the stomach and further lubricates the food mass.

Both the pancreas and the glands that are located in the duodenal mucosa secrete enzymes into the intestinal lumen that chemically digest fat, carbohydrate, and protein. Enzymes that are secreted by the intestinal cells include intestinal lipase, amino peptidase, dipeptidase, nucleotidase, nucleosidase, and enterokinase. Intestinal lipase converts fat to monoglycerides, diglycerides, glycerol, and free fatty acids. Amino peptidase breaks the peptide bond located at the N-terminal of the protein molecule, slowly releasing single amino acids from the protein chain. Dipeptidase breaks the peptide bond of dipeptides to release two single amino acid units. Both nucleosidase and nucleotidase hydrolyze nucleoproteins to their constituent bases and pentose sugars. Lastly, enterokinase converts inactive trypsinogen, a proenzyme secreted from the pancreas, to its active form. The final digestion of carbohydrate takes place at the brush border of the small intestine. The cells of the brush border secrete the enzymes maltase, lactase, and sucrase, which convert the disaccharides maltose, lactose, and sucrose to their constituent monosaccharides, glucose, fructose, and galactose.

Protease enzymes that are secreted by the pancreas include trypsin, chymotrypsin, carboxypeptidase, and nuclease. Several of these are secreted in an inactive form and are activated by other components in the small intestine after release. In addition, pancreatic lipase and amylase are released into the intestinal lumen and respectively function to hydrolyze dietary fat and starch to smaller units. Cholesterol esterase secreted by the pancreas catalyzes the formation of cholesterol esters. Free cholesterol must be esterified to fatty acids to facilitate its absorption into the body. The pancreas also secretes a large volume of bicarbonate salts into the small intestine. These salts function to neutralize the acid chyme and provide the proper pH for the digestive enzymes to function.

Bile is another important component of nutrient digestion in the small intestine. It is produced by the liver and stored in the gallbladder. Bile's primary function in the small intestine is the emulsification of dietary fat and the activation of certain lipases. These two processes result in the formation of very small, water-soluble globules called *micelles*. The formation of micelles results in an increased surface area for the action of lipase and also arranges lipid molecules into water-miscible forms that are able to gain access to the aqueous layer covering the microvilli, ultimately facilitating absorption of fat into the body.

Hormonal control of digestion in the small intestine involves several components. Secretin is produced by the mucosa of the upper portion of the duodenum in response to the entry of acidic chyme into the duodenum. It stimulates the release of bicarbonate from the pancreas and controls the rate of bile flow from the gallbladder. Cholecystokinin is also released from this portion of the intestinal mucosa in response to the presence of fat in the food mass. This hormone stimulates contraction of the gallbladder, resulting in a release of bile into the intestinal lumen. Cholecystokinin, also referred to as pancreozymin, also stimulates secretion of the pancreatic enzymes.

In dogs and cats, the chemical digestion of food is completed in the small intestine. Digestible protein, carbohydrate, and fat are hydrolyzed to amino acids, dipeptides, monosaccharides, glycerol, free fatty acids, and monoglycerides and diglycerides, respectively. As these small units are produced, they are absorbed by the body along with dietary vitamins and minerals. Absorption involves the transfer of digested nutrients from the intestinal lumen to the blood or lymphatic system for delivery to tissues throughout the body. Like digestion, the greatest proportion of absorption takes place in the small intestine.

The structure of the inner wall of the small intestine is designed to provide a high amount of surface area for the absorption of nutrients. The mucosal folds, villi, and microvilli of the mucosa produce an absorptive inner surface area that is approximately 600 times that of the outer serosal layer of the intestine. Villi are fingerlike projections that cover the convoluted folds of the mucosa. Each individual villus contains a vascular network of venous and arterial capillaries and a lymph vessel called a lacteal. These function to transport absorbed nutrients to either the portal or lymphatic circulations. The surface of each villus is covered with numerous, minute projections called microvilli. These are often collectively referred to as the brush border of the small intestine. The cells lining the luminal surface of the villi are highly specialized absorptive cells called enterocytes. These cells have a life span of only 2 to 3 days, during which they absorb nutrients from the lumen of the small intestine. Old cells are continually sloughed off and excreted in the feces, giving these cells one of the highest turnover rates of any tissue in the body.

Nutrient absorption is accomplished in the small intestine through several processes. Some small molecules are absorbed by passive diffusion according to the osmotic gradient. For example, electrolytes and water molecules both flow across the mucosa in response to osmotic pressure. Facilitated diffusion involves the transport of large molecules across the cellular membrane in concurrence with the pressure gradient. Carrier proteins located in the membrane of the enterocytes facilitate transport of these nutrients into the cells. In contrast, active transport involves the transport of nutrient

molecules across the intestinal epithelial membrane against a concentration gradient. This transport mechanism differs from passive diffusion in that more energy is required to transport materials against a concentration gradient. For example, the most common type of active transport mechanism involves a membrane protein carrier coupled with the active transport of sodium (the sodium pump).

Although some passive diffusion is believed to occur, most simple carbohydrates are absorbed by the body by an active process that is linked to sodium transport and uses a specific carrier protein. Single amino acids and some dipeptides and tripeptides are also absorbed in this manner. Small peptides that are absorbed into the cell are immediately hydrolyzed to single amino acid units before being released into the portal circulation. Sugars and amino acids are absorbed into the villus capillaries and from there enter the portal vein, which transports these nutrients to the liver. Absorption of fat involves the interaction of the fat-containing micelles with the aqueous layer surrounding the brush border. Micelles contain bile acids, monoglycerides, diglycerides, and long-chain fatty acids. Because they are water-miscible, the micelles are able to travel to the brush border where they are disrupted and their component fat particles are absorbed into the cell. The bile remains in the lumen and eventually moves down the intestine to be reabsorbed and recirculated back to the liver. Within the enterocyte, most of the fatty acids and glycerol are resynthesized into triglycerides, combined with cholesterol, phospholipid and protein, and released into the central lacteal as either chylomicrons or very-low–density lipoprotein transport particles. The central lacteal drains into the major lymph vessels and eventually enters the blood circulation near the heart.

The liver functions to further process the absorbed monosaccharides and amino acids that arrive through the portal circulation. Some monosaccharides are converted to the storage carbohydrate form, glycogen, and a certain quantity of glucose is secreted directly into the circulation. Some amino acids are released into the bloodstream, where they circulate to tissues for absorption into cells. Excess amino acids are either converted to other nonessential amino acids or are metabolized by the liver for energy.

Most minerals are absorbed by the body in an ionized form. The water-soluble vitamins are transported by passive diffusion, but some may be absorbed by an active process when the diet contains low levels. Vitamin B_{12} is unique in its requirement for an intrinsic factor for proper absorption. Fat-soluble vitamins are made soluble by combination with bile salts and are then absorbed by passive diffusion through the lipid phase of the mucosal cell membrane. In general, when there is normal fat absorption, there is normal fat-soluble vitamin absorption.

LARGE INTESTINE (COLON)

The contents of the small intestine enter the large intestine through the ileocecal valve. The *cecum* is an intestinal pocket located next to the junction of the colon and the small intestine. This portion of the intestine varies in size and functional capacity between

species of mammals. The cecum of nonruminant herbivores such as the horse and rabbit is relatively large and has a highly enhanced digestive capacity. Likewise, both the cecum and large intestine of the omnivorous pig are enlarged compared to those of the carnivorous species. Microbial digestion of dietary fiber in the cecum and colon of non-ruminant herbivores contributes significantly to nutrient intake and balance of these animals. In comparison, carnivorous species such as the cat and mink have a vestigial cecum, and the length of their large intestine is relatively short. Relative to body size, the dog's cecum is not as large as the pig's, but it is somewhat larger than the cat's.[63] This observation is consistent with the fact that the dog is adapted to consuming a diet that is more omnivorous in nature than is the diet of the cat. However, the extent to which the cecum and colon contribute bacterial digestion of dietary fiber in either of these species is probably still negligible compared to the amount that occurs in non-ruminant herbivore species. Although some volatile fatty acids (VFAs) are produced and absorbed in dogs and cats, the extent to which VFAs contribute to their energy and nutrient balance is probably negligible. There is recent evidence that the VFAs produced by bacterial digestion of fermentable fiber provides energy for intestinal mucosal cells and may contribute to intestinal health in dogs.[27]

A chief function of the large intestine in dogs and cats is the absorption of water and certain electrolytes. Unlike the small intestine, the large intestine has no villi and therefore has a lower capacity for absorption. Although it is able to efficiently absorb water and electrolytes, it has no mechanisms for active transport. Along with a large volume of water, sodium is absorbed into the body from the large intestine. As mentioned previously, the bacterial colonies of the colon are capable of digesting some of the indigestible fiber in the diet and other nutrients that have escaped digestion in the small intestine. The products of this bacterial digestion give the feces of dogs and cats their characteristic smell and color. Undigested food residues, sloughed cells, bacteria, and unabsorbed endogenous secretions make up the fecal matter that eventually reaches the rectum and is excreted from the body.

Fecal characteristics in dogs and cats can be significantly effected by the quantity and type of indigestible matter that is present in the animal's diet. Bacterial digestion of these materials produce various gases, volatile fatty acids, and other by-products. When protein reaches the large intestine in an undigested state, bacterial degradation results in the production of the amines indole and skatole. In addition, hydrogen sulfide gas is produced from the sulfur-containing amino acids of the undigested or poorly-digested protein. Hydrogen sulfide gas, indole, and skatole impart strong odors to fecal matter and intestinal gas. Certain types of carbohydrates found in legumes, such as soy beans, are resistant to digestion by the endogenous enzymes of the small intestine. These carbohydrates reach the colon and are attacked by bacteria, with the resultant production of intestinal gas (flatulence). Hydrogen, carbon dioxide, and methane gases are produced from the bacterial digestion of carbohydrates. The degree to which flatulence and strong fecal odors occur in dogs and cats that are fed poorly digested materials varies with the amounts and types that are fed and with the intestinal flora that is present in the colon of individual animals.

KEY POINTS

SECTION 1

Nutrition is the study of food, its nutrients, and other components, including an examination of the actions of specific nutrients, their interactions with each other, and their balance within a diet. The science of nutrition also studies ingestion, digestion, and absorption and use of nutrients. The six categories of nutrients—water, carbohydrates, proteins, fats, minerals, and vitamins—have specific functions and contribute to growth, body tissue maintenance, and optimal health.

Energy is needed by the body to perform metabolic work, which includes maintaining and synthesizing body tissues, engaging in physical work, and regulating normal body temperature. Because of its critical importance, energy is always the first requirement met by an animal's diet.

Although all companion animals have the ability to self-regulate their energy intake, some do not always do so, and obesity results. Free-choice feeding of highly palatable foods and a lack of appropriate exercise are frequently to blame. Portion-controlled feeding and appropriate levels of exercise are the best methods of controlling a pet's energy balance, growth rate, and weight.

The metabolizable energy (ME) of a diet or feed ingredient for a given species can be calculated by using one of three methods: (1) direct determination in feeding trials, (2) calculation method, and (3) extrapolation of data from other species. Although direct determination with feeding trials is the most accurate method, it is time-consuming and costly and requires large numbers of test animals. A quick and simple method of calculating the ME uses the minimum percentage of fat listed on the food's label in the following formula:

$$ME = 3.075 + 0.066 \text{ (Fat)}$$

Energy density (the number of calories provided by the food in a given weight or volume) is the most important factor in determining the quantity of food that a pet should eat each day. Energy density directly affects the amount of all other essential nutrients that an animal ingests.

Tip: Reading food labels and comparing contents of foods in the grocery store can be very confusing, as can be attempts to compare pet foods by reading labels. For example, when the protein content is expressed as a percentage of weight, merely reading the protein content printed on the label of a canned dog food (7% protein) and a dry dog food (27% protein) does not tell the whole story. But when a simple formula is applied to determine the protein as a percentage of calories, one can see that the protein content of the dry and canned foods in this example is almost exactly the same (see Table 1-2).

For an animal to survive, water is the single, most important nutrient for the body. Water within the cells is necessary for most metabolic processes and chemical reactions, it is important for temperature regulation, and it is an essential component of normal digestion.

Pets obtain water from food, metabolic water, and drinking water. If the water content of food is increased or decreased, most pets are naturally able to achieve water balance by increasing or decreasing their intake of drinking water.

Moderately fermentable fiber sources (as opposed to highly fermentable and non-fermentable fiber sources) that provide adequate levels of short-chain fatty acids and a source of bulk are the best fiber sources for cats and dogs. These sources contribute to the health of the large intestine.

Because carbohydrates provide an excellent energy source for the body, they should be provided adequately in the diet so that protein will be not be used for energy and can be used instead for tissue repair and growth.

Fat provides the most concentrated form of energy of all nutrients, is a source of essential fatty acids, and allows the absorption of fat-soluble vitamins. Fat also contributes to the palatability and acceptable texture of food. As fat content increases, so does the energy density of the diet. Portion-controlled feeding is usually the best method when feeding a well-balanced, energy-dense pet food containing moderate to high levels of fat (see Chapter 11).

Proteins are the major structural components of hair, feathers, skin, nails, tendons, ligaments, and cartilage. Proteins are enzymes essential for nutrient digestion, as are many hormones, such as insulin and glucagon. Blood proteins, such as hemoglobin, act as important carrier substances. The antibodies that enable the body to resist disease are composed of large protein molecules. Because the protein in the body is in a constant state of flux, a regular intake of dietary protein is necessary to maintain normal metabolic processes and provide for tissue maintenance and growth.

Like fats, protein content contributes to palatability and acceptability of food.

Tip: Although there are several laboratory tests available for evaluating the quality of protein in food, all have their limitations. In addition to the tests available, the quality of pet food protein should always be assessed by trials in which the food is fed to the animals for which it was developed. The true quality of a protein or proteins in food must also be evaluated on a long-term basis by assessing the overall health and vitality of the pet.

Most vitamins cannot be synthesized by the body and must be supplied in food. Well-balanced pet foods are formulated to provide the necessary supplementation. Vitamin C, however, is one vitamin that can be synthesized from glucose by dogs and cats. In contrast, humans must receive vitamin C from dietary sources.

Minerals are inorganic elements that comprise only about 4% of an animal's total body weight; nonetheless, the essential minerals must be present to sustain life.

An electrolyte is a substance that dissociates into ions when diffused or in solution and thus becomes capable of conducting electricity; an ionic solute.

Digestion and absorption actually begin in the mouth, with the mastication (chewing) of food and its mixture with saliva. Digestion continues throughout the gastrointestinal system and ends with the excretion of waste products and undigested food particles in the feces.

Most of the important tasks of chemical digestion and the subsequent absorption of nutrients occur in the small intestine.

In contrast to the small intestine, a primary function of the large intestine (colon) in dogs and cats is the absorption of water and certain electrolytes, especially sodium.

SECTION 1

REFERENCES

1. Cowgill GR: The energy factor in relation to food intake: experiments on the dog, *Am J Physiol* 85:45–64, 1928.
2. Durrer JL Hannon JP: Seasonal variations in caloric intake of dogs living in an arctic environment, *Am J Physiol* 202:375–384, 1962.
3. Romsos DR, Hornshus MJ, and Leveille GA: Influence of dietary fat and carbohydrate on food intake, body weight and body fat of adult dogs, *Pro Soc Exp Bio Med* 157:278–281, 1978.
4. Romsos DR, Belo PS, and Bennink MR: Effects of dietary carbohydrate, fat and protein on growth, body composition and blood metabolite levels in the dog, *J Nut* 106:1452–1464, 1976.
5. Romsos DR, Ferguson D: Regulation of protein intake in adult dogs, *J Am Vet Med Assoc* 182:41–43, 1983.
6. Edney ATB, and Smith AM: Study of obesity in dogs visiting veterinary practices in the United Kingdom, *Vet Rec* 118:391–396, 1986.
7. National Research Council: Nutrient requirements of dogs, Washington, DC, 1985, National Academy of Sciences, National Academy Press.
8. Harris LE: Biological energy interrelationships and glossary of energy terms, Washington, DC, 1966, National Academy of Sciences, National Academy Press.
9. Kendall PT, Burger IH, Smith PM: Methods of estimation of the metabolizable energy content of cat foods, *Fel Pract* 15:38–44, 1985.
10. Kuhlman G, Laflamme DP, Ballam JM: A simple method for estimating the metabolizable energy content of dry cat foods, *Fel Pract* 21:16–20, 1993.
11. National Research Council: Nutrient requirements of cats, Washington, DC, 1986, National Academy of Sciences, National Academy Press.
12. Hedhammar A: Nutrition as it relates to skeletal disease, Proceedings of the Kal Kan Symposium, Columbus, Ohio, 1980, pp 41–44.
13. Hedhammar A, Wu FM, Krook L, and others: Overnutrition and skeletal disease: an experimental study in growing Great Dane dogs, *Cornell Vet* 64(suppl 5):1–160, 1974.
14. Kasstrom H: Nutrition, weight gain and development of hip dysplasia, *Acta Radiol* 344 (suppl):135–179, 1975.
15. Lust G, Geary JC, Sheffy BE: Development of hip dysplasia in dogs, *Am J Vet Res* 34:87–91, 1973.
16. Bjorntorp P: The role of adipose tissue in human obesity. In Greenwood MRC, editor: Obesity: contemporary issues in clinical nutrition, New York, 1983, Churchill Livingstone, pp 17–24.
17. Bjorntorp P, and Sjostrom L: Number and size of fat cells in relation to metabolism in human obesity, Metabolism, 20:703–706, 1971.
18. Maynard LA, Loosli JK, Hintz HF, and others: Animal nutrition, 7, New York, 1979, McGraw-Hill.
19. Anderson RS: Water content in the diet of the dog, *Vet Ann* 21:171–178, 1981.
20. Burger IH, Blaza SE: Digestion, absorption, and dietary balance. In *Dog and cat nutrition*, ed 2, Oxford, England, 1988, Pergamon Press, pp 35–36.
21. Caldwell GT: Studies in water metabolism of the cat, *Physiol Zool*, 4:324–355, 1931.
22. Danowski TS, Elkinton JR, Winkler AW: The deleterious effect in dogs of a dry protein ration, *J Clin Invest* 23:816–823, 1944.
23. Prentiss PG, Wolf AV, Eddy HE: Hydropenia in cat and dog: ability of the cat to meet its water requirements solely from a diet of fish or meat, *Am J Physiol* 196:625–632, 1959.

24. Anderson RS: Water balance in the dog and cat, *J Sm Anim Pract* 23:588–598, 1982.
25. Wilde RO, Jansen T: The use of different sources of raw and heated starch in the ration of weaned kittens. In Burger IH, Rivers JPW, editors: *Nutrition of the dog and cat,* Cambridge, England, 1989, Cambridge University Press, pp 258–266.
26. van Soest PJ: The uniformity and nutritive availability of cellulose, *Fed Proc* 32:1804–1808, 1973.
27. Reinhart GA, Moxley RA, Clemens ET: Dietary fibre source and its effects on colonic microstructure and histopathology of beagle dogs. Abstract. Waltham Symposium on the Nutrition of Companion Animals. In Association with the 15th International Congress on Nutrition, Adelaide, Sept 23–25, 1993.
28. Sunvold GD, Fahey Jr GC, Merchen NR, and others: Fermentability of selected fibrous substrates by dog faecal microflora as influenced by diet. Abstract. Waltham Symposium on the Nutrition of Companion Animals. In Association with the 15th International Congress on Nutrition, Adelaide, Sept 23–25, 1993.
29. James WT, McCay CM: A study of food intake, activity, and digestive efficiency in different type dogs, *Am J Vet Res* 11:412–416, 1950.
30. Orr NWM: The food requirements of Antarctic sledge dogs. In Graham-Jones O, editor, *Canine and feline nutritional requirements,* London, 1965, pp 101–112.
31. Huber TL, Wilson RC, McGarity SA: Variations in digestibility of dry dog foods with identical label guaranteed analysis, *J Am Anim Hosp Assoc* 22:571–575, 1986.
32. Mead JF: Functions of the n-6 and n-3 polyunsaturated fatty acid acids. In Taylor TG, Jenkins NK, editors: *Proceedings of the XIII International Congress of Nutrition,* London, 1986, John Libbey Publishing, pp 346–349.
33. McClean JG, Monger EA: Factors determining the essential fatty acid requirements of the cat. In Burger IH, Rivers JPW, editors: *Nutrition of the dog and cat,* Cambridge, England, 1989, Cambridge University Press, pp 329–342.
34. Kane E, Morris JG, Rogers QR: Acceptability and digestibility by adult cats of diets made with various sources and levels of fat, *J Anim Sci* 53:1516–1523, 1981.
35. Brown RG: Protein in dog foods, *Can Vet J* 30:528–531, 1989.
36. Kronfeld DS: Protein quality and amino acid profiles of commercial dog foods, *J Am Anim Hosp Assoc* 18:679–683, 1982.
37. Oser BL: An integrated essential amino acid index for predicting the biological value of proteins. In *Protein and amino acid nutrition,* New York, 1959, Academic Press, pp 281–295.
38. Goodman DS: Vitamin A and retinoids in health and disease, *N Engl J Med* 310:1023–1031, 1984.
39. Hays KC: Comments on vitamin A, *Am J Clin Nutr* 22:1081–1084, 1969.
40. Gallop PM: Carboxylated calcium–binding proteins and vitamin K, *N Engl J Med* 302:1460–1465, 1980.
41. Ghosh HP, Sarkar PK, Guha BC: Distribution of the bound form of nicotinic acid in natural materials, *J Nutr* 79:451–458, 1963.
42. Belfield WO, Stone I: Megascorbic prophylaxis and megascorbic therapy: a new orthomolecular modality in veterinary medicine, *J Int Acad Prev Med* 2:10–25, 1975.
43. Innes JRM: Vitamin C requirements in the dog: attempts to produce experimental scurvy, *Report of the Cambridge Institute of Animal Pathology,* Cambridge, England, 1931, pp 143–161.
44. Naismith DH: Ascorbic acid requirements of the dog, *Proc Nutr Soc* 17:21, 1958.
45. Naismith DH, Pellett PL: The water-soluble vitamin content of blood, serum and milk of the bitch, *Proc Nutr Soc* 19:15, 1960.
46. Carvalho da Silva, A, Fajer AB, DeAngelis RC, and others: The domestic cat as a laboratory animal for experimental nutrition studies. II. Comparative growth and hematology on stock and purified rations, *Acta Physiol Latin Am* 1:26–43, 1950.
47. Grondalen J: Metaphyseal osteopathy (hypertrophic osteodystrophy) in growing dogs: a clinical study, *J Sm Anim Prac* 17:721–735, 1976.

48. Teare JA, Krook L, Kallfelz FA, and others: Ascorbic acid deficiency and hypertrophic osteodystrophy in the dog: a rebuttal, *Cornell Vet* 69:384–401, 1979.

49. Association of American Feed Control Officials: Official Publication, 1994, The Association.

50. Stewart WB, Bambino SR: Kinetics of iron absorption in normal dogs, *Am J Physiol* 201:67–77, 1961.

51. Pollack S, Balcerzak SP, Crosby WH: Transferrin and absorption of iron, *Blood,* 21:33–39, 1963.

52. Erdman JW: Oilseed phytates: nutritional implications, *J Am Oil Chem Soc* 56:736, 1979.

53. Bafundo KW, Baker DH, Fitzgerald PR: The iron-zinc interrelationship in the chick as influenced by *Eimeria acervulina* infection, *J Nutr* 114:1306–1311, 1984.

54. Hunt JR, Johnson PE, Swan PB: Dietary conditions influencing relative zinc availability from foods to the rat and correlations with in vitro measurements, *J Nutr* 117:1913–1923, 1987.

55. Sanecki RK, Corbin JE, Forbes RM: Tissue changes in dogs fed a zinc-deficient ration, *Am J Vet Res* 43:1642–1646, 1983.

56. Sousa CA, Stannard AA, Ihrke PH: Dermatosis associated with feeding generic dog food: 13 cases (1981–1982), *J Am Vet Med Assoc* 192:767–680, 1988.

57. Wolf AM: Zinc-responsive dermatosis in a Rhodesian ridgeback, *Vet Med* 82:908–912, 1987.

58. Wright RP: Identification of zinc-responsive dermatoses, *Vet Med* 80:37–40, 1985.

59. Schribner BH: Salt and hypertension, *J Am Med Assoc* 250:388–389, 1983.

60. Houston MC: Sodium and hypertension, *Arch Intern Med* 146:179–185, 1986.

61. Swales JD: Blood pressure and the kidney, *J Clin Pathol* 34:1233–1240, 1981.

62. Wilhelmj CM, Waldmann EB, McGuire TF: Effect of prolonged high sodium chloride ingestion and withdrawal upon blood pressure of dogs, *Proc Soc Exp Bio Med* 77:379–382, 1951.

63. Morris JG, Rogers QR: Comparative dog and cat nutrition. In Burger IH, Rivers JPW, editors: *Nutrition of the dog and cat,* Cambridge, England, 1989, Cambridge University Press, pp 35–66.

Nutrient Requirements of Dogs and Cats

Pets must be fed a proper diet that supplies all of the essential nutrients in their correct quantities and proportions in order to maintain health throughout all stages of life. The primary goals of feeding companion animals include maintaining optimal health, allowing a normal (but not excessive) growth rate, supporting gestation and lactation, and, in some cases, contributing to high-quality performance. Proper feeding throughout the pet's life also contributes to its long-term health, vitality, and longevity.

As a result of the advances that have been made in companion animal nutrition during the past 30 years, frank nutrient deficiencies are extremely rare in dogs and cats today. Rather, changes in nutrient status occur more often as a result of overfeeding, excessive supplementation, or exposure to inhibitory substances. It is important to recognize that individual nutrients do not function in isolation, but that interactions between essential nutrients are necessary for normal cellular metabolism. These relationships affect nutrient absorption, use, and excretion. Pet food companies use this information to formulate balanced and complete pet foods for various stages of companion animal's lives. Because of the intricate interactions between dietary components, the balance of nutrients within the diet and the absolute quantity of each individual nutrient must always be considered.

All dogs and cats require an adequate intake of nutrients every day to maintain optimal health. Requirements for energy and certain nutrients can vary significantly during the lifetime of an individual pet. Increased demands occur during growth, reproduction, and physical work. A decreased requirement for some nutrients and energy occurs as animals attain adulthood and as they age. In addition to changing needs within the life cycle, the nutrient requirements of individual animals also vary considerably. For example, the energy needs for an adult pug that spends much time dozing on the couch will be significantly lower than the energy requirement of an adult cairn terrier that weighs the same amount but inherently has a higher activity level.

Standards of nutrient requirements for dogs and cats are necessary to provide general guidelines for commercial pet food companies to use when formulating diets. Ideally these standards should report current information concerning minimum and maximum levels of nutrients, suggest nutrient requirements for different stages of life

and activity levels, and estimate the bioavailability of nutrients in commonly used pet food ingredients. Currently there are two sources of published standards that provide nutrient requirement information for dogs and cats. The National Research Council (NRC) compiles lists of minimum nutrient requirements of companion animals. A second group, the Association of American Feed Control Officials (AAFCO) has developed standards of practical nutrient profiles for dog and cat foods based on commonly used ingredients.

The recommendations of the NRC are compiled by committees of companion animal nutritionists. Two publications, the *Nutrient Requirements of Dogs* and the *Nutrient Requirements of Cats*, are issued by these committees. These publications are revised and updated as new knowledge becomes available. The nutrient recommendations for dogs were last updated in 1985, and the publication for cats was revised in 1986. These recommendations are lists of the minimum daily nutrient requirements (MDR) for dogs and cats. MDR denotes the minimum quantity of available nutrients that must be supplied in the diet each day to allow normal body metabolism. It is important to realize that the MDR recommendations of the NRC do not include safety factors that account for variability within the pet population. In addition, most of the research on which these recommendations are based was conducted using purified or semipurified diets. Such diets contain nutrients that are generally more available than those found in normal pet food ingredients. As a result, if correction factors for differences in bioavailability are not included, the use of the NRC recommendations to formulate commercial dog and cat foods can result in deficient levels of nutrients. However, no other comprehensive standard was available or acceptable to the AAFCO until late 1991, so almost all pet food companies in the United States used the NRC guidelines for dogs and cats to formulate their pet foods. The NRC recommendations were also the standards that companies were required to use to comply with regulations governing inclusion of the term "complete and balanced pet food" on their product labels (see Section 3, p. 157).

The AAFCO Nutrient Profiles were first published in 1992. These profiles provide recommendations for practical minimum and maximum levels of nutrients in commercial pet foods. The levels of nutrients listed in these reports are intended for processed

foods at the time of feeding. Minimum nutrient levels are reported for two different categories. The first category is growth and reproduction; the second is adult maintenance. Maximum nutrient levels are reported for nutrients in which there is potential for overuse or toxicosis. The Canine Nutrition Report was adopted by the AAFCO in August 1991. All pet food companies are now required to use this profile rather than the NRC recommendations when formulating dog foods to meet established nutrient levels. The Feline Nutrition Report was written in late 1991, and pet food manufacturers were required to use it starting in January 1993 (see Section 3, pp. 147–148).

CHAPTER 8

Nutritional Idiosyncrasies of the Cat

Although the dog and cat have about equal status as companion animals in our society, it is important to recognize that they belong to two separate species. This truth is evidenced by well-defined physiological, behavioral, and dietary differences. In the following chapters, differences between the cat's and the dog's nutrient requirements for a number of nutrients are discussed in detail. These differences include: the cat's unique energy and glucose metabolism; higher protein requirement; requirement for dietary taurine; sensitivity to a deficiency of the amino acid arginine; inability to convert beta-carotene to active vitamin A; and inability to convert the amino acid tryptophan to niacin.

An examination of the evolutionary relationship and current phylogeny of the domestic dog and cat offers some clues to their inherent dietary dissimilarities. Although both species are of the class Mammalia and the order Carnivora, the dog belongs to the modern day Canoidea superfamily and the cat belongs to the Feloidea superfamily.[1] Included with the dog in the Canoidea superfamily are several families with very diverse dietary habits. For example, the Ursid (bear) and the Procyonid (raccoon) families are both omnivorous, but species of the Alurid family (pandas) are strictly herbivorous. The only carnivorous species included with dogs in Canoidea are the Musetilids (weasels). The Feloidea superfamily, on the other hand, includes three families: the Viverrids (genet), the Hyaenids (hyena), and the Felids (cat) (Figure 8-1). All of the species in these families, including the cat, have evolved as strict carnivores. The evolutionary history of the dog suggests a predilection for a diet that is more omnivorous in nature. The history of the cat indicates that this species has consumed a purely carnivorous diet throughout its evolutionary development.

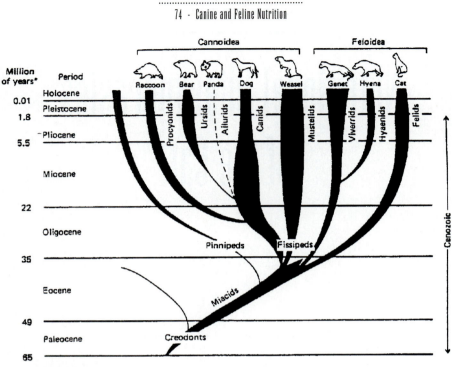

FIGURE 8-1
Phylogenic tree of the dog and cat. (From Morris J, Rogers Q. In Burger IH, Rivers JPW, editors: *Nutrition of cat and dog*, 1989, Cambridge, England, Cambridge University Press.)

The adherence of the cat to a highly specialized diet has resulted in specific metabolic adaptations that manifest themselves as peculiarities in nutritional requirements. The consequence of these changes is an animal that cannot obtain all necessary nutrients solely from plants and plant products and therefore requires the consumption of animal tissues to meet certain nutrient requirements. These specific nutritional idiosyncracies are exhibited in the domestic cat (*Felis domesticus*) but not in its frequent housemate, the domestic dog (*Canis familiaris*). This fact is of practical significance in light of the prevailing belief among some pet owners that cats may be fed as if they were small dogs.

The nutritional idiosyncracies of the cat result in more stringent dietary requirements than those of more omnivorous species, such as the dog. While all of these nutritional peculiarities are of metabolic significance, some are of greater practical

Nutritional Idiosyncrasies of the Cat

Idiosyncrasies of practical importance
High-protein requirement
Taurine requirement
Arachidonic acid requirement
Preformed vitamin A requirement

Idiosyncrasies of academic interest
Unique energy and glucose metabolism
Sensitivity to arginine deficiency
Inability to convert tryptophan to niacin

importance than others when considering the optimal nutrition and proper feeding practices of pet cats (see the box above). The domestic cat's high-protein requirement, along with its need for taurine, arachidonic acid, and preformed vitamin A, imposes a requirement for the inclusion of animal tissues in the diet of this species. Although it may be possible to develop a cereal-based ration for cats, such a formulation would require appropriate supplementation with purified forms of taurine, arachidonic acid, and preformed vitamin A.[2,3]

CHAPTER 9

Energy Balance

All animals must meet their bodies' energy needs. Energy balance is achieved when energy expenditure is equal to energy intake, resulting in minimal changes in the body's store of energy. Positive energy balance occurs when caloric intake exceeds energy expenditure. In growing and pregnant animals, excess energy is converted predominately to lean body tissue. In adult, nonreproducing animals, positive energy balance results primarily in an increase in the quantity of fat stored by the body. Negative energy balance occurs when caloric intake is lower than energy expenditure. Weight loss and a decrease in both fat and stores of lean body tissue occur during negative energy balance. The daily energy requirement of dogs and cats depends on the amount of energy that the body expends each day. Many factors can influence the energy requirement of a particular pet. These factors must all be considered when determining the number of calories and quantity of food that is required by a particular companion animal.

COMPONENTS OF ENERGY EXPENDITURE

The body's energy expenditure can be partitioned into three major components: *resting metabolic rate*, *voluntary muscular activity*, and *meal-induced thermogenesis*.[4] A fourth component, called *adaptive or facultative thermogenesis*, represents energy that is expended in response to environmental conditions and yields heat but no useful work. Adaptive thermogenesis has been shown to exist in small, warm-blooded animals and is essential for cold adaptation.[5] It is theorized that this component may also function

to increase thermogenesis during periods of overeating, thus protecting an animal from excessive weight gain. However, the importance of adaptive thermogenesis in the energy balance equation for species other than small rodents is not known.

Resting Metabolic Rate

The resting metabolic rate (RMR) contributes the greatest portion of an animal's total energy expenditure. RMR is defined as the amount of energy expended while sitting quietly in a comfortable environment several hours following a meal or physical activity. RMR represents the energy cost of maintaining homeostasis in all of the integrated systems of the body during periods of rest.[4] Homeostasis refers to the state of internal stability within the body. The slightly lower value of basal metabolic rate (BMR) is similar to RMR, but it is measured shortly after waking and following an overnight fast. The RMR accounts for approximately 60% to 75% of an animal's daily total energy expenditure. Factors influencing RMR include sex and reproductive status, thyroid gland and autonomic nervous system function, body composition, body surface area, and nutritional state.[4] Research has shown that RMR is positively correlated to the total amount of respiring cell mass present in the body. Fat-free mass or lean body mass is the closest approximation available of the total respiring cell mass. Therefore the amount of fat-free mass or lean body tissue that an animal has is the strongest predictor of its metabolic rate, followed by body surface area and body weight.[6-8] Subsequently, as a pet's lean body mass and body surface area increases, RMR increases proportionately.

Voluntary Muscular Activity

The second component of energy expenditure, voluntary muscular activity, is the most variable. Muscular activity contributes approximately 30% of the body's total energy expenditure in moderately active individuals.[9] The metabolic efficiency of performing physical work is invariable, but the total amount of energy that is expended is affected by both the duration and the intensity of the activity. In addition, any type of weight-bearing activity, such as walking or running, rises in energy cost as body weight increases. This effect is a direct result of the added energy necessary to move a greater body mass. Therefore the energy expenditure of a pet with a high activity level will depend on the duration and intensity of the exercise and the size and weight of the animal.

Meal-Induced Thermogenesis

Meal-induced thermogenesis refers to the heat produced following the consumption of a meal. The ingestion of nutrients causes an obligatory increase in heat production by the body. This increase is primarily the result of the metabolic cost of digestion, absorption, metabolism, and storage of nutrients. When a meal containing a mixture of carbohydrate, protein, and fat is consumed, meal-induced thermogenesis uses approximately

10% of the ingested calories. However, the magnitude of this heat production can be affected by the caloric and nutrient composition of the meal and the nutritional state of the individual.[9]

Adaptive Thermogenesis

Adaptive thermogenesis is an additional energy expenditure that is not accounted for by the obligatory and short-term thermogenesis of meal ingestion. Although this component is well described in several species of small mammals, the significance of adaptive thermogenesis to energy balance in larger mammals, such as dogs, cats, and humans, has not been conclusively established. Adaptive thermogenesis is manifested primarily as a change in the RMR in response to environmental stresses. These stresses include changes in ambient temperature, alterations in food intake, and emotional stress.[9] Cold adaptation in small mammals has been shown to rely on increased heat production that is disassociated from any productive work and separate from shivering thermogenesis.[5,10] Similarly, when energy intake increases, some animals are capable of increasing thermogenesis above the normal levels necessary for the metabolism of food and the maintenance of body temperature. This increased energy loss is a result of less efficient use of food calories. In the long term, the amount of weight gain that occurs during the period of overeating is significantly less than what normally would be expected from the increased caloric intake. This process may represent the body's tendency to protect the status quo of energy balance. Thus adaptive thermogenesis regulates energy expenditure in an attempt to maintain body energy balance. Although this process has been shown to occur in laboratory animals and some human subjects, its significance in maintaining energy balance in companion animals is not yet known.[11,12,10]

FACTORS AFFECTING ENERGY EXPENDITURE

A variety of factors influence a pet's total daily energy expenditure (Table 9-1). RMR is affected by body composition, age, caloric intake, and hormonal status. The RMR component of energy expenditure naturally decreases as a pet ages, which is primarily the

TABLE 9-1
Factors Affecting Components of Energy Expenditure

COMPONENT	FACTORS
Resting metabolic rate	Sex, reproductive status, hormonal status, autonomic nervous system function, body composition, body surface area, nutritional state, age
Voluntary muscular activity	Weight-bearing activity, duration of exercise, intensity of exercise, size and weight of animal
Meal-induced thermogenesis	Caloric and nutrient composition of meal, nutritional state
Adaptive thermogenesis	Ambient temperature, alterations in food intake, emotional stress

result of a gradual loss of lean body tissue. Changes in RMR can also occur as a result of food restriction. When caloric intake is decreased, an initial decrease in RMR occurs because of hormonal influences. If caloric restriction continues, the loss of lean body tissue that occurs with weight loss causes a persistent reduction in RMR. This decrease will not be corrected until normal levels of lean body tissue have been restored. Similarly, persistent overeating can lead to an increase in energy expenditure. Part of this increase is the result of the increase in lean body tissue that occurs with weight gain and increased meal-induced thermogenesis. In addition, adaptive thermogenesis may cause an increase in energy expenditure as the body attempts to maintain energy balance in the face of increased energy intake.

Changes in voluntary activity and exercise level can significantly affect energy expenditure in dogs and cats. Just like people, companion animals tend to become more sedentary as they age. This change is usually first observed when the pet becomes mature. In many breeds, play behaviors do not persist strongly into adulthood, and the onset of maturity is accompanied by a decline in physical activity. Later in life, a further decline in voluntary activity may occur because of the onset of arthritis, chronic disease, or decreased tolerance for exercise. These changes will all be reflected in a decline in the pet's total energy requirement. It follows that increasing a pet's daily exercise will result in an increased energy requirement. A portion of the higher energy expenditure occurs because of the direct calorie-consuming benefit of exercise. However, just as importantly, the long-term, cumulative effects of a regular exercise program will cause changes in body weight and composition. Regular exercise results in a higher proportion of lean to fat tissue in the pet's body. The amount of exercise necessary to decrease body fat and maintain or increase lean body tissue is related to the duration and intensity of the physical activity. As discussed previously, an increase in lean body tissue results in an increased RMR. Therefore voluntary activity not only directly burns energy but also contributes to a higher percentage of lean body tissue and to a higher RMR over the long-term.

Food and Energy Intake

The other half of the energy balance equation is energy intake. Food intake is regulated in all animals by a complex system involving both internal physiological controls and external cues. The internal signals and external stimuli that affect appetite, hunger, and satiety are presented in the following box. Little research has been conducted in dogs and cats on the internal signals that govern food intake. Information involving these signals has been collected primarily in laboratory animals and can be used to provide insight into mechanisms that may be operating in other species.

Internal Controls of Food Intake

In all mammals the natural state for the body is one of hunger. This state is held in check by the presence of food in the gastrointestinal tract, the digestion, absorption, and

Factors Affecting Energy Intake

Internal signals
Gastric distention
Physiological response to sight, sound, and smell
   of food
Changes in plasma concentrations of specific
   nutrients, hormones, and peptides

External stimuli
Food availability
Timing and size of meals
Food composition and texture
Diet palatability

metabolism of nutrients, and by the amount of nutrients stored in the body at any one time. A small number of specific compounds appear to stimulate the appetite, and a much larger number of metabolic substrates satisfy the body.[13]

The hypothalamus is known to be involved in mediating both quantitative and qualitative changes in food intake. Several different neurotransmitter substances are believed to be involved in this process. Stimulatory neurotransmitters include catecholamine, norepinephrine, and three classes of neuropeptides, opioids, pancreatic polypeptides, and galanin.[13] Injections of these components directly into the rat hypothalamus potentiates eating in both hungry and satiated animals. In addition, obesity as a result of overeating can be induced in laboratory animals by the chronic administration of norepinephrine.[13] The medial paraventricular nucleus is the area of the hypothalamus most sensitive to these neurotransmitters. Interestingly, there is evidence suggesting that these substances affect specific nutrient selection in animals, as opposed to simply increasing total caloric intake. Norepinephrine injection causes an increase in the consumption of carbohydrates, and the administration of opioids and galanin results in increased fat consumption.[13]

Substances that inhibit eating include the neurotransmitters dopamine and serotonin.[14] Synthesis of serotonin in the brain depends on the availability of the amino acid tryptophan, which is serotonin's precursor. In rats the specific action of serotonin appears to be the suppression of carbohydrate ingestion.[15] Other substances that inhibit food intake include the gut peptides cholecystokinin, glucagon, and bombesin.[16] Injections of glucagon in human subjects prior to eating causes a significant decrease in food intake.[17] The inhibitory effect of cholecystokinin on food intake has been reported in several species, including humans.[18,20,16] However, the wolf appears to be one of the few species that does not alter food intake in response to cholecystokinin.[21] Bombesin is a peptide that has been investigated recently. The exogenous administration of this gut peptide to human subjects results in decreased food intake.[22]

Insulin may be an important internal control signal for both appetite and satiety. The exogenous administration of this hormone stimulates hunger and increases food intake in human subjects. The mechanisms involved appear to be an insulin-induced decrease in the use of cellular glucose (glucoprivation) and severe hypoglycemia.[23] Insulin may also act directly on the hypothalamus to mediate this effect. Studies with rats have shown that both insulin and the adrenal glucocorticoid corticosterone function synergistically with central neurotransmitter substances to stimulate eating.[13] In human subjects, feelings of hunger are positively correlated with low levels of blood glucose.[24] However, hypoglycemia may be involved in the physiological process of hunger sensation, but excess plasma glucose does not depress food intake.[25]

Insulin may also be involved in signaling satiety and the cessation of eating. It has been theorized that the size of the fat deposit in an animal's body may be regulated by the concentration of insulin in the cerebrospinal fluid.[26] Insulin level in the cerebrospinal fluid increases and decreases proportionately as fat cells increase and decrease in size. These changes happen without the daily fluctuations that occur in plasma insulin levels. The insulin receptors of the cerebrospinal fluid, which are not accessible to the plasma insulin pool, appear to be involved in the regulation of food intake and total body adiposity. A study with rats demonstrated that when insulin was infused into the cerebrospinal fluid over a period of several weeks, food intake and body weight decreased significantly.[27] On the other hand, when the spinal pool of insulin was experimentally decreased by the injection of insulin antibodies, food intake and body weight both increased. These changes occurred independently of changes in plasma insulin concentration. Insulin levels in cerebrospinal fluid may modulate the brain's response to other internal satiety signals, such as the release of gut peptides, and may be important in long-term control of body fat stores.

A final internal control mechanism for food intake is the gastric distention that occurs following meal ingestion. Physical distention of the stomach and the lower small intestine stimulates the vagus nerve and relays satiety information to the brain. However, the presence of food in the stomach alone will not inhibit food intake until gastric distention reaches pathological proportions. This is most likely a result of the stomach's natural ability to expand greatly in size. Other internal mechanisms are probably more important in signaling postprandial satiety than are stomach fill or gastric distention.[25]

Aberrations in any of the internal control systems for appetite, hunger, and satiety can result in pathological changes in food intake. For example, lesions involving the ventromedial center of the hypothalamus will lead to overeating, but lesions of the lateral nucleus result in an inhibition of food intake. Endocrine imbalances such as insulinoma, hypopituitarism, hyperadrenocorticism, and possibly hypothyroidism may affect food intake. Any metabolic dysfunction that affects neurotransmitter substances or the gut peptides could also potentially result in changes in food intake. Little research has been conducted in dogs and cats concerning internal satiety signals. It can be speculated that such mechanisms are operating in these species, but the degree of their importance in controlling food intake in domestic pets is not known.

External Controls of Food Intake

External controls of food intake include stimuli such as diet palatability, food composition and texture, and the timing and environment of meals. The exposure to highly palatable foods is considered a primary environmental factor contributing to food over-consumption in humans, laboratory animals, and companion animals.[28,29] Studies with human subjects have demonstrated that the quantity of food consumed varies directly

with its palatability, and palatability does not appear to interact with levels of food deprivation. In other words, if food is perceived to be very appealing, an individual tends to consume more of it, regardless of the initial level of hunger.[4,30] Similarly, when rats are offered a highly palatable diet, they overeat and become obese.[31] This effect has been observed with high-fat diets, calorically dense diets, and "cafeteria type" diets that provide a large variety of palatable food items.[32]

Dogs and cats have definite preferences for certain flavors and types of pet foods. A flavor preference test for dogs showed that the majority of dogs studied preferred canned and semimoist pet food to dry food.[33] Beef appears to be the most preferred type of meat, and cooked meat is overwhelmingly preferred to uncooked meat.[34] It was theorized that early experience with cooked meat, such as that present in commercial pet foods, is the cause of the development of a strong preference for cooked compared with fresh products in dogs. Dogs also have a strong preference for sucrose, while cats do not seem to enjoy the taste of sugar.[35,36] In both species, warm food is preferred to cold food, and palatability generally increases along with the fat content of the diet.[36,37]

Palatability is an important diet characteristic that is heavily promoted in the marketing of commercial pet foods (see Section 3, p. 195). Many pet owners select a pet food based on their own perceptions of the food's appeal and their pet's acceptance of the diet, rather than on indicators of nutritional adequacy. Semimoist foods contain high amounts of simple sugars, a taste that is preferred by many dogs. Canned pet foods, on the other hand, are often very high in fat. Fat contributes both to the palatability and the caloric density of the food. Feeding pets highly palatable foods on an ad libitum basis may encourage overeating in some pets and lead ultimately to weight gain and obesity.

The timing and social setting of meals also influence eating behavior. Dogs and cats rapidly become conditioned to receiving their meals at a particular time of day. This conditioning manifests itself both behaviorally and physiologically. Pets generally show increased activity levels at mealtime, and gastric secretions and gastric motility increase in anticipation of eating. In addition, companion animals tend to increase food intake when consuming food in the presence of others.[38,25] This process is called *social facilitation*. It is not uncommon for pet owners to report that their dog or cat was quite finicky before the introduction of a second pet. In most pets, social facilitation causes a moderately increased interest in food and an increased rate of eating. In some pets, the increase in food intake that occurs in response to another animal's presence can be extreme enough to singularly cause excessive food intake.[25] In some situations the development of social hierarchies between pets has the opposite effect on food consumption. Subordinate pets may be intimidated enough by dominant animals to inhibit eating during mealtimes.

The frequency with which meals are provided affects both food intake and metabolic efficiency. Increasing meal frequency may have opposing effects on weight gain. An increase in the number of meals per day results in an increased energy loss as a result of meal-induced thermogenesis. In a study with adult dogs, a group that was fed four times per day increased oxygen consumption 30% but a second group that was fed the same amount of food in one meal daily exhibited only a 15% increase in oxygen consumption.[39] There is also evidence indicating that a decrease in lipogenesis occurs

when multiple meals are fed compared with the consumption of the same number of calories in only one or two meals.[40] In contrast, it is known that the presence of food, particularly palatable food, is a potent external cue for meal ingestion. An increased number of meal offerings each day may lead to excess consumption in individuals that are highly sensitive to external cues.[41] A study was conducted to compare the effects of free-choice feeding to portion-controlled feeding on growth and development in grow-ing puppies.[42] Puppies that had access to food throughout the day gained weight more rapidly and were heavier than were puppies that were fed using the portion-controlled regimen. However, the two groups exhibited similar amounts of skeletal growth as mea-sured by forelimb and body length. These results indicate that both groups were devel-oping maximally, but the free-choice fed group was depositing more body fat than was the portion-controlled group. Continual exposure to a highly palatable food throughout the day may lead to overconsumption and excess weight gain in some dogs and cats. This tendency to overconsume may more than compensate for the increased energy loss that results from meal-induced thermogenesis.

A final external factor that may contribute to food intake is the nutrient composi-tion of the diet. Nutrient composition affects both the efficiency of nutrient metabolism and the amount of food that is voluntarily consumed. Dietary fat and simple sugar appear to be the nutrients of greatest concern. Although most animals decrease their intake of a high-fat diet in an attempt to balance energy needs, the greater caloric den-sity of the diet and its increased palatability still can cause increased energy consump-tion in some individuals. Additionally, the metabolic efficiency of converting dietary fat to body fat for storage is higher than the efficiency of converting dietary carbohydrate or protein to body fat. Three percent of the energy content of fat is lost when it is stored as body fat. This loss can be compared with a loss of 23% of the energy content of dietary carbohydrate and protein when these nutrients are converted to body fat.[43,9] Therefore, if an animal is consuming more than its caloric requirement of a particular diet and if the excess calories are provided by fat, more weight will be gained than if the excess calories are coming from either carbohydrate or protein. This effect has been demonstrated in companion animals. Puppies that consumed a high-fat diet showed similar growth in lean body mass compared with those puppies fed diets lower in fat, but they accumulated higher amounts of body fat.[44] When adult dogs were fed either a high-fat or a high-carbohydrate diet, the dogs that were fed the high-fat diet consumed only 13% more energy than those fed the high-carbohydrate diet, but they retained 117% more energy. Even though a portion of this increased weight gain was attributed to the small difference in energy intake, there appeared to be increased efficiency of fat deposition in the dogs consuming the high-fat diet.[45]

The amount of simple sugar in a diet may also affect energy balance in some ani-mals. Rats will increase their caloric consumption of standard rat food when they are pro-vided with a water/sucrose solution to drink along with the food. Prolonged feeding of the solution will result in increased fat deposition and weight gain.[46] The mechanism respon-sible for this effect may be an insulin-induced hypoglycemia that occurs after sucrose con-sumption, resulting in increased feelings of hunger.[24] Increasing the simple sugar content of a diet increases its palatability in most species, with the exception of the cat.

A diet that is highly varied and contains calorically dense, palatable food items can also cause changes in food intake. This type of feeding regime is commonly referred to as a "cafeteria" diet and has been shown to cause dramatic increases in total food intake, meal size, meal frequency, and body weight in normal adult rats.[47] It appears that the novelty of being presented with several different types of palatable foods can override normal satiety signals.[48] A practice that is similar to the "cafeteria" diet and is occasionally observed in companion animals is the feeding of a variety of table scraps and calorically dense treats or constantly offering new types of foods. The persistent feeding of highly desirable and appealing treats to some dogs and cats may override the body's natural tendency to balance energy intake and lead to the overconsumption of energy (see Section 5, pp. 277–278).

Determination of Energy Requirement of Dogs and Cats

The total daily energy requirement of an animal is the sum of the energy that is needed for the RMR, meal-induced thermogenesis, voluntary muscular activity, and maintenance of normal body temperature when exposed to adverse weather conditions. Adult animals in a state of maintenance only require enough energy to support activity and maintain the body's normal metabolic processes and tissue stores. On the other hand, dogs and cats that are growing, reproducing, and working have increased energy requirements.

Dogs

Formulating an exact equation for the estimate of energy requirements for dogs is a difficult task because of the wide variety of body sizes and weights that occurs in this species. The amount of energy that is used by the body is correlated with total body surface area. Body surface area per unit of weight decreases as animals increase in size. As a result, the energy requirements of animals with widely differing weights are not well correlated to body weight; they are more closely related to body weight raised to a specified power, called *metabolic body weight*. Metabolic body weight accounts for differences in body surface area between animals of varying sizes. Although several different powers have been suggested, compilation of the data that is available on energy requirements for dogs indicate that the best power function to use is 0.67.[49] The allometric equation Metabolizable energy (ME) requirement $= K \times W_{kg}^{0.67}$ provides an accurate estimate of daily energy requirements for different sizes of adult dogs experiencing different activity levels. Values for K range between 130 and 300 (see the box on the following page). Two other equations can also be used to estimate ME for adult dogs. The first uses the power 0.88 in the equation ME $= 100 \times W_{kg}^{0.88}$. This equation provides a reasonable estimate of the daily energy requirements of active dogs weighing between 1 and 60 kg. However, studies have shown that this equation may overestimate the energy requirements of adult dogs that have low to normal activity levels. The third equation, ME $= 132 \times W_{kg}^{0.75}$, provides a good estimate for small and medium size

Calculation of Energy Requirements of Adult Dogs at Maintenance

Formula 1 (recommended)

ME requirement = $K \times W_{kg}^{0.67}$

K = 132 Inactive
   145 Active
   200 Very active
   300 Endurance performance (racing sled dogs)

Examples: ME requirement of a 10 kg (22 lb) dog = $145 \times (10 \text{ kg})^{0.67} = 678.2$ kcal of ME/day

ME requirement of a 40 kg (88 lb) dog = $145 \times (40 \text{ kg})^{0.67} = 1716.9$ kcal of ME/day

Formula 2

ME requirement = $100 \times W_{kg}^{0.88}$

Examples: ME requirement of a 10 kg (22 lb) dog = $100 \times (10 \text{ kg})^{0.88} = 758.5$ kcal of ME/day

ME requirement of a 40 kg (88 lb) dog = $100 \times (40 \text{ kg})^{0.88} = 2569.3$ kcal of ME/day

Formula 3

ME requirement = $132 \times W_{kg}^{0.75}$

Examples: ME requirement of a 10 kg (22 lb) dog = $132 \times (10 \text{ kg})^{0.75} = 742.3$ kcal of ME/day

ME requirement of a 40 kg (88 lb) dog = $132 \times (40 \text{ kg})^{0.75} = 2099.5$ kcal of ME/day

breeds during maintenance.[50] However, this equation may underestimate the energy needs of some of the larger breeds of dogs. Regardless which of the three equations is used to predict energy needs, the resulting number should be used only as a starting point to determine the daily energy requirement of a particular animal. Variability between individual dogs and the environmental conditions under which dogs are kept can result in a requirement that is up to 25% greater or less than the predicted amount.

The estimates provided by these equations can be adjusted according to the dog's long-term response to feeding. For example, using the first equation, an active adult dog weighing 10 kg (22 lb) would require approximately 680 kcal of ME per day. If a food containing 3800 kcal/kg (1727 kcal/lb) was fed, the dog would require 0.18 kg (180 g) of food. This is equal to 6.3 oz. One 8 oz cup of dry dog food contains 3 to 4 oz of food. Therefore the initial feeding level of this dog should be close to 2 cups of food per day (Table 9-2).

TABLE 9-2
Calculation of the Amount of Food to Feed Dogs and Cats

	ENERGY REQUIREMENT kcal of ME/kg		ENERGY DENSITY (kcal/kg)		QUANTITY (kg)				POUNDS		OUNCES		CUPS PER DAY
Dog (10 kg)	680	÷	3800	=	0.18	×	2.2	=	0.396	=	6.3	=	1.8
Cat (4 kg)	280	÷	4200	=	0.066	×	2.2	=	0.147	=	2.3	=	0.66
Puppy (10 kg)	1360	÷	3800	=	0.357	×	2.2	=	0.787	=	12.6	=	3.5
Kitten (1 kg)	250	÷	4200	=	0.059	×	2.2	=	0.129	=	2.06	=	0.58

TABLE 9-3
Energy Requirements for Different Stages of Life

STAGE	ENERGY REQUIREMENT
Dogs	
Post weaned	2 × adult maintenance ME*
40% adult body weight	1.6 × adult maintenance ME
80% adult body weight	1.2 × adult maintenance ME
Late gestation	1.25–1.5 × adult maintenance ME
Lactation	3 × adult maintenance ME
Prolonged physical work	2–4 × adult maintenance ME
Decreased environmental temperature*	1.2–1.8 × adult maintenance ME
Cats	
Post weaned	250 kcal ME/kg body weight
20 weeks	130 kcal ME/kg body weight
30 weeks	100 kcal ME/kg body weight
Late gestation	1.25 × adult maintenance ME
Lactation	3–4 × adult maintenance ME

* Adult maintenance for a dog of comparable weight.

The energy requirements predicted by these three equations are specific for adult maintenance. Stages of life that result in increased energy needs include growth, gestation, lactation, periods of strenuous physical work, and exposure to extreme environmental conditions (Table 9-3). After weaning, growing puppies require approximately 2 times the energy intake per unit of body weight as adult dogs of the same weight. An active puppy that weighs 10 kg would require 2 x 680 kcal, or 1360 kcal, per day. This would correspond to approximately 3.5 cups of food per day (Table 9-2). When puppies have reached about 40% of their adult weight, this level of food should be reduced to 1.6 times maintenance levels; it should be further reduced to 1.2 times maintenance when 80 percent of adult weight has been achieved.[49] The age at which a puppy will attain these proportions of adult weight will vary with the adult size of the dog. In gen-

eral, large breeds of dogs mature more slowly than do small breeds. Most puppies will achieve 40 percent of their adult weight between 3 and 4 months of age and 80% between 4½ and 8 months, depending on the breed. Although large breeds of dogs will not attain full adult size until they are older than 10 months of age, small breeds reach adult size at a slightly earlier age.[51]

Energy needs increase substantially for bitches during gestation and lactation. During the first 3 to 4 weeks of the 9-week gestation, energy needs remain the same as for maintenance. After the fourth week of pregnancy, energy requirements increase gradually to supply the rapidly growing fetuses with energy. A total increase of approximately 1.25 to 1.5 times the normal maintenance requirement level occurs by the end of the gestation period.[52] Lactation is one of the most energy-demanding stages of life for an animal. Depending on the size of the litter, energy needs of the bitch during lactation can increase as much as 3 times the normal maintenance requirement. Using the previous example, a bitch with a normal weight of 10 kg and maintenance energy needs of 758 kcal will require 3 × 758 kcal, or 2274 kcal, during peak lactation. This is equal to about 6 cups of food per day. The ability of a bitch to consume this amount of food may be limited by the size of her stomach. Therefore it is important to feed a food that is highly digestible and nutrient dense during this stage of life (see Section 4, pp. 220–221).

Both physical work and environmental stresses can cause increased energy needs in dogs. Short bouts of intense physical exercise may cause only a small increase in energy needs, but a regular program of prolonged exercise may cause increased needs of up to 2 to 4 times maintenance levels.[49] In addition, cold and hot weather conditions can also cause an increased energy requirement. Dogs must expend additional energy to support normal body temperature in cold conditions and to enhance body cooling mechanisms in warm conditions. Depending on the severity, living in cold conditions can cause increases of 1.2 to 1.8 times the normal maintenance needs in dogs.[53]

Cats

The mature body weight of domestic cats varies only between about 2 and 6 kg (4 and 13 lb). Because cats do not show the extreme variability in body size and weight that dogs do, it is possible to express their energy requirement on a body weight basis. It is not as important in this species to account for differences in body surface area.[54] Various estimates for the ME requirement for adult maintenance in cats have been published.[55-57] An estimate of 70 kcal/kg of body weight body weight for moderately active and 80 kcal/kg of body weight for very active adult cats provides a reasonable starting point when determining the energy needs of an individual.[58-60] Sedentary house cats receiving little or no daily exercise will require as low as 60 kcal/kg (see the box on the following page). For example, an active, adult cat weighing 4 kg (8.8 lb) would require approximately 280 kcal of ME per day. If a dry food containing 4200 kcal/kg is fed, 0.066 kg or 66 g of food should be fed. This amount is equal to about 2.3 oz of food. If a cup of this food weighs 3.5 oz, the cat should be given approximately ⅔ cup of food per day (Table 9-2).

Calculation of Energy Requirements of Adult Cats at Maintenance

Formula 1

Sedentary house cats: 60 kcal/kg × W_{kg}

Examples: ME requirement of a 4 kg cat = 60 kcal × 4 kg = 240 kcal of ME/day

ME requirement of a 6 kg cat = 60 kcal × 6 kg = 360 kcal of ME/day

Formula 2

Moderately active cats: 70 kcal/kg × W_{kg}

Examples: ME requirement of a 4 kg cat = 70 kcal × 4 kg = 280 kcal of ME/day

ME requirement of a 6 kg cat = 70 kcal × 6 kg = 420 kcal of ME/day

Formula 3

Very active cats: 80 kcal/kg × W_{kg}

Examples: ME requirement of a 4 kg cat = 80 kcal × 4 kg = 320 kcal of ME/day

ME requirement of a 6 kg cat = 80 kcal × 6 kg = 480 kcal of ME/day

Like dogs, the energy requirements of cats increase during growth, reproduction, physical activity, and extreme environmental conditions (Table 9-3). The energy and nutrient requirements of growing kittens is highest per unit of body weight at about 5 weeks of age.[59] Young, rapidly growing kittens require approximately 250 kcal of ME per kilogram of body weight. This requirement declines to 130 kcal/kg by 20 weeks of age and 100 kcal/kg by 30 weeks of age. A 3-month-old kitten weighing 1 kg (2.2 lb) would require approximately 250 kcal/day. If a dry kitten food containing 4300 kcal/kg is fed, the kitten should be given 58 g or 2 oz of food. This is equal to a little more than ½ cup of food per day.

Studies with reproducing queens have indicated that energy requirements of cats increase throughout gestation, rather than only during the last 4 to 5 weeks.[61] By the end of the 9-week gestation, an increase of about 25% above normal maintenance energy needs is usually required. It appears that the accretion of excess maternal body tissues during gestation allows the queen to prepare adequately for the intense energy demands of lactation. The queen then uses these maternal stores and additional dietary energy to meet her energy requirements during lactation. In practical situations, queens will often gain too much weight if they are allowed excess food intake during the first few weeks of gestation. As with dogs, the intake should still be strictly monitored to

assure only a moderate increase in weight during the first 4 to 5 weeks of gestation. Depending on the size of the litter, a queen's dietary energy requirement may be as high as 250 kcal/kg body weight during peak lactation.[61] Increases of approximately 120 to 180 kcal/kg body weight are typical for queens that are in good physical condition at the time of parturition.[60] Using the same adult cat as an example, this would be equal to 720 kcal/day, or about 1¾ cups of food. During all physiological stages, the energy requirement of a particular cat will vary with age, activity level, environmental temperature, body condition, and the length and thickness of the cat's coat. Therefore these estimates should be used only as a starting point when determining the exact needs of an individual animal. Evaluation of the cat's body weight and condition can then be used to adjust the initial energy requirement estimate.

WATER

The daily drinking water requirement of a dog or cat depends on several factors. Voluntary water intake will increase in response to any change that causes an increase in water losses from the body, such as increased physical activity, increased body or environmental temperature, changes in the kidney's ability to concentrate urine, or the onset of lactation. In addition, the amount of water that is present in the pet's food can significantly affect voluntary water intake. If the water content of the food is very high, both dogs and cats are able to maintain normal water balance with no additional drinking water.[62,63]

Generally, a pet's total exogenous water requirement, expressed in milliliters, for maintenance in a thermoneutral environment is equal to 2 to 3 times the dry-matter intake of food, expressed in grams.[49,58] For example, if an adult dog requires 1000 kcal/day and is given a dry food that has an energy density of 3500 kcal/kg, the dog will receive 285 g of food per day. Dry pet foods contain approximately 8% moisture. Therefore the dog will be consuming 262 g of dry matter. Multiplying this number by three gives an estimated water requirement of 785 ml of water per day. Other recommendations suggest that pets require an amount of drinking water that is roughly equal to the number of kilocalories that are consumed per day.[64] In this case, the requirement would then be equal to 1000 ml/day. The best method of ensuring adequate water intake in both dogs and cats is to provide fresh, clean water at all times, regardless of the animal's physiological state, caloric needs, or dry-matter intake.

Carbohydrate Metabolism

All animals have a metabolic requirement for glucose. This requirement can be supplied either through endogenous synthesis or from dietary sources of carbohydrate. Gluconeogenic pathways in the liver and kidney use certain amino acids, propionic acid, lactic acid, and glycerol, to produce glucose, which is then released into the bloodstream to be carried to the body's tissues. Some data suggest that gluconeogenic pathways are active at all times in carnivorous species.[65,66] For example, the cat has been shown to be able to maintain normal blood glucose levels even during prolonged periods of fasting.[65]

The dog is capable of meeting its metabolic requirement for glucose from gluconeogenic pathways throughout growth and adult maintenance, provided that sufficient fat and protein are included in the diet.[44,67] However, the need for an exogenous source of carbohydrate during the metabolically stressful periods of gestation and lactation has been debated. During gestation the bitch's needs increase because glucose provides a major energy source for fetal development. Similarly, during lactation, additional glucose is needed for the synthesis of lactose, the disaccharide that is present in milk. It is assumed that the queen's glucose requirement also increases.

An early study with dogs examined the degree of reproductive success in bitches that were fed diets with varying levels of carbohydrates. The data indicated that bitches did require a source of carbohydrate to whelp and rear healthy puppies. Females who had been fed a carbohydrate-free diet throughout gestation became hypoglycemic, hypoalanemic, and ketotic near the end of their pregnancies. Only 63% of their puppies were alive at birth, and high puppy mortality occurred shortly after birth.[52] However, this study was subsequently refuted by data from a second experiment that also examined the effects of feeding a carbohydrate-free diet to bitches throughout gestation and

lactation. This group of researchers found that a carbohydrate-free diet did not affect length of gestation, litter size, litter weight, or puppy viability.[68] The different results of the two experiments were attributed to differences in the protein levels of the diets that were used. The diet in the first study contained only 26% protein, compared with 51% and 45% protein diets that were used in the second set of experiments. It appears that the higher protein diets supplied the bitches with sufficient amounts of gluconeogenic amino acids to allow the maintenance of plasma glucose levels, despite the heavy demands of gestation and lactation. Alanine, glycine, and serine appear to be the principle gluconeogenic amino acids in the dog.[69] The fact that the dogs in the first study exhibited hypoalanemia suggests that insufficient alanine was available to allow adequate gluconeogenesis. The hypoglycemia that was observed in these bitches was probably a result of the lack of gluconeogenic precursors rather than an innate inability to synthesize sufficient glucose during gestation and lactation.

These results were further supported by a study that examined the ability of varying levels of protein in the diet to ameliorate the effects of carbohydrate-free diets on gestation and lactation.[70] The data confirmed that carbohydrate-free diets fed to pregnant and lactating bitches can cause adverse effects. However, performance was not impaired when the protein level in the diet was sufficiently high. The investigators estimated that if carbohydrate is provided in the diet, bitches require about 7 grams (g) of digestible crude protein per unit of metabolic body weight. However, if no carbohydrate is supplied in the diet, this protein requirement must be increased to approximately 12 g of protein. Lactating bitches appear to require between 13 and 18 g of protein per unit of metabolic weight when fed a diet containing carbohydrate and 30 g when fed a carbohydrate-free diet. This information tells us that although carbohydrate is physiologically essential for the dog, it is not an indispensable component of the diet, even during the metabolically demanding stages of gestation and lactation. Although specific studies have not been conducted during pregnancy and lactation in the cat, this species' unique pattern of gluconeogenesis coupled with its carnivorous nature suggests that it too can survive all stages of life while consuming a carbohydrate-free diet.

Compared with the dog and other omnivorous species, the cat has several unique mechanisms for metabolizing dietary carbohydrate. The cat's ability to maintain normal blood glucose levels and health when fed a carbohydrate-free diet is probably at least partly related to its different pattern of gluconeogenesis. In most animals, maximal gluconeogenesis for the maintenance of blood glucose levels occurs during the postabsorptive state, when dietary soluble carbohydrate is no longer available. However, carnivorous species are similar to ruminant species in that they maintain a constant state of gluconeogenesis with a slightly increased rate immediately after feeding.[71] Because the body is limited in its ability to conserve amino acids and a carnivorous diet contains low amounts of soluble carbohydrate, this immediate use of gluconeogenic amino acids for the maintenance of blood glucose levels is a distinct advantage.

The enzyme activity values in the cat's liver indicate that dietary gluconeogenic amino acids are deaminated and converted to glucose rather than being directly oxidized for energy.[72] Liver phosphoenolpyruvate carboxykinase (PEPCK), a major gluconeogenic enzyme, does not change in activity level when cats that were previously fed high-protein diets are subjected to fasting.[65] In addition, no significant changes in

hepatic PEPCK activity occurs when cats are switched from a low-protein diet (17.5%) to a high-protein diet (70%).[73] These data support the supposition that the hepatic gluconeogenic enzymes in the cat are permanently fixed at a high rate of activity, necessitating the rapid conversion of excess dietary amino acids to glucose.

There also may be differences between cats and omnivores in the relative importance of various gluconeogenic and carbohydrate metabolizing pathways. Compared with omnivorous species, the cat has a high hepatic activity of the enzyme serine-pyruvate aminotransferase and low activity of the enzyme serine dehydratase.[73,74] It appears that the cat is able to convert the amino acid serine to glucose by a route that does not involve either pyruvate or serine dehydratase. An alternate pathway has been proposed for the conversion of serine to glucose.[75] It has been observed that a high activity of the first enzyme in this alternate pathway, serine-pyruvate aminotransferase, appears to be associated with flesh-eating dietary habits in mammals.[73]

After absorption into the body, glucose must be phosphorylated to glucose 6-phosphate before it can be metabolized. The liver of most omnivorous animals, including the domestic dog, has two enzymes that catalyze this reaction, glucokinase and hexokinase. Hexokinase is active when low levels of glucose are delivered to the liver, and glucokinase operates whenever the liver receives a high load of glucose from the portal vein. The cat liver has active hexokinase but does not have active glucokinase.[76] Consequently, the rate of glucose metabolism in the liver of the cat cannot increase in response to high levels of soluble carbohydrate in the diet to the same degree as the liver of species possessing both enzymes. It can be postulated that species having both enzymes have a greater capacity to handle high glucose diets than do those that possess only hexokinase.

The fact that dogs and cats do not require carbohydrate in their diets is usually immaterial because the nutrient content of most commercial foods includes at least a moderate level of this nutrient. In general, dry pet foods contain the highest amount of carbohydrate. Commercial dry foods may include between 30% and 60% carbohydrate, and canned foods contain anywhere between 0% and 30%.[77] The largest proportion of carbohydrate in pet foods is provided by starch. Cooked starch is well digested by both dogs and cats.[44,78,79] It provides an economical and digestible energy source, and it is also essential for the extrusion process that is used in the preparation of most dry pet foods. The digestibility of dietary starch by dogs and cats is affected by heat treatment and size of the starch granules. Heating greatly increases digestibility, and finely ground starch is more digestible than coarsely ground granules.[77,80]

Although cooked starch provides an excellent energy source, certain individual disaccharides, such as sucrose and lactose, are not well tolerated by pets.[81] An animal's ability to digest and use these sugars is governed by the levels of sucrase (beta-fructofuranidase) and lactase (beta-galactosidase) found in the cells of the intestinal lumen. As in most species, the activity of lactase in dogs and cats tends to decrease with age. Queen's milk contains approximately 3% to 5% lactose, which comprises about 20% of its metabolizable energy.[82] Although kittens can digest this high level of lactose, some adult cats may exhibit diarrhea when consuming high levels of lactose. As a result of a loss of lactase activity with age, feeding adult companion animals large amounts of milk or other dairy products often results in maldigestion.[83] Small quantities of these foods can be digested by most pets, but large quantities cause diarrhea because of the osmotic effect of the sugar that escapes digestion and the volatile fatty acids that are produced by bacterial fermentation in the large intestine. Although it has not been demonstrated in dogs or cats, data in other species indicate that very young animals have low levels of sucrase activity during the first few weeks of life. For this reason, sucrose solutions should not be used as energy sources for very young or orphaned puppies and kittens.[49]

Although dietary fiber is not a required nutrient per se, the inclusion of small amounts of fiber in the diets of companion animals is necessary for the normal functioning of the gastrointestinal tract. Insoluble fiber, which is the type of fiber that is included in most pet foods, functions to increase the bulk of the diet, contributes to satiety, and maintains normal intestinal transit time and gastrointestinal tract motility. Common sources of dietary fiber in pet foods include wheat middlings, tomato, citrus and grape pomace, beet pulp, and the hulls of soybeans and peanuts. Corn, rice, wheat, and barley all contribute digestible carbohydrates and also supply small amounts of fiber. In addition, protein sources in cereal-based pet foods add varying amounts of dietary fiber to the ration. The amount of fiber in pet foods varies with the type of food and the ingredients that are included. In general, the guaranteed maximum crude fiber content of most commercial pet foods ranges between 3% and 6% of the dry matter of the diet.[84,85]

Fats

FAT AS AN ENERGY SOURCE

The fat requirement of dogs and cats depends on the animal's need for essential fatty acids and for a calorically dense diet. In pet foods, dietary fat contributes approximately 8.5 kcal of metabolizable energy per gram, and protein and carbohydrate provide about 3.5 kcal/g. In addition to its high energy content, fat is also a highly digestible nutrient. The apparent digestibility of the fats found in high-quality pet foods is usually greater than 90%.[37,80] Because of its digestibility and higher energy content, increasing the level of fat in a pet's diet appreciably increases energy density. Both dogs and cats are able to maintain health when consuming diets that contain wide ranges of fat content, provided that other nutrients are adjusted to account for the changes in energy density.[44,49,58] Because animals normally eat or are fed to meet their energy needs, consumption of a more energy-dense ration will result in decreased consumption of the total volume of food. Therefore, if nutrients are not adjusted in relation to fat, multiple nutrient deficiencies can result.

Periods of high energy demand occur during growth, gestation, lactation, and prolonged periods of physical exercise. Feeding an energy-dense, high-fat diet during these periods allows the animal to consume adequate calories without having to ingest excessive amounts of dry matter. In addition, feeding a high-fat diet during strenuous physical work may have metabolic benefits. Fatty acids are the primary source of energy that is used by the body during prolonged physical exertion. Consumption of a high-fat diet by dogs appears to result in an enhanced ability to use fatty acids for energy, ultimately contributing to improved endurance.[86,87] Most dry dog foods that are marketed for adult

maintenance contain between 5% and 13% fat.[49,85] In comparison, the fat content of dry dog foods that are formulated for gestation, lactation, or performance may be 20% or greater.[88] In general, cat foods contain slightly higher amounts of dietary fat than do most dog foods. High levels of dietary fat can be fed to both dogs and cats with no detrimental results provided that all nutrients are balanced and that the animals are fed to meet, and not exceed, their energy requirements.

Most adult pets that live relatively sedentary life-styles do not need foods containing high levels of fat. Although high-fat pet foods are capable of providing good nutrition and supporting optimal health, sedentary animals may be inclined to overconsume these diets because of their high palatability and energy density. If adult pets are fed performance diets, strict portion-controlled feeding should be used to prevent excessive energy consumption and weight gain. Likewise, feeding high-fat, energy-dense foods during periods of rapid growth should be strictly monitored. Careful monitoring is especially important in large breeds of dogs. High-fat foods that are balanced for all essential nutrients are capable of supporting a high rate of growth in dogs and cats, if they are fed *ad libitum*. However, maximal growth rate has been shown to be incompatible with proper skeletal development in dogs and other species.[89-91] Portion-controlled feeding should therefore be used to control a growing pet's weight gain, rate of growth, and body condition (see Section 4, pp. 237–239; see also Section 5, pp. 293–296).

Fat as a Source of Essential Fatty Acids

In addition to providing energy, fat is necessary in the diet of dogs and cats as a source of essential fatty acids (EFA). The fatty acids that are necessary for normal metabolism are linoleic acid and arachidonic acid of the n-6 series and, possibly, alpha-linolenic acid of the n-3 series (see Section 1, p. 23). All of these necessary fatty acids are long-chain, polyunsaturated fatty acids. Like most animals, dogs are able to meet their requirements for the n-6 fatty acids from an adequate dietary source of linoleic acid. Two key enzymes in the pathway for the synthesis of gamma-linolenic and arachidonic acid from linoleic acid are delta-6-desaturase and delta-5-desaturase. Unlike the dog, the cat is unable to synthesize arachidonic acid, because of the lack of delta-6-desaturase and low activity of delta-5-desaturase in the liver.[92-95] Recently, additional data have shown that the cat also has low levels of delta-8-, delta-5-, and delta-4-desaturase enzymes.[96,97]

When linoleic acid but not arachidonic acid is included in the diet, cats develop impaired platelet aggregation and thrombocytopenia, and queens fail to deliver viable kittens.[98,99] Interestingly, the male cat's reproductive performance is not impaired by arachidonic acid deficiency, which appears to be because of the testes' ability to produce adequate arachidonic acid from linoleate for its own use. In addition, cats that are deficient in arachidonic acid exhibit slight increases in hepatic neutral fat content and mild mineralization of the kidneys. Other clinical signs may include poor coat condition, retarded growth, impaired wound healing, and the development of skin lesions.[104,94] The addition of 0.04% ME arachidonic acid to purified diets containing adequate linoleic acid results in normal reproductive performance in female cats.[55]

Only linoleic acid is required in the diet of dogs, but a cat's diet must contain both linoleic acid and arachidonic acid. The parent fatty acid linoleate is essential for the maintenance of normal skin functions, such as the regulation of water permeability.[101] Linoleic acid also functions as the precursor for several derived fatty acids that are essential to the body for proper membrane structure, normal growth, maintenance of skin and coat condition, and lipid transport in the blood. Dietary arachidonic acid is required by the cat for functions that depend primarily on the formation of eicosanoids from arachidonic acid, such as reproductive function and platelet aggregation.[99]

DIETARY FAT AND ESSENTIAL FATTY ACID REQUIREMENTS

Dogs

The EFA requirement of the dog is usually expressed in terms of linoleic acid content because the dog's physiological requirement for EFAs can be met by sufficient dietary linoleic acid. In addition, it is of practical value to denote the requirement in this way because linoleic acid is the most prevalent EFA in most foods.[49] The National Research Council (NRC) and the Association of American Feed Control Officials (AAFCO) Canine Nutrient Profile both recommend that the canine diet for adult maintenance provide a minimum of 1% of the dry weight as linoleic acid and 5% total fat.[49,102] The AAFCO recommendations further suggest that this level be increased to 8% total fat during periods of growth and reproduction.[102]

Cats

Exact quantitative estimates for EFA requirements in cats are difficult to make because adequate levels of linoleic acid in the diet will decrease the requirement for arachidonic acid and high levels of arachidonic acid can meet some of the needs for linoleic acid.[55] One study demonstrated that dietary linoleic acid at a level of 6.7% of dietary calories is more than adequate to prevent deficiency signs in the cat.[101] Extrapolation of data on the unsaturation index of liver lipids and comparisons to data reported in the rat were used to determine a linoleic acid requirement estimate of 2.5% of the calories in the diet.[103–105] Other data demonstrated that 0.04% of the energy supplied as arachidonic acid would support adequate reproduction in queens provided that other interfering polyunsaturated fatty acids were not present in the diet.[99] Many fish oils contain n-3 fatty acids that can inhibit the body's ability to use arachidonic acid. The NRC recommends that arachidonic acid supply 0.02% of the dry weight in a diet with an energy density of 5000 kcal of ME per kilogram.[58] This recommended amount is equivalent to 0.04% of the metabolizable calories. The same group recommends that linoleic acid should supply a minimum of 1.0% of the metabolizable calories in the dry diet to meet the needs of all stages of the cat's life.[58] The AAFCO Nutrient Profile for Cats recommends 0.5% linoleic acid and 0.02% arachidonic acid in diets containing 4000 kcal/kg of metabolizable energy.[102]

DEFICIENCIES AND EXCESSES

Low amounts of fat in the diet can lead to deficiencies in both total energy and EFAs. The palatability of dog and cat diets is strongly affected by fat content. To a limit, increasing fat results in enhanced palatability. Similarly, decreasing fat below a certain level causes decreased acceptability of the diet. This effect is believed to be the result of both the consistency and the flavor that fat contributes to a pet food. Because low-fat diets may not be readily accepted by pets, their potential for causing an energy or EFA deficiency is further exacerbated by causing a decrease in food intake.

In dogs, an EFA deficiency results in a dry, dull coat, hair loss, and the eventual development of skin lesions. Over time, the skin becomes pruritic, greasy, and susceptible to infection. A change in the surface lipids in the skin alters the normal bacterial flora and can predispose the animal to secondary bacterial infections.[106] Epidermal peeling, interdigital exudation, and otitis externa have also been reported in EFA deficient dogs.[107] Because EFAs are important for the maintenance of the epidermal barrier and because skin cells have a high rate of turnover, the skin is particularly vulnerable to EFA deficiencies. Linoleic acid deficiency in cats results in similar dermatological signs. In addition, kittens will fail to grow normally, and they may develop fatty degeneration of the liver and fat deposition in the kidneys.[55,108,109]

EFA deficiencies are not common in dogs and cats. These deficiencies develop only over a long period of time. When they do occur, deficiencies are usually associated with the consumption of diets that are either poorly formulated or have been stored improperly. Most well-formulated diets contain sufficient amounts of EFAs, but exposure to high environmental temperatures and humidity for long periods of time can promote oxidation of the unsaturated fatty acids in the food. This process is commonly referred to as rancidity. If insufficient antioxidants are present, EFA activity is destroyed. As the unsaturated fats are destroyed by oxidation, not only is EFA activity lost, but so are the vitamins D, E, and biotin. EFA deficiency in dogs and cats can also occur as a complication of other diseases, such as pancreatitis, biliary disease, hepatic disease, and malabsorption.[106]

Although commercially prepared foods will not normally cause fat or EFA deficiency, many pet owners believe that supplementing their pet's diet with corn oil or some other type of fat will improve coat quality. This supplement will only be effective if the pet is truly suffering from an EFA or fat deficiency. If that is the case, completely changing the diet to a well-formulated pet food that supplies all of the essential nutrients in their correct proportions, including fat and the EFA, is recommended. Simply adding a source of fat and/or EFA to a deficient diet may or may not solve the EFA deficit and has the potential to further imbalance a diet that is already inadequate. In some cases, fatty acid supplementation may be effective in treating certain inflammatory and hyperproliferative skin diseases in companion animals. Recent research indicates that providing certain types of polyunsaturated fatty acids promotes the formation of less inflammatory agents, resulting in a lessening of clinical symptoms (see Section 6, pp. 376–381).

Excess fat intake can also be detrimental to a pet's health. Both dogs and cats are able to digest and assimilate diets containing high levels of fat.[45,110] However, providing more fat than the gastrointestinal tract can effectively digest and absorb will result in fatty stools (steatorrhea) and diarrhea. This problem is most commonly observed when pet owners provide their dog or cat with table scraps that are composed predominantly of fatty foods. In addition, the long-term consumption of diets that are very high in fat may lead to weight gain and obesity because of the high palatability and energy density of the diet. Feeding diets that are very high in fat and do not have all other nutrients balanced relative to energy density may result in the development of deficiencies in other essential nutrients. Lastly, excessive levels of polyunsaturated fatty acids in the diet cause an increase in an animal's vitamin E requirement. Vitamin E functions as an antioxidant in the body, protecting cellular membrane lipids from peroxidation. The vitamin will be preferentially oxidized before the unsaturated fatty acids, thus protecting them from rancidity. However, vitamin E is destroyed in this process. Therefore as the level of unsaturated fatty acids in the diet of an animal increases, so does its requirement for vitamin E. If a pet food contains very high levels of polyunsaturated fatty acids or if an owner is supplementing a balanced diet with high amounts of corn or vegetable oil, vitamin E in the diet must concomitantly be increased. In cats a condition called pansteatitis or "yellow fat disease" occurs when their diets are high in unsaturated fatty acids and marginal or low in vitamin E (see Section 5, pp. 303–304).

CHAPTER 12

Protein and Amino Acids

P rotein is required by the body for two major purposes: to provide the essential amino acids that may be used for protein synthesis and to supply nitrogen for the synthesis of dispensable amino acids and other essential nitrogen-containing compounds (see Section 1, p. 27). Animals do not have a dietary requirement for protein per se, but they require the essential amino acids and a certain level of nitrogen. This requirement is commonly expressed as a protein requirement because amino acids and nitrogen are most typically supplied in the diet in the form of intact protein. Adult animals require dietary protein to replace protein losses in skin, hair, digestive enzymes, and mucosal cells; protein also replaces amino acid losses from normal cellular protein catabolism. Young animals have these same maintenance requirements plus an added requirement for the growth of new tissue. If protein is deficient in the diet, adult animals will experience negative nitrogen balance and the loss of lean body tissue and immature animals will exhibit decreased weight gain or weight loss and impaired growth and development.

An animal's *protein requirement* is defined as the minimum intake of dietary protein that promotes optimal performance.[111] The criteria that have been used most often to evaluate performance when determining protein requirements in dogs and cats are nitrogen balance and growth rate. Nitrogen balance studies use the fact that protein, on the average, contains 16% nitrogen. The nitrogen content of food and excreted matter is commonly measured using an analytical test called the Kjeldahl method.[112] A measurement of nitrogen intake and excretion by the body provides a rough estimate of the body's protein status. Nitrogen balance is calculated as Nitrogen balance = Nitrogen intake – Nitrogen excretion from urine and feces. The nitrogen in the feces is made up

of unabsorbed dietary protein and nitrogen from endogenous sources. Urinary nitrogen is composed primarily of urea, which is the end product of protein catabolism. Further nitrogen losses occur from desquamated cells of the skin surface, hair, and nails. However, these losses are very difficult to measure and are usually not considered when measuring nitrogen balance in experimental studies.

Requirement studies with growing puppies use maximum positive nitrogen balance or maximum growth rate to indicate a level of protein in the diet that is adequate; studies for adult companion animals use zero nitrogen balance to indicate dietary protein adequacy. Zero nitrogen balance means that the body's daily loss of protein is replaced by intake, without a net gain or loss in total body protein. Although the vast majority of requirement studies have used zero nitrogen balance to assess the protein requirement of adult animals, it is important to recognize that diets containing this level of protein may not be adequate to promote optimal performance and health. For example, adult dogs that were fed diets containing just enough protein to attain zero nitrogen balance were found to be more susceptible to the toxicity of certain drugs.[113] In addition, higher levels of protein in the diet may be needed to maintain optimal protein reserves.[114] Although protein is not stored in the body as is fat and, to a lesser degree, carbohydrate, the term "reserves" refers to the ability of the body to mobilize protein from prioritized body tissues during periods of stress. It is possible that the requirements obtained using zero nitrogen balance may represent a minimum protein requirement for adult animals. If this is the case, it would be prudent to feed slightly higher levels of protein than this minimum amount to healthy adults, especially during periods of stress.[111]

Nitrogen equilibrium (zero balance) is the normal state for healthy adult animals during maintenance. An animal is described as being in a state of positive nitrogen balance when protein intake exceeds excretion. Positive nitrogen balance occurs when new tissue is being synthesized by the body, such as during the physiological stages of growth and gestation, or during the recovery phase after prolonged illness or injury. Negative nitrogen balance results when protein excretion exceeds intake. An animal that exhibits negative balance is losing nitrogen from tissues more rapidly than it is being replaced. This loss of nitrogen may occur for several reasons. If the animal is consuming an insufficient amount of energy, body tissues must be catabolized to provide energy to the body. If inadequate levels of available protein and/or amino acids are fed, tissue replacement cannot occur. Severe or prolonged illness or injury results in a catabolic state in animals that is evidenced by excessive breakdown of the body's tissues and negative nitrogen balance. Excess losses of nitrogen from the urine during renal failure or from the gastrointestinal tract during some types of gastrointestinal diseases can also cause negative nitrogen balance to occur (Table 12–1).

FACTORS AFFECTING PROTEIN REQUIREMENT

The determination of the exact protein requirements for dogs and cats is a difficult task because many factors can affect an individual animal's need for this nutrient. Dietary factors that affect nitrogen balance include protein quality and amino acid composition,

TABLE 12-1
States of Nitrogen Balance

STATE	BALANCE	PHYSIOLOGICAL STAGE
Zero	N* intake = N excretion	Maintenance
Positive	N intake > N excretion	Growth, gestation, recovery from illness
Negative	N intake < N excretion	Inadequate nutrition, severe illness or injury, urinary N loss during renal failure, gastrointestinal tract loss during certain diseases

*N, Nitrogen.

Factors Affecting Protein Requirement

Protein quality: As protein quality increases, protein requirement decreases.

Amino acid composition: As amino acid composition improves, protein requirement decreases.

Protein digestibility: As protein digestibility increases, protein requirement decreases.

Energy density: As energy density increases, protein requirement as a % of the diet, increases.

protein digestibility, and the energy density of the diet. In addition, an animal's activity level, physiological state, and prior nutritional status can all influence protein requirement as determined by nitrogen balance or growth rate (see the box above).

An animal's protein requirement varies inversely with the protein source's digestibility and with its ability to provide all of the essential amino acids in their correct quantities and ratios. As protein digestibility and quality increase, the level of protein that must be included in the diet to meet the animal's needs will decrease. Most of the protein requirement studies that have been conducted in dogs and cats have used either purified or semipurified diets. The protein and amino acids in these diets are highly digestible and available. However, most of the protein sources that are used in today's commercial pet foods have comparatively low digestibility coefficients. For example, protein digestibility in a semipurified diet approaches 95%, but that of high-quality, commercial diets ranges between 80% and 90%. On the other hand, low-quality, commercial pet foods can have protein digestibilities that are less than 75%.[60] As a result of these differences, requirement studies with purified or semipurified diets tend to underestimate the protein requirements of animals that are consuming mixed protein diets that contain less available nutrients.

Protein quality will also influence an animal's protein requirement. The higher the biological value of a protein, the less the amount that is needed to meet all of an animal's essential amino acid needs (see Section 1, pp. 27–28). Therefore, as the quality of the protein in the test diet increases, the estimated requirement decreases. Again, the diets that were used in most amino acid and protein requirement studies had amino acid contents that were adjusted to carefully fit the needs of the experiment. Few, if any, naturally occurring protein sources have amino acid compositions that specifically fit the requirements of companion animals. Most practical sources of protein contain excesses of some amino acids and slight or severe deficiencies of others, relative to the animal's requirement. Commercial pet foods correct for these inadequacies by using mixtures of protein sources that have complimentary profiles of essential amino acids.

Correction factors can be applied to requirement estimates that were determined using purified or high-quality protein sources. These factors account for differences in protein digestibility and quality in the sources included in commercially prepared pet foods.[49,58] However, ingredients that are used in the formulation of commercial rations can vary greatly in protein digestibility and quality.[115,116] Therefore much care must be taken when interpreting and using requirement data that have been derived from studies using purified diets. In the end, the only totally effective means of evaluating the amino acid or protein content of a particular diet is to feed the diet and thoroughly evaluate the results.

The caloric density of the diet used in the requirement study significantly affects the estimated protein requirement. The presence of nonprotein calories in a ration have a protein-sparing effect. A diet must first meet an animal's energy needs before the energy-containing nutrients can be used for other purposes. Therefore adequate nonprotein calories in the form of carbohydrate or fat will spare the protein in the diet from being metabolized for energy. If sufficient nonprotein calories are not provided, at least a portion of the dietary protein will be metabolized as an energy source. At caloric intakes that are less than the animal's energy requirement, protein will not be available for the building or replacing of body tissues because it will all be used for energy. Therefore, when a diet is limiting in both energy and protein, weight loss and a loss of lean body tissue result. Nitrogen balance studies have shown that when dietary protein level is held constant, nitrogen retention increases as caloric intake increases and approaches the animal's energy requirement.[117]

A second aspect of the relationship between protein and energy must also be examined. Assuming that adequate nonprotein energy is present in the diet, as the energy density of the diet increases, a higher total concentration of protein is required for maximal nitrogen retention. The most important factors that affect the energy density of commercial pet foods are dietary fat concentration and diet digestibility. The relationship between energy density and protein content is illustrated by the results of a study with growing dogs.[118] When a diet containing 25% crude protein and 20% fat was fed, maximal growth rate resulted. However, when the fat content of the diet was increased to 30%, 29% crude protein was necessary to support maximal growth. The reason for this change relates to an animal's tendency to eat to satisfy its energy needs. Provided that these controls are in place, an animal will naturally consume less of a more energy-dense ration. Pet owners that use portion-controlled feeding regimens usually adjust quantity according to their pet's body weight and/or growth rate. Therefore portion-

controlled feeding schedules are still regulated according to the pet's energy requirements. When lower quantities of food are fed, protein must contribute a higher proportion of the diet so that the animal will still be able to meet its total protein needs.
Although protein is the most commonly used example, this relationship with energy
also applies to all other essential nutrients.[119]

Protein requirement studies must also take into account an animal's prior nutritional status and physiological state. The amount of absorbed protein needed to produce
nitrogen equilibrium depends on the degree of protein depletion. Dogs with depleted
body protein reserves require lower levels of nitrogen to achieve nitrogen balance than
do dogs with normal reserves.[120] This effect may be the result of an increased efficiency
of absorption and use of dietary protein when in a depleted state or to a decreased rate
of protein catabolism. Ensuring that all dogs are in positive nitrogen balance and have
adequate body protein reserves by feeding a high-protein diet before the onset of a
requirement study has been used to eliminate this discrepancy. Physiological state also
directly affects nitrogen balance and will therefore affect the outcome of requirement
studies that use nitrogen balance. In growing puppies and kittens, rate of growth and,
subsequently, protein requirement decrease slightly with age.[115,121–124]

Protein Requirements of the Dog

Numerous studies have been conducted on the minimum protein requirement of the
adult dog. However, differences in protein sources, energy densities, and amino acid
balance of the experimental diets that were used have led to a great deal of confusion
regarding this requirement. Generally when diets containing very high-quality protein
sources are fed, adult dogs require between 4% and 7% of their metabolizable energy
(ME) calories to be supplied as protein.[125–127] However, when lower-quality protein
sources are included in the diet, the requirement increases to more than 20% of the ME
calories.[57,111,128] This value is equivalent to 21% protein in a typical dry dog food containing 3.5 kcal of ME per gram (g).

The protein requirement of growing puppies is significantly higher than that of adult
dogs. Early studies using mixed protein sources reported minimum protein requirements of between 17% and 22% of ME for growing dogs. These experiments used maximum weight gain as an indicator of minimum protein needs.[118,129,130] A more recent
study, which also used weight gain as the criterion, reported a slightly lower requirement.[31] However, the protein source used in this experiment was of high quality compared to that used in the earlier studies. Nitrogen balance data in this study provided a
protein requirement estimate of 20% of ME or greater.[31] It appears that weight gain in
growing dogs will be maximized at lower protein intakes than will nitrogen retention. It
has been estimated that a minimum of 19.5% of the growing dog's calories should be
supplied as high-quality protein to maximize nitrogen retention in puppies between the
ages of 8 and 17 weeks.[111] Another recent study suggested a value of 16% of ME calories as a minimum for growth in dogs.[132] However, the diets used in this study were
composed of purified amino acids, not intact protein, so they were almost 100% avail-

TABLE 12-2
Suggested Minimum Levels of Protein in the Diets of Dogs and Cats as a Percentage of ME

	NRC*	AAFCO
Dogs		
Adult maintenance	—†	18% ME
Growth and reproduction	11.4% ME	22% ME
Cats		
Adult maintenance	10% ME	23% ME
Growth and reproduction	17% ME	26% ME

*NRC 1985, 1986.
†Estimate not provided.

able. The investigators found that a level of 16% of ME supported greater T-cell responses and resulted in greater nitrogen retention in growing puppies than did a diet containing 12% protein. It was emphasized that this value should be taken as a minimum. Because all of the amino acids in the diets were highly available, there were no antagonisms resulting from amino acid excesses or imbalances and no allowances had to be made for losses due to processing or storage.[132]

The importance of considering protein digestibility and amino acid content when determining an animal's protein requirement is well illustrated by a comparison of the protein requirement estimates provided by the 1974 and 1985 National Research Council's (NRC) *Nutrient Requirements for Dogs*.[49,50] The 1985 NRC recommendations suggest a minimum protein requirement for growing dogs of 11.4% of ME calories.[49] This amount is approximately half the value that was proposed in their 1974 publication. The change in 1985 was a direct result of the publication of a number of studies that determined the dog's requirement for most of the essential amino acids. Although these studies provided valuable information concerning the minimum amino acid requirements of the dog, they were all derived from diets containing carefully controlled levels of purified amino acids. The use of these studies to derive recommendations for protein levels in practical dog foods resulted in estimates that were much lower than those based on mixed protein diets. As a result, difficulty in the interpretation and use of the 1985 recommendations led some pet food companies to return to the 1974 requirement recommendations for formulation of their pet foods. When the Canine Nutrition Expert Committee of The Association of American Feed Control Officials (AAFCO) published *Nutrient Profiles for Dog Foods* in 1992, they reinstated the original protein requirement for growth and reproduction that was published in the 1974 NRC report. The committee recommended a minimum level of 18% protein on a dry-matter basis for adult maintenance and 22% for growth and reproduction (Table 12–2).[102] These values are equivalent to 18 and 22% of ME in a food containing 3.5 Kcal/g. If the energy density of the diet is higher, appropriate adjustments in protein content must be made.

PROTEIN REQUIREMENTS OF THE CAT

Early studies of the cat's nutrient requirements showed that the cat has a protein requirement that is substantially higher than that of other mammals, including the dog.[59,122,133] When growing kittens were fed varying levels of dietary protein supplied as minced herring and minced liver, growth was reported to be satisfactory only when protein exceeded 30% of the dry weight of the diet.[122] These results were compared with requirement studies in the growing puppy that showed that puppies fed mixed diets required only 20% protein for adequate growth and development.[124] One of the first studies of the protein requirement of the adult cat reported that 21% dietary protein was necessary to maintain the cats in nitrogen balance when fed a mixed diet containing liver and white fish as the primary protein sources.[128]

More recently, experimentation using crystalline amino acids and protein isolates has allowed more precise definition of the minimum protein requirements of growing kittens and adult cats. One study reported a protein requirement of 18% to 20% (by weight) in growing kittens fed either crystalline amino acid diets or casein diets supplemented with methionine.[134] A second study reported requirements as low as 16% of ME calories when growing kittens were fed a purified diet containing all of the essential amino acids in their correct concentrations and ratios.[123] Using a similar semipurified diet, the protein requirement of adult cats was determined to be 12.5% of ME.[135] The profound effect that protein digestibility, amino acid balance, and amino acid availability have on determining an animal's dietary protein requirement is illustrated by the substantially lower values that were obtained when semipurified and purified diets were used to determine requirements. However, the comparison of these current figures with ideal minimum protein requirements of other mammals still demonstrates that the cat, together with other obligate carnivores such as the fox and the mink, has a higher requirement for dietary protein. For example, although the cat requires 20% of a 100% available, well-balanced ideal protein for growth and 12% for maintenance, the dog requires only 12% and 4% respectively.[121] It should be noted that these values are substantially lower than the protein requirement of the cat when fed a practical diet containing protein sources that are not perfectly balanced or 100% available.

The 1986 NRC recommendations for cats suggests a minimum of 240 g/kg of protein in the diets of growing kittens and 140 g/kg in the diets of adult cats. These values are calculated assuming diet energy densities of 5 kcal/g. This amount is equivalent to 24% protein, or only 17% of ME calories for growing kittens and 14% protein, or 10% of ME calories, for adults (Table 12–2). These values assume highly available and well-balanced protein sources. The NRC recommendations note that a variable proportion of the protein included in commercially prepared cat foods is indigestible and that processing methods may result in changes in the availability of certain amino acids. Therefore it is suggested that pet food companies make allowances for the amino acid composition of the proteins included in their foods and for the digestibility and availability of the protein. A value of 80% to 90% availability is suggested for high-quality ingredients and 60% to 70% for lower-quality ingredients (see Section 3, p. 195).[58]

The NRC provides recommendations for minimum nutrient requirements for dogs and cats, not recommended allowances for inclusion in pet foods. The AAFCO profiles that were established by the Feline and Canine Nutrition Expert Committees provide nutrient estimates for use in the actual formulation of pet foods. Therefore, it is not surprising that the AAFCO *Nutrient Profile for Cats* suggests a substantially higher level of protein for inclusion in commercially prepared cat foods.[102] A level of 30% of the diet (on a dry-matter basis) is suggested for growth and reproduction in diets containing 4 kcal of ME per gram of food. This value is equivalent to 26% of ME calories. A level of 26% of the diet is suggested for adult maintenance. This level is equivalent to about 23% of ME calories (Table 12–2). Other investigators have suggested a minimum level of 15% of ME calories provided by a high-quality protein for adult maintenance in cats. This level corresponds to a level of 17% (by weight) of a diet containing 4 kcal/kg.[111]

The cat's comparatively high dietary requirement for protein is the result of increased needs for the maintenance of normal body tissue rather than to increased needs for growth. Approximately 60% of the growing kitten's protein requirement is used for the maintenance of body tissues, and only 40% is used for growth.[124] The opposite is true in most of the other species that have been studied. For example, the growing rat requires only 35% of its dietary protein for maintenance and 65% for growth.[50] Similarly, the growing dog uses only 33% of its protein requirement for maintenance and 66% for growth.[121]

The elevated protein requirement for maintenance in the cat occurs as a result of the inability of the nitrogen catabolic enzymes in the cat's liver to adapt to changes in dietary protein intake.[73] When most mammals are fed diets that are high in protein, the enzymes involved in amino acid catabolism, nitrogen disposal, and gluconeogenesis will increase in activity to use surplus amino acids and to convert excess nitrogen to urea. Conversely, when low-protein diets are fed, the activity of these enzymes declines, resulting in a conservation of nitrogen.[136-138] This adaptive mechanism is of distinct advantage because it allows animals to conserve amino acids while consuming low-protein diets; it also provides a mechanism to catabolize excess amino acids when consuming high-protein diets. One study involved feeding two groups of adult cats either high-protein (70%) or low-protein (17.5%) diets for one month.[73] The activities of three urea cycle enzymes and seven nitrogen catabolic enzymes in the liver were then measured. With the exception of one transaminase enzyme, no significant differences in enzyme activity were found between the cats fed the low-protein diet and the cats fed the high-protein diet. Several gluconeogenic and lipogenic enzymes were also measured, none of which exhibited any change in activity in response to changes in dietary protein level. On the other hand, similar rat hepatic enzymes increase in activity from 2.75 fold to thirteen fold after rats are changed from a low-protein diet to a high-protein diet.[139]

In addition to the inability of the cat's protein-catabolizing enzymes to adapt to changes in dietary protein levels, the enzymes involved in nitrogen catabolism function at relatively high rates of activity.[73] This metabolic state causes the cat to catabolize a substantial amount of protein after each meal, regardless of its protein content. Thus the cat does not have the capability to conserve nitrogen from the body's general nitrogen pool. The only alternative that ensures adequate conservation of body protein stores is

the consistent consumption of a diet containing high levels of protein.[124] It can be theorized that because of the cat's strict adherence to a carnivorous diet, it experienced little selective pressure throughout its evolutionary history to develop metabolic adaptations to low-protein diets. As a result, the cat is now obligated to always consume meals that contain high amounts of dietary protein.

Another factor that contributes to an animal's dietary protein requirement is its need for essential amino acids. When the protein nutrition of the cat was first studied, it was postulated that its high dietary requirement may be the result of an unusually high requirement for one or more of the essential amino acids. The results of several experimental studies showed that with the exception of slightly higher requirements for leucine, threonine, methionine, and arginine, and a unique dietary requirement for taurine, the requirements for specific essential amino acids are not significantly greater in the cat than in the rat, dog, or pig.[105,124] Therefore elevated essential amino acid requirements are not the cause of the cat's high-protein requirement. The domestic cat does have two unique amino acid requirements, however. The first involves the cat's inability to synthesize adequate arginine for normal function of the urea cycle and protein synthesis, and the second concerns the cat's dietary requirement for taurine, an amino sulfonic acid.

Arginine Requirement

The amino acid arginine is not considered a dietary essential in most adult animals because most species can synthesize adequate amounts to meet their metabolic needs. However, arginine has been shown to be indispensable for both dogs and cats throughout life.[140,141] Arginine is needed by the body for normal protein synthesis and as an essential component of the urea cycle. Arginine functions in the urea cycle as an ornithine precursor and urea cycle intermediate. In this capacity arginine allows the large amounts of ammonia generated after the consumption of a high-protein meal to be converted to urea for excretion from the body.

The lack of arginine in the diet causes an immediate and severe deficiency response in the cat. Cats will develop severe hyperammonemia within several hours of consuming a single arginine-free meal.[142] Symptoms include emesis (vomiting), muscular spasms, ataxia, hyperesthesia (sensitivity to touch), and tetanic spasms. These symptoms can eventually lead to coma and death. Dogs show similar, but less severe, clinical signs of arginine deficiency following consumption of an arginine-free meal.[140,143]

There appear to be two basic reasons for the cat's extreme sensitivity to arginine deficiency. First of all, the cat is unable to synthesize de novo ornithine. Ornithine is an arginine precursor within the urea cycle. In most animals, the amino acids glutamate and proline act as precursors for ornithine synthesis in the intestinal mucosa. However, the cat's intestinal mucosal cells have extremely low levels of active pyrroline-5-carboxylate synthase, an essential enzyme in this pathway. The cat also has low activity of a second essential enzyme, ornithine aminotransferase.[144] In addition to being unable to synthesize ornithine, the cat is also unable to synthesize arginine from ornithine for use by extrahepatic tissues, even if dietary ornithine is provided. Work

TABLE 12-3
Arginine Synthesis

REACTION	MOST MAMMALS	CATS
Glutamate + Proline ⟶ Ornithine (Intestine)	Normal	Low
Ornithine ⟶ Citrulline (Intestine)	Normal	Little Activity
Citrulline travels to the Kidney	Does occur	Does not occur
Citrulline ⟶ Arginine (Kidney)	Does occur	Does not occur

conducted in the rat demonstrated that the normal route of arginine synthesis for use by extrahepatic tissues involves both the liver and the kidney.[145] Arginine cannot leave the liver to provide extrahepatic tissues because high activity of liver arginase prevents its accumulation to a concentration above that of the bloodstream. However, citrulline, which is produced from ornithine either in the intestinal mucosa or in the liver as a urea cycle intermediate, can travel to the kidney where it is then converted to arginine. This arginine provides the kidney and other tissues of the body with needs for normal growth and tissue maintenance. In the cat, citrulline is not produced in the intestinal mucosa (because of the inability to produce ornithine), and the citrulline produced in the liver appears to be unable to leave the hepatocyte to be converted to arginine by the kidney.[55,124] As a direct result of these two metabolic deficiencies, arginine becomes an essential amino acid for both urea cycle function and for normal growth and maintenance in the cat (Table 12–3). The importance of arginine for normal functioning of the urea cycle, coupled with the cat's high and inflexible rate of protein catabolism, causes the cat to be extremely sensitive to arginine deficiency. Like the cat, the growing dog also has a dietary requirement for arginine. However, the response of the growing dog to an arginine-deficient diet is not as severe as that observed in the immature cat.[140,143]

The growing kitten's requirement for arginine is estimated to be approximately 1.1% of a dry diet containing an ME of approximately 4.7 kcal/g.[105,140] Because arginine is found in adequate amounts in most protein sources, an arginine deficiency is not generally a practical problem in cats, provided that they are fed a diet containing adequate levels of protein.

Taurine Requirement

Taurine is a unique beta–amino-sulfonic acid that is not incorporated into proteins but is found as a free amino acid in tissues. It is synthesized by most mammals from methionine and cysteine during normal sulfur amino acid metabolism (Figure 12-1). The myocardium and retina contain high concentrations of free taurine, and these two tissues are able to concentrate taurine to levels that are 100- to 400-fold greater than those found in plasma.[146] Although taurine may be involved in many aspects of metabolism,

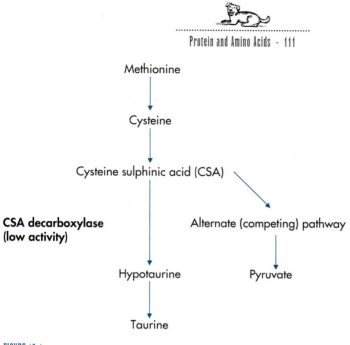

FIGURE 12-1
Taurine synthesis and metabolism in the cat

it is known to have important roles in bile acid conjugation, retinal function, and normal functioning of the myocardium.[146-148] Taurine is also necessary for normal reproductive performance in the queen.[149]

Cats are able to synthesize only small amounts of taurine.[150] This inability is presumed to be the result of the cat's low activity of an enzyme that is essential for taurine synthesis, cysteinesulfinic acid decarboxylase. In addition, a competing pathway of cysteine metabolism exists in the cat and results in the production of pyruvate rather than taurine from methionine and cysteine (Figure 12-1).[151] The cat is not unique in its limited capacity for taurine synthesis. Low levels of de novo synthesis have been reported in humans, Old World monkeys, rabbits, and guinea pigs.[152] However, the cat is the only species in which taurine deficiency occurs. This is the result of this species' unusually high metabolic demand for taurine. The domestic cat uses only taurine for bile-salt formation and, in contrast to other animals, cannot convert to conjugation of bile acids with glycine when the taurine supply is limited.[147] As a result, the cat has a continual requirement for taurine to replace fecal losses that occur from incomplete recovery by the enterohepatic circulation. Although humans and Old World monkeys also have limited capacity for taurine synthesis and prefer to conjugate bile acids with taurine, they will switch to glycine conjugation when dietary taurine is low.

Feline central retinal degeneration (FCRD) was the first clinical deficiency syndrome caused by taurine deficiency in the cat to be recognized. Taurine's primary role in the proper functioning of the retina involves the photoreceptor cells, where it regulates the flux of calcium and potassium ions across the photoreceptor pigment-epithelial cell bar-rier.[148] When taurine is absent, the photoreceptor cell membranes become disrupted and dysfunctional, eventually leading to cellular death and the loss of cells. A concomi-tant degeneration of the underlying tapetum lucidum can also occur.[153] Although abnor-malities in electroretinograms can be observed within five to six months of consuming taurine-deficient diets, visual impairment is only observed clinically when cats are in the later stages of retinal degeneration.[154-156] At this point, irreversible blindness occurs in most cats.

Taurine is also necessary for normal functioning of the myocardium. A deficiency results in the development of dilated cardiomyopathy (DCM).[146] This degenerative dis-ease has been reported in several species and causes decreased myocardial contractil-ity, which eventually leads to cardiac failure. Along with the retina, the myocardium is one of the tissues in the body that is able to concentrate taurine to levels much greater than those found in the plasma.[157] Heart studies indicate that taurine may confer a cal-cium and potassium stabilizing effect on heart tissue and may thereby ensure cationic stability and membrane integrity.[158]

One study reported data from 21 clinical cases of DCM in pet cats.[146] All of the cats were found to have significantly lower plasma taurine concentrations when compared with clinically normal cats. When the affected cats were supplemented with taurine (0.5 g, twice daily), all cats improved clinically within 2 weeks. By 3 to 4 weeks, the cats showed improved echocardiographs that eventually resulted in complete normalization of left ventricular function. When the study was published, all surviving cats were clini-cally and echocardiographically normal. In addition, two experimental cats that had been fed a purified diet containing marginally low levels of taurine for 4 years developed DCM. These cats also exhibited full recovery as a result of taurine supplementation. The authors of the study proposed that low levels of taurine in plasma and myocardial tis-sue is a major cause of the development of DCM in cats.

The dietary requirement for taurine in the cat is somewhat dependent on the level of sulfur amino acids (SAA) in the diet. Research studies have shown that the cat's tau-rine requirement increases when the SAA content of the diet is less than 1.55%.[159] Additional studies found that when weanling kittens were fed a taurine-deficient diet containing a level of SAAs near the requirement, all of the kittens developed FCRD. However, when the level of SAAs was doubled in the diet, none of the kittens developed FCRD during the 12-month study period.[55] These results are relevant to the reported occurrence of FCRD in cats that have been exclusively fed commercial dog food.[160] In general, dog foods have lower protein levels and lower SAA contents than commercial rations that have been formulated for cats.

The 1986 NRC recommended a taurine level of 500 to 750 parts per million in the dry diet of cats to prevent taurine deficiency and to maximize tissue stores.[58] However, diets formulated at these levels have been found to be inadequate.[151] A more recent report suggests adding a safety factor to previously established requirements to provide a more prudent estimate of 1000 mg/kg in dry diets and 2500 mg/kg in canned diets, on a dry-matter basis.[161-163] A higher level of taurine must be included in canned diets because recent studies have found that the taurine requirement of cats consuming

canned foods is substantially higher than that of cats consuming dry foods.[164,165] This appears to be the result of increased losses of taurine through increased enterohepatic circulation and bacterial degradation of taurocholic acid in the intestine.[165] Both the heat processing that is used to prepare canned diets and the type of protein that is included in the food are factors that contribute to the increased turnover of the body's taurine pool when cats are fed canned diets. The AAFCO *Nutrient Profiles for Cat Foods* requires that canned cat foods contain a minimum of 2000 mg/kg and that dry foods contain a minimum of 1000 mg/kg of taurine.[102]

Taurine is present only in animal tissues. High concentrations (200 to 400 mg/kg of wet weight) are found in meat, poultry, and fish. Shellfish are extremely rich sources of taurine, containing up to 2500 mg/kg.[105] Although a carnivorous diet will ensure the cat an adequate taurine intake, the consumption of a diet containing high amounts of plant products and cereal grains may not provide sufficient taurine. Of special concern are cereal-based dog foods that contain lower levels of protein and taurine. Unlike the cat, the dog does not require dietary taurine.[75] Therefore, while these diets are adequate for dogs, the practice of feeding dog foods to cats may result in taurine deficiency and the development of FCRD.[160]

Essential Amino Acids of Special Concern

The following amino acids have been identified as being essential for growing puppies and kittens: arginine, histidine, isoleucine, leucine, lysine, methionine, phenylalanine, threonine, tryptophan, and valine. Although both the dog and the cat have a dietary requirement for arginine, the cat is unusual in its immediate and severe reaction to the consumption of an arginine-free meal. The other amino acids that are of special concern in the feeding of dogs and cats are lysine and the SAAs methionine and cysteine. Of less practical concern, but of academic interest, is the cat's inability to convert the amino acid tryptophan to the B vitamin niacin.

Lysine

The growing dog's dietary requirement for lysine appears to increase as the level of total protein in the diet increases.[166] This effect has been demonstrated in other species and may be the result of amino acid imbalances and antagonisms with lysine at higher levels of protein intake.[111] This effect may be especially important because lysine is often the first limiting amino acid in cereal-based dog foods.[167] In addition, the lysine that is present in the diet is susceptible to certain types of processing damage that can occur in commercially prepared pet foods. The exposure of protein to excessive heat induces crosslinking between amino acids, resulting in decreased digestibility of the ration's total protein. Even mild heat treatment can result in a reaction between the epsilon-amino group of lysine and the amino groups of free amino acids with reducing sugars. The resultant complexes are resistant to digestion and result in a reduction in the amount of available lysine that can be supplied by the food. Therefore the lysine content of commercial pet foods must be closely monitored. The limiting amino acids in cereal proteins are lysine and tryptophan. However, meat products contain adequate amounts of these amino acids. The inclusion of meat proteins with cereal proteins in a pet food, coupled with properly controlled processing methods, will ensure that the ration contains an adequate level of available lysine. In a completely cereal-based dog food, either supplemental lysine or a meat source of lysine must be added (see Section 3, p. 176).

Methionine and Cysteine

The SAA methionine is essential for dogs and cats, but cysteine is dispensable. However, because methionine is used to synthesize cysteine by the body, approximately half of an animal's methionine requirement can be met by adequate levels of cysteine.[168,169] Therefore it is preferable to address a total SAA requirement rather than a specific methionine requirement for animals. The SAA requirement is substantially higher in the cat than it is in other mammals. Although growing dogs require a minimum of 1.06 g/1000 kcal of ME, the minimum requirement of growing cats is approximately 1.5 times this amount.[49,58] This high requirement may be a result of several factors. First, the cat is unique in its production of a compound called *felinine*. Felinine is synthesized from cysteine and is excreted in the urine of all cats. It is found in its highest concentration in the urine of adult, intact males.[170] Although its exact role is unknown, it has been suggested that felinine may be a urinary component involved in territorial marking or in the regulation of sterol metabolism in the cat species.[171] Other possible reasons for the cat's high SAA requirement are its needs for the maintenance of a thick hair coat and for increased methylation reactions necessary for the synthesis of phospholipids. Increased phospholipid synthesis is believed to be necessary for the absorption and transport of the high amount of fat that is normally included in cats' diets. Lastly, the cat's requirement for dietary taurine further adds to the cat's total requirement for SAAs in the diet.

In addition to the difference in SAA requirements between dogs and cats, there is some evidence that suggests that there may be differences in methionine requirements between breeds of dogs. One study showed that growing Labrador retrievers required higher levels of total SAAs to maximize growth and nitrogen retention than did growing beagles.[131] Methionine is usually the first limiting amino acid in most commercial pet foods that contain animal tissues and plant protein sources.[172] This fact, coupled with the high SAA requirement by cats, results in methionine being an important consideration for pet food companies during the formulation of nutritionally balanced pet foods.

The Cat's Inability to Convert Tryptophan to Niacin

The requirement for the B vitamin niacin is met in most animals through both the consumption of dietary nicotinamide and through the conversion of the essential amino acid tryptophan to nicotinic acid (Figure 12-2). The efficiency of conversion of tryptophan to niacin varies between species but is generally quite low (3%).[173] This is a result

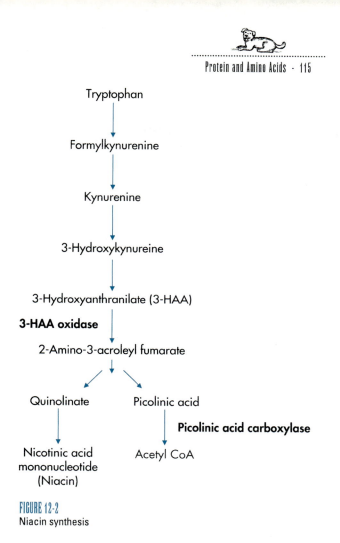

FIGURE 12-2
Niacin synthesis

of the existence of more dominant competing pathways of tryptophan metabolism. A branch point in the pathway involved in tryptophan catabolism results in the synthesis of either quinolinic acid or picolinic acid. Quinolinic acid is further metabolized to form niacin, and picolinic acid is converted to glutarate. Although most species have high levels of picolinate carboxylase activity that result in a higher production of picolinic acid, a substantial amount of niacin is still produced from the quinolinic acid branch. The activity of picolinate carboxylase in cats is 30 to 50 times higher than its activity in rats, resulting in negligible niacin synthesis from tryptophan in the cat.[173]

Animal tissues are well supplied with nicotinamide. The regular consumption of a carnivorous diet throughout evolutionary history would probably not result in selective pressure for the cat to synthesize niacin from precursor substances. However, it has been postulated that the high-protein diet of the cat would exert pressure toward a high rate of tryptophan catabolism (that is, the picolinic acid branch of the pathway). The rapid metabolism of tryptophan would prevent the accumulation of the amino acid and its intermediates, such as serotonin, to toxic levels. Animal proteins contain significantly higher levels of tryptophan than do plant proteins. Thus the high activity of picolinic carboxylase in the cat may prevent the accumulation of tryptophan and its by-products in the bloodstream following the consumption of a meal containing high amounts of animal protein.[75]

The inability of the cat to convert tryptophan to niacin is of little practical significance to the feeding management of pet cats because nicotinamide is widely distributed in feed ingredients. Sources of this vitamin in commercial pet foods include animal and fish by-products, distillers' grains and yeast, and certain oil meals. Therefore the chance of inducing a niacin deficiency through improper feeding practices are slim, regardless of the fact that the cat is unable to convert tryptophan to niacin for use by the body.

Protein Deficiency in Dogs and Cats

Signs of protein deficiency include retarded growth in young animals and weight loss and impaired reproductive and work performance in adults. A deficiency of protein commonly occurs with energy deficiency. This state is referred to as protein/calorie malnutrition (PCM). When PCM occurs, the animal exhibits lethargy, reduced digestive efficiency, and reduced resistance to infectious disease.[174] Lowered plasma protein levels occur after prolonged protein deficiency and can eventually lead to edema or ascites. There is also some evidence in other species that general undernutrition and protein deficiency during development can affect brain development and learning capabilities later in life.[175,176]

Protein deficiency is uncommon in companion animals that are fed balanced, commercial pet foods. This is probably due to the fact that the majority of commercial foods contain more protein than is needed to meet the minimum requirement.[84] When protein deficiency does occur, it is usually because owners are attempting to economize by feeding low-quality, poorly formulated rations during periods of high nutrient need, such as pregnancy or lactation. Additionally, cats that are fed cereal-based dog foods that contain marginally adequate levels of protein are at risk for the development of protein and/or taurine deficiency.

Protein Excess in the Diets of Dogs and Cats

As mentioned previously, there is some evidence suggesting that it may be beneficial to feed animals levels of protein that are higher than the minimum level necessary to maintain nitrogen equilibrium.[113,114] The additional protein may be used to provide protein reserves that contribute to the body's ability to withstand stress and infectious disease challenges. There are two possible uses for dietary protein that exceeds the body's total needs. If the animal is in zero energy balance, the excess protein will be used as an energy source. If the animal is in positive energy balance (that is, consuming more

energy than it is expending), then the excess protein will be metabolized to fat for energy storage in the body. Unlike fat and small amounts of carbohydrate, excess amino acids are not stored by the body for future use.

All companion animals have the ability to metabolize excess protein. This process results in the production of urea and its excretion in the urine. In recent years, the potential detrimental effects of excess protein intake in companion animals have interested a number of investigators. As a result of studies that were conducted with rats, it was theorized that feeding high levels of dietary protein over long periods of time to other species may contribute to the development of chronic kidney disease.[177-179] Some researchers also believe that protein excess can lead to nephropathy in animals that are already renally compromised.[177,180] Protein restriction is often used in the dietary management of companion animals with uremia that is caused by chronic kidney disease. In these cases, restriction of dietary protein to levels that meet, but do not exceed, the animal's requirement minimizes urea production and lessens some of the clinical signs that are associated with uremia.[181] However, there is no conclusive evidence showing that protein intake actually contributes to the development of kidney dysfunction in healthy animals[88] (see Section 6, pp. 392–395).

Reduced renal weight and a gradual decline in kidney function are normal occurrences of aging and have been extensively studied in humans and rats.[182-184] A study with dogs evaluated clinical changes in renal function in a colony of beagles for a period of 13 years. The data from this study indicate that normal kidney aging leads to nephron loss of up to 75% before clinical or biochemical signs occur.[185] Pets with less than 75% loss are usually clinically normal, but they may be more susceptible to renal insult than are younger animals still possessing renal reserve capacity.[185] This knowledge has led to the practice of systematically reducing the protein content in the diets of elderly animals in an attempt to prevent or minimize the progression of kidney dysfunction.[186] However, it is also important that normal geriatric dogs and cats receive adequate amounts of high-quality protein to minimize losses of body protein reserves and to satisfy maintenance protein needs. Although there is evidence that a reduction in protein intake has a significant effect on clinical signs once a high level of kidney dysfunction has occurred, there is no evidence indicating a need to systematically reduce protein levels in the diets of healthy older pets. It is recommended that the protein in the diets of geriatric dogs should not be restricted simply because of old age. Rather, elderly pets should receive diets containing adequate, but not excessive, levels of high-quality protein. If a pet is diagnosed with chronic renal disease, moderate protein restriction can then be implemented to minimize extrarenal effects.[185] The primary function of this restriction is to improve the blood chemistry aberrations and some of the clinical signs that are associated with chronic renal disease[187,188] (see Section 6, pp. 395–398).

CHAPTER 13

Vitamins and Minerals

Fat-Soluble Vitamins

Vitamins are organic dietary constituents that are necessary for growth and the maintenance of life, but they are not used by the body as an energy source or incorporated as part of tissue structure (see Section 1, p. 31). The fat-soluble vitamins include vitamins A, D, E, and K. These vitamins are absorbed from the small intestine in much the same way as dietary fat and are stored primarily in the liver.

Vitamin A

All animals have a physiological requirement for active vitamin A, or retinol. However, most mammals, including the dog but with the exception of the cat, have the ability to convert vitamin A precursors to active vitamin A (see Section 1, p. 33). Carotenoid pigments, of which beta-carotene is the most important, are cleaved by a dioxygenase enzyme in the intestinal mucosa to yield vitamin A aldehyde (retinal). Retinal is then reduced by a second enzyme to form active vitamin A (retinol). Retinol is esterified to fatty acids and absorbed into the body along with dietary fat.[189-191] The dioxygenase enzyme that is essential for the splitting of the beta-carotene molecule is either absent or grossly deficient in the domestic cat. Studies have shown that neither dietary nor intravenous beta-carotene can prevent the development of vitamin A deficiency in this species.[192] As a result, the cat must have preformed vitamin A present in the diet. The most common forms of preformed vitamin A in foods are derivatives of retinol, such as retinyl palmitate and retinyl acetate. These compounds are found in largest quantities in fish liver oils and animal livers.

Nutrient requirements for vitamin A and its content in pet foods are expressed either as International Units (IU) or as retinol equivalents. One IU of vitamin A is equal to 0.3 micrograms (µg) of retinol or 0.6 µg of beta-carotene. The 1985 National Research Council (NRC) recommendations report a minimum requirement in the growing dog of 3710 IU per kilogram of diet, in a diet containing 3.67 kilocalories of metabolizable energy per kilogram (kcal of ME/kg).[49] However, the Association of American Feed Control Officials (AAFCO) Nutrient Profile for dog foods recommends that dog foods containing an energy density of 3.5 kcal/kg should include a minimum of 5000 IU/kg for growth, reproduction, and maintenance.[102] The 1986 NRC *Nutrient Requirements of Cats* reports a vitamin A minimum requirement of 3333 IU/kg of dry diet for growing kittens and 6000 IU/kg of dry diet during pregnancy and lactation.[58] This requirement is based on a diet with a ME of 5 kcal per gram (g) of dry matter (Table 13-1). Although adequate research on the minimum daily vitamin A requirement for maintenance in mature cats has not been conducted, it is presumed that the levels provided for the growing kitten are adequate for adults during maintenance.[58] Although the levels recommended by the NRC represent the minimum requirements for cats, the AAFCO Nutrient Profiles suggests a level of 5000 IU/kg of diet on a dry-matter basis to be included in all commercially prepared cat foods.[102]

Vitamin A deficiency is rarely observed in dogs and cats because commercial pet foods contain adequate amounts and because dogs are able to convert the carotenoids found in plant matter into active vitamin A. In young, growing animals, vitamin A deficiency results in abnormal bone growth and neurological disorders. Stenosis of the neural foramina causes pinching of cranial and spinal nerves as they pass through the abnormally shaped bone. If the deficiency persists, shortening and thickening of the long bones occurs, along with abnormal development of the bones of the skull.[193,194] Vitamin A deficiency in adult animals affects reproduction, vision, and functioning of the epithelium. Clinical signs include anorexia, xerophthalmia and conjunctivitis, corneal opacity and ulceration, skin lesions, and multiple disorders of the epithelial layers in the body.[49,58]

Vitamin A toxicity is not common in the animal kingdom because the precursor for vitamin A, beta-carotene, is not a toxic substance. The intestinal mucosa regulates the hydrolysis of beta-carotene and the subsequent absorption of retinol into the body. However, the cat cannot use carotenoids and must consume all of its vitamin A as preformed retinyl palmitate or free retinol from animal tissues. The absorption of preformed vitamin A is not regulated by the intestinal mucosa, and a toxic level of this vitamin is readily absorbed by the body. The domestic cat is more likely to be fed excessive levels of vitamin A than other species of domesticated pets. If cats are fed foods that contain excessively high levels of vitamin A, they are unable to protect themselves from absorbing toxic levels. These foods include organ meats, such as liver and kidney, and various fish oils. Vitamin A toxicosis in cats results in a disorder called deforming cervical spondylosis. The effects of excess vitamin A on bone growth and remodeling cause the development of bony exostoses (outgrowths) on the cervical vertebrae. These changes eventually cause pain, difficult movement, lameness, and crippling in severe cases (see Section 5, pp. 304–307).

TABLE 13-1
Recommended Minimum Fat-Soluble Vitamin Requirements*

	VITAMIN A	VITAMIN D	VITAMIN E	VITAMIN K
Dog				
NRC	3710 IU	404 IU	22 IU	—[†]
AAFCO	5000 IU	500 IU	50 IU	—
Cat				
NRC	3333 IU	500 IU	30 IU	0.1 mg
AAFCO	5000 IU	500 IU	30 IU	0.1 mg[††]

* Per kilogram of diet.
† No requirement established.
†† For cats consuming diets containing > 25% fish (dry-matter basis).

Vitamin D

Vitamin D is essential for normal calcium and phosphorus metabolism and homeo-stasis. The actions of vitamin D on the intestine, skeleton, and kidney result in increased plasma levels of calcium and phosphorus. These increased levels allow normal mineralization and remodeling of bone and cartilage and maintain the concentration of calcium in the extracellular fluid that is necessary for normal muscle contraction and nervous tissue excitability. Many animals have the ability to synthesize vitamin D_3 from 7-dehydrocholesterol when the skin is exposed to ultraviolet (UV) radiation. The inactive form of the vitamin is then stored in the liver. Biochemical conversions, first in the liver and then in the kidney, convert vitamin D_3 to its active form when necessary (see Section 1, p. 33–36).

Dietary requirements for vitamin D depend on calcium and phosphorus levels in the diet, the ratio of these two minerals, and the age of the animal. Because of the skin's ability to produce vitamin D, adult animals that are consuming diets with adequate levels of calcium and phosphorus have very low requirements for cholecalciferol. During growth, vitamin D is important for the normal development and mineralization of bone. Even with this added need, very low levels of dietary vitamin D appear to be necessary for companion animals, provided that adequate calcium and phosphorus are present (Table 13-1).

There are conflicting data from studies that have measured the ability of companion animals to produce adequate levels of vitamin D in the skin to meet their daily needs. When a group of growing kittens were fed a diet containing adequate levels of calcium and phosphorus, normal bone growth occurred in the absence of dietary vitamin D and exposure to UV light.[195] It was speculated that the kittens in this study were able to use body stores of vitamin D that had been acquired during suckling. Another study reported that when a group of weanling English pointer and German shepherd puppies were fed a diet containing no supplemental cholecalciferol, no signs of vitamin D deficiency developed.[196] The dogs were fed the diet for 2 years and were housed in

indoor/outdoor runs. A second group was fed the same ration and supplemented with 60.5 µg of cholecalciferol per kilogram of diet. During the treatment period there were no significant differences in growth rate, body length, or serum calcium and phosphorus levels between the two groups of dogs. Periodic radiographic examinations revealed no differences in skeletal development. The authors of the study concluded that dogs that are fed practical diets and exposed to adequate sunlight do not require supplemental cholecalciferol during the first 2 years of life. It is important to note that vitamin D levels of the diets in this study were not analyzed. Therefore it is possible that adequate levels of vitamin D were present in one or more of the ingredients that were included in the basal diet.

Other data have shown that dogs and cats do not synthesize sufficient amounts of vitamin D in the skin to meet their daily requirements, even when daily irradiation with UV light is provided.[192,197] When dogs were fed a dry food to which no supplemental vitamin D had been added, both the radiated and non-radiated groups developed biochemical, radiological, and histological signs of rickets.[197] Clinical signs included broadened growth plates and bowed legs. When the vitamin D-deficient diet was replaced with a commercial dog food containing 1800 IU/kg of vitamin D, the signs resolved, normal bone mineralization was observed, and circulating levels of vitamin D metabolites increased to normal values. Vitamin D deficiency was also produced in kittens that were fed a diet containing no vitamin D and 1% calcium and phosphorus.[195] Deficiency signs were exacerbated when the diet's phosphorus level was decreased to 0.65% and calcium was increased to 2%. It appears from these data that dogs and cats depend on a dietary source of vitamin D for normal skeletal development and growth. The interrelationship between vitamin D, calcium, and phosphorus in the diet has been demonstrated by studies that have produced experimental vitamin D deficiencies in dogs and cats by limiting or imbalancing calcium and phosphorus levels in the diet.[195,198-200]

Vitamin D deficiency results in rickets in growing animals and osteomalacia in adults. Rickets is characterized by bone malformation caused by insufficient deposition of calcium and phosphorus. The long bones are affected, resulting in bowing of the legs and thickening of the joints. Osteomalacia is caused by decalcification of bone and an increased tendency of the long bones to fracture. In most animals, vitamin D deficiency develops concomitantly with deficiencies or imbalances in dietary calcium and phosphorus. Low levels of these minerals will exacerbate vitamin D deficiency and may precipitate the signs of rickets in growing animals. Excess levels of vitamin D can be toxic to dogs and cats and results in excessive calcification of soft tissues in the body. Chronic ingestion of high levels of vitamin D may eventually lead to skeletal abnormalities and deformations of the teeth and jaws in growing companion animals. Although oversupplementation with vitamin D is the most common cause of toxicity in dogs and cats, the ingestion of rodenticides that contain vitamin D has been reported to result in acute toxicity of vitamin D in several clinical cases.[201]

Vitamin E

Vitamin E functions as a biological, chain breaking antioxidant that neutralizes free radicals and prevents the peroxidation of lipids within cellular membranes. An animal's requirement for vitamin E depends on dietary levels of polyunsaturated fatty acids (PUFA) and selenium, a trace mineral. Vitamin E and selenium function synergistically. Although vitamin E protects cell membrane fatty acids by quenching the free radicals that are formed during oxidation, selenium, as a component of the enzyme glutathione peroxidase, reduces peroxide formation. This process further protects membrane fatty acids from oxidative damage (see Section 1, p. 37).

Increasing the level of unsaturated fat in the diet will cause an increase in an animal's vitamin E requirement. In commercial pet foods, vitamin E also protects unsaturated fats from destructive oxidation. The vitamin will be preferentially oxidized before the unsaturated fatty acids, thus protecting them from rancidity. However, in this process, vitamin E is destroyed. Therefore, as the level of unsaturated fatty acids in pet foods increases, the amount of vitamin E should increase.

A deficiency of vitamin E that occurs naturally is not common in dogs and cats. However, the ingestion of poorly prepared or poorly stored foods or supplementation with large amounts of PUFAs can precipitate a deficiency of this vitamin. Vitamin E deficiency in dogs has been associated with skeletal muscle degeneration, decreased reproductive performance, retinal degeneration, and impaired immunological response.[202] A deficiency of this nutrient has also been implicated in the development of certain dermatological disorders in dogs. The occurrence of demodicosis has been associated with decreased blood levels of vitamin E.[203] It has been postulated that a subclinical vitamin E deficiency causes suppression of the immune system, which in turn increases a dog's susceptibility to demodex. When a group of dogs with demodicosis was treated with supplemental vitamin E, significant levels of improvement were reported. However, other researchers have been unable to reproduce these results.[204] More controlled research is necessary before definitive conclusions can be made concerning the role of vitamin E in the control of demodectic mange. Supplementation with large amounts of vitamin E has also been shown to have antiinflammatory effects on some dogs with skin disorders.[205,206] This therapy has been used with varying levels of success in dogs with discoid lupus erythematosus, dermatomyositis, and acanthosis nigricans (see Section 6, pp. 375–376).

A condition called pansteatitis, or "yellow fat disease," occurs in cats that are fed diets containing marginal or low levels of alpha-tocopherol and high amounts of unsaturated fatty acids. Signs of pansteatitis include the presence of "swollen fat," anorexia, depression, pyrexia (fever), hyperesthesia of the thorax and abdomen, and a reluctance to move.[207,208] A diet that contains high levels of fish oil may cause a threefold to fourfold increase in a cat's daily requirement for alpha-tocopherol.[58] Early cases of pansteatitis occurred almost exclusively in cats that were fed a canned, commercial, fish-based cat food, of which red tuna was the principal type of fish. Later cases of the

disease occurred in cats that were fed diets consisting wholly or largely of canned red tuna or fish scraps. Red tuna packed in oil contains high levels of PUFAs and low levels of vitamin E. The addition of large amounts of fish products to a cat's diet appears to be the primary cause of this disease in pet cats (see Section 5, pp. 303–304).

Vitamin K

Vitamin K includes a class of compounds known as the quinones. This vitamin is necessary for normal blood coagulation because of its role in the synthesis of prothrombin (factor II) and several other clotting factors (see Section 1, p. 37). A deficiency of this vitamin is extremely rare in dogs and has never been reported in cats. Deficiencies of vitamin K in the dog have always been associated with interference with bacterial synthesis of the vitamin in the intestine or with its absorption or function. Simple dietary deficiencies of vitamin K have not been observed. This finding is believed to be the result of the ability of bacterial synthesis in the intestine to fully meet the vitamin K requirements of companion animals. Interference with vitamin K synthesis or absorption can cause a deficiency with signs of hemorrhage and decreased levels of prothrombin in the blood.

WATER-SOLUBLE VITAMINS

The water-soluble vitamins that are of importance to the dog and cat are all B-complex vitamins. Most of these vitamins are involved in the use of food and the production of energy in the body (see Section 1, p. 38). Because of the availability of well-formulated and well-balanced pet foods today, simple deficiencies of the B-complex vitamins are extremely rare in companion animals. However, there are several situations in which B-vitamin nutrition may be of concern in the nutritional management of dogs or cats. Thiamin deficiency can occur when dogs or cats are fed certain types of raw fish that contain an enzyme that destroys this vitamin, while biotin deficiency can be induced by feeding animals large amounts of raw egg whites[209-212] (see Section 5, pp. 307–308). Genetics can also play a role in B-vitamin metabolism. An inherited disorder in giant schnauzers causes malabsorption of vitamin B_{12} (see Section 6, pp. 337–339). The requirement for vitamin B_6 (pyridoxine) is directly affected by the level of protein in the diet. As protein level in the diet increases, so will the dog's or cat's requirement for vitamin B_6.[213-216]

MINERALS

As with most other nutrients, problems with mineral nutrition in dogs and cats are often a result of excesses or imbalances from interactions with other nutrients rather than a result of frank deficiencies in the diet. This section will focus on those minerals that are of most practical significance in the nutrition and feeding management of dogs and cats today.

Calcium and Phosphorus

Calcium and phosphorus are macrominerals that are necessary for the formation and maintenance of the skeleton. These nutrients are involved in a wide range of metabolic reactions (see Section 1, pp. 45–47). When considering canine and feline requirements for these nutrients, the availability of the calcium and phosphorus that is present in the diet must be taken into account. Research studies have shown that requirements for available calcium are quite low. Levels of 0.37% available calcium or 0.5% to 0.65% total calcium have been shown to be adequate for growing puppies.[49,217] The NRC's 1985 report recommends a level of 0.59% calcium on a dry-matter basis for growing dogs.[49] However, other data indicate that 0.55% total calcium may be inadequate for normal growth in large breeds of dogs.[218] Calcium requirement estimates for growth in cats are reported to vary between 200 and 400 mg/day. This amount is equivalent to approximately 0.6% to 0.8% of the diet.[58,219] However, when cats are fed purified diets, normal growth can be supported by as low as 150 to 200 mg of calcium per day.[219]

Both the NRC recommendations and the AAFCO Nutrient Profiles have established requirement estimates for calcium and phosphorus in the diets of dogs and cats.[49,58,102] The NRC recommendations set minimum requirements for available nutrients. These reports do not contain safety margins to allow for processing losses of nutrients or variability in nutrient availability. The AAFCO standards, on the other hand, provide estimates for minimum amounts of nutrients to be included in commercially prepared pet foods. Safety margins are included in all requirement estimates to account for differences in availability between ingredients. Accounting for varying levels of availability is especially important with respect to most minerals, including calcium and phosphorus. The AAFCO Nutrient Profiles for dogs recommend a minimum level of 1.0% calcium and 0.8% phosphorus for growth and 0.6% and 0.5% for adult maintenance. Recommendations for cats are 1.0% calcium and 0.8% phosphorus for growth and reproduction and 0.6% calcium and 0.5% phosphorus for adult maintenance.[102] Calcium/phosphorus ratios ranging between 1:1 and 2:1 are acceptable, with 1.2:1 to 1.4:1 being optimal in the opinions of most nutritionists.[102]

When formulating rations, pet food manufacturers must account for differences in calcium and phosphorus availability in the various ingredients that are used. Absorption coefficients for calcium have been reported to vary between 0% and 90%, depending on the composition of the diet, the age of the animal, and the total calcium content of the diet.[217,220,221] Within limits, as the calcium content of a diet decreases, the dog's efficiency of absorption tends to increase.[218] Increasing the amount of vitamin D in the diet also increases the body's ability to absorb dietary calcium and phosphorus.

Pet food ingredients vary in their ability to provide available calcium and phosphorus. In general, the calcium and phosphorus in plant products are less available than the minerals that are found in animal products. Cereal grains contain phytate, a phosphorus-containing compound that can bind other minerals, including calcium, and make them unavailable for absorption. Although phytate is very high in phosphorus, the availability of phytate phosphorus is only about 30%.[58] On the other hand, many of the animal products that are included in pet foods are very high in phosphorus but low in calcium.

These products include fresh meat or poultry, meat or fish meals, and organ meats. As a result, pet foods must be carefully formulated to ensure that both adequate levels and a proper ratio of calcium to phosphorus are maintained.

Deficiencies of calcium and phosphorus are unusual today because of the production of well-formulated pet foods. Because phosphorus is present in so many foods, a dietary deficiency of this mineral is extremely rare. However, calcium imbalance in growing dogs or cats still occurs as a result of improper feeding practices. A calcium deficiency develops most commonly when puppies or kittens are fed a "table scrap" diet consisting primarily of muscle or organ meats. This type of diet results in a syndrome called nutritional secondary hyperparathyroidism. The low calcium and extremely high phosphorus content of an all-meat diet leads to inadequate absorption of calcium and a transient hypocalcemia. The lowered blood levels of calcium stimulate the release of parathyroid hormone (PTH). PTH increases bone resorption of calcium, resulting in a restoration of normal blood calcium. When calcium is deficient in the diet, chronically elevated levels of PTH maintain blood calcium levels within a normal range. However, these elevated PTH levels lead to bone demineralization and a loss of bone mass.[222,223] In dogs the mandibles (jaw bones) show the earliest signs of bone demineralization, which leads to periodontal disease and loss of teeth. Over time, severe bone loss leads to compression of the spinal vertebrae and spontaneous fractures of the long bones. Affected dogs and cats exhibit joint pain and swelling, lameness, and a reluctance to move. Splaying of the toes, excessive sloping of the metatarsal and metacarpal bones, and lateral deviation of the carpus are also observed. Treatment involves correction of the diet through provision of a nutritionally complete and balanced ration. It is advisable to completely replace the deficient diet with a commercially prepared pet food rather than attempt to balance the current diet through the addition of calcium supplements (see Section 5, pp. 296–300).

A second problem that involves calcium homeostasis in the body is the occurrence of puerperal tetany or eclampsia in lactating bitches and queens. Eclampsia is a disease that is seen most commonly in small breeds of dogs and, less frequently, in cats. Eclampsia usually occurs immediately before or 2 to 3 weeks following parturition and is caused by the failure of the dam's calcium regulatory mechanisms to maintain serum calcium levels when there is a loss of calcium to the milk. One of the roles of ionized calcium in the body is to stabilize electrical charges across nerve and muscle cell membranes. In the absence of normal serum calcium levels, cell membranes become hyperexcitable, leading to convulsive seizures and tetany. In the case of eclampsia, serum calcium levels may decrease to less than 7 milligrams per deciliter (mg/dl). Normally, serum calcium is strictly maintained at a level of 9.5 to 10.5 mg/dl. Prompt medical care is necessary and consists of intravenous administration of calcium borogluconate.[224,225] Prognosis is very good if the disorder is treated at an early stage.

Although controlled research has not been conducted in companion animals, research in dairy cattle has demonstrated that the consumption of a diet high in calcium during pregnancy actually increases the incidence of this disorder, but moderately low intakes of calcium can prevent its occurrence.[226,227] It is believed that a relative hyper-

calcemia, caused by a high-calcium diet or calcium supplementation during pregnancy, exerts negative feedback on PTH synthesis and secretion by the parathyroid gland. This effect causes a decrease in both the body's capability to mobilize calcium stores from bone and the ability to increase calcium absorption in the intestine. When calcium is suddenly needed for lactation, the body's regulatory mechanisms are unable to adapt quickly enough to the sudden calcium loss. Calcium is diverted preferentially to milk production, and the animal's serum calcium decreases. Although a correlation between excess calcium during pregnancy and eclampsia has not been proven in dogs or cats, it is prudent to avoid calcium supplements during pregnancy in these species. If a bitch or queen is being fed a high-quality commercial food that has been formulated for feeding through gestation and lactation, calcium supplementation is not necessary and is probably contraindicated.

Just as too little calcium during growth can be detrimental to dogs and cats, so can excessive amounts. The most common cause of excess calcium in a pet's diet is supplementation of an already complete and balanced pet food with high-calcium foods or mineral supplements. Although adequate calcium is essential for normal bone growth and skeletal development, several health risks are taken when excessively high levels of calcium are added to an adequate diet. Excess calcium can produce deficits in other nutrients and has the potential for causing several serious health disorders (see Section 5, pp. 296–300).

Magnesium

Magnesium is present in both soft tissues and bone. Magnesium is essential for normal muscle and nervous tissue functioning and plays a key role in a number of enzymatic reactions (see Section 1, pp. 47–48). A deficiency of magnesium in the diet results in muscle weakness, ataxia, and eventually, convulsive seizures. However, naturally occurring magnesium deficiency is not normally seen in dogs and cats. Excess magnesium has been implicated as a risk factor in the development of feline lower urinary tract disease (see Section 6, pp. 361–363).

Copper

Copper is needed by the body for iron absorption and transport, hemoglobin formation, and normal functioning of the cytochrome oxidase enzyme system (see Section 1, pp. 49–50). The normal metabolism of copper in the body involves the passage of excess copper through the liver and its excretion in bile. Disorders that affect bile excretion often result in an accumulation of copper in the liver, sometimes to toxic levels. In these cases, liver copper toxicosis is a secondary disorder, that develops as an effect of the primary liver disease. However, a primary hepatic copper-storage disease exists in certain breeds of dogs. In these cases, the underlying cause of the disease is an accumulation of copper in the liver, that eventually results in degenerative liver disease (see Section 6, pp. 339–340).

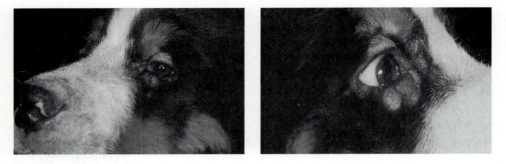

FIGURE 13-1
Zinc deficiency in a young, rapidly growing Bernase Mountain dog due to increased requirements during growth. (Reprinted with permission from Candac Sousa, D.V.M., Animal Dermatology Clinic, Sacramento, CA.)

Zinc Deficiency

With the exception of iron, zinc is the most abundant micromineral present in the body's tissues. It is important for normal carbohydrate, lipid, protein, and nucleic acid metabolism, and it is necessary for the maintenance of normal epidermal integrity, taste acuity, and immunological functioning.[228,229] The problem of zinc deficiency has been reported in a variety of animal species, including dogs and cats.[230-233] Clinical signs that are common to most species include growth retardation, abnormalities in hair and skin condition, gastrointestinal disturbances, and impaired reproductive performance.[234] The disruption of normal cellular division and maturation processes is believed to be the underlying cause of many of these symptoms.

Experimental studies of zinc deficiency in dogs and cats have found that skin and coat changes are the first clinical signs that usually develop in these species. When fed a zinc-deficient ration, dogs develop desquamating skin lesions on the foot pads, extremities, joints, and groin within 2 weeks of consuming the deficient diet. Lesions first appear as small, erythematous areas that eventually enlarge and merge into dry, crusty, brown lesions. Microscopically, the lesions show parakeratosis, hyperkeratinization, and an inflammatory infiltration of neutrophils, lymphocytes, and macrophages.[233,234] Coat changes have also been reported to occur with zinc deficiency. Affected dogs develop a dry, harsh hair coat with fading coat color.[234] When a diet containing adequate zinc is provided, these clinical signs rapidly resolve.

There are several underlying causes of naturally occurring zinc deficiency in dogs and cats. A syndrome called "generic dry dog food disease" has been described that involves the development of zinc deficiency in dogs that are fed poorly formulated, inexpensive, dry dog foods.[232,235] Young, rapidly growing dogs of the large and giant breeds seem to be most susceptible, but several cases have also been reported in adult animals (Figure 13-1)[231,232,235,236] (see Section 3, p. 191). Another dietary cause of zinc deficiency is feeding a diet that is excessively high in calcium or providing calcium supplements (see Section

5, p. 299). An inherited disorder of zinc metabolism occurs in certain breeds of dogs and also causes clinical signs of zinc deficiency (see Section 6, pp. 340–341, 381–382).

Sodium

The concern over the connection between sodium intake and essential hypertension in humans has resulted in interest in the sodium content of pet foods and its implications for companion animal health. An animal's requirement for sodium is primarily influenced by the daily unavoidable loss of this mineral from the body.[237] In adults during maintenance, these losses are usually quite low. The body's ability to conserve sodium results in a very low dietary sodium requirement in dogs and cats. Maintenance requirements of adults are estimated to range between 0.03% to 0.09% sodium in dry matter, with slight increases required during pregnancy and lactation.[102,237] Most commercial pet foods contain well above these amounts of sodium.[88]

In all animals the immediate effect of increased salt intake is increased water consumption. Sodium balance in dogs is maintained primarily through changes in urinary excretion of the mineral.[238] An increase in intake above the body's requirement is accompanied by increases in urinary water and sodium excretion. The most important risk attributed to long-term salt excess is its effect on blood pressure. Although this association has been shown to be a causal factor in the development of essential hypertension in certain human subpopulations, there are no data supporting the existence of such a relationship in dogs and cats. Essential hypertension is very rare in companion animals. Data from research studies that examined the effect of salt intake on blood pressure in dogs indicate that this species is resistant to salt retention and hypertension.[239–241] Adult dogs that were fed high-sodium diets were able to resist very high levels of salt intake without weight gain or edema, and their renal systems adjusted quickly to changes in dietary sodium.[240,241] When hypertension does occur in dogs and cats, it is usually a secondary disorder occurring as a result of renal disease.[239,242]

Although additional controlled research needs to be conducted, the dog appears to be resistant to the development of salt-induced hypertension. Although the usual levels of salt that are included in pet foods are often greater than the pet's minimum requirement, companion animals readily adapt to these levels by altering urinary excretion of sodium. It is probable that these levels are of no harm when fed to animals that are healthy and have free access to fresh water.[237]

Key Points

SECTION 2

Although equally popular as pets, the dog and cat have diverse nutritional needs. Dogs are omnivores, and cats have remained carnivores throughout their evolution. Cats cannot obtain all necessary nutrients from plants and plant products and must consume some animal tissues in order to meet their needs for high protein, taurine, arachidonic acid, and preformed vitamin A.

There are three major components comprising energy expenditure: (1) the energy expended during rest (resting metabolic rate), (2) the energy expended during voluntary muscle activity, and (3) the energy/heat produced by thermogenesis.

As pets age, regular exercise is important to maintain adequate energy expenditure. Voluntary activity burns energy, increases lean body tissue, and results in a higher resting metabolic rate.

Not surprisingly, most dogs prefer canned and semimoist pet food (rather than dry), cooked rather than uncooked meat, beef over other meats, and warm food rather than cold. To a degree, palatability increases along with the fat content of the diet.

More energy is required to convert dietary carbohydrate and protein to body fat as opposed to dietary fat. Thus if an animal consumes more than its caloric requirement and if the excess calories are provided by fat, the animal will gain more weight than if the excess calories come from carbohydrate or protein sources.

"Cafeteria" feeding, or giving a varied diet of high-calorie, palatable foods, such as table scraps, may override the body's natural tendency to balance intake and lead to overconsumption.

The energy requirements of cats and dogs are higher during growth, reproduction, physical activity, and environmental conditions. During lactation, the energy needs of dogs and cats can increase as much as three times normal, depending on litter size. Refer to Tables 9-2 and 9-3 for methods of calculating energy requirements and the amounts to feed.

As dogs and cats reach maturity, their ability to digest milk and other dairy products decreases as a result of decreased activity of lactase in the intestinal mucosa. Similarly, it is thought that very young animals have low levels of sucrase, indicating that sucrose solutions should not be given to very young or orphaned puppies and kittens.

Although deficiencies of essential fatty acids (EFA) in dogs and cats are uncommon, dermatological changes are usually the first indication of a problem. EFA deficiency usually results from poorly formulated or rancid foods, but it can occur as a complication of pancreatitis, biliary disease, hepatic disease, and malabsorption. Pay close attention to the pet's coat and skin.

Protein in the diets of adult dogs and cats and puppies and kittens is necessary for the replacement of protein losses in skin, hair, digestive enzymes, and mucosal cells, and amino acid losses from normal cellular protein catabolism. Puppies and kittens also require protein for growth. Protein-deficient adults will have a negative nitrogen balance and begin to lose lean muscle mass; puppies and kittens will experience impaired growth and development.

The protein requirement for the cat (carnivore) is significantly higher than that of the dog (omnivore), as a result of the cat's greater needs for the maintenance of normal body tissues rather than to increased needs for growth. This is because of the inability of certain catabolic enzymes in the cat's liver to adapt to changes in dietary protein intake.

Arginine deficiency in the cat has immediate and devastating effects. Severe hyperammonemia, emesis, muscle spasms, ataxia, hyperesthesia, and tetanic spasms can lead to coma and death. Taurine deficiency can lead to retinal degeneration and dilated cardiomyopathy.

Feeding cereal-based dog foods to cats can be harmful. Such foods have lower protein and taurine levels and can cause protein and taurine deficiency.

Contrary to popular belief, there is no research-based, conclusive evidence that protein ingestion contributes to the development of kidney dysfunction in healthy dogs and cats. Moreover, there is no evidence that the protein intake of geriatric dogs should be restricted just because of old age.

Vitamin A toxicity is uncommon but possible in cats. Because cats must consume preformed vitamin A and the absorption is not regulated by the intestinal mucosa, a toxic level can be absorbed. Foods with high levels of vitamin A, such as organ meats (liver and kidney) and various fish oils, should be fed sparingly. The result of vitamin A toxicosis causes the growth of bony protuberances on the cervical vertebrae that eventually cause pain, lameness, and even crippling in severe cases.

SECTION 2

REFERENCES

1. Colbert EH: Evolution of the vertebrates, ed 3, New York, 1980, John Wiley & Sons.
2. Czarnecki-Maulden GL: Nutritional idiosyncracies of the cat. In *Proceedings of the annual meeting of the American Association of Zoo Veterinarians*, Nov 2–6, Chicago, 1986 (abstract).
3. Burger I, Edney A, Horrocks D: Basics of feline nutrition, *In Practice* 9:143–150, 1987.
4. Danforth E, Landsberg L: Energy expenditure and its regulation. In Greenwood MRC, editor: *Obesity—Contemporary issues in clinical nutrition*, New York, 1983, Churchill Livingstone, pp 103–121.
5. Sellers EA, Reichman S, Thomas N, and others: Acclimatization to cold in rats: metabolic rates, *Am J Physiol* 167:651–655, 1951.
6. Ravussin E, Burnand B, Schutz Y, and others: Twenty-four hour energy expenditure and resting metabolic rate in obese, moderately obese and control subjects, *Am J Clin Nutr* 35:566–573, 1982.
7. Halliday D, Hesp R, Stalley SF, and others: Resting metabolic rate, weight, surface area and body composition in obese women, *Int J Obes* 3:1–6, 1979.
8. Forbes GB, Welle SL: Lean body mass in obesity, *Int J Obes* 7:99–107, 1983.
9. Horton ES: An overview of the assessment and regulation of energy balance in humans, *Am J Clin Nutr* 38:972–977, 1983.
10. Rothwell N, Stock MJ: Luxuskonsumption, diet-induced thermogenesis and brown fat: the case in favor, *Clin Sci* 64:19–23, 1983.
11. Sims EAH: Experimental obesity, dietary-induced thermogenesis, and their clinical implications, *Clin Endocrinol Metabol* 5:377–395, 1976.
12. Katzeff H, Danforth E Jr: Norepinephrine sensitivity and energy expenditure in response to overnutrition in lean and obese men, *Clin Res* 30:245A, 1982.
13. Leibowitz SF: Hypothalamic neurotransmitters in relation to normal and disturbed eating patterns. In Wurtman RJ, Wurtman JJ, editors: *Human obesity*, New York, 1987, New York Academy of Sciences, pp 137–143.
14. Leibowitz SF, Shor-Posner G: Brain serotonin and eating behavior, *Appetite* 7(suppl):1–14, 1986.
15. Caballero B, Finer N, Wurtman RL: Plasma amino acids and insulin levels in obesity: Response to carbohydrate intake and tryptophan supplements, *Metabolism* 37:672–676, 1988.
16. Smith GP, Gibbs J: The effect of gut peptides on hunger, satiety and food intake in humans. In Wurtman RJ, Wurtman JJ, editors: *Human obesity*, New York, 1987, New York Academy of Sciences, pp 132–136.
17. Penick SB, Hinkle LE Jr: Depression of food intake in healthy subjects by glucagon, *N Eng J Med* 264:893–897, 1961.
18. Smith GP, Jerome C, Norgren R: Afferent axons in abdominal vagus mediate satiety effect of cholecystokinin in rats, *Am J Physiol* 249:R638–R641, 1985.
19. Kissileff HR, Pi-Sunyer FX, Thornton J, and others: Cholecystokinin octapeptide (CCK-8) decreases food intake in man, *Am J Clin Nutr* 34:154–160, 1981.
20. Shaw MJ, Hughes JJ, Morley JE, and others: Cholecystokinin octapeptide action on gastric emptying and food intake in normal and vagotomized man. In Vanderhaeghen JJ, Crawley JN, editors: *Neuronal cholecystokinin*, Ann NY Acad Sci 448:640–641, 1985.
21. Morley JE, Levine AS, Plotka ED, and others: The effect of naloxone on feeding and spontaneous eating locomotion in the wolf, *Physiol Behav* 30:331–334, 1983.

22. Murrahainen NE, Kissileff HR, Thornton J, and others: Bombesin: another peptide that inhibits feeding in man, *Soc Neurosci* 9:183, 1983 (Abstract).

23. Silverstone T, Besser M: Insulin, blood sugar and hunger, *Postgrad Med J* 47:427–429, 1971.

24. Geiselman PJ, Novin D: The role of carbohydrates in appetite, hunger and obesity, *Appetite* 3:203–223, 1982.

25. Houpt KA, Hintz HF: Obesity in dogs, *Can Pract* 5:54–577, 1978.

26. Itallie TB, van Kissileff HR: The physiologic control of energy intake: an econometric perspective, *Am J Clin Nutr* 38:978–988, 1983.

27. Woods SC, Porte D Jr, Bobbioni E: Insulin: its relationship to the central nervous system and to the control of food intake and body weight, *Am J Clin Nutr* 42:1063–1071, 1985.

28. Vasselli JR, Cleary MP, van Itallie TB: Modern concepts of obesity, *Nutr Rev* 41:361–373, 1983.

29. Houpt KA: Ingestive behavior problems of dogs and cats, *Vet Clin North Am Small Anim Pract* 12:683–690, 1982.

30. Hill SW: Eating responses of humans during meals, *J Comp Physiol Psychol* 86:652–657, 1974.

31. Scalafani A, Springer O: Dietary obesity in adult rats: similarities to hypothalamic and human obesity syndromes, *Physiol Behav* 17:461–471, 1976.

32. Slattery JM, Potter RM: Hyperphagia: a necessary precondition to obesity?, *Appetite* 6:133–142, 1985.

33. Kitchell RL, Baker GG: Taste preference studies in domestic animals. In Swan H, Lewis D, editors: Proceedings of the 6th nutritional conference, Nottingham, England, 1972, Churchill Livingstone, pp 156–202.

34. Lohse CL: Preferences of dogs for various meats, *J Am Anim Hosp Assoc* 10:187–192, 1974.

35. Bartoshuk LM, Harned MA, Parks LTD: Taste of water in the cat: effect of sucrose preference, *Science* 171:699–701, 1971.

36. Houpt KA, Smith SL: Taste preferences and their relation to obesity in dogs and cats, *Can Vet J* 22:77–81, 1981.

37. Kane E, Morris JG, Rogers QR: Acceptability and digestibility by adult cats of diets made with various sources and levels of fat, *J Anim Sci* 53:1516–1523, 1981.

38. Edelman B, Engell D, Bronstein P, and others: Environmental effects on the intake of overweight and normal-weight men, *Appetite* 7:71–83, 1986.

39. Leblanc J, Diamond P: The effect of meal frequency on postprandial thermogenesis in the dog, *Fed Proc* 44:1678, 1985 (abstract).

40. Fabry P, Tepperman J: Meal frequency—a possible factor in human pathology, *Am J Clin Nutr* 23:1059, 1970.

41. Rodin J: The externality theory today. In Stunkard AJ, editor: *Obesity*, Philadelphia, 1980, WB Saunders, pp 226–239.

42. Alexander JE, Wood LLH: Growth studies in Labrador Retrievers fed a calorie-dense diet: time-restricted versus free choice feeding, *Can Pract* 14:41–47, 1987.

43. Danforth E Jr: Diet and obesity. *Am J Clin Nutr* 41:1132–1145, 1985.

44. Romsos DR, Belo PS, Bennink MR, and others: Effects of dietary carbohydrate, fat and protein on growth, body composition and blood metabolite levels in the dog, *J Nutr* 106:1452–1464, 1976.

45. Romsos DR, Hornshus MJ, Leveille GA: Influence of dietary fat and carbohydrate on food intake, body weight and body fat of adult dogs, *Proc Soc Exp Biol Med* 157:278–281, 1978.

46. Kanarek RB, Marks-Kaufmann R: Developmental aspects of sucrose-induced obesity in rats, *Physiol Behav* 23:881–885, 1979.

47. Rogers PJ, Blundell JE: Meal patterns and food selection during the development of obesity in rats fed a cafeteria diet, *Neurosci Biobehav Rev* 8:441–453, 1984.

48. Rolls BJ, Rowe EA, Turner RC: Persistent obesity in rats following a period of consumption of a mixed energy diet, *J Physiol (Lond)* 298:415–427, 1980.

49. National Research Council: *Nutrient requirements of dogs*, Washington, DC, 1985, National Academy of Sciences, National Academy Press.

50. National Research Council: *Nutrient requirements of dogs*, Washington, DC, 1974, National Academy of Sciences, National Academy Press.

51. Allard RL, Douglass GM, Kerr WW: The effects of breed and sex on dog growth, *Compan Anim Pract* 2:15–19, 1988.

52. Romsos DR, Palmer HJ, Muiruri KL, and others: Influence of a low carbohydrate diet on performance of pregnant and lactating dogs, *J Nutr* 111:678–689, 1981.

53. Blaza SE: Energy requirements of dogs in cold conditions, *Can Pract* 9:10–15, 1982.

54. Kendall PT, Blaza SE, Smith PM: Comparative digestible energy requirements of adult beagles and domestic cats for bodyweight maintenance, *J Nutr* 113:1946–1955, 1983.

55. MacDonald ML, Rogers QR, Morris JG: Nutrition of the domestic cat, a mammalian carnivore, *Ann Rev Nutr* 4:521–562, 1984.

56. Gisler DB, Ewing DE: A free access dry ration for cats, *Lab Anim Care* 14:91–93, 1964.

57. Burger IH, Blaza SE, Kendall PT, and others: The protein requirement of adult cats for maintenance, *Feline Pract* 14:8–14, 1984.

58. National Research Council: *Nutrient requirements of cats*, Washington, DC, 1986, National Academy of Sciences, National Academy Press.

59. Miller SA, Allison JB: The dietary nitrogen requirements of the cat, *J Nutr* 64:493–499, 1958.

60. Carey D: Iams Technical Center data, Lewisburg, Ohio, 1993, The Iams Company.

61. Loveridge GG, Rivers JPW: Bodyweight changes and energy intakes of cats during pregnancy and lactation. In Burger IH, Rivers JPW, editors: *Nutrition of the dog and cat*, New York, 1989, Cambridge University Press, pp 113–132.

62. Danowski TS, Elkinton JR, Winkler AW: The deleterious effect in dogs of a dry protein ration, *J Clin Invest* 23:816–823, 1944.

63. Prentiss PG, Wolf AV, Eddy HE: Hydropenia in the cat and dog: ability of the cat to meet its water requirements solely from a diet of fish or meat, *Am J Physiol* 196:625–632, 1959.

64. Lewis LD, Morris ML, Hand MS: Nutrients. In *Small animal clinical nutrition*, ed 3, Topeka, Kan, 1987, Mark Morris Associates, pp 1:1–1:25.

65. Kettlehut IC, Foss MC, Migliorini RH: Glucose homeostasis in a carnivorous animal (cat) and in rats fed a high-protein diet, *Am J Physiol* 239:R115–R121, 1978.

66. Migliorini RH, Linder C, Moura JL, and others: Gluconeogenesis in a carnivorous bird (black vulture), *Am J Physiol* 225:1389–1392, 1973.

67. Belo PS, Romsos DR, Leveille GA: Influence of diet on glucose tolerance, on the rate of glucose utilization and on gluconeogenic enzyme activities in the dog, *J Nutr* 106:1465–1472, 1976.

68. Blaza SE, Booles D, Burger IH: Is carbohydrate essential for pregnancy and lactation in dogs? In Burger IH, Rivers JPW, editors: *Nutrition of the cat and dog*, New York, 1989, Cambridge University Press, pp 229–242.

69. Brady LJ, Armstrong MK, Muriuri KL, and others: Influence of prolonged fasting in the dog on glucose turnover and blood metabolites, *J Nutr* 107:1053–1061, 1977.

70. Kienzle E, Meyer H: The effects of carbohydrate-free diets containing different levels of protein on reproduction in the bitch. In Burger IH, Rivers JPW, editors: *Nutrition of the dog and cat*, New York, 1989, Cambridge University Press, pp 113–132.

71. Morris JG, Rogers QR: Nutritionally related metabolic adaptations of carnivores and ruminants. International Symposium on Plant, Animal and Microbial Adaptations to Terrestrial Environments, Man and the Biosphere, Halkidiki, Greece, 1982.

72. Beliveau GP, Freedland RA: Metabolism of serine, glycine and threonine in isolated cat hepatocytes (*Felis domestica*), *Comp Biochem Physiol* 71B:13–18, 1982.

73. Rogers QR, Morris JG, Freedland RA: Lack of hepatic enzymatic adaptation to low and high levels of dietary protein in the adult cat, *Enzyme* 22:348–356, 1977.

74. Rowsell EV, Carnie JA, Wahbi SD, and others: L-serine dehydratase and L-serine-pyruvate aminotransferase activities in different animal species, *Comp Biochem Physiol* 63:543–555, 1979.

75. Morris JG, Rogers QR: Metabolic basis for some of the nutritional peculiarities of the cat, *J Sm Anim Pract* 23:599–613, 1982.

76. Ballard FJ: Glucose utilization in mammalian liver, *Comp Biochem Physiol* 14:437–443, 1965.

77. De Wilde RO, Jansen T: The use of different sources of raw and heated starch in the ration of weaned kittens. In Burger IH, Rivers JPW, editors: *Nutrition of the cat and dog*, New York, 1989, Cambridge University Press, pp 259–266.

78. Trudell JI, Morris JG: Carbohydrate digestion in the cat, *J Anim Sci* 41:329, 1975.

79. Pencovic TA, Morris JG: Corn and wheat starch utilization by the cat, *J Anim Sci* 41:325, 1975.

80. Morris JG, Trudell J, Pencovic T: Carbohydrate digestion by the domestic cat (*Felis catus*), *Br J Nutr* 37:365–373, 1977.

81. Burger IH: A basic guide to nutrient requirements. In Edney, ATB, editor: *Dog and cat nutrition*, ed 2, Oxford, England, 1988, Pergamon Press, pp 9–34.

82. Keen CR, Lonnerdal B, Fisher GL: Age-related variations in hepatic iron, copper, zinc and selenium concentrations in beagles, *Am J Vet Res* 42:1884–1887, 1981.

83. Mundt HC, Meyer H: Pathogenesis of lactose-induced diarrhea and its prevention by enzymatic splitting of lactose. In Burger IH, Rivers JPW, editors: *Nutrition of the cat and dog*, New York, 1989, Cambridge University Press, pp. 267–274.

84. Kallfelz FA: Evaluation and use of pet foods: general considerations in using pet foods for adult maintenance, *Vet Clin North Am Sm Anim Pract* 19:387–403, 1989.

85. Huber TL, Wilson RC, McGarity SA: Variations in digestibility of dry dog foods with identical label guaranteed analysis, *J Am Anim Hosp Assoc* 22:571–575, 1986.

86. Downey RL, Kronfeld DS, and Banta CA: Diet of beagles affects stamina, *J Am Anim Hosp Assoc* 16:273–277, 1980.

87. Hammel EP, Kronfeld DS, Ganjam VK, and others: Metabolic responses to exhaustive exercise in racing sledge dogs fed diets containing medium, low and zero carbohydrate, *Am J Clin Nutr* 30:409–418, 1976.

88. Kallfelz FA, and Dzanis DA: Overnutrition: an epidemic problem in pet animal practice?, *Vet Clin North Am Sm Anim Pract* 19:433–446, 1989.

89. Reiland S, Stromberg B, Olsson SE, and others: Osteochondrosis in growing bulls, *Acta Radiol* 358 (suppl):179–196, 1978.

90. Saville PD, Leiber CS: Increases in skeletal calcium and femur thickness produced by under nutrition, *J Nutr* 99:141–144, 1969.

91. Hedhammar A, Wu F, Krook L, and others: Overnutrition and skeletal disease: an experimental study in growing Great Dane dogs, *Cornell Vet* 5 (suppl 64):1–159, 1974.

92. Rivers JPW, Sinclair AJ, Crawford MA: Inability of the cat to desaturate essential fatty acids, *Nature* (London), 258:171–173, 1975.

93. Rivers JPW, Hassam AG, Alderson C: The absence of delta-6-desaturase activity in the cat, *Proc Nutr Soc* 35:67a–68a, 1976.

94. Rivers JPW, Sinclair AJ, Moore DP, and others: The abnormal metabolism of essential fatty acids in the cat, *Proc Nutr Soc* 35:66a–67a, 1976.

95. Hassam AG, Rivers JPW, Crawford MA: The failure of the cat to desaturate linoleic acid: its nutritional implications, *Nutr Metabol* 21:321–328, 1977.

96. Sinclair AJ, Slattery W, McLean JG, and others: Essential fatty acid deficiency and evidence for arachidonate synthesis in the cat, *Br J Nutr* 46:93–96, 1981.

97. Davidson BC, and Traher CS: The importance of essential fatty acid evaluation and supplementation in feline diets, *J South Afric Vet Assoc* 58:39–41, 1987.

98. MacDonald ML, Anderson BC, Rogers QR, and others: Essential fatty acid requirements of cats: pathology of essential fatty acid deficiency, *Am J Vet Res* 45:1310–1317, 1984.

99. MacDonald ML, Rogers QR, Morris JG: Effects of linoleate and arachidonate deficiencies on reproduction and spermatogenesis in the cat, *J Nutr* 114:719–726, 1984.

100. Rivers JPW, Frankel TL: Fat in the diet of cats and dogs. In Anderson RS, editor: *Nutrition of the dog and cat*, Oxford, England, 1980, Pergamon Press, pp 67–99.

101. MacDonald, ML, Rogers QR, Morris JG: Role of linoleate as an essential fatty acid for the cat, independent of arachidonate synthesis, *J Nutr* 113:1422–1433, 1983.

102. Association of American Feed Control Officials: *Official Publication*, 1994, AAFCO.

103. Holman RT: Biological activity of and requirements for polyunsaturated acids, *Prog Chem Fats Lipids* 9:607–682, 1971.

104. Mohrhauer H, Holman RT: The effect of dose level of essential fatty acids upon fatty acid composition of the rat liver, *J Lipid Res* 4:151–159, 1963.

105. O'Donnell JA III, and Hayes KC: Nutrition and nutritional disorders. In Holzworth J, editor: *Diseases of the cat: medicine and surgery*, Philadelphia, 1987, WB Saunders, pp 15–42.

106. Codner EC, Thatcher CD: The role of nutrition in the management of dermatoses, *Semin Vet Med Surg (Sm Anim)* 5:167–177, 1990.

107. Hansen AE, Wiese HF: Fat in the diet in relation to nutrition of the dog. I. Characteristic appearance and changes of animals fed diets with and without fat, *Tex Rep Biol and Med* 9:491–515, 1951.

108. Sinclair AJ, McLean JG, Monger EA: Metabolism of linoleic acid in the cat, *Lipids* 14:932–936, 1979.

109. Rivers JPW: Essential fatty acids in cats, *J Sm Anim Pract* 23:563–576, 1982.

110. Humphreys ER, Scott PP: The addition of herring and vegetable oils to the diets of cats, *Proc Nutr Soc* 21:XVIII, 1962.

111. Schaeffer MC, Rogers QR, Morris JG: Protein in the nutrition of dogs and cats. In Burger IH, Rivers JPW, editors: *Nutrition of the dog and cat*, New York, 1989, Cambridge University Press, pp 159–205.

112. Bradstreet RB: *The Kjeldahl method for organic nitrogen*, New York, 1965, Academic Press.

113. Allison JB, Wannemacher RW, Migliarese JF: Diet and the metabolism of 2-aminofluorene, *J Nutr* 52:415–425, 1954.

114. Wannemacher RE, McCoy JR: Determination of optimal dietary protein requirements of young and old dogs, *J Nutr* 88:66–74, 1966.

115. Case LP, Czarnecki-Maulden GL: Protein requirements of growing pups fed practical dry-type diets containing mixed-protein sources, *Am J Vet Res* 51:808–812, 1990.

116. Mabee DM, Morgan AF: Evaluation by dog growth of egg yolk protein and six other partially purified proteins, some after heat-treatment, *J Nutr* 43:261–279, 1951.

117. Allison JB: Optimal nutrition correlated with nitrogen retention, *Am J Clin Nutr* 4:662–672, 1956.

118. Ontko, JA, Wuthier RE, Phillips PH: The effect of increased dietary fat upon the protein requirement of the growing dog, *J Nutr* 62:163–169, 1957.

119. Hilton JW, Atkinson JL: High lipid and high protein dog foods, *Can Vet J* 29:76–78, 1988.

120. Allison JB, Seeley RD, Brown JH, and others: The evaluation of proteins in hypoproteinemic dogs, *J Nutr* 31:237–242, 1946.

121. Payne PR: Assessment of the protein values of diets in relation to the requirements of the growing dog. In Graham-Jones O, editor: *Canine and feline nutritional requirements*, 1965, London, Pergamon Press, pp 19–31.

122. Dickinson CD, Scott PP: Nutrition of the cat. II. Protein requirements for growth of weanling kittens and young cats maintained on a mixed diet, *Br J Nutr* 10:311–316, 1956.

123. Anderson PA, Baker DH, Sherry PA, and others: Nitrogen requirement of the kitten, *Am J Vet Res* 41:1646–1649, 1980.

124. Rogers QR, Morris JG: Why does the cat require a high protein diet? In Anderson RS, editor: *Nutrition of the dog and cat*, New York, 1980, Pergamon Press, pp 45–66.

125. Arnold A, Schad JS: Nitrogen balance studies with dogs on casein or methionine-supplemented casein, *J Nutr* 53:265–273, 1954.

126. Kade CF Jr, Phillips JH, Phillips WA: The determination of the minimum requirement of the adult dog for maintenance of nitrogen balance, *J Nutr* 36:109–121, 1948.

127. Melnick D, Cowgill GR: The protein minima for nitrogen equilibrium with different proteins, *J Nutr* 13:401–424, 1937.

128. Greaves JP, Scott PP: Nutrition of the cat. III. Protein requirements for nitrogen equilibrium in adult cats maintained on a mixed diet, *Br J Nutr* 14:361–369, 1960.

129. Heiman V: The protein requirements of growing puppies, *J Am Anim Hosp Assoc* 111: 304–308, 1947.

130. Gessert CG, Phillips PH: Protein in the nutrition of the growing dog, *J Nutr* 58:415–421, 1956.

131. Burns RA, LaFaivre MH, Milner JA: Effects of dietary protein quantity and quality on the growth of dogs and rats, *J Nutr* 112:1843–1853, 1982.

132. Sheffy BE: The 1985 revision of the National Research Council nutrient requirements of dogs and its impact on the pet food industry. In Burger IH, Rivers JPW, editors: *Nutrition of the dog and cat*, New York, 1989, Cambridge University Press, pp 11–26.

133. Jansen GR, Deuth MA, Ward GM, and others: Protein quality studies in growing kittens, *Nutr Rep Int* 11:525–536, 1975.

134. Smalley KA, Rogers QR, Morris JG: The nitrogen requirement of the kitten using crystalline amino acid diets or casein diets. Proceedings of the twelfth International Congress on Nutrition, San Diego, 1981, p 117 (abstract).

135. Burger IH, Blaza SE, Kendall PT: The protein requirement of adult cats, *Proc Nutr Soc* 40:102a, 1981.

136. Harper AE: Effect of variations in protein intake on enzymes of amino acid metabolism, *Can J Biochem* 43:1589–1597, 1965.

137. Kaplan JH, Pitot HC: The regulation of intermediary amino acid metabolism in animal tissues. In Munro HN, editor: *Mammalian protein metabolism*, vol 4, New York, 1970, Academic Press, pp 388.

138. Schimke RT: Adaptive characteristics of urea cycle enzymes in the rat, *J Biol Chem* 237:459–467, 1962.

139. Szepesi B, Freedland RA: Alterations in the activities of several rat liver enzymes at various times after initiation of a high protein regimen, *J Nutr* 93:301–310, 1967.

140. Burns RA, Milner JA, Corbin JE: Arginine: an indispensable amino acid for mature dogs, *J Nutr* 111:1020–1024, 1981.

141. Anderson PA, Baker DH, Corbin JE: Lysine and arginine requirements of the domestic cat, *J Nutr* 109:1368–1372, 1979.

142. Morris JG, Rogers QR: Ammonia intoxication in the near-adult cat as a result of a dietary deficiency of arginine, *Science* 199:(4327):431–432, 1978.

143. Czaenecki GL, Baker DH: Urea-cycle metabolism in the dog with emphasis on the role of arginine, *J Nutr* 114:581–586, 1984.

144. Costello MJ, Morris JG, Rogers QR: The role of intestinal mucosa in endogenous arginine biosynthesis in ureotelic mammals. Proceedings of the twelfth International Congress on Nutrition, San Diego, Aug 16–21, 96:538, 1981 (abstract).

145. Featherston WR, Rogers QR, Freedland RA: Relative importance of kidney and liver in synthesis of arginine by the rat, *Am J Physiol* 224:127–129, 1973.

146. Pion PD, Kittleson MD, Rogers, QR, and others: Myocardial failure in cats associated with low plasma taurine: a reversible cardiomyopathy, *Science* 237:764–768, 1987.

147. Rabin AR, Nicolosi RJ, Hayes KC: Dietary influence of bile acid conjugation in the cat, *J Nutr* 106:1241–1246, 1976.

148. Hayes KC, Sturman JA: Taurine in metabolism, *Annu Rev Nutri* 1:401–420, 1981.

149. Sturman JA, Gargano AD, Messing JM, and others: Feline maternal taurine deficiency: effect on mother and offspring, *J Nutr* 116:655–657, 1986.

150. Knopf K, Sturman JA, Armstrong M, and others: Taurine: an essential nutrient for the cat, *J Nutr* 108:773–778, 1978.

151. Morris JG, Rogers QR: Why is the nutrition of cats different from that of dogs?, *Tijdschr Diergeneesk* 1:64S–67S, 1991.

152. Hayes KC: Nutritional problems in cats: taurine deficiency and vitamin A excess, *Can Vet J* 23:2–5, 1982.

153. Wen GY, Sturman JA, Wisniewski HM, and others: Tapetum disorganization in taurine-depleted cats, *Invest Ophthalmol Vis Sci* 18:1201–1206, 1979.

154. Schmidt SY, Berson EL, Hayes KC: Retinal degeneration in cats fed casein. I. Taurine deficiency, *Invest Ophthalmol* 15:47–52, 1976.

155. Sturman JA, Rassin DK, Hayes KC, and others: Taurine deficiency in the kitten: exchange and turnover of [^{35}S] taurine in brain, retina and other tissues, *J Nutr* 108:1462–1476, 1978.

156. Barnett KC, Burger IH: Taurine deficiency retinopathy in the cat, *J Sm Anim Pract* 21:521–526, 1980.

157. Hayes KC: A review of the biological role of taurine, *Nutr Rev* 34:161–165, 1976.

158. Huxtable R, Barbeau A: *Taurine*, 1976, New York, Raven Press, pp 121–134.

159. O'Donnell JA, III, Rogers QR, and Morris JG: Effect of diet on plasma taurine in the cat, *J Nutr* 111:1111–1116, 1981.

160. Aguirre GD: Retinal degeneration associated with the feeding of dog food to cats, *J Am Vet Med Assoc* 172:791–796, 1978.

161. Miller TM, Blackwell CP: Gulf menhaden by-products, *Pet Food Ind* 31:22–26, 1989.

162. Burger IH, Barnett KC: The taurine requirement of the adult cat, *J Sm Anim Pract* 23:533–537, 1982.

163. Carey DP, Strieker MJ: Taurine essentials and clinical management, Iams Technical Report, Lewisburg, Ohio, 1993, The Iams Company.

164. Hickman MA, Rogers QR, Morris JG: Effect of processing on the fate of dietary [^{14}C] taurine in cats, *J Nutr* 120:995–1000, 1990.

165. Hickman MA, Morris JG, Rogers QR: Intestinal taurine and the enterohepatic circulation of taurocholic acid in the cat, *Adv Exp Med Biol* 315:45–54, 1992.

166. Milner JA: Lysine requirements of the immature dog, *J Nutr* 111:40–45, 1981.

167. Brown RG: Protein in dog foods, *Can Vet J* 30:528–531, 1989.

168. Teeter RG, Baker DH, Corbin JE: Methionine and cystine requirements of the cat, *J Nutr* 108:291–297, 1978.

169. Burns RA, Milner JA: Sulfur amino acid requirements of the immature beagle dog, *J Nutr* 111:2117–2122, 1981.

170. Roberts RN: A study of felinine and its excretion by the cat, doctoral dissertation, Buffalo, 1963, State University of New York.

171. Shapiro IL: In vivo studies on the metabolic relationship between felinine and serum cholesterol in the domestic cat, doctoral dissertation, Newark, Del, 1962, University of Delaware.

172. Rogers QR, Morris, JG: Protein and amino acid nutrition of the cat, American Animal Hospital Association Proceedings, 1983, pp 333–336.

173. Ikeda M, Tsuji H, Nakamura S, and others: Studies on the biosynthesis of nicotinamide adenine dinucleotide. II. A role of picolinic carboxylase in the biosynthesis of nicotinamide adenine dinucleotide from tryptophan in mammals, *J Biol Chem* 240:1395–1401, 1965.

174. Maynard LA, Loosli JK, Hintz HF, and others: The proteins and their metabolism, In *Animal nutrition*, ed 7, New York, 1979, McGraw-Hill, pp 136–185.

175. Levitsky DA, Massaro TF, Barnes RH: Maternal malnutrition and the neonatal environment, *Fed Proc* 32:1709–1719, 1973.

176. Barnes RH: Effect of postnatal dietary protein and energy restriction on exploratory behavior in young pigs, *Dev Psychobiol* 9:425–435, 1976.

177. Brenner BM, Meyer TW, and Hostetter TH: Dietary protein intake and the progressive nature of renal disease: the role of hemodynamically mediated glomerular injury in the pathogenesis of progressive glomerular sclerosis in aging, renal ablation, and intrinsic renal disease, *N Eng J Med* 307:652–657, 1982.

178. Murphy DH: Too much of a good thing: protein and a dog's diet, *Int J Stdy Anim Prob* 4:101–107, 1983.

179. Saxton JA, Kimball GC: Relation of nephrosis and other diseases of albino rats to age and to modifications of diet, *Arch Pathol* 32:951–965, 1941.

180. Lalick JJ, Allen JR: Protein overload nephropathy in rats with unilateral nephrectomy, *Arch Pathol* 91:373–382, 1971.

181. Polzin DJ, Osborne CA: Conservative medical management of canine chronic renal failure: concepts and controversies, *Proc Am Coll Vet Int Med* 1:4–55 to 4–58, 1986.

182. Lowenstein LM: The rat as a model for aging in the kidney, In Gibson DC, Adelman RC, Finch C, editors: *Development of the rodent as a model system of aging*, US Department of Health, Education, and Welfare, 1978.

183. Goldman R: Aging of the excretory system: kidney and bladder. In Finch EE, Hayflick L, editors: *Handbook of the biology of aging*, New York, 1977, Van Nostrand Reinhold.

184. Kaufman GM: Renal function in the geriatric dog, *Compend Cont Ed Pract Vet* 6:108–109, 1984.

185. Cowgill LD, Spangler WL: Renal insufficiency in geriatric dogs, *Vet Clin North Am Sm Anim Pract* 11:727–749, 1981.

186. Branam JE: Dietary management of geriatric dogs and cats, *Vet Tech* 8:501–503, 1987.

187. Leibetseder JL, Neufeld KW: Effects of medium protein diets in dogs with chronic renal failure, *J Nutr* 121:S145–S149, 1991.

188. Polzin DJ, Osborne CA, Hayden DW, and others: Influence of reduced protein diets on morbidity, mortality and renal function in dogs with induced chronic renal failure, *Am J Vet Res* 45:506–517, 1984.

189. Glover J, Goodwin TW, Morton RA: Conversion of beta-carotene into vitamin A in the intestine of the rat, *Biochem J* 41:XLV, 1947.

190. Goodman DS, Huang HS, Kanai M, and others: The enzymatic conversion of all-trans beta-carotene into retinal, *J Biol Chem* 242:3543–3554, 1967.

191. Thompson SY, Braude R, Coates ME, and others: Further studies on the conversion of beta-carotene to vitamin A, *Br J Nutr* 4:398–420, 1960.

192. Gershoff SN, Andrus SB, Hegsted DM, and others: Vitamin A deficiency in cats, *Lab Invest* 6:227–239, 1957.

193. Mellanby E: The experimental production of deafness in young animals by diet, *J Physiol* 94:316–321, 1938.

194. Hayes KC: On the pathophysiology of vitamin A deficiency, *Nutr Rev* 29:3–6, 1971.

195. Rivers JPW, Frankel TL, Juttla S, and others: Vitamin D in the nutrition of the cat, *Proc Nutr Soc* 38:36A, 1979.

196. Kealy RD, Lawler DF, Monti KL: Some observations on the dietary vitamin D requirement of weanling pups. In Morris JG, Finley D, Rogers Q, editors: *Proceedings of the Waltham International Symposium on the Nutrition of Small Companion Animals,* Sept 4–8, University of California, Davis, Calif, 1990, pp S66–S69.

197. Hazewinkel HAW: Nutrition in relation to skeletal growth deformities, *J Sm Anim Pract* 30:625–630, 1989.

198. Campbell JR, Douglas TA: The effect of low calcium intake and vitamin D supplements on bone structure in young growing dogs, *Br J Nutr* 19:339–347, 1965.

199. Brickman AS, Chilumula RR, Coburn JW, and others: Biologic action of 1,25-dihydroxy-vitamin D_3 in the rachitic dog, *Endocrinology* 92:728–734, 1973.

200. Kelly PJ: Bone remodeling in puppies with experimental rickets. *J Lab Clin Med* 70:94–105, (1967).

201. Livezey KL, Dormann DC, Hooser SB, and others: Hypercalcemia induced by vitamin D_3 toxicosis in two dogs, *Can Pract* 16:26–31, 1991.

202. Scott DW, Sheffy BE: Dermatosis in dogs caused by vitamin E deficiency, *Comp Anim Pract* 1:42–46, 1987.

203. Figueriredo C: Vitamin E serum contents, erythrocyte and lymphocyte count, PCV, and hemoglobin determinations in normal dogs, dogs with scabies, and dogs with demodicosis: Proceedings of the Annual American Academy of Veterinary Dermatologists and the American College of Veterinary Dermatology, 1985, pp 8.

204. Miller WH: Nutritional considerations in small animal dermatology, *Vet Clin North Am Sm Anim Pract* 19:497–511, 1989.

205. Scott DW, Walton DK: Clinical evaluation of oral vitamin E for the treatment of primary canine acanthosis nigricans, *J Am Anim Hosp Assoc* 21:345–350, 1985.

206. Ayres S, Mihan R: Is vitamin E involved in the autoimmune mechanism? *Cutis* 21:321–325, 1978.

207. Cordy DR: Experimental production of steatitis (yellow fat disease) in kittens fed a commercial canned cat food and prevention of the condition by vitamin E, *Cornell Vet* 44:310–318, 1954.

208. Gaskell, CJ, Leedale AH, Douglas SW: Pansteatitis in the cat: a report of five cases, *J Sm Anim Pract* 16:117–121, 1975.

209. Smith DC, Proutt LM: Development of thiamine deficiency in the cat on a diet of raw fish, *Proc Soc Exp Biol Med* 56:1–5, 1944.

210. Houston D, Hulland TJ: Thiamine deficiency in a team of sled dogs, *Can Vet J* 29:383–385, 1988.

211. Pastoor FJH, Herck H, van Klooster A, and others: Biotin deficiency in cats as induced by feeding a purified diet containing egg white, *J Nutr* 121:S73–S74, 1991.

212. Shen CS, Overfield L, Murthy PNA, and others: Effect of feeding raw egg white on pyruvate and propionyl Co A carboxylase activities on tissues of the dog, *Fed Proc* 36:1169, 1977.

213. Miller EE, Baumann CA: Relative effects of casein and tryptophan on the health and xanthurenic acid excretion of pyridoxine deficient mice, *J Biol Chem* 157:551–562, 1945.

214. Gries CL, Scott ML: The pathology of pyridoxine deficiency in chicks, *J Nutr* 102:1259–1268, 1972.

215. Linkswiler HM: Vitamin B-6 requirements of men. In *Human vitamin B-6 requirements*, Washington, DC, 1978, National Academy of Science, pp 279–290.

216. Bai SC, Sampwon DA, Morris JG, and others: The level of dietary protein affects the vitamin B-6 requirement of cats, *J Nutr* 121:1054–1061, 1991.

217. Jenkins KJ, Phillips PH: The mineral requirements of the dog. II. The relation of calcium, phosphorus and fat levels to minimal calcium and phosphorus requirements, *J Nutr* 70:241–246, 1960.

218. Hazewinkel HAW, Van Der Brom WE, van Klooster AT, and others: Calcium metabolism in Great Dane dogs fed diets with various calcium and phosphorus levels, *J Nutr* 121:S99–S106, 1991.

219. Scott PP: Minerals and vitamins in feline nutrition. In Graham-Jones O, editor: *Canine and feline nutrition requirements*, Pergamon Press, London, 1965, pp 75.

220. Hedhammer A: Nutrition as it relates to skeletal disease. In Proceedings of the Kal Kan Symposium, Columbus, Ohio, 1980, Kal Kan, pp 41–44.

221. Schmidt M: Dissertation in veterinary medicine, Hanover Veterinary School, Hanover, Germany, 1977.

222. Bennett D: Nutrition and bone disease in the dog and cat, *Vet Rec* 98:313–320, 1976.

223. Hintz HF, Schryver HF: Nutrition and bone development in dogs, *Comp Anim Pract* 1:44–47, 1987.

224. Austad R, Bjerkas E: Eclampsia in the bitch, *J Sm Anim Pract* 17:793–798, 1976.

225. Bjerkas E: Eclampsia in the cat, *J Sm Anim Pract* 15:411–414, 1974.

226. Boda JM, Cole HH: The influence of dietary calcium and phosphorus on the influence of milk fever in dairy cattle, *J Dairy Sci* 37:360–372, 1954.

227. Wiggers KD, Nelson DK, Jacobson NL: Prevention of parturient paresis by a low-calcium diet prepartum: a field study, *J Dairy Sci* 58:430–431, 1975.

228. Catalanotto FA: The trace metal zinc and taste, *Am J Clin Nutr* 31:1098–1103, 1978.

229. Miller WH, Griffin CE, Scott DW, and others: Clinical trial of DVM Derm Caps in the treatment of allergic disease in dogs: a nonblinded study, *J Am Anim Hosp Assoc* 25:163–168, 1989.

230. Kane E, Morris JG, Rogers QR, and others: Zinc deficiency in the cat, *J Nutr* 111:488–495, 1981.

231. Wolf AM: Zinc-responsive dermatosis in a Rhodesian Ridgeback, *Vet Med* 82:908–912, 1987.

232. Van den Broek AHM, Thoday KL: Skin disease in dogs associated with zinc deficiency: a report of five cases, *J Sm Anim Pract* 27:313–323, 1986.

233. Sanecki RK, Corbin JE, Forbes RM: Tissue changes in dogs fed a zinc-deficient ration, *Am J Vet Res* 43:1642–1646, 1982.

234. Banta CA: The role of zinc in canine and feline nutrition. In Burger IH, Rivers JPW, editors: *Nutrition of the dog and cat,* New York, 1989, Cambridge University Press, pp 317–327.

235. Sousa CA, Stannard AA, Ihrke PJ: Dermatosis associated with feeding generic dog food: 13 cases (1981–1982), *J Am Vet Med Assoc* 192:676–680, 1988.

236. Fadok VA: Zinc responsive dermatosis in a Great Dane: a case report, *J Am Anim Hosp Assoc* 18:409–414, 1982.

237. Mitchell AR: Salt intake, animal health and hypertension: should sleeping dogs lie? In Burger IH, Rivers JPW, editors: *Nutrition of the dog and cat,* New York, 1989, Cambridge University Press, pp 275–292.

238. Smith RC, Haschem T, Hamlin RL, and others: Water and electrolyte intake and output and quantity of faeces in the health dog, *Vet Med Sm Anim Clin* 59:743–748, 1964.

239. Spangler WL, Gribble DH, Weiser MG: Canine hypertension: a review, *J Am Vet Med Assoc* 170:995–998, 1977.

240. Ladd M, Raisz LG: Response of the normal dog to dietary sodium chloride, *Am J Physiol* 159:149–152, 1949.

241. Wilhelmj CM, Waldmann EB, McGuire TF: Effect of prolonged high sodium chloride ingestion and withdrawal upon blood pressure of dogs, *Proc Soc Exp Biol Med* 77:379–382, 1951.

242. Anderson LJ, Fisher EW: The blood pressure in canine interstitial nephritis, *Res Vet Sci* 9:304–313, 1968.

Pet Foods

he previous sections examined basic principles of nutrition and the specific nutrient requirements of dogs and cats. The practical application of this information is the provision of optimal nutrition to companion animals throughout life. This section provides information that enables pet owners and professionals to thoroughly evaluate and select the appropriate foods for dogs or cats. The history and current regulation of commercial pet foods is examined, with special attention paid to current labeling requirements and measurements of nutritional adequacy. A study of the nutrient content of pet foods provides an overview of ingredients that are included in commercial pet foods and the methods that are used to measure nutrient content. Chapter 17, which examines the various types of pet foods that are available, facilitates easy categorization of foods for comparison purposes. Also, detailed information regarding the evaluation of pet foods allows owners and professionals to efficiently assess commercial products and select appropriate foods for individual animals.

CHAPTER 14

History and Regulation of Pet Foods

Pet owners generally have two options available when choosing the type of diet to feed their companion animals. They either regularly prepare a homemade diet, or they can purchase a commercially prepared dog or cat food. Today the majority of pet owners feed their companion animals commercially prepared foods. The popularity of commercial products is evidenced by the growth of the pet food industry over the past 35 years. In 1958 total pet food sales in the United States were estimated to be $350 million. This amount increased to $1.43 billion in 1972 and to $5.1 billion in 1986.[1] By 1992 U.S. retail pet food sales reached $8.1 billion.[2] The Pet Food Industry's directory of pet food manufacturers currently lists 320 companies, and it is estimated that there are more than 3200 different brands of pet food products.[3] Given the enormous variety of types, flavors, and nutritional claims of pet foods, choosing a proper diet for a pet can be a confusing process. This section provides information about the history and regulation of commercial pet foods, types of pet foods, and the differences between them; it also provides methods that pet owners can use to evaluate products and select the pet food that best fits their needs and the needs of their companion animal.

History of Pet Foods

Before the middle of the nineteenth century, diets for dogs and cats were not commercially prepared. Owners fed their pets table scraps or homemade formulas made from human foods and leftovers. The first commercial dog food to be marketed was in the form of a biscuit. It was produced and sold in 1860 by James Spratt, an American living in London.[4] Following success in England, Spratt began selling his product in the United States. In the early 1900s several other groups observed Spratt's success and began to develop and sell pet foods. The Chappel brothers of Rockford, Illinois were responsible for producing the first batches of canned food. The Chappels named their product Ken-L-Ration dog food and followed it with the introduction of a dry product in the 1930s. Around the same time, Samuel Gaines broke into the market with a new type of dog food called a "meal." The meal consisted of a number of dried, ground ingredients that were mixed together and sold in 100 lb bags. Pet owners enjoyed the convenience of this new product because they were able to buy fairly large quantities at one time and very little preparation of the food was necessary before feeding.

In the early 1900s, pet foods were marketed only through feed stores. The National Biscuit Company (Nabisco), which purchased Milk Bone in 1931, was the first group to attempt to sell its product in grocery stores. Selling pet food in human food markets initially met with much resistance. Because most pet foods were made from by-products of humans foods, customers and store owners considered it unsanitary to sell such products next to foods that were meant for human consumption. However, Nabisco persisted, and Milk Bones finally made it into the supermarket. The convenience and economy of purchasing pet foods at grocery stores rapidly overcame customer concerns. Improved distribution and availability resulted in increased sales and popularity of commercial pet foods. By the mid 1930s many brands were sold in grocery stores. At this time, although some dry biscuits and meal products were available, canned pet foods were still the most popular type of pet food product sold in the United States.

With the onset of World War II, a shortage of metal resulted in fewer cans available for the processing of pet food. The pet food industry responded by producing and selling a larger proportion of dry foods. However, once the war was over, canned foods again became more popular with pet owners. It was not until the development of the extrusion process that dry pet foods began to increase in popularity. The extrusion process and expanded pet foods were first developed by researchers at Purina laboratories in the 1950s. Extrusion involves cooking and mixing all of the pet food ingredients together and then forcing the mixture through a dryer under conditions of pressure and heat. This process causes a rapid expansion of the bite-sized food particles, resulting in increased digestibility and palatability of the food. After extrusion and drying, a coating of fat or other palatability enhancer is usually sprayed onto the outside of the food pieces. In 1957 Purina Dog Chow, an expanded product, was first introduced to grocery stores. One year later, this new product had become the best selling dog food in the United States. Today the majority of dry pet foods that are sold in the United States are extruded products, and dry dog food makes up the largest proportion of the pet food market.

Because little was known about the nutrient requirements of dogs and cats when pet foods were first manufactured, the same food was commonly marketed for both species. Manufacturers merely labeled the cans or bags differently. However, as more knowledge was acquired about the different nutrient needs of dogs and cats, separate pet foods were formulated for each. In 1990 dry dog food held the highest retail sales, followed by canned cat food. Canned dog food and dry cat food ranked third.[2] As more

TABLE 14-1
Governing Agencies of Commercial Pet Foods

AGENCY	FUNCTION
Association of American Feed Control Officials (AAFCO)	Sets standards for substantiation claims and provides an advisory committee for state legislation
National Research Council (NRC)	Collects and evaluates research and makes nutrient recommendations
Food and Drug Administration (FDA)	Specifies permitted ingredients and manufacturing procedures
United States Department of Agriculture (USDA)	Regulates pet food labels and research facilities
Pet Food Institute (PFI)	Trade organization representing pet food manufacturers
Canadian Veterinary Medical Association (CVMA)	Administers voluntary product certification

knowledge becomes available about canine and feline nutrition, companies are developing diets that are designed for specific stages of life, physiological states, and health problems.[4] Although not all of these products are beneficial or necessary, they represent a response to the pet owning public's desire to supply their companion animals with the best nutrition possible during all stages of life. The public's increased interest in nutrition and health, coupled with the large number of commercial products that are available, has led many pet owners, hobbyists, and professionals to critically evaluate the types of foods that they select for their animals. An increasing number of pet owners are now interested in learning more about the regulation of the foods that they buy and the formulation and nutrient content of these foods.

GOVERNING AGENCIES

A number of agencies and organizations regulate the production, marketing, and sales of commercial pet foods in the United States. Each agency has different and sometimes overlapping responsibilities and has varying degrees of authority. Although some regulations are mandatory, others are suggested but optional. The following discussion identifies the major agencies and their roles in pet food regulation and provides an overview of the current regulations that govern the production and sale of pet foods in the United States (Table 14-1).

Association of American Feed Control Officials

The Association of American Feed Control Officials (AAFCO) is the most instrumental agency involved in the regulation of commercial pet foods. AAFCO was first formed in 1909 and is an association of state and federal feed control officials that acts in an advisory capacity to provide models for state legislation. For example, AAFCO's Uniform Feed Bill specifies labeling procedures and ingredient nomenclature for all animal feeds. Because AAFCO is an association and not an official regulatory body, its policies must be

voluntarily accepted by state feed control officials for actual implementation. Pet food regulations can vary somewhat between states, and AAFCO's policy statements and regulations promote uniformity in feed regulations throughout the United States.

AAFCO's involvement in the pet food industry began in the 1960s. The Pet Food Institute, a trade organization, worked with AAFCO to develop a set of policy statements and, eventually, regulations. Today AAFCO ensures that nationally marketed pet foods are uniformly labeled and nutritionally adequate.[5] These services include providing interpretations of AAFCO's pet food regulations and suggestions for uniform enforcement. A large proportion of AAFCO's regulations specifies the type of information that companies are allowed to include on their pet food labels. The Pet Food Committee of AAFCO also regularly reviews labels as a voluntary service for industry and state officials. Although a majority of the states follow AAFCO regulations for pet foods, not all states have a mechanism for inspection and enforcement of the regulations.

An important accomplishment of AAFCO in recent years has been the development of practical nutrient profiles to be used as standards for the formulation of dog and cat foods. Committees consisting of canine and feline nutritionists from universities and the pet food industry worked together to establish two sets of standard nutrient profiles: one for dogs and one for cats. The profiles are based on ingredients that are commonly included in commercial foods, and nutrient levels are expressed for processed foods at the time of feeding. Minimum nutrient levels to be included in the pet food are provided for two categories: (1) growth and reproduction and (2) adult maintenance. Maximum levels are suggested for nutrients that have been shown to have the potential for toxicity or when overuse is a concern. AAFCO Nutrient Profiles have replaced the previously used National Research Council (NRC) recommendations as the recognized authority for the substantiation of label claims (see p. 157). Although the goal of the NRC is to compile information concerning the basic nutrient requirements of dogs and cats, the AAFCO Nutrient Profiles provide practical minimum and maximum levels of nutrients for inclusion in commercial pet foods. Therefore the AAFCO Nutrient Profiles are more functional for the commercial pet food industry than were the NRC recommendations.

National Research Council

The NRC is a private, nonprofit organization that collects and evaluates research that has been conducted by others. The NRC functions as the working arm of the National Academy of Sciences, National Academy of Engineering, and Institutes of Medicine, and it conducts services for the federal government, the scientific community, and the general public.[6] The NRC includes a standing committee on animal nutrition that identifies problems and needs in animal nutrition, recommends appointments of scientists to subcommittees, and reviews reports. Two NRC subcommittees have been established for dog and cat nutrition. These groups develop reports that provide recommendations for the nutrient requirements of dogs and cats throughout various stages of life. Signs of nutrient deficiency and excess in these species are also included in these reports. The current NRC recommendations for dogs and cats, published in 1985 and 1986 respec-

tively, are based primarily on research using purified or semipurified diets that contained nutrients in highly available forms. Although these studies provide valuable information about the minimum requirements of available nutrients for dogs and cats, they cannot be used as guidelines for the formulation of commercial pet foods without the inclusion of safety margins. Safety margins are needed to account for the decreased availability of nutrients in practical ingredients, variability of nutrient availability between ingredients, and loss of nutrients of processing.

Before the development and acceptance of AAFCO's Nutrient Profiles, the NRC reports on nutrient requirements for dogs and cats were used as the recognized authorities for pet food formulation and substantiation of label claims on commercial pet foods. Because the 1985 and 1986 editions of the NRC requirements provided estimates only for available nutrients and did not include safety margins, pet food manufacturers were using the 1974 and 1978 NRC publications as their standards for pet food formulation. In the early 1990s, AAFCO's Dog and Cat Food Nutrient Profiles replaced the NRC recommendations as the standard to be used by pet food manufacturers. In addition to providing suggested levels of nutrients to be included in foods, rather than the minimum nutrient requirements of the animals, AAFCO's Nutrient Profiles also include maximum levels for selected nutrients.

Currently the NRC has no regulatory responsibilities to the pet food industry. In 1991 the agency requested that their recommendations not be used to substantiate nutritional adequacy in dog and cat foods. However, the periodic revisions of the NRC's *Nutrient Requirements for Dogs* and *Nutrient Requirements for Cats* are a valuable resource of information for all groups that are involved in pet nutrition. These reports review current research concerning essential nutrient requirements of companion animals, signs of toxicity and deficiency, and interactions that can occur between nutrients within diets. Although these standards are not of practical use for the formulation of commercial pet foods, they do provide a compilation of pertinent research on the topic of companion animal nutrition.

Food and Drug Administration

All pet food manufacturers must follow the Food and Drug Administration (FDA) rules that specify permitted ingredients for pet foods and describe acceptable manufacturing procedures. Feed control officials within each state are usually relied on to inspect facilities and enforce these regulations, although the FDA is authorized to take direct action, if necessary. The FDA also regulates the inclusion of health claims on pet food labels. A health claim is defined as the assertion or implication that the consumption of a food may help in the treatment, prevention, or reduction of a particular disease or diseases. The Center for Veterinary Medicine (CVM), a department of the FDA, has primary regulatory authority over health claims on pet food labels.

If a health statement is considered a "drug claim," the CVM will not allow its use on the label.[7] All new drugs are subjected to an FDA approval process before being marketed. New foods, on the other hand, are not required to undergo similar pre-market testing. Therefore the inclusion of any health claims on pet foods that indicate that the

consumption of the product will treat or prevent a specific disease constitutes a drug claim, and this product would be subject to the same series of tests required of all new drugs. For example, the FDA has decreed that the word "hypo-allergenic" cannot be used on pet food labels because this term may misrepresent the product. Similarly, the FDA's influence has led AAFCO to disallow inclusion of the term "low ash" on cat food labels because the statement may imply that the product has an effect on feline lower urinary tract disease.

The recent passing of the Nutrition Labeling and Education Act (NLEA) of 1990 has led to changes in medical claims allowances for human food labels. Specifically this act allows certain health claims on labels of human foods that relate the intake of a certain food or nutrient to a reduced risk of a disease, without automatically categorizing the product as a drug. The NLEA also specifically exempts medical foods from several of the labeling requirements that are required of other human foods. To ensure that such products are adequately regulated, the FDA is currently developing new regulations that place medical foods in a separate category from other human foods.[8]

The definitions used by the NLEA were developed for foods for human consumption. However, the CVM refers to these regulations in its decisions regarding approval of veterinary medical foods or "prescription diets." These foods are marketed and sold exclusively to veterinary practitioners and are intended to be fed as the sole source of nutrition to pets that have been diagnosed with specific medical disorders. In the past, these foods were exempt from AAFCO requirements for the substantiation of the "complete and balanced" claim. However, recent changes require that these products substantiate nutritional adequacy using the same AAFCO protocols as those used for all other pet foods. Interestingly, medical diets that contain the label designation "use under the direction of a veterinarian" are exempt from including feeding directions because it is presumed that directions will be prescribed by the veterinarian. Currently the CVM does not allow any health claims or diagnostic information on the label of veterinary medical pet foods, but it does allow companies to include intended use and contraindication information in brochures and other promotional materials that are provided to veterinarians. In all cases, the wording of these materials must be very precise to avoid a drug claim as opposed to a claim of nutritional support for a specific disease.

United States Department of Agriculture

The United States Department of Agriculture (USDA) is responsible for ensuring that pet foods are clearly labeled to prevent human consumers from mistaking these products for human foods. This role includes the inspection of meat ingredients that are used in pets foods to ensure proper handling and to guarantee that such ingredients are not included in the human food supply. A second important role that the USDA plays in the pet food industry is to inspect and regulate research facilities. All kennels and catteries that are operated by pet food companies, private groups, or universities must fulfill USDA requirements for physical structure, housing and care of animals, and sanitation. Once these facilities have passed initial certification, they are regularly inspected by USDA officials. Although some pet food companies maintain their own kennels, others

contract their feeding trials out to private research kennels or universities. Long-term feeding trials make up a large component of the testing that is conducted on quality, commercial pet foods. It is important that the facilities in which these tests are conducted maintain proper care of their animals and conform to sound sanitation practices.

Pet Food Institute

The Pet Food Institute (PFI) is a trade organization that represents manufacturers of commercially prepared dog and cat foods. The PFI works closely with the pet food committee of AAFCO to evaluate current regulations and make recommendations for changes. However, as a group, PFI does not have any direct regulatory powers over the production of pet foods, pet food testing, or statements included on labels. Perhaps the most important work of PFI in recent years is its involvement in the revision of the AAFCO's Policy Statement 21 (PS 21) and the development of the Nutrition Assurance Program (NAP) (see pp. 159–161).

Canadian Veterinary Medical Association Pet Food Certification Program

Like the PFI, the Canadian Veterinary Medical Association (CVMA) is not a regulatory agency. However, it administers a voluntary product certification program for pet food manufacturers in Canada. This program has been in operation since 1977 and involves two phases—an initial certification followed by an ongoing monitoring program. To achieve initial certification, a manufacturer must prove that the pet food is capable of meeting the nutritional needs of dogs or cats throughout all stages of life. The product must be tested using both feeding trials and laboratory analyses of nutrient levels. After a product has passed initial certification, its production is monitored every 2 months and digestibility trials are conducted every 6 months. Like the PFI's NAP program, involvement in the CVMA certification program is not mandatory. Rather, it provides a method of voluntary enforcement of certain standards for pet foods and is considered to be the CVMA's "seal of approval" for certified pet food products in Canada. Currently AAFCO does not allow the CVMA seal on Canadian pet foods that are shipped to the United States for sale.

OVERVIEW OF CURRENT PET FOOD REGULATIONS

Most of the control over the nutrient content of pet foods, ingredient nomenclature, and label claims is relegated to AAFCO. As stated previously, AAFCO is not a regulatory agency per se, but rather it acts in an advisory capacity to state feed control officials. The Uniform Feed Bill that AAFCO has developed and implemented is a model for state legislation and specifies labeling procedures and ingredient nomenclature. Pet food regulations still vary somewhat from state to state, but adherence to AAFCO's regulations minimizes these differences. Each year AAFCO publishes an official document that includes a section containing the current regulations for pet foods. These regulations

govern the terms and definitions, label format, brand and product names, nutrient guarantee claims, types of ingredients, and drug and food additives that are used with or included in commercial pet foods.

The definitions and terms section of AAFCO's pet food regulations defines the format to be used in the principal display panel and sets rules for ingredient and guaranteed analysis statements that are included on labels. Statements that are allowed on labels are described and strictly regulated. These are called statements of nutritional adequacy or purpose of the product. For example, the commonly used "complete and balanced nutrition for all stages of life" claim must be substantiated through one of two possible methods that are defined by AAFCO. The first method (option 1) involves demonstrating through a series of feeding trials that the pet food satisfactorily supports health in a group of dogs or cats throughout gestation, lactation, and growth. The tests that the manufacturer uses must follow a set of feeding trial protocols that have been established and sanctioned by AAFCO. The second method (option 2) requires that the food is formulated to contain ingredients in quantities that are sufficient to provide the estimated nutrient requirements for all stages of life for the dog or cat. If this second option is used, AAFCO Nutrient Profiles for Dog and Cat Foods are used as the standard against which to measure nutrient content. The large-scale difference between the thoroughness of these two methods has led other agencies and some pet food companies to encourage AAFCO to make changes in these requirements (see pp. 159–161).

Limited label claims must be substantiated for the particular stage of life for which they are formulated. Most commonly, limited claims signify feeding for adult maintenance only. In these cases, the food must either be shown to meet the AAFCO Nutrient Profile for adult maintenance or must have passed AAFCO's feeding trials for maintenance. Foods that contain the statement "intended for intermittent or supplemental use" do not meet requirements of either "complete and balanced" or for a limited claim and are therefore not expected to provide complete nutrition. AAFCO also requires that all products labeled with the "complete and balanced" claim include specific feeding directions on the product label.

Brand and product names are also regulated. For example, if a pet food includes a flavor designation in its name, that flavor must be shown to be detectable by a recognized testing method. Similarly, the use of the term "all" or "100%" must mean that only the designated ingredient and an amount of water necessary for processing is present in the product. The inclusion of one or more ingredient names in the product name is allowed only if the ingredients constitute a minimum of 25% of the pet food, singularly or in combination. If in combination, none of the named ingredients can be less than 3% of the formula. For example, the use of the terms "lamb and rice" in a product name requires that 25% or greater of the formula is lamb meat and rice, with rice making up the lesser of the two ingredients while still providing at least 3% of the formula. Artificial color may be added to pet foods only if it has been shown to be harmless to pets. These additives are approved and listed by the FDA. Health claims are regulated by AAFCO through FDA state officials or through the FDA directly. As discussed previously, some health claims are acceptable, but others are considered to be drug claims and are therefore not allowed.

CHAPTER 15

Pet Food Labels

The pet food label is a very important component of commercial pet foods because many consumers rely primarily on the label for information about the product's nutritional adequacy and palatability. Current regulations require that all labels of pet foods that are manufactured and sold in the United States contain the following items: product name; net weight; name and address of the manufacturer; guaranteed analysis for crude protein, crude fat, crude fiber, and moisture; list of ingredients in descending order of predominance by weight; the words "dog or cat food"; and a statement of nutritional adequacy or purpose of the product. Pet food manufacturers must also include a statement that indicates the method that was used to substantiate the nutritional adequacy claim, either through the Association of American Feed Control Officials (AAFCO) feeding trials or by formulating the food to meet AAFCO nutrient profiles (Figure 15-1).

WHAT CONSUMERS CAN LEARN FROM THE PET FOOD LABEL

Guaranteed Analysis Panel

Most pet owners first look at the guaranteed analysis panel of the pet food because this gives them information regarding the amount of protein and fat contained in the product. Manufacturers are required to include minimum percentages for crude protein and fat and maximum percentages for moisture and fiber for dog and cat foods. It is important to recognize that these numbers represent only minimums and maximums and do

Wuf-Wuf Dog Food
Net wt. 8 lb

Feeding instructions	Cups per day
Toy breeds	0.5–1 cups
Small breeds	2–4 cups
Medium breeds	4–7 cups
Large breeds	7–9 cups
Giant breeds	9–11 cups

Guaranteed analysis

Crude protein	Not less than 26%
Crude fat	Not less than 15%
Crude fiber	Not less than 5%
Moisture	Not less than 12%

Ingredients: meat and bone meal, ground corn, ground wheat, wheat middlings, corn gluten meal, animal fat (preserved with BHA), salt, spray-dried blood, choline chloride, vitamin A, D_3, E, B_{12}, B_2 supplements, calcium pantothenate, biotin, folic acid, zinc oxide, sodium selenite.

Manufactured by Wuf-Wuf Inc., city, state

FIGURE 15-1
Typical commercial pet food label

not reflect the exact amounts of these nutrients in the product. For example, a pet food that has a label claim of "minimum crude fat: 11%" cannot have less than 11% fat, but may have more. Although one product with this claim may contain 13% fat, another carrying the same claim may have 11.5% fat. Assuming all other nutrients are comparable, the 1.5% difference in fat content can make a significant difference in the product's caloric density and palatability.

The terms crude protein, crude fat, and crude fiber all refer to specific analytical procedures that are used to estimate these nutrients in foodstuffs. On the average, protein contains 16% nitrogen. Crude protein is the estimate of total protein in a foodstuff that is obtained by multiplying analyzed levels of nitrogen by a constant. Slight inaccuracies in this estimate are caused by variations in nitrogen content between proteins and by the presence on nonprotein nitrogen compounds in the foodstuff. Crude fat is an estimate of the lipid content of a food that is obtained through extraction of the food with ether. In addition to lipids, this procedure also isolates certain organic acids, oils,

pigments, alcohols, and fat-soluble vitamins. On the other hand, some complex lipids, such as phospholipids, may not be isolated with this method. Crude fiber represents the organic residue that remains after plant material has been treated with dilute acid and alkali solvents, and after the mineral component has been extracted. Although crude fiber is used to report the fiber content of many commercial products, it usually underestimates the level of true dietary fiber in a product. It has been determined that the crude fiber method recovers only 50% to 80% of the cellulose, 10% to 50% of the lignin, and less than 20% of the hemicellulose in a given sample.[9] Consequently, crude fiber may be a measurement of most of the cellulose in a sample, but it underestimates all of the other dietary fiber components. Consumers can use the guaranteed analysis panel to provide a rough estimate of protein, fat, fiber, and moisture content in a particular pet food. However, these numbers should only be considered as a starting point when comparing different products or brands, and they should not be assumed to represent the actual levels of these nutrients in the food.

When examining the guaranteed analysis panel of a pet food, consumers must always take into account the moisture (water) content of the product. The amount of water in a food will significantly affect the values that are listed in the guaranteed analysis table because most pet foods display nutrient levels on an "as fed" (AF) basis, rather than a dry-matter basis (DMB). AF means that the percentages of nutrients were calculated directly, without accounting for the proportion of water in the product. Pet foods can vary greatly in the amount of water that they contain. For example, dry cat and dog foods usually contain between 6% and 10% water, but some canned foods contain up to 82% water.[10] In order to make valid comparisons of nutrients in foods with different amounts of moisture, it is necessary to first convert nutrients to a DMB. Similarly, the caloric content of a pet food will also affect the interpretation of the guaranteed analysis panel. Caloric density must always be considered when comparing levels of protein, fat, carbohydrate, and other nutrients in different pet foods (see pp. 197–198).

Ingredient List

The ingredient list is often the second place on the label that consumers look for information about the food that they are buying. The list of ingredients must be arranged in decreasing order of preponderance by weight. Terms that are used must be names assigned by AAFCO when applicable, or they must be the name that is commonly accepted as standard by the feed industry. In no case can any single ingredient be given undue emphasis, nor can designations of the quality of ingredients be included. The ingredient list can be used to indicate whether the principal components of a pet food come from animal products or from plant products. In general, if an ingredient from an animal source is listed first or second in a canned pet food or within the first three ingredients of a dry pet food, the food can be assumed to contain animal products as its principal protein source.

Most popular brands and generic brands of pet food are formulated as "variable formula diets." This means that the ingredients used in the food will vary from batch

to batch, depending on the availability and market prices of ingredients. In contrast, most of the premium foods that are sold at feed stores, pet stores, and through veterinarians are produced using fixed formulas. In this case, the company will not change the formulation in response to changes in market prices. Checking the ingredient list of several bags of a particular pet food over a period of time can indicate whether the company is using fixed or variable formulation. Although the pet owner may pay slightly more for a fixed formulation diet, the consistency between batches of food is a distinct advantage to the dog or cat that is consuming the food (see p. 190). When pet food manufacturers make decisions to change the formulation of a pet food, AAFCO's regulations require that ingredient changes are reflected on the label within a 6-month period. This grace period is provided to allow companies to use existing packaging supplies. After 6 months, all packages must denote the ingredients of the new formulation.

Although the ingredient list can provide general information about the type of ingredients that are included in a food, it does not provide information about the quality of its components. Ingredients that are used in pet foods vary significantly in digestibility, amino acid content and availability, mineral availability, and in the amount of indigestible by-products that they contain. For example, terms such as "meat by-products" and "cereal grain products" are impossible to evaluate because there can be considerable variation in the quality of these ingredients. Most premium foods, in addition to using a fixed formulation, include high-quality ingredients that are highly digestible and available. On the other hand, some generic foods and lower priced popular brands will contain ingredients that are significantly lower in quality. Unfortunately, there is usually no way of determining the quality of the ingredients that are used from the ingredient list. In fact, some premium foods with high-quality, highly available ingredients may have an ingredient list that is almost identical to that of a generic food that contains poor-quality ingredients with low digestibility and nutrient availability. Therefore the ingredient list alone should never be used to compare two pet foods because the differences in the qualities of ingredients are impossible to know from this information.

Like the guaranteed analysis, the list of ingredients can be deceptive in some cases because manufacturers are not required to list the ingredients on a DMB. This is usually not a problem in dry pet foods because most of the ingredients included in these diets have a relatively low moisture content. However, canned products may contain ingredients with vastly different amounts of moisture. As a result, an ingredient that actually contributes a low proportion of nutrients to the food may be listed first if it has a high water content, but an ingredient that contributes a large proportion of the nutrients to the food may be lower on the ingredient list if it has a low moisture content. A common example involves the use of textured vegetable protein (TVP) in canned pet foods. TVP is composed of extruded soy flour that is dyed and shaped to resemble meat products. The actual meat ingredients in a product that contains TVP can be listed high on the ingredient list because they are added in a wet form. However, TVP is added to the formulation in a dry form and therefore appears to contribute very little on an AF basis. In reality, most of the protein in the food is coming from the TVP and not from the first-listed, animal-source ingredients.

A second way that the ingredient list can be misleading is the manner in which certain ingredients are presented. Manufacturers may separate different forms of similar ingredients so that they can be listed separately on the label and appear further down the list. For example, an ingredient list may include kibbled wheat, ground wheat, wheat flour, flaked wheat, wheat middlings, and wheat bran. These ingredients are called "split ingredients" and they may in some cases represent two or more forms of the same product. Examples of split ingredients are ground wheat and wheat flour, which differ only in the fineness of the grind that is used during processing. Individually these ingredients comprise only a small fraction of the diet and therefore can be listed low on the ingredient list. As a whole, wheat actually constitutes a large proportion of this diet. Consumers should be aware that listing different forms of the same ingredient suggests a purposeful but legal misrepresentation of the product's ingredient content on the part of the manufacturer.

Nutritional Adequacy

A final item that consumers may read on the pet food label is the claim of nutritional adequacy. With the exception of treats and snacks, the label of all pet foods that are in interstate commerce must contain a statement and validation of nutritional adequacy. When the "complete and balanced nutrition" claim is used, manufacturers must indicate the method that was used to substantiate this claim. Currently, AAFCO regulations require that the manufacturer either performs AAFCO-sanctioned feeding trials on the food (option 1), or formulates the diet to meet the AAFCO Nutrient Profiles for Dog or Cat Foods (option 2). The first option, testing the food through a series of feeding trials, is the most thorough and reliable evaluation method. The suggested terminology for labels of pet foods that have passed these tests is as follows: "Animal feeding tests using AAFCO procedures show that (brand) provides complete and balanced nutrition for (life stages)."[11] The inclusion of the terms "feeding tests," "AAFCO feeding test protocols," or "AAFCO feeding studies" in a label claim all validate that the product has undergone a complete series of feeding tests with dogs or cats. However, if the substantiation claim states only that the food has met the AAFCO Nutrient Profiles (option 2), this indicates that AAFCO feeding trials were not conducted on the food. Although most companies that use option 2 will measure the level of certain nutrients in the food through laboratory analysis, the best way to test the nutritional adequacy of a pet food is still through actual feeding trials.

Consumers should be aware that the use of feeding trials is not required if manufacturers use the second method of substantiation. This method is commonly referred to as the "calculation method" because it allows manufacturers to substantiate the "complete and balanced" claim by merely calculating the nutrient content of the formulation for the diet using standard tables of ingredients, and without having to conduct laboratory analyses or actually feeding the food to any animals. Although some manufacturers using this method of substantiation may still conduct some of their own feeding trials, there is no way of knowing this from the label unless they have used the AAFCO feeding trial protocols (see the box on the following page).

Label Claims of Nutritional Adequacy and How to Interpret Them

Claim 1: "Wuf-Wuf is formulated to meet the nutrient levels established by AAFCO's Canine Nutrition Expert Subcommittee's Nutrient Profiles of Dog Foods for all life stages."
Interpretation: This dog food has not been subjected to AAFCO feeding tests. Although the food has been formulated to meet the AAFCO's Nutrient Profiles, there is no way of knowing from this substantiation claim whether or not feeding studies have been conducted on this food.

Claim 2: "Wuf-Wuf is guaranteed nutritionally complete and balanced for your dog's entire life. The food meets the nutritional requirements that are established by AAFCO feeding studies."
Interpretation: This dog food has been subjected to the complete series of AAFCO feeding studies, including gestation, lactation, and growth. This substantiation method shows that the food is complete for all life stages.

Claim 3: "Wuf-Wuf provides complete and balanced nutrition for adult dog maintenance, based on the AAFCO protocol feeding studies."
Interpretation: This food has undergone AAFCO feeding protocol studies for maintenance only and has not been tested for gestation, lactation, or growth. Feeding studies have been conducted, but the food has not been shown to be nutritionally complete for life stages other than maintenance.

THE "IDEAL" PET FOOD LABEL

Recent changes in human food labeling and an increased awareness of the general public about the importance of proper nutrition has resulted in increased concern of pet owners about their pets' diets. Consumers are now demanding to know more about the food that they are feeding to their companion animals. One of the ways in which this information can be provided is through the pet food label.

AAFCO has made some recent changes and is continuing to study ways in which to improve the current pet food label so that it more adequately represents the food that is contained in the package. For example, in 1992 a new regulation was passed that required all dog and cat foods that are labeled "complete and balanced for any or all stages of life" to include feeding directions on the product label. At a minimum, these instructions must state "Feed (weight per unit of product) per (weight unit) of dog or cat."[12] Before 1994 the inclusion of a caloric density statement on pet food labels was prohibited. In 1993 recommendations were made to AAFCO for the measurement of metabolizable energy (ME) and the inclusion of ME values on pet food labels. This new provision was accepted in 1994, making the inclusion of a caloric density statement on the label optional for pet food manufacturers. The inclusion of such a statement, along with a breakdown of the percentage of calories that are contributed by fat, carbohydrate, and protein, provides information about the suitability of the food for different stages of a pet's life. For example, hard-working dogs may benefit from a diet with an increased proportion of ME calories supplied by fat. In addition, it is much more accurate to compare foods according to the percentage of calories that are contributed by carbohydrate, protein, and fat than to compare them by the percentage of these nutrients by weight (see pp. 170–173).

Information Provided by the Pet Food Label

The pet food label *does* provide information about:
Net weight of product
Name and location of manufacturer or distributor
Minimum crude protein and crude fat content
Maximum moisture and crude fiber content
List of ingredients
Nutritional adequacy statement
Method of substantiation of adequacy claim
Feeding instructions
Caloric density (optional)

The pet food label *does not* provide information about:
Exact levels of nutrients
Digestibility and nutrient availability
Quality of the ingredients

Information about additional nutrients on the guaranteed analysis panel would also be beneficial to consumers. As discussed previously, current regulations require that only crude protein, crude fat, fiber, and moisture be included on this panel. Expanding this to include ash, calcium, phosphorus, and perhaps sodium and magnesium would give consumers more information to use when selecting a food. Changing this panel to include actual amounts of these nutrients (i.e., proximate analysis) rather than the minimums and maximums that are now required would also be expedient. As AAFCO continues to review, evaluate, and revise its current regulations, it is probable that many of these changes will occur, resulting in a pet food label that can provide consumers with a greater amount of helpful information (see the box above).

NUTRITION ASSURANCE PROGRAM OF THE PET FOOD INSTITUTE

A substantial portion of AAFCO's regulations involves the methods of substantiation that are used for label claims of nutritional adequacy. Policy Statement 21 (PS 21) of the AAFCO pet food regulations specifically addresses this matter and has been a pivotal issue for AAFCO, PFI, and pet food manufacturers. In 1986 PFI proposed revisions to PS 21 that would have changed the methods that were used to verify label claims. The objectives of these revisions were to add substance to the "complete and balanced" claim on labels and to assure consumers that a product with this label claim would actually meet a pet's nutrient needs over the course of its life span. The most important proposed change was the elimination of the calculation method as an acceptable method for substantiation of label claims. PFI believes that this method is not adequate for nutrition verification. The calculation method means that table values of nutrient levels in pet food ingredients are used to formulate the food to meet AAFCO Nutrient Profiles for dogs or cats. Neither laboratory nutrient analysis, digestibility trials, nor feeding trials are required to be performed on the diet. Because of differences in processing methods, bioavailability of nutrients, diet digestibility, and nutrient interactions within diets, this

method cannot unequivocally support the claim of complete and balanced nutrition. In addition, the levels of nutrients that are actually present in the ingredients that are used can vary greatly from the levels that are reported in standard tables. Because many pet foods are developed to provide the sole nutrition for an animal from weaning into old age, it is extremely important that adequate testing is conducted on these products.

As a replacement of the calculation method, PFI proposed that pet food companies that did not conduct AAFCO feeding trials (option one for label substantiation) must conduct laboratory analyses of nutrient levels in the pet food after processing. Along with these analyses, companies would also be required to feed the food to a number of dogs or cats and to conduct digestibility trials. In 1987 the AAFCO accepted these changes. However, in 1990, before the new regulation was put into effect, they reversed this decision and PS 21 reverted back to its original version. AAFCO officials stated that difficulty in finding acceptable and consistent laboratory methods for analyzing nutrient levels in pet foods was the reason for this decision. In 1992 and 1993 the only change that was made to PS 21 was the replacement of the NRC nutrient recommendations with the AAFCO Nutrient Profiles. Currently, AAFCO regulations do not require pet food companies to conduct laboratory analysis on the food or to conduct digestibility trials. If AAFCO feeding trials are not used to verify claims (option one), then the calculation method alone is sufficient for the label to claim nutritional adequacy (option two).

PFI's commitment to developing a policy or program that would adequately validate label claims and improve consumer confidence in commercial pet foods led the organization to develop the Nutrition Assurance Program (NAP). The NAP is a voluntary, self-enforcement program that provides a supplemental means for pet food companies to demonstrate the nutritional adequacy of their products. The objectives of the program include the clear communication of information to consumers regarding the degree of testing that was conducted on a particular product. Because the NAP is not formally accepted by AAFCO, a NAP designation cannot be included on the label of pet foods that participate in the program. However, products that have passed this certification can be labeled that the product has fulfilled AAFCO's feeding protocol requirements, because this is a basic requirement of the NAP. The PFI also maintains a toll free phone number for consumers to call and obtain information about the NAP and about specific pet foods that have passed NAP certification. The phone number is 1-800-851-0769.

There are several major components to the NAP. Because the most reliable method of proving the nutritional adequacy of a pet food is through actual feeding trials, the NAP recognizes only one method for substantiating a claim of nutritional adequacy. Pet food companies are required to test their product using AAFCO protocol feeding tests. In addition to these tests, the manufacturer must also conduct digestibility trials and laboratory analyses of nutrients in the finished product. It is important to note that manufacturers are not required to conduct this testing on each individual product that they produce. Rather, they are required to group their products into "families." A family consists of products that contain similar ingredients, use the same processing method, and are intended to have the same label claim. The product with the most basic nutritional profile within a family must then go through complete protocol testing. This product is

called the "lead product." If this product passes, it is assumed that the other products within the family will also pass because they all either meet or exceed the nutrient profile of the lead product. Once a particular nutritional claim is established for the lead product, pet foods within the same family are entitled to make the same nutritional claim. For the remaining products, only laboratory analyses of a select number of nutrients must be conducted.

PFI has established a secretariat who is responsible for collecting affidavits for products that pass this testing. The affidavit is a legally binding declaration that is completed by the manufacturer and submitted once testing of a product has been completed. The secretariat also acts as a liaison between PFI and pet food manufacturers on all matters regarding the NAP certification. When a product family has been certified by the NAP, relisting is necessary every 2 years or whenever significant formula changes are made to the product. The routine biennial retesting of a product involves only laboratory analyses and digestibility trials. In the case of a change in formulation, if the change is made to the lead product, complete retesting, including feeding trials, is necessary. Periodic, unannounced verification is also made of all of the supporting certification documents that the pet food manufacturer holds. During this evaluation, the secretariat reviews the results of the AAFCO feeding studies, digestibility trials, and laboratory analyses.

The NAP provides consumers with additional assurance about the testing that has been completed on a particular pet food product. The program is intended to supplement, not replace, the testing that is currently required by AAFCO. Although present AAFCO regulations cannot ensure that adequate and complete feeding trials have been conducted on all products, the NAP does provide this verification. Consumers are encouraged to use the NAP to provide guarantees that the food they choose for their companion animal has been proven through AAFCO feeding trials to provide complete and balanced nutrition.

Pet Food Advertising

Pet food manufacturers are in a unique situation when they consider the marketing techniques used to sell their products. Although it is the dog or the cat that is consuming the food and the animal's health that is directly affected by the product's quality, it is the pet owner who is making the decision to buy the product. Therefore manufacturers must not only consider what is the most nutritious food to feed to dogs and cats, they must also consider the pet owner's perception of the best food to feed his or her companion animal. Most of today's marketing strategies are aimed toward convincing pet owners that a particular food offers some benefit to the pet that is above and beyond that of all other products. Because most foods now carry the "complete and balanced" label claim, offering complete nutrition is not perceived by many owners to be a strong selling point. Rather, acceptability and palatability, cost, feeding convenience, digestibility, and suitability of the food for the pet's life style, age, or physiological state are all important considerations for today's owner. In recent years, as knowledge about canine and feline nutrition has increased, pet food companies have started to produce foods that specifically meet the needs of companion animals during different stages of life and for pets that live different life styles. Examples of these foods include high-performance diets for working dogs, growth diets for young dogs and cats, and maintenance diets for adult pets. The sale of these foods is accompanied by educational programs for pet owners about the nutrient needs of their companion animals.

The needs and perceptions of the pet owner are of primary concern when marketing a pet food. Identifying these needs is often the first task for pet food manufacturers. Although some pet owners are concerned primarily with providing the best nutrition for their companion animals, others are more interested in the cost of the food, its availability in stores, or the convenience of feeding it. In today's market there are products that appeal to all of these needs and to the many different types of pet owners.

Because there is no way to determine by examining it or by feeding it a few times, whether or not a food contains superior nutrition, many pet owners rely on a product's palatability and acceptability as their chief selection criteria. Palatability is a subjective measure of how well an animal likes a particular food, and acceptability is an indication of whether the amount of food that is eaten will be enough to meet the animal's caloric requirements.[13] These are both important considerations, because regardless of a food's nutritional value, it cannot nourish an animal if it is not eaten. Palatability and acceptability are also very powerful marketing tools. Most pet owners enjoy giving their companion animal a food that is eagerly accepted and eaten, and they will be inclined to buy a food that they know their pet relishes. However, many highly palatable foods are high in fat and as a result are energy dense. This increased palatability, coupled with high energy density, can lead to overeating and obesity if the food is fed on a free-choice basis. In recent years the prevalent use of palatability as a marketing tool for pet foods has probably contributed to the increasing problem of obesity in dogs and cats in the United States. Owners should certainly pick a food that their pet enjoys, but they should be aware that extremely palatable foods can induce overeating.

In today's busy society, convenience and ease of preparation are also important to many pet owners. The convenience of feeding dry pet foods and the availability of these foods in supermarkets contributed greatly to their initial success. Dry foods keep well after opening, do not require refrigeration, and require little if any preparation before feeding. Packaging foods in portion-sized bags is another technique that attracts pet owners who desire convenience. Many canned cat foods and semimoist pet foods are marketed to provide one meal per package, therefore eliminating even the need to measure out a portion of food before feeding.

Although it is not the chief consideration of most pet owners, to some the cost of the food is very important. There are a number of commercial foods available today that are advertised as being more economical to feed yet still provide superior nutrition. However, it is important for pet owners to know that to produce a low-cost product, ingredients that are of lower quality, and thus lower cost, must be used. Therefore a cheaper product is invariably going to be a lower quality food, even though the guaran-

teed analysis panel may not reflect this. In addition, when considering the price of a pet food, the actual cost of feeding the animal must be calculated, not the cost per unit weight of the food. Most low-quality, cheap ingredients have significantly lower digestibilities than the ingredients that are used in premium foods. A greater quantity of a food with low digestibility must be fed to an animal to provide the same amount of nutrition as a food with higher digestibility and nutrient availability. As a result, owners may find that they have to feed significantly larger portions of the cheaper food to their pet. Also, companies that produce inexpensive dog and cat foods do not have the funds or capability to conduct thorough testing of their products. In most cases, these foods are not tested using AAFCO feeding protocols because this testing will cost extra money. In general, when pricing dog and cat foods, it is safe to assume that buyers usually "get what they pay for." Premium products cost more primarily because they contain higher quality ingredients and because they have been subjected to more rigorous testing than cheaper generic and name-brand products. Marketing techniques that promote cheaper foods as being equivalent in value to more costly products usually mislead the consumer into believing that the food offers the same benefits as a premium food but at a substantially lower cost.

In recent years a new technique that has been used to increase sales of pet foods is "niche marketing."[4] This concept involves developing, marketing, and selling products that are designed for specific age groups, physiological states, activity levels, and health problems. As more knowledge has become available, nutritionists and pet food manufacturers have realized that optimum nutrition is often best provided through specialized products that are formulated for different stages of life or even for certain disease states. In general, more consumer education is necessary with these products; most are sold only through feed stores, veterinarians, and pet supply stores. These products can be contrasted to the "all-purpose" pet foods that are developed and marketed for sale in grocery stores. Although specialized foods are marketed to appeal to involved pet owners who are interested in providing the best nutrition to their pets, the "all-purpose" foods are attractive to the pet owner who wishes to have a food that is balanced, fairly economical to feed, and convenient to buy.

Other commonly used marketing tools for pet foods include the development of products that resemble foods consumed by humans. This obviously appeals to the sense of taste of the pet owner, more so than that of the animal that will be eating the food. These products are varied and creative. Some foods have the appearance of chunks of meat, and others look like stews, containing a variety of meat and vegetables. The actual content of these foods is usually not the ingredient that they are made to resemble. For example, TVP can be shaped and dyed to resemble chunks of meat. Flavor varieties are also a strong selling tool. Because owners enjoy variety in their diets, they believe that this is also important for their pets. Almost all of the pet foods and treats that are sold in grocery stores come in a variety of flavors. Although these differences may appeal to owners, it is unknown whether individual pets have strong preferences between flavors. Nonetheless, it is the owner who buys the food, and some will be induced to buy a food that looks like ground steak or pronounces to be "liver-flavored."

Promoting the addition or deletion of a particular ingredient in a pet food is another tactic that is used to increase sales. Whether or not this information is grounded in fact is a moot point because there is always a segment of the pet-owning population that is willing to believe in the value or hazard of a given ingredient. For example, some owners believe that soy is a poor-quality ingredient. Pet foods that are marketed as containing no soy capitalize on this belief, whether or not it is founded in fact. Similarly, the pet-owning public can be convinced that the presence of a particular ingredient may contribute to a superior product. The use of fish and fish meal in cat foods is an example. Cats are actually desert animals by ancestry and probably had very little access to fish in their original diets. However, the use of clever and cute advertisements has convinced pet owners that all cats inherently love the taste of fish. The presence of fish in certain cat foods is then promoted as a distinct benefit. Although it is true that cats enjoy the taste of fish, this ingredient is no more palatable to most cats than are several other high-protein ingredients that are included in cat foods.

CHAPTER 16

Nutrient Content of Pet Foods

T he most important consideration in choosing a commercial pet food for a companion animal is its nutrient content. This term refers not only to the exact levels of nutrients in the food but also to the digestibility and availability of all essential nutrients. Nutrients can be supplied in commercial pet foods by a large number of different ingredients. Commonly used pet food ingredients can vary greatly in form and quality. It is this diversity that can make the selection of a suitable dog or cat food a difficult task. The methods that are used to determine and express nutrient content in pet foods and a review of commonly used pet food ingredients and additives are included in this chapter.

METHODS USED TO DETERMINE NUTRIENT CONTENT

Laboratory Analysis

When pet food manufacturers formulate and produce pet foods, there are two possible ways that they can determine the level of nutrients that are present in the product. The first and most accurate way is to conduct a laboratory analysis of the finished product. Proximate analysis is a commonly used panel of tests that provides information about a select group of nutrients. The laboratory procedures involved in proximate analysis provide the percentages of moisture, protein, fat, ash (minerals), and fiber that are contained in the food. Nitrogen-free extract (NFE), which represents a rough estimate of the soluble carbohydrate fraction of the food, can be calculated by subtraction (see Section 1,

p. 11). The guaranteed analysis panel of the pet food label does not report actual levels of nutrients. Rather, the guaranteed analysis panel is generated from the proximate analysis results and reports only maximum or minimum levels of a very limited number of nutrients.

Pet food companies that are producing high-quality products and that are interested in the education of pet owners will provide consumers with information about the exact nutrient content of their foods. Because regulations do not allow the inclusion of these details on the pet food container itself, they are usually supplied to pet owners in the form of informational brochures and pamphlets. These publications can be obtained through the feed store, pet supply store, or veterinarian's office where the food is purchased or by contacting the pet food company directly. In addition to the proximate analysis of the food, the content of essential minerals and vitamins and the energy density of the food are also usually included in these reports.

Calculation

A second method that manufacturers may use to determine nutrient content is calculation from the average nutrient content of the food's ingredients using values that are reported in standard tables. The amount of essential nutrients that are contributed by each ingredient in the food are then summed. Standard tables contain average levels of essential nutrients in common feed ingredients. Although this method of nutrient determination is certainly less costly and less time-consuming than laboratory analysis, there are several significant problems with using calculation alone to determine the nutrient content of pet foods. First, there is a lack of complete and accurate data for levels of nutrients in many of the ingredients that are included in commercial pet foods. As a result, manufacturers must rely on tables that contain approximations of the types of ingredients that they are using. The quality of ingredients can affect levels and availability of nutrients in finished pet foods. Standard tables represent averages and cannot reflect differences in ingredient quality. The processing of a pet food will also affect nutrient content and availability. Calculating nutrient content from a formulation on paper does not account for losses that occur during processing or storage. Pet foods are processed in a variety of different ways, each of which may affect the level and availability of certain nutrients. No data are currently available that accurately predict these losses.[14] As a result, the only accurate means of determining nutrient content of a pet food is through laboratory analyses of the processed, finished product. Even in this case, the information that is provided does not account for either the digestibility or availability of the food, which can only be obtained through actual feeding studies with animals.

Determination of Digestibility

Current Association of American Feed Control Officials (AAFCO) regulations do not require that companies determine the digestibility of their foods (see pp. 152, 159–161). However, the digestibility of a pet food must always be considered. Digestibility provides a measure of the diet's quality because it directly determines the proportion of

TABLE 16-1
Variability in Pet Food Digestibility*

	DIET		
	A	B	C
Protein digestibility (%)	70.25	80.99	85.86
Fat digestibility (%)	82.70	90.42	90.72
Fiber digestibility (%)	17.44	48.53	61.48
Fecal score	3.95	4.47	4.48
Fecal volume	162.38	89.18	46.48

Data provided by Iams Technical Center, Lewisburg, Ohio, 1993.
*Based on a 1–5 rating. 1 = loose, watery; 5 = firm. Scores of 4 to 5 are considered normal.

nutrients in the food that is available for absorption into the body. Pet food companies evaluate the digestibility of their products through feeding studies. The disappearance of nutrients as they pass through the gastrointestinal tract and are absorbed into the body is measured. The test diet is fed to the animals for a pretest period of 5 to 7 days to allow acclimation to the diet. Following this period, the amount of food that is consumed and the amount of fecal matter that is excreted are recorded for 3 to 5 days. The fecal matter that is collected represents the undigested residue of the food that was consumed. Laboratory analyses of both feed and fecal matter are conducted to provide the levels of nutrients in each, and amounts of digested nutrients are calculated by subtraction. The expression of these figures as percentages are called "digestion coefficients." In this type of study, the figures that are derived are called "apparent" digestibility coefficients because the fecal matter also contains metabolic waste products that originated from the animal and not from the food (Table 16-1).

True digestibility can be determined by deducting the normal metabolic loss of the nutrient from the amount of the nutrient that is measured in the fecal matter. True digestibility trials are most commonly conducted for protein. The animals are fed a protein-free or very low-protein diet for a short period of time, and a baseline level of protein excretion is measured. This figure can then be used to account for the metabolic loss of protein in the feces that is endogenous in origin when the digestibility trial is conducted. It can be argued that apparent digestibility is actually a better indication of a diet's ability to supply nutrients than is true digestibility. The endogenous losses that occur in the fecal matter represent cellular and enzymatic losses that are the result of the cost of digesting and absorbing food. These losses represent the "cost" to the animal of digestion. Therefore apparent digestibility represents the actual net gain to the animal from the digestion of the food.[15]

Information about the nutrient content of a diet means little if the product's digestibility is not known. For example, laboratory analyses of two different dry dog foods reveal that they each contain 28% protein. If the protein digestibility of diet A is 70.25%, this means that the food actually provides less than 20% digestible protein. On the other hand, if the digestibility of diet C is 85.8%, it provides about 24% digestible protein (Table 16-1; see also the accompanying box). The amount of protein that is

Effect of Different Digestibilities on the Amount of Protein Available to the Dog

Diet A:
28% protein
70.25% of the protein is digestible

Therefore 70.25% of 28% protein = 0.7025 × 28 = **19.67%** digestible protein

Diet C:
28% protein
85.9% of the protein is digestible

Therefore 85.9% of 28% protein = 0.859 × 28 = **24.05%** digestible protein

available to the animal is higher in diet C than in diet A, even though laboratory analyses indicate that they have similar total protein contents. Digestibility also affects fecal volume and form, and defecation frequency (Table 16-1). As a diet's digestibility increases, fecal volume will decrease significantly. In addition, a highly digestible pet food produces firm and well-formed feces. Although manufacturers are not required to conduct digestibility trials on their feeds, reputable companies that produce quality products always conduct these trials to ensure that their foods contain levels of nutrients that will meet animals' daily requirements upon absorption into the body.

DETERMINATION OF METABOLIZABLE ENERGY

The metabolizable energy (ME) of a pet food is another important consideration when selecting a diet (see Section 1, pp. 10–12). ME indicates the amount of energy in a pet food that is available to the animal for use. Although digestible energy (DE) measures the amount of energy that is absorbed across the intestinal wall, ME accounts for digestibility and for losses of energy in the urine and through expired gases (flatus). Although expired gases account for a significant proportion of energy in most farm animals, it is an insignificant energy loss in dogs and cats. Therefore the analysis of the ME of foods for dogs and cats includes only urinary losses of energy.

ME is the preferred unit for analyzing energy content of pet foods because unlike gross energy, which is a measure of the total energy in the diet, ME provides an accurate representation of the amount of energy that is actually available to the animal. ME can be determined either through feeding trials or, less accurately, by calculation using standard energy values for protein, carbohydrate, and fat. A rough estimate of the ME of a pet food can also be calculated using the values that are provided in the guaranteed analysis panel on the label (see Section 1, pp. 10–12).

The new AAFCO regulation (PS7) that allows, but does not require, the inclusion of caloric claims on pet food labels stipulates that ME must be expressed as kilocalories per kilogram of product. Additional units such as kilocalories per cup or pound may be listed also. Like the "complete and balanced" statement on the pet food label, the ME statement must be accompanied by a substantiation claim. AAFCO regulations allow manufacturers to determine ME content by one of three possible ways:

1. Calculation using Modified Atwater factors and values for crude protein, crude fat, and NFE obtained from proximate analysis. (Samples must be taken from at least four production batches of the product.)
2. Calculation from digestible nutrients or digestible energy. (Data are obtained from digestibility trials without urine collection.)
3. Direct determination from digestibility trials including urine collection.

Although the inclusion of ME values on pet food labels will help pet owners to select appropriate products for their pets, there is still some controversy regarding the methods of substantiation that are required.[16] The use of modified Atwater factors for the calculation of ME in commercial pet foods has been shown to overestimate the ME content for some foods. In contrast, calculation from DE using a correction factor for urine energy losses closely approximates ME values obtained through direct measurement.[16,17] This discrepancy means that companies using either direct measurement of ME or calculation of ME from digestibility trial data will accurately represent the product's ME on the label. However, as with the "complete and balanced" claim, when the calculation method is used, the stated ME value may be less accurate. Ironically, the standard that is currently used to verify direct measurement and digestibility trial calculation methods for ME determination is the calculation method. The AAFCO requires that if digestibility trials are used to obtain ME values, the value on the label must not exceed or understate the value that is determined using the calculation method by more than 15%.[12] Therefore, just as with the "complete and balanced" claim, pet food consumers should always make note of the method that was used to determine the ME value when selecting a pet food.

EXPRESSION OF NUTRIENT CONTENT

The guaranteed analysis panel of a pet food usually reports nutrient levels on an "as fed" (AF) basis. This means that the nutrient content in the diet is measured directly, without accounting for the amount of water in the product. This type of measurement is called "as fed" because it represents the level of nutrients in the food as it is consumed by the animal. For example, if 10 ounces (oz) of a semimoist cat food contains 2.5 oz of protein, it contains 25% (($2.5 \div 10$) $\times$ 100) protein on an AF basis. Similarly, if 10 oz of a dry cat food also contains 2.5 oz of protein, it too has a protein content of 25%, on an AF basis. Comparing these two foods on an AF basis would indicate that they contribute similar levels of protein to the cat. However, because of the large range in moisture content between different types of pet foods, the diluting effect of water makes comparisons between pet foods on an AF basis difficult to interpret.

Animals eat or are fed to meet their caloric needs. Therefore a food with a high water content has its nutrients essentially "diluted" compared with a food containing a

Converting Nutrients from As Fed (AF) to Dry-Matter (DM) Basis

Formula
Percentage of nutrient on an AF basis ÷ Proportion of DM in the diet

Example
Semimoist food contains: 25% protein
                         75% DM

Dry food contains: 25% protein
                   90% DM

For semimoist food: $(25 \div 75) \times 100 = $ **33%** protein on a DMB

For dry food: $(25 \div 90) \times 100 = $ **28%** protein on a DMB

---

lower amount of water. Regardless of the amount of moisture in the diet, an animal will still need to eat a certain amount of dry matter to meet its daily caloric requirement. Conversion of nutrient data to a dry-matter basis (DMB) allows more accurate comparisons to be made between different types of pet foods. For example, the semimoist cat food discussed earlier contains 25% water and 75% dry matter and the dry food contains 10% water and 90% dry matter. The percentage of protein on a DMB can be calculated by dividing the percentage of the nutrient on an AF basis by the proportion of dry matter in the diet. The protein content of the semimoist food on a DMB is approximately 33%, but the protein content of the dry diet is 28% (see the box above). Therefore, although their label guarantees indicate similar protein contents, the semimoist food actually contains a higher level of protein than does the dry food on a DMB.

One of the most accurate ways to compare foods is by calculating the levels of nutrients as a proportion of ME. Energy-containing nutrients such as protein, fat, and carbohydrate are expressed as percentage of ME. The nutritional standard for nutrients that do not contain energy (vitamins and minerals) is units per 1000 kilocalories (kcal) of ME. Because all animals eat or are fed to meet their energy needs, the amount of food consumed and thus the amount of nutrients taken in depends directly on the caloric content of the food. For example, diet A and diet B contain the same amount of protein (26%) on a DMB; diet A contains 4000 kilocalories per kilogram (kcal/kg) and diet B contains 3500 kcal/kg. A greater quantity of diet B will need to be consumed to meet a particular animal's caloric needs. A dog that requires 2000 kcal/day would consume 500 g of diet A, or approximately 570 g of diet B. If the two diets contain the same percentage of protein on a weight basis, the dog would consume more total protein when he was fed diet B compared with diet A (Table 16-2). If the protein level was sufficiently high, this would mean that excess protein would be consumed when the dog was fed diet B. Excess protein will invariably be used directly for energy or converted to fat for the storage of energy. On the other hand, if the diets contained marginal levels of protein, the dog may be deficient in protein when consuming diet A, which had a higher

TABLE 16-2
Protein Intake Relative to Dietary ME

	ENERGY REQUIREMENT (KCAL)		DIET ENERGY DENSITY (KCAL/G)		FOOD INTAKE (G)		PROTEIN IN DIET (%)				PROTEIN CONSUMED (G)
Diet A	2000	÷	4.0	=	500	×	26	÷	100	=	130
Diet B	2000	÷	3.5	=	571	×	26	÷	100	=	148.5

caloric density. This example illustrates the need to increase nutrient density as the caloric density of a diet increases. Although protein is a commonly used example, this concept applies to all of the essential nutrients. Because an animal will be fed less of a calorically dense food, the percentage of nutrients by weight in these foods must be higher so that the animal can still meet its needs for all essential nutrients while eating a lower quantity of food. Nutrient level in pet foods must be carefully balanced so that when caloric requirements are satisfied, the requirements for all other nutrients will be met at the same time.

The simplest way to solve the confusion of differences in caloric densities is to express nutrients as a percentage of ME or as units per 1000 kcal of ME, rather than as a percentage of weight. This is certainly the most accurate way to present nutrient content data and to compare different foods. Nutrient densities of foods with different moisture contents can be compared because water does not contribute any calories to the distribution. In addition, foods with differing caloric contents are equalized using this method, allowing for accurate representation of nutrient levels. Although using dry-matter calculations will eliminate distortions that are the result of differences in moisture content, such comparisons do not take into consideration the calories of the foods or the amounts that must be consumed by the animal to meet energy needs. Comparisons using nutrient densities that are calculated on a caloric basis can be used with foods of different dry-matter content, energy content, and with different weights or volumes.

The three nutrient groups that contribute energy to the diet are protein, carbohydrate, and fat. The relative contributions that each of these groups make to a diet's energy content is an important consideration in choosing a suitable pet food for a particular animal. For example, a hard-working dog requires sufficient protein to supply needs for muscle development and maintenance and increased calories to supply the necessary energy for work. Diets for working dogs should contain adequate protein and a fairly high proportion of fat. A suggested caloric distribution expressed as a percentage of ME calories for protein, fat, and carbohydrate is 29%, 59%, and 12%, respectively.[18] In contrast, a diet that is formulated for less active, adult animals should have a lower proportion of fat and an increased proportion of soluble carbohydrates. A suggested distribution is 22%, 30%, and 48% of ME calories from protein, fat, and carbohydrate, respectively.[18] A maintenance diet with this caloric distribution has an energy balance that is shifted from fat to carbohydrate. This profile better meets the

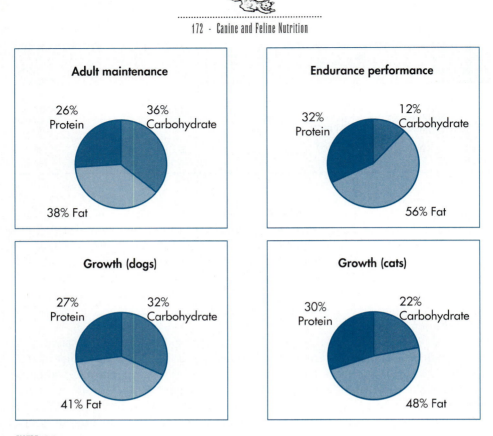

Adult maintenance

26% Protein

36% Carbohydrate

38% Fat

Endurance performance

32% Protein

12% Carbohydrate

56% Fat

Growth (dogs)

27% Protein

32% Carbohydrate

41% Fat

Growth (cats)

30% Protein

22% Carbohydrate

48% Fat

FIGURE 16-1
Recommended caloric distribution of pet foods

reduced energy needs of a sedentary dog and makes weight gain less likely. A typical profile of ME distribution for growing dogs is 27% protein, 41% fat, and 32% carbohydrate, and a profile for growing cats is 30% protein, 48% fat, and 22% carbohydrate (Figure 16-1).

Pet food companies that provide nutritional information about their products to consumers in the form of brochures will often include caloric distribution information in these materials. If the information is not available, pet owners can calculate a rough estimate of the food's ME and caloric distributions of protein, fat, and carbohydrate from the food's proximate analysis. If proximate analysis is not known, the guaranteed analysis panel on the label can be used, although it is much less accurate. Calculations that can be used to estimate total ME per kilogram are provided in Section 1, pp. 10–12. The example used is a dry dog food that contains this guaranteed analysis:

• Crude protein: Not less than 26%
• Crude fat: Not less than 15%
• Crude fiber: Not more than 5%

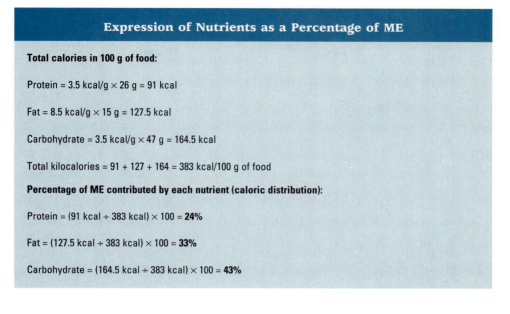

Expression of Nutrients as a Percentage of ME

Total calories in 100 g of food:

Protein = 3.5 kcal/g × 26 g = 91 kcal

Fat = 8.5 kcal/g × 15 g = 127.5 kcal

Carbohydrate = 3.5 kcal/g × 47 g = 164.5 kcal

Total kilocalories = 91 + 127 + 164 = 383 kcal/100 g of food

Percentage of ME contributed by each nutrient (caloric distribution):

Protein = (91 kcal ÷ 383 kcal) × 100 = **24%**

Fat = (127.5 kcal ÷ 383 kcal) × 100 = **33%**

Carbohydrate = (164.5 kcal ÷ 383 kcal) × 100 = **43%**

Mineral content is estimated to be about 7% and carbohydrate content is determined by subtraction: 100 – 26 – 15 – 5 – 7 = 47%. Modified Atwater factors can be used to calculate the number of calories that are contributed by each nutrient in 100 g of food (see Table 1-3, p. 12). The total calories in 100 g of food equals 383. The total calories of ME per kilogram of this food is 3830, or 1741 kcal/lb of food. The percentage of ME calories contributed by protein equals approximately 24%. The proportions of calories that are contributed by fat and carbohydrate are 33% and 43%, respectively (see the box above). This pet food has a distribution that would be appropriate for an adult dog during maintenance that is not working hard.

If a pet food's caloric distribution is calculated from the guaranteed analysis panel, it is important to recognize that the calculated numbers represent only a rough estimate and not the actual caloric distributions of the food. Companies that produce quality products and that are aware of the importance of proper nutrient density will publish ME and caloric distribution information for companion animal professionals and consumers. Because the calculation method can misrepresent a food by up to 15%, the determination of these data is best accomplished through actual animal feeding studies.[19]

COMMON PET FOOD INGREDIENTS

The ingredient list on a pet food label contains all of the food sources that are included in the formulation of the diet. Pet food regulations require the actual ingredients in each food to conform to the label, and the ingredient list cannot contain any reference to the quality of the ingredients that were used. Every ingredient that is part of a commercial pet food is included for a specific purpose. A few of the major ingredients may contain only one

major nutrient or nutrient group, and others may contribute several essential nutrients to the diet. For example, corn is an excellent source of starch and is the principal source of digestible carbohydrate in many dry pet foods. Although corn contains a small percentage of protein, the amount of protein that is contributed to the total diet is small. Therefore corn is considered to be primarily a source of digestible carbohydrate when included in pet foods. Chicken contains high levels of protein and fat and is considered to be a source of both of these nutrients. A good rule for determining whether or not an ingredient in a pet food is a protein source is to compare the level of protein in the ingredient with the level of the ingredient in the food. Anything that has a protein content that is greater than its percentage in the diet is considered to be a source of protein for that ration. For example, if a pet food contains 20% chicken by-product meal that has a protein content of 65%, chicken by-product meal constitutes a protein source for that food.

When the ingredient list of a pet food is examined, the nutrient or nutrients that are contributed by each ingredient should be a primary concern. Both the amount and quality of the ingredient in the product will determine how efficiently the ingredient can provide nutrition to animals that are consuming the complete diet. It is also important to consider that a pet food is made up of a number of ingredients, not just the first three or four that are provided at the start of the list. Nutrients that are contributed by all ingredients must be considered when evaluating a pet food. The following discussion reviews common pet food ingredients and the major nutrients that they contribute to commercial pet foods (see the box on the following page).

Protein Sources

The protein in dog and cat foods can be supplied by animal sources, plant sources (grains), or a combination of the two. In general, high-quality animal source proteins provide superior amino acid balances for companion animals, compared with the amino acid balances that are supplied by grain proteins. However, animal protein sources can range from excellent quality to poor quality. Characteristics of the ingredient such as digestibility and amino acid availability can only be determined through feeding trials. This information cannot be conveyed through the information presented on the pet food label. In contrast, grain protein sources are comparatively consistent in quality and ability to supply amino acids. The protein in grains is not as balanced or available as the protein in high-quality animal sources, but it is higher in these characteristics than are poor-quality animal protein sources.

Animal protein sources that are commonly included in commercial pet foods include beef, chicken, chicken by-product meal, chicken meal, dried egg, fish and fish meal, meat and bone meal, meat by-products, and meat meal. In recent years lamb, lamb meal, and rabbit have also been included in some dog and cat foods. The term "meat" can represent any species of slaughtered mammal. Most commonly, this includes the striated muscle of pork, beef, sheep, or horse meat. When the term "by-product" is included in the ingredient name, this means that secondary products are included with the ingredient in addition to the principal product. For example, when an ingredient is listed as "poultry," this means that it includes the clean combination of flesh and skin with or without bone

Common Pet Food Ingredients

Primary Nutrient Contribution

Protein	Carbohydrate	Fat	Dietary Fiber
Beef	Alfalfa meal	Animal fat	Apple pomace
Brewer's dried yeast	Barley	Chicken fat	Barley
Chicken meal	Brewer's rice	Corn oil	Beet pulp
Chicken liver meal	Brown Rice	Flax seed (full fat form)	Cellulose
Chicken by-product meal	Dried kelp	Poultry fat	Citrus pulp
Chicken	Dried whey	Safflower oil	Oat bran
Chicken by-products	Flax seed	Soybean oil	Peanut hulls
Corn gluten meal	Flax seed meal	Sunflower oil	Pearled barley
Dried eggs	Ground corn	Vegetable oil	Rice bran
Fish	Ground rice		Soybean hulls
Fish meal	Ground wheat		Soybean mill run
Lamb	Molasses		Tomato pomace
Lamb meal	Oat meal		
Meat by-products	Pearled barley		
Meat meal	Rice flour		
Meat and bone meal	Wheat		
Poultry by-product meal	Wheat flour		
Soy flour			
Soybean meal			

derived from part or whole carcasses of poultry, exclusive of feathers, heads, feet, and entrails.[12] On the other hand, poultry by-product, refers to the clean parts of carcasses of slaughtered poultry, which may contain bone, heads, feet, and viscera. Because of the inclusion of heads and feet, poultry by-product meal may be lower in nutritional value than fresh poultry or poultry meal. Depending on the supplier, by-products can vary greatly in the amount of indigestible material that they contain. This is one of the factors contributing to the variability that is seen between animal protein sources. Another common term that is often part of an ingredient's name is "meal." This term simply refers to any ingredient that has been ground or otherwise reduced in particle size.

Some animal protein sources contain varying amounts of bone. If meat and bone meal is included as an ingredient, the amount of bone that is contained in the product can affect its quality as a protein source, as well as the mineral balance of the entire diet. The matrix of bone is composed of the protein collagen. Collagen is very poorly digested by dogs and cats yet will be analyzed as protein in the pet food. All muscle meats are very low in calcium content and have calcium/phosphorus ratios of between 1:15 and 1:26.[20] When bone is included with a meat ingredient, the calcium level of the product is increased and the calcium/phosphorus ratio may be normalized. However, inexpensive meat and bone meals often contain excess levels of minerals. In this case, the problem becomes one of supplying too much calcium, phosphorus, and magnesium to the diet, rather than an insufficient amount of these nutrients. An excessively high calcium level in a pet food that contains meat and bone meal, poultry meal, or fish meal is an indication that the meal included in the product was of poor quality and contained excessively high amounts of bone.

Grain protein sources that are used in pet foods include corn gluten meal, soy flour, soy grits, soybean meal, alfalfa meal, brewers dried yeast, flax seed meal, and wheat germ. Pet foods that contain grain products as the major source of protein usually include a combination of soy products and corn gluten meal. Corn gluten meal is the dried residue that remains after most of the starch and germ-containing portions of the grain have been removed and the bran has been separated and removed. As a protein source, corn gluten meal is relatively consistent in quality. This protein source is not as digestible as high-quality animal protein ingredients, but its protein is often more available than some of the poorer quality animal products.[21] On a dry-weight basis, corn gluten meal contains a high proportion of protein, but its protein is deficient in the essential amino acids lysine and tryptophan. Soybean products have been included in pet foods for a number of years. Defatted soybean meal, flour, or grits are the forms that are usually included in dry pet foods, and textured vegetable protein (TVP) is the form that is often found in semimoist and canned foods. Soy protein can complement corn gluten meal in a plant-based pet food because it contains adequate to high levels of all of the essential amino acids, with the exception of methionine, a sulfur amino acid.

Raw soy contains phytate and several metabolic inhibitors that affect an animal's ability to digest and absorb other nutrients.[22,23] These inhibitor substances are destroyed during the heat processing of pet foods, but phytate is capable of interfering with the absorption of certain minerals even after processing.[24] Therefore pet food manufacturers must account for the effects of phytate when balancing the mineral component of soy-containing foods. Like most legumes, soybeans contain several complex carbohydrates and simple sugars that cannot be digested by enzymes of the small intestine. These carbohydrates pass undigested into the large intestine, where bacterial fermentation results in the production of intestinal gas and flatulence. The degree to which this problem occurs in companion animals seems to depend on the amount of soy in the food and on an individual animal's susceptibility.

Carbohydrate Sources

Ingredients that contribute digestible carbohydrates to commercial pet foods include various forms of corn, rice, wheat, and oats. Barley, carrots, flax seed, molasses, peas, and potatoes may also be included, but usually in lesser amounts. With the exception of molasses, all of these ingredients contribute complex carbohydrates in the form of starch. Cooking starch greatly enhances its digestibility. Therefore heat treatment of these ingredients is necessary during the processing of the food to ensure maximal use by companion animals. In dry pet foods, a certain proportion of the diet must be made up of starch to allow for proper expansion of the food pellets. During expansion, temperatures within the extruder reach close to 150°C. This temperature increases the size of the starch granules and improves digestibility and palatability.

Although it is not a digestible nutrient, dietary fiber is categorized with carbohydrates. Dietary fiber is not digested by intestinal enzymes, but it is required in the diet

to allow normal gastrointestinal tract functioning. Sources of indigestible fiber in commercial pet foods include beet pulp, rice bran, apple and tomato pomace, peanut hulls, citrus pulp, the bran of oats, rice, and wheat, and cellulose. Bran is a milling by-product that consists of the outer coarse coat (pericarp) of the cereal grain. During the production of flour, this portion is removed from the grain and separated. Pulp is the solid residue that remains after juices are extracted from fruits or vegetables; pomace specifically refers to the pulp of fruit.

Fat Sources

The fat in a pet food contributes calories and essential fatty acids and enhances palatability. Commonly used sources of fat in commercial pet foods include various types of animal fats and vegetable oils. The general term "animal fat" refers to fat that may come from the tissues of mammals and/or poultry. Animal fat must contain a minimum of 90% total fatty acids, not more than 2.5% unsaponifiable matter, and not more than 1% insoluble impurities.[12] Saponification is the combination of a fatty acid with a cation, resulting in the formation of a soap. The unsaponifiable matter of a fat is the portion that contains lipid compounds other than triglycerides and fatty acids. These compounds can include sterols, pigments, fatty alcohols, and fat-soluble vitamins. If the product is made up completely of a single type of fat, such as poultry or beef fat, a descriptive term denoting the species of the animal source must be used. Chicken fat and poultry fat are the two most common types of animal fat included in dog and cat foods. Therefore, if the ingredient list includes animal fat, the consumer must assume that the fat contains fats from several different types of mammals and/or poultry. Similarly, the term "vegetable fat" or "oil" is the product obtained from the extraction of the oil from seeds and must contain the same levels of fatty acids, unsaponifiable matter, and insoluble impurities as animal fat. If a specific plant source is the exclusive source of the oil, this must be indicated on the label. Most commonly, corn, safflower, and soybean oils are used in commercial pet foods. In addition to specific fat sources, ingredients such as chicken and poultry and various meat products also contribute a significant amount of fat to pet foods. If an antioxidant has been added to the fat source as a preservative, this must be indicated following the listing of the product on the ingredient list.

Vitamin and Mineral Sources

Almost all of the major ingredients that were discussed earlier also contribute vitamins and minerals to the diet. When a balanced ration is formulated, vitamin and mineral levels are made adequate through the addition of purified or semipurified forms of these nutrients. Because only small amounts of vitamins and minerals are required by animals and because other ingredients also supply these nutrients, purified forms of vitamins and minerals are present in small amounts in pet foods and are listed low on the ingredient list of the label.

Minerals vary greatly in their bioavailability, and many factors can affect the mineral availability within a diet. It is important not only to have adequate amounts of each mineral relative to the animal's requirement but also to consider the relationship between minerals and the overall balance of the ration. Excess levels of any mineral may adversely affect the ability of the body to absorb other minerals in the diet. For example, excess levels of calcium, copper, and possibly vitamin D can all inhibit the absorption of zinc in dogs.[25] Manufacturers must always consider these relationships when balancing the mineral component of their pet foods.

One of the biggest concerns about vitamins in commercial pet foods is their loss during processing and storage. Adequate quantities of vitamins that account for losses during processing and storage must be added to pet foods to ensure that sufficient levels are present at the time of feeding. The high heat and pressure that is used in the canning process result in losses of the B vitamins, thiamin, and folic acid. Compensatory levels of these vitamins must be added to maintain adequate post-processing levels. In dry, extruded pet foods, there are considerable losses of vitamin A, riboflavin, folic acid, niacin, and biotin. However, if vitamin A is added as part of the fat coating that is sprayed onto the food after extrusion, there is little to no loss of the vitamin during storage. In semimoist foods, slight losses of vitamin A and riboflavin have been observed.[26] Studies have provided recommendations for levels of vitamins to add to preprocessed pet food to ensure that levels after processing and storage are still sufficient to meet the animal's nutrient needs.[26] In addition, manufacturers who assure thorough testing of their products conduct nutrient analyses of their finished products. This testing may not be done by manufacturers who use calculation as their method of nutritional adequacy substantiation.

Ingredients that contribute vitamins and minerals to pet foods must be balanced in terms of their overall quantities, their bioavailability, and their relationships to each other. Commonly included sources of minerals in commercial pet foods include potassium chloride, calcium carbonate, dicalcium phosphate, monosodium phosphate, manganese sulfate or manganous oxide, copper sulfate or copper oxide, zinc oxide, sodium selenite, potassium iodide, ferrous sulfate, and cobalt carbonate. Examples of sources of vitamins include choline chloride, D-activated animal sterol (a source of vitamin D), alpha-tocopherol, thiamin or thiamin mononitrate, niacin, calcium pantothenate, pyridoxine hydrochloride, riboflavin, folic acid, biotin, menadione dimethylpyrimidinol (a source of vitamin K), vitamin A acetate, and vitamin B_{12}.

Preservatives and Additives

One of the chief concerns in the production of commercial pet foods is safety. A product must be proven to be both nutritious and safe for consumption by companion animals throughout its designated shelf life. The manufacturer must ensure that the food remains free of bacterial contamination and harmful toxins and is protected from degradation and the loss of nutrients during storage. The method of preservation that is used for a pet food depends to some degree on the type of food. The low moisture content

of dry pet foods inhibits the growth of most organisms. The heat sterilization and anaerobic environment of canned foods kills all microbes. Semimoist pet foods often have a low pH and contain humectants that bind water within the product, making it unavailable for use by invading organisms. Frozen pet foods, although less common, are protected by storage at extremely low temperatures.

Many commercial foods also contain added compounds that aid in the preservation process. Potassium sorbate prevents the formation of mold and yeasts; glycerol and certain sugars act as humectants. Some examples of additives that do not protect the food, but which are added to contribute color, flavor, or aroma to the food are artificial colors approved by the United States Department of Agriculture (USDA), onion and garlic powders and artificial flavors approved by the Food and Drug Administration (FDA).

A primary nutrient in pet foods that requires protection during storage is dietary fat. In recent years the inclusion of high levels of fat in dry pet foods has resulted in the need for methods of protecting these fats from oxidative destruction during storage. Foods that are formulated for dogs and cats contain vegetable oils, animal fats, and the fat-soluble vitamins A, D, E, and K. These nutrients all have the potential to undergo oxidative destruction during storage. This oxidative degradation, called lipid peroxidation, occurs as a three-stage process.[27] Initiation occurs when a free radical, usually oxygen, attacks a polyunsaturated fatty acid and results in the formation of a fatty acid radical. Exposure of the fat to heat, ultraviolet radiation, or certain metal ions such as iron and copper will accelerate this process. The fatty acid radical continues to react with oxygen, resulting in the formation of peroxides. Peroxides react with other fatty acids to form more fatty acid radicals and hydroperoxides (Figure 16-2). This second phase is called propagation because the reaction is autocatalyzed and increases geometrically in rate. The reaction is only terminated when all of the available fatty acids and vitamins have been oxidized. The subsequent decomposition of the hydroperoxides that were produced produces offensive odors, tastes, and changes in the texture of the food. In addition, auto-oxidation of lipids in pet foods results in the formation of toxic forms of these peroxides, which can be harmful to the health of companion animals if consumed.

Pet food manufacturers include antioxidants in commercial pet foods to prevent the auto-oxidation process. The FDA defines antioxidants as substances that aid in the preservation of foods by retarding deterioration, rancidity, or discoloration that is the result of oxidative processes.[28] Various types of antioxidants have been accepted for use in human and animal foods since 1947.[29] These compounds do not reverse the effects of oxidation once it has started but rather retard the oxidative process and prevent destruction of the fat in the food. Therefore, to be effective, antioxidants must be included in the diet when it is initially mixed and processed. The inclusion of antioxidant compounds in commercial pet foods prevents rancidity, maintains the food's flavor, odor, and texture, and prevents the accumulation of the toxic end products of lipid degradation.

Antioxidants can be categorized into two basic types, natural products and synthetic products. Natural antioxidants are commonly found in certain grains and vegetable oils. Vitamin E is probably the most widely distributed natural antioxidant.

No Antioxidant

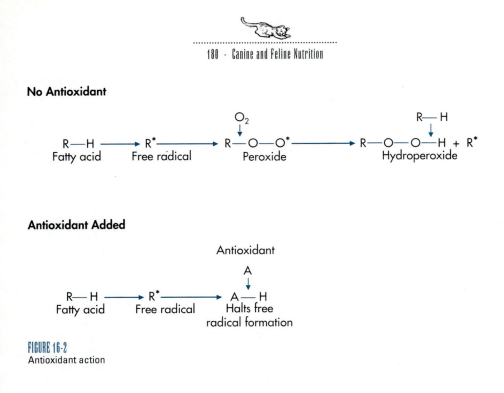

Antioxidant Added

FIGURE 16-2
Antioxidant action

Physiologically, vitamin E functions as an antioxidant in body tissues, and it will also function to protect fats in the diet from oxidative destruction. There are several forms in which vitamin E, or the tocopherols, exists in nature. Alpha-tocopherol has the strongest biological function in tissues of the body. In contrast, gamma- and delta-tocopherol both have low biological activity, but they are more effective than alpha-tocopherol as feed antioxidants.[30] Because of the high market demand for physiologically active vitamin E, commercial preparations contain primarily alpha-tocopherol. This form has lower value as a feed antioxidant, and commercial preparations have often been modified to improve their delivery to the body. These changes may render the compound even less effective as a protector of fat within a pet food.[28] Mixed tocopherols, containing both delta- and gamma-tocopherol, are the most effective natural antioxidants and show the greatest efficacy in the protection of animal fats in pet foods. However, the broad use of tocopherols as antioxidants in pet foods is usually precluded by the low availability and high cost of these preservatives.

A second natural antioxidant that may be included in pet foods is ascorbic acid (vitamin C). Ascorbic acid functions naturally as an antioxidant by scavenging oxygen. However, it is a water-soluble compound and is not easily solubilized with the lipid fraction of foods, which limits its function as an antioxidant for the fat in commercial pet foods. Vitamin C has been shown to work synergistically with other antioxidants, such as vitamin E and butylated hydroxytoluene, and it is often included in pet foods for this reason.[31] Ascorbyl palmitate is a compound that is similar in structure to ascorbic acid. Although ascorbyl palmitate is not normally found in nature, its hydrolysis yields ascor-

bic acid and the free fatty acid palmitic acid, both of which are natural compounds. The antioxidant function of ascorbyl palmitate is the result of the ascorbic acid portion of the molecule.

In general, the use of natural compounds as the primary antioxidants in commercial pet foods has limited value. The level of these antioxidants that must be included to provide an adequate level of protection is very high. Commercial pet foods undergo rigorous processing procedures that can include exposure to high heat, steam, and pressure, and then they must be protected from damaging oxidative reactions during varying lengths of storage. In addition, most natural antioxidants have poor "carry through." This term refers to the stability of the compound and its ability to retain its antioxidant functions after being subjected to the high heat, pressure, and moisture of food processing. Most natural antioxidants do not have good carry through, so an excess amount of the additive must be included in the food to compensate for high losses during processing. These additions are inefficient and add to the cost of the food.

When natural antioxidants are used in pet foods, the products of choice are the mixed tocopherols, usually in combination with ascorbic acid.[27] However, in most cases, these natural ingredients are used primarily to supplement the actions of the synthetic antioxidants that are also included in the food. Because these natural compounds tend to be significantly more expensive than synthetic antioxidants, it is difficult to attain the necessary level of natural antioxidants without becoming cost prohibitive.

Effective synthetic antioxidants for pet foods include butylated hydroxyanisole (BHA), butylated hydroxytoluene (BHT), tertiary butylhydroquinine (TBHQ), and ethoxyquin. BHA and BHT are probably the most common synthetic antioxidants in use today. These two compounds are approved for use in both human foods and animal feeds and have a synergistic antioxidant effect when used together. BHA and BHT have good carry through and high efficacy in the protection of animal fats, but they are slightly less effective when used with vegetable oils.[27] TBHQ is an effective antioxidant for most fats and is approved for use in human and animal foods in the United States. However, this compound has not been approved in Canada, Japan, or by the European Economic Community, so it is not usually used in pet foods that have an international market.[27] Ethoxyquin has been approved for use in animal feeds for more than 30 years and is approved for limited use in human foods. Like BHT and BHA, ethoxyquin has good carry through, and it has a high efficacy in the protection of fats. Ethoxyquin is slightly more efficient as an antioxidant than BHA or BHT, which allows lower levels of the compound to be included in the feed. It is especially effective in the protection of oils that contain high levels of polyunsaturated fatty acids.[28]

In recent years there has been some concern about the safety of synthetic antioxidants, specifically ethoxyquin, in pet foods. One of the arguments against the use of this additive was the fact that ethoxyquin is used as an antioxidant in the rubber industry. The biochemical mechanism through which ethoxyquin prevents oxidation of rubber is exactly the same manner in which it works to protect the fat in pet foods. Similarly, BHA and BHT were both originally used to protect petroleum products from the oxidative

TABLE 16-3
Common Antioxidants Used in Pet Foods

	COST	AVAILABILITY	CARRY THROUGH	EFFECTIVENESS
Natural				
Tocopherols	High	Low	Poor	Low
Ascorbic acid	High	Low	Poor	Low
Ascorbyl palmitate	High	Low	Poor	Low
Synthetic				
Butylated hydroxyanisole	Low	Moderate	Good	High
Butylated hydroxytoluene	Low	Moderate	Good	High
Tertiary butylhydroquinine	Low	Poor	Good	High
Ethoxyquin	Low	Good	Excellent	High

changes that led to gumming.[28] The fact that a compound acts as an antioxidant in other situations does not preclude it from being an effective antioxidant in foods. Like most compounds, ethoxyquin, BHA, and BHT have multiple uses. A second criticism of ethoxyquin originated from the observation that in outdated editions of the *Merck Chemical Index*, ethoxyquin was listed as an insecticide and herbicide. The possible functions of this compound were included by the manufacturer in a broad screening process that attempts to identify all possible applications of new products. Ethoxyquin has never been promoted or sold as an insecticide or herbicide, and the company eliminated these as possible uses for the product in 1983.[32]

Ethoxyquin has been included in feeds for animals since 1959, and its safety in foods has been extensively studied in rabbits, rats, poultry, and dogs. The original studies on which the FDA based approval for the inclusion of ethoxyquin in animal feeds included a 1-year chronic toxicity study in dogs. Data from this and other studies were used to determine a "safe tolerance level" of 150 parts per million (150 milligrams per kilogram [mg/kg]) of food.[33] Subsequently, the manufacturer of ethoxyquin conducted a 5-year, multi-generational study in dogs. The data from this study failed to show any adverse side effects of ethoxyquin when it was fed at a level of 300 mg/kg of the diet.[34] At this time, no studies are found in the literature which support the contention that ethoxyquin is responsible for the variety of health problems that have been reported by pet owners to the FDA. The maximum allowable concentration of ethoxyquin in all animal feeds is 150 mg/kg of the finished product. Pet foods that contain this additive must include it in the list of ingredients, as a preservative.

It is important for pet owners to recognize that almost all products that humans and animals consume will become toxic when consumed at high enough levels. The inclusion of synthetic antioxidants in commercial pet foods is necessary for the protection of dietary fat from detrimental oxidative changes. The proper use of these compounds prevents the occurrence of rancidity and the production of toxic compounds in pet foods. In most cases, synthetic antioxidants are the best compounds to use because of their efficacy, good carry through, and cost. In contrast, poor carry through, instability, and high levels needed for effective protection make natural antioxidants difficult to use as the only type of antioxidant (Table 16-3).

CHAPTER 17

Types of Pet Foods

The majority of pet owners in the United States feed their companion animals commercially prepared pet foods instead of homemade diets.[35] Commercial products are available in several forms that vary according to the processing methods used, ingredients included, and methods of preservation. Foods can also be categorized according to nutrient content, the purpose for which they are formulated, and the quality of ingredients that they contain. One of the broadest classifications of commercial pet foods divides products according to processing method, methods of preservation, and moisture content. These categories are the dry, canned, and semimoist foods. Commercial products can be further categorized according to their quality and the marketing methods that are used to sell them. The following sections examine the various types of commercial pet foods, advantages and disadvantages of each, and the use of homemade diets.

DRY PET FOODS

Dry pet foods contain between 6% and 10% moisture and 90% or more dry matter.[10] This category of pet foods includes kibbles, biscuits, meals, and expanded products. Ingredients that are commonly used in dry pet foods include cereal grains, meat, poultry or fish products, some milk products, and vitamin and mineral supplements. A certain level of starch must be included in expanded products to allow proper processing of the product.

Kibbles and biscuits are prepared in much the same manner, although the shape of the product differs. In each case, all of the ingredients are mixed into a homogeneous dough, which is then baked. When biscuits are made, the dough is formed or cut into the desired shapes and the individual biscuits are baked much like cookies or crackers. When a kibble is produced, the dough is spread onto large sheets and baked. After cooling, the large sheets are broken into bite-size pieces and packaged. Many dog and cat treats are baked biscuits, and a few companies still produce complete and balanced kibbles. Dry meals, the major type of dry pet food sold before to 1960, are prepared by mixing together a number of dried, flaked, or granular ingredients.

The development of the extrusion process resulted in the almost complete replacement of meals and kibbles with extruded pet foods. The extrusion process produces expanded pet foods. This procedure involves mixing all of the ingredients together to form a dough, which is then cooked in an extruder and forced through a dye under pressure and high heat. This procedure causes rapid cooking of the starches within the product, resulting in increased digestibility and palatability. After cooling, a coating of fat or another palatability enhancer is usually sprayed on the expanded pellets, and hot air drying reduces the total moisture content of the product to 10% or less. Expanded products represent the most common type of dry pet food that is currently produced and sold in the United States.

The cooking process of extruded and baked dry foods improves the digestibility of the complex carbohydrates in the product and enhances the food's palatability. Heat treatment and storage can result in minor losses of some vitamins, so compensatory amounts of these nutrients are included by most manufacturers when the diet is formulated. The heat that is used in the extrusion process also sterilizes the product, and the low amount of moisture that is present in dry foods aids in the prevention of contamination with bacteria or fungus.

The caloric density of dry pet foods ranges between 3000 and 4500 kilocalories of metabolizable energy (kcal of ME) per kilogram (kg), or between 1300 and 2000 kcal per pound on a dry-weight basis. Dry cat foods are often slightly higher in energy density than are dog foods. The energy density of dry pet foods is somewhat limited by the processing and packaging methods that are used. However, the majority of dry pet foods can fully supply the energy needs of the majority of companion animals. Products that are formulated for adult maintenance will only be bulk limited if fed to hard-working or stressed dogs that have very high energy requirements. In these cases, "high performance" pet foods have been developed to meet the energy requirements of working dogs. Depending on the purpose of the food, the dry-matter content of dry dog foods contains between 8% and 22% fat and between 18% and 32% protein (Table 17-1). Cat foods of all types contain slightly higher levels of protein than dog foods.

Dry dog foods are the most common type of pet food that pet owners buy in the United States.[2,36] In general, these products are more economical to feed than semimoist or canned foods, and they store well because of their low moisture content. Large quantities of these products can be bought at one time, and dry products have a reasonably long shelf life when stored under proper conditions. Many pet owners prefer feeding dry foods because they can leave a bowl of food available to their pet at all times without worrying about spoilage. In some cases, dogs and cats can be easily fed free-

TABLE 17-1
Nutrient Content of Dry, Semimoist, and Canned Dog Foods

	AF BASIS	DM BASIS
Dry		
Moisture (%)	6–10	0
Fat (%)	7–20	8–22
Protein (%)	16–30	18–32
Carbohydrate (%)	41–70	46–74
ME (kcal/kg)	2800–4050	3000–4500
Semimoist		
Moisture (%)	15–30	0
Fat (%)	7–10	8–14
Protein (%)	17–20	20–28
Carbohydrate (%)	40–60	58–72
ME (kcal/kg)	2550–2800	3000–4000
Canned		
Moisture (%)	75	0
Fat (%)	5–8	20–32
Protein (%)	7–13	28–50
Carbohydrate (%)	4–13	18–57
ME (kcal/kg)	875–1250	3500–5000

AF, As fed; DM, dry matter; ME, metabolizable energy.

choice with a dry food and they will not overconsume. However, the high fat content and palatability of some of the foods that are marketed today precludes free-choice feeding for many dogs and cats. Dry pet food may also offer some dental hygiene advantages. The chewing and grinding that accompanies eating dry biscuits or pet food may aid in the prevention of plaque and calculus accumulation on teeth.[37]

A potential disadvantage of dry pet foods, when compared with semimoist or canned foods, is that dry foods may be less palatable to some dogs and cats. This disadvantage is especially true of foods that are low in fat or that contain poorly digestible ingredients. However, in recent years, dry pet foods that contain high-quality ingredients and moderate to high levels of fat have been developed and marketed. These foods are nutrient dense and are highly palatable to most companion animals. Because of their high caloric density and digestibility, lower amounts of these diets need to be fed, which results in lower stool volume. This factor, plus the enhanced palatability, have made these new, higher fat dry foods popular with many pet owners.

Because ingredients that are primarily low in moisture are used to formulate dry pet foods, harsh or improper drying of the ingredients can cause a reduction in nutrient availability and the loss of nutrients. As a result, poor-quality dry foods may have very low digestibilities and nutrient availabilities. Companies that manufacture high-quality, premium products will use only properly treated ingredients to ensure that the digestibilities of their products remain high after processing.

CANNED PET FOODS

There are two primary types of canned pet foods, those that provide complete and balanced nutrition and those that provide a dietary supplement in the form of a canned meat or meat by-product. Complete and balanced canned foods may contain blends of ingredients such as muscle meats, poultry or fish by-products, cereal grains, textured vegetable protein, and vitamins and minerals. Some of these products contain only one or two types of muscle meat or animal by-products with enough supplemental vitamins and minerals to make the ration nutritionally complete. The second type of canned food, often referred to as canned meat products, consists of the same types of meat listed earlier but without supplemental vitamins and minerals. These foods are not formulated to be nutritionally complete and are intended to be used only as a supplement to an already complete and balanced diet. For example, some pet owners add a small amount of canned pet food to their pet's complete and balanced dry food every day. The high fat content of the canned supplement enhances the texture and palatability of the pet's diet. Although many complete and balanced dry foods will also be highly palatable and provide a balanced diet, some pet owners believe that feeding a dry diet alone becomes boring or bland to their pet. Adding a spoonful or two of a product that looks like meat or a stew makes many owners believe that they are making the meal more enjoyable for their pet.

Canned pet foods are prepared by cooking and blending all of the wet ingredients together, canning and cooking the mixture, and pressure sterilizing the sealed can. Cooking occurs in two stages. Steam injection begins the process during mixing of the formulation and is followed by the retort (pressure cooking) phase. Temperatures and times for retorting vary with the product and can size, but typically, cans are held at around 250° for 60 minutes.

From a processing standpoint, there are three types of canned foods, loaf, chunks or chunks in gravy, and a chunk-in-loaf combination. Depending on the ingredients that are used, these products can vary greatly in nutrient content, digestibility, and availability.[38] In general, canned foods are more palatable and digestible than many dry pet foods, and they contain a higher dry-weight proportion of protein and fat (Table 17-1). The high heat and pressure involved in processing canned foods kills harmful bacteria and causes some nutrient losses. The manufacturers of high-quality products conduct the research that is necessary to determine the extent of these losses and then adjust their formulations to compensate for them. However, some companies may not properly consider the nutrient losses that occur during the canning process. Manufacturers that use the calculation method to substantiate their label claims are not required to account for these losses because the calculation method is completed before processing.

When measured on a dry-weight basis, the caloric content of canned pet foods generally ranges between 3500 and 5000 kcal/kg or about 1600 and 2300 kcal/lb. The fat content of canned pet foods ranges between 20% and 32%, and protein levels are usually between 28% and 50%. Most canned products contain a relatively small proportion of digestible carbohydrate compared with other types of pet foods (Table 17-1). Canned foods are often more expensive than are dry pet foods. Although expense is often not a

concern for owners of cats or small dogs, it can become significant when feeding large dogs or multiple pets. Nutrient and price comparisons between canned and dry pet foods should always be made on either a dry-weight basis or a caloric-density basis because canned foods contain a very large proportion of water (see pp. 169–173). In the United States the moisture content of pet foods can be as high as 78%, or equal to the natural moisture content of the ingredients that are used, whichever is greater.[12] On the average, canned pet foods contain about 75% water. This amount can be compared with dry pet foods that contain approximately 6% to 10% moisture.[10]

Some advantages of canned pet foods include their extremely long shelf life and high acceptability. The sterilization and sealing of the cans allows these products to be kept for long time periods before opening, without the need for special storage considerations. Because of their nutrient content and texture, canned foods tend to be highly palatable to dogs and cats. However, this can be a disadvantage for some companion animals. Dogs and cats that have moderate to low energy requirements may be predisposed to the development of obesity when exclusively fed canned pet foods. If fed free-choice, the high palatability of these products can override an animal's inherent tendency to eat to meet its caloric requirements, resulting in the overconsumption of energy.

In recent years, gourmet-type canned cat foods have become especially popular. These products may or may not be nutritionally complete and contain primarily animal tissues such as fish, shrimp, tuna, or liver. These foods are often sold in small, one-to two-serving cans, and appeal to owners' desires to give their cat "something special." There may be an inherent danger to the exclusive feeding of these products to some cats. More so than dogs, cats are susceptible to the development of fixed food preferences if fed a diet that contains a single type of ingredient for a long period of time. Some cats will eventually only accept this one food item and will refuse to eat any other type or flavor of food.[39,40] If the food is not complete and balanced, nutrient imbalances may occur. Therefore, if canned foods are used with cats, it is advisable to feed complete and balanced rations that contain more than one principal ingredient. The gourmet products can be used as supplemental feeding, but they should not make up the entire diet. The high fat content of canned foods also makes these products calorically dense. Dogs and cats with increased energy needs may benefit from the increased energy that can be obtained in a lower volume of food.

SEMIMOIST PET FOODS

Semimoist pet foods contain 15% to 30% water, and they include fresh or frozen animal tissues, cereal grains, fats, and simple sugars as their principal ingredients. These products are softer in texture than dry pet foods, which contributes to their acceptability and palatability. Several methods of preservation are used to prevent contamination and spoilage of semimoist foods and to permit an extended shelf life. The inclusion of humectants such as simple sugars, glycerol, or corn syrup bind water molecules in the food and make them unavailable for use by invading organisms. Until 1992 propylene glycol was also used as a humectant in semimoist pet foods. However, the Food and Drug Administration (FDA) determined that this compound was a potential risk to cats and has prohibited its use in cat foods. Further protection is provided by preservatives such as potassium sorbate, which prevents the growth of yeasts and molds. Small amounts of organic acids may also be included to decrease the pH of products and to inhibit bacterial growth.

The high simple sugar content of many semimoist pet foods contributes to the palatability and digestibility of these products. Although dogs have been shown to enjoy the taste of simple sugars, cats are less likely to select sweet foods.[41,42] Semimoist pet foods that contain a high proportion of simple carbohydrates have digestibility coefficients that are similar to those of canned foods. However, because of their lower fat content, the caloric density of semimoist foods is usually less. The ME content of semimoist foods ranges between 3000 and 4000 kcal/kg on a dry-weight basis, or about 1400 to 1800 kcal/lb. Semimoist foods contain between 20% and 28% protein and between 8% and 14% fat on a dry-weight basis. The proportion of carbohydrate in semimoist foods is similar to that of dry foods (Table 17-1). However, the carbohydrate in semimoist pet foods is largely in the form of simple carbohydrates with a relatively small proportion of starch.

Semimoist pet foods appeal to some pet owners because they generally have less odor than canned foods and many come in convenient single-serving packages. These foods are also available in a large variety of shapes and textures that often resemble different types of meat products, such as ground beef, meat patties, or chunks of beef. Although these different forms do not reflect nutrient content or palatability for the pet, they do appeal to the tastes of many pet owners. Semimoist foods do not require refrigeration before opening and have a relatively long shelf life. The cost of these foods when compared on a dry-weight basis is usually between the cost of dry and canned products. However, products sold as single-serving packages are often comparable in price to canned pet foods. Because they are lower in energy density than canned foods, semimoist diets can be fed free-choice to some pets. However, these products will dry out and lose appeal when left in the pet's bowl for an extended period of time.

SNACKS AND TREATS

Snacks and treats have become increasingly popular with pet owners in recent years. A survey conducted in 1965 showed that Nabisco's Milk Bones dominated the treat market, and the choice of snacks at that time was extremely limited. However, in less than 20 years, almost every major pet food company began marketing some type of dog or cat snack.[43] This increase can be theorized to reflect some of the changing roles that dogs and cats have had in our society within the last few decades. Pet owners purchase treats not because of their nutritional value but as a way of showing love and affection for their pets. Feeding and caring for a pet is a nurturing process, and giving pets "special" snacks generates the positive feelings that accompany nurturing. Owners are gratified by the pleasure that they see their companion animal receiving from the treats.

A treat can be defined as something special and unexpected that the pet relishes. Therefore palatability to the pet is of chief importance. Owners are less concerned with the nutritional value of a snack than they are with its appearance and palatability. In the

early years, all dog treats were in the form of baked biscuits. Over time, different shapes, sizes, and flavors of these biscuits were developed and marketed. Because treats are usually impulse buys, owners are more likely to try a new flavor or type of treat than they are to completely switch dog or cat food. To capitalize on this, manufacturers have continued to develop new types of dog and cat snacks. A variety of semi-moist treats are now available, and rawhide chews and treats have also become popular. Many of these products resemble foods that humans normally eat, such as hamburgers, sausage, bacon, cheese, and even ice cream.

Although treats and snacks do not have to be nutritionally complete, a significant proportion of these products are formulated to be complete and balanced, and some carry the same nutritional label claims as dog and cat foods. In general, treats and snacks are highly palatable and cost significantly more than other types of pet foods when compared on a weight basis. Although some snacks and treats can provide complete nutrition, they are not required to be nutritionally complete and are not intended for this purpose.

Popular, Premium, and Generic Brands of Pet Foods

Popular

Brands of commercial pet foods can be classified into three general categories, popular, premium, and generic. The popular brands include foods that are marketed nationally or regionally and sold in grocery store chains. The companies that produce these foods devote a substantial amount of energy and finances to advertising, which results in high name recognition of their products. The principal marketing strategies that are used to sell these products are the diet's palatability and its appeal to the pet owner.

Most popular brands are produced using variable formulations. This means that the ingredients included in a particular brand will vary from batch to batch, depending on ingredient availability and cost to the manufacturer. For example, poultry meal may be the primary protein source in Happy Pal dog food the first time that a pet owner purchases a bag. However, because of changes in market prices, the second bag may include poultry by-product meal or even a cereal grain as the principal protein source. When variable formulation is used, the guaranteed analysis panel will not change, but the source and the quality of the ingredients can be altered without notice. This alteration can result in variable product quality and digestibility and may cause gastrointestinal upsets in some pets when a new bag of food is fed.

Some of the nationally marketed popular brands carry label claims that are verified through the Association of American Feed Control Officials (AAFCO) feeding trials. However, smaller manufacturers that only produce and sell foods regionally often use the calculation method to validate label claims (see p. 157). In general, popular brands of pet food have lower digestibilities than most premium brands of foods, but they contain higher quality ingredients and have higher digestibilities than do the generic or private label pet foods.

Premium

The term "premium pet foods" refers to products that are developed to provide optimal nutrition for dogs and cats during different stages of life. These foods are targeted toward companion animal owners, hobbyists, and professionals who are very involved in their animal's health and nutrition. In general, quality ingredients that are highly digestible and have good to excellent nutrient availability are used in these products.[38] Manufacturers of most premium pet foods formulate and market products for different stages of life and life styles. For example, dog foods have been developed for hard-working dogs (performance diets), adult dogs during maintenance, growing dogs, and bitches during lactation and gestation. The companies that produce these products provide educational materials about companion animal nutrition and feeding to pet owners and professionals, and their foods are usually only available through pet supply stores, feed stores, or veterinarians.

In contrast to popular brands, most premium brands of pet food are produced using fixed formulations. This means that the manufacturer guarantees that the ingredients that are used will not fluctuate in response to ingredient availability or market price. In addition, most manufacturers of these foods validate their label claims through AAFCO feeding studies, as opposed to the calculation method. This validation guarantees the pet owner that the food has been adequately tested through actual feeding studies with animals. Premium pet foods are usually more costly on a "per weight" basis because of the higher quality ingredients that are used and the level of testing that is conducted on the products. However, because these products are usually very digestible and nutrient dense, smaller amounts need to be fed and the cost per serving is often comparable to many popular brands of pet food.

Generic/Private Label

Generic pet foods are products that do not carry a brand name. These products are usually produced and marketed locally or regionally. The most important consideration of the manufacturers of generic foods is producing a low-cost product. For this reason, cheap, poor-quality ingredients may be used, and little, if any, feeding tests are conducted. These products almost exclusively use the calculation method rather than AAFCO feeding trials to validate label claims of nutritional adequacy. Some products have not been formulated to be nutritionally complete and will not even carry a label claim.[44] Feeding studies with dogs have shown that generic products have significantly lower digestibilities and nutrient availabilities than popular and premium brands of food.[44] Poor-quality ingredients and low fat content result in low palatability. Generic products represent the least expensive and the poorest quality of pet foods that are commercially available to pet owners.

Private-label pet foods are products that carry the house name of the grocery store chain or other store in which they are sold. Like generic pet foods, these products are usually produced on a least cost basis. The only difference is that private-label foods are produced (or simply packaged and labeled) under a contract with the grocery store

whose name they carry. Most are produced by the same companies that make generic products and may be similar in quality to generic pet foods. Private-label foods often claim to be comparable to premium foods, although they sell for a much lower price. Like any industry, "clone" products are marketed that may imitate the name, packaging, bag colors, and/or ingredient lists of premium foods.

Although the low cost may be appealing to some pet owners, there are several problems that may occur with generic and private-label pet foods. Because these foods are produced using cheap ingredients and because minimal testing is conducted, low nutrient availability can result in a product that is not actually complete and balanced. A study with growing puppies compared the effects of feeding a nationally produced, popular brand of dog food to three price brand (generic and private-label) foods.[44] The puppies that were fed the price brands required between 19% and 40% more food for each pound of body weight gained than those that were fed the national brand. Moreover, at the end of the 10-week growth study, puppies that were fed one of the price brands developed graying of the hair coat and had significantly reduced growth rates compared to the other groups. These puppies also had significantly lower hemoglobin, packed cell, and serum albumin levels than the dogs that were fed the national brand. The graying of the hair coat was presumed by the investigators to be indicative of a deficiency in one or more essential nutrients. Digestibilities of diet dry matter, crude protein, crude fat, and nitrogen-free extract (an estimate of carbohydrate content) were lower in two of the price brand products compared with the national brand. Protein digestibility was especially low, indicating that poor-quality protein sources were used and possibly that excessive heat caused damage to dietary protein during processing. Other studies have reported the occurrence of zinc-responsive dermatosis in dogs that were fed generic pet foods.[45,46,47] It is believed that the high proportion of plant products and phytate in generic foods binds dietary zinc, making it unavailable for absorption by the body. The inclusion of poor-quality meat and bone meals containing high amounts of calcium may exacerbate this problem because high levels of calcium will inhibit zinc absorption.[46] Problems with ingredient quality and variability, nutrient balance and availability, and the uncertainty of adequate testing and quality control generally make generic and private-label foods a poor choice for pet owners when selecting a commercial pet food.

HOMEMADE DIETS

Although the majority of pet owners in the United States enjoy the convenience, economy, and reliability of commercially produced pet foods, some owners still prefer to prepare homemade diets for their pets. If a homemade diet is going to be fed, the recipe that is used must be guaranteed to produce a ration that is complete and balanced. One of the problems with preparing homemade pet foods is that many of the recipes that are available have not been adequately tested for nutrient content and availability. Once an adequate recipe is found, the ingredients that are purchased should conform as closely as possible to the recipe and should be consistent between batches of food. Most recipes allow the owner to prepare a relatively large volume at one time and freeze small portions for extended use. Ingredients should never be substituted or eliminated from the recipe because of the danger of imbalancing the ration. Pet owners should also be aware of the dangers of feeding single food items in lieu of a prepared diet. Foods that owners enjoy are not necessarily the most nutritious foods to feed to their pets. Homemade diets can provide adequate nutrition to companion animals provided that a properly formulated recipe is used, the correct ingredients are included, and the recipe is strictly adhered to on a long-term basis.

CHAPTER 18

Evaluation of Commercial Pet Foods

The large variety of commercial pet foods that are produced and sold in the United States can make the selection of a proper diet a complex and confusing process. The information presented earlier in this section illustrates the need for pet owners to critically evaluate a product before feeding it to their pets. Because many pet foods are intended to provide the only source of nutrition for a pet throughout its life, it is extremely important that owners select a product that is capable of providing optimal nutrition and promoting the long-term health of their pet. The following chapter provides tools that companion animal owners and professionals can use to evaluate commercial pet foods. These criteria aid in distinguishing between products that are inadequate, acceptable, or superior in their ability to provide proper nutrition to a companion animal (see the box on the following page).

COMPLETE AND BALANCED

The phrase "complete and balanced" means that a food contains all of the essential nutrients at levels that meet a pet's requirements. Because animals eat or are fed to meet their energy requirements, nutrient levels in the diet must be balanced so that when an animal meets its caloric needs, its requirements for all other nutrients are fulfilled at the same time. Regulations of the Association of American Feed Control Officials (AAFCO) allow pet food manufacturers to include the complete and balanced claim on their label if they have substantiated it through one of two possible methods. Option one requires that the pet food has been successfully evaluated through a series of AAFCO-

Factors to Consider in the Evaluation of Pet Foods

Complete and balanced nutrition
Palatability
Digestibility
Metabolizable energy content
Feeding cost
Reputation of manufacturer
Dental health contribution
Taurine content (cats only)
Urine-acidifying ability (cats only)

sanctioned animal feeding trials. Option two requires only that the food is formulated to meet the minimum and maximum levels of nutrients that have been established by the AAFCO's Nutrient Profiles for Dog and Cat Foods (see p. 157). It is a common misconception that every pet food that carries the complete and balanced label claim has been proven to provide optimum nutrition through rigorous animal testing.[5] A pet food that has only been formulated on paper to meet AAFCO standards (option two) may not actually be complete and balanced when fed. Animal testing of pet foods is currently the best way to assess nutrient availability. These tests are capable of detecting problems and inadequacies of products that could not be detected when only chemical analysis or calculations are used.[48]

The first criterion that a pet owner should use when evaluating a food is a check for the "complete and balanced" claim. The life stages of the claim should correspond to the owner's intended use for the food (i.e., adult maintenance, all life stages, performance). Pet food manufacturers are currently required to include the method of substantiation that was used for the complete and balanced claim on the pet food label. If a statement that AAFCO feeding trials were conducted is included, this means that the food was adequately tested through feeding trials with dogs and cats. However, if the statement merely claims that the food meets AAFCO Nutrient Profiles, this signifies that AAFCO feeding tests were not conducted. In these cases, the owner has no way of knowing whether or not the pet food in question has been adequately tested through feeding trials before it was marketed. Pet owners can contact the manufacturer directly and request information regarding the type of testing that has been conducted on the product. If the manufacturer does not support the complete and balanced claim through feeding trials that measure the long-term effects of feeding the food, then a product should not be considered adequate for long-term feeding. The Nutrition Assurance Program (NAP) certification can also be used to validate the complete and balanced claim. In addition to AAFCO feeding trials, digestibility studies and laboratory analyses for nutrient content must be conducted on all pet foods that pass NAP certification. Pet owners can call a toll free phone number that is maintained by the Pet Food Institute (PFI) to verify if a particular pet food has passed NAP certification. The phone number is 1-800-851-0769.

PALATABILITY

The palatability and acceptability of a pet food are important because a food must be acceptable to the pet in order for it to provide optimum nutrition. The companion animal must be willing to eat an adequate amount of the food to receive its required calories and level of essential nutrients. An unpalatable food will be rejected by a dog or cat, regardless of the level or balance of nutrients that it contains. Similarly, a diet can be palatable but still not contain adequate levels of some nutrients. Dogs and cats are not capable of detecting nutrient deficiencies or imbalances in their diets. Companion animals will continue to consume an imbalanced diet until the physiological effects of nutrient deficiencies or excesses cause illness or a reduction in food intake. Because of the marketing value of highly palatable foods, most of the products that are currently sold are highly acceptable to pets. In fact, problems of overconsumption and weight gain are much more common than are problems of diet rejection. Although palatability is important, it should never be used as the sole criterion when evaluating a food and should not be considered an indication of the foods nutritional adequacy.

DIGESTIBILITY

The digestibility of a pet food is an important criterion because it directly measures the proportion of nutrients in the food that are available for absorption. True and apparent digestibility can only be measured through controlled feeding trials (see p. 167). The results of these trials provide digestibility coefficients for the food's dry matter, crude protein, crude fat, and nitrogen-free extract (NFE), which is a measure of the carbohydrate fraction in a food. Studies of popular brands of dog foods reported that the average digestibility coefficients for crude protein, crude fat, and NFE were 81%, 85%, and 79%, respectively.[49] A similar study with cats reported that popular brands of commercial cat foods have average digestibility coefficients of 78%, 77%, and 69% for crude protein, crude fat, and NFE, respectively. Premium pet foods usually have slightly higher digestibility coefficients than these values, and generic products have substantially lower digestibilities.[38,44] Digestibilities as high as 89%, 95% and 88% percent for crude protein, crude fat, and carbohydrate, respectively, can occur in dry-type premium pet foods. In general, the ingredients that are used in pet foods are lower in digestibility than are most foods consumed by humans. As the quality of ingredients that are included in the food increases, so will the food's dry matter and nutrient digestibility.

A pet food that is low in digestibility contains a high proportion of ingredients that cannot be digested by the enzymes of the gastrointestinal tract. These components pass through to the large intestine, where they are partially or completely fermented by colonic bacteria. Rapid or excessive bacterial fermentation leads to the production of gas (flatulence), loose stools, and occasionally, diarrhea. In addition to these side effects, a greater quantity of a poorly digested food must be fed to the animal because the pet is absorbing a smaller proportion of nutrients from the feed. As the quantity of food that

is consumed increases, rate of passage through the gastrointestinal tract also increases. The more rapid passage of food through the intestines exacerbates the poor digestibility of the diet and further contributes to poor digestibility, high stool volume, and gas production. A pet food's digestibility is decreased by the presence of high levels of dietary fiber, ash, phytate, and poor-quality protein. Improper processing or excessive heat treatment can also adversely affect the digestibility of the diet. In contrast, pet food digestibility is increased by the inclusion of high quality ingredients, increased levels of fat, and the use of proper processing techniques.

In general, dogs and cats digest foods of animal origin better than those of plant origin. This difference is primarily the result of the presence of lignin, cellulose, and other components of fiber in plant ingredients. However, it is important for owners and professionals to recognize that low-quality animal products that contain high amounts of skin, hair, feathers, and connective tissue are also not well digested by dogs and cats. Although a pet food that contains high-quality animal products will have a higher digestibility than a plant-based food, pet foods that contain poor-quality animal ingredients may have lower digestibilities than plant-based products with similar nutrient profiles.[21]

Several studies have shown that dogs have significantly higher apparent digestibilities of the major organic nutrients in commercial pet foods than cats.[50,51] Both the dog and the cat belong to the order Carnivora and are classified as simple-stomached carnivores. The cat is a very strict carnivore, but the dog is more omnivorous in nature. This difference is reflected in the abilities of the two species to digest certain types of dietary components. A study that compared the digestive capabilities of dogs and cats found that when fed the same dog or cat food, dogs had higher apparent digestibility coefficients and obtained more digestible nutrients per unit of food eaten than cats for almost all nutrients and types of foods.[51] It was suggested that some of these differences could be explained by a greater ability of the dog to digest dietary fiber, compared with the cat. For example, other data have shown that dogs are capable of digesting lignocellulose and hemicellulose with limited efficiency, but cats appear to have no ability to digest cellulose.[52,53]

Regardless of differences in the digestive capabilities of dogs and cats, it is important to be aware that commercial pet foods can differ significantly in digestibility and nutrient availability. The labels of two products may have the same ingredient lists and guaranteed analysis panels, but when they are fed, they may have different digestibilities. This variability will directly affect the ability of each diet to provide adequate levels of nutrients to an animal. A greater quantity of a poorly digested diet must be fed to an animal in order to meet its nutrient requirements. This fact is illustrated by a study with growing dogs that compared two commercial dry dog foods (R1 and R2) using feeding trials that followed the AAFCO feeding test protocols.[54] Chemical analysis of the two diets showed that they contained identical levels of nutrients. However, when fed to a group of dogs, the effect of each diet on growth and development was significantly different. Dogs that were fed the R2 diet grew significantly less and ate less food than did the R1 dogs. The R2 dogs became anorexic, had significantly lower body weights and body lengths, and showed poor coat quality and greying of the hair coat. These dogs

also had depressed hemoglobin and hematocrit values and lower serum cholesterol, alkaline phosphatase, calcium, and phosphorus levels. The authors of the study concluded that the R2 diet had lower palatability and that its nutrients were less available than those in diet R1. Subsequent digestibility trials found that diet R2 was 18% lower in apparent digestibility than diet R1. In another study, digestibility trials of four commercial dog foods with identical guaranteed analysis panels showed that the national brand of food had a significantly higher digestibility than did the three price brands that were examined.[44] It is important to note that in both of these studies the analytical values that were obtained through chemical analysis provided no information that would indicate differences in the digestibility of the foods.

Currently, AAFCO's regulations do not allow pet food manufacturers to include quantitative or comparative digestibility claims on their labels.[12] This information can only be obtained by actually feeding the food. Some pet food companies include digestibility data with the literature that they provide about their foods. Many manufacturers of premium brands of foods include this information with the educational materials they give to the retailers, pet supply stores, and veterinarians who sell their foods. The PFI's NAP also requires digestibilty trial data for all foods that undergo NAP certification. However, most popular brands of pet food that are sold through grocery store chains do not provide information regarding digestibility. If digestibility information is not readily available, this information can be obtained by writing or calling the company directly. Pet owners should choose foods that have a dry-matter digestibility of 80% or greater and should reject any foods that have digestibilities lower than 75%.

Buying a package of pet food and actually feeding it to a pet can also provide valuable information about a food's digestibility. A product that is highly digestible will produce low stool volumes and well-formed and firm feces. In addition, the fecal matter will not contain mucous, blood, or any recognizable components of the pet food. Defecation frequency should be relatively low and bowel movements should be regular and consistent. Normal growth rates and body weight should be easily maintained by the food without the need to feed excessive quantities, and long-term feeding should result in a healthy skin and hair coat. Although these observations do not provide quantitative information about digestibility, they are a reasonably accurate measure of a diet's ability to supply absorbable nutrients to a companion animal.

METABOLIZABLE ENERGY CONTENT

The metabolizable energy (ME) of a pet food represents the amount of energy that is available to the animal for use (see p. 168). The energy density of pet foods is typically expressed as kilocalories (kcal) of ME per unit weight (kilogram [kg] or pound). ME can be determined either through feeding trials or, less accurately, by calculation using standard energy values for protein, carbohydrate, and fat (see Section 1, pp. 8–9; see also Section 2, p. 169).

Energy density should be considered when evaluating a pet food because it will directly affect the quantity of food that must be fed to meet the pet's energy require-

TABLE 18-1
Determination of Cost Per Serving

	ME REQUIREMENT		KCAL/KG		QUANTITY/DAY	PRICE/KG	PRICE/LB	COST/DAY
Diet A	4500	÷	4500	=	1 kg (2.2 lb)	28 ¢	12.7 ¢	28 ¢
Diet B	4500	÷	3600	=	1.25 kg (2.75 lb)	25 ¢	11.4 ¢	31 ¢

ment. For example, two dry dog foods that are advertised as performance diets for working dogs have ME values of 4500 kcal/kg (diet A) and 3600 kcal/kg (diet B). If a sled dog that is training in mild weather conditions requires 4500 kcal/day, it will need to consume 1 kg of diet A or 1.25 kg of diet B (Table 18-1). The consumption of 25% more of diet B is necessary to meet this dog's daily caloric requirement. Hard-working dogs and lactating bitches and queens all have high energy requirements. These requirements are often best met by feeding a food that is relatively high in energy and nutrient density. On the other hand, a diet with a lower energy density facilitates weight maintenance and the prevention of obesity in adult pets that lead sedentary life styles. However, if the ME content of a pet food is too low, the quantity of food that the pet needs to eat in order to meet its requirement may exceed the physical capacity of the gastrointestinal tract. The consumption of an excessive quantity of food leads to increased rate of passage through the gastrointestinal tract and decreased digestibility. In general, pet owners should select a pet food that contains between 3000 and 5000 kcal/kg on a dry-matter basis, depending on the needs of the animal.

Before 1994, AAFCO regulations prohibited the inclusion of statements of caloric density on pet food labels. In 1994 the AAFCO passed a regulation allowing voluntary label claims of ME content. The new regulation requires companies that include ME claims to substantiate ME content through either a calculation method using modified Atwater factors or through data collected from a series of digestibility trials with animals. As in the case of the complete and balanced claim, the method that the company uses to substantiate the ME claim must be stated (see pp. 168–169). In addition to knowing the caloric density of the pet food, it is also helpful for pet owners to know the relative energy contributions that are provided by carbohydrate, protein, and fat in the diet. The dietary proportion of fat should be higher for hard-working animals and lower for sedentary adult or elderly animals. Similarly, the proportion of calories that are supplied by soluble carbohydrate should be increased in diets that are intended for adult maintenance or for elderly animals.

FEEDING COST

As the quality of the ingredients that are included in a pet food increases, so does the cost to the manufacturer. Therefore, as a product's quality increases, so does its price

per unit weight. When making price comparisons between foods, it is important to consider the cost of actually feeding the food as opposed to the cost per unit weight. The cost per serving of a high-quality product is often equal to or lower than that of an inferior product because a smaller quantity of the high quality pet food is fed. Using the previous example, the price of diet A is $25 for a 40-lb bag and the price of diet B is $22 for a 40-lb bag. Although diet A is actually more expensive than diet B, the cost of feeding diet B is higher because of its lower energy density (Table 18-1). When evaluating a food for the first time, owners can record the purchase date and the price of the food. When the package is empty, dividing the cost of the product by the number of days that the bag lasted will provide the cost per day to feed that particular food. A second product with the same net weight can then be compared in the same manner.

REPUTATION OF THE MANUFACTURER

The reputation of the pet food manufacturer should always be considered when selecting a pet food. Companies that have a national reputation for producing consistent, high-quality products and devote resources to consumer education about proper nutrition for companion animals should be selected. The inclusion of a toll free phone number on the product's package indicates a company that welcomes inquiries about their products. In addition, the manufacturer's response to all inquiries should be timely, thorough, and direct. A pet food manufacturer should be expected to readily supply information about the pet food's level of testing, digestibility data, ME content, and nutrient content. Pet food manufacturers that produce quality products are concerned with their reputations and with serving the needs and concerns of the pet owners who buy their pet foods. This concern will be evidenced by the company's accessibility to consumers and their response to questions about their products.

OTHER FACTORS

Several other factors may be considered when evaluating commercial pet foods. A cat food's taurine content should be assessed. The availability of taurine in a diet is influenced by a number of factors, including other nutrients and the type of processing that is used. Therefore the adequacy of the taurine level of a diet can only be assessed through actual feeding trials. Pet food manufacturers should be able to show that their product will maintain normal blood taurine levels in cats when fed on a long-term basis. Whole blood taurine should be maintained in adult cats at a level of 250 nanomole per milliliter or greater.[48,55] Generally, extruded dry foods that contain greater than 1000 mg/kg and canned cat foods that contain greater than 2000 to 2500 mg/kg on a dry-matter basis are adequate.[48,56]

Cat foods also should be evaluated with regard to their ability to produce an acidified urine. A urinary pH of 7 or greater is currently believed to be an important risk factor for the development of feline lower urinary tract disease (FLUTD) in cats.[57] Feeding

a diet that maintains a urinary pH of between 6 and 6.6 when fed ad libitum prevents the development of the struvites that cause this disorder. However, a diet that produces an overly acidified urine (less than 6) can put the cat at risk of metabolic acidosis and skeletal decalcification. Pet owners should select a diet that has been shown through feeding trials to produce a urine pH of between 6 and 6.6. Although magnesium was once implicated as an important risk factor for FLUTD, it is now known that magnesium levels in the diet only become significant when urinary pH is maintained at too high a level.[55,57] However, it is still wise to avoid products that have magnesium contents that are greater than 0.1% of the diet's dry matter. Currently, pet food manufacturers in the United States are not allowed to include information about urinary pH on the cat food label. This information can be obtained through educational literature produced by the company or by contacting the manufacturer directly.

Another factor that may be assessed is a pet food's ability to contribute to dental health in dogs and cats. It has been speculated that dry pet foods can contribute to dental health because the abrasion involved in chewing reduces plaque and calculus formation. However, there are only a limited number of studies that have examined this claim.[37] Although dry pet foods and feeding hard biscuits as treats may contribute to dental health and reduce calculus formation, feeding dry pet food should not be considered an alternate to regular dental care and teeth cleaning.

The overall best judge of a commercial pet food is the animal itself. Once a pet food has been evaluated and selected, pet owners should feed the product for a minimum of 2 months before evaluating its total effect on their pet's health. A diet that provides good nutrition and adequate energy supports normal weight gain or weight maintenance, healthy skin, a shiny and healthy coat, normal fecal volume and consistency, and overall vitality in the pet. Signs of a poor diet include weight loss or poor growth, poor coat quality, the development of skin problems, and a lack of vigor. Whenever any of these signs are observed, a thorough examination by a veterinarian should be conducted. Although changing the diet may be warranted, other medical causes of these problems should always be investigated.

KEY POINTS

SECTION 3

The pet food industry has grown tremendously since commercial pet foods were introduced in the United States in the early 1900s. In 1992, pet food retail sales amounted to $8.1 billion, and today there are over 300 companies producing an estimated 3200 brands of pet food. It is easy to see how choosing a proper diet for a pet can be confusing!

There are six regulatory agencies involved in the pet food industry. These agencies have various roles. Some have regulatory authority, and others have advisory responsibility (see Table 14-1).

Statements and claims made on pet food labels, and even the name of the food itself, are regulated by the Association of American Feed Control Officials (AAFCO). For example, AAFCO requires that such claims as "complete and balanced nutrition for all stages of life" must be substantiated either through feeding trials or by formulating the food to meet AAFCO Nutrient Profiles for Dog and Cat Foods. If a product uses a flavor in its name (for example, "Beefy Stew"), that flavor must have been detected by a recognized testing method.

When looking at the pet food label, most consumers first read the guaranteed analysis panel. Here manufacturers report the *minimum percentages* of crude protein and fat, and the *maximum percentages* of moisture and crude fiber. Consumers should be aware that these percentages do not represent actual amounts of protein and fat, and using these percentages to compare different products or brands can be misleading.

The ingredient list can tell consumers the principal components of the pet food and whether the components are from plant or animal sources. Usually if an animal-source ingredient is listed first or second in a canned pet food or within the first three ingredients of a dry food, the food can be assumed to contain animal products as its principal protein source. However, the ingredient list does not provide information about the quality of the ingredients.

Tip: If different forms of the same ingredient are listed separately (that is, kibbled wheat, ground wheat, wheat flour, flaked wheat, wheat middlings, wheat bran), consumers should be aware that the collective "wheat" content may be very high and actually make up a large percentage of the food's content.

Tip: The Nutrition Assurance Program (NAP) of the Pet Food Institute (PFI) maintains a toll-free phone number that consumers can call to obtain information about the degree of testing that was conducted on a particular product through the voluntary NAP testing program. The number is 1-800-851-0769.

Caveat emptor: Purchasing a low-cost pet food may seem economically practical, but low-cost pet foods usually contain lower-quality, less-digestible ingredients. Therefore more food must be fed to the animal to provide adequate nutrition than if the animal were being fed a high-quality, highly digestible food with greater nutrient availability. Thus the per-meal cost of the cheaper food may be higher. Also, companies producing low-cost pet foods generally do not test the foods using AAFCO feeding protocols. Remember, buyers usually "get what they pay for."

Tip: Additional information about the nutrient content of high-quality pet foods can be found in pamphlets obtained from the pet supply store or veterinarian where the food was purchased, or it can be obtained directly from the manufacturer. Reputable manufacturers will readily supply information, and many have toll-free telephone numbers listed on the package.

Dry dog foods are the most common type of pet food purchased by consumers in the United States. Dry foods are economical, easy to store and feed, and may be beneficial to dental hygiene. High-quality dry foods have high caloric density and digestibility, meaning that less food can be fed, more nutrients will be absorbed and used, and stool volume will decrease.

Tip: There are two primary types of canned pet foods—those that provide complete and balanced nutrition and those that do not. Complete and balanced canned foods contain vitamins and minerals, in addition to muscle meats, poultry or fish by-products, cereal grains, and/or textured vegetable protein. Those foods that are not complete and balanced do not contain the vitamins and minerals and should be considered as a dietary supplement only. Make sure you read the labels to determine if the canned food is complete and balanced.

Caution: Feeding cats one type of "gourmet" cat food exclusively may result in the cat's refusal to eat any other type or flavor of food. Because these "gourmet" foods may or may not be nutritionally complete, nutrient imbalances may occur. When feeding your cat canned food, feed complete and balanced rations that contain more than one principal ingredient.

Although generic or private label (store brand) foods may appeal to owners because of the low cost, owners are cautioned that the cost is a reflection of the cheap, low-quality ingredients used and the lack of feed-trial testing. A study comparing the effects of feeding generic and private label foods versus a nationally produced popular brand to puppies showed that the puppies fed the generic and private label foods had graying of the hair coat and significantly reduced growth rates, as well as significant abnormalities of some blood values.

Digestibility represents the proportion of nutrients in a food that is available for absorption into the animal's body. Commercial pet foods can differ significantly in digestibility and nutrient availability even if two products have the same ingredient lists and guaranteed analysis panels. If digestibility information is not readily available about a food, pet owners should contact the company directly. Choose foods that have a dry-matter digestibility of 80% or greater.

SECTION 3

REFERENCES

1. Enterline WR: The production of extruded pet foods, *Pet Food Ind* July/August; pp 26–30, 1986.
2. Maxwell JC Jr: Maxwell report, *Pet Food Ind* July/Aug, pp 4–8, 1993.
3. Phillips T: Top ten retail US pet food sales, *Pet Food Ind* Jan/Feb, pp 4–8, 1990.
4. Lazar V: Dog food history, *Pet Food Ind* Sept/Oct, pp 40–44, 1990.
5. Pet Food Industry: The big picture: AAFCO's Richard Sellers talks about regulatory philosophy, health claims and PS 21, *Pet Food Ind* March/April, pp 4–9, 1991.
6. Phillips T: NRC profile *Pet Food Ind* March/April, pp 10–18, 1992.
7. Phillips T: Regulatory drama, *Pet Food Ind* March/April, pp 10–11, 1991.
8. Dzanis DA: Health claims: a regulatory perspective, *Pet Food Ind* Sept/Oct, pp 44–47, 1993.
9. Van Soest PJ: The uniformity and nutritive availability of cellulose, *Fed Proc* 32:1804–1808, 1973.
10. Burger IH, Blaza SE: Digestion, absorption and dietary balance. In *Dog and cat nutrition*, ed 2, Oxford, England, 1988, pp 35–56.
11. Pet Food Institute: *Nutrition assurance program: PFI handbook*, Washington, DC, 1992, The Institute.
12. Association of American Feed Control Officials: Pet food regulations. In *AAFCO official publication*, Atlanta, 1994, The Association of Feed Control Officials.
13. Lewis LD, Morris ML, Hand MS: Pet foods. In *Small animal clinical nutrition*, ed. 3, Topeka, Kan, 1987, Mark Morris Association, pp 2-1 to 2-28.
14. Phillips T: PS 21: stop or go?, *Pet Food Ind* Sept/Oct, pp 14–26, 1989.
15. Kendall PT, Smith PM, Holme DW: Factors affecting digestibility and in vivo energy content of cat foods, *J Sm Anim Pract*, 23:538–554, 1982.
16. Shields RG, Kigin PD, Izquierdo JA, and others: Counting calories: caloric claims—measuring digestibility and metabolizable energy, *Pet Food Ind* Jan/Feb, pp 4–10, 1994.
17. Kendall PT, Burger IH, Smith PM: Methods of estimation of the metabolizable energy of cat foods, *Fel Pract*, 15:38–41, 1985.
18. Carey D: Metabolizable energy, The Iams Company, Lewisburg, Ohio, Unpublished report, 1991.
19. Carey D: Nutrient density, The Iams Company, Lewisburg, Ohio, Unpublished report, 1992.
20. Rainbird AL: A balanced diet. In Edney ATB, editor: *Dog and cat nutrition*, ed 2, Oxford, England, 1988, Pergamon Press, pp 57–74.
21. Case L, and Czarnecki GL: Protein requirements of growing pups fed practical dry-type diets containing mixed-protein sources, *Am J Vet Res* 51:808–812, 1990.
22. Rackis JJ: Biological and physiological factors in soybeans. *Am Oil Chem Soc J* 51:161A–174A, 1974.
23. Czarnecki GL: Bioavailability of nutrients in feed ingredients, *Pet Food Ind* Jan/Feb, pp 18–20, 1986.
24. Banta CA: The role of zinc in canine and feline nutrition. In Burger IH, Rivers JPW, editors: *Nutrition of the dog and cat*, Cambridge University Press, New York, 1989, pp 317–327.
25. Kunkle GA: Zinc-responsive dermatoses in dogs. In Kirk RW, editor: *Current veterinary therapy VII*, Philadelphia, 1980, WB Saunders, pp 472–476.
26. Adams CR: Stability of vitamins in processed dog food, *Pet Food Ind* Jan/Feb, pp 20–21, 1981.

27. Papas AM: Antioxidants: which ones are best for your pet food products?, *Pet Food Ind* May/June, pp 8–16, 1991.

28. Hilton JW: Antioxidants: function, types and necessity of inclusion in pet foods, *Can Vet J* 30:682–684, 1989.

29. Dziezak D: Preservatives: antioxidants—the ultimate answer to oxidation, *Food Tech* 9:94–102, 1986.

30. Cort WM: Anti-oxident activity of tocopherol, ascorbic acid and their mode of action, *J Am Oil Chem Soc*, 51:321–325, 1974.

31. Packer JE, Slater TF, Willson RL: Direct observation of a free radical interaction between vitamin E and vitamin C, *Nature* 278:737–738, 1979.

32. Phillips T: Ethoxyquin: fact and fiction, *Pet Food Ind* Nov/Dec, pp 16–17, 1989.

33. Dzanis DA: Safety of ethoxyquin in dog foods, *J Nutr* 121:S163–164, 1991.

34. Monsanto Chemical Company: A five-year chronic toxicity study in dogs with santoquin: report to FDA, 1964.

35. Doyle Dane Bernback International: DDB study documents belief in animal rights, *Pet Food Ind* March/April pp 20–22, 1984.

36. Pet Food Industry: Better homes and gardens: inquiry on pets, *Pet Food Ind* Nov/Dec, pp 12–18, 1985.

37. Samuelson AC, Cutter GR: Dog biscuits: an aid in canine tartar control, *J Nutr* 121:S162, 1991.

38. Kallfelz FA: Evaluation and use of pet foods: general considerations in using pet foods for adult maintenance, *Vet Clin North Am Sm Anim Pract* 19:387–403, 1989.

39. Munson TO, Holzworth J, Small E, and others: Steatitis ("yellow fat") in cats fed canned red tuna, *Am Vet Med Assoc* 133:563–568, 1958.

40. Griffiths RC, Thornton GW, and Willson JE: Pansteatitis (yellow fat) in cats, *J Am Vet Med Assoc* 137:126–128, 1960.

41. Bartoshuk LM, Harned MA, Parks LTD: Taste of water in the cat: effect of sucrose preference, *Science* 171:699–701, 1971.

42. Houpt KA, Smith SL: Taste preferences and their relation to obesity in dogs and cats, *Can Vet J* 22:77–81, 1981.

43. Willard TR: Treats and new products, *Pet Food Ind* Sept/Oct, pp 18–24, 1984.

44. Huber TL, Wilson RC, McGarity SA: Variations in digestibility of dry dog foods with identical label guaranteed analysis, *J Am Anim Hosp Assoc* 22:571–575, 1986.

45. Miller WH Jr: Nutritional considerations in small animal dermatology. *Vet Clin North Am Sm Anim Pract* 19:497–511, 1989.

46. Wolf AM: Zinc-responsive dermatosis in a Rhodesian Ridgeback, *Vet Med* 82:908–912, 1987.

47. Sousa CA, Stannard AA, Ihrke PJ, and others: Dermatosis associated with feeding generic dog food: 13 cases (1981–1982). *J Am Vet Med Assoc* 192:676–680, 1988.

48. Morris JG, Rogers QR: Evaluation of commercial pet foods, *Tijdschr Diergeneesk* 1:67S–70S, 1991.

49. Kendall PT, Holme DW, Smith PM: Methods of prediction of the digestible energy content of dog foods from gross energy value, proximate analysis and digestible nutrient content, *J Sci Food Ag* 3:823–828, 1982.

50. Kendall PT: Comparable evaluation of apparent digestibility in dogs and cats, *Proc Nutr Soc* 40:45a, 1981.

51. Kendall PT, Holme DW, Smith PM: Comparative evaluation of net digestive and absorptive efficiency in dogs and cats fed a variety of contrasting diet types, *J Sm Anim Pract* 23:577–587, 1982.

52. Visek WJ, Robertson JB: Dried brewer's grains in dog diets. *Proc Cornell Nutr Conf* pp 40–49, 1977.

53. Morris JG, Trudell J, Pencovic T: Carbohydrate digestion by the domestic cat (*Felis catus*), *Br J Nutr* 37:365–370, 1977.

54. Sheffy BE: The 1985 revision of the National Research Council nutrient requirements of dogs and its impact on the pet food industry. In Burger IH, Rivers IPW, editors: *Nutrition of the dog and cat*, Cambridge University Press, New York, 1989, pp 11–26.

55. Pet Food Industry: DVM recommendations: does your cat food earn them?, *Pet Food Ind* July/August, pp 4, 1990.

56. Morris JG, Rogers QR: Why is the nutrition of cats different from that of dogs?, *Tijdschr Diergeneesk* 1:64S–67S, 1991.

57. Tarttelin MF: Feline struvite urolithiasis: factors affecting urine pH may be more important than magnesium levels in food, *Vet Rec* 121:227–230, 1987.

Feeding Management Throughout the Life Cycle

t he previous sections have examined basic nutritional principles, the nutrient requirements of dogs and cats, and the different types of diets that can be fed to companion animals. Although knowledge of nutrient requirements and pet foods is essential, an understanding of feeding methods, feeding behavior, and dietary management is also necessary for the provision of optimal nutrition and care. This section provides practical guidelines for feeding healthy dogs and cats throughout all stages of life. Proper dietary management and care that begins at birth and continues throughout life supports optimal health and vitality in companion animals and ultimately contributes to a quality life and a rewarding human/companion animal relationship.

This section examines feeding management for each stage of life and different levels of physical activity. Guidelines are provided that help pet owners to properly select the best food for their particular dog or cat during each stage of life. These recommendations provide a starting point for feeding dogs and cats. However, it is important to remember that every dog and cat is an individual. For example, two adult animals of the same breed, age, and relative size in the same household may have significantly different energy and nutrient needs. Pet owners should use general guidelines coupled with regular assessments of their pet's weight, health status, and vigor to evaluate the best way to feed their particular dog or cat.

Feeding Regimens for Dogs and Cats

Normal Feeding Behavior

An examination of the way that the wild ancestors of the dog and cat hunted and consumed food provides insight into the normal eating behaviors exhibited by domesticated pets. Although both dogs and cats are classified in the order Carnivora, only cats are true carnivores. Dogs are more omnivorous in nature. This difference is manifested by unique anatomical and metabolic characteristics, as well as in the differing ways the two species obtain and ingest food (see Section 2, pp. 73–75).

The dog's wild relative, the wolf, obtains much of its food supply by hunting in a pack. Cooperative hunting behaviors allow the wolf to prey on large game that would otherwise be unavailable to a wolf hunting alone. As a result, most wolf subspecies tend to be intermittent eaters, gorging themselves immediately after a kill and then not eating again for an extended period of time. Competition between members of the pack at the site of a kill leads to the rapid consumption of food and the social facilitation of eating behaviors. Wolves and other wild canids also exhibit food hoarding behaviors. Small prey or the remainder of a kill is buried when food is plentiful and later dug up and eaten when food is not readily available.

Like their ancestors, domestic dogs tend to eat rapidly. This tendency can be a problem for some dogs because it may predispose them to choke or swallow large amounts of air. If social facilitation (competitive eating behavior) is the cause of rapid eating, feeding the dog separately from other animals, thus removing the competitive aspect of mealtime, often normalizes the rate of eating. In other cases, changing the diet to a food that is less palatable or to one that is difficult to consume rapidly solves

Practical Feeding Tips: Methods To Decrease the Rate of Eating

Feed a less palatable diet.
Feed a dry pet food.
Add water to the dry food just before serving.
Train adults to eat only from their own bowl.
Feed puppies from several pans.

the problem. For example, some dogs will readily gorge themselves on canned or semi-moist foods but will return to eating at a normal rate when fed a dry diet. If a dog attempts to eat dry food too quickly, adding water to the diet immediately before feeding decreases the rate of eating and minimizes the chance of swallowing large amounts of air.

Social facilitation is observed in domestic dogs that are fed together as a group. The presence of another animal at mealtime can stimulate a poor eater to consume more food. For example, pet owners often comment that their dog was a poor eater until a second dog was introduced into the family. Studies have shown that puppies and dogs will usually consume more food when fed as a group, compared with when they are fed alone.[1] If food is available at all times, the effects of social facilitation eventually become minimal. On the other hand, if dogs are meal fed as a group, dominance interactions may occur. As a result, dominant animals obtain most of the food, and the subordinate pets receive less than their required amount. Training adult dogs to eat only from their own bowls or feeding young puppies with several pans of food is a way to eliminate this problem (see the box above).

Vestiges of the wolf's food hoarding behaviors are often observed in domestic dogs. It is not uncommon for dogs to bury bones in yards or, much to the owner's chagrin, to hide coveted food items in furniture or under beds. However, unlike their wild ancestors, many domestic dogs forget about these hidden caches and never return to dig them up.

Although the dog's ancestry suggests that an intermittent feeding schedule would be best, dogs are capable of adapting to a number of different feeding regimens. These regimens include portion controlled feeding, time-controlled feeding, or free-choice (ad libitum) feeding. These regimens, and the advantages and disadvantages of each, are discussed later in this chapter.

It is common to think of the domestic cat as a descendant of the wild felids that prey on large, grazing animals. However, the immediate ancestor of the cat is actually the small, North African cat. This cat's primary prey are small rodents about the size of field mice.[2] Therefore the immediate ancestor of the cat is not an intermittent feeder like the larger wild cats, but rather it is an animal that feeds frequently throughout the day by catching and consuming a large number of small rodents. Like the majority of wild felids, the North African cat is a solitary animal, living and hunting alone for much

of its life and interacting with others of its species only during mating season. This solitary nature has resulted in an animal that eats slowly and is uninhibited by the presence of other animals.

Most domestic cats consume their food slowly and do not exhibit social facilitation. If fed free-choice, cats will nibble at the food throughout the day, as opposed to consuming a large amount of food at one time. Several studies of eating behavior in domestic cats have shown that if food is available free-choice, cats will eat frequently and randomly throughout a 24-hour period.[1,3,4] It is not unusual for a cat to eat between 13 and 16 meals per day, with each meal having a caloric content of only about 23 kilocalories (kcal).[3,4] Interestingly, the caloric value of a small field mouse is approximately 30 kcal. It has been suggested that the eating behaviors observed in domestic cats are similar to those of feral domestic cats eating rodents or other small animals.[2-4]

WHAT TO FEED

Pet owners have a choice of feeding one of three types of commercially prepared foods or a homemade formula. Most pet owners prefer the convenience, cost-effectiveness, and reliability of feeding commercial products. The decision of whether to feed a canned, semimoist, or dry commercial pet food can be made with an understanding of the advantages and disadvantages of each type of food (see Section 3, pp. 183–188). If a homemade diet is fed, care must be taken to ensure that a complete and balanced ration is prepared and that there is consistency of ingredients and nutrient content between batches of food. Surveys have shown that more than 90% of pet owners in the United States feed commercially prepared pet foods as the primary component of their pet's diet.[5] Therefore most of the discussion in this section will concern feeding commercial diets to pets; reference will be made to homemade diets in special situations.

One of the most important considerations when choosing a dog or cat food is the pet's stage of life and life style. Nutrient and energy needs differ according to an animal's age, activity level, and reproductive status. As knowledge about these needs has been acquired, specific diets have been developed by pet food companies to efficiently meet the needs of pets during different ages and physiological states. Several important factors must be considered when selecting a food for dogs and cats during all physiological states. Nutrient content and bioavailability are of primary importance. The food should provide all of the essential nutrients in adequate amounts and in proper balance to meet the needs of the pet's life style and stage of life. The food must also supply sufficient energy to maintain ideal body weight or to support optimal tissue growth. Caloric needs must be met when the food is fed in an amount that is well within the limits set by the animal's appetite and by the storage and digestive capacity of its gastrointestinal tract. The food must be appetizing to the pet and should be acceptable when fed as the primary diet over an extended period of time. The form and texture of the food must be appealing and should be easily chewed and ingested. Feeding the pet food for extended periods of time should support proper gastrointestinal tract functioning and

Factors To Consider When Selecting a Pet Food

Nutrient content and bioavailability	Caloric density
Palatability and acceptance	Diet digestibility
Effect on gastrointestinal tract functioning	Long-term feeding effects

should consistently result in the production of regular, firm, and well-formed stools. Lastly, the long-term effects of feeding the food must be assessed. The food should support those measurements of vitality and health that are somewhat subjective, such as good coat quality, healthy skin condition, proper body physique and muscle tone, and high energy level (see the box above).

When and How To Feed: Feeding Regimens

There are three types of feeding regimens that may be used when feeding dogs and cats. These regimens are called free-choice (also called ad libitum or self-feeding), time-controlled feeding, and portion-controlled feeding. One method of feeding may be preferred over another, depending on the owner's daily schedule, the number of animals that are being fed, and acceptability of the method by the pet.

Free-choice feeding involves having a surplus amount of food available at all times. The pet is able to consume as much food as desired at any time of the day. This type of feeding relies on the animal's ability to self-regulate food intake so that energy and nutrient needs are met. Dry pet food is most suitable for this type of feeding because it will not spoil as quickly as canned food or dry out as easily as semimoist products. However, even if dry food is used, the food bowl or dispenser should be cleaned and refilled with fresh food daily.

Compared with other feeding methods, free-choice feeding requires the least amount of work and knowledge on the part of the owner. The food and water supply is replenished only one time daily, and it is not necessary to determine the pet's exact daily requirements. If dogs are fed free-choice in a kennel setting, the kennel noise that usually occurs in response to mealtime is decreased or eliminated. This fact is considered a distinct advantage by many kennel owners. In addition, the constant presence of food in the kennel can help to relieve boredom that may be associated with confinement and can help to minimize undesirable behaviors such as coprophagy and excessive barking. Using free-choice feeding with a group of dogs that are housed together and have access to the same food dispenser ensures that even the most subordinate dogs will be able to consume adequate food because there is always surplus food available.

When dogs are fed free-choice they tend to consume frequent, small meals throughout the day. This pattern may have an energy balance advantage because a greater meal-induced energy loss occurs when many small meals are consumed, compared with when one or two large meals are eaten per day.[6] However, this loss is usu-

ally more than compensated for by the tendency of dogs that are fed free-choice to increase their total daily food intake. This effect of a free-choice regimen can be an advantage for dogs or cats that are "poor keepers" and will not eat enough to meet their energy needs when fed one or two meals per day. Animals with very high energy needs may also benefit from consuming frequent meals on a free-choice regime. Feeding numerous small meals per day is often prescribed for pets with dysfunctions in the ability to digest, absorb, or utilize nutrients, and for dogs who have a history of gastric dilatation. However, because free-choice feeding allows the animal rather than the owner to decide when to eat, animals that require frequent feeding as a treatment for medical conditions are better fed on a portion-controlled, rather than free-choice, basis.

Although free-choice feeding is convenient for the owner, problems such as anorexia or overconsumption may go undetected with this method. If an animal is sick, or if dominance hierarchies result in a submissive dog not being allowed to eat, a change in feed intake may not be noticed until the dog has lost substantial weight. If the decreased intake is the result of a medical problem, valuable time may be lost before the problem is diagnosed. The opposite situation, overconsumption and the development of obesity, is fairly common in pets that are fed free-choice. Although almost all animals are capable of eating to meet their caloric needs, the regulatory mechanisms that control food intake can be overridden if an animal is leading a relatively sedentary life style and is fed a highly palatable and energy-dense pet food. In this situation, a dog or cat often consumes more energy than required to meet its daily needs. In growing animals this can result in accelerated growth rate and increased deposition of body fat; in adult animals it will lead to obesity.

Most dogs and cats will overconsume when they are first introduced to a free-choice feeding regime. However, over time many animals adjust their intake to meet caloric needs. It is advisable to begin free-choice feeding by setting out a dish of food immediately after the dog or cat has consumed a meal. This extra food will help to prevent engorgement by the pet the first time that a surplus amount of food is available. The ability to adapt to free-choice feeding will depend on the physiological state, energy level, temperament, and life style of the pet. Although some adult dogs and cats maintain optimal weight and condition on this type of regimen, others will habitually overeat and should not be fed free-choice.

Meal feeding involves controlling either the portion size or the amount of time that the pet has access to food. Similar to a free-choice regimen, time-controlled feeding relies somewhat on the pet's ability to regulate its daily energy intake. At mealtime, a surplus of food is provided and the pet is allowed to eat for a predetermined period of time. Most adult dogs and cats that are not physiologically stressed are able to consume enough food to meet their daily needs within 15 to 20 minutes. Although one meal per day can be sufficient for feeding adult pets during maintenance, providing two meals per day is healthier and more satisfying. There is some evidence that feeding once daily can lead to gastric changes that are associated with gastric dilatation in large breeds of dogs.[7] Moreover, feeding two times per day reduces hunger between meals and minimizes food associated behavior problems such as begging and stealing food.

As in the case of free-choice feeding, there are some dogs and cats that will not adapt well to time-controlled feeding. Pets that are very fastidious may not consume enough food within the allotted time period. In contrast, other pets will use the opportunity to eat voraciously throughout the allotted time period. A time-controlled feeding program may actually exacerbate gluttonous behavior because pets quickly learn that they have to "beat the clock" whenever a meal is offered.

Portion-controlled feeding is the feeding method of choice in most situations. This procedure allows the owner the greatest amount of control over the pet's diet. One or several meals are provided per day, and they are premeasured to meet the pet's daily caloric and nutrient needs. As in the case of time-controlled feeding, many adult pets can be maintained on one meal per day, but providing two or more daily meals is preferable. Portion-controlled feeding enables the owner to carefully monitor the pet's food consumption and immediately observe any changes in food intake or eating behavior. The pet's growth and weight can be strictly controlled with this method by adjusting either the amount of food or the type of food that is fed. As a result, conditions of underweight, overweight, or inappropriate growth rate can be corrected at an early stage.

A disadvantage to portion-controlled feeding is that it demands the greatest time commitment and knowledge on the part of the owner. Guidelines for feeding are provided on the bags or containers of most pet foods; these can be used as a starting point when determining the amount to feed. Additional advice can be obtained from veterinarians, breeders, and pet food companies. The time commitment of portion-controlled feeding is usually not an issue with most pet owners unless a very large number of animals is involved. Most owners coordinate their pets' meals with their own and find that mealtime becomes an enjoyable routine for both their pet and themselves.

DETERMINING HOW MUCH TO FEED

In all animals, food intake is governed principally by energy requirement. When companion animals are fed free-choice, the underlying control over the amount of food that is consumed is primarily the pet's need for energy. Although highly palatable or energy-dense foods can override the natural tendency to eat to meet energy needs, energy is still the dietary component that most strongly governs the amount of food consumed. When companion animals are fed on a portion-controlled basis, owners will select a quantity of food based primarily on the pet's weight response, thereby feeding to meet energy needs. If the pet gains too much weight (energy surplus), the owner will decrease the amount that is fed. Conversely, if weight is lost, an increased amount of food is provided.

Commercial pet foods are formulated to contain the proper amount of essential nutrients when a quantity is fed that meets the pet's energy requirement. Balancing energy density with nutrient content ensures that when an animal's caloric needs are met, its needs for all other essential nutrients will be met by the same quantity of food. Therefore the best way to determine how much to feed a particular animal is to first estimate the animal's energy needs and then calculate the amount of a particular pet food that must be fed to meet that need.

TABLE 19-1

Determination of Quantity To Feed during Maintenance and Gestation of a 15-kg Dog

	ENERGY REQUIREMENT (KCAL ME)		ENERGY† DENSITY (KCAL/KG)		QUANTITY (KG)				POUNDS		OUNCES				CUPS PER DAY
Maintenance	890	÷	4500	=	0.198	×	2.2	=	0.44	=	7.0	÷	3.5*	=	2.0
Gestation	1112	÷	4500	=	0.247	×	2.2	=	0.54	=	8.6	÷	3.5	=	2.5

* An 8-oz measuring cup contains approximately 3.5 oz of dry food
† Energy density can be obtained from product literature or by contacting the pet food manufacturer
†† ME, metabolizable energy

A number of factors affect a pet's energy requirement. These factors include age, reproductive status, body condition, level of activity, breed, temperament, and environmental conditions. When determining a pet's energy requirement, these factors are accounted for by adding or subtracting calories from the quantity of food that is determined to support the maintenance energy requirement of the adult pet. The maintenance requirement refers to the amount of kilocalories (kcal) of energy per day necessary to support a moderately active adult animal that is not reproducing and is living in a temperate climate. For example, energy needs during the latter stage of gestation in dogs and cats increase from 1.25 to 1.5 times the female's maintenance requirement. If an active 15-kilogram (kg) (33 lb) bitch normally required 890 calories per day for maintenance, she would require approximately 1112 to 1335 kcal/day at the end of gestation. If a food containing 4500 kcal/kg was fed, this would correspond to approximately 2½ cups of food per day (Table 19-1). Information presented in this section provides estimates for accounting for these factors when estimating the energy requirements of a given animal.

Another way to determine the amount to feed a dog or cat is to use the guidelines that are included on the commercial pet food label. All pet foods that carry the complete and balanced claim are required to include feeding instructions on the product label.[8] These guidelines usually provide estimates of the quantity to feed for several different ranges in body size. Such instructions provide only a rough estimate that can be used as a starting point when first feeding a particular brand of food. Adjustments in these estimates should be made based on the owner's knowledge of the individual animal and on the animal's response to feeding.

CHAPTER 20

Pregnancy and Lactation

The proper feeding and care of reproducing animals is necessary for the health and condition of the dam and sire and for the viability, health, and growth of their offspring. It has been observed that successful gestation and lactation in companion animals is the result of a combination of factors. These factors include selection of healthy breeding animals, application of correct breeding management techniques, maintenance of a healthy environment, and the consistent and long-term provision of a proper diet.[9] Ideally, the correct feeding and management of reproducing animals begins during growth and development of the dam and sire and continues throughout mating, gestation, and lactation (see the accompanying boxes).

PREBREEDING FEEDING AND CARE

The selection of breeding animals should include screening for any faults or anomalies that are believed to be genetically transmissible. All animals should also undergo a thorough assessment of temperament, structure, and health before being admitted into a breeding program. Conformation shows and various types of working trials can be used by breeders to evaluate their animals and to compare them to established breed standards. Once an adult dog or cat has been selected for breeding, a complete physical examination should be given, including a fecal check for internal parasites and the administration of any required vaccinations.

Before breeding, both the sire and the dam should be in excellent physical condition, well exercised, and not overweight or underweight. It is especially important that

Practical Feeding Tips: Gestation

Feed a diet that is highly digestible and energy and nutrient dense.
Do not increase feed intake until the fifth or sixth week of gestation.
Provide several small meals per day during late gestation.
Increase feed intake to approximately one and one quarter to one and one half times maintenance by the end of gestation.
Dams should gain no more than 15% to 25% of their body weight by the end of gestation.
Dams should weigh 5% to 10% above their normal body weight after whelping.

Practical Feeding Tips: Lactation

Feed a diet that is highly digestible and energy and nutrient dense.
Provide adequate calories to prevent excess weight loss.
Feed two to three times maintenance during peak lactation.
Provide free-choice feeding or several small meals per day during peak lactation.
Slowly reduce the dam's intake after the fourth week of lactation.
Provide clean, fresh water free-choice.

the dam be at optimum weight and in prime condition. If the dam is underweight, she may be unable to consume enough food during gestation to provide for her own nutritional needs, as well as the needs of her developing fetuses. Lack of proper nutrition in the dam can result in decreased birth weight and increased neonatal mortality. Conversely, overweight conditions in dams can lead to the development of very large fetuses and dystocia.

The queen or bitch should be fed a high-quality, highly digestible food that is adequate for gestation and lactation. If a change in diet is required, the new food should be introduced as soon as signs of proestrus are observed. Pet foods that have increased nutrient density are appropriate because of the increased nutrient requirements of reproduction. These needs can then be met without excess food consumption, thus avoiding the likelihood of gastrointestinal upsets or weight loss. Changing to this diet early during the dam's reproductive cycle allows her to be fully adjusted to the new food when breeding takes place and prevents the need to abruptly change diets during either gestation or lactation.

During estrus, many bitches exhibit a slight depression in appetite. A study of 129 bitches showed an average decrease in food intake of 17% during estrus, with the lowest level of intake occurring at or around ovulation.[10] In most dogs, appetite usually returns to normal within several days. This short-term loss of appetite is natural and does not appear to affect fertility or litter size in normal bitches.

Feeding Management During Gestation and Parturition

Bitches

In pregnant dogs, less than 30% of fetal growth occurs during the first 5 to 6 weeks of pregnancy. Although the fetuses are developing rapidly, they are very small until the last third of the 9-week gestation. As a result, there is only a slight increase in the dam's weight and nutritional needs during the first 5 to 6 weeks of gestation.[11] After the fifth week, fetal weight and size increase greatly for the remaining 3 to 4 weeks of gestation. In the dog, more than 75% of weight and at least half of fetal length is attained between the fortieth and fifty-fifth day of gestation.[12] Therefore optimal nutrition is imperative during the last few weeks of gestation to ensure optimal fetal growth and development.

If a bitch is at ideal weight at the time of breeding, no increase in food intake is necessary for the first 4 to 5 weeks. Contrary to popular belief, a bitch should not receive a greater amount of food immediately after she has been bred. An increase of food at this time is unnecessary and could lead to excessive weight gain during pregnancy. It is not unusual for bitches to undergo a transient period of appetite loss at approximately 3 weeks of gestation. Like appetite depression that occurs during estrus, this change lasts for only a few days. After the fourth or fifth week of pregnancy, the bitch's food intake should be increased gradually so that at the time of whelping her daily intake is approximately 25% to 50% higher than her normal maintenance needs, depending on the size of the litter and the size of the bitch.[11] Her body weight should increase by approximately 15% to 25% by the time of whelping. Using the previous example, a bitch whose optimum weight is 15 kilograms (kg) (33 lb) should weigh between 17 and 19 kg (37 and 41 lb) at the end of her pregnancy.

As the developing puppies increase in size, there will be a reduction in the abdominal space that is available for expansion of the bitch's digestive tract after a meal. Therefore it is helpful to provide several small meals per day during the last few weeks of gestation so that abdominal space does not limit the bitch's ability to consume an adequate quantity of food. It is important to provide enough food during this period because dams that are underweight during mid and late gestation may have difficulty maintaining body condition and milk production after parturition. On the other hand, it is just as important not to overfeed pregnant bitches. Excessive intake and weight gain will be reflected in heavier fetuses and may result in complications at the time of whelping.

Mammary gland development and milk production occur 1 to 5 days before parturition, and many bitches will refuse all food approximately 12 hours before whelping. A slight drop in body temperature, occurring 12 to 18 hours before the start of labor, is a fairly reliable indicator of impending parturition.

Once the bitch has whelped the litter, expelled all of the fetal placentas, and her puppies are resting normally, she should be provided with fresh water and food. Most bitches will begin eating within 24 hours of whelping. If necessary, the dam's appetite

can be stimulated by moistening her food with warm water. Adding water to the food also ensures that adequate fluid is consumed. If the bitch has been adequately prepared for lactation, she should have a postwhelping weight that is 5% to 10% above her pre-breeding maintenance weight.

Queens

The weight gain pattern that occurs in pregnant queens is slightly different from that observed in bitches.[13] Although most of the bitch's weight increase occurs during the last third of gestation, pregnant queens exhibit a linear increase in weight beginning around the second week of gestation. A second difference between bitches and queens involves the type of weight that is gained during pregnancy. In dogs, almost all of the preparturition gain is lost at whelping.[14] In contrast, weight loss immediately following parturition in the cat accounts for only 40% of the weight that was gained during pregnancy. The remaining 60% of the queen's weight gain is body fat and is gradually lost during lactation. Thus it appears that the queen is able to prepare for the excessive demands of lactation by accumulating surplus body energy stores during gestation.

The guidelines that were described for the gestating bitch apply to the pregnant queen. The queen should be fed a diet that is intended for reproduction throughout gestation and lactation. The amount of food that she receives should be gradually increased starting during the second week of gestation and continued until parturition. At the end of gestation, the queen should be receiving approximately 25% to 50% more food than her normal maintenance needs. Because most cats adapt well to free-choice feeding, this is often the best way to provide the pregnant queen with adequate nutrition during pregnancy. The queen's weight gain should be monitored closely to prevent excessive weight gain during this time period.

FEEDING MANAGEMENT DURING LACTATION

The most important nutritional consideration during lactation for both bitches and queens is the provision of adequate calories. Ample energy intake allows sufficient milk production and prevents drastic weight loss in the dam. Adequate water intake is also important for the production of a sufficient volume of milk. The stress that lactation imposes on the bitch or queen depends on the dam's nutritional status and weight at parturition, her litter size, and her stage of lactation. Dams with large litters, and dams that have minimal body energy stores at parturition are at greatest risk for excessive weight loss and malnourishment during lactation.

Depending on the size of the litter, a bitch or queen will consume two to three times their maintenance energy requirement during lactation. A general guideline is to feed one and one half times maintenance during the first week of lactation, two times maintenance during the second week, and two and one half to three times maintenance during the third to fourth week of lactation.[15] Another general rule of thumb for dogs suggests adding 100 kilocalories (kcal) of metabolizable energy per day to the bitch's

normal maintenance diet for each pound of litter.[16] Peak lactation occurs at 3 to 4 weeks postpartum and is followed by the introduction of solid or semisolid food to the litter. After the fourth week, the amount of milk that is consumed by the puppies and kittens will decrease as their solid food intake gradually increases.

Lactation represents one of the greatest nutritional challenges to the animal. Many pet foods formulated for adult maintenance do not provide sufficient nutrient density for a bitch or queen during lactation. Research with lactating bitches found that when a diet containing approximately 4200 kcal/kg (1900 kcal/lb) was fed, little or no weight loss occurred during the entire period of lactation. However, bitches with four or more puppies fed a diet with a lower energy density (3100 kcal/kg) lost weight during lactation.[17] In addition to causing weight loss in the dam, energy deficiency during lactation may also affect the quantity of milk that is produced. If milk quantity is affected, compromised puppy and kitten growth and an increased risk of neonatal morbidity can result.

A highly digestible, nutrient-dense diet should be fed to all lactating queens and bitches, regardless of litter size. Even when a premium-quality food is fed, the quantity of food that the dam requires during peak lactation may exceed the capacity of her gastrointestinal tract. Therefore the daily ration should be divided into several meals or should be fed free-choice. After 3 weeks, it is advisable to feed the bitch and queen separately from the litter to prevent the puppies and kittens from consuming the dam's food.

Water is also of utmost importance during lactation. Inadequate fluid intake will lead to a significant decrease in the quantity of milk that is produced. Fresh, cool water should always be readily accessible to the lactating queen and bitch.

By 3 to 4 weeks of age, puppies and kittens begin to be interested in solid food. At the same time, the dam's interest in nursing starts to decline. As this occurs, the dam's daily food intake should be slowly reduced. By the time that the puppies and kittens are of weaning age (7 to 8 weeks), the dam's food consumption should be less than 50% above her normal maintenance needs.

FEEDING THE DAM DURING WEANING

Queens and bitches begin to wean their puppies and kittens at approximately 6 to 10 weeks of age. Most breeders impose complete weaning by 7 to 8 weeks of age so that the puppies and kittens can be transferred to their new homes. Puppies and kittens that begin eating solid food at 3 to 4 weeks of age are usually consuming the major portion of their diet in the form of solid food by the time they are 7 to 8 weeks old.

If the dam continues to produce milk immediately before weaning, several days of limited feeding will aid in decreasing milk production. If milk production is allowed to continue at a high level during weaning, there is an increased chance for the dam to develop mastitis. All food should be withheld from the dam on the day of weaning, provided she is in good physical condition. The dam's daily ration should then be gradually reintroduced at 25%, 50%, 75% and, finally, 100% of her maintenance level on successive postweaning days.

In general, bitches and queens will lose some weight during lactation, but the amount should not exceed 10% of their normal body weight.[11] Proper feeding and management during gestation and lactation will ensure that weight loss is minimized, even when large litters are raised. The condition of the bitch and queen at the time of breeding will influence their ability to withstand the stresses of gestation and lactation and will significantly affect their body condition at the end of the reproductive cycle. An animal who was in poor condition when bred will lose greater amounts of weight than is desirable and will require an extended period of repletion after weaning. The repletion period allows the dam's body to regain stores of nutrients that were lost during gestation and lactation. In these cases, an energy- and nutrient-dense, highly digestible food should be fed until the queen or bitch has returned to optimal body condition.

SUPPLEMENTATION DURING GESTATION AND LACTATION

Some breeders regularly supplement their bitch's or queen's diet with calcium or calcium-containing foods, such as cottage cheese or other dairy products, during gestation and lactation. The added mineral is believed to ensure healthy fetal development during pregnancy and to aid in milk production during lactation. It is also thought that calcium may prevent the onset of eclampsia after parturition.

Supplementation with calcium or any other mineral during pregnancy is not necessary for healthy fetal development, as long as the dam is consuming a well-balanced, high-quality, commercial ration. In fact, some researchers claim that excessive supplementation with calcium or vitamin D during pregnancy may cause soft-tissue calcification and physical deformities in the developing fetuses.[18] Although calcium needs are high during both gestation and lactation, the bitch and queen normally obtain the additional nutrient requirements through consumption of higher amounts of the normal diet (see Section 5, pp. 299–300).

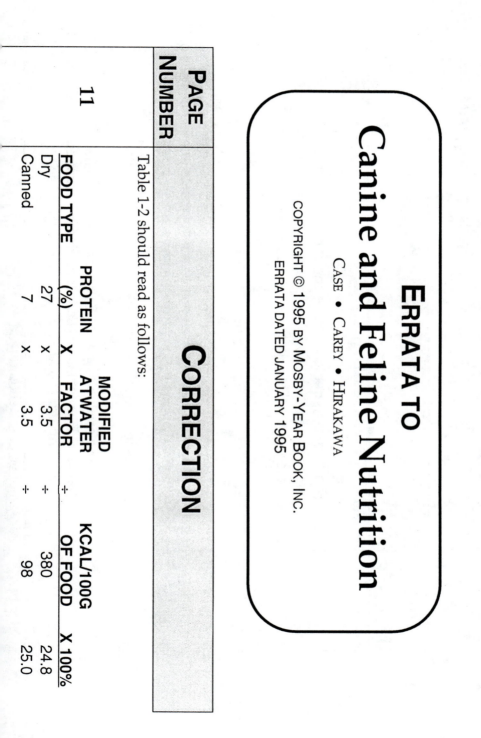

ERRATA TO
Canine and Feline Nutrition

CASE • CAREY • HIRAKAWA

COPYRIGHT © 1995 BY MOSBY-YEAR BOOK, INC.

ERRATA DATED JANUARY 1995

PAGE NUMBER	CORRECTION
11	Table 1-2 should read as follows:

FOOD TYPE	PROTEIN (%)	X	MODIFIED ATWATER FACTOR	÷	KCAL/100G OF FOOD	X 100%
Dry	27	x	3.5	÷	380	24.8
Canned	7	x	3.5	÷	98	25.0

PAGE NUMBER	CORRECTION
63	Paragraph 1 should read as folows: Tip: Reading **pet** food labels and comparing contents of foods in the grocery store can be very confusing. **[deletion]** For example, when the protein content is expressed as a percentage of weight . . . . Paragraph 4 should read as folows: Moderately fermentable fiber sources (as opposed to highly fermentable and non-fermentable fiber sources) that provide adequate levels of short-chain fatty acids **in the large intestine** and a source of bulk . . . Paragraph 7 should read as folows: Proteins are the major structural components of hair, feathers, skin, nails, tendons, ligaments, and cartilage. **Enzymes essential for nutrient digestion are proteins,** as are many hormones. . .
131	Paragraph 3, Line 3 should read as folows:

... cellular protein catabolism.

Page	Correction
146	Paragraph 3, Line 8 should read as folows: . . . together and then forcing the mixture through a **dye** under conditions of pressure . . .
154	Figure 15-1 should read as folows: Crude fiber . . . . **Not more** than 5% Moisture . . . . **Not more** than 12%
394	Paragraph 3, Line 11 should read as folows: . . . maintenance needs (see **Section 4**, pp. 255-256). Restricting protein when it is not necessary . . .

18	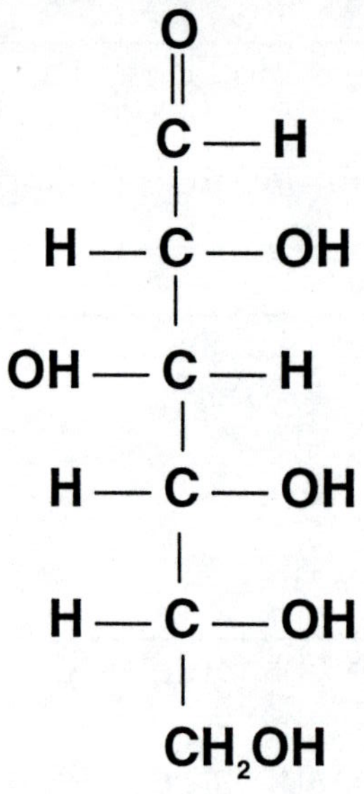 Glucose
26	Figure 4-1 Dipeptide chain structure should be: 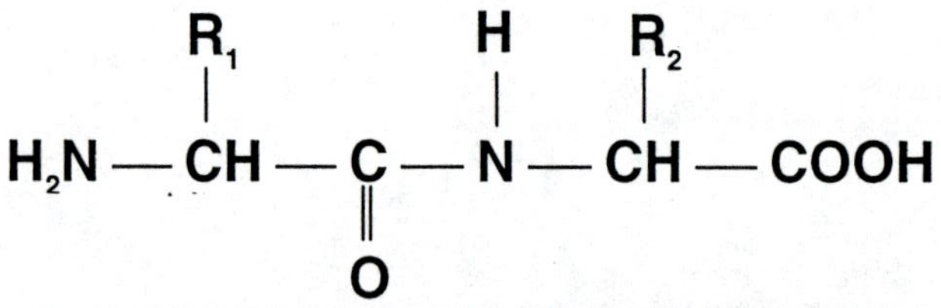

CHAPTER 21

Nutritional Care of Neonatal Puppies and Kittens

The first 36 hours of a puppy's or kitten's life is a critical time period nutritionally. At birth, puppies and kittens are physiologically and neurologically immature. The process of birth and the sudden environmental changes that newborns experience are very stressful. Therefore every effort should be made during this time to minimize stress and variations in the environment. A quiet, warm whelping/queening area should be provided, and human visitors outside of the immediate family should be prevented from disturbing the litter during the first few days.

COMPOSITION OF NATURAL MILK

Immediately after parturition, the dam produces a special type of milk called *colostrum*. Colostrum is vitally important for the provision of passive immunity to newborn puppies and kittens. Passive immunity is provided in the form of immunoglobulins and other immune factors that are absorbed across the intestinal mucosa of the newborn puppy and kitten. Most of these factors are large, intact proteins. Once absorbed into the body, these factors offer protection from a number of infectious diseases to the litter.

In older neonates and adult animals, normal digestive processes would result in the complete digestion of these compounds, making them unavailable to the body as immune mediators. However, the intestinal mucosa of newborn dogs and cats is capable of absorbing the intact immunoglobulins that are provided by colostrum. The time period during which the newborn's gastrointestinal tract is permeable to the intact immunoglobulins in colostrum is very short. The term "closure" refers to the change in

TABLE 21-1
Nutrient Composition of Colostrum and Mature Milk in the Dog

	COLOSTRUM	MATURE MILK
Protein (%)	4.3	7.53
Sugar (%)	4.4	3.81
Fat (%)	2.4	9.47
Total Solids (%)	12	22.7
Gross energy (kcal/100g)	64	146

Modified from Oftedal AT: *J. of Nutr.*, 114:803–812, 1984 and Bebiak DM et al, *Vet Clin of North Am Sm Anim Pract* 17:505–533, 1987.

the gastrointestinal tract's absorptive capacity that precludes further absorption of large intact proteins. In puppies, closure occurs after 24 hours and it is presumed that the time period is similar in kittens.[19] Therefore it is vitally important that newborn puppies and kittens receive adequate colostrum during the first 24 hours of life.

In addition to the immunological and nutritional benefits of colostrum, it has also been postulated that the volume of fluid ingested immediately following birth contributes significantly to postnatal circulating volume.[19] This indicates that a lack of adequate fluid intake shortly after birth may contribute to circulatory failure in newborns.

Like the milk of many mammalian species, the milk of dogs and cats changes during lactation to effectively meet the needs of their developing young. Several forms of colostrum are produced during the first 24 to 72 hours after birth, after which the composition slowly transforms to mature milk. The nutritional composition of colostrum is lower in total solids, fat, and protein than is mature milk (Table 21-1).[10] The mature milk of dogs and cats also has a relatively high iron concentration. These two species are similar to the rat and several marsupial species in their ability to concentrate iron in their milk at a level that is substantially higher than the concentration found circulating in plasma.[20,21] The high iron content in milk may reflect a high requirement for this mineral during the first few weeks of life. Studies have shown that the concentration of iron is strongly influenced by the stage of lactation, with values decreasing with time.[21,22] The concentrations of protein and calcium in milk are highly correlated during lactation. This correlation is explained by the fact that casein, a protein with a high calcium binding capacity, is one of the principal proteins found in canine and feline milk.[20,21]

Normal Development of Puppies and Kittens

During the first few weeks of life, puppies and kittens should nurse at least four to six times per day. Infrequent or weak nursing often signifies chilling, illness, or congenital problems and should be attended to immediately by a knowledgeable breeder or veterinarian. The two primary activities of all newborns are eating and sleeping. The eyes of puppies and kittens open between 10 and 16 days after birth and their ears begin to

function between 15 and 17 days after birth. Normal body temperature for puppies is 94° to 97°F for the first 2 weeks of life. Normal kitten temperature during this time is about 95°F. By 4 to 5 weeks of age, body temperatures have reached the normal adult temperature in both species.

Because puppies and kittens have no shivering reflex for the first 6 days of life, an external heat source is necessary. The dam is the best source of this warmth. After 6 days the puppies and kittens are able to shiver, but they are still very susceptible to chilling. Keeping the environment warm and free from drafts is of utmost importance during the first few weeks of life to prevent hypothermia. It is recommended that the environmental temperature be kept at 70°F during this period, assuming that the dam is providing an adequate amount of warmth and protection to the newborns.[19] Newborns should be weighed daily during the first 2 weeks and then every 3 to 4 days until weaning. A helpful guideline is for puppies to gain between 1 and 2 grams (g) per day for every pound of anticipated adult weight for the first 3 to 4 weeks of life. For example, if the anticipated adult weight of a dog is 25 pounds, the puppy should be gaining between 25 and 50 g/day (0.9 to 1.8 oz). Kittens usually weigh between 90 and 110 g at birth and should gain between 50 and 100 g per week up until they are 5 to 6 months of age.

In healthy puppies and kittens, the dam's milk will support normal growth until approximately 4 weeks of age.[22] Supplemental feeding with commercial milk replacer should only be necessary with unusually large litters. After 4 weeks, milk alone will no longer provide adequate calories or nutrients for continued normal development. At approximately the same time, puppies and kittens become increasingly interested in their environment and begin to spend more time awake and playing with each other. The time at which the dam's milk is no longer solely able to meet the nutrient needs of the offspring corresponds to the time at which the young are becoming interested in trying new foods.

INTRODUCTION OF SOLID FOOD

Supplemental food should be introduced at 3 to 4 weeks of age. For puppies, this supplement should be a thick gruel made by mixing a small amount of warm water with the bitch's food. Cow's milk should not be used to make the gruel because it has a higher lactose content than bitch's milk and may cause diarrhea. A similar gruel can be made for kittens by using either water or milk. Unlike puppies, kittens are able to tolerate the lactose content of cow's milk and will often readily consume a mixture of milk and cat food. Puppies and kittens should not be fed a homemade "weaning formula." Although the foods that are used to make these formulas are of high nutrient value, homemade formulas are usually not nutritionally balanced or complete. The use of this type of formula should be avoided unless its exact nutrient composition is known.

The semisolid food should be provided in a shallow dish, and puppies and kittens should be allowed access to fresh food several times per day. At first, little food will be consumed, and the litter's major food source will continue to be the dam's milk.

Practical Feeding Tips: Introducing Solid Food to Puppies and Kittens

Begin introducing semi-solid food at 3 to 4 weeks of age.
Feed a gruel of growth/maintenance dry diet mixed with water (puppies/kittens) or milk (kittens).
Place the gruel in a shallow dish.
Feed puppies and kittens several times per day.
Begin feeding dry food at 6 weeks of age.

However, by 5 weeks of age, the young should be readily consuming semisolid food. The deciduous teeth erupt between 21 and 35 days after birth. By 5 to 6 weeks of age, puppies and kittens are able to chew and consume dry food. Nutritional weaning is usually complete by 6 weeks of age, although some bitches and queens will continue to allow their young to nurse until 7 to 8 weeks of age or longer (see the box above). Complete weaning (behavioral weaning) is not complete until puppies and kittens are at least 7 to 8 weeks of age.

NUTRITIONAL CARE OF ORPHANS

The bitch and queen normally supply warmth, stimulus for elimination and circulatory functions, passive immunity, nutrition, maternal attention, and security to their puppies and kittens. Technically, an orphan is any young animal that does not have access to the milk or care of its mother. Circumstances that may render young puppies and kittens orphans include the death of the dam, the production of an inadequate quantity or quality of milk, or rejection of the young by the dam. Whatever the underlying cause, once puppies or kittens are orphaned they depend on humans for the provision of maternal care, proper nutrition, and a suitable environment. Although it is difficult, if not impossible, to fully compensate for the absence of the dam, the use of proper management and feeding techniques can result in the development of normal, healthy puppies and kittens.

Maintaining the Proper Environment

Orphaned animals must be kept in a warm, draft-free, and clean environment. Maintaining the appropriate temperature is of utmost importance because chilling can decrease the survivability of newborns. When a bitch or queen is present, her body heat provides an excellent heat source and protection against drafts. In her absence, the ambient temperature must be increased. For the first week of life, the ambient temperature should be kept between 85° and 90°F. This temperature can be decreased slightly to between 80° and 85°F during the second to fourth weeks and to 70° to 75°F during the fifth week. After the litter reaches 5 to 6 weeks of age, a room temperature of approximately 70°F can be maintained (Table 21-2). Generally, newborn kittens and

TABLE 21-2 Proper Room Temperature for Orphan Puppies and Kittens	
AGE (WEEKS)	**TEMPERATURE**
0–1	85°–90° F
2–4	80°–85° F
5–6	70°–75° F
>6	70° F

small puppies require slightly higher ambient temperatures than do large puppies. A heating pad or heat lamp may be used to provide heat, although a pad is often preferred because it allows for the maintenance of a normal day/night light cycle. Regardless of the type of heater that is used, the heat source should provide a temperature gradient within the whelping box so that the puppies and kittens can move to warmer or cooler areas as needed. Humidity must also be considered. If the environment is too dry, neonates are subject to dehydration. If dry heat is used to keep the whelping box warm, pans of water should be placed near the heaters to maintain room humidity. A relative humidity of approximately 50% is effective in preventing dehydration and maintaining moist nasal and respiratory passages in newborn puppies and kittens.[23] Drafts in the room can be controlled by providing a whelping box or incubator with high sides.

What to Feed

One of the greatest challenges involved in raising orphaned puppies and kittens is providing them with adequate nutrition. Because the best possible nutrition for young animals comes from their dam, foster mothering is the best solution for orphaned newborns. Unfortunately, a foster mother of the same species is usually not available. The alternative is to provide nutrition through a well-formulated milk replacer. A milk replacer will nourish the puppies and kittens for the first few weeks of life, until their digestive and metabolic functions develop to the point at which solid food can be introduced. It is important that the chosen formula closely approximates the composition of the natural milk of the bitch or queen. Feeding a formula that is not similar in composition to the species' natural milk can result in diarrhea and digestive upsets and has the potential to compromise growth and development.

Several commercially produced canine and feline milk replacers are available. Most of these products are composed of cow's milk that has been modified to simulate the composition of bitch's and queen's milk. A comparison of the compositions of the milk of different species shows that bitch's milk has a large proportion of calories from fat and a low percentage from lactose, with protein intermediate. Queen's milk, on the other hand, contains a larger percentage of calories from lactose and a lower percentage from fat than bitch's milk. The milk of cows and goats has a relatively high percentage of calories from lactose and less from protein and fat.[24] Additionally, the lower

TABLE 21-3
Nutrient Composition of Milk from Various Species (%)

SPECIES	FAT (%)	PROTEIN (%)	LACTOSE (%)	DRY MATTER (%)
Dog	9.8	8.1	3.5	22.8
Cat	5.1	8.1	6.9	18.5
Cow	3.8	3.3	4.7	12.4
Goat	4.5	3.3	4.6	13.0

Modified from Baines FM.: *J of Sm Anim Pract* 22:555–578, 1981.

percentage of total solids in cow's and goat's milk indicates that these milks are more dilute than either bitch's or queen's milk (Table 21-3).

Unaltered cow's milk is too low in energy, protein, fat, calcium, and phosphorus for young puppies and kittens.[25] On a caloric basis, the lactose content of cow's milk is nearly three times that found in bitch's milk. For this reason, puppies that are fed straight cow's milk will develop severe diarrhea.[19] Evaporated cow's milk is occasionally recommended for raising orphans because it has a level of protein, fat, calcium, and phosphorus that is similar to bitch's milk. However, the lactose content of evaporated milk is still much too high for young puppies.[25] The deficient levels of protein and fat in cow's milk can be improved by the addition of appropriate amounts of a food substance that is high in these nutrients, such as egg yolk.

There are numerous recipes available for the formulation of homemade milk replacers for puppies and kittens. However, pet owners should be advised that most homemade recipes were originally developed through trial and error techniques, and their actual nutrient compositions are unknown. A published analysis of several commonly used homemade formulas reported that these recipes contain a wide range of nutrient compositions. Some formulas are adequate for feeding puppies and kittens, but others contain a nutrient composition that is drastically different from that of natural bitch's and queen's milk.[25] A homemade formula should only be used if its nutrient composition is known and if the formula has been proven to be safe and effective for raising orphaned puppies or kittens.

In most cases, commercial milk replacers are the preferred source of nutrition for orphans. Commercially prepared formulas closely approximate natural bitch's and queen's milk, and they have been thoroughly tested for the specific purpose of raising neonatal puppies and kittens. In addition, unlike homemade formulas, the nutrient content and the biological integrity of commercial preparations is guaranteed. It is important to note that even a well-formulated commercial milk replacer cannot provide newborns with the antibodies that are normally found in colostrum. Therefore, if newborns are orphaned before they have received colostrum, extra care must be taken to maintain a clean environment and to prevent the transmission of disease.

TABLE 21-4
Calculating the Volume of Formula to Feed an Orphan

AGE	VOLUME TO FEED (PER 100 G OF BODY WEIGHT)		BODY WEIGHT		VOLUME/DAY		NO. OF FEEDINGS/DAY		VOLUME FEEDING
10 days	15 ml /100 g	×	200 g	=	30 ml	÷	5	=	6 ml
20 days	20 ml /100 g	×	300 g	=	60 ml	÷	5	=	12 ml

How Much to Feed

Calorie and fluid intake must be adjusted so that the puppies and kittens are able to consume enough formula to meet their nutrient needs for growth and, at the same time, they must not underconsume or overconsume fluid volume. During the first few weeks, the food intake of the neonate is largely limited by stomach volume. Most newborn puppies can handle only 10 to 20 milliliters (ml) of milk per feeding. Kittens are able to handle approximately one third to one half of this amount.[25,26] Therefore the concentration of the formula is extremely important. The milk replacer for puppies should have a caloric value of between 1000 and 1300 kcal of metabolizable energy (ME) per liter, a concentration that is similar to that of bitch's milk.[12,22] Queen's milk has a caloric density of approximately 1000 kcal ME per liter.[25] If the energy concentration is lower than this, more feedings per day will be necessary to meet the neonate's needs. In this case, the intake of excess fluid would adversely affect water balance and may stress the immature kidneys. Conversely, if the energy density of the formula is too high, digestive upsets and diarrhea may occur.[27] There are various estimates of the caloric needs of newborn puppies. A generally accepted guideline suggests that during the first 3 weeks of life, orphaned puppies receive between 130 and 150 kcal of ME per kilogram (kg) of body weight per day. After 4 weeks of age, caloric needs increase to 200 to 220 kcal/kg of body weight.[22,25] Less is known about the optimal energy intake of newborn kittens, but the guidelines provided for newborn puppies can be used as a starting point. In all cases, these figures should be used only as guidelines because the individual requirements of puppies and kittens can vary greatly. Orphans should be weighed daily to ensure that they are receiving enough nourishment to support normal weight increases.

If the commercial milk replacer has an energy value similar to that of the bitch's or queen's milk, between 13 and 17 ml/100 g of body weight per day should be fed for the first 2 weeks. This amount is increased to 20 to 22 ml/100 g of body weight per day for the third and fourth weeks.[22] For example, a 10-day-old kitten, weighing 200 g (7 oz) should be fed approximately 30 ml of formula. The total volume of formula should be divided equally among the daily feedings. If feedings are provided five times each day, each feeding should contain 6 ml. When the kitten is 20 days old and weighs 300 g (10.5 oz), it should receive approximately 60 ml of formula per day (Table 21-4). If the

concentration of the formula is correct, neonates that are bottle-fed should be able to self-regulate their formula intake. Feeding orphans four to five times per day is usually practical, with feedings spaced at even time intervals. This schedule is often reasonable for human caretakers, and it also allows the neonates to obtain their needed hours of uninterrupted sleep.

Methods of Feeding

Two possible methods may be used to feed orphaned puppies: bottle-feeding with a small animal nursing bottle or delivering the formula directly into the stomach using a stomach tube. If the puppies and kittens are bottle-fed, they should be held in an upright position with the head tilted forward and slightly upward. The bottle should be held in a manner that minimizes air intake by the puppy or kitten. When bottle-fed, orphans will usually reject the bottle when their stomachs are full. However, the correct volume of formula should still be estimated and measured for each feeding. This step will aid in record keeping and will minimize the risk of overfeeding.

Many breeders prefer to use a feeding tube with orphans. This method of feeding is faster and, if conducted properly, reduces the risk of formula aspiration. However, improper tube placement or too rapid a rate of delivery can result in injury. Overfeeding is also more likely with tube feeding because puppies and kittens are unable to self-regulate their intake. Therefore proper training is necessary if tube feeding is used.

Fresh formula should be made up daily and warmed to approximately 100°F before feeding. A slightly restricted quantity of formula should be fed for the first two to three feedings of the orphans; this allows gradual adjustment to the milk replacer. If puppies and kittens are overfed during the first few days, diarrhea may result, leading to dehydration and increased susceptibility to infection. After each feeding and several times daily, the anal/genital area of the newborns should be massaged gently with a damp cloth. This action simulates the dam's licking and stimulates urination and defecation. Grooming, cleaning, and feeding of the orphans should be conducted on a regular basis, and the litter box should be cleaned several times per day.

Orphans should be weighed regularly. There may be a small decrease in body weight during the first 2 to 3 days because of the restricted feeding of the new formula. The growth rate of puppies raised on a milk replacer for the first 2 weeks of life, and for kittens the first 3 weeks of life, will be slightly less than that of neonates raised naturally.[24] This is a normal occurrence. If raised properly, orphans will be developmentally equal to naturally raised puppies and kittens by the time that they are consuming solid food.

The orphans will show an increased demand and tolerance for food once their eyes open and they are on their feet. At this time, a shallow bowl of formula should be provided before each bottle-feeding. The puppies and kittens should be encouraged to lap formula from the bowl. Once the litter readily initiates lapping at each meal, they can begin to take entire feedings from the bowl. In general, puppies adjust to lapping at an earlier age and more rapidly than kittens. A gruel can be made using the milk replacer

Practical Feeding Tips: Orphan Puppies and Kittens

Provide a warm and clean environment that is free from drafts.
Feed a commercial milk replacer.
Estimate correct amount of formula based on the animal's age and weight.
Divide the formula into four and five equal feedings per day.
Bottle-feed or use a feeding tube.
Weigh orphans regularly—one time per day for the first week and one to two times per week thereafter.
Introduce semi-solid food at 3 to 4 weeks of age.
Wean to dry pet food by 6 to 10 weeks of age.

and dry dog or cat food when the puppies and kittens are 3 to 4 weeks old. Once semi-solid food is introduced, fresh water should be available at all times. The thickness of the gruel can be gradually increased with time. This gradual change allows the puppies and kittens to become accustomed to chewing and swallowing solid food and enables their gastrointestinal tracts to adapt to the new food. By 6 to 7 weeks of age, puppies should be consuming normal dry dog food. Kittens can consume normal kitten food by approximately 8 to 10 weeks of age and should be fully adapted to regular kitten food by no later than 11 to 12 weeks of age[23] (see the box above).

Growth

Most puppies and kittens are fully weaned from their dam and are ready to be placed in their new homes by 7 to 9 weeks of age. For puppies, this represents an ideal time to enter a new home because the primary socialization period occurs between 5 and 12 weeks of age. At 7 weeks of age the puppies have spent sufficient time with their litter to allow proper canine socialization. The remainder of this important developmental period can then be spent bonding to their new owners. It is believed that cats also undergo a primary socialization period at approximately the same age. Although this period is not as well defined in kittens as it is in puppies, 7 to 9 weeks appears to be the best age for kittens to begin positive relationships with their new human companions.

DIETARY REQUIREMENTS OF GROWING DOGS AND CATS

The most rapid period of growth in dogs and cats occurs during the first 6 months of life. Large breeds of dogs attain their mature size by approximately 10 to 16 months of age; smaller breeds and cats reach adult size by 6 to 12 months.[28,29] When they reach maturity, most dogs and cats have increased their birth weight by forty- to fiftyfold. Thus an enormous amount of growth and development is taking place in a relatively short period of time. Supplying a balanced diet during growth is crucial for adequate development and the attainment of normal adult size (Figure 22-1).

FIGURE 22-1
A, Golden retriever at 6 months of age. **B–D,** Same dog at 33, 54, and 88 months of age.
(C. H. Sun Dances Fibber MacGee, bred and owned by Sun Dance Kennels, Lisa and Jerry Halcomb.)

Puppies and kittens should be fed a diet that has been formulated for growth. The pet food should be guaranteed to be nutritionally adequate for growth or for all stages of life proven by the use of Association of American Feed Control Officials (AAFCO) feeding trials (see Section 3, pp. 152, 157). Growth represents a period of rapid tissue accretion and development that is reflected primarily by increased needs for energy and essential nutrients. It is important to realize that the additional nutrient needs for growth are readily supplied through the increased quantity of food that the animal consumes to meet its high energy requirement. There is no evidence that growing dogs and cats have requirements for nutrients that are not needed by adults. There is also no evidence that indicates the existence of any requirement differences between the various breeds of dogs and cats during growth.

Energy

Nutrient and energy needs during growth exceed those of any other stage of life, with the exception of lactation. The energy needs of growing puppies are approximately twice those of adult dogs of the same size.[30] After 6 months of age, these needs begin to decline as the animal's growth rate decreases. A general guideline suggests that a young dog's energy intake should be approximately two times its maintenance level until 40% of adult weight has been reached. At this point, intake should be decreased to approximately 1.6 times maintenance level, and further decreased to 1.2 times maintenance level when the pet has reached 80% of adult weight.[31,32] Similarly, growing cats have energy needs that are significantly higher than are the maintenance needs of adult cats. Although moderately active adult cats require approximately 70 kcal metabolizable energy (ME) per kilogram of body weight, growing kittens need a minimum of 160 kcal of ME per kilogram of body weight during peak growth.[33,34] (See Section 2, pp. 88–90).

Protein

The protein requirement of growing puppies and kittens is higher than the protein requirement of adult animals. In addition to normal maintenance needs, young animals also need more protein to build the new tissue that is associated with growth. Because young animals consume higher amounts of energy and thus higher quantities of food than adult animals, the total amount of protein that they consume is naturally higher. Pet foods that are fed to growing puppies and kittens should contain slightly higher protein levels than foods that are developed for maintenance only. More importantly, the protein that is included in the diet should be of high quality and should be highly digestible. This type of protein ensures that sufficient levels of all of the essential amino acids are being delivered to the body for use in growth and development. The actual percentage of protein that is in the diet is not as important as is the balance between protein and energy. The minimum proportion of energy that should be supplied by protein in the diet for a growing dog is 22% of the ME kilocalories, and the minimum for growing cats is 26.25%.[8]

Calcium and Phosphorus

Contrary to popular belief, diets containing excessively high amounts of calcium and phosphorus should not be fed to growing dogs.[35] The AAFCO Nutrient Profiles recommend that dog and cat foods that are formulated for growth contain a minimum of 1.0% calcium and 0.8% phosphorus on a dry-matter basis.[8] Research studies have shown that the dog's requirements for calcium and phosphorus are actually less than these amounts.[36,37] However, the AAFCO Nutrient Profiles include safety factors that account for differences in the availability of nutrients in pet foods and for individual differences

between animals. Therefore this level ensures that all growing dogs and cats will receive adequate levels of these essential nutrients. Many commercially available pet foods contain slightly more than the recommended levels of calcium and phosphorus, so they will supply more than adequate amounts of calcium and phosphorus to growing pets.[38]

Contrary to the belief of many breeders and pet owners, growing companion animals have no need for a level of calcium or phosphorus in their diets above that which is contained in a balanced, commercial food. Feeding excessive amounts of calcium during growth is not only unnecessary, it can contribute to the development of certain skeletal disorders in large and giant breeds of dogs.[35,39] For this reason the AAFCO Nutrient Profiles include a maximum level of calcium and phosphorus that should not be exceeded in commercial dog foods.[8] As a rule, dietary supplements should never be added to a balanced, complete pet food that has been formulated for growing dogs or cats (see Section 5, pp. 297–299).

Pet Food Digestibility and Energy Density

Diet digestibility and energy density are important considerations when feeding growing pets because of the quantity of food necessary to meet requirements for growth and development. Growing dogs and cats have higher requirements for energy and essential nutrients than adults, but they also have less digestive capacity, smaller mouths, and smaller and fewer teeth.[40] These differences limit the amount of food that a young animal can consume and digest within a meal or time period. If a diet is low in digestibility or energy density, a larger quantity must be consumed. The effects of low digestibility are exacerbated by the fact that as increasing amounts of a food must be fed, diet digestibility decreases further. When a poor-quality food with a low energy density is fed to growing puppies and kittens, the limits of the pet's stomach may be reached before adequate nutrients have been consumed. The result is compromised growth and impaired muscle and skeletal development. Young animals will benefit from eating a food that is energy- and nutrient-dense because the volume of food intake need not be excessive and intake will not be limited by the size of the animal's stomach.

It is equally important that growing dogs and cats not be overfed. Mild overfeeding during growth leads to an accelerated growth rate and can predispose the animal to obesity later in life. In large breeds of dogs, an accelerated growth rate can contribute to the development of certain skeletal disorders.[41,42] One of the most common causes of overnutrition in growing puppies and kittens is the addition of supplemental foods to a balanced diet that has been formulated for growth. Supplementation is unnecessary and may be detrimental (see Section 5, pp. 293–301).

Feeding Procedures During Growth

Once a puppy or kitten has been placed in a new home, the owner may wish to feed a pet food that is different from the food that was fed to the litter. If the pet's diet is going to be changed, the new food should be introduced very gradually. No dietary change should be made at all within the first few days that the puppy or kitten is in the new home. Moving to a new home and leaving the dam and littermates is very stressful, and providing a brand new diet at the same time can exacerbate this stress. Most breeders will send a small package of food along with the puppy or kitten. This food should be fed for the first few days that the animal is in the new home. After 2 or 3 days, the new food can be introduced by mixing it in quarter increments with the original diet. The proportion of the new food should be increased for 4 successive days until the puppy or kitten is consuming only the new diet.

Growing Dogs

Proper feeding of young dogs will support normal muscle and skeletal development and a typical rate of growth for the dog's particular breed. Generally, small breeds of dogs mature earlier than large breeds of dogs. Overfeeding for maximal growth rate and early maturity should be avoided. Studies with rats have shown that overnutrition early in life results in increased fat cell number and higher total body fat during adulthood.[43,44] In contrast, other studies have shown that mild restriction of calories during growth results in significantly increased longevity.[45] Rapid growth rates have also been shown to be incompatible with optimal skeletal development in dogs, rats, humans, and several other species.[41,42,46-50]

When obesity occurs in a young animal there is often an increase in both the size and number of fat cells in the body. This condition, called *hyperplastic obesity*, is believed to be more resistant to treatment than is *hypertrophic obesity*, which involves only an increase in fat cell size.[51,52] The presence of additional numbers of fat cells results in a higher percentage of body fat, even if the animal is not yet overweight. Thus an animal with fat cell hyperplasia will have a higher percentage of total body fat than an animal that weighs the same amount but has a normal number of fat cells.[43,53] Normal adipocyte hyperplasia occurs during specific critical periods of development in growing animals.[54,55] The exact age that these periods occur in dogs and cats is not known. However, data in other species indicate that adipose tissue growth normally occurs during either infancy or adolescence.[43,56,57] If these data are true for the dog and cat, it is probable that the level of nutrition provided to growing pets is of importance in determining the number of fat cells that the animal has at maturity.

It has been postulated that superfluous fat cell hyperplasia during the critical periods of adipose tissue growth may produce a long-term stimulus to gain excess weight in the form of excess adipocytes that require lipid filling.[58] The existence of excess numbers of adipocytes results in both an increased predisposition toward obesity in adulthood and in increased difficulty in maintaining weight loss when it occurs. This theory has been supported by several studies with laboratory animals showing that early overnutrition results in increased fat cell number and total body fat throughout adult life.[43,44] The use of proper feeding techniques that allow judicious control of a growing dog's weight are therefore important for long-term weight control.

A second reason that overfeeding for maximal growth rate and development is not desirable relates to its potential to affect skeletal development. A concern for skeletal development is important when feeding large and giant breeds of dogs, which generally exhibit a higher incidence of developmental bone disorders. Some commonly diagnosed skeletal diseases in young dogs include hypertrophic osteodystrophy (metaphyseal osteopathy), osteochondrosis, and hip dysplasia.[59,60,61] Genetics plays a role in each of these disorders, but heredity is not completely responsible for their existence. For example, hip dysplasia has been estimated to have a hereditary component of approximately 40%, with environmental factors playing an important role in the expression of the disease.[62] Several studies support the theory that nutrition is one of the environmental factors that influences the development of these diseases. Supplementation with certain nutrients and/or feeding an energy- and nutrient-dense diet at a level that supports maximal growth rate have been implicated as contributing factors[39,41,42] (see Section 5, pp. 293–296).

In contrast, feeding growing dogs moderately restricted levels of a well-balanced diet does not affect final body size or development.[41,63,64] Dogs that are fed restricted levels of food that support a slower growth rate will still attain normal adult size, but they will do so at a later age. It is advisable to feed growing dogs to attain a growth rate that is average, rather than maximal, for the dog's particular breed. This goal can best be achieved through strict portion-controlled feeding and the frequent assessment of weight gain and body condition. A high-quality, highly digestible food that is formulated for growth should be fed on a portion-controlled basis. Three to four small meals per day should be provided until the dog is 4 to 6 months of age, after which two meals per day should be fed. As adults, dogs can be fed one or two meals per day. However, most dogs, especially the large breeds, adapt best to two meals per day.

Free-choice feeding is not recommended for growing dogs because most of the foods that are formulated for growth are quite energy dense and highly palatable. Although some growing dogs are able to self-regulate their intake, many will overconsume these diets. Dogs should be fed on a portion-controlled basis until they have reached at least 80% to 90% of their adult weight.[18,31] If a pet owner eventually wishes to switch the dog to a free-choice regimen, this should be done only after the dog has achieved mature size.

In addition to controlling food intake, owners should also provide regular periods of vigorous exercise to their growing dog. Exercise aids in the achievement of proper energy balance and supports normal muscle development. Young dogs should be exercised at a level that maintains a lean, well-muscled body condition throughout their growing period. Daily running, swimming, or retrieving for 20 to 40 minutes is adequate for most dogs. Care should always be taken to avoid excessive periods of exercise involving prolonged concussion to developing joints in growing dogs, especially dogs of the large or giant breeds.

Practical Feeding Tips: Growing Dogs and Cats

Feed a highly digestible, nutrient-dense food that has been formulated for growth.
Meal feed using a portion-controlled regimen.
Feed three to four meals per day until the pet reaches 4 to 6 months of age: feed 2 meals per day after 6 months of age.
Feed to achieve average rate of growth for the pet's breed *and* to support a lean body condition.
Avoid overfeeding or feeding to promote maximal growth rate.
Provide regular daily exercise.
Do not add nutrient supplements to the pet's balanced diet.

Growing Cats

Like dogs, growing cats should be fed to achieve normal growth and development. A high-quality, commercial cat food that has been proven to be adequate for growth through AAFCO feeding trials is recommended. Supplementation of this diet is not necessary and can be detrimental. Normal feline feeding behavior results in the frequent consumption of many small meals throughout the day.[3,4] If adequate exercise is provided, most growing cats can self-regulate their energy intake when fed free-choice and will not overeat. In general, excessive caloric intake and accelerated growth rate are not common problems in growing cats. However, if inadequate exercise is provided or a highly palatable diet is fed, excessive weight gain can result. In these situations, portion-controlled feeding should be used (see the accompanying box).

Adult Maintenance

A dog or cat that has reached mature adult size and is not pregnant, lactating, or working strenuously is defined as being in a maintenance state. This category includes most of the dogs and cats that are kept as house pets in the United States. The major nutritional concerns during this period of life are the provision of a nutritionally complete and balanced diet that supplies the pet's daily nutrient needs. Feeding proper amounts of a high-quality, well-formulated diet throughout a pet's adult life contributes to optimal health and the maintenance of ideal body weight and condition.

Adult dogs should be fed a high-quality food that has been formulated for adults and has been proven to be adequate for maintenance through long-term feeding trials. Although canned, semimoist, or dry food can be fed, dry foods are often preferred for this stage of life. In general, canned and semimoist foods have higher caloric densities on a dry-matter basis than dry foods. When canned or semimoist foods are fed to adult dogs, they may contribute to the development of obesity if intake is not closely monitored. Dry dog foods are less calorically dense, and they can also help to maintain proper tooth and gum hygiene. Dry foods are also easier and more economical to feed to large groups of dogs than are other types of foods.

The availability of highly palatable pet foods coupled with the sedentary lives of many dogs has resulted in a high incidence of obesity in the adult dog population. Results of a survey conducted in England found that 24.3% of all dogs visiting veterinary clinics were either obese or grossly obese. In contrast, only 1.9% of the dogs were judged to be thin.[65] No recent survey pertaining to the occurrence of obesity in companion animals in the United States has been reported. However, given the similarities in animal keeping patterns, it is reasonable to assume that the occurrence of obesity in dogs in the United States is comparable to that reported in Great Britain.

The two most effective ways to prevent obesity in adult dogs are to provide daily exercise and to closely regulate food intake. Exercise can be in the form of daily walks or runs or several sessions of vigorous games such as fetch or hide and seek. Swimming is also an excellent form of exercise. Most dogs enjoy swimming if introduced to water at an early age and in a gradual manner. Monitoring an adult dog's daily food intake is best accomplished through portion-controlled feeding. Some dogs are able to self-regulate their food intake when fed free-choice. However, many dogs tend to overconsume and gain weight. Providing two premeasured meals at regular times each day is a simple way to carefully regulate a dog's food intake. The guidelines that are printed on pet food labels provide an estimate of the amount needed to feed an average adult dog that is living indoors and provided with a moderate amount of exercise. Alternatively, an estimate of the amount to feed can be calculated using the pet's ideal body weight (see Section 2, pp. 86–87; see also Table 9-2). Although each of these approximations can be used as a starting point, every dog should be fed as an individual. Adjustments can be made, depending on the pet's activity level, temperament, body condition, and weight status.[66]

It is not necessary to feed a wide variety of foods to adult dogs. Most dogs are best maintained on a constant diet of a balanced pet food and a constant supply of fresh water. Changing the diet frequently can result in gastrointestinal tract upsets, with resulting diarrhea and/or vomiting. If a pet's diet is to be changed, the new food should be introduced slowly by mixing it in increasing amounts with the dog's original food over a period of several days.

Like dogs, adult cats should be fed a food that has been proven to be adequate for maintenance. Cats are nonvoracious feeders and prefer to eat many small meals frequently throughout the day.[3,4] Many cats will adapt to free-choice feeding and can maintain their normal body weight on this type of regime. Although any type of food can be fed to adult cats, dry cat foods are best suited for free-choice feeding because they keep fresh longer than other foods. In addition, cats are less likely to overconsume dry foods when fed free-choice. In general, cats that live entirely indoors have less opportunity or inclination to exercise than do cats who have access to outdoors. As a result, indoor cats are more prone to obesity. If an adult cat cannot maintain normal body condition on a free-choice regime, portion-controlled feeding should be instituted.

CHAPTER 24

Performance and Stress

D ogs work with people in a variety of capacities, including acting as aids for the blind and the physically disabled, pulling sleds on arctic expeditions and races, herding and guarding sheep, hunting, and performing protection and drug detection tasks for the police and military. The type of training, level of exercise, and daily routine that a dog experiences will vary with the type of work. In general, all working dogs have higher energy requirements than adult dogs during periods of normal maintenance. Depending on the type and intensity of work, modifications in the nutrient composition of the diet and changes in the daily feeding regimen of the working dog may be necessary.

ENDURANCE PERFORMANCE

Sled dogs working in cold environments engage in high intensities of exercise for long periods of time. For this reason, these dogs have often been used in studies of the nutritional needs of working dogs during endurance events.[67-71] The type of work that occurs during endurance competitions differs from that performed during short races or sprinting events, such as greyhound racing or lure coursing. Although greyhounds engage in brief, intense bouts of high-speed running, sled dogs pull for several hours at a time at slower speeds. Metabolically, the energy that is necessary for short sprints is obtained primarily through anaerobic pathways, and energy for long endurance events is derived from predominantly aerobic metabolism.

The energy requirement of a working dog depends on the intensity and duration of the exercise and the environmental conditions in which the animal is working. A general

guideline suggests that energy needs increase to between 1.5 and 2.5 times maintenance requirements when working in ambient temperatures. Working in cold weather can further increase energy needs by an additional 50% or more.[72,73] It is generally accepted that sled dogs training in cold environments have higher energy needs than any other type of working dog.[68,73] Recent data indicate that a sled dog performing in the Alaskan bush under race conditions expends from 9000 to 10,000 kilocalories (kcal) per day.[70,74] However, other types of prolonged work such as guarding, herding, aiding the disabled, and scenting for drugs or explosives will also result in increased energy requirements. When feeding working dogs it is important that the precise level and frequency of the animal's work is accurately assessed. Commercial diets that have been formulated for performance are invariably energy dense and highly palatable. Overfeeding this type of ration or feeding it to a dog that is not working hard enough to need it can lead to a loss of condition and the development of obesity.

An examination of the types of muscles that are involved in endurance exercise provides information about the energy sources that are needed. The skeletal muscles of dogs contain three main types of muscle fibers: type I (slow twitch) and types IIa and IIb (fast twitch). Slow-twitch fibers have a high capacity for aerobic metabolism, and fast-twitch fibers can use both oxidative (aerobic) and anaerobic pathways.[75] The slow-twitch fibers use fatty acids and glucose for fuel and are believed to be important for endurance events. Although these fibers are found in all skeletal muscles, their numbers predominate in antigravity muscles such as the dog's anconeus and the quadratus muscles.[76] In general, endurance athletes have higher numbers of well-developed, slow-twitch fibers, and athletes involved in high-speed sprinting events have a higher proportion of fast-twitch fibers.[75,77] Diet may be important with respect to its ability to supply the correct form of fuel to the particular types of muscles that are being used during exercise.

Although it is generally accepted that energy is the nutrient of most concern for working dogs, there has been much debate about the best way to supply the energy in the diet. Increasing stamina and strength are goals for the nutritional programs of many human athletes. As a result, a great deal of research has been conducted concerning ways to supply fuel to long distance runners and bikers, which will improve performance.[78,80] Studies with humans have shown that an important limiting factor in prolonged exercise is the amount of glycogen present in the working muscles, and that the onset of fatigue is highly correlated with muscle glycogen depletion.[81,82] In addition, endurance for submaximal exercise can be increased by raising muscle glycogen stores and decreased by lowering muscle glycogen.[82] Therefore a major goal when feeding human endurance athletes is to either increase muscle glycogen stores or to delay muscle glycogen depletion during periods of exercise.

The procedure of "glycogen loading" (also called carbohydrate loading) was developed for human athletes with the intent of increasing muscle glycogen stores before periods of prolonged exercise. Glycogen loading is accomplished by first depleting muscle glycogen through exhaustive exercise and then consuming a high carbohydrate diet for 4 to 7 days.[83,84] The preliminary glycogen depletion phase results in "glycogen supercompensation" when the subject consumes a diet that is high in starch for several

subsequent days. Glycogen stores in working muscles are significantly increased above normal levels when this regimen is followed by human athletes.[85–87] The beneficial effects that higher initial glycogen stores have on endurance are believed to be the result of the availability of larger amounts of glycogen for anaerobic energy metabolism in the working muscles.[88]

There is also evidence that endurance can be effectively improved by increasing the availability of fatty acids for oxidation by working muscle.[89] Increased metabolism of fatty acids spares the use of muscle glycogen and thus delays glycogen depletion and fatigue.[90] Research has shown that the consumption of a high-fat, low-carbohydrate diet increases the use of fatty acids and intramuscular triglycerides by working muscles, but it also results in lowered muscle glycogen stores.[79,91] However, the results of long-term studies with rats and humans have shown that adaptation to this type of diet over several weeks results in either sustained or improved endurance, despite lowered glycogen stores.[79,92] Therefore it appears that two nutritional strategies are beneficial to improving endurance and delaying fatigue, feeding to increase muscle glycogen stores and feeding to enhance the ability of working muscles to use fatty acids for energy.

In the dog, approximately 70% to 90% of the energy for sustained work is derived from fat metabolism, and only a small amount of energy is derived from carbohydrate metabolism.[93,94] In addition, results of field studies with sled dogs and laboratory studies with beagles suggest that the ability to use fatty acids through aerobic pathways for energy may be more important than the use of muscle glycogen through anaerobic pathways during strenuous exercise.[67,71,88,95] Although limited research has been conducted, it is believed that the practice of glycogen loading is not effective in dogs. Some authors even suggest that glycogen loading may be responsible for the occurrence of exertional rhabdomylosis in racing dogs.[70,73] Exertional rhabdomyolysis is a disorder that is caused by rapid anaerobic metabolism of muscle glycogen, resulting in an accumulation of lactic acid. Lactic acid accumulation can have several adverse side effects, including damage to muscle-tissue membranes, edema, and inhibition of lipolysis and glycolysis.[96]

Dietary fat, on the other hand, appears to be an important component in the diet of working dogs. Energy density and diet digestibility have been shown to be the two most important nutritional factors affecting performance in working dogs.[69,95,97] The most efficacious way to supply this energy is in the form of fat. A study with beagles measured endurance of dogs running on a treadmill; the dogs were fed either a commercial, dry diet that was formulated for maintenance or one of three highly digestible, high-fat diets. The dogs that were fed the maintenance diet experienced exhaustion after 103 minutes, but the dogs that were fed the more energy-dense, highly digestible diets did not experience exhaustion until they had run for a significantly longer time period (137 minutes). Analysis of these data showed that performance level in the beagles was positively correlated with intake of digestible fat. It appears that highly digestible, high-fat diets can supply the extra energy that is needed by working dogs and contribute positively to endurance performance.

The distinctive features of the maintenance diet that caused poor endurance were lower energy density and lower diet digestibility.[95] An animal with increased energy needs must consume a great deal of food to meet those needs. If the diet is low in digestibility, a large amount of dry matter must be ingested. The amount of dry matter that can be consumed during a meal is limited by the dog's gastric capacity and its ability to digest and assimilate large boluses of food. Therefore, in addition to the need for high fat content as an energy source, high digestibility is necessary to limit the total amount of food that the dog must consume at each meal. Although some maintenance diets can supply enough energy if consumed in great enough quantities by working dogs, they may become bulk limiting and thus limit performance.

Although high digestibility and high energy density improve stamina, some data indicate that carbohydrate intake is negatively correlated with endurance performance in dogs.[98] However, these results more likely reflect the fact that carbohydrate displaced fat from the poorly performing diets, rather than being a direct effect of carbohydrate content. An experiment with racing sled dogs compared diets containing either 0%, 23%, or 38% of the energy from carbohydrate and varying levels of fat and protein. No difference in performance was observed between the diets, although the dogs receiving the carbohydrate-free diet did experience diarrhea.[67] The three performance diets that were used in the endurance experiment with beagles contained between 4% and 26% carbohydrate, yet no difference in performance was observed between these diets. Carbohydrate intake has been positively correlated with performance in human athletes because of its enhancing effect on muscle glycogen stores. A source of carbohydrate is probably beneficial in the diets of working dogs to allow the maintenance of normal muscle glycogen levels. However, the carbohydrate in these diets must be highly digestible and must not limit the energy density of the ration by replacing fat.

It has been claimed that high-protein diets are also beneficial for working dogs.[99] However, there is no experimental evidence that demonstrates enhanced performance as a result of increased protein intake. One study that is used to support this theory did not actually measure performance. Several hematological parameters were monitored in sled dogs that consumed diets containing varying levels of protein, fat, and carbohydrate. The dogs that were fed diets containing increased levels of protein had higher hematocrit levels than other dogs in the study.[99] The higher hematocrit levels in these dogs may have been a result of several factors, including the diet's higher fat, lower carbohydrate, and higher protein contents. More importantly, the significance of high hematocrit levels and their underlying cause was not determined. It is not known whether these high values were a result of increased erythropoiesis, decreased red blood cell loss, or increased dehydration. Moreover, the relationship between increased hematocrit levels and performance is unknown. At this time, there is no evidence that working dogs have a higher protein requirement than do dogs during maintenance, beyond the increase that occurs as a result of increasing energy intake.

The provision of adequate amounts of water during work is even more important than providing adequate energy. Dogs lose water primarily through respiration and, to a much lesser degree, through perspiration. These water losses can increase by tenfold to twentyfold during exercise.[18,70,100] Therefore it is important that dogs are provided with water at frequent intervals throughout a session of work. Even mild dehydration can lead to reduced work capacity, decreased strength, and hyperthermia.[72,100] Working dogs should be given frequent opportunities to drink small amounts of fresh

Practical Feeding Tips: Endurance Performance

Feed a highly digestible, energy-dense, high-fat diet.
Provide continual access to clean, fresh water.
Feed two or more meals per day on a portion-controlled basis.
Feed the largest meal of the day after the day's training is complete.
Provide a meal ½ to 2 hours before training or an endurance event.
Provide small amounts of food frequently throughout endurance events.

water during periods of extended work. This practice will prevent the development of even mild dehydration. Cool water is preferable because it is more palatable to most dogs, and it is more effective in helping to cool the body.[101]

Feeding practices that are best suited for hard-working dogs are designed to minimize gastrointestinal expansion during bouts of work and to maintain a high work capacity throughout the session of exercise. Dogs should be fed on a portion-controlled basis so that the trainer can strictly regulate the timing and the size of meals. The main meal of the day should be fed to a working dog after the period of exercise to allow adequate digestion of food.[40] Generally, at least two to three meals should be provided per day, and a small meal should be provided 1.5 to 2 hours before endurance activity.

Studies conducted with humans have shown that when a meal containing carbohydrates is ingested immediately before an endurance race, plasma insulin levels are significantly increased at the start of the race. This elevated insulin response, coupled with the increased insulin sensitivity that is naturally induced by exercise, results in a rapid fall in blood glucose levels and in significantly greater rates of muscle glycogen use.[102] In addition, insulin suppresses lipolysis, thereby opposing effective fatty acid use during exercise. It is believed that these metabolic changes may hasten the onset of fatigue and exhaustion in human endurance athletes.[103] Although no research of this nature has been conducted in dogs, it seems reasonable to assume that this species will exhibit a similar response to feeding a carbohydrate snack within the last hour before a race.

In contrast, feeding small amounts to dogs during the endurance event may be beneficial. Studies with humans have found that hyperinsulinemia is prevented and fatigue is postponed if a food containing carbohydrate is provided during, rather than before, exercise.[80,104] However, because dogs primarily use fat during endurance exercise, a carbohydrate snack is not recommended. If the dog is adapted to a high-fat endurance diet, feeding a high-fat–high-protein snack during endurance performance is preferable. Feeding small amounts of food to dogs during prolonged endurance events may be helpful in sustaining performance over long periods of time (see the box above).

SPRINT RACING PERFORMANCE

The exercise that sprint racing dogs engage in is substantially different from that required of sled dogs and dogs that work for long periods of time. Greyhound races are extremely

short, sprinting events. In the United States, racing takes place on an oval tract and involves distances between $\frac{5}{16}$ and $\frac{3}{8}$ of a mile. During a race, dogs reach speeds of 36 to 38 miles per hour, but they maintain this speed for only 30 to 40 seconds.[18] It is known that brief, intense periods of exercise preclude the mobilization and delivery of fatty acids and the adequate oxygenation of tissue necessary for aerobic metabolism.[105] As a result, the primary source of energy for this type of exercise is the anaerobic metabolism of carbohydrate. Both muscle glycogen and circulating blood glucose supply energy to muscles during brief bouts of intense work.[106] This process differs from endurance exercise, in which both fat and carbohydrate supply energy to the working muscles. Postrace biochemical data collected from racing greyhounds indicate that the greyhound relies primarily on anaerobic metabolism for energy. Blood lactate levels increase dramatically from prerace values of 8 milligrams per deciliter (mg/dl) to postrace values of 220 mg/dl, reflecting the significant contribution of anaerobic metabolism of carbohydrate to the energy demands of the race.[107] It appears that the greyhound is well adapted to this type of work, because both lactate levels and blood pH return to normal values within 1 hour after the race.[108] Training also increases the body's ability to metabolize accumulated lactic acid following an intense bout of exercise.[109]

Studies with human athletes have indicated that dietary modification is more effective in influencing endurance athletes than sprinters. This may be a result of the fact that two factors that influence endurance during prolonged periods of exercise are the body's ability to use fat for energy and the quantity of glycogen stored in the working muscles.[84] As discussed previously, both of these factors can be somewhat influenced by diet. Sprinters, on the other hand, rapidly use muscle glycogen and circulating glucose through anaerobic metabolism. A study with human runners showed that although the practice of glycogen loading increased exercise time to exhaustion, it did not appear to influence running speed at the beginning of the race.[78]

Although short-term, anaerobic energy metabolism may not be readily influenced by diet, it is still important that racing dogs receive diets that are energy dense and highly digestible. Feeding a diet that has been formulated for performance will ensure that dry-matter intake during racing or training is not excessive. The diet that is fed to racing greyhounds should also contain a reasonable amount of highly digestible carbohydrate to ensure that body glycogen stores are maintained at an optimal level and can be adequately restored following intensive periods of training or racing.

WEATHER EXTREMES

Adverse weather conditions, in the form of extreme cold or heat, result in increased energy needs in dogs and cats. This increase can be quite substantial, depending on the severity of the weather. A study of dogs living in an Arctic environment showed that an increase in energy intake of 70% to 80% was necessary for the dogs to maintain normal body temperatures without experiencing weight loss.[110] Dogs are capable of a significant level of cold-induced thermogenesis, a mechanism involving an increase in metabolic rate during exposure to a cold environment. The increased metabolic rate produces additional body heat that is used to maintain body temperature.

Although the increased energy needs of dogs in Arctic environments are very great and result in large increases in daily energy intake, dogs housed outside during moderately cold weather also experience a degree of cold-induced thermogenesis. A study with Labrador retrievers and beagles showed that as environmental temperatures decreased from 59°F (thermal neutral zone) to 47°F, the dogs' metabolizable energy (ME) intake increased and remained high until the ambient temperature was increased. During the cold period, there was a slight decrease in mean body weight despite increased energy intake. Results from this study indicate that an average increase in ME intake of 25% is necessary to maintain body weight in dogs housed in cool conditions.[111] This figure can be used as a general guide for increasing the ME intake of dogs that are housed outdoors during the winter months. However, factors such as the dog's size, coat type and length, the type of shelter that is provided, and weather conditions such as wind and drifting snow will significantly influence the amount of food needed by dogs that are housed in cold environments.[112] For example, a study with beagles, Labrador retrievers and Siberian huskies found that the ME requirements of Siberian huskies were less affected by fluctuations in environmental temperature than were the ME intakes of beagles and Labrador retrievers. It appears that the double coat of huskies acts as a protective barrier to insulate them against large fluctuations in environmental temperature.[113]

The energy needs of dogs and cats also increase with high environmental temperature and humidity. The exposure to high ambient temperature causes an increase in the amount of energy that must be used to cool the body. Working dogs in humid environments experience slight increases in energy needs, and at the same time they often exhibit a reduction in appetite.[97] Therefore it is important to provide dogs that are working in hot environments with a diet that is high in caloric and nutrient density so that nutritional needs may be met without the consumption of large quantities of food. It is also important that cool water be provided continuously in warm environments. Water is especially important for dogs that are required to work in warm or humid conditions.

STRESS

Working animals are exposed to a variety of stresses, such as intense physical exertion, weather extremes, and psychological strain. Although repeated, low levels of tolerable stresses are believed to be a necessary component of training and improved performance, severe stress can result in a breakdown in performance.[88] Signs of severe stress in dogs include apathy, depression, anorexia, and a reluctance to work.[88] It has been suggested that some of the side effects of severe stress in working dogs include diarrhea and dehydration, exertional rhabdomyolysis, lower bowel bleeding, anemia, and metatarsal fractures.[66] However, no controlled research studies have been conducted with working dogs to substantiate these claims.

External influences such as training regimen, housing conditions, environmental temperature and humidity, and the type of training methods that are used will greatly influence the degree of stress that an individual animal experiences. Internal influences on stress include an animal's temperament, age, physical capabilities, and nutritional

status. The provision of a well-balanced, high-quality diet that has been formulated for working dogs will help to prevent the onset of severe stress, but it cannot compensate for other adverse conditions in the dog's life. In other words, a sound nutritional program is extremely important for hard-working animals, but it will never counteract the detrimental effects of stress that are produced by poor training or care.

The major nutritional considerations for working dogs experiencing stress are energy density and diet digestibility. In addition to these dietary modifications, many breeders, exhibitors, and trainers believe that stressed dogs must also receive supplements of certain vitamins and minerals. However, there is no evidence to suggest that working dogs require higher amounts of these nutrients. Supplemental vitamin C was first advocated as an aid in the relief of various stress conditions in human athletes because plasma ascorbate levels were found to decline during stress.[88] This practice was then extended to working animals. However, several controlled studies with human athletes have demonstrated that vitamin C supplementation has no beneficial effect on either anaerobic or aerobic work capacity.[114] Studies examining the effects of supplementation with other vitamins have shown a similar lack of results.[114] Research investigating the specific effects of supplemental vitamins and minerals on performance in working and stressed dogs must be conducted before any valid recommendations can be made. If a diet is nutritionally balanced and the dog is consuming enough to meet its energy needs during work, supplemental vitamins and minerals should not be necessary.

Geriatrics

I mprovements in the control of infectious diseases and in the nutrition of dogs and cats in recent years has resulted in a gradual increase in the average life span of companion animals. It is believed that the maximum life span of a given species remains relatively fixed, but average life span can be affected by genetics, health care, nutrition, and mature body size. The maximum life span of the dog is estimated to be about 27 years, and the average life span is approximately 13 years.[115] In general, the large and giant breeds of dogs tend to die at younger ages than do the small and toy breeds. The average life span of the domestic cat is approximately 14 years, and its maximum life span may be as high as 25 to 35 years.[115] The increased number of geriatric pets and the understanding that most of these dogs and cats have been cherished family members for many years necessitates increased attention to the care and proper nutrition of this portion of the companion animal population.

NORMAL PHYSIOLOGICAL CHANGES THAT OCCUR WITH AGING

The effect of aging on the body is observed as a gradual decline in the functional capacity of organs, beginning shortly after the animal has reached maturity. Different systems of the body age at different rates, and the degree of compromised function that must occur before clinical signs are seen depends on many factors in the pet's life. Although one pet may exhibit severe pathological effects of aging by 7 years, another may exhibit no clinical signs even at 12 years. It is also not unusual for more than one chronic dis-

ease to be present in a single geriatric pet. This variability necessitates that older animals be assessed as individuals, using functional changes in body systems rather than chronological age to categorize them with the elderly population.

Metabolic Effects of Aging

An animal's resting metabolic rate (RMR) naturally slows as the animal ages. Changes in body composition include a decrease in the percentage of lean body tissue (muscle) and an increase in the percentage of body fat. The loss of lean tissue causes a substantial decrease in the RMR. In addition, most pets voluntarily reduce their physical activity as they become older. Total daily energy requirements may decrease by as much as 30% to 40% during the last one third of a pet's life span as a result of decreased metabolic rate and physical activity.[116]

Changes in the Integument

The skin loses elasticity and becomes less pliable with age as a result of increased calcium content and pseudoelastin in the elastic fibers. This loss of elasticity is often accompanied by hyperkeratosis of both the skin and the follicles. Follicles may atrophy, resulting in areas of hair loss. The loss of pigment cells in the hair follicles results in the production of white hairs, often observed around the muzzle and face of older dogs and cats. The incidence of skin neoplasia also increases with age. The median age for the development of skin tumors is about 10.5 years in dogs and 12 years in cats.[117]

Changes in the Alimentary System

The effect of aging on the alimentary system may directly affect a pet's ability to consume, digest, or metabolize food. Dental calculus, periodontal disease, the loss of teeth, and a decline in the amount of functional salivary tissue may all contribute to a decrease in food intake. In addition, normal decreases in colonic motility with age can predispose some older pets to constipation.

Changes in the Urinary System

Renal failure is one of the four leading causes of death in old dogs and is a major cause of illness and mortality in geriatric cats.[118,119] A study that evaluated clinical changes in renal function in a colony of beagles for 13 years found that nephrosclerosis was the most frequently diagnosed kidney lesion in older dogs.[120] The data from this study suggest that normal kidney aging may lead to nephron loss of up to 75% before clinical or biochemical signs occur in older dogs. Pets with less than 75% loss are usually clinically normal but may be more susceptible to renal insult than younger animals still possessing renal reserve capacity.[121] These observations are of major importance when determining the timing and degree of dietary modification that is to be used in the treatment of renal disease in geriatric dogs and cats (see Section 6, pp. 395–400).

Renal disease in older pets directly affects nutrition and dietary management because clinical kidney insufficiency is associated with weight loss, muscle wasting, altered plasma protein profiles, decreased caloric and nutrient intake, intestinal malabsorption, and reduced assimilation and use of nutrients. The accumulation of the metabolic products of protein, of which urea is the most abundant, is believed to further contribute to the development of the clinical and physiological abnormalities of renal failure. Dietary modification attempts to minimize the accumulation of these end products in the bloodstream while still supplying adequate energy and protein to maintain weight and minimize the muscle wasting associated with old age and compromised renal function.

Changes in the Musculoskeletal System

Old age is accompanied by a decline in the percentage of lean body mass and bone mass. Both the number and size of muscle cells decrease with age and the cortices of the long bones become thinner, dense, and brittle. This may be due in part to inadequate absorption of calcium in the intestine of some older pets. Arthritis commonly occurs in older pets and obesity can compound the effects of arthritis. The presence of joint pain may also affect the pet's desire and ability to eat. Decreased appetite, leading to weight loss, is occasionally observed in severely arthritic pets.

Changes in the Cardiovascular System

Heart-related disease is a fairly common cause of morbidity in older pets and is estimated to occur in up to 30% of aged dogs.[122] The incidence in cats is not known, but it is thought to occur less frequently.[123] Cardiac output decreases by as much as 30% between midlife and old age.[116] Maximal heart rate and oxygen consumption during exercise also decrease significantly. In animals with adult onset heart disease, fibrosis and myocardial necrosis will eventually interfere with normal conduction pathways and result in arrhythmias. Normal vascular changes of aging include hyaline thickening of the media of the blood vessels and increased deposition of calcium in the intima of the aorta and the media of the peripheral arteries. All of these changes contribute to a progressive increase in the workload of the heart, which can eventually lead to the development of congestive heart disease or heart failure.

Changes in the Special Senses

Old age may result in a general reduced reaction to stimuli and partial loss of the sensations of vision, hearing, and taste. Nuclear sclerosis or cataracts of the lens are frequently seen in older dogs and cats. A decrease in taste acuity may lead to decreased interest in food, reduced intake, and weight loss in some older pets.

Behavioral Changes Associated with Aging

The most common behavioral problems that occur in old dogs and cats are related to or secondary to degenerative disease and other geriatric changes.[124] Several of these behavioral changes may affect the pet's ability or desire to obtain adequate nutrition. For example, pets suffering from the chronic pain of arthritis may become increasingly irritable and reluctant to engage in any type of activity, including eating. On the other hand, the development of diabetes mellitus in dogs is often accompanied by a ravenous appetite. Because diabetic pets are usually overweight to begin with, the desire to consume large amounts of food further exacerbates this condition.

Depression or pathological mourning as a result of the loss of a beloved housemate or owner can result in severe anorexia in older pets. If prolonged, this anorexia can lead to weight loss and increased susceptibility to illness. Changes in the social structure of the family, usually because of the introduction of another pet, may also cause elderly dogs or cats to change their eating patterns. In some instances, social facilitation may cause an abrupt increase in intake, predisposing the pet to obesity. In other cases, intimidation by the new pet may cause the older animal to suddenly decrease food intake.

One of the most noticeable changes in the behavior of geriatric pets is their resistance to a change in daily routine. A move to a new residence, the introduction of a new pet, or a change in the owner's work schedule may be met with depression, alterations in elimination patterns, and/or changes in eating habits. It is important to be aware that geriatric cats are particularly predisposed to behavior problems when their environment is altered.[124] Introducing changes gradually and allowing the elderly pet sufficient time to adapt is often effective in minimizing stress and preventing the occurrence of behavior problems.

NUTRIENT CONSIDERATIONS FOR THE OLDER PET

The aging pet has a need for the same nutrients that were required during earlier physiological states. However, quantities of nutrients required per unit of body weight may change, and the way in which nutrients are provided to the pet may require modification. Such changes usually depend on the presence or degree of degenerative disease. Nutrients that may be of specific concern in aging dogs and cats are discussed in the following sections.

Energy

The reduction in the metabolic rate and physical activity of geriatric pets results in a decreased total daily energy requirement. Inactivity alone may cause a decrease of up to 20% of the pet's total daily energy requirement.[123] This decrease, coupled with the natural slowing of basal metabolic rate, can result in a total reduction in energy needs of up to 30% to 40%.[116] Elderly pets will vary greatly in their energy needs, depending on individual temperament, the presence of degenerative disease, and the amount of daily exercise that the pet receives. Caloric intake should be carefully monitored in older pets to ensure adequate intake of calories and nutrients while at the same time preventing the development of obesity.

Protein and Amino Acids

The decrease in lean body mass that occurs with aging results in a loss of the protein reserves that can normally be used by the body during reaction to stress and illness. Stress triggers nervous, metabolic, and hormonal adaptations that allow the body to adapt to aversive stimuli. The mobilization of body protein is a characteristic physiological response to stress. Older animals are subject to a high incidence of disease and stress and are therefore especially vulnerable if their ability to react is compromised. It is important that geriatric pets be provided with high-quality protein at a level that is sufficient to supply the essential amino acids needed for body maintenance needs and to minimize losses of lean body tissue.

Studies conducted with human subjects have shown that the efficiency of protein use is slightly lower in the elderly than in young adults. The amount of available energy in the form of egg protein required for nitrogen balance was reported to be 4% in young men, but it increased to 6% in elderly men.[125] These data indicate that the dietary protein intake of older adults should be increased slightly to compensate for decreased use.

A study with dogs compared the protein requirements in young and old animals.[126] The ratio of liver and muscle protein to deoxyribonucleic acid (DNA) was measured and used as an estimate of body protein reserves. Results showed that protein/DNA ratios were maximized when young adult dogs were fed a semipurified diet containing 12.4% protein. Old dogs, on the other hand, required 18.8% protein to maximize body protein reserves. In contrast, another study compared the digestive capabilities of 12-year-old dogs to 1-year-old dogs over a 2-year period. No difference was observed in the ability of old dogs to use protein and other nutrients from four different diets compared with young adult dogs.[127]

Aging pets should be fed diets with a lower percentage of calories from protein than those used for growth but with higher than the minimum that is necessary for adult maintenance.[127] In addition to having diminished protein reserves, the decreased total energy needs of the older pet may result in the need to slightly increase the percentage of protein calories in the diet. Premium pet foods that are formulated for adult maintenance contain high-quality protein sources and therefore can provide an adequate level and quality of protein to the older pet (see Section 3, pp. 189–191). However, pet food brands that contain minimal amounts of protein from poor-quality sources may not be capable of providing adequate protein nutrition.

Much controversy exists concerning dietary protein and renal function in older animals. It is an accepted fact that decreased renal functioning is a normal occurrence with aging. As a direct result of this knowledge, and because of a series of studies that were conducted in rats, some investigators have recommended that all elderly pets receive

moderately reduced protein diets in an attempt to prevent or minimize the progression of kidney dysfunction.[128] However, it is also important that healthy, geriatric dogs and cats receive adequate amounts of high-quality protein to minimize losses of body protein reserves and to satisfy maintenance protein needs. Although there is evidence that a reduction in protein intake has a significant effect on clinical signs of chronic renal failure, once a certain level of dysfunction has occurred, there is no evidence to support a systematically reduced protein level in the diets of healthy older pets. It is recommended that the protein in the diet of geriatric dogs should not be restricted simply because of old age. Rather, elderly pets should receive diets containing adequate levels of high-quality protein. If chronic renal disease is diagnosed, moderate protein restriction can be implemented as needed.[129] (See Section 6, pp. 395–398.)

Fat

It has been theorized that the increase in the percentage of body fat that occurs with aging is partially a result of an increasing inability of the body to metabolize lipids.[127] Slightly decreasing the amount of fat in the diet may benefit geriatric dogs and cats, provided that the fat that remains in the diet is both highly digestible and rich in essential fatty acids.

Vitamins and Minerals

No controlled research has been conducted that examines the vitamin requirements of geriatric dogs and cats. However, it has been suggested that moderate increases in requirements for the B vitamins and fat-soluble vitamins A and E may occur because of the normal digestive and metabolic changes that occur with aging.[27] There are currently no data available that support this theory. The development of decreased glucose tolerance with age may cause a slight increase in the requirement of B vitamins necessary for carbohydrate use. However, a deficiency of these vitamins has never been demonstrated in older pets. Adequate levels of vitamins are contained in most commercial pet foods, and supplementation should not be necessary for elderly pets.

Supplemental dietary phosphorus should not be fed to older pets. Diets high in this mineral have been shown to contribute to kidney damage in human subjects by increasing blood flow and filtration through the glomerulus and promoting calcium and phosphorus deposition in the kidney.[130,131] There is some evidence in dogs that excess phosphorus in the diet contributes to the progression of kidney disease.[132,133] Excess phosphorus may also indirectly contribute to an increase in parathyroid hormone levels in healthy dogs by causing a reduction in serum calcitriol levels.[123] Although the effects of high-phosphorus diets on kidney function in healthy geriatric dogs and cats is not known, it is prudent to avoid an excess of this mineral in the diet[129,131] (see Section 6, pp. 394–395).

Sodium in dog and cat foods has received attention because of the concern about this nutrient in human diets. Some commercial pet foods contain as high as 2% sodium, even though the actual sodium requirement of dogs and cats is much lower than this.

However, at levels of 2% or greater, intake of the diet is self-limiting. Pets will not consume diets that contain excessively high amounts of sodium.[8] At levels below 2%, sodium has not been shown to cause disease in healthy dogs. Therefore the sodium content in the diet of healthy elderly pets should not be of concern, provided the level is within the recommended range of 1% or less on a dry-matter basis.

Feeding Management and Care of the Older Pet

Major objectives of the feeding and care of geriatric dogs and cats should be to maintain health and optimum body weight, slow or prevent the development of chronic disease, and minimize or improve clinical signs of diseases that may already be present. Routine care for geriatric pets should involve the adherence to a consistent daily routine, regular attention to normal health care procedures, and periodic veterinary examinations for assessment of the presence or progression of chronic disease. Stressful situations and abrupt changes in daily routines should be avoided. If a drastic change must be made in an older pet's routine, attempts should be made to minimize stress and to accomplish the change in a gradual manner.

Optimal body weight can be maintained and obesity prevented through the judicious control of caloric intake and adherence to a regular exercise schedule. Although many adult dogs and cats are able to maintain normal body weights when fed free-choice, this may no longer be possible as the pet "slows down." Decreasing energy needs may lead to obesity in some older pets if a free-choice regimen is continued. It is recommended that geriatric dogs and cats be fed at least two to three small meals per day, rather than one large meal. Feeding several small meals per day promotes improved nutrient use and may decrease feelings of hunger between meals.[134] The timing and size of meals should also be strictly regulated. A regular schedule minimizes alimentary stress and supports normal nutrient digestion and use. Fresh water should be available at all times to older dogs and cats.

Geriatric cats and some older dogs may become very particular about their eating habits. The pet's willingness to eat new foods may decrease. It may be necessary for owners to provide an especially strong-smelling or highly palatable food to their older cat.[134] Other dogs and cats may accept only one particular brand or flavor of food. If possible, pet owners should accommodate these needs, provided that the preferred food can provide adequate nutrition to the pet.

Unless a disease state that requires specific nutrient alterations is present (such as diabetes, renal disease, or congestive heart failure), older, healthy pets should not require special "geriatric diets." Many of the commercially available premium pet foods contain quality ingredients that provide nutrients in a highly available form. Lower quality pet foods are not generally recommended for elderly pets because some of these products provide poorly available nutrients.[123]

Proper care of the teeth and gums is important for the geriatric pet. If an owner is unable or unwilling to regularly examine and brush the pet's teeth, yearly descaling by

Practical Feeding Tips: Elderly Companion Animals

Provide regular health checkups (at least twice a year).
Avoid sudden changes in the daily routine or diet.
Provide a highly digestible diet that contains high-quality protein.
Use portion-controlled feeding to prevent obesity; feed to maintain ideal body weight.
Provide a moderate level of regular exercise.
Maintain proper care of the teeth and gums.
When necessary, provide a therapeutic diet to manage or treat disease.

a veterinarian is necessary to prevent buildup of dental calculus and the development of periodontal disease. Dental problems can lead to decreased food intake, anorexia, and systemic disease if not treated promptly in older animals.

Regular and sustained periods of physical activity help to maintain muscle tone, enhance circulation, improve alimentation, and prevent excess weight gain. The level and intensity of exercise should be adjusted to the individual pet's physical and medical condition. Many dogs, if healthy and maintained in good condition, can enjoy running and playing active games with their owners well into old age. Almost all older dogs will benefit from and enjoy two 15- to 30-minute walks per day. Although most cats do not readily accept walking on a lead, playing games with older cats can be an acceptable form of exercise (see the box above).

KEY POINTS

SECTION 4

Competitive (rapid) eating, a characteristic of the dog's ancestor, the wolf, can cause choking or excessive food intake in domestic dogs. Feeding dogs alone or changing the diet can help.

In contrast to dogs, most cats eat slowly. If fed free-choice, cats will eat frequently and randomly throughout a 24-hour period.

The type of feeding regimen used depends on several factors: the owner's schedule, the number of animals being fed, and the pet's acceptability of the feeding method. Portion-controlled feeding is the method of choice in most situations.

Although free-choice feeding has some advantages, owners should evaluate pets fed by this method for the development of problems, such as anorexia, overconsumption, or problems due to social hierarchies within groups of dogs.

Commercial pet foods balance nutrient content and energy density, thus assuring that when an animal's caloric needs are met, its needs for all other essential nutrients will also be met.

Determining how much to feed a dog or cat is based on age, reproductive status, body condition, level of activity, breed, temperament, and environmental conditions. Commercial pet food labels provide general guidelines, but every pet must be evaluated and fed as an individual.

During pregnancy, supplementation with calcium or any other mineral is not necessary if a well-balanced, commercial ration is fed.

Within the first 24 hours of birth, colostrum provides intact immunoglobulins, thereby protecting the puppies and kittens from a number of infectious diseases. The nutrient content of colostrum differs significantly from mature milk, and its intact immunoglobulins provide passive immunity to the neonates.

Orphaned puppies and kittens represent a challenge to the owner. Once orphaned, they must depend on humans for maternal care, proper nutrition, and a suitable environment. Maintaining proper warmth, normally provided by body heat from the bitch or queen, is critical to assure survival of the newborn puppies and kittens. Pay close attention to temperature guidelines and methods of providing a warm environment.

Although there are a number of well-formulated, commercial milk replacements available, they do not provide the immune protection of colostrum. Thus, if the animals were orphaned before they received colostrum (within the first 24 hours of birth), they will be more susceptible to infectious disease.

To support the growth of new tissues, pet foods for growing puppies and kittens should have a slightly higher protein content than foods fed for adult maintenance.

Contrary to popular belief, calcium and phosphorous supplements are not necessary for growing pets and can be harmful in large and giant breeds of dogs, contributing to the development of certain developmental skeletal disorders.

Hyperplastic obesity is an increase in both the size and number of fat cells. Hypertrophic obesity is an increase in fat-cell size. As has been found in other species, it is possible that if young, growing animals are overnourished, they may be predisposed to obesity at maturity.

Although heredity certainly plays a role in the development of certain skeletal disorders, studies have identified diet supplementation with certain nutrients and/or feeding an energy- and nutrient-dense diet at a level that supports maximal growth rate as environmental contributing factors.

An endurance study showed that a highly digestible, high-fat diet can provide the extra energy needed by working dogs and contribute positively to endurance performance.

It is well known that carbohydrate intake, or "loading," in humans provides the necessary energy for performing athletes. However, a similar effect has not been observed in working dogs. In addition, there is no evidence that increased protein intake leads to increased performance in working dogs.

Working dogs should be fed using the portion-controlled method, with the main meal of the day provided after the period of exercise. In general, hard-working dogs should be fed two to three meals per day, with one small meal fed 1.5 to 2 hours before the exercise.

In contrast to working dogs, racing greyhounds draw energy from the anaerobic metabolism of carbohydrates; muscle glycogen and circulating blood glucose fuel muscles during their brief periods of intense work. Although such short-term energy metabolism may not be strongly influenced by diet, racing dogs should be fed energy-dense, highly digestible diets that have been formulated for performance.

As a general guideline, an average increase of 25% of a dog's metabolizable energy (ME) intake is necessary to maintain body weight in dogs housed in cool conditions (less than 59°F).

Advances in health care and nutrition are leading to increased longevity for companion animals. Paralleling the events of aging in humans, geriatric cats and dogs experience many of the same changes. The functioning efficiency of body systems and organs declines, resting metabolic rate decreases, and pets reduce their physical activity. As a result, energy requirements may decrease by as much as 30% to 40%.

The protein controversy: Contrary to popular belief, protein in the diets of geriatric dogs should not be restricted simply because the dog is old. Attempts to prevent or minimize the natural decline in kidney function associated with aging by reducing protein consumption may lead to negative nitrogen balance and losses of body protein reserves. Although protein reduction does have a significant positive effect on clinical signs of chronic renal failure once a certain level of dysfunction has occurred, protein should not be arbitrarily restricted in a generally healthy older pet.

Tip: Exercise and nutrition can be adapted to fit a geriatric pet's needs. More frequent feedings (two or more times a day) will help digestion and avoid feelings of hunger. Fast games of fetch can be replaced by one or two 15- to 30-minute walks each day.

SECTION 4

REFERENCES

1. Mugford RA: External influences on the feeding of carnivores. In Kare MR, Maller O, editors: *The chemical senses and nutrition*, New York, 1977, Academic Press.
2. Hart BL, Hart LA: *Canine and feline behavioral therapy*, Philadelphia, 1985, Lea & Febiger, pp 161–165.
3. Kane E, Morris JG, Rogers QR: Acceptability and digestibility by adult cats of diets made with various sources and levels of fat, *J Anim Sci* 53:1516–1523, 1981.
4. Kanarek RB: Availability and caloric density of diet as determinants of meal patterns in cats, *Physio Behav* 15:611–618, 1975.
5. Doyle Dane Bernback International: DDB study documents belief in animal rights, *Pet Food Ind* Mar/Apr, pp 20–22, 1984.
6. Leblanc J, Diamond P: The effect of meal frequency on postprandial thermogenesis in the dog, *Fed Proc* 44:1678, 1985 (abstract).
7. Wingfield WE: *Proceedings of the Colorado State University Annual Conference for Veterinarians*, 1978, pp 85–88.
8. Association of American Feed Control Officials: *Official publication*, 1994, The Association of American Feed Control Officials.
9. Lawler DF, Bebiak DM: Nutrition and management of reproduction in the cat, *Vet Clin North Am Sm Anim Pract* 16:495–519, 1986.
10. Bebiak DM, Lawler DF, Reutzel LF: Nutrition and management of the dog, *Vet Clin North Am Sm Anim Pract* 17:505–6533, 1987.
11. Moser D: Feeding to optimize canine reproductive efficiency, *Probl Vet Med* 4:545–550, 1992.
12. Sheffy BE: Nutrition and nutritional disorders, *Vet Clin North Am Sm Anim Pract* 8:7–29, 1978.
13. Loveridge GG: Bodyweight changes and energy intake of cats during gestation and lactation, *Anim Tech* 37:7–15, 1986.
14. Holme DW: Practical use of prepared foods for dogs and cats. In *Dog and cat nutrition*, New York, 1982, Pergamon Press, pp 47–59.
15. Kronfeld DS: Nature and use of commercial dog foods, *J Am Vet Med Assoc* 166:487–493, 1975.
16. Mosier JE: Nutritional recommendations for gestation and lactation in the dog, *Vet Clin North Am Sm Anim Pract* 7:683–692, 1977.
17. Ontko JA, Phillips PH: Reproduction and lactation studies with bitches fed semi-purified diets, *J Nutr* 65:211–218, 1958.
18. Lewis LD, Morris ML, Hand MS: Dogs: feeding and care. In *Small animal clinical nutrition*, Topeka, Kan, 1987, Mark Morris Associates, pp 3–1 to 3–32.
19. Fisher EW: Neonatal diseases of dogs and cats, *Br Vet J* 138:277–284, 1982.
20. Lonnerdal B, Keen CL, Hurley LS, and others: Developmental changes in the composition of beagle dog milk, *Am J Vet Res* 42:662–666, 1981.
21. Keen CL, Lonnerdal B, Clegg MS, and others: Developmental changes in composition of cats' milk: trace elements, minerals, protein, carbohydrate and fat, *J Nutr* 112:1763–1769, 1982.
22. Oftedal OT: Lactation in the dog: milk composition and intake by puppies, *J Nutr* 114:803–812, 1984.
23. Monson WJ: The care and management of orphaned puppies and kittens, *Vet Tech* 8:430–434, 1987.

24. Monson WJ: Orphan rearing of puppies and kittens, *Vet Clin North Am Sm Anim Pract* 17:567–576, 1987.
25. Baines FB: Milk substitutes and the hand rearing of orphan puppies and kittens, *J Sm Anim Pract* 22:555–578, 1981.
26. Mapletoft RJ, Schutte AP, Coubrough RI, and others: The perinatal period of dogs: nutrition and management in the hand rearing of puppies, *J South Afr Vet Med Assoc* 45:183–194, 1974.
27. Mosier JE: *Canine and feline geriatrics*, Proceedings of the American Animals Hospital Association, 1978, pp 153–160.
28. Douglass GM, Kane E, Holmes EJ: A profile of male and female cat growth, *Comp Anim Pract* 2:9–12, 1988.
29. Allard RL, Douglass GM, Kerr WW: The effects of breed and sex on dog growth, *Comp Anim Pract* 2:15–19, 1988.
30. Arnold A, Elvehjem CA: Nutritional requirements of dogs, *J Am Vet Med Assoc* 95:187–193, 1939.
31. Sheffy BE: Meeting energy-protein needs of dogs, *Compen Cont Ed Sm Anim Pract* 1:345–354, 1979.
32. National Research Council: *Nutrient requirements of dogs*, Washington, DC, 1985, National Academy of Sciences.
33. Kendall PT, Blaza SE, Smith PM: Comparative digestible energy requirements of adult beagles and domestic cats for bodyweight maintenance, *J Nutr* 113:1946–1955, 1983.
34. Loveridge GG: Factors affecting growth performance in male and female kittens, *Animal Technology* 38:9–18, 1987.
35. Hazewinkel HAW, Goedegebuure SA, Poulos PW, and others: Influences of chronic calcium excess on the skeletal development of growing Great Danes, *J Am Anim Hosp Assoc* 21:377–391, 1985.
36. Jenkins KJ, Phillips PH: The mineral requirements of the dog. II. The relation of calcium, phosphorus and fat levels to minimal calcium and phosphorus requirements, *J Nutr* 70:241–250, 1960.
37. Gershoff SN, Legg MA, Hegsted DM: Adaptation to different calcium intakes in dogs, *J Nutr* 64:303–311, 1958.
38. Kallfelz FA, Dzanis DA: Overnutrition: an epidemic problem in pet practice?, *Vet Clin North Am Sm Anim Pract* 19:433–466, 1989.
39. Hazewinkel HA: Calcium metabolism and skeletal development of dogs. In Burger IH, Rivers JPW, editors: *Nutrition of the dog and cat*, Cambridge University Press, Cambridge, England, 1989, pp 293–302.
40. Earle KE: Calculations of energy requirements of dogs, cats and small psittacine birds, *J Sm Anim Pract* 34:163–183, 1993.
41. Hedhammer A, Wu F, Krook L, and others: Overnutrition and skeletal disease: an experimental study in growing Great Dane dogs, *Cornell Vet* 64:(suppl 5):1–159, 1974.
42. Kealy RD, Olsson SE, Monti KL, and others: Effects of limited food consumption on the incidence of hip dysplasia in growing dogs, *J Am Vet Med Assoc* 201:857–863, 1992.
43. Faust IM, Johnson PR, Hirsch J: Long-term effects of early nutritional experience on the development of obesity in the rat, *J Nutr* 110:2027–2034, 1980.
44. Johnson PR, Stern JS, Greenwood MRC, and others: Effect of early nutrition on adipose cellularity and pancreatic insulin release in the Zucker rat, *J Nutr* 103:738–743, 1973.
45. Ross MH: Length of life and caloric intake, *Am J Clin Nutr* 25:834–838, 1972.
46. Saville PD, Lieber CS: Increases in skeletal calcium and femur thickness produced by undernutrition, *J Nutr* 99:141–144, 1969.
47. Dluzniewska KA, Obtulowicz A, Koltek K: On the relationship between diet, rate of growth and skeletal deformities in school children, *Folia Med Cracov* 7:115–126, 1965.

48. Wise DR, Jennings AR: Dyschondroplasia in domestic poultry, *Vet Rec* 91:285–286, 1972.
49. Reiland S: The effect of decreased growth rate on frequency and severity of osteochondrosis in pigs: an experimental investigation, *Acta Radiol* 358:179–196, 1978.
50. Wyburn RS: A degenerative joint disease in the horse, *N Zealand Vet J* 25:321–322, 335, 1977.
51. Hirsch J, Knittle JL, Salans LB: Cell lipid content and cell number in obese and non-obese human adipose tissue, *J Clin Invest* 52:929–934, 1966.
52. Bjorntorp P, Sjostrom L: Number and size of fat cells in relation to metabolism in human obesity, *Metabolism* 20:703–706, 1971.
53. Faust IM, Johnson PR, Stern JS, and others: Diet-induced adipocyte number increase in adult rats: a new model of obesity, *Am J Physiol* 235:E279–E286, 1978.
54. Bertrand HA, Lynd FT, Masoro EJ, and others: Changes in adipose mass and cellularity through the adult life of rats fed ad libitum or a life–prolonging restricted diet, *J Gerontol* 35:827–835, 1980.
55. Hirsch J, Knittle JL: Cellularity of obese and non-obese adipose tissue, *Fed Proc* 29:1516–1521, 1970.
56. Etherton TD, Wangsness PJ, Hammers VM, and others: Effect of dietary restriction on carcass composition and adipocyte cellularity of swine with different propensities for obesity, *J Nutr* 112:2314–2323, 1982.
57. Lewis DS, Bertrand HA, Masoro EJ: Pre-weaning nutrition on fat development in baboons, *J Nutr* 113:2253–2259, 1983.
58. Vasselli JR, Cleary MP, van Itallie TB: Modern concepts of obesity, *Nutr Rev* 41:361–373, 1983.
59. Grondalen J: Arthrosis in the elbow joint of young rapidly growing dogs. VI. Interrelation between clinical, radiographical and pathoanatomical findings, *Nord Vet Med* 34:65–75, 1982.
60. Lust G, Geary JC, Sheffy BE: Development of hip dysplasia in dogs, *Am J Vet Res* 34:87–91, 1973.
61. Grondalen J: Metaphyseal osteopathy (hypertrophic osteodystrophy) in growing dogs: a clinical study: *J Sm Anim Pract* 17:721–735, 1976.
62. Willis MB: Hip scoring: a review of 1985–1986, *Vet Rec* 118:461–462, 1986.
63. Kendall PT, Burger IH: The effect of controlled and appetite feeding on growth and development in dogs, Proceedings of the Kal Kan Symposium on Canine Nutrition, Sept 29–30, Leicestershire, England, 1979.
64. Lavelle RB: The effects of the overfeeding of a balanced complete commercial diet to a group of growing Great Danes. In Burger IH, Rivers JPW, editors: *Nutrition of the dog and cat*, Cambridge University Press, Cambridge, England, 1989, pp 303–315.
65. Edney ATB, Smith AM: Study of obesity in dogs visiting veterinary practices in the United Kingdom, *Vet Rec* 118:391–396, 1986.
66. Rainbird AL: Feeding throughout life. In Edney ATB, editor: *Dog and cat nutrition*, Oxford, England, 1988, Pergamon Press, pp 75–96.
67. Hammel EP, Kronfeld DS, Ganjam VK, and others: Metabolic responses to exhaustive exercise in racing sledge dogs fed diets containing medium, low and zero carbohydrate, *Am J Clin Nutr* 30:409–418, 1976.
68. Kronfeld DS: Diet and the performance of racing sledge dogs, *J Am Vet Med Assoc* 162:470–473, 1973.
69. Orr NWM: The feeding of sledge dogs on Antarctic expeditions, *Br J Nutr* 20:1–11, 1966.
70. Hinchcliff KW, Reinhart GA, Burr JR, and others: Ultimate athletes? Metabolizable energy intake and sustained metabolic scope in Alaskan sled dogs. Manuscript submitted for publication, 1994.

71. Reynolds, AJ: The effect of diet and training on energy substrate storage and utilization in trained and untrained sled dogs, In *Nutrition and physiology of Alaskan sled dogs*, Abstracts of a symposium held at the College of Veterinary Medicine, The Ohio State University, Sept 5, 1992.

72. Gannon JR: Nutritional requirements of the working dog, *Vet Ann* 21:161–166, 1981.

73. Orr NWM: The food requirements of Antarctic sledge dogs, In Graham-Jones O, editor: *Canine and feline nutritional requirements*, England, 1964, Pergamon Press, pp 101–112.

74. Iams Pet Food Company: Data provided by the Iams Technical Center, Lewisburg, Ohio, 1993.

75. Barrette D: Feeding the sporting dog, *Can Vet J* 30:440–441, 1989.

76. Armstrong RB: Distribution of fiber types in locomotory muscles of dogs, *Am J Anat* 163:87–98, 1982.

77. Guy PS, Snow DH: Skeletal muscle fibre composition in the dog and its relationship to athletic ability, *Res Vet Sci* 31:244–248, 1981.

78. Karlsson J, Saltin B: Diet, muscle glycogen and endurance performance, *J Appl Physiol* 31:203–206, 1971.

79. Phinney SD, Bistrian BR, Evans WJ, and others: The human metabolic response to chronic ketosis without caloric restriction: preservation of submaximal exercise capability with reduced carbohydrate oxidation, *Metabolism* 32:769–776, 1983.

80. Coyle EF, Hagberg JM, Hurley BF, and others: Carbohydrate feeding during prolonged strenuous exercise can delay fatigue, *J Appl Physiol* 55:230–235, 1983.

81. Hermansen L, Hultman E, Saltin B: Muscle glycogen during prolonged, severe exercise, *Acta Physiol Scand* 71:129–139, 1967.

82. Bergstrom J, Hermansen L, Hultman E, and others: Diet, muscle glycogen and physical performance, *Acta Physiol Scand* 71:140–150, 1967.

83. Sherman WM, Costill DL, Fink WJ, and others: Effect of exercise-diet manipulation on muscle glycogen and its subsequent utilization during performance, *Int J Sports Med* 2:114–118, 1981.

84. Evans WJ, Hughes VA: Dietary carbohydrates and endurance exercise, *Am J Clin Nutr* 41:1146–1154, 1985.

85. Ivy JF, Miller W, Power V: Endurance improved by ingestion of a glucose polymer supplement, *Med Sci Sports Exerc* 15:466–471, 1983.

86. Bergstrom J, Hultman E, Roch-Norlund AE: Muscle glycogen synthetase in normal subjects: basal values, effect of glycogen depletion by exercise and of a carbohydrate rich diet following exercise, *Scand J Clin Lab Invest* 29:231–236, 1972.

87. Bergstrom J, Hultman E: Muscle glycogen synthesis after exercise: an enhancing factor localized to the muscle cells in man, *Nature* 210:309–310, 1966.

88. Kronfeld DS, Adkins TO, Downey RL: Nutrition, anaerobic and aerobic exercise, and stress. In Burger IH, Rivers JPW, editors: *Nutrition of the dog and cat*, Cambridge University Press, Cambridge, England, 1989, pp 133–145.

89. Hickson RC, Rennie MJ, Conlee RK, and others: Effects of increased plasma fatty acids on glycogen utilization and endurance, *J Appl Physiol* 43:829–833, 1977.

90. Newsholme EA: Control of metabolism and the integration of fuel supply for the marathon runner. In Knuttgen HG, Vogel JA, Poortmans J, editors: *Biochemistry of exercise*, Champaign, Ill, 1983, Human Kinetic Publishers, pp 144–150.

91. Jansson E: Diet and muscle metabolism in man, *Acta Physiol Scand* Suppl:487, 1980.

92. Miller WC, Bryce GR, Conlee RF: Adaptations to a high-fat diet increases endurance in male rats, *J Appl Physiol* 56:78–83, 1984.

93. Therriault DG, Beller GA, Smoake JA, and others: Intramuscular energy sources in dogs during physical work, *J Lipid Res* 14:54–61, 1973.

94.   Paul P, Issekutz B: Role of extramuscular energy sources in the metabolism of the exercising dog, *Am J Physiol* 22:615–622, 1976.

95.   Downey RL, Kronfeld DS, Banta CA: Diet of beagles affects stamina, *J Am Anim Hosp Assoc* 16:273–277, 1980.

96.   Sahlin K: Effect of acidosis on energy metabolism and force generation in skeletal muscle. In Knuttgen HG, Vogel JA, Poortmans J, editors: *Biochemistry of exercise*, Champaign, Ill, 1983, Human Kinetics Publishers, pp 151–160.

97.   McNamara JH: Nutrition for military working dogs under stress, *Vet Med Sm Anim Clin* 67:615–623, 1972.

98.   Kronfeld DS, Hammel EP, Ramberg CF Jr, and others: Hematological and metabolic responses to training in racing sled dogs fed diets containing medium, low, or zero carbohydrate, *Am J Clin Nutr* 30:419–430, 1977.

99.   Adkins TO, Kronfeld DS: Diet of racing sled dogs affects erythrocyte depression by stress, *Can Vet J* 23:260–263, 1982.

100.   Gisolfi CV: Water and electrolyte metabolism in exercise. In Fox EL, editor: *Nutrient utilization during exercise*, Columbus, Ohio, 1983, Ross Laboratories, pp 21–25.

101.   Fink WJ, Greenleaf JE: Fluid intake and athletic performance. In Haskell W, Scala J, and Whittam J, editors: *Nutrition and athletic performance, Proceedings of a conference on nutritional determinants of athletic performance*, 1981, pp 33–66.

102.   Costill DL, Coyle E, Dalsky G, and others: Effects of elevated plasma FFA and insulin on muscle glycogen usage during exercise, *J Appl Physiol* 43:695–699, 1977.

103.   Foster C, Costill DL, Fink WJ: Effects of pre-exercise feedings on endurance performance, *Med Sci Sports* 11:1–5, 1979.

104.   Ivy JL, Costill DL, Fink WJ, and others: Influence of caffeine and carbohydrate feedings on endurance performance, *Med Sci Sports* 11:6–11, 1979.

105.   Askew EW: Fat metabolism in exercise. In Fox EL, editor: *Nutrient utilization during exercise*, Columbus, Ohio, 1983, Ross Laboratories, pp 13–21.

106.   Saltin B, Karlsson J: Muscle glycogen utilization during work of different intensities. In *Muscle metabolism during exercise*, Vol II, New York, 1971, Plenum Press, pp 289–300.

107.   Bjotvedt G, Weems CW, Foley K: Strenuous exercise may cause health hazards for racing greyhounds, *Vet Med* 79:1481–1487, 1984.

108.   Rose RJ, Bloomberg MS: Responses to sprint exercise in the greyhound: effects on hematology, plasma biochemistry and muscle metabolics, International Greyhound Symposium, Orlando, Fla, 1983.

109.   Donovan DM, Brooks GA: Endurance training affects lactate clearance not lactate production, *Am J Physiol* 244:E83–E92, 1983.

110.   Durrer JL, Hannon JP: Seasonal variations of intake of dogs living in an arctic environment, *Am J Physiol* 202:375–378, 1962.

111.   Blaza SE: Energy requirements of dogs in cool conditions, *Can Pract* 9:10–15, 1982.

112.   Campbell IT, Donaldson J: Energy requirements of antarctic sledge dogs, *Br J Nutr* 45:95–98, 1981.

113.   Finke MD: Evaluation of the energy requirements of adult kennel dogs, *J Nutr* 121:S22–S28, 1991.

114.   Williams MH: Vitamin supplementation and physical performance. In Fox EL, editor: *Nutrient utilization during exercise*, Columbus, Ohio, 1983, Ross Laboratories, pp 13–21.

115.   Brace JJ: Theories of aging, *Vet Clin North Am Sm Anim Pract* 11:811–814, 1981.

116.   Mosier JE: Effect of aging on body systems of the dog, *Vet Clin North Am Sm Anim Pract* 19:1–13, 1989.

117.   MacDonald J: Neoplastic diseases of the integument. Proceedings of the American Animal Hospital Association, 1987, pp 17–20.

118.   Debartola SP, Rutgers HC, Zack PM: Clinicopathologic findings associated with chronic renal disease in cats: 4 cases (1973 – 1984), *J Am Vet Med Assoc* 190:1196–1202, 1987.

119. Polzin DJ: Topics in general medicine: general nutrition; the problems associated with renal failure, *Vet Med* 82:1027–1035, 1987.
120. Cowgill LD, Spangler WL: Renal insufficiency in geriatric dogs, *Vet Clin North Am Sm Anim Pract* 11:727–749, 1981.
121. Kaufman GM: Renal function in the geriatric dog, *Comp Cont Ed Pract Vet* 6:108–109, 1984.
122. Hamlin RL: Managing cardiologic disorders in geriatric dogs, Proceedings of the Geriatric Medicine Symposium, 1987. pp 14–18.
123. Markham RW, Hodgkins EM: Geriatric nutrition, *Vet Clin North Am Sm Anim Pract* 19:165–185, 1989.
124. Houpt KA, Beaver B: Behavioral problems of geriatric dogs and cats, *Vet Clin North Amer Sm Anim Pract* 11:643–652, 1981.
125. Zanni E, Calloway DH, Zezulka AY: Protein requirements of elderly men, *J Nutr* 109:513–524, 1979.
126. Wannemacher RW, McCoy JR: Determination of optimal dietary protein requirements of young and old dogs, *J Nutr* 88:66–74, 1966.
127. Sheffy BE, William AJ: Nutrition and the aging animal, *Vet Clin North Am Sm Anim Pract* 11:669–675, 1981.
128. Branam JE: Dietary management of geriatric dogs and cats, *Vet Tech* 8:501–503, 1987.
129. Garvey M: Topics in geriatric medicine: general nutrition; the problems associated with renal failure, *Vet Med* 82:1027–1035, 1987.
130. Hostetter TH, Rennke HG, Brenner BM: Compensatory renal hemodynamic injury: a final common pathway of residual nephron destruction, *Am J Kidney Dis* 1:310–314, 1982.
131. Walser M: Does dietary therapy have a role in the predialysis patient?, *Am J Clin Nutr* 33:1629–1637, 1980.
132. Finco DR, Brown SA, Crowell WA, and others: Effect of phosphorus/calcium-restricted and phosphorus/calcium-replete 32% diets in dogs with chronic renal failure, *Am J Vet Res* 53:157–163, 1992.
133. Brown SA, Crowell WA, Barsanti JA: Beneficial effects of dietary mineral restriction in dogs with marked reduction of functional renal mass, *J Am Soc Nephrol* 1:1169–1179, 1991.
134. Feline Practice, Care of old cats, *Feline Practice,* 13:3–40, 1983.

Feeding Practices: Problems, Fads, and Fallacies

Previous sections have examined the nutrient requirements of dogs and cats, types of pet foods that can be fed, and proper feeding management practices throughout the lifetime of the healthy pet. Several decades ago, before much was known about the nutritional needs of dogs and cats and before nutritionally balanced pet foods were produced, nutrient deficiencies were a common occurrence in companion animals. Today, pet foods that provide complete nutrition and have the potential to promote optimal health are readily available to pet owners and professionals. As a direct result of advances in scientific knowledge and in the formulation of commercial pet foods, the occurrence of serious nutrient deficiencies in companion animals has become extremely rare. Feeding management problems are now more likely to result in problems of overnutrition rather than undernutrition. The provision of surplus calories, supplementation with excess amounts of certain vitamins and minerals, and feeding young dogs to promote a rapid rate of growth are all practices that can result in developmental disease and chronic health problems. Less commonly, deficiencies or toxicities of certain vitamins can occur because of the presence of inhibitory substances in the food or improper feeding practices. This section focuses on problems and fallacies of feeding management that can cause nutrient imbalances and impair the health of growing and mature companion animals. These problems include obesity, feeding for a high rate of growth, supplementation with certain nutrients, deficiencies and excesses of certain vitamins, feeding inappropriate food items to pets, and common nutrition myths.

Development and Treatment
of Obesity

O besity is currently the most common nutritional disorder that occurs in companion animals in the United States. Surveys have reported incidence rates of between 24% and 34% in adult dogs.[1-4] It can be theorized that the incidence of obesity has increased because a sedentary lifestyle has become the norm rather than the exception for many dogs. In addition, the provision of highly palatable and energy-dense foods further contributes to the energy imbalance that leads to obesity.

Less information is available on the incidence of obesity in cats. A survey conducted in the 1970s reported an incidence rate of only 9% in pet cats.[1] However, a recent study involving 233 cats reported that 40% of the cats were either overweight or obese.[5] The increased popularity of the cat as a house pet, decreased daily activity of cats that are confined indoors, and increased availability of highly palatable cat foods are all factors that may be responsible for the dramatic increase in the incidence of obesity in cats in the United States.

Effects

Obesity is defined as the excessive accumulation of fat in the adipose storage areas of the body.[6] A body weight that is 20% or more above normal is generally considered to be indicative of obesity, and health problems in human subjects begin to increase when weight reaches 15% or greater above ideal body weight.[1,7,8] It is probable that this applies to dogs and cats. Dogs and cats that are overweight have an increased risk of chronic health problems, such as the development of hyperinsulinemia, glucose intolerance, and diabetes.[9] Obese dogs with type III diabetes exhibit glucose intolerance and elevated basal insulin and insulin response curves. When body weight is reduced, glucose intolerance usually improves to near normal values.[10] It has been postulated that obesity in dogs, as in humans, modulates glucose and insulin homeostasis, resulting in hyperinsulinemia and various degrees of glucose intolerance. It is very likely that persistent hyperinsulinemia caused by obesity is an important factor in the eventual development of diabetes mellitus in overweight pets.

Obesity may also contribute to the development of pulmonary and cardiovascular disease. Excess weight puts a strain on the circulatory system because an increased cardiac workload is required to perfuse an increased tissue mass. This increased workload may cause additional strain on a heart that is already weakened by fatty infiltration. The physical effects of carrying excess weight also contribute to exercise and heat intolerance, joint and locomotor problems, and the development of arthritis.[11] Dogs and cats that are obese have an increased surgical and anesthetic risk, and they experience an increased incidence of morbidity and mortality following surgical procedures.

TYPES OF OBESITY

The basic problem of obesity involves an increased mass of body fat produced either by an enlargement of fat cell size alone (hypertrophic obesity) or by an increase in both fat cell size and fat cell number (hyperplastic obesity). Pets that develop hyperplastic obesity are generally believed to be difficult to treat and have a poor long-term prognosis. Normal adipocyte hyperplasia occurs during specific critical periods of development. In most species, these periods occur during early growth and occasionally during puberty.[12-14] Once adulthood is reached, fat cell number does not normally increase further. Overfeeding during adulthood results in an increase in fat cell size, but no change in fat cell number. Although conditions of extreme and prolonged overfeeding can result in fat cell hyperplasia in some animals, the majority of cases of adult onset obesity are a result of fat cell hypertrophy alone.[15,16]

The body has the capacity to add new adipocytes, but it is not able to reduce its existing adipocyte number. This phenomenon, called the "ratchet effect," indicates that body fat can always increase, but it cannot decrease below a minimum level that is set by the total number of adipocytes and their need to remain lipid filled. This fact is of importance when considering growth rate and weight gain in young, developing dogs and cats. Data from several studies with laboratory animals show that overnutrition during growth results in increased fat cell number and total body fatness during adulthood.[17,18] Superfluous fat cell hyperplasia during the critical periods of adipose tissue growth may produce a long-term stimulus to gain excess weight in the form of excess adipocytes.[7] The greater number of fat cells results in both an increased predisposition toward obesity in adulthood and increased difficulty in maintaining weight loss when it occurs. Therefore the reason that hyperplastic obesity is difficult to treat is that the excess fat cells maintain a stimulus for lipid deposition and are resistant to reductions in fat content below a certain level. Persistent overnutrition during development in growing dogs and cats may result in both hypertrophy and hyperplasia of adipocytes,

Factors Contributing to Obesity in Companion Animals	
Endogenous Factors	**Exogenous Factors**
Age, sex, and reproductive status	Voluntary activity level
Presence of hormonal abnormalities or	External influences on food intake
hypothalamic lesions	Diet composition and palatability
Genetic predisposition	Living environment and type of life-style

leading to the development of obesity. The potential for an animal to produce excess numbers of fat cells during specific critical periods illustrates the importance of proper weight control throughout growth.

CAUSES OF OBESITY

The fundamental underlying cause in all cases of obesity is an imbalance between energy intake and energy expenditure that results in a persistent energy surplus. Excess energy is stored primarily as fat, resulting in weight gain and a change in body composition. Although the problem of obesity appears very simple in terms of energy balance, a multitude of underlying causes for the imbalance exist, not all of which are completely understood. Moreover, the development of obesity in an individual dog or cat can be the result of several separate influencing factors occurring simultaneously (see the accompanying box).

Factors that may contribute to the development of obesity can be classified as having either endogenous or exogenous origin. Endogenous factors include the animal's age, sex and reproductive status, hormonal abnormalities, hypothalamic lesions, and genetic predisposition. Exogenous factors include voluntary activity level, external influences on food intake, diet composition, food palatability, and type of life-style. Most cases of companion animal obesity are a result of overfeeding, under exercising, or a combination of the two.[10,19,20] It is important to recognize that each of these situations may be a result of either external or internal aberrations. For example, a dog may consume excess food because the diet that is being fed is highly palatable and of high caloric density (exogenous stimuli). On the other hand, the cause would be of endogenous origin if overeating was in response to lesions involving the satiety center located in the ventral medial hypothalamus.[21,22] The various causative factors that may be involved in the development of obesity are discussed in the following section.

DECREASED ENERGY EXPENDITURE

An animal's energy expenditure can be divided into three major components, resting metabolic rate (RMR), voluntary muscular activity, and meal-induced thermogenesis (see Section 2, pp. 77–79). Although the importance in companion animals is not known, a fourth component, called adaptive thermogenesis, may also contribute to energy expenditure. The existence of an abnormally low RMR, meal-induced thermogenesis, or adaptive thermogenesis have all been studied as possible causes of weight gain in animals and humans. Studies measuring the RMR have not supported the claim that obese individuals gain weight because they possess abnormally low RMR values.[23-25] In fact, the RMR of most obese subjects is actually higher than that of normal weight subjects. Although the state of obesity is characterized primarily by excessive amounts of body fat, overweight animals also have increased amounts of lean body tissue. The elevated RMR accompanying obesity is accounted for by this increased, respiring tissue mass.[26] When the RMR is expressed in relationship to the total amount of lean body mass in obese animals, it is within a normal range.[23,24]

Subnormal, meal-induced thermogenesis in an animal would result in lower energy expenditure than would normally be expected after the ingestion of a meal.[27] The long-term result of such a deficit would be a slightly positive energy balance, leading to an increased propensity toward weight gain. Although such a defect in a pre-obese animal would account for only a small number of calories per day, it may have the potential to affect long-term energy balance and contribute to the development of obesity. However, studies with human subjects have shown that a defect in meal-induced thermogenesis could not singularly account for the large increases in weight that are seen in obese subjects.[28]

Lastly, the existence of adaptive thermogenesis in several species of small mammals is widely accepted. However, the inference that other species can adapt to periods of overconsumption by increasing energy expenditure through changes in adaptive thermogenesis is still very controversial. If adaptive thermogenesis is present in species other than small rodents, it is possible that a defect in the response to overfeeding may be of importance in the development of obesity in some individuals. However, the paucity of well-controlled studies, coupled with the publication of conflicting results, leads to the conclusion that adaptive thermogenesis in response to overeating is probably not a major contributing factor to the development of obesity in companion animals.

Reduced voluntary activity is the most important contributor to decreased energy expenditure in overweight companion animals. In today's society, most dogs are kept as companions and house pets rather than as active, working partners to their human owners. Cats are also experiencing decreased activity levels. Many cats lead sedentary, indoor lives rather than having the roam of farms and neighborhoods as in the past. Additional factors that influence the voluntary activity level of dogs and cats are breed, temperament, age, type of life-style, reproductive status, and the presence of certain chronic illnesses or developmental disorders. In normal animals experiencing moderate levels of exercise, physical activity contributes approximately 30% of the body's total energy expenditure.[29] Decreased voluntary activity results in a direct reduction of this energy expenditure and can also affect a pet's daily food intake. Research studies have shown that completely sedentary animals actually consume more food and gain more weight than do animals that experience moderate activity levels.[30] It appears that inactivity below a certain level cannot be entirely compensated for by an adequate decrease in food intake. As a result, animals that are maintained at or below this minimum activity level will consume more than their energy needs and inevitably gain weight.

Endocrine Disorders

Two endocrine disorders that may influence body weight in companion animals are hypothyroidism and hyperadrenocorticism. The condition of hypothyroidism results in a decreased RMR, which in turn may cause a predisposition for obesity. This disorder is diagnosed when clinical signs are observed and plasma levels of one or both of the thyroid variants (T_3 and T_4) are found to be below normal. Idiopathic atrophy of the thyroid gland is the most common cause of hypothyroidism in the dog.[31] This disorder occurs most frequently in middle-aged and older dogs, and certain breeds show a higher incidence of it than the general population. These breeds include golden retrievers, Irish setters, English bulldogs, basenjis, and some spaniel breeds.[31] Hypothyroidism can occur in cats, but it is much less common and has not been well documented.[32] Clinical signs of hypothyroidism include lethargy, dulled mental attitude, and easy fatigability. Skin changes that are commonly seen include alopecia, the development of a dry, coarse coat, and hyperpigmentation of skin.[33] Cold sensitivity and weight gain are two clinical signs that directly result from the decreased RMR associated with hypothyroidism. However, only a small percentage of dogs exhibit either or both of these signs.[33,34] Assessment of thyroid hormone levels should always be included in the differential diagnosis of obesity in companion animals. However, hypothyroidism is probably responsible for only a small percentage of cases of overt obesity in pets.

Hyperadrenocorticism (Cushing's syndrome) can also result in increased body size. This disorder is caused by the production of excess corticosteroids by the adrenal cortex. It is seen most commonly in middle-aged and older dogs; and breed predilections have been observed in poodles, dachshunds, boxers, Brussels griffons, and Boston terriers.[31] Cushing's syndrome can occur in cats, but it is quite rare.[32] The primary clinical signs of this disorder include polyuria, polydypsia, lethargy, hair loss, and the development of a pendulous abdomen.[32,35] True obesity occurs in approximately 50% of the cases, although the presence of an enlarged abdomen may be perceived to be obesity by some pet owners. Diagnosis is based on adrenal function tests and can be used to differentiate between Cushing's-induced obesity and obesity as a result of other causes.

Effects of Neutering

Obesity is more prevalent in neutered than in intact companion animals. Survey studies have found that neutered male and female dogs are more likely to be overweight than are intact dogs.[3-5] Veterinarians usually encourage clients to castrate or spay their pets before they become sexually mature. As a result, many dogs and cats are neutered between 6 months and 1 year of age. This time period corresponds to a natural decrease in the pet's growth rate and energy needs. If owners are not aware of this change and continue to feed their pet the same amount of food, excess weight gain will result. Because spaying and neutering often occur just before maturity, the change in sexual status may be erroneously blamed for a weight gain that was actually the result of diminished energy needs and excess food intake.

Increasing age and a change in sexual status are also associated with a decrease in voluntary physical activity. In general, puppies and kittens are more active than adult animals. If an individual dog or cat naturally decreases its activity level as it reaches maturity, the consumption of the same quantity of food will result in weight gain. In addition, intact animals display sexually motivated behaviors that increase the amount of energy expended as physical activity. Male dogs and cats have an inclination to roam and fight with other males, and intact females increase their physical activity and roaming behavior during estrus.[36]

Certain reproductive hormones may affect voluntary food intake. Many animals will spontaneously decrease food intake during estrus, and the cause of this change has been attributed to the female sex hormone, estrogen.[37] A study with dogs examined the influence of estrus on voluntary food intake in 12 beagle bitches. Results showed that there was a tendency for females to decrease food consumption during the week that they were in estrus. Another study examined food intake patterns in ovariohysterectomized and sham-operated bitches. Over a period of 90 days, the ovariohysterectomized bitches gained significantly more weight and consumed greater amounts of food than did the sham-operated controls. The authors of this study attributed the difference in weight gain to an increase in food intake and a decrease in voluntary activity.[37]

Similarly, a study comparing intact to neutered male cats found that neutered males ate less but gained more weight than did intact males. This difference was theorized to be the result of decreased physical activity and increased efficiency of energy use that occurred with the loss of testosterone in the neutered animals.[38]

Old Age

As an adult animal ages, lean body mass declines, resulting in a decreased RMR and total daily energy needs. The loss of lean body mass is exacerbated if aging is accompanied by a decrease in voluntary activity. The total daily energy needs of an average size, 7-year-old dog may decrease by as much as 20% compared with when it was a young adult.[36] If food intake does not decrease proportionately with decreasing energy needs as an animal ages, weight gain will result.

Genetic Predisposition

Several types of genetic obesity have been shown to exist in laboratory animals.[7] Studies have also indicated that there is a genetic component to obesity in some human subjects.[39–41] The fact that certain breeds of dogs have a disproportionately high incidence of obesity indicates that genetics may be a contributing factor in this species as well. Cocker spaniels, Labrador retrievers, Shetland sheepdogs, and several of the small terrier breeds have a higher incidence of obesity than the general population of dogs. In contrast, boxers, German shepherd dogs, fox terriers, and the sight hound breeds have a low incidence of obesity.[2,4] It is theorized that the genetic tendency toward obesity originally had survival value for the dog in its wild state because those animals who effi-

ciently stored excess energy as fat were better able to tolerate long periods of food deprivation.[42] No data have been reported concerning breed predilections to obesity in pet cats, but such predilections may also exist in this species.

Alterations in Food Intake

Food intake is regulated in all animals by a complex system involving both internal physiological controls and external cues. Internal signals that affect appetite, hunger, and satiety include mechanical stimulation from the gastrointestinal tract; physiological responses to the sight, sound, and smell of food; and changes in plasma concentrations of specific nutrients, hormones, and peptides. External stimuli include factors such as food availability, presence of other animals, timing and size of meals, food composition and texture, and diet palatability (see Section 2, pp. 82–85). It appears that the external cues that affect food intake are most important in the regulation of food intake and development of obesity in companion animals.[27]

External controls of food intake include stimuli such as diet palatability, food composition and texture, and the timing and environment of meals. The most important of these factors is feeding pets highly palatable diets that may induce some animals to overconsume. Studies with laboratory animals have shown that when rats are offered a highly palatable diet, they overeat and become obese.[43] This effect has been observed with high-fat diets, calorically dense diets, and cafeteria-type diets, which provide a large variety of highly palatable food items.[44] Moreover, the long-term exposure to highly palatable foods in human subjects leads to permanent increases in body weight, fat cell size, and fat cell number.[7] Although an endogenous predisposition to obesity and increased efficiency of weight gain may occur in some animals, the largest portion of weight gain that is observed when animals are fed highly palatable diets is a direct result of overconsumption.[44] Studies with human subjects have demonstrated that the quantity of food consumed varies directly with its palatability, and palatability does not appear to interact with levels of food deprivation. In other words, if food is perceived to be very appealing, an individual tends to eat more of it regardless of the initial level of hunger.[45]

Palatability is an important diet characteristic that is heavily promoted in the marketing of commercial pet foods. Many pet owners select a product based on their own perceptions of the food's appeal and their pet's acceptance of the diet, rather than on indicators of nutritional adequacy. Semi-moist foods contain variable amounts of simple sugars and other humectants that contribute to palatability. Canned pet foods and some premium dry foods are very high in fat content. Fat contributes both to the palatability and caloric density of the food. Feeding pets highly palatable foods on an *ad libitum* basis may contribute to both the development and the maintenance of obesity because many pets readily overconsume these foods. Similarly, the common practice of feeding a variety of table scraps and other appealing treats to dogs and cats can induce many pets to overeat and gain excessive amounts of weight. Most of the table scraps that are fed to pets also contain a high proportion of their calories from fat, and so can further contribute to a caloric imbalance.

The social setting of meals also influences eating behavior. Most pets will increase food intake when consuming food in the presence of other animals.[22,46] This process is called social facilitation and is usually more pronounced in dogs than in cats. In most pets, social facilitation causes a moderate increase in food intake and an increased rate of eating. In some, the increase in food intake in response to another animal's presence can be extreme enough to singularly cause weight gain.[22]

Similarly, meal frequency affects both food intake and metabolic efficiency. An increase in the number of meals per day results in an increased energy loss to meal-induced thermogenesis (see Section 2, pp. 83–84). There is also evidence in humans indicating that a decrease in lipogenesis (fat tissue synthesis) occurs when multiple meals are fed compared with consuming the same number of calories in only one or two meals.[47] However, if several meals are provided per day, portions must be strictly controlled. Increased feeding frequency often causes increased voluntary intake, thereby offsetting any metabolic benefits of multiple meals.

A final external factor that may be a contributing cause of obesity in companion animals is the nutrient composition of the diet. Nutrient composition affects both the efficiency of nutrient metabolism and the amount of food that is voluntarily consumed. When fed *ab libitum*, high-fat diets will promote weight gain and obesity.[48] Although most animals decrease the volume of intake of a high-fat diet in an attempt to balance energy needs, the greater caloric density of the diet and its increased palatability usually cause a total increase in energy intake. Additionally, the metabolic efficiency of converting dietary fat to body fat for storage is higher than is the efficiency of converting dietary carbohydrate or protein to body fat (see Section 2, p. 84). Therefore, if an animal is consuming more than its caloric requirement of a particular diet and if the excess calories are provided by fat, more weight will be gained than if the excess calories are coming from either carbohydrate or protein.

The caloric distribution of fat, carbohydrate, and protein is very important in determining a diet's potential contribution to weight imbalance in dogs and cats. As the percentage of metabolizable energy (ME) calories from fat increases in a pet food, the ability of the diet to meet high-energy demands of a hard-working dog also increases. However, if this diet is fed to a dog that does not need it, weight gain may occur if intake is not strictly monitored. A diet that contains a low percentage of ME from fat will aid in weight loss and/or in the maintenance of normal body weight in a sedentary adult animal. The selection of a pet food should therefore match the proportion of ME contributed by fat to the animal's life-style and activity level (Figure 26-1).

DEVELOPMENT OF OBESITY

Two stages occur during the development of obesity: the dynamic phase and the static phase. During the initial dynamic phase, an animal consumes more energy than it expends and the surplus energy is deposited as both body fat and lean body tissue. As the dog or cat gains weight, its RMR increases proportionately to the increase in lean

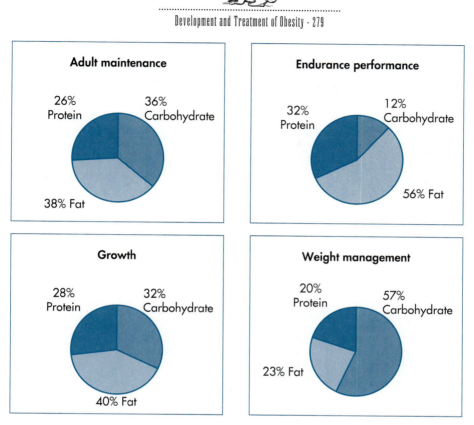

FIGURE 26-1
Recommended caloric distribution of dog foods (expressed as % of ME calories)

body mass. Eventually the increased RMR, coupled with the increased energy expenditure that is needed to move a larger body size, will offset the caloric surplus. At this point, zero energy balance is achieved and the animal stops gaining weight. The static phase of obesity occurs when the animal is no longer gaining weight but achieves energy balance and maintains its overweight condition for a prolonged period of time.

If the initial, dynamic phase occurs at a young age or if the energy surplus is extreme, fat cell hyperplasia occurs along with fat cell hypertrophy. Research in other species has shown that hyperplastic obesity is more resistant to treatment than is simple hypertrophic obesity.[17,18] The presence of additional numbers of fat cells results in a higher percentage of body fat. Therefore an animal with fat cell hyperplasia will have a higher proportion of body fat than will an animal that weighs the same amount but has a normal number of fat cells. This difference affects energy expenditure and the ability to lose weight and maintain this loss when it occurs.

TABLE 26-1
Standard Weights of Popular Breeds of Dogs (lb)

BREED	MALE	FEMALE
Basset hound	65–75	50–65
Beagle (13")	13–18	13–16
Beagle (15")	17–22	15–20
Boxer	55–70	50–60
Chihuahua	2–6	2–6
Chow chow	45–50	40–50
Cocker spaniel	25–30	20–25
Collie	65–75	50–65
Dachshund, miniature	8–10	8–10
Dachshund, standard	16–22	16–22
Dalmation	50–65	45–55
Doberman pinscher	65–80	55–70
English springer spaniel	49–55	40–45
German shepherd dog	75–90	65–80
Golden retriever	65–75	55–65
Labrador retriever	65–80	55–70
Maltese	4–6	4–6
Miniature schnauzer	16–18	12–16
Pekingese	10–14	10–14
Pomeranian	4–7	3–5
Poodle, standard	50–60	45–55
Poodle, miniature	17–20	15–20
Poodle, toy	7–10	7–10
Rottweiler	80–95	70–85
Shetland sheepdog	16–22	14–18
Shih Tzu	12–17	10–15
Siberian husky	45–60	35–50
Yorkshire terrier	4–7	3–6

DIAGNOSIS OF OBESITY

The diagnosis of obesity in companion animals should always include an examination for the presence of edema, ascites, hypothyroidism, hyperadrenocorticism, and diabetes mellitus. After these diseases have been ruled out, a comparison of the pet's current weight with previous weight measurements or with its weight shortly after reaching adulthood may be indicative of abnormal weight gain. In some cases involving purebred dogs and cats, a comparison of the pet's body weight with the weights suggested by the breed's standard may also be a useful guideline for determining ideal body weight (Table 26-1; see also Appendix 2).

Estimating the percentage of body fat is the most accurate method of diagnosing obesity. Ultrasound provides a noninvasive, rapid method for measuring subcutaneous fat, but is not yet practical in most clinical settings.[27,49] Likewise, measurements of total body density are very accurate, but are usually not feasible.[3] The most practical method used to assess excess body fat and obesity in dogs and cats is palpating the thickness of tissue overlying the rib cage and along the ventral abdomen.[3,19,50,51] If a dog or cat is too thin, the ribs will be easily seen. An animal of normal weight will have barely visi-

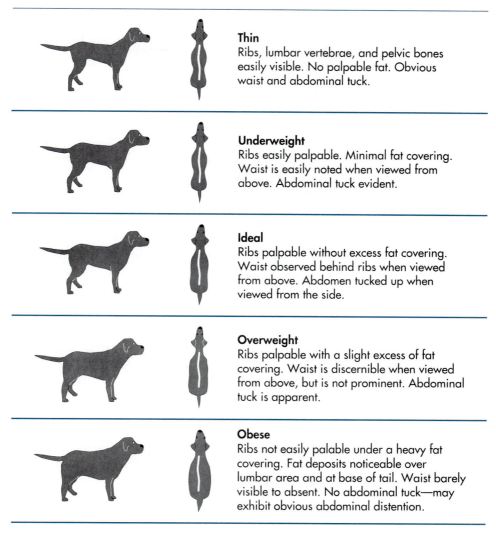

Thin
Ribs, lumbar vertebrae, and pelvic bones easily visible. No palpable fat. Obvious waist and abdominal tuck.

Underweight
Ribs easily palpable. Minimal fat covering. Waist is easily noted when viewed from above. Abdominal tuck evident.

Ideal
Ribs palpable without excess fat covering. Waist observed behind ribs when viewed from above. Abdomen tucked up when viewed from the side.

Overweight
Ribs palpable with a slight excess of fat covering. Waist is discernible when viewed from above, but is not prominent. Abdominal tuck is apparent.

Obese
Ribs not easily palable under a heavy fat covering. Fat deposits noticeable over lumbar area and at base of tail. Waist barely visible to absent. No abdominal tuck—may exhibit obvious abdominal distention.

FIGURE 26-2
Visual assessment of body condition in the dog.

ble ribs that can be easily felt when palpated. An overweight animal's ribs will not be visible and an overlying layer of fat can be felt. The pet is diagnosed as grossly obese if the ribs cannot be felt at all.[51]

Visual assessment of the pet provides additional support for the diagnosis of obesity. An animal at normal weight should have an hourglass shape when viewed from above (Figure 26-2).[36] The loss of a waist as a result of excess fat between the muscles of the abdominal wall, and the presence of a pendulous abdomen as a result of fat accumula-

tion in intraabdominal sites are both indicative of excess body fat.[19] Dogs have a tendency to develop fat deposits around the base of the tail, but cats often accumulate fat just anterior to the inguinal region. Subjective evaluation of the animal's gait, exercise tolerance, and overall appearance can also be used to support a diagnosis of obesity.

Management of Obesity

The short-term goal of the treatment of obesity is to reduce body fat stores. This goal relies on the induction of a negative energy balance. Negative energy balance can be accomplished by restricting dietary intake, stimulating total energy expenditure, or a combination of the two.[52] The long term goal of treatment is for the pet to attain its ideal body weight and to maintain this weight for the remainder of its life.

Dogs and cats that are 15% or more above their ideal body weight should be placed on a strict weight loss program. When initiating such a program, the determined rate of weight loss should be high enough to ensure a noticeable change within several weeks, yet low enough to minimize excessive hunger and the loss of lean body tissue. Because of the large variation in size and degree of obesity in individual animals, a recommended percentage of body weight loss per week should be used rather than a set quantity of weight loss. Depending on the degree of obesity and the age and health of the pet, a weight loss of 1% to 3% of the animal's total body weight per week is recommended.[36] For example, an adult dog with an ideal body weight of 25 kilograms (kg) (55 lbs) that actually weighs 30 kg (66 lbs) should lose between 0.3 and 0.9 kg (0.7 to 1.9 lbs) per week. A midpoint of 0.6 kg (1.3 lbs) can be used as a target loss when calculating this dog's energy needs for the weight loss program (Table 26-2 and the box on p. 284).

Three important components should be included in all weight reduction programs. These are behavior modification, exercise, and dietary modification. Dietary modification and exercise will create an energy deficit that will result in weight loss. Behavior modification can be helpful in changing the owner's behavior and the pet's behavior, which will aid in weight loss and the prevention of weight regain.

Behavior Modification

Behavior modification techniques are designed to change habits of the owner that may have contributed to the pet's initial weight gain. Such activities include providing the pet with high-calorie table scraps, self-feeding a highly palatable and energy-dense food, encouraging or allowing begging, and frequently feeding dog biscuits and treats.[20] Some changes that can be instituted include keeping the pet out of the kitchen while meals are being prepared, decreasing the number of treats that are given per day, breaking treats into small pieces and giving only a small piece at a time to the pet, providing attention and petting instead of food treats, keeping the pet out of the dining room during mealtimes, eliminating all "people foods" from the diet, and maintaining the pet on a portion-controlled feeding regimen.[20, 51] Establishing a strictly regulated schedule so that all meals are provided at the same time each day can also help to eliminate begging at times.[20, 53]

TABLE 26-2
Energy Requirements for Weight Loss in Dogs and Cats

CURRENT WEIGHT (LB)	CURRENT WEIGHT (KG)	ME* (KCAL/DAY)	60% OF ME (KCAL/DAY)	AMOUNT† (CUP/DAY)
Dogs				
5	2.3	246	148	½
10	4.5	400	240	⅔
15	6.8	525	315	1
20	9.1	636	382	1
25	11.4	739	443	1¼
30	13.6	835	501	1½
35	15.9	926	556	1⅔
40	18.2	1012	607	1¾
45	20.5	1095	657	1⅞
50	22.7	1175	705	2
55	25.0	1253	752	2⅛
60	27.3	1328	797	2¼
65	29.5	1401	841	2⅓
70	31.8	1473	884	2½
75	34.1	1542	925	2⅔
80	36.4	1611	967	2¾
85	38.6	1677	1006	2⅞
90	40.9	1743	1046	3
95	43.2	1807	1084	3
100	45.5	1870	1122	3¼
105	47.7	1933	1160	3⅓
110	50.0	1994	1196	3½
115	52.3	2054	1232	3½
120	54.5	2113	1268	3⅔

CURRENT WEIGHT (LB)	CURRENT WEIGHT (KG)	ME* (KCAL/DAY)	60% OF ME (KCAL/DAY)	AMOUNT† (CUP/DAY)
Cats				
4	1.8	126	88	¼
5	2.3	161	113	⅓
6	2.7	189	132	⅓
7	3.2	224	157	½
8	3.6	252	176	½
9	4.1	287	201	⅔
10	4.5	315	220	⅔
11	5.0	350	245	¾
12	5.4	378	265	¾
13	5.9	413	289	⅞
14	6.4	448	314	⅞
15	6.8	476	333	1
16	7.3	511	358	1
17	7.7	539	377	1
18	8.2	574	402	1⅛
19	8.6	602	421	1¼
20	9.1	637	446	1¼

*Dogs: ME = 145 x (BWkg)$^{0.67}$ Cats: ME = 70 x (BWkg)
†Calculated for a pet food with a caloric density of 3500 kcal/kg and weight density of 3.5 oz/cup. Adjustments must be made for foods with higher or lower densities.

Calculation of Energy Needs for a Weight Loss Program

Target Weight Loss Per Week

Ideal body weight = 25 kg (55 lbs)

Actual body weight = 30 kg (66 lbs)

Target weight loss per week = 30 kg × 2% = 0.6 kg/week (1.3 lbs)

This dog should lose approximately 1.3 lbs per week when placed on a weight loss program.

Caloric Requirement for Weight Loss

ME requirement (moderately active adult) = $145 \times W_{kg}^{0.67}$

$(30 \text{ kg})^{0.67} \times 145 = 1415.9$ (approximately 1416 kcal/day)

Caloric restriction for weight loss = 1416 × 0.60 = 850 kcal/day

Volume of food to feed

   Diet A (400 kcal/cup) = 850/400 = 2.1 cups per day

   Diet B (350 kcal/cup) = 850/300 = 2.8 cups per day

Exercise

The inclusion of moderate, regular exercise in the treatment of obese pets affects body weight in several ways. Increased activity has the direct benefit of raising daily energy expenditure and thus contributing to the energy deficit that is necessary for weight loss. An increase in exercise also aids in the regulation of food intake. Studies with animals and humans have shown that caloric intake varies proportionally with energy expenditure during moderate to high levels of exercise. However, reduction of activity to a completely sedentary level results in increased food intake and eventual weight gain.[54, 55] It appears that the normal physiological regulators of caloric intake do not function properly below a certain minimum level of physical activity, and an uncoupling of the relationship between energy expenditure and energy intake occurs. Even a small change in an overweight pet's activity level may be beneficial because of the possibility that normal physiological controls of food intake may be restored when activity increases.

Lastly, exercise causes desired changes in body composition. Regular and continued exercise results in a higher proportion of lean to fat tissue. Because an animal's RMR is directly related to the amount of lean body tissue that it has, increasing lean tissue contributes to the maintenance of a normal RMR during weight loss. A decline in RMR naturally occurs in response to caloric restriction, resulting in a decreased rate of weight loss over time. This decrease occurs as a direct result of the loss of lean body mass that accompanies the consumption of a hypocaloric diet.[52] The inclusion of regu-

lar exercise along with caloric restriction minimizes or completely eliminates this decline in the RMR, allowing continued weight loss throughout the program and aiding in the prevention of weight regain.[56,57]

Physical activity should always be initiated at a low level with animals that are accustomed to a completely sedentary life-style. Twenty minutes of legitimate exercise three to five times per week is a good start. Daily exercise is ideal. Both the duration and the intensity of the exercise can be increased as the animal begins to lose weight and increases its exercise tolerance. Daily walking, running, or playing fetch and other games are recommended forms of exercise for dogs. Although it is difficult to induce an increase in physical activity in some cats, many will enjoy walking outside on a harness or chasing and playing with toys. Whatever the chosen activity, it is important that the exercise program is regular and continues throughout the life span of the pet.

Diet

The third and most important component of a weight loss program for dogs and cats is caloric restriction. The first step to be taken when planning a diet is to weigh the pet and set a goal for weight reduction (see Table 26-2 and the box on calculating energy needs for a weight loss program). An estimate of the pet's caloric requirement should then be determined. Providing a diet that provides 60% to 70% of the calories necessary to maintain current body weight usually results in adequate weight loss.[11,36] Even though dogs can lose weight and maintain health on energy deficits as low as 40% of maintenance requirements, cats should never be fed less than 60% of their energy requirement. At a level of 60% to 70% of metabolizable energy, most pets will lose between 1% and 2% of their total body weight per week. For example, the estimated daily caloric requirement of a 66-lb dog is 1416 kilocalories (kcal). Caloric restriction to 60% of this requirement equals 850 kcal/day. If a food that contains 400 kcal per 8-ounce cup is fed, this dog should receive slightly more than 2 cups of food per day. A caloric deficit of 3500 kcal is necessary to lose 1 lb of body fat. Therefore this amount of food should result in a loss of approximately 1.1 lb per week. If exercise is included in the program, additional energy deficit will be accounted for through increased energy expenditure and a slightly greater weight loss will be seen (see Table 26-2 and the box on p. 284).

During the weight loss program, the pet should be weighed once each week and a record or graph of weight loss should be kept. Caloric intake can be adjusted as the pet loses weight (Table 26-2). If possible, follow-up veterinarian visits should be made every 2 to 3 weeks to record progress. Portion-controlled feeding should be used, even if a commercially prepared, reducing diet is fed. Portion-controlled feeding allows strict monitoring of a pet's total food intake and removes the opportunity for the pet to spontaneously increase its intake of a food with a low energy density. It may also be helpful to feed several small meals per day rather than one or two large meals. This practice may decrease signs of hunger and increase the energy losses of meal-induced thermogenesis.[58] Once the goal weight has been reached, the daily volume of food can be slowly increased until an amount that maintains ideal body weight is provided.

Types of Diets for Weight Loss

Some pet owners include a great number of treats and table scraps in their pet's daily ration. When this is the case, simply eliminating all of the extra tidbits and restricting the pet's intake to 70% to 80% of its body weight requirement will lead to adequate weight loss. This is the preferred method to use with pets who are only slightly overweight, are exercised regularly, and have well-motivated owners.

When instituting this type of caloric restriction, pets will naturally be hungrier than usual and begging behaviors may increase proportionately. In addition, weight loss may be relatively slow due to the smaller caloric deficit. The lower limit of this type of dietary regimen, in terms of the caloric deficit, is set by the nutrient requirements of the dog or cat. Because a normal maintenance diet is being fed, it is imperative that the quantity provided is sufficient to meet the pet's total nutrient requirements. Commercial pet foods that are formulated for adult maintenance contain adequate amounts of protein, fat, vitamins, and minerals to meet the needs of an animal at normal weight and consuming adequate calories. If the volume of a maintenance diet is reduced too drastically in an effort to limit calories, nutrient deficiencies may develop.[19] Commercially prepared foods with a low energy density are formulated to contain adequate levels of nutrients while supplying less calories. Therefore, in cases of moderate to severe obesity or when owners are not strongly motivated to change their habits, a change of diet to a commercially prepared diet with a low energy density is recommended for weight reduction.

Several commercial pet foods that meet total nutrient requirements have been formulated to provide fewer calories than other adult maintenance foods. These reduced-calorie diets are divided into two distinct types: those that are low in fat and high in digestible, complex carbohydrate and those that are low in fat and high in indigestible fiber (Tables 26-3 and 26-4).

Dietary fat promotes weight gain and obesity because it increases the caloric density and palatability of the diet and promotes increased metabolic efficiency of body fat deposition.[29,48,59] Decreasing the fat content of a pet food results in a decreased caloric density and may decrease palatability. Commercial, low-fat diets contain between 8% and 11% fat on a dry-matter basis. This percentage is equivalent to 18% to 26% of the calories in a diet with an energy density of 3500 kcal/kg. The decreased proportion of fat is low enough to reduce the caloric density of the food but high enough to still provide adequate palatability and the required amounts of essential fatty acids. All pet foods that are marketed for weight reduction or for sedentary pets have decreased levels of fat. However, significant differences occur in the amounts of indigestible fiber, digestible carbohydrate, and protein that these foods provide (Table 26-4). Some products replace fat with primarily digestible carbohydrate, and other products contain high levels of indigestible fiber.

Adult maintenance diets for pets with normal activity levels contain between 30% and 50% of their calories from digestible carbohydrate. Diets that are formulated for the weight maintenance of inactive dogs or weight reduction for overweight dogs contain levels that are greater than 50%. High-quality, digestible carbohydrate provides an

TABLE 26-3
Low Fat/High Fiber vs. Low Fat/High Carbohydrate Reducing Diets

	FAT (%)	CRUDE FIBER (%)	ENERGY DENSITY (KCAL/CUP)	ME ENERGY (% OF GE)	FECAL SCORE (1–5)*	FECAL VOLUME (G/DAY)
Diet A	7	14.2	250	67.3	3.9	162.4
Diet B	9.7	3	270	87.8	4.5	46.5

* Fecal Score: 1 = Watery, diarrhea; 5 = Firm, compact.
Data provided by Iams Technical Center, Lewisburg, Ohio, 1993.

TABLE 26-4
Nutrient Compositions of Several Reduced Calorie Dog Foods

FOOD	CARBOHYDRATE*	FAT*	PROTEIN*	FIBER†	ME (KCAL/KG)	COMMENTS
A	57	21	22	14	2800	↑↑ Fiber, ↓ Fat
B	70	14	16	10	3000	↑ Fiber, ↓↓ Fat, ↓ Protein
C	66	13	21	4	3300	↓↓ Fat
D	62	21	17	10	3300	↑↑ Fiber, ↓ Fat, ↓ Protein
E	36	37	27	4	3400	↔ Fat, ↓ CHO
F	66	20	14	5.5	3500	↑ Fiber, ↓ Fat, ↓ Protein
G	48	30	22	3.5	3500	↓ Fat
H	57	23	20	2.0	3800	↓ Fat, ↓ Fiber

* Percentage of ME kcal.
† Percentage by weight.

excellent source of energy in low-fat pet foods and has less than half of the caloric density of fat. Raising the proportion of carbohydrate in the diet has the added advantage of inducing a higher dietary thermogenic response.[59-61] In other words, a high proportion of dietary carbohydrate contributes to higher energy expenditure by increasing the amount of heat loss as a result of meal ingestion. Pet foods that replace fat with complex carbohydrate without adding additional fiber retain the level of digestibility of the higher fat products, but they contain less total calories (Table 26-3 and Figure 26-1). Corn and rice are both excellent sources of digestible carbohydrate for pet foods. An added advantage to a low-fat diet that is high in complex carbohydrates is that, unlike reducing diets that are high in dietary fiber, it does not result in increased fecal volume or defecation frequency (Table 26-3, diet B).

An alternate way that the caloric density of a diet can be decreased is by diluting calories through the addition of indigestible fiber (Table 26-3, diet A; Table 26-4). Several commercial reducing diets are marketed that contain low levels of fat and unusually high amounts of dietary fiber. The rationale behind these products is that the increased bulk and decreased digestibility of the diet will cause a decrease in voluntary energy consumption and assimilation leading to weight loss. However, there are limited data to support this theory in companion animals, and results of studies examining the use of fiber for weight reduction in humans are inconsistent. Although dietary fiber does increase feelings of satiety in humans on a per meal basis, if allowed, most subjects will spontaneously overconsume high fiber diets to meet their energy needs.[62–64]

A recent study examined the effect of dietary fiber on caloric intake in adult dogs.[65] The test diets consisted of a commercial, low-calorie diet to which 2% dietary fiber was added. Five sources of fiber were tested: wheat bran, arbocell, almond-shell flour, pea fiber, and lentils. A group of six dogs was fed each of the six diets (one control plus the five fiber sources) for a 12-day test period. The diets were fed in an amount that corresponded to the food allowance calculated for weight reduction. On two occasions during the 12-day period, each dog was offered a "challenge meal" 3 hours after eating. This meal consisted of a standard canned dog food and was offered free-choice for a period of 15 minutes. The level of intake of the challenge meal was recorded. A comparison of the increased-fiber diets to the control diet showed no influence of dietary fiber on intake of the challenge meal or on intake during the subsequent 6-day transition period between tests. The type of fiber also had no effect on the level of intake. The investigators concluded that the consumption of moderate levels of dietary fiber in dogs had no effect on either food intake or the prevention of hunger during the 12-day test periods used in this study.

One study that did show decreased caloric consumption and weight loss in obese pets consuming high-fiber diets used experimental diets that were both high in dietary fiber and low in fat.[66] Caution must be used in the interpretation of these results because the separate effects of high fiber and low fat cannot be isolated in these studies. Because the advice to increase fiber is usually accompanied by a recommended decrease in dietary fat, it is not yet clear that any weight loss can be attributed specifically to increased fiber consumption.

A certain level of fiber is necessary in the diets of companion animals. Optimal levels are needed for proper functioning of the gastrointestinal tract. However, the weight-reducing effect of high levels of indigestible fiber in the diet is questionable, and excessive fiber intake can produce a number of adverse side effects. High intakes of dietary fiber cause decreases in nutrient digestion and availability. Specifically, fiber interferes with the absorption of lipids, calcium, zinc, and iron, and it results in increased fecal energy and nitrogen excretion.[67–71] If a diet is simultaneously high in indigestible fiber and low in fat and/or other nutrients, it is possible that long-term feeding may result in nutrient deficiencies in some animals. Excess fiber consumption also leads to increased gas production, fecal volume, and defecation frequency. Although not actually a health risk, these latter side effects are certainly disagreeable to most pet owners (Table 26-3).[72]

Although dietary fiber may induce satiety as a result of its bulking effect, it appears that within limits, this effect will be overridden by an animal's drive to eat to meet its energy needs. High-fiber diets may be effective in weight control if portions are strictly controlled, but the undesirable side effects of these diets and their potential to decrease the availability of essential nutrients may make them a poor choice for long-term caloric restriction. On the other hand, a weight loss diet that contains a reduced level of fat and a high proportion of digestible carbohydrate achieves the desired reduction in caloric density without sacrificing diet digestibility or nutrient availability (Table 26-3, diet B).

The significantly reduced protein content of some low-calorie pet foods may also be of concern (Table 26-4, diets B, D, and F). Research in humans has shown that fecal nitrogen increases with increasing levels of dietary fiber.[68,70] Fractionization studies indicate that the increased nitrogen is largely associated with bacterial mass, either as bacterial products, mucosal cell debris, or unabsorbed intestinal secretions. Another source of the increased fecal nitrogen may be unavailable protein complexes that are present within the fiber itself. The cooking and processing of high-fiber foods can result in the formation of Maillard complexes, polymerization products of certain carbohydrates and amino acids that become unavailable for absorption.

Research conducted in the dog and cat has shown that some types of fiber also significantly decrease apparent nitrogen digestibility in these species.[69,72] In one study, as levels of the soluble fiber carrageenan were increased in the diet from 0% to 20%, apparent crude protein digestibility decreased from 89.3% to 77.3% in dogs and from 85.6% to 77.2% in cats.[69] On the other hand, increasing the level of dietary cellulose did not affect protein digestibility in either groups of animals. Additional data have shown that purified cellulose had a slightly negative effect on protein digestibility in adult dogs. When increasing levels of cellulose were added to a complete and balanced diet, no significant differences in protein digestibility occurred between individual diets, but there was a significant linear relationship between increasing dietary cellulose and apparent nitrogen digestibility.[72]

As discussed previously, a major goal of a weight loss program for pets is to minimize the loss of lean body tissue while supporting the loss of body fat. Limiting dietary protein below maintenance needs in an overweight pet will contribute to the loss of lean body tissue. Data from several studies indicate that certain types of dietary fiber interfere with protein metabolism in dogs and cats. Therefore diets that contain increased levels of indigestible fiber and reduced levels of protein are not recommended for weight loss or for long-term weight maintenance of sedentary dogs and cats.

When any type of reduced-calorie foods is used for weight loss in dogs and cats, strict portion-controlled feeding should always be used. Most dogs and cats, if given the opportunity, will merely increase the volume of food that they eat in an effort to keep energy intake the same. The advantage of feeding a reducing diet is that lower calories can be consumed in a larger volume of food and there is less risk of causing a nutrient imbalance during restricted feeding of the diet. For example, if a reducing pet food that contains 300 kcal/cup is fed, the dog used in the previous example would receive 3½ cups of food a day rather than 2½ cups. This larger volume of food may result in a greater feeling of satiety and less tendency to beg or steal food. Moreover, these pet foods are specifically formulated by pet food manufacturers to provide balanced nutrition while lowering the amount of calories being consumed.

Total Fasting as a Treatment for Weight Loss

Total fasting or starvation is another type of caloric restriction that can be used for weight reduction in dogs. However, fasting can have both immediate and long-term negative consequences. These consequences include excessive losses of lean body tissue, decreased intestinal mass surface and activity, and the potential for increased proportion of body fat if weight is regained in the long term.[11] Because owners and veterinarians are capable of exerting total control over a pet's daily caloric intake, there are very few situations in which fasting as a cure for obesity is warranted. In addition, it is important to recognize that unlike dogs, cats are incapable of tolerating starvation. Fasting obese cats results in excessive losses of lean body tissue and increased hepatic fat deposition, which may lead to hepatic lipidosis (see Section 6, pp. 401–403). Therefore this type of dietary restriction should never be used with obese cats and only in extreme cases with obese dogs.

Metabolic changes that occur during fasting are adaptive processes that shift the brain's substrate use from primarily glucose to ketones.[73] In humans these metabolic shifts are accompanied by the development of ketosis, metabolic acidosis, accelerated urinary excretion of ammonia, and hyperuricemia.[74,75] These changes are responsible for many of the adverse side effects and health complications that accompany total fasting in human subjects. However, dogs do not develop ketosis, increase urinary ammonia excretion, or show a change in uric acid metabolism during prolonged starvation.[76] A study with adult dogs reported that blood ketone concentrations in fasted animals were less than 0.5 millimole per liter (mmole/l) following a total fast of 2 weeks. In contrast, blood ketone levels in fasted human subjects increase from 5 to 8 mmole/l within only 1 week.[77,78] Liver function tests also remained normal in dogs during prolonged fasting.[77] The ability of the dog to greatly increase gluconeogenesis from glycerol and consequently maintain normoglycemia may be responsible for the dog's ability to adapt very quickly and efficiently to starvation and to develop fewer adverse side effects.

Fasting as a treatment should only be considered when the degree of obesity poses a significant health risk to the dog and the owner is poorly motivated to institute any type of caloric restriction. Hospitalization is required and may continue for as long as 6 to 8 weeks, depending on the severity of the pet's condition.[51] During the fast, daily vitamin and\or mineral supplements should be provided to prevent nutrient deficiencies, and water should always be available. When desired body weight has been attained, refeeding to a maintenance level can be introduced slowly over a period of several days. Follow-up veterinary visits should be scheduled so that weight maintenance can be monitored and, if necessary, the pet's daily ration readjusted.

There are several disadvantages to the use of fasting as a weight loss method, and these should always be considered before its implementation. Many pet owners are opposed to the use of starvation because they feel that it is inhumane. Others may not want to incur the cost of hospitalization. The effect that starvation has on body composition is also an important consideration. Although dogs can metabolically tolerate fasting, they still lose a greater proportion of lean body tissue when starvation is used for weight reduction compared with the use of moderate caloric restriction.[78,79] A study with obese human subjects found that protein loss was two- to five-fold greater in fasted subjects than in subjects who were fed a restricted calorie diet for weight loss.[80] This loss of lean body tissue is not selective. Unrestricted expenditure of lean tissue for energy can result in tissue damage, particularly to the heart muscle.[11,81] In addition to

this health risk, the loss of excessive amounts of lean body tissue during starvation may also predispose the dog to later weight regain. Physiological pressure to regain lean body mass can stimulate increased hunger and food intake, leading to the repletion of fat stores along with lean tissue stores.[79] Because the owner is not directly involved in the weight loss process, obesity recurrence is more likely after a program of starvation than if a more conservative, in-home treatment was used. As stated previously, fasting as a treatment for obesity is not recommended in the majority of cases and should only be used as a "last resort" measure.

Maintaining the Reduced State after Weight Loss

The dietary and exercise habits that were established during the treatment of obesity must be maintained for dogs and cats even after caloric restriction for weight loss has ended. The pet should be fed a well-balanced, complete food designed for adult maintenance and should continue with the level of daily exercise that was included in the weight loss program. Pet owners should avoid reverting to old habits such as feeding table scraps, providing a large number of treats, or allowing begging behaviors. Some pets can be fed a normal adult maintenance pet food once they have reached ideal body weight. However, others will easily gain weight when fed these foods. A low-fat diet that is high in complex carbohydrates containing less calories but adequate nutrients for adult maintenance is suggested for weight maintenance in these pets. In all cases, portion-controlled feeding, twice daily, is the feeding schedule that should be used.

Prevention of Obesity

Although a variety of different factors may contribute to the development of obesity, the two most important causes are overfeeding and under exercising.[19] Obesity in pets can be successfully treated. However, the ideal situation is to prevent its occurrence in the first place.

In human subjects, hyperplastic obesity, signified by the presence of an abnormally high number of adipose cells, is difficult to treat and has a poor long-term prognosis. The development of hyperplastic obesity usually takes place during growth and often leads to obesity in adult life. Although hyperplastic obesity has not been extensively studied in dogs and cats, it is assumed that the prognosis is similar to that in other species. It is possible that overnutrition in a young dog or cat sets the stage for a lifelong battle with obesity. It is imperative that adequate nutrients and calories for optimal growth be provided to the young dog and cat. However, feeding excess amounts of a calorically dense food may stimulate adipocyte hyperplasia and lead to an abnormally high rate of growth and weight gain. Growing pets should be fed an amount of food that promotes normal growth rate and a lean body condition. Some pets are able to self-feed and will not overeat. However, many young dogs and cats will overeat as a result of boredom, competition with other animals, or the availability of a highly palatable food.

Practical Feeding Tips: Treatment of Obesity in Dogs and Cats

Develop a program that will produce a target weight loss of 1% to 3% of the total body weight per week.
Select an appropriate diet for weight loss.
Restrict caloric intake to 60% to 70% of metabolizable energy for current body weight.
Eliminate all table scraps and treats; change feeding habits that contribute to overeating and obesity.
Include a program of moderate, daily exercise.
After desired weight loss has been achieved, adjust intake to maintain ideal body weight.
Prevent weight regain by continuing regular exercise and strictly monitoring caloric intake.

In the majority of cases, portion-controlled feeding should be used and the pet's weight and rate of gain should be strictly monitored. Daily exercise should be started when pets are young, and it should be continued throughout life.

During adulthood, portion-controlled feeding, regular exercise, and avoiding the development of bad habits are the conditions necessary to prevent obesity. As pets age, their energy requirements naturally decrease. Exercise tolerance also decreases as pets get older, and these changes may predispose older pets to weight gain. Maintaining moderate levels of exercise and possibly changing the pet's diet to a ration that is low in energy density can help to prevent obesity in later years (see the box above).

CHAPTER 27

Overnutrition and Supplementation

Effects of Overnutrition During Growth

Improper feeding practices during growth are associated with several developmental skeletal disorders in dogs. Specifically, free-choice feeding of diets that are nutrient and energy dense and/or supplementation with certain nutrients during growth have been shown to be significant factors in the etiology of these disorders. Skeletal diseases are most prevalent in the large and giant breeds, and their onset is usually associated with periods of rapid growth. The most common of these disorders are canine hip dysplasia, osteochondritis dissecans, and hypertrophic osteodystrophy, also called metaphyseal osteopathy.

Canine hip dysplasia (CHD) is a biomechanical disease characterized by incongruity between the femoral head of the thigh and the acetabulum of the hip joint. The degree of subluxation and joint laxity determines the severity of the disease, and affected dogs may range from being asymptomatic throughout life to being severely crippled at a young age. It is generally accepted that the etiology of canine hip dysplasia is multifactorial, involving a strong genetic component and a number of potential environmental factors.[82] The animal's diet and the growth rate that it influences are believed to be important environmental factors.

Osteochondritis dissecans (OCD) is characterized by impaired maturation of cartilage at multiple points throughout the dog's skeleton. The primary lesion occurs when a segment of articular (joint) cartilage is separated from the underlying bone. The shoulder, elbow, stifle, and hock are the most commonly affected joints in the dog. As with CHD, the etiology of OCD appears to be multifactorial. Genetic predisposition, rapid growth rate, and excessive weight gain appear to be important causal factors.

Hypertrophic osteodystrophy (HOD) occurs primarily in the large and giant breeds of dogs and is characterized by excessive bone deposition and retarded bone resorption. The distal ulna, radius, and tibia are the bones that are most commonly affected. Radiographically, an irregular, radiotranslucent zone initially appears in the metaphysis and is separated from the growth plate by an excessively dense band of bone. As the disease progresses, additional bone is deposited outside of the periosteum, and soft-tissue swelling and subperiosteal hemorrhages develop around affected metaphyseal areas. The dog exhibits acute pain and swelling in the affected areas, intermittent pyrexia, and occasional anorexia.

Most forms of developmental skeletal disease are influenced by genetics, but heredity cannot fully explain their occurrence. For example, a heritability coefficient of 40% has been suggested for CHD.[83] This means that approximately 60% of the influencing factors are environmental in nature. Although it is difficult to identify all of the environmental components that are involved in these disorders, research studies have indicated that nutrition plays an important role. A number of nutrients have been examined. These nutrients include energy, protein, vitamin C, fat, carbohydrate, and calcium. The data indicate that the two most important nutritional factors in the development of skeletal disease are excess caloric intake during growth and high calcium intake (see p. 296).

Excess energy intake during growth commonly occurs as a result of feeding a high-quality, growth diet to a young dog on a free-choice basis or feeding excess amounts of food on a portion-controlled basis. Some owners believe that puppies should be kept "plump" in appearance and that a rotund puppy is a healthy puppy. However, when puppies are fed excessive amounts of a balanced diet, growth rate will be maximized before excess weight in the form of fat is gained. As a result, a growing dog that appears to be slightly overweight is usually growing at a maximal rate. Studies with dogs, humans, and other species have shown that the consumption of excess calories resulting in maximal or above-average growth rate is not compatible with optimal skeletal development.[84-86]

An extensive study conducted with growing Great Danes found that generalized overnutrition contributed to the development of orthopedic problems in this breed.[86] Two groups of growing puppies were fed a highly palatable, energy-dense food throughout growth. The first group was fed free-choice, and the second group was fed amounts of food that were restricted to two-thirds of the intake of the first group. The dogs that were fed free-choice grew significantly faster than did the dogs that were fed restricted amounts of food. Moreover, bone tissue was significantly affected by the rapid growth rate. A variety of skeletal abnormalities were observed in the dogs that were fed free-choice, including enlargement of the costochondral junctions and the epiphyseal-metaphyseal regions of long bones, hyperextension of the carpus, and sinking of the metacarpophalangeal and metatarsophalangeal joints. The affected dogs exhibited varying degrees of lameness and pain when palpated. It was concluded that generalized overnutrition, in the form of excess energy, protein, calcium, and phosphorus, caused an increased growth rate in these dogs that contributed to abnormal skeletal development.[86]

Additional work has been conducted with growing dogs of several other large breeds, including German shepherd dogs, golden retrievers, and Labrador retrievers. In one study, a group of puppies that had high parental frequencies of hip dysplasia were examined. Data showed that the incidence and severity of dysplasia was greater in puppies that had rapid growth rates as a result of increased caloric intake, compared with those that were fed restricted amounts of food.[87] Similarly, when a group of puppies was hand-reared at a reduced rate of growth, they developed a very low incidence of hip dysplasia. In contrast, a control group that was fed to allow a much higher growth rate showed a very high incidence of hip dysplasia.[88,89] A recent, well-controlled study with a group of 48 Labrador retrievers reported that growing dogs that were fed 25% less food than their counterparts fed free-choice had significantly less hip joint laxity at 30 weeks of age and a lower incidence of hip dysplasia at 2 years of age. The dogs in the study were fed a balanced diet that was formulated for growth for the entire 2-year study. Radiographic criteria established by the Orthopedic Foundation of America (OFA) were used to evaluate the dog's hips. Results showed that 16 of 24 dogs in the group fed free-choice were dysplastic while only 7 of the 24 dogs in the limited-fed group were dysplastic.[90]

It is theorized that abnormal skeletal development during periods of rapid growth is the result of overloading the growing skeleton with prematurely increased muscle mass and body weight.[91] This theory is supported by the fact that rapidly growing male dogs of the large and giant breeds are more frequently affected than are smaller females. There also appears to be a correlation between increasing body size and the occurrence of the lesions associated with osteochondrosis.[91] A comparison between the bones of large and small breeds of dogs during periods of rapid growth show that the bones of large breeds are relatively less dense than are the bones of small breeds at similar stages of development. Bones of large breeds have a thinner cortex, larger medullary cavity, and a less dense spongiosa.[92] It appears that the bones of large dogs during growth are not as strong as are those of smaller dogs during the same period. This may be the basis for the genetic predispositions toward skeletal abnormalities that are seen in the large and giant breeds.

The accelerated growth rate caused by free-choice feeding results in higher body weight and increased deposition of muscle and fat tissue. Recent studies have shown that overnutrition also stimulates accelerated skeletal growth. Great Dane puppies were fed a diet formulated for growth from weaning until they were 6 months of age. Puppies in one group were fed free-choice (ad libitum) and puppies in the second group were restricted to 70% to 80% of the amount consumed by the first group. As in previous studies, dogs fed ad libitum weighed significantly more than the restricted group at 6 months of age. Bone measurement data showed that accelerated skeletal growth, in the form of increased size and volume of bone, contributed significantly to the increased weight. The male dogs that experienced overnutrition also showed an increased rate of bone remodeling, resulting in enlarged bones with relatively low densities and low resistance to the greater weight that they were required to bear.[92] It appears that if a large dog is allowed to attain its maximal growth rate by feeding it excess amounts of a balanced diet, the accelerated growth rate creates a rapidly growing skeleton that is less

Practical Feeding Tips: Feeding Growing Dogs to Decrease the Risk of Developmental Skeletal Disease

Select a complete and balanced dog food that has been formulated for growth.
Feed this food throughout the first 1 to 2 years of life.
Use a portion-controlled feeding regimen and carefully measure the amount of food that is fed each day.
Provide an amount of food that will support an average rate of growth for the dog's breed.
Provide an amount of food that will maintain a lean body condition throughout growth.
Strictly monitor weight gain and body condition until the dog reaches maturity.
Do not supplement the diet with minerals, vitamins, or additional foods.

strong and less able to withstand the biomechanical stresses of the greater muscle mass and body weight that are put on it. Not only do these dogs weigh more, but their bones are less able to handle the added weight. The end result is the development of aberrations in ossification, damage to developing cartilage and growth plates, and premature closure of growth plates. Most often this manifests as osteochondrosis, but these changes may also be involved in the onset of several other developmental skeletal diseases.[86,92]

The final skeletal height of a dog is strongly influenced by genetics. Providing adequate, but not excessive, amounts of a balanced diet enables an animal to achieve its potential size but at a slower rate than if excess food is provided.[93] Feeding an energy-dense, nutrient balanced food at a level that promotes a high rate of growth will decrease the time that it takes the dog to attain adult size and can contribute to abnormal skeletal development. However, feeding restricted amounts of a balanced food to achieve a slower growth rate results in an animal of the same size but at a later point in time. Allowing the skeleton to develop slowly eliminates the biomechanical stresses of excess weight and the changes in bone development that are seen when rapid growth occurs. The best way to support a normal growth rate is to feed growing dogs adequate, but not excessive, amounts of a balanced diet, using a portion-controlled regimen. A pet food that has been formulated for growth should be fed throughout the first 1 to 2 years of life, depending on the rate of maturation of the particular breed. Body weight should be strictly monitored, and a lean body condition should be maintained throughout growth (see the box above).[90]

CALCIUM SUPPLEMENTATION

Supplementing a pet's diet during growth and other periods of physiological stress is a common practice. Calcium is a nutrient that is often added to dog's diets and, less commonly, to the diets of cats. The reason most often cited for calcium supplementation relates to its essential role in normal skeletal growth and development. Supplements such as dicalcium phosphate and bone meal are added to a growing dog's diet during growth spurts or when problems such as hyperextension of the carpus or sinking of the metacarpophalangeal joints occur. Some professional breeders may encourage all of their puppy buyers to routinely supplement the pet's diet with calcium during the entire

first year of life as a prophylactic measure. Some breeders believe that calcium supplementation is not only necessary for proper bone development but that it will also prevent the development of certain skeletal disorders. In addition, dogs' diets are occasionally supplemented with minerals during gestation and lactation. Supplemental calcium and phosphorus are believed by some to ensure healthy fetal development during pregnancy, to aid in milk production during lactation, and to prevent the onset of eclampsia after parturition. Regardless of the good intentions, there are potential risks when excessively high levels of calcium are added to an adequate and balanced diet. Excess calcium in the diet can produce deficiencies in other nutrients and has the potential for causing several serious health disorders in the dog.

Supplementation During Growth

Research has shown that normal growth in puppies can be supported by a calcium intake of 0.37% available calcium or 0.6% total calcium.[94] The Association of American Feed Control Officials (AAFCO) Nutrient Profile for Dog Food sets minimum levels for calcium of 0.8% for growth and reproduction and 0.5% for adult maintenance. The profile also mandates a maximum level of 2.5% calcium in all dog foods. This maximum level was included because published data have indicated that excess calcium during growth may contribute to abnormal skeletal development.[95,96] Studies indicate that a high level of calcium in the diet is associated with the occurrence of OCD, enlarged joints, dropped hocks, splayed feet, angular limb deformities, wobbler's syndrome, and stunted growth.[86,95,97]

In 1985 a study was undertaken with the purpose of determining the role of supplemental calcium in the occurrence of osteochondrosis in growing Great Danes.[95] An experimental diet was formulated that met the recommendations of the 1974 National Research Council (NRC) Nutrient Requirements for Dogs. Both the control group and the experimental group of dogs received this diet throughout growth. In addition, the experimental group received calcium carbonate supplementation to achieve a level of 3.3% in the diet, which is three times the amount recommended by the NRC.[98,99] Results showed that excessive calcium intake resulted in chronic hypercalcemia and hypophosphatemia. Skeletal differences between the control and experimental dogs included a higher percentage of total bone volume, retarded bone maturation, retarded bone remodeling, and a decreased number of osteoclasts (bone resorption cells) in the dogs receiving calcium supplementation. This group also showed a higher incidence and severity of the cartilage irregularities associated with osteochondrosis at the distal and proximal humeral cartilages. Clinically, calcium-supplemented dogs exhibited retained cartilage cones, severe lateral deviation of the feet, and the radius curvus syndrome that was previously described by another researcher.[100]

The mechanism through which calcium exerts these effects relates to the homeostatic control of blood calcium and phosphorus levels. Studies have shown that excessive calcium intake in young dogs results in a transient hypercalcemia and hypophosphatemia.[95] The hormone calcitonin is secreted in response to elevated serum calcium and lowers plasma calcium to normal levels. Calcitonin produces its effects by decreasing bone resorption and retarding cartilage maturation in developing bone. The

chronic suppression of bone resorption results in a gradual thickening and increased density of cortical bone. In growing dogs, this change interferes with normal bone remodeling. The deposition of excessive subperiosteal bone that results may cause the clinical signs of HOD and wobbler's syndrome, and the chronic effects of calcitonin on cartilage maturation may result in the eventual detachment of the articular cartilage that is seen in OCD.[95] Because of their rapid periods of growth and their predisposition to skeletal disorders, large and giant breeds of dogs are especially susceptible to the pathological effects of excess calcium consumption. However, it is postulated that these changes also occur in smaller breeds at a subclinical level, resulting in infrequent diagnosis of disease.[101]

One group of investigators examined the effects of excess dietary calcium and endogenous vitamin D formation on the calcitonin-producing cells of the thyroid gland. Growing beagles were given 2.3 grams of supplemental calcium per day and exposed to daily sunlight. After 70 days, the thyroid glands of the supplemented dogs contained significantly increased proportions of calcitonin-producing C-cells and decreased proportions of thyroid follicles, compared with those of control dogs. The authors of the study concluded that high dietary calcium intake caused thyroid C-cell hyperplasia, which would suggest the occurrence of chronic hypercalcitoninism in these dogs.[102] Additionally, examination by electron microscope of the thyroid C-cells of dogs fed excess calories, protein, and calcium showed that these cells were releasing larger amounts of calcitonin than were the C-cells of dogs fed restricted diets.[86] Under the influence of calciotropic hormones (calcitonin), excess calcium is routed largely to the skeleton, and resorption of mineral from bone also decreases.

A complicating factor involved in calcium nutrition for growing dogs is that they do not appear to have a mechanism that will protect them from absorbing large amounts of calcium when there are excessive levels in the diet. Dietary calcium is absorbed across the intestinal epithelium through either active transport or passive diffusion. The active transport mechanism is saturable, carrier-mediated, and depends on the animal's vitamin D status. The second mechanism is nonsaturable, diffusional transfer that is directly dependent on the concentration of available calcium in the intestinal lumen. Studies of humans and laboratory animals have shown that nonsaturable passive diffusion is the predominant pathway for calcium absorption in neonates and young animals.[103] In adults, the percentage of calcium that is absorbed from the diet varies between 10% and 90%, depending on the composition of the food, calcium content of the diet, and physiological state of the animal.[96,97,104]

A study with growing dogs found that 45% of dietary calcium was absorbed when a normal level of calcium was fed (1.1% of the diet dry matter). The percent of calcium absorption increased to 80% when the level of calcium was decreased to 0.55%. However, when the calcium level was increased to 3.3%, 45% of the calcium was still absorbed. As a result, calcium balance was significantly more positive in the dogs fed a high level of the mineral compared with the dogs that were fed either normal or low levels. Mineral content of cortical and cancellous bone was greater in the high-calcium dogs and there was decreased bone turnover and remodeling of the skeleton. As dogs age and reach maturity, they appear to be able to adapt to high calcium intakes by decreasing the proportion that is absorbed.[97] Therefore young dogs are especially susceptible

to the adverse effects of high dietary calcium because of their rapidly developing and changing skeletons and because of their inability to decrease calcium absorption in response to excess levels in the diet.

Diets containing excessively high amounts of calcium are also capable of causing a relative zinc deficiency in dogs.[105,106] High levels of calcium and other minerals, such as iron and copper, interfere with zinc absorption, possibly through competition for absorption sites or by acting as intestinal ligands.[107,108] Although adult animals can be affected, these effects have been most frequently observed in growing dogs. A controlled study found that puppies fed balanced diets containing excess supplemental calcium developed zinc deficiency within 2 to 3 months.[105] Clinical signs included impaired growth rate, anorexia, conjunctivitis, and the development of a dull, coarse hair coat. Desquamating skin lesions that are characteristic of zinc deficiency were also observed on the abdomen and extremities.[105] Clinical cases of zinc deficiency have also been reported. Three separate litters of puppies developed zinc-responsive dermatosis when fed diets containing two to three times the NRC requirement for calcium. When supplemented with oral zinc, all puppies showed dramatic improvement within 7 to 10 days.[106]

Studies with growing dogs indicate that adding excessive amounts of calcium or calcium-containing foods to a balanced diet can contribute to the development of the skeletal disorders that owners are attempting to prevent. This practice may also lead to subclinical or clinical zinc deficiency. If a growing dog is fed an appropriate amount of a high-quality pet food that is formulated for growth, supplementation with calcium is unnecessary and contraindicated. If a pet owner is feeding their pet a food that appears to contain inadequate or unavailable levels of calcium, switching the dog to an adequate commercial diet is safer than attempting to correct the imbalance in the poor diet through supplementation.

Supplementation During Gestation and Lactation

Supplementation with calcium or any other mineral is not necessary for normal fetal development during pregnancy or for normal milk production during lactation. Although calcium needs do increase during these two physiological states, the dam's requirements are met by consuming increased amounts of a complete and balanced diet. In addition to being unnecessary for fetal bone development and milk production, supplemental calcium is also not effective in the prevention of puerperal tetany.

Puerperal tetany, or eclampsia, is a disease that most commonly occurs in small breeds of dogs at parturition or 2 to 3 weeks later. The disease is caused by a failure of the bitch's calcium-regulatory mechanisms to maintain serum calcium levels when there is a loss of the mineral to the milk during lactation. Serum calcium decreases to less than 7 milligrams per deciliter (mg/dl) and ataxia, muscular tetany, and convulsive seizures occur. Standard treatment is intravenous administration of calcium boroglu-conate.[109]

A similar, hypocalcemic syndrome occurs post parturition in cows. It has been shown in this species that the consumption of a diet that is high in calcium during preg-

nancy actually increases the incidence of the disorder, but that a diet that is moderate to low in calcium decreases its incidence.[110,111] It is believed that a relative hypercalcemia resulting from high calcium intake during pregnancy exerts negative feedback on parathyroid hormone synthesis and secretion by the parathyroid gland. This feedback causes a decrease in both the body's ability to mobilize calcium stores from bone and the ability to increase calcium absorption in the intestine. When calcium is suddenly needed for lactation, these regulatory mechanisms are unable to adapt quickly enough to the sudden calcium loss. The calcium that is available is diverted preferentially to milk production, and serum calcium decreases. Although additional research concerning the effect of supplemental calcium during pregnancy on the incidence of this disorder needs to be conducted in dogs, it is currently recommended that if a bitch is being fed a high-quality, commercial food that has been designed for feeding through gestation and lactation, calcium supplementation is not necessary and is probably contraindicated.

Ascorbic Acid (Vitamin C) Supplementation

Companion animals do not have a requirement for dietary ascorbic acid. Like most species, dogs and cats produce endogenous ascorbic acid in the liver from either glucose or galactose. Therefore, unless there is a high metabolic need or inadequate amounts are being synthesized by the body, a dietary source of ascorbic acid is unnecessary in these species. The body requires ascorbic acid for the hydroxylation of the amino acids proline and lysine in the formation of the structural protein collagen. Collagen is the primary constituent of osteoid, dentine, and connective tissue fibers, and it is produced in quantity by osteoblasts during skeletal growth and development.

The practice of supplementing the diets of growing dogs with ascorbic acid can be traced back to a report that compared the development of HOD in young dogs with the bone abnormalities that are associated with scurvy (vitamin C deficiency) in humans.[112] It was theorized that an endogenous deficiency of ascorbic acid in dogs was responsible for the development of HOD. HOD occurs primarily in rapidly growing puppies of large breeds of dogs. It is characterized by excessive bone deposition and retarded bone resorption and occurs most often in the distal ulna, radius, and tibia. Affected dogs exhibit acute pain and swelling in the metaphyseal regions of the long bones, intermittent pyrexia, and occasionally anorexia.[113]

Radiographic examination of dogs with HOD and humans with scurvy both show radiotranslucent zones in affected metaphyses and eventual subperiosteal hemorrhages. Studies adding supportive evidence for a role of ascorbic acid in HOD have found decreased levels of ascorbic acid in the plasma and urine of dogs with HOD.[114–116] However, later evidence showed that a very crucial difference between HOD in the dog and scurvy in the human had been overlooked by the early investigations. HOD is characterized by osteopetrosis, involving excess bone deposition in the

metaphysis and periosteum and retarded bone resorption. Scurvy, on the other hand, is an osteoporotic condition, involving the demineralization of bone that is caused by impaired collagen formation by osteoblasts in the developing skeleton. This major difference provides strong evidence that the two conditions are not the same disorder.

More importantly, controlled studies of the efficacy of supplemental ascorbic acid as a therapeutic treatment for HOD have not supported the claim that low levels of ascorbic acid are a causal agent in HOD in dogs.[115] A study with growing Labrador retrievers found that supplementation with 500 mg/day of ascorbic acid from weaning to 4½ months of age had no effect on the development of skeletal disorders. Both groups of dogs in the study were fed a highly palatable, energy-dense diet on a free-choice regimen. Dogs in both the supplemented and the nonsupplemented groups developed skeletal lesions indicative of HOD. In addition, supplemented dogs were found to have higher levels of circulating serum calcium. It was postulated that this "relative hypercalcemia" may have led to elevated calcitonin levels. As discussed previously, persistent hypercalcitoninism has the potential to contribute to the bone changes that are observed in many of the developmental skeletal disorders in young dogs. It was concluded that supplemental ascorbic acid has no preventive effect, and it may even exacerbate the development of certain skeletal lesions in growing dogs.[117] Additional research has indicated that HOD is more likely to be caused by overnutrition leading to a high rate of growth than to an endogenous lack of ascorbic acid[86] (see pp. 293–296).

Although the original attention awarded to ascorbic acid status in the dog pertained specifically to HOD, this association was expanded, without scientific support, to include several other developmental bone disorders. These disorders included CHD and OCD. As a result, many breeders and professionals habitually began supplementing their growing dogs' diets with ascorbic acid in hopes of preventing the onset of these diseases. However, there is no evidence to support the claim that supplemental ascorbic acid can prevent the development of either of these disorders in growing dogs.

Some research has been conducted concerning the role of supplemental ascorbic acid in the development of OCD in growing pigs. A group of pigs was supplemented with ascorbic acid at a level of 100 mg per kilogram of body weight per day until attainment of slaughter weight. The control group was raised in identical conditions and was fed the same diet but did not receive supplemental ascorbic acid. Examination of bones after slaughtering revealed no significant differences in either the incidence or the degree of osteochondrotic lesions in the elbow joint, distal epiphyseal plate of the ulna, or the medial condyle of the femur. The supplemented and the nonsupplemented groups of pigs showed equal incidence of these bone lesions.[118]

In addition to being unwarranted, ascorbic acid supplementation in dogs and cats may be detrimental. Excess ascorbic acid is excreted in the urine as oxalate, and high concentrations of oxalate have the potential to contribute to the formation of calcium oxalate uroliths in the urinary tract. Highly selective breeding practices, attaining moderate growth rates in puppies, and feeding a high-quality, balanced, commercial ration without added supplements is a more practical and scientifically supported route to preventing the development of skeletal diseases in dogs.

CHAPTER 28

Vitamin Deficiencies and Excesses

Although serious deficiencies of vitamins are highly unusual in pets today, select deficiencies and toxicities can occur as a result of improper feeding practices. Feeding excessive levels of foods that contain marginal levels of vitamin E and high amounts of polyunsaturated fatty acids can lead to vitamin E deficiency in cats. On the other hand, feeding cats foods that contain too much vitamin A can lead to toxicity. Thiamin deficiency can be induced by feeding raw fish, and biotin deficiency can be caused by feeding raw egg whites. Both raw fish and raw egg whites contain inhibitory substances. These problems are described in detail in the following chapter.

Vitamin E Deficiency in Cats: Pansteatitis

A condition called *pansteatitis* (yellow fat disease) occurs in cats that are fed diets containing marginal or low levels of alpha-tocopherol (vitamin E) and high amounts of unsaturated fatty acids. An animal's vitamin E requirement is directly affected by the level of unsaturated fatty acids that are present in the diet. As the level of polyunsaturated fatty acids increases, the need for vitamin E will also increase. For example, a diet that contains high levels of fish oil may cause a threefold to fourfold increase in a cat's daily requirement for alpha-tocopherol.[119] If inadequate amounts of vitamin E are fed, dietary and body fat undergo oxidative degradation, leading to the formation of peroxides and hydroperoxides. The accumulation of reactive peroxides in the cat's adipose tissue results in pansteatitis, which is characterized by chronic inflammation and yellow-brown discoloration of body fat.

Signs of Pansteatitis in Cats

Depression, anorexia
Hyperesthesia (sensitivity to touch) of the chest and abdomen
Reluctance to move, decreased agility
Presence of abnormal fat deposits under the skin and in the abdomen
Dietary history includes items that are high in unsaturated fats and low in vitamin E

Clinical signs of pansteatitis in the cat include anorexia, depression, pyrexia, and hyperesthesia of the thorax and abdomen. The cat may demonstrate a change in behavior and agility and develop a poor or roughened hair coat.[120,121] Palpation of subcutaneous and intraabdominal fat depots is painful to the cat and reveals the presence of granular or nodular fat deposits. Information concerning the animal's dietary history should be involved in the diagnosis, but confirmation of diagnosis is provided by histological examination of a fat biopsy sample. The fat of cats with pansteatitis is very firm and deep yellow to orange in color with a diffuse inflammatory response.[120,122] The orange pigment (commonly referred to as ceroid) is believed to be an intermediate polymerization product of unsaturated fatty acids that have undergone peroxidation. The peroxidation occurs as a result of insufficient intracellular antioxidants, specifically vitamin E (see the box above).

Early cases of pansteatitis occurred almost exclusively in cats that were fed a canned, commercial, fish-based food made primarily of red tuna.[120,123] Later cases occurred in cats that were fed diets consisting wholly or largely of canned red tuna or fish scraps.[121,124] Red tuna packed in oil contains high levels of polyunsaturated fatty acids and low levels of vitamin E. The addition of large amounts of fish products to a cat's diet appears to be the primary cause of pansteatitis in pet cats.

Treatment of pansteatitis involves the elimination of fish from the cat's diet and its replacement with a well-balanced, high-quality, commercial cat food. Dietary changes may be difficult in cats that have become accustomed to eating only a singular food item. This problem has been most commonly reported in cats that received only red tuna as the principal component of their diet for an extended period of time.[122,123] Along with correction of the diet, vitamin E (alpha-tocopherol) should be administered orally at a dose of 10 to 25 International Units (IU) twice daily for 5 to 7 days.[121,125] Corticosteroid therapy may also be used to decrease inflammation and reduce pain. Prognosis for recovery from pansteatitis is usually very good, but it may be slow in advanced cases.

VITAMIN A TOXICOSIS IN CATS: DEFORMING CERVICAL SPONDYLOSIS

Feeding excess amounts of the fat-soluble vitamins can be toxic to dogs and cats. This is not generally seen as a practical problem, except in the case of vitamin A. Vitamin A

Signs of Deforming Cervical Spondylosis in Cats

Anorexia and weight loss
Increased lethargy and reluctance to move
Persistent lameness in one or both front legs
Decreased ability to self-groom
Decreased ventriflexion of the head
Posture changes by adopting a "marsupial-like" sitting position
Dietary history includes items that contain a high concentration of vitamin A

toxicosis has been reported most often in cats that are fed diets composed exclusively of liver or other organ meats. Although it is no longer a common practice because of the availability of commercial pet foods, some pet owners still feed their cats a diet consisting exclusively of liver, milk, and various table scraps. This practice is usually the result of well-meaning but poorly informed pet owners believing that cats, being carnivores, will thrive on an all-meat or liver diet. Although many nutrients in these diets are imbalanced, one of the most serious problems that can occur is vitamin A toxicosis.

The pathological result of vitamin A excess in cats is the development of a syndrome called *deforming cervical spondylosis*. The effects of vitamin A on bone growth and remodeling result in the development of bony exostoses (outgrowths) along the muscular insertions of cervical vertebrae and the long bones of the forelimbs. Over time, these bony processes cause pain and difficult movement.[126] Vitamin A-induced skeletal disease is not a practical problem in dogs, but it has been produced experimentally. Studies have shown that extremely high intakes of vitamin A in growing dogs result in decreased length and thickness of long bones, premature closure of epiphyseal growth plates, and the development of osteophytes and periosteal reactions.[127]

Initial clinical signs of deforming cervical spondylosis in cats include anorexia, weight loss, lethargy, and an increasing reluctance to move. Cats become unkempt in appearance and are less interested or able to groom themselves. As the disease progresses, a very characteristic postural change is observed. Cats will adopt a marsupial-like sitting position, holding the front legs elevated off of the ground. They also often walk with their hind limbs flexed, and ventri-flexion of the head is decreased or altogether absent. A fixed-stare expression is often observed, probably as a result of the cats inability to turn its head to see. Lameness in one or both of the front limbs is seen in the later stages.[126,128] Development of exostoses occurs primarily in the first three joints of the cervical vertebrae and joints of the forelegs. It has been theorized that the normal movements involved in a cat's regular licking and grooming practices result in these predilection sites. Chronic intoxication with vitamin A appears to increase the sensitivity of the periosteum to the effects of low levels of trauma and repetitive movements that would normally be insufficient to cause an inflammatory response (see the box above).[128]

Experimental studies show that the level of vitamin A required to produce skeletal lesions within only a few months time is between 17 and 35 micrograms per gram

(μg/g) of body weight.[128] A 1-kilogram (kg) (2.2 lb) kitten would have to consume a minimum of 17,000 μg (56,000 IU) of vitamin A per day to attain this level. According to the National Research Council's current *Nutrient Requirements of Cats*, a 1-kg kitten requires approximately 50 μg of vitamin A per day (1000 μg/kg of dry diet).[119] The toxic dose of vitamin A necessary to produce acute toxicity is therefore more than 300 times the kitten's daily requirement. An adult cat weighing 5 kg (11 lbs) would have to consume at least 85,000 μg of vitamin A daily to reach this toxic level. The daily vitamin A requirement for an active 5-kg adult cat is approximately 80 μg/day. Therefore an adult cat would have to consume 1000 times its daily requirement of vitamin A to achieve toxic levels. It is indisputable that a cat will never consume this level if it is receiving a nutritionally balanced, commercial pet food.

It would also be difficult for a cat to consume this high a level of vitamin A while being fed an all-liver diet. Beef liver contains approximately 160 μg (530 IU)/g.[129] An adult cat consuming 6 ounces of liver per day would be ingesting only 27,200 μg of vitamin A per day, quite a bit less than the levels described by researchers.[128] However, all of the case studies that are reported in the literature found that deforming cervical spondylosis developed in cats that were fed liver diets.

There are two possible explanations for this discrepancy. First, it is known that the livers of production animals vary greatly in vitamin A content.[129] The level of 160 μg/g of vitamin A in beef liver is an average, not an absolute, value. Second, and more importantly, all of the case studies that have been reported occurred in adult cats that had been fed liver diets for long durations of time.[130,131] The experimental work that has been conducted involved much higher levels of vitamin A and produced signs of toxicity in very short periods of time. At lower doses of vitamin A, cervical spondylosis appears to develop slowly over the lifetime of the cat, and clinical signs of the disease do not become evident until much later in adult life. This conclusion is supported by the fact that the average age for the diagnosis of cervical spondylosis in pet cats is 4.25 years.[126] Therefore the reported level of vitamin A required to produce toxicity in the cat (17 to 35 μg/g of body weight) may be realistic for the experimental production of acute toxicity, but the level that can produce deforming cervical spondylosis if excess vitamin A is consumed by pet cats for long durations of time is probably substantially lower.

Regular supplementation of a cat's diet with liver, even if it is added to a balanced diet, has the potential to cause skeletal problems if the practice is continued for several years. When liver is fed exclusively, vitamin A toxicosis may occur concurrently with nutritional secondary hyperparathyroidism because of the low calcium and high phosphorus contained in organ meats.[131] Cod liver oil fed as a supplement also has the potential to induce vitamin A toxicity. Adding 1 tablespoon of cod liver oil to a cat's food twice daily will result in an intake of approximately 10,000 μg of additional vitamin A per day. Fish liver oils are also excessively high in vitamin D, and excessive supplementation may result in the combined effects of vitamins A and D toxicosis.

The treatment of vitamin A toxicosis in cats includes the removing of the source of excessive vitamin A from the diet, replacing the source with a complete and balanced pet food, and providing supportive therapy. The prognosis is guarded because resolu-

tion of skeletal lesions may never be complete. In addition, if the cat has been fed a liver diet for a long time, the change to a balanced pet food may be difficult since many cats develop a fixed food preference and refuse to eat any other diet.

Thiamin Deficiency

Certain types of fish contain an enzyme, called *thiaminase*, that destroys thiamin (vitamin B_1). Consumption of these types of fish has been shown to cause thiamin deficiency in a variety of species. Experimental studies with cats have produced signs of thiamin deficiency within 23 to 40 days of consuming diets composed solely of raw carp or raw salt-water herring.[132] The subcutaneous administration of thiamin to affected cats resulted in recovery in all cases. Although both carp and herring can cause thiamin deficiency, perch, catfish, and butterfish do not show thiaminase activity. Other common types of fish that contain thiaminase include whitefish, pike, cod, goldfish, mullet, shark, and flounder. However, it is not known whether the thiaminase levels present in these fish are sufficient to produce deficiency in animals.[133] Thiaminase is a heat-labile enzyme and is denatured by normal cooking temperatures. As a result, the potential for thiamin deficiency exists only when uncooked fish is fed.

Although thiamin deficiency is uncommon in dogs and cats, clinical cases have been reported. Cats appear to be more susceptible because of their high requirement for this vitamin in the diet and because of the tendency of pet owners to feed cats unconventional diets.[132,134] Most cases have been the result of feeding cats diets that contained a large proportion of raw fish.[132,135] Similarly, a group of sled dogs that was fed a diet consisting of frozen, uncooked carp developed clinical signs of thiamin deficiency after a 6-month period. The addition of oatmeal, a dry dog food, and 100 milligrams of thiamin per day to the affected dogs resulted in complete recovery within 2 months.[136]

Because thiamin is essential for normal carbohydrate metabolism, the central nervous system is severely affected by a deficiency of this vitamin. Initial clinical signs of deficiency include anorexia, weight loss, and depression. As the deficiency progresses, neurological signs of ataxia, paresis, and, eventually, convulsive seizures are present. The terminal stage is characterized by severe weakness and prostration and eventually leads to death.[136,137] Diagnosis of thiamin deficiency in dogs and cats is made based on clinical signs and the dietary history of the animal. Elevated plasma pyruvate and lactate concentrations are also useful in confirming a diagnosis.

Treatment includes elimination of raw fish from the diet, its replacement with a well-balanced, commercial pet food, and thiamin therapy. Thiamin should be administered intravenously or subcutaneously at a dose of 75 to 100 milligrams twice daily until neurological signs subside.[134] Oral thiamin supplementation should also be administered for several months following the initial clinical episode.[136] In most affected pets, these clinical signs will decrease within several days. However, if severe neurological damage has occurred, the pet may never make a full recovery. A permanent intolerance of physical exercise and some degree of persistent ataxia occasionally occurs in animals that have recovered from thiamin deficency.

Biotin Deficiency

Biotin is essential as a coenzyme for a number of carboxylation reactions involved in fatty acid, amino acid, and purine metabolism (see Section 1, p. 40). Dietary deficiencies of this vitamin are not generally a problem in dogs and cats because it is believed that these species are able to obtain most, if not all, of their requirement through synthesis by intestinal microbes.[99,119] However, deficiencies have been produced experimentally through prolonged antibiotic therapy or by feeding a diet containing raw egg white.[138-140] Egg white contains avidin, a secretory protein that is produced by the hen's oviduct during formation of the egg. When consumed, avidin combines with biotin in the intestine and prevents biotin absorption. The avidin in egg white is so effective in this capacity that feeding raw egg white has been used to experimentally induce biotin deficiency in laboratory animals.

Signs of biotin deficiency in dogs and cats include the development of scaly dermatitis, alopecia, and, eventually, diarrhea and anorexia.[139,141] Although egg white has the capacity to induce a biotin deficiency in companion animals, the danger of this occurring is slight. The fact that the yolk of the egg contains large quantities of biotin offsets the potential risk of causing a biotin deficiency when the entire egg is fed.

Furthermore, cooking denatures avidin and destroys its biotin-binding ability. Practically speaking, the only potential danger to companion animal nutrition would be regular supplementation of a pet's diet with only the white of the raw egg. Although egg is an excellent source of protein and provides a number of essential nutrients, it is wise to limit the amount fed to companion animals.

CHAPTER 29

Common Nutrition Myths

L ike any science, a number of "old wives tales" and myths exist about the nutrition and feeding of dogs and cats. Some of these myths and feeding fads have their origins in scientific fact, but the facts have been exaggerated, obscured, or misapplied. Other myths have arisen from nutritional misinformation perpetuated by a lack of scientific proof or disproof and by the pervasive desire to find easy solutions to medical or behavioral problems through diet. Although some nutritional myths cause no harm to the pet, others have the potential to adversely affect health or contribute to a dietary imbalance. A number of commonly held myths are discussed, along with scientific research that addresses these beliefs (Table 29-1).

FEEDING "PEOPLE FOODS" TO DOGS AND CATS

Some pet owners enjoy feeding their dogs and cats "people foods" for the same reasons that they like to give them treats and snacks. Providing a special treat is a way of showing affection and love. Adding table scraps and other choice food items to a pet's diet is believed to enhance the pet's enjoyment of the meal. Although some human foods are unsuitable for companion animals and should not be fed at all, others only become detrimental if they make up too high a proportion of the pet's diet. Some pet owners insist on feeding at least small amounts of "people foods" to their companion animals. If these foods are to be fed, proper guidelines should always be followed (see the box on the following page).

TABLE 29-1
Summary of Common Nutritional Myths

MYTH	SUPPORTING RESEARCH	DISPUTING RESEARCH	CONCLUSION (TRUE/FALSE)
Feeding brewer's yeast or thiamin repels fleas	Human studies that were poorly controlled	Two studies with dogs	False
Feeding garlic or onion repels fleas	None reported	None reported; Reports of onion toxicity in dogs	False
Diet causes acute, moist dermatitis ("hot spots")	None reported; diet may play indirect role in some cases	Supportive evidence for other causes	False
Certain diets cause the coat to turn red in dogs	None reported	Supportive evidence for other causes	Probably false
Components in the diet cause GDV	None reported	Yes	False
Ethoxyquin causes health problems	None reported	Several long-term studies in dogs and other species	False
High-fat pet foods cause hyperlipidemia	None reporting diet as a primary cause	Supportive evidence for other causes	False

Practical Feeding Tips: Adding "People Foods" to a Pet's Diet

The addition of extra foods should be limited to no more than 5% to 10% of the pet's daily caloric requirement.

Any meat, fish, or poultry that is fed should be well cooked and all bones should be removed.

The use of milk and cheese should be strictly monitored. Some adult dogs and cats are lactose intolerant and cannot efficiently digest dairy products.

The exclusive use of any single food item should be avoided, even when adding it to the pet's diet in very small amounts.

Correction of the nutrient imbalances of a poor diet should not be attempted by adding table scraps.

Vitamin and/or mineral supplements are unnecessary when a complete and balanced pet food is fed, and they can be detrimental to health.

Pet owners should be aware of the development of unwanted behavior problems, such as begging during mealtimes and stealing food.

The addition of all extra foods should be discontinued if weight gain, gastrointestinal tract upset, or signs of nutrient imbalance are seen.

Table Scraps

The amount of table scraps that are added to a pet's diet should be strictly limited. Although the owner may eat a very nutritious and well-balanced diet, the nutritional requirements of dogs and cats are not the same as a human's. In addition, most owners add only the choice scraps from their meals to their pet's dinner bowl, such as fat trimmings and leftover meat, and they leave the vegetables and grains behind. The table

TABLE 29-2
Nutrient Composition of a Performance Dry Dog Food with Added Proportions of Beef (Dry-Matter Basis)*

NUTRIENT	DRY DOG FOOD	75% DOG FOOD/25% BEEF†	50% DOG FOOD/50% BEEF	25% DOG FOOD/75% BEEF
Protein	34%	39%	46%	55%
Fat	23%	24%	25%	26%
Carbohydrate	35%	30%	23%	14%
Crude Fiber	1.9%	1.6%	1.3%	0.75%
Calcium	1.3%	1.1%	**0.87%**	**0.53%**
Phosphorus	1.0%	0.89%	**0.73%**	**0.53%**
Ca:P ratio	1.3:1	1.2:1	1.2:1	1:1
Potassium	0.87%	0.89%	0.92%	**0.96%**
Sodium	0.60%	0.53%	0.44%	0.31%
Magnesium	0.11%	0.09%	0.08%	**0.06%**
Iron	215 mg/kg	183 mg/kg	142 mg/kg	**85 mg/kg**
Vitamin A	21,700 IU/kg	18,500 IU/kg	14,400 IU/kg	8600 IU/kg
Vitamin D	1950 IU/kg	1670 IU/kg	1290 IU/kg	**770 IU/kg**
Vitamin E	153 IU/kg	130 IU/kg	100 IU/kg	**60 IU/kg**
Thiamin	19.5 mg/kg	16.7 mg/kg	13 mg/kg	7.7 mg/kg
Riboflavin	25 mg/kg	21 mg/kg	16.5 mg/kg	10 mg/kg
Niacin	64 mg/kg	55 mg/kg	42 mg/kg	25 mg/kg
Metabolizable energy	4700 kcal/kg	4800 kcal/kg	5000 kcal/kg	5200 kcal/kg
Caloric Distribution				
Protein	27%	31%	35%	41%
Fat	45%	45%	47%	48%
Carbohydrate	28%	24%	18%	10%

*Imbalanced nutrients are expressed in bold print. Nutrient levels were compared to the AAFCO nutrient profiles and corrected for differences in energy density.
† Beef = Fresh ground round.

scraps that end up in the pet's bowl may be very tasty (and much appreciated), but they usually do not provide balanced nutrition. If table scraps are fed to pets, they should never make up more than 5% to 10% of the pet's total daily caloric intake.

Meat and Poultry

Some owners believe that because the cat and the dog are carnivorous in nature, they should be able to survive on an all-meat diet. However, the muscle tissue of meat and poultry alone cannot supply complete nutrition to companion animals. Both of these high-protein foods are deficient in calcium, phosphorus, sodium, iron, copper, iodine, and several vitamins. It is true that, in the wild, the ancestors of dogs and cats survived on freshly killed meat. However, the fact that they consumed their *entire* prey, including bones, organs, and intestinal contents, is often overlooked. Like other supplemental foods, the addition of meat and poultry to the diet should be strictly limited because of their potential to imbalance the pet's diet (Table 29-2).

Fish

Most cats and some dogs love the taste of fish. Advertising campaigns used by some pet food companies have convinced people that cats prefer the taste of fish over many other food items. In reality, cats enjoy fish to about the same degree that they enjoy several other high-protein foods. Although fish is a good source of protein for dogs and cats, it does not supply complete nutrition. In general, most types of deboned fish are deficient in calcium, sodium, iron, copper, and several vitamins. Some types of fish also contain small bones that are difficult to remove before cooking. These bones may easily lodge in a pet's throat or gastrointestinal tract and cause perforation or obstruction.

Tuna is a type of fish that is commonly fed to cats because it is readily available and inexpensive. Canned tuna packed in oil contains high levels of polyunsaturated fatty acids. The excessive intake of these oils can result in a vitamin E deficiency as a result of their high polyunsaturated fat and low vitamin E content. In the cat, this eventually manifests as a condition called pansteatitis or "yellow fat disease." Signs of pansteatitis include decreased appetite, lethargy, elevated temperature, and tenderness and pain in the chest and abdomen.[121-123] Treatment includes eliminating fish from the cat's diet and replacing it with a well-balanced, high-quality commercial cat food (see pp. 303–304).

Raw fish should never be fed to pets. Certain types of fish, such as carp and herring, contain a compound that destroys thiamin, a B vitamin, and may cause a thiamin deficiency,[132,133] (see p. 307). There is also the potential for parasite transmission when raw fish is fed. If any type of fish is added to a companion animal's diet, it should always be well cooked and only very small amounts should be fed.

Liver

Liver is an excellent source of iron, protein, copper, vitamin D, and several B vitamins. However, like other single food items, it is not a nutritionally complete food. Liver is severely deficient in calcium and excessively high in vitamin A. Both of these nutritional imbalances can cause bone disorders. Vitamin A toxicity has been shown to develop slowly over a period of years in cats that were regularly fed fresh liver as their primary dietary protein source.[142-144] The bone deformities of vitamin A toxicity form gradually and may go undetected for several years. Severe and irreversible crippling eventually occurs, and diagnosis is often too late to be of any help (see pp. 304–307).[145,146] Although small amounts of liver added to a cat's diet are not harmful, liver as a primary component of a cat's diet should be avoided.

Milk and Dairy Products

Almost all cats and dogs love the taste of milk. Although milk and dairy products are excellent sources of calcium, protein, phosphorus, and several vitamins, excessive intake may cause diarrhea in young and adult pets. Milk contains the simple sugar lactose. Lactose requires breakdown in the intestinal tract by the enzyme lactase. Some cats and dogs do not produce sufficient amounts of lactase to handle the large quantity

of lactose present in milk. Lack of sufficient lactase results in an inability to completely digest milk and will subsequently cause digestive upsets and diarrhea. Dairy products such as cheese, buttermilk, and yogurt contain slightly lower levels of lactose. Even though these products may be more easily tolerated, they still have the potential for causing diarrhea and dietary imbalances. Most pets can tolerate and enjoy an occasional bowl of milk, but like all supplementation, the practice of feeding milk should be strictly limited.

Dairy products should not be used as a supplemental source of calcium or protein. As discussed previously, excess dietary calcium can contribute to the development of skeletal disorders in growing dogs and is not helpful in preventing eclampsia in lactating dams (see Chapter 26, pp. 296–300). Although dairy products do supply high-quality protein, they contain deficiencies and excesses of other nutrients and may contribute to a dietary imbalance if large amounts are added to an otherwise adequate diet.

Oils and Fats

Cod liver oil, vegetable oils, and animal fats are occasionally added to pets' diets to improve the taste of the diet or to supply additional vitamins. It is true that fish oils are excellent sources of vitamin A, vitamin D, and the omega-3 fatty acids. However, both of these vitamins are toxic when consumed in excess. Because vitamins A and D are stored in the liver, the effects of excess intake are cumulative and develop over long periods of time. The daily addition of 1 or 2 tablespoons of cod liver oil (or other vitamin A supplement) to a small pet's diet has the potential of eventually developing into a toxicity problem. In addition, oversupplementation with fat may result in either obesity or in an eventual decrease in the quantity of food that is consumed. A decrease in intake may occur because energy needs will be met with a lower quantity of food. Deficiencies of other nutrients may then develop. Excessive intake of dietary fat may also cause digestive problems in some pets.

Some owners add fat to their pets' diets with the intention of improving coat quality. Dogs have a requirement for the essential fatty acid linoleic acid, and cats require linoleic and arachidonic acid. Animals that are deficient in essential fatty acids will develop poor coat quality and skin problems. Pet food of inferior quality or foods that have been stored too long may contain inadequate levels of these fatty acids. However, if a high-quality pet food is being fed, adding fat or oil should not be necessary. In most cases, diet is not the principle cause of skin problems or poor coat quality in companion animals. More probable causes of skin disorders include internal and external parasitic infections, allergies, and various hormonal imbalances. If a coat or skin problem persists in a dog or cat, even when a high-quality food is fed, a veterinarian should be consulted.

Chocolate

Most dogs enjoy sweet flavors, including the taste of chocolate. Cats, on the other hand, are much less likely to find sweet foods palatable.[42] Chocolate contains a methylxan-

thine called theobromine, which is toxic to dogs when consumed in large quantities. Three methylxanthine compounds are commonly found in human foods. These are caffeine, theophylline, and theobromine. Caffeine is most abundant in coffee, tea, and cola beverages, and theophylline is found primarily in tea. Theobromine is the most abundant methylxanthine that is found in cocoa and chocolate products. The main sites of action of xanthine compounds in the body are the central nervous system, the cardiovascular system, the kidneys, smooth muscle, and the skeletal musculature. Theobromine in particular acts as a smooth muscle relaxant, coronary artery dilator, diuretic, and cardiac stimulant.

Although it is not a common clinical problem, theobromine toxicity in dogs can be life threatening when it occurs. Toxicity studies have shown that compared with several other species, the dog is unusually sensitive with the physiological effects of theobromine. This sensitivity appears to be the result of a lower rate of theobromine metabolism, resulting in a longer half-life in the bloodstream and tissues. After a single dose, the half-life of theobromine in the plasma of adult dogs is approximately 17.5 hours.[147] In comparison, theobromine's half-life in human subjects is only 6 hours, and in rats it is 3 hours.[148,149] It has been theorized that the extended half-life in dogs may potentiate acute toxicity reactions to theobromine after the consumption of foods containing chocolate.[147]

Signs of theobromine toxicity in dogs include vomiting, diarrhea, panting, restlessness, increased urination or urinary incontinence, and muscle tremors. These signs usually occur about 4 to 5 hours after the dog has consumed the food containing chocolate. The onset of generalized motor seizures signifies a poor prognosis in most cases and often results in death.[150-152] Theobromine toxicity is treated by inducing vomiting as soon as possible. An activated charcoal "shake" given by gastric lavage may aid in decreasing the quantity of the drug that is absorbed into the bloodstream. Unfortunately, there is no specific systemic antidote for theobromine poisoning.

Although few controlled studies of the level of theobromine that constitutes a toxic dose have been conducted in dogs, data from long-term studies and case reports indicate that toxicity can occur when a dog consumes a dose of 90 to 100 milligrams per kilogram (mg/kg) of body weight or greater.[152] Factors such as individual sensitivity to theobromine, mode of theobromine administration, presence of other foods in the gastrointestinal tract at the time of ingestion, and variations in theobromine content between chocolate products cause wide variations in the susceptibility of individual dogs to chocolate poisoning. Chocolate products differ greatly in their theobromine content and, therefore, in their ability to produce theobromine poisoning. Chocolate liquor, commonly called baking or cooking chocolate, is the base substance from which all other chocolate products are produced.

The average level of theobromine in baking chocolate is about 1.22%.[153] A one-ounce square contains approximately 346 mg of theobromine. Therefore, if a medium-sized dog weighing 25 pounds (11 kg) consumed 3 ounces of baking chocolate, a potentially fatal dose of 94 mg/kg theobromine would be ingested. Commercial cocoa (unsweetened) has an average theobromine content of 1.89%, the highest theobromine content of all commonly consumed chocolate products. However, dogs are less likely to consume baking chocolate or cocoa powder than other, sweeter chocolate products. The addition of sugar, cocoa butter, and milk solids to baking chocolate to produce sweet

chocolates results in a significant dilution of theobromine content. For example, the level of theobromine in semisweet chocolate pieces is 0.463%. A 25-pound dog would have to consume approximately ½ pound of semisweet chocolate to reach a potentially toxic level of 95 mg/kg. Similarly, milk chocolate contains 0.153% theobromine. The ingestion of approximately 1.5 pounds of milk chocolate would result in a potentially lethal dose for a 25-pound dog.

Dogs generally love the taste of chocolate, and owners occasionally give chocolate candy or foods containing chocolate to their dogs as a special treat. If a dog's intake of chocolate is strictly limited to occasional small treats, there is no danger of theobromine toxicity. All of the published case studies of theobromine toxicity in dogs have been the result of a pet accidentally ingesting a large amount of chocolate.[150-152] If given the opportunity, many pets will readily overconsume chocolate. Therefore all chocolate foods should be stored in areas inaccessible to pets.

Myth: Feeding Brewer's Yeast or Thiamin Repels Fleas

The use of either brewer's yeast or one of its components, the B-vitamin thiamin, as a repellent for external parasites has been advocated for many years. This practice can be traced back to several studies with human subjects that were conducted during the 1940s. In one study, when subjects were given oral doses of 100 to 200 mg of thiamin per day, it was reported that they experienced lower numbers of mosquito bites and decreased severity of dermatological reactions.[154] Another early study reported that benefits were observed when infants and children with severe flea infestations were treated with 10 mg of thiamin per day.[155] However, neither of these studies were well controlled, and several subsequent studies with humans have failed to show any significant effect of thiamin supplementation on insect infestations.[156]

Companion animal owners and professionals, anxious to find safe and convenient means for controlling flea and mite infestations, quickly adapted this practice for use in dogs and cats. However, there is no evidence to indicate that feeding thiamin or brewer's yeast has a repellent effect on fleas or mites in these species. Two controlled studies have reported that neither brewer's yeast nor thiamin repelled fleas or mosquitos in dogs. In the first study, dogs that were fed 14 grams per day of active or inactive brewer's yeast had the same weekly flea counts as did a group of dogs that was not supplemented.[157] In the second study, neither flea counts nor the number of flea bites on dogs were affected by supplementation with 100 mg of thiamin per day.[156] Although supplementing pet's diets with brewer's yeast is probably not harmful, it is not effective in either repelling or controlling flea populations in homes or on the skin of companion animals.

Myth: Feeding Garlic or Onion Repels Fleas

Feeding either of these two food items will certainly make a pet's breath smell, but it will not have any effect on fleas. Moreover, feeding large amounts of onion to dogs or cats can be toxic. Excess consumption of onions results in the formation of Heinz bod-

ies on circulating red blood cells, which ultimately results in the development of hemolytic anemia. In severe cases, this anemia can be fatal.[158-160] The toxic compound in onions that is responsible for this effect is n-propyl disulfide. Signs of the hemolytic anemia that is produced by onion toxicity include diarrhea, vomiting, depression, elevated temperature, and dark-colored urine. Although vomiting and diarrhea may be immediate, the remaining signs usually appear 1 to 4 days following the ingestion of the onion. If onion toxicity is suspected, veterinary care should be sought immediately. Many dogs love the taste of onions and may overconsume if given the opportunity. Therefore onion-containing foods should only be fed in small amounts to dogs and cats, and they certainly should not be expected to have an effect on flea infestations.

MYTH: DIET CAUSES ACUTE MOIST DERMATITIS ("HOT SPOTS")

Acute moist dermatitis is a condition that is commonly referred to as "hot spots" because it frequently occurs during warm months of the year and because the lesions that develop are inflamed and feel hot to the touch. This disease is most commonly seen in breeds of dogs that have very dense, heavy coats, and it may be related to poor ventilation of the skin or improper grooming to remove matted hair and debris. Hot-spot lesions can develop within just a few hours. The lesions are usually first noticed as a patch of missing hair. A round, red, moist area that is extremely painful rapidly develops. The area often has a yellowish center surrounded by a reddened ring of inflammation. Self-trauma occurs in the form of biting and scratching at the affected area because the lesions are usually intensely pruritic. If not treated, the spots can spread to other areas of the body.

Any factor that causes irritation, pruritus, and/or self-trauma can lead to acute moist dermatitis. Allergic reactions, external parasites, skin infections, an unhealed injury, or improper grooming can all initiate self-trauma and the development of a hot spot. It is believed by some pet owners that a diet that is too "rich" or too high in protein is the cause of hot spots. However, there is no evidence that a relationship exists between acute moist dermatitis and protein levels in the diet.[161] Diet may play a role if it produces a severe fatty acid deficiency or if the pet has a food-induced allergy. Fatty acid deficiencies can occur when improperly formulated or improperly stored pet foods are fed and are characterized by a number of dermatological signs (see Section 2, pp. 98–99). Food-induced allergies may indirectly cause a hot spot to develop because allergies typically cause intense pruritus, which in turn may lead to self-trauma and the development of hot spots (see Section 6, pp. 384–385). However, both of these causes occur very infrequently. The most common underlying cause of acute moist dermatitis in dogs appears to be flea-bite hypersensitivity and other allergic skin diseases.[161]

MYTH: CERTAIN DIETS CAUSE COAT COLOR TO TURN RED IN DOGS

In recent years, dog show enthusiasts have become concerned with a problem that is commonly called red coat. This term refers to a perceived change in coat color from

almost any normal base color to a red or reddish brown. This change is of greatest concern to, and in fact has only been reported by, individuals who exhibit and/or breed dogs. It is the belief of some that a component or components in the diet is the cause of this malady. Several different brands of premium dog foods have been implicated. The specific brand that is targeted apparently depends on the part of the country that the owner lives in and the breed of dog that is being discussed.

One of the difficulties in investigating this problem has been the inconsistency and infrequency of its occurrence. Interestingly, when pet food companies have attempted to investigate red coat, they have found that very few of the cases are first-person complaints. In most cases, the complainant did not actually own the dog or dogs that turned red but had heard of a case through friends or breeders. Secondly, there is still no precise definition of the red coat problem. The condition that one owner observes and calls red coat may not be the same that another interprets as the same problem. Although the perceived occurrence of red coat among dog show enthusiasts is quite high, the actual occurrence of the problem in dogs is extremely low. As a result, the number of actual dogs that have been available for investigators to study has been very small.

An understanding of normal coat color development is necessary to completely understand the potential causes of a change in coat color in a dog. An individual hair takes between 6 and 8 weeks to grow. Once mature, the hair enters a resting phase and remains dormant for weeks or months before being shed to make room for a new hair. The color of a dog's hair is determined by the type and amount of pigment that is deposited in the growing hair while it is in the hair follicle. Specialized, pigment-producing cells within the follicle secrete either yellow-red pheomelanin or black-brown melanin that is deposited within the actual hair. Other genetic factors affect the distribution of pigment within the hair shaft, the dilution or masking of color, and the distribution of color in different areas of the body. These factors result in the wide variety of coat colors that are seen in different breeds of dogs. In addition to genetics, other factors that may affect the color of the hair during either its growth or resting cycle include medications, topical substances, aging, environment, and diet.

A change in the color of a hair may be affected in one of two possible ways. A systemic factor may cause a change in the color of hairs while they are still in the hair follicle (that is, a change in the pigment-producing cells). Within the hair, this type of change would be expected to extend from the skin surface and outward toward the hair tip, and the portion of the hair that is affected would depend on the length of time that the influencing factor was in effect. For example, if the change was only in effect for 2 weeks, the color change would appear as a band of color on the length of the hair shaft. Because individual hairs within the entire coat are at different stages of development, the red color in the hair coat would be dispersed throughout the coat at different levels on each hair shaft. By definition, this type of change in coat color would take weeks to months to appear or disappear. Also, because hair growth occurs at random throughout the coat, it would be expected that any change in color would not be uniform, but would occur in only the hairs that were growing at the time that the influencing factor was present. Resting hairs would not be affected by any factor that affected a change in coat color in the growing hair.

The second way that a change in coat color can occur is through the deposition of a substance on the outside of the hair shaft. This change could involve substances that are either applied by the dog's owner, secreted by the dog's skin, or licked onto the hair by the dog. This type of change would involve the entire length of the hair shaft, and all of the hairs within a region would be affected. Therefore the appearance of this type of coat-color change would be significantly different from the appearance of the coat if a systemic factor was in effect.

There are several known factors that can affect hair coat color in dogs and could be responsible for imbuing a red hue to the coat. Aging of hair naturally causes a change in color. As a hair approaches the end of its resting period and is ready to be shed, black hairs will turn reddish to reddish brown. This change occurs primarily near the tip of the hair, with the base of the hair remaining black. However, in some cases, especially when hairs are retained for a long period of time without shedding, the entire shaft may turn red. When the dog sheds its coat, these hairs are removed, and a return to normal color is seen. In addition to age of the hair, exposure to sunlight can also cause black hairs to turn red. When this occurs, the change in color usually affects variable portions of the ends of the hairs. The color of the hair at the base (near the dog's skin) remains black.

Topically applied dips or shampoos that contain insecticides can also turn hair a red hue. This effect can be seen with any natural coat color, but it will be most noticeable in white or light-colored dogs. When an applied agent is the cause, the change in color will be uniform throughout the hair shaft. Similarly, frequent shampooing, using certain types of rinses, and blow drying can all alter hair coat color.

Lastly, a commonly observed cause of coat-color change in dogs is porphyrin staining. Porphyrin is a substance found in the tears and the saliva of dogs that turns red when exposed to sunlight. It is a normal end product of hemoglobin metabolism and is the substance that is responsible for the reddish staining that is seen around the eyes of some breeds of dogs. Dogs that lick excessively will also deposit porphyrins on their coat, causing these areas to stain red. Licking that is associated with allergic reactions or other dermatological problems may cause reddening of the coat. In these cases, the entire length of the hair in certain regions of the body will be affected.

Although a number of different factors are known to cause coat-color changes in dogs, a connection between diet and red coat has never been demonstrated. Copper deficiency can cause hypopigmentation of the coat that may manifest as a reddening or graying of the hairs. However, other clinical signs accompany this deficiency, including anemia, skin lesions, and the development of a rough, dull hair coat.[162] The anemia of copper deficiency will eventually cause clinical illness in affected dogs. It is highly unlikely that a dietary imbalance of any nutrient is the cause of the red coat problem in dogs. When a nutrient is deficient or in excess, multiple systems of the body are usually involved, and clinical signs other than just a change in coat color will develop.

The few number of actual cases of red coat that have been examined have been found to have an identifiable underlying cause. These causes have included exposure to sun, staining with porphyrin, the presence of old hairs that have not been shed, and a

coexisting dermatological disease.[163] Although more research involving coat-color changes in dogs and cats needs to be conducted, it appears that nutrition is not the cause of the red coat problem in dogs that have been studied.

Myth: Type of Diet or Components in the Diet Cause Gastric Dilatation Volvulus

Gastric dilatation volvulus (GDV), commonly referred to as bloat, is a life-threatening disorder that is characterized by rapid and abnormal distention of the stomach (dilatation). This disorder is often, but not always, accompanied by rotation of the stomach along its long axis (volvulus). Dilatation occurs when gas and secretions accumulate within the stomach and are not expelled because of the occlusion of both the cardiac and pyloric sphincters. The condition rapidly worsens as the distended and rotated stomach places pressure on the major abdominal blood vessels. This pressure causes a loss of blood flow to the stomach and other vital organs, decreased cardiac output, and the development of shock. At this point the dog's condition will rapidly deteriorate and if the GDV is not corrected quickly, shock and tissue damage become severe, and death ensues. The time course of GDV is quite variable between dogs, but this disorder should always be treated as a medical emergency.

Bloat most often affects large, deep-chested dogs. The breeds that have been identified as being most susceptible include the German shepherd dog, Great Dane, Saint Bernard, Irish setter, bloodhound, and borzoi.[164] Although rare, the disorder can also occur in small breeds of dogs and cats.[164,165] Bloat typically occurs shortly after the dog has consumed a meal and has then either consumed a large volume of water or has engaged in strenuous exercise. However, GDV has also occurred in the absence of these conditions. Dogs that are developing GDV will exhibit acute abdominal pain and distention and will often whine, pace, salivate, and appear anxious. The dog may attempt to vomit but is unable to regurgitate any stomach contents. As the problem progresses, shock occurs and is characterized by pale mucous membranes, a rapid and weak pulse, increased heart rate, and weakness. In all cases, veterinary care must be provided immediately.

Initial treatment of GDV involves decompression of the stomach and treatment for shock. Surgical intervention is usually also necessary and involves derotation and repositioning of the stomach, followed by prophylactic measures that help to prevent recurrence. Surgery also allows assessment of the damage to the stomach and other organs. Despite rapid treatment, 38% to 68% of initial GDV cases are fatal.[166] Death occurs either during surgery because of irreversible shock or within several days of surgery as a result of cardiac or metabolic complications or gastric necrosis.[167]

The underlying cause of GDV is not known, but a number of theories have been proposed. Factors that have been examined include a genetic predisposition, dietary management practices, diet type and composition, and intrinsic abnormalities such as elevated serum gastrin or altered gastric motility. Research studies have examined most of these theories and a growing body of evidence is available concerning the underlying cause or causes of this disorder. Because a pet's diet is the one factor that owners have some measure of control over, the theories that identify diet as an underlying cause have received an inordinate amount of publicity and attention. In addition, the results of studies that have examined the role of diet in GDV have often been misinterpreted or misrepresented. The end result is much confusion for pet owners, breeders, and some professionals about the actual role of various factors in the onset of GDV.

Genetics certainly play a role in GDV to the degree that body type and structure are inherited characteristics. However, it is not known if there are additional heritable factors within breeds or family lines that can increase the susceptibility of a dog to this disorder. The study of the genetics that are involved in GDV is complicated by the fact that it is often difficult or impossible to separate the effects of genetics from influences of the environment, such as husbandry practices, medical care, and feeding management. Although dogs that inherit a large, deep-chested body type have an increased susceptibility to this disease, additional influences of genetics are not known at this time.

Several feeding management practices appear to affect a susceptible dog's chances of developing GDV. Specifically, the size and number of meals that the dog receives per day may be important, as are the timing of exercise and exposure to stress. It has been observed that although the role of overeating or overdrinking is difficult to determine, the majority of cases of GDV occur when the dog has a full stomach.[167] A study with Irish setters reported that dogs that were fed one large meal per day throughout growth developed larger, heavier stomachs than did dogs that were fed three meals per day during the same time period. The dogs that were fed once daily also had greater gastric distention than did the dogs that were fed multiple meals, but no differences in gastric motility were seen between the two groups. The investigators concluded that feeding one time per day opposed to feeding multiple small meals per day may contribute to changes associated with GDV in susceptible dogs.[168] It has also been postulated that strenuous exercise, stress, or excitement may also be contributing factors, especially before or after a meal or a large volume of water is consumed.[167]

Composition of the diet or type of diet that is fed has received much attention as a possible cause of GDV, but there are little actual data to support this theory. Dry dog foods have been implicated because of the belief that they absorb water and expand while in the stomach, causing an abnormal amount of gastric distention. Another theory proposes that cereal-based, dry diets delay gastric emptying when consumed and contribute to the accumulation of gas in the stomach. The presence of soybean products in pet foods has also been proposed as a causative factor. It has been theorized that soy provides a fermentative substrate for *Clostridia* species bacteria within the stomach, which produces the gas that is responsible for GDV. A study with large breeds of dogs compared the effects of feeding a dry cereal-based, canned meat, or canned, cereal-based diet on gastric motility and the rate of gastric emptying. Results showed that there was no significant effect of diet on gastric function in any of the dogs that were studied.[169]

Another study reported that intragastric moistening of ingested, dry dog food also failed to produce the stomach distention that is characteristic of GDV.[170] A clinical study

involving 240 dogs that had been treated for GDV did not find any correlation between the type of food that was fed and the occurrence of GDV.[171] Lastly, the fermentation theory has been largely refuted by the observation that the gas found in the stomachs of GDV dogs is made up primarily of atmospheric gas, indicating that swallowed air is the source of the gas, not fermented stomach contents.[172] Production of fermentative gas in the stomach of dogs with GDV can occur after death and may lead to the erroneous conclusion that this gas was the initial cause of the disorder. Studies of postmortem tissue decomposition have been unable to demonstrate that the presence of *Clostridia* species bacteria in the stomach is primary to disease rather than secondary. Currently, the studies that are available support the conclusion that GDV is not a dietary disorder and its development is not related to any component in pet foods nor to the type of food that is fed.

The final group of theories that have been investigated involve intrinsic factors that affect gastric motility and gastric emptying. Delayed emptying of the stomach occurs in dogs that have had GDV.[173] One theory proposed that chronically elevated levels of the hormone gastrin could contribute to these changes in gastric function. Delayed gastric emptying is a direct effect of gastrin. However, studies with dogs that had been treated for GDV found that there were no differences in serum gastrin levels between these dogs and healthy control dogs.[166] Other studies have shown that the stomachs of dogs that have recovered from GDV have electrical (neural) activity that results in abnormal muscular contractions. These abnormal contractions lead to premature closure of the pylorus, gastric retention of solids, and delayed gastric emptying.[166] It is currently proposed that GDV may be the result of a functional defect that prevents normal gastric motility and emptying. This inherent defect may predispose the dog to an atonic stomach and, possibly, to the stretching of the gastrohepatic ligament that is necessary for the development of GDV. Other contributing factors may include a hereditary predisposition, exercise before or after eating, overeating, and possibly stress.

Although the types of diet and components within the diet are not causal factors in GDV, several feeding management practices can be used that can help to prevent bloat in dogs that are susceptible or have a history of bloat. In other words, although what the dog eats does not appear to affect the occurrence of GDV, how the dog is fed and the environment in which he is fed can be managed to minimize the chances of GDV. Portion-controlled meal feeding should be used, and several small meals should be fed per day, as opposed to one large meal, to prevent overfilling of the stomach. Similarly, although fresh water should be available at all times, dogs should not be allowed to drink a large volume of water before or after eating or after exercise. Because dogs will often increase their rate of eating or the amount that they eat when in the presence of other dogs, all susceptible dogs should be fed separately, and any stress that may be associated with the feeding environment should be minimized. If possible, feeding times should be scheduled so that the dog is supervised and can be observed for 1 to 2 hours after meals. Lastly, exercise should always be withheld for 1 hour before and at least 2 hours following feeding. All dogs that have a susceptible body type or that have a history of GDV should be carefully monitored for signs of GDV. If signs are seen, veterinary care should be sought immediately (see the box on the following page).

Practical Tips: Prevention of GDV in Susceptible Dogs

Use portion-controlled meal feeding as the feeding regimen.
Feed several small meals per day to prevent overfilling of the stomach.
Do not allow the consumption of a large volume of water immediately before or after eating or exercise.
Feed susceptible dogs separately from other animals. If possible, supervise mealtimes.
Do not provide exercise for 1 hour before and 2 hours after meals.
If signs of GDV are observed, seek veterinary assistance immediately.

MYTH: ETHOXYQUIN CAUSES REPRODUCTIVE PROBLEMS, AUTOIMMUNE DISEASE, AND CANCER IN DOGS

Ethoxyquin is a synthetic antioxidant that is included in animal foods and some human foods as a preservative to protect fats and fat-soluble vitamins from oxidative degradation (see Section 3, pp. 181–182). Without the inclusion of antioxidants in pet foods, oxidative processes lead to rancidity of the product. Rancid fat is offensive in odor and flavor and includes compounds that are toxic when consumed. The inclusion of antioxidants in commercial pet foods ensures the safety, nutritional integrity, and flavor of the product during the time that it will be fed to companion animals.

Although ethoxyquin has been approved by the Food and Drug Administration and used in foods for more than 30 years, this compound has recently been erroneously identified by some companion animal owners and breeders as a potentially dangerous agent in pet foods. Depending on the source, ethoxyquin is identified as being responsible for reproductive problems, autoimmune disorders, and/or various types of cancers in dogs and cats. All of these reports are anecdotal in nature and do not provide a method of establishing an exact role of diet or any dietary components in the onset of disease. However, there are numerous short-term and long-term studies that have been conducted with a variety of species that confirm the safety of ethoxyquin at the levels that are included in human and pet foods. Currently, there is no scientific evidence indicating that ethoxyquin can cause health problems when included at approved levels in pet foods.[174]

MYTH: HIGH-FAT PET FOODS CAUSE HYPERLIPIDEMIA

Most people are aware of the relationship of dietary fat and cholesterol to the development of atherosclerosis and heart disease in humans and of the importance of limiting these nutrients in their diet. In recent years, this knowledge has led some pet owners to apply these same nutritional principles to the diet of their companion animals. However, there exist some very basic differences between these species in the ways in

which dietary fat is assimilated and metabolized. Unlike humans, dogs and cats are capable of consuming a wide range of dietary fat and still maintaining normal blood lipid levels. This is presumably because dogs and cats first evolved as carnivorous predators with a diet that normally contained a high proportion of animal fat. The capability to consume, digest, and assimilate a high-fat diet has remained with these species throughout the domestication process.

Both hyperlipidemia and atherosclerosis are rare conditions in dogs and cats. When cases of these conditions do occur, they are either of genetic origin or they develop secondarily to other disease states. For example, an inherited defect in lipoprotein lipase activity in cats causes elevated triglyceride and cholesterol levels in affected cats. The disorder eventually leads to the development of severe peripheral nerve paralysis. It is proposed that an autosomal recessive mode of inheritance, similar to that of an analogous disease in humans, is responsible for this disorder.[175] There is also some evidence for the existence of an inherited defect in lipid metabolism in miniature schnauzers and possibly also in Brittany spaniels[176,177] (see Section 6, pp. 341–346). A second cause of hyperlipidemia in companion animals is the presence of certain preexisting disorders. Diseases that may cause secondary hyperlipidemia include diabetes mellitus, hypothyroidism, pancreatitis, nephrotic syndrome, and liver disease.[177] Certain medications such as glucocorticoids and immunosuppressant drugs may also result in transient increases in blood lipid levels in some pets.

When they occur, elevated triglyceride levels in dogs and cats may produce clinical signs of anorexia, lethargy, abdominal pain, seizures, vomiting, diarrhea, and lipid-laden aqueous humor. Hypercholesterolemia, on the other hand, may be related to the development of atherosclerotic lesions, lipemia retinalis, and lipid opacification of the cornea.[177] Traditionally, the dietary treatment for hyperlipidemia in dogs and cats has been a low-fat diet. Both primary and secondary hyperlipidemia appear to respond well to the strict adherence to low-fat, low-calorie diets in these species.[175-177] However, feeding a low-fat diet to healthy pets with the intention of preventing hyperlipidemia and elevated cholesterol levels is unnecessary. Balanced, low-fat diets can be used for the treatment of obesity and for weight maintenance in adult pets that lead sedentary life-styles. However, the concerns that humans have with dietary lipids and heart disease do not apply to our companion animals, except in the specific circumstances that are discussed above.

KEY POINTS

SECTION 5

Canine and feline couch potatoes? Unfortunately, like contemporary American humans, increasing numbers of cats and dogs are obese. Recent surveys report obesity rates from 24% to 34% among dogs and 40% among cats. It can be theorized that a sedentary life-style along with overfeeding highly palatable and energy-dense foods may be responsible.

It is known that health problems in humans begin to increase when a person's weight is 15% or more above their ideal weight. Similarly, health problems among dogs and cats probably increase with obesity. Such problems include hyperinsulinemia, glucose intolerance, diabetes, pulmonary and cardiovascular disease, exercise and heat intolerance, and orthopedic problems. Surgical risk is higher, and the incidences of postoperative morbidity and mortality increase.

Once new fat cells are added to the body, their number cannot be decreased below a minimum level. Understandably, to avoid obesity in adulthood, it is important to provide pets with proper weight control throughout their periods of growth.

Although the cause of obesity seemingly could be explained by simple mathematics (that is, more energy is taken in than is expended), there are many underlying causes for such an imbalance, not all of which are completely understood.

The notion that an individual or animal is obese because of "low metabolism" is a fallacy. In fact, research in humans has shown that the resting metabolic rate of obese subjects is actually higher than that of normal weight subjects.

It is commonly believed that neutering a pet leads to obesity. Although it is true that obesity is more common among neutered pets, a contributing cause is that the age of the pet at neutering (between 6 months and 1 year of age) corresponds with a natural decrease in the pet's growth rate and energy needs. Thus owners should decrease the amount of food during this period in the pet's development.

External stimuli, such as diet palatability, food composition and texture, and the timing and environment of meals, appear to be the most important factors leading to overconsumption and obesity.

Just like their human counterparts, animals will tend to eat more, regardless of their initial level of hunger, when the food is highly palatable and presented in a social setting with others present.

More weight will be gained when the excess calories are provided by fat than by protein or carbohydrate sources.

The benefits of exercise, which are well known to human athletes, also can have a positive effect on overweight pets. Exercise can positively affect an animal's normal physiological control of food intake and supports a higher proportion of lean to fat tissue, which contributes to maintaining a normal resting metabolic rate during weight loss.

All commercial pet foods formulated for weight loss or for consumption by sedentary pets have decreased levels of fat. However, some replace fat with digestible carbohydrates, such as corn and rice, and some use indigestible fiber, which results in increased fecal volume and defecation frequency.

Tip: Many of the preventive and causative factors for obesity are the same for humans and animals. Lowering both your own and your pet's intake of fat and increasing the amount of exercise will benefit you both. Take more walks and team up with your pet to improve your health and maintain ideal weight.

Heredity is not completely responsible for many forms of developmental skeletal disease, such as canine hip dysplasia. Environmental factors, such as nutrition, are also responsible. Research has shown that excess caloric intake during growth and high calcium intake are two important nutritional factors in the development of skeletal disease. Therefore the well-intentioned efforts of some owners to maximize the growth rate of puppies by feeding excessive amounts of a balanced diet can actually lead to orthopedic problems.

During certain periods of growth, the bones of large dogs are thinner and weaker than those of smaller dogs, and this may partially explain the predisposition for skeletal abnormalities among large and giant breeds.

Caution: Although some breeders recommend routine calcium supplementation for growing puppies, this practice is unnecessary and can sometimes lead to several serious health disorders. Excess calcium has been shown to lead to many orthopedic problems, ironically the type of problem that the supplementation was supposed to avoid.

Calcium supplementation during pregnancy and lactation is generally contraindicated. Feeding a high-quality, commercial pet food formulated for feeding through gestation and lactation is recommended.

Although frank deficiencies of vitamins are highly unusual in pets today, select deficiencies and toxicities can occur as a result of improper feeding practices. Feeding excessive levels of foods that contain marginal levels of vitamin E and high amounts of polyunsaturated fatty acids can lead to vitamin E deficiency in cats. On the other hand, feeding cats foods that contain too much vitamin A can lead to toxicity. Thiamin deficiency can be induced by feeding raw fish, and biotin deficiency can be caused by feeding raw egg whites. Both raw fish and raw egg whites contain inhibitory substances.

Supplementing a cat's diet with liver, cod liver oil, or other fish liver oils can cause vitamin A and D toxicosis. Certain fish (raw carp and saltwater herring) have been shown to produce thiamin (vitamin B_1) deficiency. Feeding a diet containing raw egg white can cause biotin deficiency.

Tip: Resist the temptation to give a large amount of human foods to pets. Many problems can result, such as obesity, deficiencies of minerals and vitamins, parasite transmission, toxic levels of some vitamins and minerals, orthopedic deformities, digestive upsets, and diarrhea.

Caution: Although small amounts of chocolate given occasionally as special treats are not harmful, death has been reported to occur when dogs ingest larger quantities of chocolate (theobromine toxicity). Because dogs generally love the taste of chocolate, be sure to keep chocolate out of a pet's reach; approximately 1.5 pounds of milk chocolate could be lethal for a 25-pound dog.

Contrary to popular belief, there is no evidence that adding brewer's yeast to pet foods repels fleas or mites.

Although many hypotheses have been advanced for the cause of gastric dilatation volvulus (GDV or"bloat"), no dietary causes have been identified. Development of GDV is not related to any component in pet foods or to the type of food that is fed. However, it is thought that large, deep-chested dogs might be predisposed to developing this often-fatal disorder.

S E C T I O N   5
REFERENCES

1. Markwell PJ, Erk W, Parkin GD, and others: Obesity in the dog, *J Sm Anim Pract* 31:533–537, 1990.
2. Mason E: Obesity in pet dogs, *Vet Rec* 86:612–616, 1970.
3. Anderson RS: Obesity in the dog and cat, *Vet Ann* 14:182–186, 1973.
4. Edney ATB, Smith AM: Study of obesity in dogs visiting veterinary practices in the United Kingdom, *Vet Rec* 118:391–396, 1986.
5. Sloth C: Practical management of obesity in dogs and cats, *J Sm Anim Pract* 33:178–182, 1992.
6. Davidson S, Passmore R: *Human nutrition and dietetics*, ed. 4, Edinburgh, 1969, Churchill Livingstone p 367.
7. Vasselli JR, Cleary MP, van Itallie TB: Modern concepts of obesity, *Nutr Rev* 41:361–373, 1983.
8. van Itallie TB: Morbid obesity: a hazardous disorder that resists conservative treatment, *Am J Clin Nutr* 33:358–363, 1980.
9. Mattheeuws D, Rottiers R, Kaneko JJ, and others: Diabetes mellitus in dogs: relationship of obesity to glucose tolerance and insulin response, *Am J Vet Res* 45:98–103, 1984.
10. Mattheeuws D, Rottiers R, Baeyens D, and others: Glucose tolerance and insulin response in obese dogs, *J Am Anim Hosp Assoc* 20:287–290, 1984.
11. Edney ATB: Management of obesity in the dog, *Vet Med Sm Anim Clin* 69:46–49, 1974.
12. Bertrand HA, Lynd FT, Masoro EJ, and others: Changes in adipose mass and cellularity through the adult life of rats fed ad libitum or a life-prolonging restricted diet, *J Gerontol* 35:827–835, 1980.
13. Hirsch J, Knittle JL: Cellularity of obese and non-obese adipose tissue, *Fed Proc* 29:1516–1521, 1970.
14. Knittle JL, Fellner FG, Brown RE: Adipose tissue development in man, *Am J Clin Nutr* 30:762–766, 1977.
15. Bjorntorp P: The role of adipose tissue in human obesity. In Greenwood MRC, editor: *Obesity—contemporary issues in clinical nutrition*, New York, 1983, Churchill Livingstone, pp 17–24.
16. Lemonnier D: Effect of age, sex and site of cellularity of the adipose tissue in mice and rats rendered obese by a high fat diet, *J Clin Invest* 51:2907, 1972.
17. Faust IM, Johnson PR, Hirsch J: Long-term effects of early nutritional experience on the development of obesity in the rat, *J Nutr* 110:2027–2034, 1980.
18. Johnson PR, Stern JS, Greenwood MRC, and others: Effect of early nutrition on adipose cellularity and pancreatic insulin release in the Zucker rat, *J Nutr* 103:738–743, 1973.
19. Sibley KW: Diagnosis and management of the overweight dog, *Br Vet J* 140:124–131, 1984.
20. Kaufman E: Obesity in dogs, *Vet Tech* 7:5–8, 1986.
21. Leibowitz SF: Hypothalamic neurotransmitters in relation to normal and disturbed eating patterns. In Wurtman RJ, Wurtman JJ, editors: *Human obesity*, New York, 1987, New York Academy of Sciences, pp 137–143.
22. Houpt KA, Hintz HF: Obesity in dogs, *Can Pract* 5:54–57, 1978.
23. Ravussin E, Burnand B, Schutz Y, and others: Twenty-four hour energy expenditure and resting metabolic rate in obese, moderately obese and control subjects, *Am J Clin Nutr* 35:566–573, 1982.

24. Halliday D, Hesp R, Stalley SF, and others: Resting metabolic rate, weight, surface area and body composition in obese women, *Int J Obes* 3:1–6, 1979.

25. Hoffmans M, Pfeifer WA, Gundlach BL, and others: Resting metabolic rate in obese and normal weight women, *Int J Obes* 3:111–118, 1979.

26. James WPT, Davies HL, Bailes J, and others: Elevated metabolic rates in obesity, *Lancet* 1:1122–1125, 1978.

27. Ashwell M: Brown adipose tissue — relevant to obesity?, *Hum Nutr App Nutr* 30:763–770, 1983.

28. Nair KS, Halliday D, Garrow JS: Thermic response to isoenergetic protein, carbohydrate or fat meals in lean and obese subjects, *Clin Sci* 65:307–312, 1983.

29. Horton ES: An overview of the assessment and regulation of energy balance in humans, *Am J Clin Nutr* 38:972–977, 1983.

30. Applegate EA, Upton DE, Stern JS: Food intake, body composition and blood lipids following treadmill exercise in male and female rats, *Physio Behav* 28:917–920, 1982.

31. Meyer DJ: Clinical manifestations associated with endocrine disorders, *Vet Clin North Am Sm Anim Pract* 7:433–441, 1977.

32. Randolph JF, Jorgensen LS: Selected feline endocrinopathies, *Vet Clin North Am Sm Anim Pract* 14:1261–1270, 1984.

33. Nesbitt GH, Izzo J, Peterson L, and others: Canine hypothyroidism: a retrospective study of 108 cases, *J Am Vet Med Assoc* 177:1117–1122, 1980.

34. Anderson RK: Canine hypothyroidism, *Sm Anim Pract* 1:103–109, 1979.

35. Peterson ME: Hyperadrenocorticism, *Vet Clin North Am Sm Anim Pract* 14:731–749, 1984.

36. Branam JE: Dietary management of obese dogs and cats, *Vet Tech* 9:490–493, 1988.

37. Houpt KA, Coren B, Hintz HF, and others: Effect of sex and reproductive status on sucrose preference, food intake and body weight of dogs, *J Am Vet Med Assoc* 174:1083–1085, 1979.

38. Duch DS, Chow FHC, Hamar DW, and others: The effect of castration and body weight on the occurrence of the feline urological syndrome, *Fel Pract* 8:35–40, 1978.

39. Brook CGD, Huntley RMC, Slack J: Influence of heredity and environment in determination of skin fold thickness in children, *Br Med J* 2:719–721, 1975.

40. Bouchard C: Body composition in adopted and biological siblings, *Hum Biol* 57:61–75, 1985.

41. Stunkard AJ, Sorensen TIA, Hanis C, and others: An adoption study of human obesity, *N Engl J Med* 314:193–198, 1986.

42. Houpt KA, Smith SL: Taste preferences and their relation to obesity in dogs and cats, *Can Vet J* 22:77–81, 1981.

43. Scalafani A, Springer O: Dietary obesity in adult rats: similarities to hypothalamic and human obesity syndromes, *Physiol Behav* 17:461–471, 1976.

44. Slattery JM, Potter RM: Hyperphagia: a necessary precondition to obesity?, *Appetite* 6:133–142, 1985.

45. Hill SW: Eating responses of humans during meals, *J Comp Physiol Psychol* 86:652–657, 1974.

46. Edelman B, Engell D, Bronstein P, and others: Environmental effects on the intake of overweight and normal-weight men, *Appetite* 7:71–83, 1986.

47. Fabry P, Tepperman J: Meal frequency—a possible factor in human pathology, *Am J Clin Nutr* 23:1059, 1970.

48. Blundell JE: Nutritional manipulation for altering food intake. In Wurtman RJ, Wurtman JJ, editors: *Human obesity*, New York, 1987, New York, Academy of Sciences, pp 144–155.

49. Wilkinson MJA, McEwan NA: Use of ultrasound in the measurement of subcutaneous fat and prediction of total body fat in dogs, *J Nutr*, 121:S47–S50, 1991.

50. Joshua JO: The obese dog and some clinical repercussions, *Sm Anim Pract* 11:601–606, 1970.

51. Lewis LD: Obesity in the dog, *J Am Anim Hosp Assoc* 14:402–409, 1978.

52. Ravussin E, Burnand B, Schutz Y, and others: Energy expenditure before and during energy restriction in obese patients, *Am J Clin Nutr* 41:753–759, 1985.

53. Darke PGG: Obesity in small animals, *Vet Rec* 102:545–546, 1978.

54. Mayer J, Marshall NB, Vitalle JJ: Exercise, food intake and body weight in normal rats and genetically obese adult mice, *Am J Physio* 177:544–548, 1954.

55. Pi-Sunyer FX: Exercise effects on calorie intake. In Wurtman RJ, Wurtman JJ, editors: *Human obesity*, New York, 1987, New York Academy of Sciences, pp 94–103.

56. Schultz CK, Bernauer E, Mole PA: Effects of severe caloric restriction and moderate exercise on basal metabolic rate and hormonal status in adult humans, *Fed Proc* 39:783, 1980 (abstract).

57. Scheuer J, Tipton CM: Cardiovascular adaptations to physical training. *Ann Rev Physiol* 39:221–251, 1977.

58. Leblanc J, Diamond P: The effect of meal frequency on postprandial thermogenesis in the dog, *Fed Proc* 44:1678, 1985 (abstract).

59. Danforth E Jr: Diet and obesity, *Am J Clin Nutr* 41:1132–1145, 1985.

60. Schwartz RS, Ravussin E, Massari M, and others: The thermic effect of carbohydrate versus fat feeding in man, *Metabolism* 34:285–293, 1985.

61. Acheson KJ, Ravussin E, Wahren J, and others: Nutritional influences on lipogenesis and thermogenesis after a carbohydrate meal, *Am J Physiol* 246:E62–E70, 1984.

62. Porikos K, Hagamen S: Is fiber satiating? Effects of a high fiber preload on subsequent food intake of normal-weight and obese young men, *Appetite* 7:153–162, 1986.

63. Levine AS, Tallman JR, Grace MK, and others: Effect of breakfast cereals on short-term food intake, *Am J Clin Nutr* 50:1303–1307, 1989.

64. Burley VJ, Leeds AR, Blundell JE: The effect of high and low fibre breakfasts on hunger, satiety and food intake in a subsequent meal, *Int J Obes* 1(suppl):87–93, 1987.

65. Butterwick RF, Markwell PJ: Effect of level and source of dietary fibre on food intake in the dog. Waltham Symposium on the Nutrition of Companion Animals, Sept 23, 25, 1993 (abstract).

66. Hand MS: Treating and preventing obesity in small animals. In *Managing fiber-responsive diseases*, Hill's Pet Products, Topeka, Kansas, 1988, Veterinary Medicine Publishing Company.

67. Eastwood MA, Brydon WG, Tadesse K: Effect of fiber on colon function. In Spiller GM, Kay RM, editors: *Medical aspects of dietary fiber*, New York, 1980, Plenum Press, pp 1–16.

68. Vahouny GV, Cassidy MM: Dietary fibers and absorption of nutrients, (review) *Proc Soc Exp Biol Med* 180:432–446, 1985.

69. Leibetseder J: Fibre in the dog's diet. In Anderson RS, editor: *Nutrition and behavior in dogs and cats*, Oxford, England, 1984, Permagon Press, pp 71–77.

70. Cummings JH: Nutritional implications of dietary fiber, *Am J Clin Nutr* 31:S21–S29, 1978.

71. Fernandez R. Phillips SF: Components of fiber impair iron absorption in the dog, *Am J Clin Nutr* 35:107–112, 1982.

72. Burrows CF, Kronfeld DL, Banta CA, and others: Effects of fiber on digestibility and transit time in dogs, *J Nutr* 112:1726–1732, 1982.

73. Brady LJ, Armstrong MK, Muiruri KL: Influence of prolonged fasting in the dog on glucose turnover and blood metabolites, *J Nutr* 107:1053–1061, 1977.

74. Rapoport A, From GLA, Husdan H: Metabolic studies in prolonged fasting. I. Inorganic metabolism and kidney function, *Metabolism* 14:31–46, 1965.

75. Rapoport A, From GLA, Husdan H: Metabolic studies in prolonged fasting. II. Organic metabolism, *Metabolism* 14:47–64, 1965.

76. Lemieux G, Plante GE: The effect of starvation in the normal dog including the dalmatian coach hound, *Metabolism* 17:620–630, 1968.

77. Bruijne JJ, De Altszuler N, and Hampshire J: Fat mobilization and plasma hormone levels in fasted dogs, *Metabolism* 30:190–194, 1981.

78. Owen OE, Felig P, Morgan A: Liver and kidney metabolism during prolonged starvation, *J Clin Invest* 48:574–583, 1969.

79. Stunkard AJ: Conservative treatments for obesity, *Am J Clin Nutr* 45:1142–1154, 1987.

80. Fidanza F: Effects of starvation on body composition, *Am J Clin Nutr* 33:1562–1566, 1980.

81. Isner JM, Sours HE, Paris AL: Sudden, unexpected death in avid dieters using the liquid-protein-modified-fast diet, *Circulation* 60:1401–1412, 1979.

82. Riser WH: Canine hip dysplasia: cause and control, *J Am Vet Med Assoc* 165:360–362, 1974.

83. Willis MB: Hip scoring: a review of 1985-1986, *Vet Rec* 118:461–462, 1986.

84. Saville PD, Lieber CS: Increases in skeletal calcium and femur thickness produced by undernutrition, *J Nutr* 99:141–144, 1969.

85. Dluzniewska KA, Obtulowicz A, Koltek K: On the relationship between diet, rate of growth and skeletal deformities in school children, *Folia Med Craco,* 7:115–126, 1965.

86. Hedhammer A, Wu F, Krook L, and others: Overnutrition and skeletal disease—an experimental study in growing Great Dane dogs, *Cornell Vet* 64 (suppl 5): 1–159, 1974.

87. Kasstrom H: Nutrition, weight gain and development of hip dysplasia, *Acta Radiol* 334(suppl):135–179, 1975.

88. Lust G, Geary JC, Sheffy BE: Development of hip dysplasia in dogs, *Am J Vet Res* 34:87–91, 1973.

89. Lust G, Rendano VT, Summers BA: Canine hip dysplasia: concepts and diagnosis, *J Vet Med Assoc* 187:638–640, 1985.

90. Kealy RD, Olsson SE, Monti KL, and others: Effects of limited food consumption on the incidence of hip dysplasia in growing dogs, *J Am Vet Med Assoc* 201:857–863, 1992.

91. Olsson SE, Reiland S: The nature of osteochondrosis in animals, *Acta Radiol Scand* 358 (suppl) :299–306, 1978.

92. Dammrich K: Relationship between nutrition and bone growth in large and giant dogs, *J Nutr* 121:S114–S121, 1991.

93. Alexander JE, Wood LLH: Comparative growth study, Tech Rep, Lewisburg, Ohio, 1990, The Iams Company.

94. Association of American Feed Control Officials: Pet food regulations. In *AAFCO official publication*, Atlanta, 1992, The Association, pp 87–108.

95. Hazewinkel HAW, Goedegebuure SA, Poulos PW, and others: Influences of chronic calcium excess on the skeletal development of growing Great Danes, *J Am Anim Hosp Assoc* 21:377–391, 1985.

96. Hazewinkel HA: Calcium metabolism and skeletal development of dogs. In Burger IH, Rivers JPW, editors: *Nutrition of the dog and cat*, Cambridge, England, 1989, Cambridge University Press, pp 293–302.

97. Hazewinkel HAW, Brom WE, van den Klooster AT, and others: Calcium metabolism in Great Dane dogs fed diets with various calcium and phosphorus levels, *J Nutr,* 121:S99–S106, 1991.

98. National Research Council: Nutrient requirements of dogs, National Academy of Sciences, Washington, DC, 1974, National Academy Press.

99. National Research Council: *Nutrient requirements of dogs*, National Academy of Sciences, Washington, DC, 1985, National Academy Press.

100. Carrig CB: Comparative radiology: dysplasia in the canine forelimb. In Potchem ET, editor: *Current concepts in radiology*, vol. 3, St. Louis, 1977, Mosby, pp 217–260.

101. Richardson DC: The role of nutrition in canine hip dysplasia, *Vet Clin North Am Sm Anim Pract* 22:529–541, 1992.

102. Stephens LC, Norrdin RW, Benjamin SA: Effects of calcium supplementation and sunlight exposure on growing beagle dogs, *Am J Vet Res* 466:2037–2042, 1985.

103. Allen LH: Calcium bioavailability and absorption: a review, *Am J Clin Nutr* 35:783–808, 1982.

104. Hedhammer A, Krook L, Schrijver HF, and others: Calcium balance in the dog. In Anderson RS, editor: *Nutrition of the dog and cat*, Oxford, England, 1980, Pergamon Press, pp 119–127.

105. Robertson BT, Burns MJ: Zinc metabolism and zinc-deficiency syndrome in the dog, *Am J Vet Res* 24:997–1002, 1963.

106. Kunkle GA: Zinc responsive dermatoses in dogs. In Kirk RW, editor: *Current veterinary therapy VII: small animal practice*, Philadelphia, 1980, WB Saunders, pp 472–476.

107. Hunt JR, Johnson PE, Swan PB: Dietary conditions influencing relative zinc availability from foods in the rat and correlations with in vitro measurements, *J Nutr* 117:1913–1923, 1987.

108. Pecoud A, Donzel P, Schelling JL: Effect of foodstuffs on the absorption of zinc sulfate, *Clin Pharmacol Ther* 17:469–474, 1975.

109. Austad R, Bjerkas E: Eclampsia in the bitch, *J Sm Anim Prac* 17:793–798, 1976.

110. Boda JM, Cole HH: The influence of dietary calcium and phosphorus on the influence of milk fever in dairy cattle, *J Dairy Sci* 37:360–372, 1954.

111. Wiggers KD, Nelson DK, Jacobson NL: Prevention of parturient paresis by a low-calcium diet prepartum: a field study, *J Dairy Sci* 58:430–431, 1975.

112. Gratzl E, Pommer A: Moller-Barlow's disease in the dog, *Wien Tierarztl Mschr* 28:481–492, 513–519, 531–537, 1941.

113. Stogdale L: Foreleg lameness in rapidly growing dogs, *J South Afr Vet Assoc* 50:61–68, 1979.

114. Meier H, Clark ST, Schnelle GB, and others: Hypertrophic osteodystrophy associated with disturbance of vitamin C synthesis in dogs, *J Am Vet Med Assoc* 130:483–491, 1957.

115. Grondalen J: Metaphyseal osteopathy (hypertrophic osteodystrophy) in growing dogs. A clinical study, *J Sm Anim Prac,* 17:721–735, 1976.

116. Holmes JR: Suspected skeletal scurvy in the dog, *Vet Rec* 74:801–813, 1962.

117. Teare JA, Krook L, Kallfelz A, and others: Ascorbic acid deficiency and hypertrophic osteodystrophy in the dog: a rebuttal, *Cornell Vet* 69:384–401, 1979.

118. Milton JL: Osteochondritis dissecans in the dog, *Vet Clin North Am Sm Anim Pract* 13:117–133, 1983.

119. National Research Council: *Nutrient requirements of cats*, National Academy of Sciences, Washington, DC, 1986, National Academy Press.

120. Cordy DR: Experimental production of steatitis (yellow fat disease) in kittens fed a commercial canned cat food and prevention of the condition by vitamin E, *Cornell Vet* 44:310–318, 1954.

121. Gaskell CJ, Leedale AH, Douglas SW: Pansteatitis in the cat: a report of five cases, *J Sm Anim Pract* 16:117–121, 1975.

122. Munson TO, Holzworth J, Small E, and others: Steatitis ("yellow fat") in cats fed canned red tuna, *J Am Vet Med Assoc* 133:563–568, 1958.

123. Griffiths RC, Thornton GW, Willson JE: Pansteatitis (yellow fat) in cats, *J Am Vet Med Assoc* 137:126–128, 1960.

124. Watson ADJ, Porges WL, Huxtable CR, and others: Pansteatitis in a cat, *Aust Vet J* 49:388–392, 1973.

125. Lewis LD, Morris ML, Hand MS: Renal failure. In *Small animal clinical nutrition*, ed 3, Topeka, Kan, 1987, Mark Morris Associates, pp 8–1 to 8–51.

126. English PB, Seawright AA: Deforming cervical spondylosis of the cat, *Aust Vet J* 40:376–381, 1964.

127. Cho DY, Frey RA, Guffy MM, and others: Hypervitaminosis A in the dog, *Am J Vet Res* 36:1597–1603, 1975.

128. Seawright AA, English PB, Gartner RJW: Hypervitaminosis A and deforming cervical spondylosis of the cat, *J Comp Pathol* 77:29–38, 1967.

129. United States Department of Agriculture: *Nutritive value of foods*, Home and Garden Bulletin No 72, Washington, DC, 1981, US Government Printing Office.

130. Lucke VM, Bardgett PL, Mann PGH, and others: Deforming cervical spondylosis in the cat associated with hypervitaminosis A, *Vet Rec* 82:141–142, 1968.

131. Riser WH, Brodey RS, Shirer JF: Osteodystrophy in mature cats: a nutritional disease, *J Am Radiol Soc* 9:37–46, 1968.

132. Smith DC, Proutt LM: Development of thiamine deficiency in the cat on a diet of raw fish, *Pro Soc Exp Bio Med* 56:1–5, 1944.

133. Jubb KV, Saunders LZ, Coates HV: Thiamine deficiency encephalopathy in cats, *J Comp Pathol* 66:217–227, 1956.

134. Loew FM, Martin CL, Dunlop RH, and others: Naturally occurring and experimental thiamine deficiency in cats receiving commercial cat food, *Can Vet J* 11:109–113, 1970.

135. Jarrett J: Thiaminase-induced encephalopathy, *Vet Med Sm Anim Clin* 65:705–708, 1970.

136. Houston D, Hulland TJ: Thiamine deficiency in a team of sled dogs, *Can Vet J* 29:383–385, 1988.

137. Everett GM: Observations on the behavior and neurophysiology of acute thiamin deficient cats, *Am J Physio* 141:139–149, 1944.

138. Shen CS, Overfield L, Murthy PNA, and others: Effect of feeding raw egg white on pyruvate and propionyl Co A carboxylase activities on tissues of the dog, *Fed Proc* 36:1169, 1977.

139. Greve JH: Effects of thyroid and biotin deficiencies on canine demodicosis. *Dissert Abstr* 24:1757, 1963.

140. Pastoor FJH, van Herck H, van Klooster A, and others: Biotin deficiency in cats as induced by feeding a purified diet containing egg white, *J Nutr* 121:S73–S74, 1991.

141. Carey CJ, Morris JG: Biotin deficiency in the cat and the effect on hepatic propinyl CoA carboxylase, *J Nutr* 107:330–334, 1977.

142. Baker JR, Hughes IB: A case of deforming cervical spondylosis in a cat associated with a diet rich in liver, *Vet Rec* 83:44–45, 1968.

143. Seawright AA, Hrdlicka J: Severe retardation of growth with retention and displacement of incisors in young cats fed a diet of raw sheep liver high in vitamin A, *Aust Vet J* 50:306–315, 1974.

144. Seawright AA, Steele DP, Clark L: Hypervitaminosis A of cats in Brisbane, *Aust Vet J* 44:203–206, 1968.

145. Clark L, Seawright AA, Hrdlicka J: Exostoses in hypervitaminotic A cats with optimal calcium-phosphorus intakes, *J Sm Anim Pract* 11:553–561, 1970.

146. Fry PD: Cervical spondylosis in the cat, *J Sm Anim Pract* 9:59–61, 1968.

147. Gans JH, Korson R, Cater MR, and others: Effects of short-term and long-term theobromine administration to male dogs, *Toxicol Appl Pharmacol* 53:481–496, 1980.

148. Welch RM, Hsu SY, DeAngelis RL: Effect of arvelor 1254, phenobarbital and polycyclic aromatic hydrocarbons on the plasma clearance of caffeine in the rat, *Clin Pharmacol Ther* 22:791–798, 1977.

149. Drouillard DD, Vesell ES, Dvorchick BN: Studies on theobromine disposition in normal subjects, *Clin Pharmacol Ther* 23:296–302, 1978.

150. Hoskam EG, Haagsma J: Chocolate poisoning terminating in the death of two dachshunds, *Tijdschr Diergeneesk* 99:523–525, 1974.

151. Decker RA, Meyers GH: Theobromine poisoning in a dog, *J Am Vet Med Assoc* 161:198–199, 1972.

152. Glauberg A, Blumenthal PH: Chocolate poisoning in the dog, *J Am Anim Hosp Assoc* 19:246–248, 1983.

153. Zoumas BL, Kreiser WR, Martin RA: Theobromine and caffeine content of chocolate products, *J Food Sci* 45:314–316, 1980.

154. Shannon WR: Thiamine chloride: an aid in the solution of the mosquito problem, *Minn Med* 26:799–803, 1943.

155. Eder HL: Flea bites: prevention and treatment with thiamine hydrochloride, *Arch Ped* 62:300, 1945.

156. Halliwell REW: Ineffectiveness of thiamine (vitamin B_1) as a flea-repellent in dogs, *J Am Anim Hosp Assoc* 18:423–426, 1982.

157. Baker NF, Farver TB: Failure of brewer's yeast as a repellent to fleas on dogs, *J Am Vet Med Assoc* 183:212–214, 1983.

158. Farkas MC, Farkas JN: Hemolytic anemia due to ingestion of onions in a dog, *J Am Anim Hosp Assoc* 10:65–66, 1974.

159. Spice RN: Hemolytic anemia associated with ingestion of onions in a dog, *Can Vet J* 17:181–183, 1976.

160. Kay JM: Onion toxicity in a dog, *Mod Vet Prac* 64:477–478, 1983.

161. Muller GH, Kirk RW, Scott DW: *Small animal dermatology*, ed 4, Philadelphia, 1989, WB Saunders, Philadelphia, pp 796–806.

162. Kirk RW: Nutrition and the integument, *J Sm Anim Pract* 32:283–288, 1991.

163. The Iams Company: Data provided by the Iams Technical Center, Lewisburg, Ohio, 1993.

164. Tordoff RJ: Gastric dilatation-volvulus, *Comp Cont Ed Pract Vet* 1:142–149, 1979.

165. Key DM: Dilatation and torsion of the stomach in a cat, *Fel Prac* 7:38–39, 1977.

166. Hall JA: Canine gastric dilatation volvulus update, *Sem Vet Med Surg Sm Anim* 4:188–193, 1989.

167. Carey D: Canine gastric dilatation volvulus: a review, Presented at the AMVEPE Annual Meeting, May, 1991, Iams Company Technical Report, The Iams Company, Lewisburg, Ohio, 1993.

168. Van Kruiningen HJ, Wojan LD, Stake PE, and others: The influence of diet and feeding frequency on gastric function in the dog, *J Am Anim Hosp Assoc* 23:145–153, 1987.

169. Burrows CF, Bright RM, Spencer CP: Influence of dietary composition on gastric emptying and motility in dogs: potential involvement in acute gastric dilatation, *Am J Vet Res* 46:2609–2612, 1985.

170. Burrows CF, editor: Bloat panel report, Proceedings of a meeting, June 10–11, 1987.

171. Cott B, Shelton M, DeYoung DW: Preliminary report on a GDV questionnaire, *Purebred Dogs: Am Kennel Gaz* 92:76–77, 1975.

172. Caywood D, Teague HD, Jackson DA: Gastric gas analysis in the canine gastric dilatation-volvulus syndrome, *J Am Anim Hosp Assoc* 13:459–462, 1977.

173. Leib MS, Wingfield WE, Twedt DC, and others: Plasma gastrin immunoreactivity in dogs with acute gastric dilatation-volvulus, *J Am Vet Med Assoc* 185:205–208, 1984.

174. Dzanis DA: Safety of ethoxyquin in dog foods, *J Nutr* 121:S163–S164, 1991.

175. Jones BR, Johnstone AC, Cahill JI, and others: Peripheral neuropathy in cats with inherited primary hyperchylomicronaemia, *Vet Rec* 119:268–22, 1986.

176. Rogers WA, Donovan EF, Kociba GJ: Idiopathic hyperlipoproteinemia in dogs, *J Am Vet Med Assoc* 166:1087–1091, 1975.

177. Hubert B, Braun JP, La Farge F, and others: Hypertriglyceridemia in two related dogs, *Comp Anim Pract* 1:33–35, 1987.

Nutritionally Responsive Disorders

utrition is a vital component to the health of all companion animals. Section 5 presents information about the results of feeding imbalanced diets and inappropriate food items or providing excess calories during growth and adulthood. Another way that nutrition affects the health of an animal is through inherited disorders of nutrient metabolism. There are several diseases in companion animals that are genetic in origin and affect an animal's ability to either digest, absorb, or metabolize certain nutrients. These disorders are examined in Chapter 30. Dietary management, when effective, is discussed.

Nutrition also affects health when diet is used to either manage or treat disease. Dietary therapy plays an important role in the treatment of a number of chronic diseases in dogs and cats, even though the underlying cause of the disease may be unrelated to diet. For example, dietary therapy has been proven to be efficacious in the management of diabetes mellitus, feline lower urinary tract disease, chronic kidney disease, certain skin disorders, and feline hepatic lipidosis. Although dietary intervention is occasionally used with a number of other canine and feline diseases, only those disorders for which dietary management has been proven to be effective in companion animals through controlled research are included in the chapters of this section.

CHAPTER 30

Inherited Disorders of Nutrient Metabolism

C linical disease can occur in some companion animals as a result of the inability to absorb, assimilate, or metabolize specific nutrients. In some cases, breed predisposi-tions can be found, and the disorder appears to have a genetic basis. Five specific examples in dogs involve lipid metabolism, purine metabolism, and the nutrients vitamin B_{12}, copper, and zinc. Although inherited disorders of metabolism are less well documented in cats, a familial hyperlipidemia has been reported in this species (Table 30-1).

MALABSORPTION OF VITAMIN B_{12} IN GIANT SCHNAUZERS

Vitamin B_{12} (cobalamin) is required by the body as a coenzyme for several metabolic reactions and for normal deoxyribonucleic acid (DNA) synthesis and erythropoiesis. A deficiency results in macrocytic anemia and neurologic impairment. Absorption of B_{12} from the diet requires the presence of a compound called intrinsic factor (IF). In the dog, IF is produced by the gastric mucosa and the pancreas and binds to cobalamin as it passes through the gastrointestinal tract.[1] The IF-B_{12} complex then attaches to specific receptor sites on cells lining the intestinal mucosa and is absorbed into the body. Without the presence of IF, cobalamin absorption is severely impaired.

Like other species, dogs require very small amounts of dietary vitamin B_{12} because of naturally low requirement, efficient conservation, and the body's ability to store adequate amounts of B_{12} in the liver for long periods of time. In addition, efficient reabsorption of excreted vitamin B_{12} through the enterohepatic circulation results in efficient conservation of this nutrient. As a result, naturally occurring deficiencies of vitamin B_{12} are not common in the canine species.

TABLE 30-1
Selected Inherited Disorders of Nutritional Metabolism

DISORDER	BREEDS AFFECTED	TREATMENT
Malabsorption of vitamin B_{12}	Giant schnauzer	Intramuscular injections of B_{12}
Copper-storage disease	Doberman pincher Bedlington terrier West Highland white terrier Cocker spaniel	Copper-restricted diet, zinc acetate supplementation
Lethal acrodermatitis	Bull terrier	None
Zinc malabsorption	Siberian husky Alaskan malamute Great Dane Doberman pincher	Zinc supplementation
Hyperlipidemia	Miniature schnauzers, cats	Restricted fat/calorie diet
Abnormal purine metabolism	Dalmatians	Reduced purine diet, production of alkaline urine, adequate hydration, allopurinol

An inherited disorder of vitamin B_{12} malabsorption has been recognized in giant schnauzers.[2] Although the exact mode of inheritance of this disorder is not known, examination of the familial distribution of vitamin B_{12} malabsorption in the breed suggests a simple autosomal recessive inheritance.[2] This disorder appears to be limited to giant schnauzers and has not yet been identified in other breeds. The incidence rate in giant schnauzers is not known.

Clinical signs develop early in life and include failure to thrive, lethargy, loss of appetite, neutropenia (decreased white blood cells), and nonregenerative anemia. Diagnosis can be confirmed through analysis of serum B_{12} levels, response to parenteral administration of the vitamin, and the presence of elevated levels of methylmalonic acid in the urine. Methylmalonic acid is only excreted when the normal metabolism of certain amino acids, fatty acids, and cholesterol is blocked because of the lack of a necessary B_{12}-containing coenzyme. Normally, dogs excrete less than 10 milligrams (mg) of methylmalonic acid per gram (g) of creatine in the urine. Giant schnauzers with vitamin B_{12} malabsorption excrete between 4000 and 6000 mg/g of creatine.[2]

Tests for concurrent intestinal malabsorption of other nutrients in affected dogs have shown that normal absorption occurs, with the exception of vitamin B_{12}. Moreover, oral administration of vitamin B_{12}, with or without IF, is not effective in resolving clinical symptoms or in raising serum B_{12} levels. These results indicate that the defect may be located at the level of the cell receptor in the small intestine. It has been hypothesized that affected giant schnauzers have either a defect in the specific receptor that binds the IF-B_{12} complex or have defective transport of the complex across the enterocyte once binding has occurred.[2] Long-term treatment involves the regular administration of intramuscular injections of vitamin B_{12}. This injection bypasses the

intestine and provides tissues with the necessary vitamin. Complete resolution of clinical signs has been reported with a dosage as low as 1 mg every 4 to 5 months. In other cases, a weekly dosage of 0.5 mg has been used.[2]

Copper-Storage Disease

Copper is needed by the body for iron absorption and transport, hemoglobin formation, and normal functioning of the cytochrome oxidase enzyme system (see Section 1, pp. 49–50; Section 2, p. 127). The normal metabolism of copper in the body involves the passage of excess copper through the liver and its excretion in bile. Disorders that affect bile excretion often result in an accumulation of copper in the liver, sometimes to toxic levels. In these cases, copper toxicosis in the liver is a secondary disorder that develops as an effect of the primary liver disease. However, a primary, hepatic copper-storage disease exists in certain breeds of dogs. In these cases, the underlying cause of the disease is an accumulation of copper in the liver that eventually results in liver disease. This disorder has been named copper-associated liver disease or copper-storage disease and occurs most prevalently in Bedlington terriers, West Highland white terriers, Doberman pinchers, and cocker spaniels.[3]

Copper-storage disease involves the impaired removal of copper from the liver, resulting in accumulation of the mineral as the dog ages. Its development is independent of diet and eventually causes chronic, degenerative liver disease. The mode of inheritance in Bedlington terriers is a simple, autosomal recessive gene that shows no sex predilection.[4] The disease in West Highland white terriers is similar, but the mode of inheritance has not been completely established.[3] The mode of inheritance in other breeds is not known.

Normal liver copper concentration in dogs ranges between 200 and 400 parts per million (ppm) of dry weight, and this level remains constant throughout life.[5] Dogs with copper-storage disease begin to accumulate the mineral shortly after birth. Biopsies of the livers of affected puppies show increased copper in the hepatocytes as early as 5½ months of age.[6] During the first few months of life, while copper is accumulating, there is no liver damage and serum levels of liver enzymes remain within normal range. When hepatic copper reaches a toxic level of approximately 2000 ppm, centrolobular hepatitis with concomitant elevation of liver enzymes develops. Dogs vary significantly in the age at which toxic levels are reached. Even after toxicity occurs, levels continue to accumulate, reaching as high as 10,000 ppm.[7]

Serum chemistry profiles are useful preliminary screening tools in individuals of affected breeds that are less than 1 year of age. Liver biopsies should be taken if elevated levels of the liver enzyme alanine amino transaminase are observed. Clinical signs of disease are usually not manifested until the dog is between 4 and 8 years old, although some may show signs as early as 1 year or as late as 11 years of age.[3] Widespread liver necrosis and post-necrotic cirrhosis begin to cause clinical signs that are associated with liver disease. Lethargy, anorexia, vomiting, abdominal pain, and, occasionally, ascites and icterus are observed. Some dogs suffer acute tubular necrosis

in the kidney and show polyuria and polydypsia in addition to signs of liver disease.[3] Acute episodes of liver necrosis may cause sudden death in a small number of affected dogs.

Because symptoms of copper-storage disease cannot be differentiated from other forms of liver disease, the only method for definitive diagnosis of this disorder is a liver biopsy. Treatment involves lifelong feeding of a copper-restricted diet and the administration of medications that either decrease intestinal absorption or increase urinary excretion of copper.[3,8] Two chelating agents, penacillamine and trientine, have been used in dogs with copper-storage disease and act by increasing urinary excretion of copper.[7,9,10] However, despite the reported use of these drugs, controlled efficacy and treatment regimen studies have not been conducted in this species, and penicillamine may be toxic in some animals.[3,8] Recent evidence shows that zinc acetate, which functions to block the intestinal absorption of copper, may be the treatment of choice for dogs with copper-storage disease.[8] Results of a study that examined the efficacy of zinc acetate in the treatment of copper-storage disease in Bedlington terriers and West Highland white terriers found that administration of zinc acetate at dosages that resulted in plasma zinc concentrations of 200 to 500 micrograms per deciliter (µg/dl) suppressed hepatic inflammatory disease and reduced hepatic copper concentrations. It appeared that hepatic function could be restored by the long-term administration of zinc acetate in affected dogs. The administration of 100 mg of zinc acetate twice daily is recommended for the first 3 months of treatment. After this time period, the dosage can be reduced to 50 mg twice daily. For maximum effectiveness, the zinc should not be administered with the dog's food. Plasma zinc concentrations should be measured every 2 to 3 months to determine that the level has increased appropriately and does not exceed 1000 µg/dl. Affected dogs require lifelong therapy. Copper status must be monitored closely to guard against the potential for copper deficiency.[3]

Zinc Malabsorption

Although zinc deficiency and zinc-responsive dermatosis can be caused by feeding an imbalanced diet, another potential cause involves an inherited predisposition of impaired zinc absorption. Several breeds of dogs appear to be affected by zinc malabsorption, and varying levels of severity of this disorder have been reported. The most severe zinc-related disorder is lethal acrodermatitis in bull terriers. This genetic disease is inherited as an autosomal recessive gene and results in an inability to absorb dietary zinc, even when high levels of the mineral are added to the diet.[11] A cell-mediated immunodeficiency also occurs in affected dogs. Growth is stunted and severe skin lesions develop by the time the puppies are 10 weeks old.[12] The immunodeficiency results in increased susceptibility to pyoderma and multiple infections throughout the body. This disorder is invariably fatal and has a median survival age of only 7 months.[11]

A less severe zinc-responsive disorder occurs in Alaskan malamutes, Siberian huskies (see Figure 30-1), and, occasionally, Great Danes and Doberman pinchers.[13-16] Research has shown that Alaskan malamutes afflicted with inherited chondrodysplastic

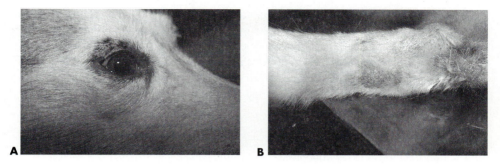

FIGURE 30-1
Inherited zinc malabsorption in a Siberian Husky. **A**, Face and **B**, hock. (Reprinted with permission from Candance Sousa, D.V.M., Animal Dermatology Clinic, Sacramento, CA.)

dwarfism have an impaired ability to absorb intestinal zinc.[16] Dwarfism in this breed has a simple autosomal recessive inheritance, and zinc malabsorption appears to be a component of this disorder. However, impaired zinc absorption has also been described in malamutes that are not afflicted with chondrodysplasia.[14]

The onset of this syndrome usually occurs at puberty, and some dogs show signs only during times of physiological stress, such as pregnancy or exposure to weather extremes. Dermatological signs include crusting, scaling, and underlying suppuration around the face, elbows, scrotum, prepuce, and vulva. In chronic cases, hyperpigmentation of the affected skin surface is seen. The dogs are usually not pruritic until the lesions have become extensively crusted. Mild to moderate weight loss and a dull, dry coat are also observed. Histopathological examinations of skin biopsies show diffuse parakeratotic hyperkeratosis.

Oral supplementation with zinc results in rapid resolution of the skin lesions within 7 to 10 days. In most dogs, supplementation is required throughout life to prevent recurrence of clinical signs.[14] A therapeutic dose of 100 mg of zinc sulfate, administered twice daily, is recommended.[14] Zinc sulfate can cause emesis in some dogs, but this can be prevented in most cases by giving the mineral with the dog's food. In a small proportion of cases supplementation is necessary only during periods of stress. Although unusual, similar cases have also been reported in growing Great Danes.[15,17] The mode of inheritance of this disorder in all breeds is currently unknown.

HYPERLIPIDEMIA

The term hyperlipidemia is used interchangeably with hyperlipoproteinemia and refers to elevated levels of triglycerides and/or cholesterol in animals that have been fasted for at least 12 hours.[18] Most of the cases of hyperlipidemia that are seen in companion animals occur secondary to another underlying disorder that affects lipid metabolism. Diseases that may cause secondary hyperlipidemia include diabetes mellitus, hypothyroidism, pancreatitis, nephrotic syndrome, and liver disease.[19] In addition, certain medications such as glucocorticoids and immunosuppressant drugs may cause transient increases in blood lipid levels. Familial, or primary, hyperlipidemia refers to cases in which a heritable basis for hyperlipidemia can be found. Two well-documented, inherited disorders of lipid metabolism occur in dogs and cats, hyperlipidemia in miniature schnauzers and lipoprotein lipase deficiency in cats.

Lipoprotein Metabolism

A basic understanding of the mechanisms of lipid transport in the blood is necessary for an examination of hyperlipidemia. Because lipids are insoluble in water, transport in the blood requires complexing with more soluble molecules, such as proteins and phospholipids. Free fatty acids are carried in the bloodstream by albumin, a serum protein. Triglycerides and cholesterol esters are carried by lipoproteins, which are spherical, macromolecular complexes made up of a lipid core surrounded by a thin, outer membrane. The proteins that are present in the lipoprotein's outer membrane, called apoproteins, are recognition sites for target tissues and as enzyme cofactors in lipid metabolism reactions.[20]

Lipoproteins can be categorized according to their lipid components and resultant aqueous densities. Like humans, dogs have four major classes of lipoproteins, each of which has a principal lipid component and one or more transport functions. Chylomicrons are synthesized in response to the absorption of fat from the intestine, and function in the transport of dietary triglyceride to extrahepatic tissues and cholesterol to the liver. Chylomicrons appear in the blood approximately 2 hours postprandially, causing a transient increase in plasma triglyceride concentration. When they are delivered to tissues, the triglycerides are hydrolyzed to fatty acids and glycerol by the enzyme lipoprotein lipase (LPL). The second category of lipoproteins, called very low-density lipoproteins (VLDL), transport endogenous triglycerides from the liver to extrahepatic tissues for use as an energy source or for storage in adipose tissue. In contrast to chylomicrons, VLDLs are produced continually so that in the fasting state VLDLs are the main carriers of endogenously produced triglyceride. Low-density lipoproteins (LDL) transport cholesterol from the liver to extrahepatic tissues for incorporation into cell membranes and for steroid hormone synthesis. Lastly, the high-density lipoproteins (HDL) also transport cholesterol, but they are responsible for moving excess cholesterol out of extrahepatic cells back to the liver for excretion in bile, a process called "reverse cholesterol transport."

Postprandial hyperlipidemia is a natural occurrence that reflects a transient rise in chylomicrons and normally resolves within 6 to 10 hours following consumption of a meal. However, persistent hyperlipidemia in a fasted dog or cat is an abnormal response and is associated with a number of health risks. In dogs, fasting serum triglyceride concentrations greater than 150 mg/dl and/or total cholesterol concentration greater than 300 mg/dl are considered hyperlipidemic. Values for cats are fasting triglyceride and/or cholesterol values of greater than 100 mg/dl or 200 mg/dl, respectively.[21]

A number of health problems may be caused by persistent hyperlipidemia in companion animals. Hypertriglyceridemia, especially when severe, is associated with abdominal pain, vomiting, diarrhea, anorexia, seizures, hepatomegaly, and the abnormal deposition of lipid in certain tissues.[18,21,22] Like some hereditary hypertriglyceridemias in humans, elevated triglyceride levels in dogs and cats may also increase risk for the development of acute pancreatitis.[20,23] Hypercholesterolemia is not common in dogs and cats and when it does occur is not associated with as many health risks as is hypertriglyceridemia. Corneal lipid depositions have been reported in dogs as a result of elevated blood cholesterol.[24] In contrast to humans, the development of atherosclerosis in response to hypercholesterolemia is rare in dogs and cats, and when it is seen is usually the result of congenital or spontaneous hypothyroidism.[25]

Hyperlipidemia in Miniature Schnauzers

Hyperlipidemia in miniature schnauzers is a well-documented disorder.[23,26,27] It is reported that many clinically normal dogs of this breed are found to have persistent fasting hyperlipidemia during routine veterinary examinations.[23] There is no sex predilection, and the disorder is usually first seen in schnauzers that are greater than 4 years of age.[23] The hyperlipidemia is caused by elevated triglycerides and is typically characterized by chylomicron excess.[23] Serum cholesterol levels are either normal or slightly increased.[20] Increased serum lipase and amylase activities have been recognized in hyperlipidemic miniature schnauzers that are presented with acute pancreatitis. In these cases, the pancreatitis is believed to be caused by the hypertriglyceridemia.

Affected dogs are either asymptomatic or have recurrent episodes of abdominal pain or distress, vomiting, and/or diarrhea. Seizures have also been associated with persistent hyperlipidemia in this breed.[26] Owners may report that episodes of abdominal distress last several days, followed by spontaneous recovery. In many cases, the clinical signs and history are similar to that of dogs with acute pancreatitis, but radiographic and laboratory evidence do not often support this diagnosis. This syndrome has been termed "pseudo pancreatitis" by one investigator.[23] Hyperlipidemia in miniature schnauzers is believed to be hereditary because of the high breed predisposition and because most affected miniature schnauzers lack evidence of diseases that cause secondary hyperlipidemia.[20]

The underlying cause of primary hyperlipidemia in miniature schnauzers is not known. However, it is theorized that either a familial deficiency of the enzyme LPL or the absence of an apoprotein that functions to activate LPL may be responsible. The enzyme LPL is located in capillary and endothelial tissue and hydrolyzes the triglycerides that are transported by chylomicrons and VLDLs for transport into cells. A defect in the synthesis or activity of this enzyme prevents the delivery of dietary triglycerides to tissues and leads to the retention of chylomicrons and impaired VLDL metabolism. The absence of an important apoprotein called apo C-II would have a similar effect. Apo C-II is normally a component of chylomicrons and VLDL and is a cofactor for LPL. In humans, individuals with an apo C-II deficiency have clinical symptoms similar to individuals with LPL deficiency.[28]

Feline Lipoprotein Lipase Deficiency

An inherited deficiency of lipoprotein lipase is the cause of a hyperchylomicronemia that is well recognized in the cat and has been shown to be inherited as an autosomal recessive trait.[29–34] The hyperlipidemia is caused by markedly elevated fasting triglyceride concentrations as a result of increased chylomicrons and, to a lesser extent, VLDLs.[35] Clinical signs may or may not be present, and the severity of clinical disease is not well correlated with the degree of hyperlipidemia. The age of onset of clinical signs varies from as young as 3 weeks to middle age.[35] When cats are presented with clinical disease, the most common signs include the development of subcutaneous xanthomas (lipid deposits) and lipemia retinalis. The xanthomas occur most often in areas of the body where trauma caused damage to capillaries, leading to extravasation of lipids. Variable peripheral neuropathies are seen in some cases. The signs of nerve damage develop slowly and are characterized by the loss of conscious proprioception and motor function, with retention of sensation of pain. These neuropathies are thought to be caused by compression of nerves by lipid granulomata at sites of trauma.[20]

Investigations of this disorder have shown that the plasma of affected cats has significantly reduced LPL activity after heparin administration compared with the plasma of normal cats.[29,31,33] Heparin administration stimulates the release of active lipoprotein lipase and is used as a measure of LPL activity. Another study of a family of cats reported that the affected cats produced an abnormal LPL protein that failed to bind normally to vascular endothelium, rendering it inactive.[33] These results support the theory that an inherited disorder of lipid metabolism involving a deficiency of active LPL occurs in the cat.

Diagnosis of Primary Hyperlipidemia

In cases of hyperlipidemia, all causes of secondary hyperlipidemia must be ruled out before a diagnosis of primary hyperlipidemia can be made. A 16-hour, fasting blood sample should be taken, and cholesterol and triglyceride concentrations should be measured.[18] If there is a history of recurrent abdominal pain, vomiting, or diarrhea, serum amylase and lipase activities should be measured to monitor pancreatic pathology. The pet's breed, family lineage, age, and clinical history can be used to support a diagnosis.

Quantification of the plasma concentrations of each lipoprotein class may assist in the differential diagnosis of hyperlipidemia. A rough estimate of the lipoprotein pattern can be obtained through electrophoresis. Recently, an electrophoretic technique used for human lipoprotein analysis was adapted and validated for use in the dog.[36] However, electrophoresis separation of lipoproteins is not a disease-specific technique and cannot always differentiate between functional classes of elevated lipoproteins.[20] Laboratory techniques that can accurately identify lipoproteins that are not adequately differentiated by electrophoresis are not conducted by most diagnostic laboratories and must be referred to research laboratories.[20] In the case of the cat, if a LPL deficiency is suspected, the determination of plasma activity of this enzyme is suggested. LPL activity can be indirectly assayed by collecting plasma before and after the administration of

heparin. However, this technique does not differentiate between hepatic lipase and lipoprotein lipase. Special procedures can be used to differentiate between these two enzymes for diagnostic purposes.[37]

Dietary Treatment of Primary Hyperlipidemia

The aim of treatment in primary hyperlipidemia is to reduce and maintain plasma lipid concentrations to levels that no longer predispose the dog or cat to health risks. Dietary intervention is recommended in animals that have fasting hypertriglyceridemia of greater than 500 mg/dl or hypercholesterolemia greater than 750 mg/dl.[21,22] Miniature schnauzers that have fasting hypertriglyceridemia but no clinical signs should be treated if the hyperlipidemia persists for two consecutive samples taken several weeks apart.[23]

In both the dog and cat, a diet that is restricted in fat and calories is recommended. Feeding less fat will decrease the influx of triglyceride-containing chylomicrons into the bloodstream, reduce the load on LPL, and promote the clearance of chylomicrons and VLDLs. A diet containing between 8% and 12% fat on a dry-matter basis is recommended as a starting point. Follow-up blood samples should be taken several weeks after switching to the new diet.[23] It is imperative that the restricted fat diet is the animal's only source of food. All table scraps and extra treats must be discontinued. Owners should be cautioned that dogs with hyperlipidemia may be susceptible to acute pancreatitis and that a single, high-fat meal may result in the onset of this disease. If a fat-restricted diet normalizes blood triglyceride levels, dietary management should be continued for the remainder of the pet's life.

Feeding a low-fat diet to cats with LPL deficiency has been shown to normalize blood lipid levels and cause a regression of xanthomas and peripheral neuropathies within 12 weeks of lowering plasma lipid concentrations.[29,38] Similarly, clinical signs in miniature schnauzers usually resolve when serum triglyceride levels are normalized.[26] Most miniature schnauzers with hyperlipidemia can be successfully managed by diet, but more drastic fat reduction may be necessary as the pet ages. If any clinical signs of acute pancreatitis develop, periodic follow-up examinations should be conducted and veterinary care should be sought immediately.

In some cases, reducing the level of fat in the diet is not sufficient to reduce blood lipid levels. There are several lipid-lowering drugs that are approved for use in humans but not in dogs or cats. Although there are some reports of success using drugs such as clofibrate, gemfibrozil, and pharmacological doses of niacin, the efficacy of these therapies has not been proven and these drugs are not licensed for use in either dogs or cats. Marine fish oils, containing high amounts of n-3 fatty acids, have also been used as an adjunct therapy for hyperlipidemia in dogs.[18,29] Studies with humans have shown that these oils reduce plasma triglyceride and cholesterol concentrations by decreasing the production of VLDLs.[39] Improved triglyceride levels have been reported in hyperlipemic dogs receiving supplemental marine oil at doses up to 30 to 60 mg per kilogram a day, with no clinical or biochemical side effects.[18,22,40] Although not effective for all dogs, marine oil supplementation may help to normalize blood lipid levels in animals that are not responding adequately to dietary fat restriction alone.

The amelioration of clinical signs is the best indicator of long-term prognosis in pets with primary hyperlipidemia. The animal's health is invariably improved if dietary fat restriction is strictly enforced and blood lipid levels can be lowered to normal or near normal concentrations. Naturally, the presence of any secondary, underlying disorders that could contribute further to hyperlipidemia, such as insulin-dependent diabetes or hypothyroidism, increase the health risks and make long-term management more difficult in these pets.

PURINE METABOLISM IN DALMATIANS

Purines are components of the nucleic acids that are found in the nucleus of plant and animal cells. All mammals are capable of synthesizing purines for tissue growth and maintenance. Purines are also obtained through the reuse of dietary or endogenous nuclear material. Nuclear material that is ingested and hydrolyzed contains purine bases that can be converted back into nucleotides to be used for growth and maintenance by the body. Normal cellular turnover and tissue maintenance, along with the digestion of excess dietary purines, results in purine catabolism. A primary end product of purine catabolism is uric acid. If the liver enzyme uricase is present, uric acid is further degraded to form the compound allantoin. Uric acid that is not converted to allantoin is present in body tissues as its salt, monosodium urate.

Most mammals, with the exception of humans, the higher apes, and dalmatians, convert most uric acid to allantoin, and as a result excrete very little urate in the urine. Dalmatians are unique in that they excrete both urate and allantoin in their urine as end products of purine metabolism.[41,42] Compared with other breeds of dogs, dalmatians have increased levels of urate and decreased levels of allantoin in the bloodstream and in the urine.[43] Other breeds of dogs excrete 10 to 60 mg of urate per 24-hour period, and their serum urate concentration is approximately 0.25 mg/dl.[42,44,45] In contrast, dalmatians excrete approximately 400 to 600 mg of urinary urate in a 24-hour period.[41,43,46] However, these values can range from less than 200 mg to greater than 1 g of uric acid. The mean serum urate concentration in dalmatians is about 0.5 mg/dl with a range of 0.3 to 4.0 mg/dl, approximately twofold to fourfold greater than values in other dog breeds.[42,44]

There appear to be two separate, underlying mechanisms that are responsible for the dalmatian's high production of uric acid and low production of allantoin. In the liver a defective uric acid transport system results in decreased oxidation of uric acid to allantoin by the enzyme uricase.[47] The second problem involves the kidney. Compared with other species and other breeds of dogs, dalmatians have reduced renal tubular reabsorption of urate.[42] In other breeds, 98% of the uric acid in the glomerular filtrate is reabsorbed in the proximal tubules and returned to the liver for further oxidation to allantoin. Dalmatians have a greatly reduced ability to reabsorb uric acid in the proximal tubules, resulting in increased urinary excretion of urate. Although few research studies have examined the mode of inheritance of these defects in the dalmatian, it has been suggested that altered purine metabolism in this breed is the result of an autosomal recessive gene.[48]

Altered purine metabolism in dalmatians does have some medical significance. Although allantoin is highly soluble, urate has a low aqueous solubility. As a result, its accumulation in the body can result in the precipitation of urate crystals out of the serum or urine. In humans, crystallization occurs in body tissues when serum urate values are greater than 6.5 mg/dl.[49] The presence of urate crystals causes the medical affliction that is commonly called "gout," and is characterized by inflammation, swelling, and painful joints. Interestingly, although dalmatians do not convert uric acid to allantoin, their serum does not attain levels that are high enough to cause gout. Rather, because of the reduced reabsorption of urate in the renal tubules, dalmatians excrete large amounts of urate in the urine, preventing buildup in the serum. Although this capability appears to protect dalmatians from developing signs of gout, the shift of excess urate from the serum to the urine carries with it other problems.

The presence of a high concentration of urate in the urinary tract of dalmatians appears to predispose dogs of this breed to the development of urate urolithiasis. In dogs, urate uroliths or calculi are composed primarily of ammonium urate, and a sufficiently high concentration of both urate and ammonium in the urine are necessary for the formation of these uroliths. Studies show that although urate calculi account for only 5% of calculi found in dogs, 45% to 65% of those that are seen come from dalmatians. Furthermore, 75% to 100% of calculi found in dalmatians are composed completely or partially of urate.[50-52] Urate urolithiasis is also significantly more common in male dalmatians than in females.[46,52,53] The anatomical differences between the urethras of males and females may partially explain this disparity. The small, rounded urate crystals are expected to pass readily through the wider female urethra, but may tend to lodge in the male urethra as it enters the narrow groove in the os penis. However, others have reported that female dogs that are not dalmatians are more likely to form urate-containing calculi than males.[46] Therefore it appears that additional factors may be responsible for the higher incidence or urate urolithiasis that is seen in male dalmatians.

Clinical signs of urolithiasis in the dog, regardless of the type of urolith that is present, are dependent on the duration of the urolithiasis, the size of the uroliths, their location in the tract, and the presence or absence of a concomitant urinary tract infection. General signs include frequent urination and the voiding of small amounts of urine, the appearance of pain or straining during urination, and hematuria. As with other types of urolithiasis, urethral obstruction is characterized by anuria, depression, anorexia, vomiting, and/or diarrhea. Complete obstruction always constitutes a medical emergency.

Although high urinary uric acid excretion is a major predisposing factor for the development of urate urolithiasis in dalmatians, it is not the sole cause. Most dalmatians excrete urate in the urine at a concentration above its solubility limits. However, not all dalmatians develop urate uroliths, and dalmatians that do have not been shown to excrete urate in greater excess than those that do not.[54] Other predisposing factors that may be involved include urinary ammonium concentration, urinary pH, the presence of a urinary tract infection, and dietary purine intake. The incidence of urate urolithiasis in the dalmatian breed is not known, but it has been suggested that the majority of dogs never experience clinical signs of this disease and that the incidence rate may be as low as 1%.[55]

Treatment for urate urolithiasis in dogs usually requires surgical removal of the calculi. Prophylactic measures for dalmatians that are predisposed to urate urolithiasis include feeding a diet that promotes an alkaline urine and is low in purines and ensuring adequate hydration.[46] A reduced purine diet decreases the amount of urate precursors that are present in the urine, and the production of an alkaline urine increases the solubility of urate uroliths. The diet should provide moderate to low levels of high-quality protein. Moderate restriction of protein results in decreased ammonium ion production from the catabolism of excess protein. Ingredients that are high in protein content also tend to be high in purines. The moderate restriction of protein therefore also reduces purine intake. Oral administration of sodium bicarbonate is effective in changing the alkalinity of the urine. It is hypothesized that the control of any concomitant urinary tract infections may also aid in preventing recurrence.[54]

Daily administration of the drug allopurinol is often used as a prophylactic method in dalmatians that are predisposed to urate urolithiasis. Allopurinol is an inhibitor of the enzyme xanthine oxidase, which is necessary for the degradation of purines. Administration of this drug results in a decrease in uric acid production. However, this can result in increased levels of xanthine in the urine and lead to urinary calculi that contain xanthine. An increased incidence of this type of calculi has been reported in dalmatians that have received this drug.[52,56]

Diabetes Mellitus

D iabetes mellitus is a chronic endocrine disorder that occurs in both dogs and cats. It is caused by the relative or absolute deficiency of the hormone insulin, which is produced by the beta-cells of the pancreas. Insulin stimulates the transport of glucose and other nutrients across cell membranes for cellular use and is involved in a number of anabolic processes within the body. A lack of insulin activity leads to elevated blood glucose levels (hyperglycemia) and an inability of tissues to receive the glucose that they need (glucoprivation). Primary clinical signs include polyuria, polyphagia, polydypsia, and, in some cases, weight loss. Diagnosis is usually made using the initial signs of the disorder, which are the presence of a persistent hyperglycemia and a persistent or concurrent glycosuria.[57,58]

Incidence and Clinical Signs

It is estimated that diabetes occurs in 0.5% of dogs and 0.12% of cats seen by veterinarians in the United States.[59] A large proportion of these diabetic pets are obese. Other factors that appear to be related to the development of diabetes in dogs are hormonal abnormalities such as hypothyroidism and Cushing's syndrome, pancreatic islet-cell destruction, stress, and genetic predisposition.[58] Diabetes in cats is less common and may be related to obesity, stress, or the administration of progestins.[60,61]

Two primary forms of diabetes mellitus have been identified in companion animals. Insulin-dependent diabetes mellitus (IDDM), also referred to as type I diabetes, is characterized by an inability of the beta-cells of the pancreas to produce or secrete insulin.

TABLE 31-1
Forms of Diabetes Mellitus

FORM	UNDERLYING CAUSE	INCIDENCE	TREATMENT
Insulin-dependent diabetes mellitus (Type I)	Inability of beta-cells to synthesize or secrete insulin	70%–80% of cases	Require exogenous insulin and dietary management
Non-insulin-dependent diabetes mellitus (Type II)	Insensitivity of peripheral tissues to insulin and impaired beta-cell response	20%–30% of cases	Weight loss, dietary management, and/or hypoglycemic agents

As a result, the animal must be given exogenous insulin-replacement therapy to maintain glycemic control. Insulin-dependent diabetes is the most common form of diabetes in companion animals, accounting for more than 70% to 80% of the cases that are diagnosed.[60,62,63] Noninsulin-dependent diabetes mellitus (NIDDM), or type II diabetes, occurs when there is a relative deficiency of insulin. In these cases, the beta-cells of the pancreas are still able to produce insulin, but peripheral insulin insensitivity and impaired beta-cell responsiveness to stimuli cause sustained hyperglycemia and cellular glucoprivation. This type of diabetes is almost always associated with obesity, and glycemic control can often be improved simply through weight loss and attainment of normal body weight.[64] Oral hypoglycemic agents are also used to control blood glucose concentration in pets with NIDDM[65–67] (Table 31-1).

All of the clinical symptoms that are observed in pets with diabetes mellitus are associated with the short- or long-term effects of hyperglycemia. Polydypsia, polyuria, and/or weight loss are usually the first signs that are observed. The microvascular effects of diabetes contribute to the development of cataracts and renal disease. Polyneuropathy develops in some cases and can manifest as weakness, depression, or urinary and bowel incontinence. Bacterial infections are common in animals with poor glycemic control. All of these complications can be minimized or prevented through stringent control of blood glucose levels in diabetic animals. The therapeutic goal in both IDDM and NIDDM is to maintain blood glucose levels within a normal range and to minimize postprandial (after-meal) fluctuations. This goal can be achieved through exogenous insulin administration, oral hypoglycemic agents, diet, exercise, and the control of concurrent illness.

Dietary goals for dogs and cats with IDDM are to improve regulation of blood glucose by delivering nutrients to the body during periods when exogenous insulin is active and to minimize postprandial fluctuations in blood glucose levels. Dietary therapy will not eliminate the need for insulin replacement therapy, but it can be used to improve glycemic control. Dietary treatment for pets with NIDDM can be instrumental in improving glycemic control and preventing the need to institute exogenous insulin therapy. Factors that must be considered when developing an appropriate diet for a diabetic pet include the consistency and type of diet, its nutritional adequacy and nutrient composition, and the pet's caloric intake and feeding schedule.

CONSISTENCY AND TYPE OF DIET

When exogenous insulin therapy is used, it is imperative that the type and quantity of nutrients that are delivered to the body remain consistent from day to day. The proportions of calories in the diet that are supplied by carbohydrate, protein, and fat should stay constant, and these nutrients should always be supplied by the same ingredients. The provision of a consistent diet allows the insulin dosage to be adjusted to closely fit the needs of the animal. Changes in the ingredients or nutrient composition of a diet can disrupt the tight coupling of blood glucose levels with insulin activity that is needed for proper glycemic control. Therefore only pet foods that are prepared using a fixed formulation should be selected for diabetic pets (see Section 3, p. 190). Manufacturers that use fixed formulations assure that the nutrient composition and ingredients remain consistent between batches of food. In contrast, manufacturers that use variable formulations will change ingredients depending on availability and market prices. If information about the formulation type is not readily available, it can be obtained by contacting the manufacturer directly. Homemade diets should also be avoided with diabetic pets because of difficulties with maintaining nutrient consistency.

The type of commercial product that is fed is also of importance. Semimoist pet foods are not an appropriate choice for diabetic pets. Postprandial blood glucose and insulin responses have been shown to be highest when dogs are fed semimoist foods compared with when they are fed either canned or dry pet foods.[68] This increase appears to be because of the high level of simple carbohydrate that is found in semimoist products. These nutrients require minimal digestion in the small intestine and are rapidly absorbed following a meal. In contrast, the digestible carbohydrates that are found in dry and canned foods are made up primarily of complex carbohydrates (starch). Starches require enzymatic digestion to simple sugars before they can be absorbed into the body. This process slows the rate of delivery of glucose to the bloodstream. Complex carbohydrates also cause a decreased rate of food passage through the gastrointestinal tract and slow absorption of other nutrients in the diet.[68] Dry pet foods generally contain higher levels of both complex carbohydrates and plant fiber than semimoist or canned foods.

NUTRITIONAL ADEQUACY AND NUTRIENT COMPOSITION

In almost all cases, the treatment of diabetes involves lifelong dietary management. Therefore the diet must be nutritionally complete and balanced and must supply optimum levels of all essential nutrients that are required by the pet. Methods that are discussed in Section 3 can be used to determine the nutritional adequacy of a commercial product. As discussed previously, the label on the product will indicate if feeding trials have been conducted on the food or if it has merely been formulated to meet Association of American Feed Control Officials (AAFCO) Nutrient Profiles. A food that has been adequately tested using the AAFCO's animal feeding test protocols should be selected.

Ideal protein, carbohydrate, and fat levels in diets for diabetic dogs and cats have not been thoroughly investigated. A low-fat diet that is high in complex carbohydrates and fiber is currently advocated for human diabetics. Current recommendations for humans include limiting fat to less than 30% of calories and consuming 50% or greater of calories as complex carbohydrates.[69] The diet should also contain a relatively high proportion of soluble plant fiber. One of the most frequently used classification schemes divides fiber into one of two broad categories, soluble or insoluble fiber. Soluble fibers include pectin, gums, mucilages, and a few of the hemicelluloses. These fibers have great water-holding capacities, delay gastric emptying, and are almost completely digested by colonic bacteria. Most of their effects are exerted on the small intestine rather than on the large intestine. Insoluble fibers include cellulose, lignin, and most of the hemicelluloses. These fibers have less initial water-holding capacity, cause a decrease in gastrointestinal transit time, and are less efficiently digested by gastrointestinal bacteria. The consumption of insoluble fiber results in increases in fecal weight, fecal water volume, and defecation frequency. The primary effects of insoluble fibers occur in the large intestine.[70]

Research in humans indicates that a diet containing a high proportion of complex carbohydrate and soluble fiber dampens postprandial changes in blood glucose levels and aids in glycemic control.[69,71,72] Fiber promotes the slowed digestion and absorption of dietary carbohydrate, which results in a flattening of the glucose response curve after meals. The type of fiber that is used appears to be important. Studies with humans have found that postprandial hyperglycemia is reduced when both soluble and insoluble fibers are fed, but the viscous (soluble) fibers have the most pronounced effect.[73,74] Other studies have confirmed that a positive relationship exists between the viscosity of fiber solutions that are included in the diet and the degree of flattening of the glycemic response curve.[75,76] Soluble fiber also has the added benefit of causing a decrease in the low-density lipoprotein fraction of blood cholesterol in human subjects.[77]

Some investigators have suggested that dietary fiber has a similar effect in dogs and cats. When groups of dogs with experimentally induced diabetes mellitus were fed diets containing 15% fiber, significant reductions in 24-hour blood glucose fluctuations and in urinary glucose excretion were reported.[78] A slight reduction in monthly insulin requirements and blood-glycosylated hemoglobin concentration were also observed. These effects occurred when either insoluble fibers (cellulose) or soluble fibers (pectin) were used as the diet's primary fiber source. However, it is important to note that the experimental diets used in this study were created by adding supplemental fiber or carbohydrate to a balanced diet, resulting in dilution of the original diet. These diets were compared with a high-carbohydrate, low-fat control diet that was not diluted. As a result, the control diet differed from the experimental diets not only in its fiber content, but also in fat content, caloric density, and nutrient density. These confounding factors make it impossible to separate effects that were directly the result of dietary fiber from any effects that resulted from other dietary variables.

In a second study, a group of dogs with naturally occurring IDDM were fed a commercial, canned diet that was diluted by the addition of either 20 grams of wheat bran (insoluble fiber) or 20 grams of guar (soluble fiber).[79] When the dogs consumed the

canned food without added fiber, they all developed hyperglycemia within 60 minutes of eating, followed by development of a relative hypoglycemia between 90 and 240 minutes. The addition of guar to this diet abolished the postprandial hyperglycemia in four of six dogs and significantly reduced it in the remaining two dogs. The addition of wheat bran also reduced the maximal postprandial peak in blood glucose, but to a lesser extent. These effects were observed in both diabetic dogs and the healthy controls. Again, as in the previous study, the effect of dietary dilution results in differences in all nutrient levels and in the caloric density between the experimental and control diets.

The potential adverse side effects of dietary fiber must be addressed when examining the use of high-fiber diets for diabetic pets. Diets containing high amounts of soluble fiber can be very sticky in consistency and difficult for dogs to consume.[78] In addition, the long-term consumption of a diet containing 15% soluble fiber caused diarrhea and the development of a dry, brittle, and lusterless coat in some dogs.[80,81] These effects may have been the result of decreased availability of fatty acids and/or other essential nutrients.

Fiber can interfere with the absorption of dietary lipids, calcium, zinc, and iron, and can result in increased fecal energy and nitrogen excretion. Diets that contain high amounts of soluble fiber have also been shown to cause damage to the gastrointestinal tracts of laboratory animals and humans.[82,83] These effects must always be considered when manufacturers formulate diets that contain increased levels of dietary fiber. Simply adding fiber to a commercial product that has been formulated for adult maintenance is contraindicated. The added fiber may bind nutrients within the diet, eventually resulting in a nutrient deficiency. A diet that contains additional fiber should not be fed to diabetic pets that are underweight. Because of the low energy density of these foods, they are not suitable for pets that need to gain weight. Management requires reestablishment of glycemic control through insulin therapy and the feeding of a high-calorie, nutrient-dense food that is low in fiber to allow weight gain.

Other side effects of dietary fiber include excess gas production and flatulence, increased frequency of defecation, and increased quantity of fecal dry matter. Although these changes do not impose a health risk to animals, they are still undesirable effects that may be of considerable concern to pet owners. One study reported that when a group of dogs was switched from a normal, commercial diet to a diet containing 14% crude fiber, defecation frequency increased from two to four times per day and fecal dry matter and water excretion increased significantly.[84] These side effects should be considered when determining the level of dietary fiber to include in the diet of a diabetic pet. Often, diet palatability and level of tolerance of the pet and of the owner will dictate the level of fiber that can be included in a pet's food.

Although soluble and insoluble fiber may have a beneficial effect in modulating postprandial fluctuations in blood glucose levels of diabetic companion animals, the lack of long-term, well-controlled studies necessitates caution in the use of dietary fiber in the management of diabetic pets. Previous studies have divided dietary fiber into two types based on physical properties: soluble and insoluble. Recent evidence indicates that other fiber attributes should also be considered when studying physiological effects of fiber. These attributes include the degree of fermentability in the gastrointestinal

Dietary Management of Diabetes Mellitus: Diet Characteristics

Nutritionally complete and balanced
Consistent proportion of carbohydrate, fat, and protein
Consistency in ingredients (fixed formulation)
Greater than 40% of calories supplied by complex carbohydrate
Moderate in fiber content (if the pet is of normal or greater weight)
High-quality protein source
Moderately restricted in fat (≤ 20% of calories)

tract, the type of short-chain fatty acids that are produced from fermentation, and the presence of other dietary components[85,86] (see Section 1, pp. 18–19). Moderate levels of dietary fiber are necessary for normal gastrointestinal tract functioning and should be included in the diets of diabetic companion animals. However, the use of diets containing high levels of dietary fiber for long periods of time is not recommended.

Research concerning the level of protein to include in diets for diabetic pets is lacking. However, it is prudent to advise that diabetic dogs and cats should be fed high-quality protein at a level that meets their daily requirements. Cats have higher protein requirements that will somewhat limit the amount of digestible complex carbohydrate that can be included in the diet. If chronic renal failure develops as a complication of diabetes, protein must be restricted accordingly to control azotemia. The digestion of complex carbohydrates provides glucose to the bloodstream at a slower rate than simple carbohydrates, and so complex carbohydrates should supply most of the diet's carbohydrate. As a general rule, complex carbohydrate should provide 40% or greater of the calories in diets for diabetic pets. Fat intake by diabetic dogs and cats should also be moderately restricted if the pet is overweight. Alterations in lipid metabolism can cause the development of hypercholesterolemia and hepatic lipidosis in some animals. Restricted fat intake helps to prevent or minimize these changes and facilitates weight loss or weight management. As a general rule, the fat content of pet foods for diabetic pets should not exceed 20% of the metabolizable energy calories in the diet (see the box above).

CALORIC INTAKE AND WEIGHT CONTROL

The relationship between obesity and NIDDM in humans is well documented. Studies with dogs and cats have shown that a similar relationship exists in these species.[87-89] Baseline plasma insulin level and insulin response to a glucose load increase linearly in dogs as a function of their degree of obesity. This effect occurs in both healthy and diabetic animals that are overweight.[88] Similarly, a study with cats found that healthy but obese cats had normal fasting plasma glucose concentrations, but they had abnormal results to glucose tolerance tests. The obese cats also had slightly higher baseline serum

insulin concentrations. Results of an intravenous glucose tolerance test showed a significant delay in initial insulin response followed by a substantially increased insulin response at a later phase of the test.[89] Decreased tissue sensitivity to insulin and impaired beta-cell responsiveness to stimuli are believed to be the cause of these changes in obese animals. The tissue of obese animals has decreased numbers of cellular insulin receptors, and the receptors that are present have reduced binding affinity.[90,91] In some cases, a post-receptor, intracellular defect in insulin action also occurs.[92] Ultimately these changes decrease the body's ability to respond to insulin. Over time, beta-cell hyperresponsiveness develops, and baseline insulin and insulin secretion increase in an attempt to compensate for the obesity-induced resistance to cellular insulin.

Weight reduction and control is an important aspect of the dietary management of all diabetic animals that are overweight. When obesity is reduced in dogs and cats with abnormal, insulin-secretory responses, glucose tolerance often improves.[88] In addition, weight loss in pets with IDDM can result in enhanced tissue sensitivity to insulin, resulting in lowered daily insulin requirements. When the diabetic pet is overweight, caloric intake should be designed for weight loss and the eventual maintenance of ideal body weight. A diet that contains a high proportion of complex carbohydrates and reduced fat provides decreased energy density. However, a diet that is low in energy density must also contain adequate levels of all nutrients in forms that are available for digestion and absorption. As discussed previously, a commercial diet that is formulated to be complete and balanced while containing moderate fiber, increased complex carbohydrates, and reduced fat should be used. Adding complex carbohydrate or fiber to a normal diet in an attempt to decrease energy density can lead to nutrient imbalances. When weight loss is instituted with pets that have IDDM, adjustments in insulin will be required as glucose tolerance improves.

TIMING OF MEALS

The feeding schedule of pets with diabetes should be planned so that nutrients are delivered to the body during peak periods of exogenous insulin activity. This span will be determined by the type of insulin that is used and the time of day that it is administered. Several small meals should be provided throughout the period of insulin activity, as opposed to feeding a single, large meal. Feeding several small meals helps minimize postprandial fluctuations in blood glucose levels. Other factors that affect the degree of hyperglycemia that occurs following a meal include the composition of the meal and the type of insulin that is administered.

If insulin is administered early in the morning, the first meal should be given immediately before the insulin injection. If the pet refuses to eat on any occasion, the insulin injection can be withheld, thereby preventing the subsequent onset of hypoglycemia. The remaining three or four meals in the day can be given at approximately 4- to 5-hour intervals, depending on the action of the insulin that is used. Taking blood samples and

measuring blood glucose levels every 1 to 2 hours throughout a 24-hour period will indicate if the feeding schedule coincides adequately with insulin activity. If postprandial blood glucose levels rise above 180 milligrams per deciliter (mg/dl), the time interval between feeding and insulin administration should be decreased. If hyperglycemia still occurs, the size of the meal should be decreased and/or the number of meals that are provided per day increased. Likewise, a meal should always be provided within 1 to 2 hours following the lowest blood glucose level.[81,93]

Once an appropriate diet and feeding schedule have been selected, the program should be strictly adhered to. Pets that have previously been fed free-choice should be gradually switched to the new regimen. Although most dogs will adapt quickly, cats can be very resistant to changes in their feeding routine and in the type of food that is fed. This resistance can make dietary managment of the diabetic cat difficult for some pet owners. Mixing the new food into the cat's previous food and changing to a meal-feeding regimen over a period of several weeks can help to decrease these problems.[94] Supplemental foods should not be given and feeding times should vary as little as possible. Periodic monitoring of blood glucose levels can be used to adjust the diet as the pet loses weight, changes the amount of exercise that it receives, or requires adjustments in insulin dosage.

CHAPTER 32

Feline Lower Urinary Tract Disease

F eline lower urinary tract disease (FLUTD) is a generally accepted term that describes a collection of diseases with diverse etiologies in the lower urinary tract of the domestic cat. The syndrome has previously been referred to as feline urologic syndrome (FUS), but that term should be avoided because the term FLUTD more adequately describes the disorder.[95] When a cat develops FLUTD, mucosal irritation of the urinary tract results in clinical signs of dysuria (painful urination), hematuria (presence of blood in the urine), increased frequency and decreased volume of urination, and, occasionally, urethral obstruction. Urinary tract irritation may be caused by the presence of infectious agents, tumors, urethral plugs, uroliths, or crystals in the tract. In the case of FLUTD, bacteria and viruses are rarely found to be the source of irritation, while uroliths (also referred to as calculi) are most commonly observed.[96] In a substantial number of cases, however, no specific cause of the disorder can be identified.[97–99]

When urolithiasis is the cause of FLUTD, the crystals or uroliths that are found may contain various mineral compositions. In many cases, the uroliths are composed primarily of struvite, small concretions containing magnesium, ammonium, and phosphate. In the past, the vast majority of FLUTD cases were attributed to struvite urolithiasis. However, recent evidence indicates that struvite as a cause of FLUTD may be on the decline.[99] Calcium oxalate uroliths are the second most common type of urolith that are found in cases of FLUTD, and they may be increasing in prevalence[100] (see the box on the following page).

Potential Causes of Feline Lower Urinary Tract Disease

Urolithiasis, with uroliths composed of the following:
   Struvite
   Calcium oxalate
   Calcium phosphate
   Uric acid
Urinary tract infections
Urethral plugs
Neoplasia
Trauma
Anatomic abnormalities

INCIDENCE

A survey of the occurrence of FLUTD in the household cat population of the United States estimates the incidence of initial diagnosis to be approximately 0.85% per year.[101] This estimate is slightly higher than the figure of 0.34% to 0.52% reported in an earlier study of household cats in Great Britain and may suggest an increase in the diagnosis in the domestic cat population.[102] A recent, unpublished study reported that 9.6% (26 out of 270) of feline veterinary hospital admissions were presented with signs of FLUTD.[103]

FLUTD represents a major health concern to veterinarians and cat owners. There is a high probability of recurrence of symptoms following the initial episode of FLUTD.[104] Although both male and female cats develop the disease equally, FLUTD can be life threatening for male cats because of an increased tendency toward complete urinary obstruction. One study reported that blockage recurred in 45% of male cats within 6 months of their first obstruction, with death occurring in 16% of all previously obstructed cats.[105]

CLINICAL SIGNS

Initial signs of FLUTD include frequent urination, dribbling of urine, and/or urination in inappropriate places. Hematuria and a strong odor of ammonia in the urine are often observed. Pet owners may report additional signs of dysuria, such as prolonged squatting or straining following urination (often confused with constipation), and frequent licking of the urogenital region. These signs are usually the only signs observed in female cats. Male cats, on the other hand, have an increased tendency to develop partial or complete urethral obstruction, presumably because of their longer and narrower urethra and the sudden narrowing of the urethra at the bulbourethral glands as it enters the penis. Obstruction may occur suddenly or over a period of weeks. If obstruction is complete, uremia develops rapidly and is characterized by depression, anorexia, dehydration, and, periodically, vomiting and diarrhea. Increased back pressure of urine can cause renal

Signs of Feline Lower Urinary Tract Disease

Frequent urination	Dribbling of urine
Urination in inappropriate places	Depression
Prolonged squatting or straining following urination	Anorexia
Hematuria	Vomiting and diarrhea
Licking of urogenital region	Dehydration

ischemia, ultimately resulting in permanent renal damage. In severe cases the distended bladder may rupture, causing a transitory relief of signs, followed rapidly by the development of peritonitis and death. Uremia alone will lead to coma and death within 2 to 4 days, and so it represents a medical emergency (see the box above).

Struvite Urolithiasis as a Causative Factor in FLUTD

The clinical signs of FLUTD are caused by the presence and irritating effects of crystals, uroliths, urethral plugs, or other factors in the urinary tract. When uroliths are the cause, they may be found in the bladder, the urethra, and/or the kidney, but they are rarely located in the ureters. Although uroliths can be up to several millimeters in diameter, most are the size of a grain of sand or even microscopic. Uroliths are typically polycrystalline concretions that contain approximately 95% inorganic crystalloids and 5% organic matrix.[106] When obstruction occurs, a variable mixture of struvite and this proteinaceous colloidal matrix forms a plug that molds itself to the shape of the urethral lumen.[107] The vast majority of uroliths observed in cats are located in the urinary bladder, with the most common site for obstruction in male cats occurring in the region of the penile urethra.[106,108]

Early studies reported that more than 95% of the urinary uroliths in cats with FLUTD were composed of struvite.[108,109] However, recent research indicates that the proportion of struvite cases may be decreasing and those that are caused by calcium oxalate may be increasing.[100,110] A recent study reported that 64.5% of uroliths found in cats with FLUTD contained 70% to 100% struvite. Calcium oxalate was the second most common mineral found, representing approximately 20% of the uroliths.[111] Much less frequently, uroliths composed of calcium phosphate or ammonium urate are found.

Because struvite crystals have been found to be the most prevalent cause of FLUTD in cats, most research has focused on preventing these crystals from forming in the urine and on the development of effective dietary management of cats with struvite FLUTD. Although it now appears that a significant proportion of cases may have other causes, prevention of the formation of struvite crystals is still an important and effective treatment regimen for the management of FLUTD in many cats. However, it is imperative that cases of FLUTD be individually assessed. Dietary management that promotes

struvite dissolution can be used when struvite urolithiasis or struvite-containing ure-theral plugs are shown to be a causative factor.

Several conditions are necessary for the formation of struvite crystals in the urinary tract.[112] A sufficient concentration of the composite minerals magnesium, ammonium, and phosphate must be present in the urine. In addition, these minerals must remain in the tract for an adequate period of time to allow crystallization to occur. Lastly, and most importantly, a pH that is favorable for crystal precipitation must exist within the urinary tract environment.[112] Struvite is soluble at a pH below 6.6 and struvite crystals will form at a pH of 7.0 and above.[113] The presence of the colloidal proteins that are often associated with the struvite crystals may also be important. Although most attention has been focused on the properties of struvite, the protein component of FLUTD uroliths may also play a role in the etiology of this disease.[114]

PRESENCE OF URINARY TRACT INFECTIONS

One of the early explanations for the occurrence of FLUTD was the presence of either a bacterial or viral infection in the bladder, with the microbes serving as the nidus, or seed, for urinary crystals. However, this theory has been refuted by data showing that FLUTD is rarely accompanied by urinary tract infections.[115] Additionally, a consistent correlation between the presence of microbes in the urinary tract and the development of uroliths in adult cats has never been demonstrated.[109] Although one group of researchers presented data to support the theory of a cell-associated herpesvirus as a causative agent, others have been unable to either repeat this work or to isolate a herpesvirus from naturally occurring cases of FLUTD.[95,116,117] Recent studies have shown that the inoculation of a cell-associated herpesvirus can cause viral urinary tract infections in laboratory cats.[118] A group of researchers has also identified "virus-like" particles in the urethral plugs of obstructed male cats.[119] However, there is still no evidence that the presence of a virus is a causal agent involved in naturally occurring FLUTD.

Although urinary tract infections do not appear to be a common cause of FLUTD, they are occasionally diagnosed as a complicating factor.[98] Some bacterial infections may be iatrogenic, occurring as a sequela to the use of indwelling catheters for relief of urinary tract obstruction.[120] When bacterial infection does occur, it should be treated with appropriate antimicrobial therapy.

DIAGNOSIS

Diagnosis of FLUTD can be reached using medical history, clinical signs, and abdominal palpation. Radiography or sonography can be used to localize sites of obstruction or to detect large uroliths, but they will not usually detect uroliths that are less than 3 millimeters in diameter.[106] Urinalysis, determination of urolith composition, and urine cultures can confirm the diagnosis.

Factors Influencing the Development of FLUTD

Cat	Diet
Age	Urine-acidifying properties
Sex	Digestibility and caloric density
Activity level	Magnesium level
Weight status	Availability (feeding schedule)

Dietary Factors Involved in FLUTD

FLUTD is generally believed to have a multifactorial etiology.[121,122] The disease is rarely seen in cats younger than 1 year of age, with a peak incidence occurring between 2 and 6 years. Reduced activity caused by household confinement, obesity, and/or neutering may increase a cat's chance of developing FLUTD. Studies that have examined breed predilections have found that compared with domestic shorthair cats, Siamese cats have a decreased risk, and Persian cats have an increased risk of developing the disease.[123,124] However, it should be noted that breed characteristics such as lethargy and a tendency toward obesity in Persian cats may actually be the factors that contributed to the differences that were observed. Male and female cats have an equal chance of developing the urethritis or cystitis of FLUTD. However, because of anatomical differences, male cats are much more likely to obstruct and exhibit life-threatening clinical signs.[125]

Diet and feeding practices represent important risk factors for FLUTD (see the box above). These factors include acidifying properties of the food, the level of magnesium in the diet, fluid balance (as affected by diet digestibility and caloric density), and the cat's feeding schedule. More than any of the other risk factors involved, these are elements of a cat's life over which pet owners have some control. For this reason, these factors and their significance in the cause, management, and prevention of FLUTD will be discussed in detail. Because struvite urolithiasis has been found to be a common underlying cause of FLUTD, dietary management is aimed primarily at preventing the development of struvite uroliths in the urinary tract of susceptible cats. However, it is important to recognize that the measures adopted for management of struvite urolithiasis may not be appropriate for cases in which another underlying cause has been identified.

Magnesium Intake

One of the factors necessary for the formation of struvite in urine is the presence of sufficient concentrations of three composite minerals, magnesium, ammonium, and phosphate. Feline urine always contains high amounts of ammonium because of the cat's high protein requirement and intake. Urine phosphate in the healthy cat is also usually

high enough for struvite formation, regardless of dietary phosphorus intake. The concentration of urine magnesium, on the other hand, is normally quite low and can be directly affected by diet.[126]

Early investigations of FLUTD focused on dietary magnesium as a causal agent. The manipulation of magnesium to produce or prevent phosphate urolithiasis had previously been well documented in rats and sheep.[127,128] This work was used to suggest a role of this mineral in the etiology of FLUTD in domestic cats. One of the first studies showed that urethral obstruction and bladder uroliths could be induced in adult male cats when they were fed a diet containing either 0.75% or 1.0% magnesium and 1.6% phosphate.[129] The obstructing uroliths were composed primarily of magnesium and phosphate. Subsequent work showed that high levels of dietary phosphorus were not necessary for urolith development, but they did increase the risk for urolith formation when dietary magnesium was also high. However, if magnesium intake was low, the incidence of urolith formation was low regardless of the level of phosphorus.[130] In a later study by the same group, cats were fed diets containing 0.75%, 0.38%, or 0.08% magnesium on a dry-matter basis (DMB). Seventy-six percent of the cats that were fed the highest level, 70% of the cats that were fed 0.38%, and 0% of the cats that were fed the lowest level of magnesium developed urolithiasis and obstructed within 1 year or less.[131] Similarly, when random-source and specific, pathogen-free cats were fed diets containing either high magnesium or high magnesium and high phosphorus, urethral obstruction was induced. The obstructing material was identifiable as struvite by radiographic crystallography in one of the seven affected cats.[132]

These studies demonstrate the relationship between increasing magnesium in the diet and an increased rate of urolith formation and urethral obstruction in cats. However, the significance of these data to the role of dietary magnesium in naturally occurring FLUTD has been questioned. The levels of dietary magnesium that were used in these studies were all substantially higher than those that are normally found in commercial cat foods. The domestic cat requires only 0.016% available magnesium for growth and maintenance.[133] The Association of American Feed Control Officials (AAFCO) Nutrient Profile requires cat foods to contain a minimum of 0.04% magnesium.[134] Most commercial cat foods contain slightly higher than this amount but less than 0.1%. Although the magnesium in naturally occurring ingredients is not 100% available, these levels invariably supply cats with their magnesium requirement. The amount of magnesium in cat foods is higher than the cat's requirement for magnesium, but it is still substantially lower than the levels that have been used in experimental studies to induce struvite formation (0.40% to 1.0%).

A second problem with some of the experimental data involves the composition of experimentally produced uroliths. Epidemiological data have revealed that the majority of uroliths found in naturally occurring cases of FLUTD are composed of struvite (magnesium ammonium phosphate). However, the uroliths that were experimentally induced by some studies were actually made up of magnesium phosphate, with no detectable ammonium.[129,130] The composition of urethral plugs that caused obstruction in cats fed experimental diets was also different from the composition of urethral plugs

of cats that have spontaneous disease. Although the experimentally induced plugs were composed almost exclusively of struvite crystal aggregations, the plugs that are found in spontaneous disease are composed of struvite crystals and varying proportions of a mucogelatinous protein matrix.[135,136]

The most important confounding factor involves the form of magnesium that was added to the diets in the experimental studies. A group of investigators examined the effects of two different forms of supplemental dietary magnesium on urine pH of adult cats.[137] The data showed that the addition of 0.45% magnesium chloride to a basal diet resulted in a significant lowering of urine pH. In contrast, when the cats were fed the same basal diet supplemented with 0.45% magnesium oxide, a significantly higher, alkaline pH was produced. In a free-choice feeding regime, mean urine pH in cats fed the basal diet was 6.9, and urine pH of cats fed the magnesium chloride and magnesium oxide supplemented diets were 5.7 and 7.7, respectively. When urine samples were examined microscopically, crystal formation was observed in cats fed the basal diet and the magnesium oxide diet but not in cats fed the magnesium chloride diet. Therefore, at the same level of magnesium intake, urine pH and the formation of crystals were affected by the form of magnesium that was included in the diet. The observations that high levels of magnesium result in increased struvite formation are confounded by the effect of magnesium chloride versus magnesium oxide on urine pH. It can be concluded that similarities exist between the experimentally induced struvite urolithiasis and naturally occurring FLUTD, but the presence of significant differences and confounding factors indicates that magnesium intake is not singularly responsible for the natural development of the disease. Recent evidence indicates that dietary magnesium is less significant than urine pH and water balance as a dietary risk factor for FLUTD.

Ash Content as an Indicator of Magnesium Content

Ash consists of all of the noncombustible materials in a diet. Magnesium is the primary component of ash that has been implicated in the development of FLUTD. Because the level of magnesium in the food is not always stated on pet food labels, ash content has been widely used by pet owners as an indicator of magnesium level. However, this is not an accurate inference because the level of magnesium does not always correlate with the level of ash in commercial cat foods. Although most foods that are high in ash are also high in magnesium, a low-ash diet is not necessarily also low in magnesium. Diets that are low in ash may be so because of a reduced calcium content, not reduced magnesium. Although magnesium is a component of ash, the level of ash in a commercial cat food should not be used as a measure of the food's magnesium content.

Urine-Acidifying Properties of the Diet

Struvite is more soluble in acid than in alkaline medium. As a result, the pH of a cat's urine can have a profound effect on the formation of struvite crystals and the development of FLUTD. Struvite crystals will form in feline urine with a pH of 7.0 or greater, and they are soluble at a pH of 6.6 or less.[113] Normal, healthy cats typically have an acid urine with a pH of between 6.0 and 6.5, except after meals.[131] In all animals, the consumption of a meal results in a rise in urine pH within 4 hours. This effect, called the postprandial alkaline tide, is caused by kidney compensation for the loss of gastric acids that are secreted during digestion of the meal. To compensate for the loss of acid and to maintain normal pH in body fluids, the kidneys excrete alkaline ions, resulting in an increased urine pH. The magnitude of the alkaline tide is directly proportional to the size of the meal and to the acidifying or alkalinizing components within the meal. Depending on the nature of the diet and the size of the meal, the postprandial alkaline tide in cats can result in a urine pH as high as 8.0.[138]

Several studies have demonstrated the importance of urine pH in the formation of struvite crystals in the cat.[137-141] One report examined the effects of feeding either a canned diet, a dry diet, or the dry diet supplemented with a urine acidifier (1.6% ammonium chloride) on urine pH and struvite formation in adult male cats.[139] Data showed that urine pH was highest in cats that were fed the dry diet (7.55) and showed a significant decrease to 5.97 with the addition of ammonium chloride. A urine pH of 5.82 was produced by consumption of the canned diet. The most significant findings of this study concerned urine struvite formation. Struvite crystals were present in 78% of the cats fed the dry diet and in only 9% of the cats fed the dry diet plus the urine acidifier. Intakes of dry matter, magnesium, and other minerals were the same for cats fed each of the dry diets. None of the cats that were fed the canned diet developed urinary struvite crystals. In addition, when urine samples of all cats were adjusted to a pH of 7.0 using 0.5 M sodium hydroxide, 46% of the cats fed the canned diet and 100% of the cats fed the ammonium chloride-supplemented, dry diet showed typical struvite formation. These results show that at similar levels of energy, dry matter, and magnesium intake, the most important factor affecting feline struvite formation is urine pH.

Regardless of the level of magnesium intake by the cat, the dietary manipulation of urine pH consistently affects struvite formation. When a dry diet containing a high level of magnesium (0.37%) was fed to adult male cats, the addition of 1.5% ammonium chloride resulted in a urine pH of 6.0 or less.[140] Cats that were fed the diet without supplemental ammonium chloride produced urine with a pH of 7.3. Seven of the 12 non-supplemented cats formed struvite uroliths and obstructed on two occasions, but only two of the cats that were fed the acidifying diet obstructed on a single occasion. When the diets of the seven obstructed cats were supplemented with ammonium chloride, they experienced no further episodes of struvite formation or obstruction. Radiographic examination revealed visible uroliths, which dissolved after 3 months of consuming the acidifying diet. Similar results have been reported when diets containing levels of magnesium that are commonly found in commercial pet foods were fed. When adult cats were fed a purified diet containing only 0.045% magnesium, struvites formed and the cats showed clinical signs of FLUTD when the diet produced an alkaline urine.[138] However, if ammonium chloride was added as an acidifying agent, clinical signs disappeared within 4 days and did not recur while the acidifying diet was fed.

The domestic cat is a carnivorous mammal. Compared with an omnivorous or herbivorous diet, a true carnivorous diet has the effect of increasing net acid excretion and decreasing urine pH.[142,143] This urine-acidifying effect is primarily a result of the high level of sulfur-containing amino acids that are contained in meats. The oxidation of these amino acids results in the excretion of sulfate in the urine and a concomitant decrease in urine pH.[144] In addition, a diet that contains a high proportion of meat is lower in potassium salts than is a diet containing high amounts of cereal grains, which has been shown to produce an alkaline urine when metabolized.[145,146]

It has been postulated that the inclusion of high amounts of cereal grains and low amounts of meat products in some brands of commercial cat food may be a contributing factor to the development of FLUTD. For example, the struvite-producing, commercial, dry diet that was used in one study contained 46% cereal grains, primarily in the form of wheat meal.[139] Although a certain amount of cereal is necessary for the extrusion and expansion process of dry foods, high amounts of these products may contribute to the production of an alkaline urine. Conversely, the inclusion of high amounts of meat products in cat foods usually contributes to the production of a more acid urine.

As pet food manufacturers search for ingredients to include in cat foods that will naturally produce an acid urine, each ingredient must be separately evaluated for its effect on urine pH. For example, a recent study compared the urine-acidifying effects of corn gluten meal, poultry meal, and meat and bone meal when diets containing these ingredients were fed to cats. Results showed that of the ingredients tested, corn gluten meal had the strongest acidifying effect on urine. Unlike most plant protein sources, corn gluten meal contains higher concentrations of sulfur-containing amino acids than either poultry meal or meat and bone meal. Corn gluten meal is unusual in that it is a cereal protein that produces an acid urine when fed to cats.[147]

Although the maintenance of an acid urine with a pH of 6.0 to 6.6 is an effective way of preventing the formation of struvite crystals and the clinical signs of FLUTD in many cases, this is not conclusive proof that struvite formation is the underlying cause of the disorder. Some investigators have suggested that changing the pH of the urine merely manages the disease and does not address the underlying problem. Other factors that have been identified as possible causes include the presence of other types of uroliths, the synthesis of the protein component of the urethral plugs within the urinary tract, and the presence of viral or bacterial agents.[107,136] Further research is necessary to determine the importance of other factors in FLUTD. However, at this time, effective management of this disorder in many cats can be achieved through maintenance of a properly acidic urine.

Danger of Overacidification

Even though the maintenance of a urine pH of 6.6 or lower will prevent the formation of struvite crystals, the production of a urine that is too acidic can be detrimental to the cat's health. If more acid is consumed than an animal is capable of excreting, metabolic acidosis will occur. Acidosis causes a variety of health problems, including depletion of body potassium stores, renal dysfunction, impairment of normal bone homeostasis, and increased risk of calcium oxalate urolithiasis.[110]

The consumption of an acidifying diet or urine-acidifying agents that cause even a mild acidosis will result in increased urinary losses of potassium and calcium and may compromise electrolyte balance.[144] When acid intake is too high, the body will reestablish acid-base balance at a decreased blood bicarbonate concentration. Carbonate and phosphate are resorbed from bone to supply cations, and the calcium that is resorbed is excreted in the urine. Prolonged losses of calcium as a result of renal acidosis may eventually lead to bone demineralization and osteoporosis.[148,149] Urinary acidifying agents have been shown to have detrimental effects on bone mineralization in cats. When a diet containing 3% ammonium chloride was fed to growing kittens, urine pH was significantly decreased but the kittens also exhibited impaired growth, decreased blood pH, increased urine calcium excretion, and bone demineralization of the caudal vertebrae.[148] Similar changes were reported when adult cats were fed a diet containing 1.5% ammonium chloride.[150]

Studies have also shown that when cats are fed a severely acidifying diet for several months, they develop decreased levels of serum potassium and depletion of body potassium stores.[138,151] Although serum calcium may be maintained, it is theorized that this is a result of bone resorption. Other studies indicate that the long-term feeding of highly acidifying diets containing marginal levels of potassium cause hypokalemia and kidney disease in some cats.[152,153] A recent study showed that three out of nine cats fed an acidifying diet containing 40% protein and marginal levels of potassium developed chronic renal failure within 2 years.[151]

A final effect of an acidified urine may be to promote the formation of another type of urolith. Although struvite is soluble in an acid urine, an acid pH may increase the likelihood of calcium oxalate formation. The prolonged feeding of a highly acidified diet leads to loss of calcium in the urine, making this mineral available for the formation of calcium-containing uroliths. In addition, feeding a low-magnesium diet can exacerbate this problem because urine magnesium appears to inhibit calcium oxalate formation.[154] Reports show that the proportion of calcium oxalate urolithiasis in cats diagnosed with FLUTD has increased during the past several years.[110,155] However, it is not known whether this change represents a true increase in the number of oxalate cases or if the proportion of total FLUTD cases caused by calcium oxalate has merely increased because widespread use of acidifying diets has led to a decrease in the number of cases that are caused by struvite. It has been theorized that the widespread feeding of acidifying diets that contain low levels of magnesium may be a contributing factor to this trend.[110,154] However, it is also possible that inherent differences between cats result in some cats that are "struvite formers" and others that are "oxalate formers." As yet, there are no data available that address any of these possibilities, and feeding a diet that causes a moderately acidified urine and contains a low but adequate level of magnesium is the dietary treatment of choice in most cases.

Cats are capable of acidifying their urine to a pH as low as 5.5. Therefore diets should be formulated to maintain a urine pH above 6.0 but below 6.5 to prevent the for-

mation of struvite crystals and to prevent the ill effects of excessive acidification. When calcium oxalate uroliths are known to be the cause of FLUTD, urine acidification is not an appropriate treatment.[98,156] Unfortunately, dietary regimens for the dissolution or prevention of oxalate uroliths in cats have not yet been developed.

Fluid Balance and Urine Volume

Decreased urine volume may be a contributing factor in FLUTD in some cats. Diets that cause a decrease in total fluid turnover can result in decreased urine volume and increased urine concentration, both of which may contribute to struvite formation. It was originally suggested that dry cat foods contribute to decreased fluid intake and urine volume. One study showed that cats that were fed a dry cat food had decreased total water intake compared with cats consuming similar energy levels from canned food.[157] Cats did increase voluntary water intake when fed the dry food, but not in sufficient amounts to fully compensate for the lower moisture content of the food. In a subsequent experiment, adult cats were fed a semipurified, basal diet containing varying levels of moisture.[114] The cats consuming a diet containing 10% moisture had an average daily urine volume of 63 milliliters (ml). This volume increased to 112 ml/day when the moisture content of the ration was increased to 75%. Urine specific gravity was also slightly higher in cats that were fed the low-moisture food. In both of these studies, the differences in urine volume were attributed to lower total water intake in the cats that were consuming low-moisture foods.

However, in contrast to these studies, two other groups of investigators found no difference in water consumption between cats fed dry diets and those fed canned diets.[158,159] It appears that diet composition, especially fat content and caloric density, may actually be the factors affecting water turnover in cats fed different types of commercial diets.[158] A study examined the effects of diet type, composition, and digestibility on water-excretory patterns in cats.[126] A comparison of three canned diets showed that when cats were fed diets containing high levels of fat (34% and 28% of dry matter), significantly less dry matter was consumed than when cats were fed a canned diet containing a relatively low level of fat (14%). The results were less fecal dry matter and volume and less water excreted in the feces of cats fed the high-fat diets. Because total water intake was the same for all cats, the cats consuming the high-fat diets excreted significantly higher volumes of water in their urine to achieve water balance. Further evidence supporting the importance of caloric density and fat content is demonstrated by a comparison of the low-fat canned food to the three dry cat foods in this study. Water volume in urine and feces was similar between cats fed the low-fat, canned ration and cats fed the three dry diets. Other than the large difference in water content, the nutrient content of the low-fat, canned food was very similar to that of the dry diets. Energy digestibility of the canned ration was also equivalent to that of the dry diets (79.3% and 78.7%, respectively) and was significantly lower than the digestibility of the high-fat, canned diets (90.3%). Statistical analysis of these data revealed that the percentage of water that is excreted in the urine of cats is directly related to the fat and energy content of the diet, with correlation coefficients of 0.96 and 0.94, respectively.

The water content of the commercial diet is probably not an important factor in determining a ration's capacity to contribute to urine volume and the development of FLUTD. Rather, caloric density, fat content, and digestibility are more important factors to consider. The consumption of a cat food that is energy dense and highly digestible will result in lower total dry-matter intake. This decrease will be accompanied by decreased fecal volume and fecal water and increased urine volume. These effects may be beneficial in preventing FLUTD in cats because urine will contain a lower concentration of the mineral components that cause FLUTD. In addition, an increase in urine volume also stimulates an increased frequency of urination, thus decreasing the time available for struvite formation.

Method of Feeding

The postprandial alkaline tide occurs as a result of meal ingestion and the subsequent excretion and loss of gastric acids. Both the size of a meal and the frequency of eating will have an effect on the duration and magnitude of the urinary alkaline tide. Domestic cats are nibblers by nature. When fed on free-choice basis, most cats will eat small meals every few hours throughout the day.[160,161] Many pet owners who feed dry cat food provide it to their cats on a free-choice basis. Depending on the alkalizing effects of the diet, this feeding regimen may create a continuous alkaline tide of low magnitude.

In one study, cats were fed a dry, commercial food, either on a free-choice basis or one time daily. The urine pH of cats fed ad libitum was maintained between 6.5 and 6.9 throughout the day. The mean urine pH of cats that were fed the same ration one time daily significantly increased 2 hours after the meal to a peak pH value of 7.7 and then gradually decreased for the remainder of the day, becoming acidic several hours before the next meal.[141] Another group of researchers fed cats two dry foods and three canned foods on an ad libitum basis and recorded urine pH throughout a 24-hour period.[131] One of the dry foods and two of the canned foods maintained constant urine pH values of less than 6.3. However, one dry and one canned food produced pH values that ranged from 6.5 to higher than 7.0. When the same foods were meal fed one time daily, all of the foods except one dry and one canned product caused peak urine pH values of greater than 7.0 within 4 hours after the start of the meal. These values all declined to less than 6.5 by approximately 16 hours after the meal. One dry food and one canned diet maintained pH values of 6.6 or less, even when meal fed.

Lastly, a study that examined the relationship between method of feeding, food and water intake, urine volume, and urine composition in cats found that the period of highest urinary excretion of magnesium and phosphorus occurred preprandially and, therefore, did not coincide with the daily alkaline tide.[162] Although these results indicate that the highest concentration of composite minerals does not occur during the time they would be most likely to precipitate, this may not be a necessary condition for struvite formation. Recent research has shown that urine pH is directly related to the size of the meal, and this relationship can be described by a simple linear model. In other words, as the size of the meal increases, so does postprandial urine pH. The data also showed

that as postprandial urine pH increased, the presence of struvite crystals increased accordingly. Struvite did not form when urine pH was maintained at less than 6.6.[163]

Determination of the best feeding schedule to use is largely dependent on the diet that is fed. The effect of nibbling creates a continuous, slightly elevated urine pH. A diet that produces a postprandial pH of 6.5 to 7.0 would be expected to maintain a pH of less than 6.5 during ad libitum feeding and would be an appropriate diet to choose for an ad libitum feeding schedule.[163] In contrast, a diet that produces a higher postprandial rise in urine pH would be expected to maintain a urine pH of greater than 6.5 during ad libitum feeding. In this case, the maintenance of an alkaline urine for extended periods of time would predispose the cat to the formation of struvite crystals. Therefore, with this diet, meal feeding may be preferable in order to reduce the duration of exposure to the alkaline urine.

DIETARY MANAGEMENT

In clinical cases in which obstruction has occurred, immediate care involves stabilization of the cat's condition, fluid replacement therapy, and relief of bladder distention and urethral obstruction. Removal of the obstruction can usually be accomplished by either flushing the urolith or urethral plug out of the urethra or by cystocentesis. Bacterial urinary tract infections, if present, should be managed by appropriate antimicrobial therapy. Cats should remain hospitalized for 5 to 7 days after treatment because of the high rate of recurrence during this time period. Long-term dietary management involves the removal or dissolution of any remaining struvite uroliths and feeding an appropriate diet that prevents struvite formation. When obstruction is caused by urethral plugs, and if the mineral component of the plug is struvite, dietary modification in the form of acidification is used in long-term management. However, it is not known if dietary manipulation will have an effect on the formation of the colloidal matrix of these plugs.[156]

Remaining struvite uroliths that are present in the urinary tract can be removed either through surgical means or diet-induced dissolution. Surgical intervention provides immediate relief to the animal followed by recovery within 3 to 7 days. On the other hand, dietary dissolution is a noninvasive procedure but can take several months to be effective. When dietary intervention is used, the diet should be formulated to reduce the urinary concentration of magnesium and to produce an acid urine with a pH of approximately 6.0. Although sodium chloride may also be present in the diet in an attempt to induce diuresis, this has not been proven to be effective.[164] Depending on the size and number of uroliths that are present, complete dietary dissolution usually takes between 5 and 7 weeks.[165]

Although there are diets available that are specifically formulated for the dissolution of feline struvite, an effective diet can also be created by adding a urine acidifier to a low-magnesium cat food.[166] Adding 800 milligrams (mg) of ammonium chloride per day to a high-quality, commercial cat food will result in the elimination of the postprandial

alkaline tide and the maintenance of a urine pH of 6.0 or less.[167] Similar results were reported when cats were fed a commercial, dry cat food containing 1.6% ammonium chloride.[139,140] However, the addition of excessive amounts of ammonium chloride can be toxic.[168] Adding amounts of ammonium chloride as low as 1000 mg/day to the diet has been shown to cause anorexia, vomiting, and diarrhea in some cats.[168] Therefore the ammonium chloride dosages should be strictly monitored, and cats should be observed closely for signs of toxicity.

The amino acid, dl-methionine, is also an effective urine acidifier when included in the diet. The recommended dose is 1 gram per day or 1% to 2% of the dry matter of the diet.[138] However, methionine toxicity has been shown to occur at levels only slightly above this dose.[138,169] When levels of 2.8% to 5.5% of the dry matter of the diet were fed, cats developed hemolytic anemia, methemoglobinemia, and Heinz body formation.[170] Therefore ammonium chloride or a combination of ammonium chloride and dl-methionine is preferable to using dl-methionine alone.

Regardless of the method that is used to achieve an appropriate diet, the urine pH of cats fed the diet should be monitored 4 to 8 hours after initial consumption to ensure that adequate (but not excessive) acidification is occurring. A urine pH of approximately 6.0 is desirable. Only the prescribed diet should be fed, with no additional supplements or other cat foods. During the dissolution phase of treatment, cats should be monitored for struvite dissolution, using either palpation or radiography, at 2- to 4-week intervals. Periodic evaluation of urine sediment for crystalluria may be helpful in assessing progress, but because many healthy, normal cats develop urine struvite crystals, the presence of crystalluria should not be interpreted as persistent FLUTD.[110,147] The diet should be continued for at least 1 month following complete dissolution of struvite.[171] After this time period, cats can be changed to a maintenance diet that has been demonstrated to be effective in the prevention of FLUTD.

Diets that produce highly acidified urine should only be used therapeutically for struvite dissolution. These diets should not be fed during growth, reproduction, or for adult maintenance. In addition, urinary acidifiers are contraindicated with any commercial cat foods that have been specifically formulated to be calculolytic. Highly acidifying diets should not be fed to cats with any type of cardiac dysfunction, hypertension, or acidemia. Prolonged urinary acidification, even in healthy animals, can compromise electrolyte balance and lead to urinary losses of calcium and potassium[144] (see pp. 365–367).

The maintenance diet that is fed to prevent the recurrence of FLUTD should produce a slightly acidified urine, be high in caloric density and digestibility, and contain a relatively low level of magnesium. A urine pH of 6.6 or less will prevent the formation of struvite crystals. Dietary ingredients that have the effect of increasing urinary acid excretion include proteins of animal origin (because of their high sulfur-amino acid content) and compounds that result in an elevated absorption of chloride, phosphate, or sulfate.[146] Conversely, most cereal grains contain high levels of potassium salts that have the effect of producing an alkaline urine.[139] The exception is corn gluten meal, which produces an acidic urine because of its high concentration of sulfur-amino acids.[147] Most commercial cat foods that contain high amounts of cereal grains should be avoided.

Practical Feeding Tips: Prevention of Struvite FLUTD

Diet should be highly digestible and calorically dense.
Diet should produce a slightly acidified urine (pH 6.0 to 6.5).
Diet should contain a relatively low level of magnesium (≤0.1% on a dry-matter basis).
Diet should contain animal products as the primary protein source.

Diets that are high in caloric density and are highly digestible will be consumed in smaller amounts, thus lowering both dry-matter intake and magnesium intake. The lower dry-matter intake will result in decreased fecal matter and fecal water and in increased urine volume. Decreased magnesium intake will result in lower concentrations of urine magnesium, which is necessary for struvite formation. Thus the percentage of magnesium in the diet is not as important as the total amount of magnesium that the cat consumes. Although some researchers believe that magnesium concentration in the diet should be 0.1% or less on a DMB, others maintain that FLUTD risk is only increased when magnesium levels reach 0.25% or greater.[110,166,172]

There are several high-quality, nutritionally complete commercial cat foods that meet the criteria discussed above. Although many grocery store brands of dry cat food may contain relatively low concentrations of magnesium, they are often also low in fat and digestibility and too high in cereal grains. A commercial cat food should not be selected only on the basis of its ash or magnesium content. The food's caloric density, digestibility, and urine-acidifying properties should all be considered when selecting a commercial cat food for the prevention of FLUTD (see the box above).

CHAPTER 33

Nutritionally Responsive Dermatoses

The skin (integument) is a metabolically active organ system that provides sensory input, protects the body from physical and infectious injury, functions in temperature control and immunoregulation, and serves as a reservoir for some nutrients.[173] The health of a pet's skin and hair coat can be affected by nutrient imbalances that involve protein, vitamin A, vitamin E, the essential fatty acids, or zinc. Dogs and cats that are consuming high-quality, complete, balanced pet foods are unlikely to suffer from a serious deficiency or excess of any of these nutrients. However, feeding a poorly formulated or stored commercial food or preparing a homemade diet that is not correctly balanced can lead to skin disorders. In addition, any metabolic or functional disorder that affects a pet's ability to digest, absorb, or use nutrients can cause secondary nutrient imbalances that can manifest as dermatoses. A third way nutrition can affect the health of the skin is through the development of a food allergy or hypersensitivity. The development of a hypersensitivity to one or more components in the diet can be the cause of inflammatory dermatoses in dogs and cats. Dermatoses caused by both nutrient imbalances and food hypersensitivities are discussed in this chapter.

PROTEIN DEFICIENCY

Protein deficiency in dogs and cats causes changes to the skin and hair coat. Protein deficiency leads to abnormal keratinization of skin and hair, depigmentation of the hair shafts, and changes in sebaceous and epidermal lipids. Hairs become brittle and break off easily, and coat growth will slow or stop. The lipid layer of the epidermis is also

abnormal and loses its function as a protective barrier. The skin becomes scaly, greasy, and susceptible to secondary bacterial infections. Today dermatoses that are induced by protein deficiency are very rare in dogs and cats. Cases of extreme protein/calorie malnutrition or starvation can result in dermatological signs, but other clinical signs of malnutrition will also be observed. When healthy pets are fed balanced, complete pet foods, signs of protein deficiency are highly unlikely.

Vitamin A-Responsive Dermatosis

Vitamin A is necessary for normal epithelial cell differentiation and maintenance and for the process of keratinization (see Section 1 pp. 32–33, Section 2 pp. 119–120). Either a deficiency or an excess of this vitamin causes skin lesions in dogs and cats. Signs include hair loss and poor coat condition, hyperkeratinization of the epidermis and hair follicles, scaling of the skin, and an increased susceptibility to secondary bacterial infections of the skin.[173] Toxicity is most commonly caused by feeding an all-liver diet or by oversupplementation with cod liver oil. More commonly, certain types of skin disorders are responsive to treatment with supplemental vitamin A.

The administration of vitamin A and the retinoids (natural and synthetic analogs of vitamin A) appear to have both a physiological and a pharmacological effect. These compounds have been used successfully in humans and animals to treat cases of idiopathic seborrhea that are not caused by a vitamin A deficiency. Seborrhea is a general term that describes the overproduction of oils and other protective secretions by the sebaceous glands in the skin. The skin usually becomes flaky, greasy, or both. Because the epidermal lipid layer is abnormal, the animal becomes prone to secondary bacterial skin infections that can cause pruritus and further damage to the skin. Treatment of seborrhea in companion animals is usually directed toward determining the underlying cause and correcting it. However, in a substantial number of cases, an underlying cause cannot be identified and treatment is directed primarily toward the relief of clinical signs.

Although many cases of seborrhea in dogs and cats do not respond to vitamin A supplementation, a small proportion do respond favorably and can be kept in permanent remission through the long-term administration of vitamin A or one of its analogs. In particular, cocker spaniels with idiopathic seborrhea have been shown to respond to vitamin A supplementation.[174,175] Two similar cases have also been reported in a Labrador retriever and a miniature schnauzer.[175,176] Vitamin A-responsive dermatosis is characterized by dry and scaly skin, which progresses to oily changes. The dog eventually develops large, hyperkeratotic plaques composed of sebum and keratin and marked follicular plugging. Lesions are most prominent on the underside of the chest and abdomen. Hair loss and skin changes are accompanied by secondary bacterial folliculitis. Pruritus and inflammation may or may not be present.[174,176] Almost all reported cases also showed moderate to severe otitis externa.[174,176]

Cases of vitamin A dermatoses do not respond to the traditional treatments for seborrhea, which include medicated shampoos, antibiotic therapy, and/or glucocorticoid therapy. Although clinical signs can be used to support a diagnosis, conclusive diagno-

sis of vitamin A-responsive dermatoses can only be confirmed through favorable response to supplementation. A dose of 10,000 International Units (IU) per day is suggested, although levels as high as 50,000 IU/day have been used.[174-176] A decrease in clinical signs is usually seen within 4 weeks, with complete remission within 2 to 6 months.[174,176] Attempts to reduce the level of vitamin A or to withdraw therapy result in a relapse of clinical signs, indicating that lifelong therapy is necessary. The dosages that are used represent six to ten times the dog's normal requirement for vitamin A. However, no signs of vitamin A toxicity have been observed in the reported cases, even after several years of therapy. Other studies have indicated that much higher levels of vitamin A are necessary to induce clinical signs of toxicity in the dog.[177,178]

It is important to note that this condition is not caused by a vitamin A deficiency. In all reported cases, the dogs were being fed a high-quality, complete and balanced, commercial dog food. Moreover, serum levels of vitamin A were normal and no other signs of vitamin A deficiency were observed. One group of investigators also reported that the skin changes that were seen in cases of vitamin A responsive dermatosis differed significantly from those seen with a true vitamin A deficiency.[176] It is likely that the effect of vitamin A is the result of a pharmacological action of the vitamin on epithelial cells, rather than through the vitamin's role as an essential nutrient.[174] The prevalence in cocker spaniels suggests a genetic basis for the disease in that breed.

VITAMIN E-RESPONSIVE DERMATOSIS

It has been suggested that vitamin E may play a role in certain skin disorders in dogs. The occurrence of demodicosis (skin lesions caused by the demodectic mange mite, *Demodex canis*) has been associated with decreased blood levels of vitamin E. It has been theorized that a subclinical vitamin E deficiency causes suppression of the immune system, which in turn increases a dog's susceptibility to the demodex mite. In one study, a group of dogs with demodicosis were treated with supplemental vitamin E and significant levels of improvement were observed.[179] However, other studies have reported that vitamin E supplementation has no effect on demodicosis.[12] More controlled research is necessary before definitive conclusions can be made concerning the role of vitamin E in the control of this disorder in dogs.

Supplementation with large amounts of vitamin E has been shown to control primary acanthosis nigricans in dachshunds. This disorder is characterized by hair loss and extreme hyperpigmentation (blackening) and thickening of the skin. As the disease progresses, varying degrees of greasiness, crusting, rancid odor, and secondary bacterial infections develop. Pruritus is usually absent or mild during the early stages of the disorder, but it may become more pronounced as secondary infections occur.

In one study, a group of eight dachshunds with acanthosis nigricans were given 200 IU of alpha-tocopherol daily, and all eight dogs showed improvement within 60 days. The inflammation, crusting, and pruritus completely subsided, although hyperpigmentation did not improve. Clinical signs did not reappear in any of the dogs after follow-up periods of 7 months to 3 years. All of the dogs were maintained on the vitamin E sup-

TABLE 33-1
Vitamin E-Responsive Dermatoses

DISORDER	BREEDS	SUCCESS OF VITAMIN E SUPPLEMENTATION
Dermodicosis	All	Variable
Primary acanthosis nigricans	Dachshunds	Yes
Discoid lupus erythematosus	All	Variable
Dermatomyositis	Collies, shetland sheepdogs	Variable

plementation throughout this time.[180] None of the owners ever attempted to decrease the dose or to withdraw the supplementation, so it is not known if long-term vitamin E supplementation is necessary in all cases.

A medium sized, adult dog (20 kilograms [kg]) has a minimum daily requirement for vitamin E of about 10 IU.[181] Most commercial pet foods will supply a 20-kg dog with between 20 and 50 IU/day. The levels that were fed in this study represent four to ten times the dog's normal daily intake of vitamin E. No toxicity signs were observed in any of the eight dogs. The authors concluded that vitamin E may offer a therapeutic alternative for some cases of primary canine acanthosis nigricans.[180] In all cases the disorder is chronic and persistent, and therapy is directed toward control rather than cure. Many dogs with acanthosis nigricans respond favorably to treatment with systemic glucocorticoids. However, concern with the immediate and long-term side effects of glucocorticoid therapy dictates the need to find alternative treatments, one of which may be supplementation with vitamin E.

Vitamin E therapy has also been used with varying levels of success in dogs with discoid lupus erythematosus and dermatomyositis.[12,182,183] Further research needs to be conducted to substantiate these studies and to determine effective doses of vitamin E. In contrast, studies of the efficacy of vitamin E supplementation for treatment of atopic dermatitis (allergic dermatitis) have shown that vitamin E is not effective as an antiinflammatory agent and does not provide relief from pruritus[183] (Table 33-1).

ESSENTIAL FATTY ACIDS AND SKIN DISEASE

As components of cell-membrane phospholipids and precursors for a variety of regulatory compounds, the essential fatty acids (EFA) maintain the health and integrity of epithelial tissue in the body. Because of its high cell turnover rate, the skin is especially susceptible to EFA deficiencies.[184] The dog requires a dietary source of linoleic acid, and the cat requires linoleic plus arachidonic acid (see Section 2, pp. 96–97). In dogs, an EFA deficiency results in a dry, dull coat, hair loss, and the eventual development of skin lesions. Over time the skin becomes pruritic, greasy, and susceptible to infection. A change in the surface lipids in the skin alters the normal bacterial flora and predisposes the animal to secondary bacterial infections.[13,185] Epidermal peeling, interdigital exuda-

tion, and otitis externa have also been reported in EFA-deficient dogs. Linoleic acid deficiency in cats results in similar signs.

Naturally occurring skin disease as a result of EFA deficiency is rare in companion animals today. When a deficiency does occur, it is usually the result of feeding a diet that is either poorly formulated or that has been stored improperly. Healthy companion animals that are fed high-quality foods are not at risk of developing an EFA deficiency. If the food has been stored at high temperatures or beyond the stated expiration date, there is a risk of EFA loss as a result of oxidative changes to the food. When an EFA deficiency is suspected, it is better to change the diet to one that is well formulated and has been stored properly, rather than to attempt to correct a deficiency by adding supplemental fatty acids.

EFA supplementation and the dietary manipulation of EFA metabolism appear to have some efficacy in the treatment of certain skin disorders that are not the result of a dietary deficiency of EFAs. The polyunsaturated fatty acids are divided into several series, based on the distance of the first double bond in the carbon chain from the terminal methyl group. For example, the n-3 (or omega-3) fatty acids have the first double bond, located at the third carbon atom (see Section 2, p. 23). The series that are of interest in the treatment of skin disease are the n-3 and n-6 fatty acids. Algae synthesize high amounts of n-3 fatty acids. As a result, most marine animals contain high concentrations of n-3 fatty acids in their tissues. Sources of n-3 fatty acids in pet foods include fresh, cold-water fish oils, and whole-fat flax. Land animals, in contrast, have high concentrations of the n-6 fatty acids because most plants that are consumed by terrestrial animals contain greater amounts of n-6 than n-3 fatty acids.[40] Sources of n-6 fatty acids in pet foods include corn, safflower, sunflower, cottonseed, and soy oils. Although animals are capable of elongating and further desaturating these fatty acids after they have been consumed, interconversion between the n-3 and n-6 series is not possible within the body. However, the metabolic pathways for the conversion of n-3 and n-6 fatty acids to inflammatory agents share several enzymes.[185] The desaturation and elongation process produces arachidonic acid from linoleic acid (of the n-6 series) and eicosapentaenoic acid (EPA) from linolenic acid (of the n-3 series) (Figure 33-1). These two compounds are the most biologically active polyunsaturated fatty acids.

Arachidonic acid (n-6 series) and EPA (n-3 series) exist in the body as components of cell membranes and as part of the metabolic fatty-acid pool. Both are precursors for a group of compounds known as the eicosanoids. The prefix "eico" is Greek for twenty; indicating that the eicosanoids are metabolites of 20-carbon fatty acids such as arachidonic acid and EPA. These include the prostaglandins, leukotrienes, prostacyclins, and thromboxanes. These compounds all have local hormone-like effects and are involved in inflammatory reactions, immunoregulation, and epidermal cell proliferation.[12] When cellular injury occurs, membranes release their component fatty acids, which will then be metabolized to their respective eicosanoids. The specific eicosanoids that are formed from EPA and arachidonic acid each have different physiological effects. In general, the EPA-derived eicosanoids are much less potent inducers of inflammation than are the arachidonic acid-derived eicosanoids. Arachidonic acid is converted to the two- and four-series of eicosanoids that participate in inflammatory and hypersensitiv-

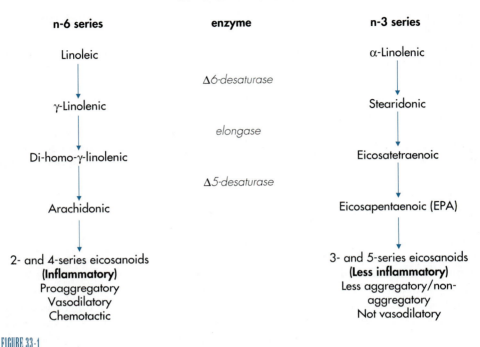

n-6 series	enzyme	n-3 series
Linoleic		α-Linolenic
↓	Δ6-desaturase	↓
γ-Linolenic		Stearidonic
↓	elongase	↓
Di-homo-γ-linolenic		Eicosatetraenoic
↓	Δ5-desaturase	↓
Arachidonic		Eicosapentaenoic (EPA)
↓		↓
2- and 4-series eicosanoids **(Inflammatory)** Proaggregatory Vasodilatory Chemotactic		3- and 5-series eicosanoids **(Less inflammatory)** Less aggregatory/non-aggregatory Not vasodilatory

FIGURE 33-1
Metabolism of n-3 and n-6 series fatty acids

ity (allergic) reactions. In contrast, EPA and other n-3 fatty acids are metabolized to the three- and five-series eicosanoids, which are believed to be less inflammatory[185-187] (see Figure 31-1).

The ratio of n-6 to n-3 fatty acids in an animal's tissues can be manipulated by diet, and these manipulations influence the inflammatory response in a dog's skin. Because the two-series fatty acids compete for the same initial enzyme system, providing a diet that contains an increased proportion of n-3 fatty acids and a decreased proportion of n-6 fatty acids results in changes in the types of inflammatory metabolites that are produced in the skin. A recent study showed that feeding dogs a diet with an n-6 to n-3 ratio of between 5:1 and 10:1 resulted in the skin's production of significantly lower levels of leukotriene B_4 and significantly higher levels of the less inflammatory metabolite, leukotriene B_5, compared with the levels that were produced when the dogs were fed a diet with a ratio of 28:1.[188]

It appears that feeding certain types of fish oils and other compounds that contain high levels of n-3 fatty acids such as EPA will have the effect of decreasing inflammatory and hypersensitivity responses in some pets. Allergic skin diseases are common in companion animals and are characterized by extreme pruritus, self-trauma to the skin, and secondary bacterial infection. Allergic cats may also exhibit miliary dermatitis, symmetrical truncal alopecia, and/or eosinophilic plaques and granuloma.[189] One of the most common allergic skin disorders is atopic dermatitis. Dogs and cats with atopy have

a genetic predisposition to produce excessively high levels of reaginic (IgE) antibodies. As a result, they often respond to common antigens in their environment by manifesting an allergic response. Inhaled allergens such as pollens or molds are often responsible, but other causes such as certain food components, external parasites, chemicals, or topical irritants are also seen. When exposed to the offending antigen, mast cells present in the pet's skin release a number of inflammatory agents, including several of the metabolites of the n-6 fatty acids (arachidonic acid).

Dietary manipulation of fatty acid metabolism in an attempt to decrease the proportion of n-6 fatty acids and increase the proportion of n-3 fatty acids in cell membranes has been used as a treatment for inflammatory dermatoses in dogs and cats. One study treated 93 dogs that had been diagnosed with atopic dermatitis with a commercial fatty acid supplement containing 15 milligrams (mg) of EPA per capsule.[187] A dose of one capsule per 9 kg (30 lb) body weight was given. One third of the dogs showed good to excellent response to the supplement. Another study using the same supplement reported that after 4 to 5 weeks of treatment, 11% of dogs with atopy, food allergy, or flea-bite allergy were adequately controlled by the supplement alone, with no other treatment necessary.[190]

The mechanism of action of EPA appears to be a change in the type of eicosanoid that is produced. Because arachidonic acid and EPA compete for the same enzymes, when the level of EPA is increased in cell membranes, production of the less inflammatory three- and five-series are increased and production of the two- and four-series eicosanoids are decreased.[188] Because there are a number of different agents that mediate inflammation and pruritus in dogs with allergic dermatitis, this manipulation cannot be expected to work in all cases.[13,185,187]

A second method of manipulating fatty acid metabolism has been used in conjunction with n-3 fatty acid supplementation for the treatment of inflammatory skin diseases in dogs. Gamma-linolenic acid is a fatty acid that is produced from linoleic acid, an EFA. In the body, gamma-linolenic acid is first converted to dihomo-gamma linolenic acid and then to either the monoenoic prostaglandins or to arachidonic acid (Figures 33-1 and 33-2). The more active pathway for metabolism of dihomo-gamma linolenic acid is toward the production of the monoenoic prostaglandins. Like the eicosanoids that are produced from EPA, these prostaglandins are less inflammatory than the dienoic prostaglandins that are synthesized from arachidonic acid. Providing gamma-linolenic acid in the diet bypasses the rate-limiting step from linoleic acid to linolenic acid, which requires the delta-6-desaturase enzyme. This promotes the formation of dihomo-gamma linolenic acid and the monoenoic prostaglandins, rather than the formation of arachidonic acid and its inflammatory metabolites. Evening primrose oil is a concentrated source of gamma-linolenic acid.

When dogs' diets are supplemented with evening primrose oil, plasma levels of dihomo-gamma linolenic acid have been shown to increase.[191] Similarly, when dogs with atopy that had been controlled by evening primrose oil and fish oil were fed a supplement containing only olive oil (a poor source of both n-3 and n-6 fatty acids), plasma levels of dihomo-gamma linolenic acid subsequently decreased. A return of clinical signs in these dogs parallelled the reduction in dihomo-gamma linolenic acid.[192] It has been

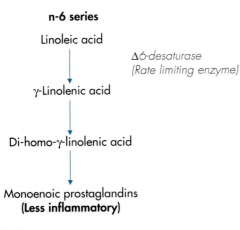

n-6 series

Linoleic acid

Δ6-desaturase
(Rate limiting enzyme)

γ-Linolenic acid

Di-homo-γ-linolenic acid

Monoenoic prostaglandins
(Less inflammatory)

FIGURE 33-2
Production of γ -linolenic acid metabolites

postulated that atopic disease in some dogs may be a manifestation of a deficiency of the enzyme delta-6-desaturase. Providing gamma-linolenic acid effectively bypasses the delta-6-desaturase step of fatty acid metabolism and provides substrate for the production of the monoenoic prostaglandins.[193]

Recent studies have shown that supplements containing a combination of evening primrose oil and fish oil are effective in the long-term control of atopy in dogs and cats.[184,192,194-196] When 33 dogs were treated with this supplement, 18% of the dogs needed no other treatment and 7% showed a significant reduction of clinical signs.[184] Similar results have been reported in cats. When the diets of 14 cats that were diagnosed with miliary dermatosis were supplemented with various combinations of evening primrose oil and fish oil, improvements in clinical signs were observed when the cats were fed either evening primrose oil alone, or a combination of evening primrose oil and fish oil.[195] Supplementation with fish oil alone (n-3 fatty acids) was not effective. After 12 weeks of treatment, 11 of 14 cats showed a favorable response to the combination of 80% evening primrose oil and 20% fish oil. A second study with cats found that 40% of cats with non-lesional pruritus and 67% of cats with eosinophilic granuloma complex responded favorably to dietary supplementation with a product containing EPA, gamma-linolenic acid, decahexaenoic acid, safflower oil, natural glycerin, and vitamin E.[189] It has been speculated that cats may differ from dogs in their response to n-3 fatty acids because cats have been shown to lack n-3 fatty acid activity in the skin and because of the cat's decreased activity of the enzyme delta-6-desaturase[195] (see Section 2, pp. 96–97).

Supplementation with marine oils containing high levels of EPA, other n-3 fatty acids, and gamma-linolenic acid appear to be an effective treatment for some dogs and cats with various types of allergic dermatitis. These compounds may provide a safe alternative or adjunct therapy to long-term corticosteroid therapy in animals that show

a favorable response. No severe side effects have been reported, although a very small percentage of pets may show vomiting or diarrhea when supplemented with these oils.[189,190] Positive results to fatty acid supplementation may be observed after 2 weeks, but they usually take 6 to 8 weeks to become apparent.[197] Although a small percentage of pets requires no other therapy, many benefit from the concurrent use of antihistamines or low dosages of prednisolone. In many cases, fatty acid supplementation as a treatment for allergic dermatitis allows significant reduction in the dose and/or frequency of other antiinflammatory drugs that were being used.[198-200]

Documentation of appropriate dosages of supplements and ratios of fatty acids to include in pet foods is lacking. Experimental data show that changes in skin concentrations of fatty acids are maximized after 3 to 12 weeks of supplementation or feeding the new diet. However, great variability is seen with the type and ratio of fatty acids that are used.[188,201] Although dosages of supplements that are added to the pet's diet have not been identified, a recent study showed that feeding a diet that contains an n-6 to n-3 ratio between 5:1 and 10:1 results in desired changes in skin leukotriene concentrations.[188] Because controlled dosage studies are still lacking, current recommendations are to select products that supply both EPA and gamma-linolenic acid, and administer the supplement at the manufacturer's recommended dosage for a minimum of 6 to 8 weeks before assessing the animal's response.[197] If a new pet food is selected, one that contains a source of n-3 fatty acids and a ratio of n-6 to n-3 fatty acids between 5:1 and 10:1 is recommended. This ratio will meet dog and cat's essential fatty acid requirements (n-6 fatty acids), while providing a lipid base that is noninflammatory.

ZINC DEFICIENCY

Zinc deficiency may occur in companion animals for a number of reasons. Genetic disorders are responsible for impairment of zinc absorption and metabolism in several breeds of dogs. A defect in the mucosal transfer system of zinc in the small intestine occurs in Alaskan malamutes and Siberian huskies; and bull terriers with lethal acrodermatitis have an inability to absorb dietary zinc (see pp. 340–341). Zinc deficiency can also result from inadequate levels of the mineral in the diet and from the presence of other nutrients or components that interfere with zinc absorption.[14,202–204] Naturally occurring cases of zinc-responsive dermatoses have been associated with feeding diets that contain either marginal levels of zinc and/or high levels of components that interfere with zinc absorption, such as phytate or calcium.[202,203] Supplementation of the diets of growing dogs with calcium also has the potential to result in a dermatoses associated with zinc deficiency.[13,185,204]

The skin lesions of zinc deficiency first occur over pressure points and on the foot pads, but they will eventually spread over the entire body. Affected areas are characterized by hair loss, redness, inflammation, and crusting. Secondary skin infections are also seen. Diagnosis is usually made by diet history, physical examination, and skin

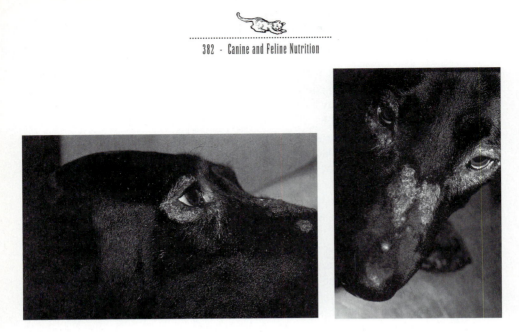

FIGURE 33-3
Zinc deficiency in an adult male Labrador retriever caused by a diet of generic dog food. (Reprinted with permission from Candace Sousa, D.V.M., Animal Dermatology Clinic, Sacramento, CA.)

biopsy. Positive response to oral zinc supplementation without changing the diet can be used to confirm a diagnosis.[202] A dose of 10 mg/kg/day of zinc sulfate or 1.7 mg/kg/day of zinc methionine is recommended.[13,202] Skin lesions will show a rapid response to supplementation, with complete healing within 2 weeks. Zinc supplementation confirms a diagnosis and aids in rapid recovery. However, in most cases a correction of the diet to a complete and balanced food that supplies adequate levels of zinc and does not include inhibitory substances is recommended. Continued supplementation with zinc after correction of the diet should not be necessary, except in cases in which the dermatoses were caused by an inherited problem with zinc metabolism.

DIETARY HYPERSENSITIVITY (ALLERGY)

Dogs and cats can have adverse reactions to dietary ingredients for a number of reasons (see the accompanying box). Dietary hypersensitivity occurs when an animal develops a specific immunological reactivity (allergy) to one or more components in the diet. Hypersensitivities differ significantly from food intolerances, in which the animal responds adversely to its diet, but there is no evidence of an immune-mediated response. Intolerances include problems such as a lack of the intestinal enzyme lactase, resulting in an inability to digest lactose; food toxicities; and pharmacological reactions to dietary ingredients.[205] Because dietary hypersensitivity usually manifests as a dermatosis, the discussion included in this section will be limited to this type of dietary problem.

Causes of Adverse Food Reactions in Dogs and Cats

Immunological	Nonimmunological
Food allergy	Food intolerance
	Metabolic adverse reaction
	Toxicity
	Pharmacological reaction

Description and Incidence

In most dogs and cats, dietary hypersensitivities manifest as allergic dermatoses. Studies have shown that 97% of allergic companion animals show dermatological signs alone and 10% to 15% develop gastrointestinal disease with or without skin disease.[206-208] It has been estimated that food-induced allergic dermatitis constitutes 1% of all dermatoses that are seen by small animal veterinarians and 10% of the inflammatory dermatoses that are diagnosed.[209,210] However, other researchers report that dietary hypersensitivities account for between 23% and 62% of all nonseasonal allergic dermatoses.[211,212] Although the estimated incidence rates vary considerably, it is generally accepted that dietary hypersensitivity ranks third in incidence to inhalant allergies and flea bite allergies as a cause of pruritic skin disease in dogs and cats.[206]

Dietary hypersensitivity can develop at any age. Unlike inhalant allergies (atopy) and flea bite dermatitis, which often take several years to develop, dietary hypersensitivity can first occur in pets that are less than 1 year of age. In two reports, 19% and 33% of the cases first developed clinical signs when they were less than 1 year of age.[207,213] A recent study of 25 dogs diagnosed with food allergy found that the median age of initial onset was 1 year.[214] These data suggest that a food allergy should always be considered when an immature pet exhibits a nonseasonal allergic dermatitis.

The onset of dietary allergy can be seen at any time of the year and is not typically associated with a recent diet change. In one study, 68% of the dogs had been fed the offending diet for 2 years or more before clinical signs developed.[209] No significant sex or age predilections have been observed. Although the presence of a genetic component has not been proven, one study did find that among purebred dogs, German shepherd dogs and golden retrievers appeared to be over-represented when compared with a general hospital population. This difference was not significant but suggests the possibility of a genetic predilection in these breeds.[214] Other breeds that appear to be at increased risk include the soft-coated Wheaton terrier, dalmatian, West Highland white terrier, collie, Chinese Shar Pei, Lhasa Apso, cocker spaniel, English springer spaniel, miniature schnauzer, and Labrador retriever.[215]

Some investigators have reported that, unlike atopy and flea bite allergy, dietary hypersensitivity does not respond well to corticosteroid treatment.[173,208] However, other studies have found that a significant number of cases show a decrease in clinical signs when treated with systemic glucocorticoids.[213,214] In one study, 72% of the dogs that were diagnosed with food allergy had either partial or complete response to corticosteroid therapy.[214] A favorable response to the administration of systemic glucocorticoids should therefore not be taken as an indication that food allergy is not an underlying cause of clinical signs.

Etiology

The immunological mechanisms that cause dietary hypersensitivity are incompletely understood. Affected animals usually have an allergic response to only one or two specific ingredients in the diet and, less commonly, they demonstrate multiple sensitivities.[206,209] The disorder is currently considered to be the result of Type I and/or Type III immediate hypersensitivity response. A Type I response is responsible for the severe pruritus that is seen after ingesting the offending dietary antigen. A Type III response, on the other hand, is thought to be responsible for the acute intestinal signs (diarrhea) that are seen in a small number of animals.[206] Antigens are generally large proteins, lipoproteins, or glycoproteins with molecular weights of 10,000 or greater. It is possible that some of the processing procedures that are used to produce commercial pet foods increase the antigenicity of certain dietary components.[208,216] This would explain the observation that some allergic pets tolerate homemade diets but develop an allergic response to commercial diets that contain the same ingredients.[207] Beef and dairy products are the cause of 80% or more of the cases of food allergy in dogs and cats.[206,214,217] Other dietary ingredients to which dogs and cats become allergic include cereal grains, pork, chicken, egg, and fish.

It has been proposed that early weaning of puppies or kittens may predispose some pets to the development of food allergies later in life.[217] In healthy animals, the small intestine possesses a protective barrier that limits the absorption of macromolecules. In young puppies and kittens, this protective barrier is not completely functional. When foreign food proteins are introduced to the immature gut, some may pass across the intestinal barrier, penetrate the lymphoid tissue, and trigger an immunological response. Disease states that disrupt the small intestine's immunological barrier may have a similar effect. This theory is speculative at this time but may explain the early onset of food allergies in some pets. Further research must be conducted to determine the exact role that early weaning and/or the disruption of the intestine's protective barrier may play in the development of dietary hypersensitivities.

Clinical Signs

The most common dermatological sign of dietary hypersensitivity in dogs and cats is an intense pruritus.[12,205,218] Initially, this usually occurs between 4 and 24 hours of ingesting the offending antigen. Over time, chronic cases show constant pruritus, with no evident association between eating and an exacerbation of signs.[206] The onset of pruritus is not accompanied by other skin changes. However, the pet's intense scratching, biting, and self-trauma quickly lead to secondary lesions. In dogs, the areas of the body that are most often affected are the feet, the arm pits, and the groin.[206,219] Cats are affected most intensely around the head, neck, and ears.[217] In severe cases in both

Signs of Dietary Hypersensitivity in Dogs and Cats

Dogs	Cats
Intense pruritus (feet, armpits, groin)	Intense pruritis (head and neck)
Self-induced trauma	Self-induced trauma
Chronic inflammation of skin	Ulcerative dermatitis
Papular eruptions	Miliary dermatitis
Hair loss	Hair loss
Hyperpigmentation/scaling	Cutaneous hyperesthesia
Otitis externa	Seborrhea
Secondary bacterial infections (recurrent pyodermas)	Vomiting/diarrhea (common)
Vomiting/diarrhea (10% to 15% of cases)	

species, generalized pruritus over the entire body is seen.[205] Excessive scratching and licking leads to hair loss and reddening of the skin. The presence of papular eruptions occur in approximately 40% of reported cases, and secondary bacterial infections are seen in about 20% of reported cases.[205] Other secondary changes may include chronic inflammation, crusting, seborrhea, and hyperpigmentation.

A persistent otitis externa, with or without infection, is often seen in dogs, and in some cases is the only presenting sign. A small number of cases have also been reported that showed only a recurrent pyoderma that was not associated with pruritus. The pyoderma subsided with antibacterial therapy but continued to recur until the diet was changed.[214] Skin disease caused by a dietary hypersensitivity is usually nonseasonal. However, if multiple sensitivities are present (that is, dietary allergy plus atopy or flea bite allergy), the dietary sensitivity may not manifest clinically until another sensitivity is also triggered and the dog or cat reaches its pruritic threshold. This situation can cause the signs to appear to be seasonal in nature[205,217] (see the box above).

Diagnosis and Treatment

Diagnosis of dietary hypersensitivity involves first ruling out other causes of the allergic dermatosis. These causes include atopy, flea bite dermatitis, and drug hypersensitivities. Obtaining a full diet history is equally important. When a food allergy is suspected, the standard method of diagnosis involves three steps: feeding an elimination diet and demonstrating an amelioration of clinical signs, challenging the pet with the original diet and observing a return of clinical signs, and feeding select ingredients to identify the specific offending dietary antigens (see the box on the following page). Intradermal skin testing and serologic testing have been shown to be unreliable in diagnosing food allergies in dogs and cats.[216,220]

By definition, an elimination diet contains protein and carbohydrate sources to which the pet has not previously been exposed. In many cases, lamb and rice provide acceptable protein and carbohydrate sources. Whole lamb, rather than ground lamb, should be used because ground lamb meat may be contaminated with ground beef,

Three Stages of Dietary Hypersensitivity Diagnosis

Feeding the Elimination Diet
The diet should consist of ingredients that the animal has not been previously exposed to and should contain a ratio of 1:2 to 1:4 parts protein to carbohydrate. The animal should be introduced to the diet over a 4-day period. Improvement in clinical signs is usually observed within 3 weeks, but may take up to 10 weeks.

Feeding a Challenge Diet to Confirm
Refeed a diet that is known to cause an allergic reaction in the animal. If pruritus occurs within 4 hours to 14 days, a diagnosis of dietary hypersensitivity is confirmed.

Identifying the Offending Dietary Ingredients
Add one suspected offending ingredient to the elimination diet. Monitor the animal for signs of allergic response. Repeat for all suspected ingredients.

making it unsuitable for use in an elimination diet.[216] The recent increase in the inclusion of lamb meat in commercial pet foods may eventually cause this protein source to lose its suitability in elimination diets for some pets. Fresh chicken, fish, or tofu may be suitable alternative protein sources; potato can also be used as an alternate carbohydrate source.[13,205,208]

A homemade pet food is best for the elimination phase of diagnosis because some pets with food hypersensitivity will still react to commercial diets. For example, 20% of dogs that were asymptomatic when fed a homemade diet of lamb and rice became pruritic again when fed a commercial preparation containing the same ingredients.[207] Another controlled study showed that 16% of dogs with diagnosed food hypersensitivity developed allergic reactions to a commercial diet that was manufactured as an elimination diet for the diagnosis of dietary hypersensitivity.[216] These differences provide evidence that the processing of commercial pet foods may enhance the antigenicity of some food components. In cases in which the preparation of a homemade elimination diet is cost prohibitive or in which there is poor owner compliance, a commercially prepared hypoallergenic diet should be used. Commercially prepared elimination diets have the benefits of economy, convenience, and assurance of consistency and nutritional adequacy. However, the owner must be aware that some pets with food allergy still react to commercial, hypoallergenic diets. In these cases an amelioration of clinical signs will not be seen and a definitive diagnosis cannot be made.

A ratio of 1:2 to 1:4 parts protein to carbohydrate source can be used to prepare the homemade elimination diet, and the pet's diet should be gradually changed to this diet over a period of 3 to 4 days. The elimination diet should then be fed exclusively, with no additional treats or table scraps. In addition, all chew toys that are made of animal products must be removed, and chewable vitamins or heartworm medication must be replaced with pure forms of medication. Some dogs and cats will show improvement after eating the elimination diet for only 3 weeks, but an 8- to 10-week trial period should be used to establish a diagnosis.[205] A recent study of 51 dogs with food allergy reported that only 25% of the dogs responded to an elimination diet after 3 weeks of feeding, and

greater than 90% of the dogs had responded by 10 weeks.[215] In general, a 50% or greater reduction of pruritus and skin disease is accepted as a diagnosis for a dietary hypersensitivity.[210] Some pets may have a dietary hypersensitivity occurring concomitantly with other pruritic dermatoses, such as flea bite allergy or atopy. When this occurs, feeding an elimination diet will often cause a decrease in pruritus and skin disease but will not result in the complete resolution of signs. If pruritus is not diminished during the elimination phase, then either food allergy is not the diagnosis, or the elimination diet that is being used still contains an ingredient to which the pet is allergic.

A conclusive diagnosis can be made when the pet's former diet is reintroduced as a challenge diet, and a return of pruritus is seen within 4 hours and 14 days.[206,214] The final phase, identification of specific antigens, is accomplished by adding single food items to the elimination diet and assessing for a return of clinical signs. Because beef and dairy products account for the majority of dietary hypersensitivities in dogs and cats, these ingredients should be tested first. Adding powdered milk at a level of ½ to 2 tablespoons per meal provides exposure to the antigens found in dairy products.[219] If no return of signs is seen after 10 to 14 days, the next ingredient can be tested.[214] Food items that are readily available to pet owners can be easily tested. Cooked beef, wheat flour, and soy meal can each be tested by adding ½ to 2 tablespoons per meal. Only one new substance should be added and tested at a time, and if a food causes an allergic reaction, the elimination diet should be fed until all signs are resolved before proceeding to another item. If no clinical signs are observed within 14 days of adding a test ingredient, the pet is probably not allergic to that food. Fortunately most pets are shown to be allergic to only one or two specific dietary ingredients.[209,214,217]

The identification phase of diagnosis can be very tedious and time-consuming for many pet owners. In addition, some owners are reluctant to risk the reoccurrence of clinical signs in their pet. After completing the elimination and challenge phases and arriving at a diagnosis of food allergy, some pet owners choose to simply find a diet that their pet tolerates without attempting to identify the specific ingredients to which the pet reacts. Simply changing to a new, commercial pet food will rarely be effective because most commercial foods contain similar ingredients. Diets should be selected that contain protein and carbohydrate sources to which the pet has not been exposed and are not expected to cause a reaction. Feeding the elimination diet as the long-term maintenance diet is acceptable if this diet has been determined to be complete and balanced.

The lifetime nutritional management of pets with dietary hypersensitivity requires feeding a diet that is palatable, complete and balanced, and that does not contain the offending antigen or antigens. Although homemade diets are recommended for the elimination phase of diagnosis, balanced commercial products are preferred for long-term maintenance. Commercial products offer economy and convenience and, unlike most homemade diets, are guaranteed to be nutritionally complete and balanced. Lamb is traditionally used as the protein source in these diets. However, the increased use of this product as a protein source in commercial pet foods has resulted in an increasing number of allergic pets who will not tolerate it.

Some pets with diagnosed food hypersensitivities will eventually develop additional sensitivities to ingredients in the new diet.[205] In these cases, the identification phase

must be repeated and another suitable diet must be found. Similarly, it is possible for the original sensitivity to become diminished and allow the pet to once again consume a diet containing that ingredient.[205] Because dietary hypersensitivity is not always responsive to corticosteroid therapy and because of the long-term side effects of corticosteroids, emphasis is placed on strict adherence to dietary management rather than on drug therapy. In either case, the therapeutic objective is management of the disorder because dietary hypersensitivity can never be cured. Any small dietary indiscretion on the part of the owner or the pet does not cause direct harm but may lead to damage from pruritus and self-induced trauma. In some cases, repeated failures to adhere to the new diet decrease the chance of obtaining relief when fed an elimination diet. It is therefore very important that pet owners are aware of the need for strict compliance in order to control clinical signs.

CHAPTER 34

Chronic Kidney Disease

DESCRIPTION AND CLINICAL SIGNS

Chronic renal failure in dogs and cats is characterized by an irreversible and progressive loss of kidney function and the development of clinical signs that reflect the kidney's decreasing ability to perform normal regulatory and excretory functions. There are many potential causes for the initial kidney damage that leads to chronic disease. These causes include, but are not limited to, trauma, infection, immunological disease, neoplasms, renal ischemia (decreased blood flow to the kidney), genetic anomalies, and toxins. In most cases the initial underlying cause is no longer present when the pet develops chronic kidney failure. This is due to the ability of the kidney to compensate for large proportions of functional tissue loss. However, over time these compensatory mechanisms may break down, leading to progressive loss of kidney function and signs of chronic disease.

Nephrons are the functional units of the kidney. Each nephron consists of a glomerulus and a system of tubules within which reabsorption and excretion occur. The glomerulus is a tuft of capillaries where waste products and electrolytes from the blood are filtered. The tubules originate at the base of the glomerulus and selectively reabsorb many of the blood components that are present in the filtrate. When the filtrate reaches the final portion of the tubule, it contains only those compounds that are going to be excreted as waste in the urine. The healthy kidney contains thousands of nephrons and has a substantial functional reserve.

Blood flow through the kidneys is very high, with approximately one fourth of cardiac output filtered through the kidneys each minute. The waste products of protein catabolism, such as urea, creatinine, uric acid, and ammonia, are removed and excreted

in the urine. In addition, electrolytes and trace minerals are filtered, reabsorbed, and selectively excreted. The kidney is also important in the normal regulation of fluid balance, pH, and blood pressure, and for the production of the hormone erythropoietin and the active form of vitamin D. The progressive loss of these functions leads to functional loss and eventual clinical signs of chronic kidney disease.

The compensatory mechanisms of the healthy nephrons that remain after initial renal injury allow the kidney to function normally even after the loss of a large proportion of tissue. A loss of at least 70% to 85% of functional capacity usually occurs before a pet begins to show clinical signs of renal failure.[221-223] One of the first signs that most pet owners notice is increased water consumption and increased urination. This effect is caused by a reduced capacity of dogs to concentrate their urine, resulting in an increased volume of urine and increased frequency of urination. Some dogs may appear to regress in their housebreaking or may involuntarily empty their bladder while sleeping. Polydypsia accompanies the increased urination because the dog compensates to maintain fluid balance. Polyuria and polydypsia are less commonly observed in cats because cats will usually become uremic before they lose the ability to concentrate urine.[224] In addition, owners of indoor cats that use litter boxes are less likely to notice increased urination even when it does occur.

Other clinical signs that are seen in dogs and cats with advanced renal failure are thought to be associated with the degree of azotemia or uremia that is present. Azotemia refers to the accumulation of nitrogenous waste products in the blood, composed primarily of urea nitrogen and/or creatinine. The term uremia technically means elevated concentrations of urea in the blood, but commonly refers to the collection of clinical signs that are associated with renal failure. These signs include decreased appetite or anorexia, vomiting, depression, electrolyte and pH disturbances, mucosal ulcers, and weight loss. Some pets will develop chronic diarrhea and neurological signs. Aberrations in phosphorus and calcium metabolism lead to secondary renal hyperparathyroidism, which causes renal osteodystrophy (bone demineralization) and deposition of calcium phosphate in soft tissues. In many cases of chronic renal failure, the inability of the kidney to produce erythropoietin and a reduced life span of red blood cells lead to anemia[225] (see box on the following page).

Diagnosis of chronic renal disease in dogs and cats is based on medical history, clinical signs, serum chemistry, and urinalysis. General indicators of renal dysfunction are elevated blood urea nitrogen (BUN) levels and elevated plasma creatinine levels. Plasma creatinine levels of between 1.5 and 4 milligrams per deciliter (mg/dl) are indicative of mild to moderate renal disease.[225] Levels higher than 4 mg/dl usually indicate severe failure or end-stage renal disease.[225,226] Plasma creatinine is a sensitive indicator of renal dysfunction and is not affected by dietary protein intake. In contrast, BUN is strongly affected by the consumption of a protein-containing meal. Therefore all samples should be taken 12 hours postprandial. A fasting BUN of greater than 35 mg/dl is usually an indication of some level of kidney dysfunction. Elevated serum phosphorus (greater than 5 mg/dl) also provides supportive evidence for a diagnosis of chronic renal failure.[225]

Measurement of an animal's glomerular filtration rate (GFR) is the most accurate procedure for diagnosis of chronic renal disease. This test requires 24-hour urine col-

Signs of Chronic Kidney Disease

Polyuria	Anorexia
Increased frequency of urination	Weight loss
Polydipsia	Anemia
Depression	Renal osteodystrophy
Diarrhea	Neurological impairment
Vomiting	

lection by a veterinarian and measures the rate at which blood is filtered through the kidneys and waste products are removed and excreted.[225] An accurate estimate of GFR can also be obtained by measuring the renal clearance of exogenous creatine.[227,228] With chronic renal disease, the eventual decline in GFR is responsible for the inability of the kidney to filter and excrete waste products efficiently.

THE PROGRESSIVE NATURE OF CHRONIC KIDNEY DISEASE

The occurrence of chronic renal failure is preceded by some type of renal insult or injury that causes a loss of nephrons. Following this initial episode, the kidneys undergo structural and functional compensatory adaptations. Specifically, these changes include increased glomerular capillary hypertension, increased single nephron glomerular filtration rate (SNGFR), and renal hypertrophy (growth of remnant nephrons).[229-233] The increase in GFR in the surviving nephrons causes the kidney's total GFR to be higher than that which would be predicted following the reduction in renal mass. These changes enable the damaged kidney to compensate and to function for variable and extended periods of time at normal or near normal capacity. During this compensatory phase, clinical signs of renal disease are not evident.

Depending on the extent of the damage to the kidney and on other factors that can influence the progression of disease, renal function may eventually begin to decline. When this occurs, the progressive and irreversible loss of functioning nephrons causes a gradual reduction in total GFR and in the kidney's ability to excrete waste products from the body. The inability to excrete waste products and the compromised regulatory functioning of the kidney lead to clinical signs of kidney failure. Renal failure can progress to end-stage disease even after the initial cause of injury has been resolved and in the absence of active renal disease. It appears that the loss of a certain critical mass of nephrons can result in self-perpetuating, progressive renal disease. Studies in dogs have indicated that between ¾ and ¹⁵/₁₆ of renal mass must be destroyed before progression of renal disease occurs.[222] However, great variability is seen among individuals. Some dogs and cats never develop progressive disease, even when an extremely high proportion of renal mass has been destroyed.[234]

Many factors may contribute to the progression of renal disease in dogs and cats. Evidence from early studies with rats suggested that the alterations that compensate for

the initial loss of active tissue may eventually contribute to progressive deterioration of the remaining tissue.[232,235] These studies led to the hypothesis that hyperfiltration and hypertension of surviving nephrons ultimately would cause cellular injury, resulting in progressive glomerularsclerosis and a loss of nephron function. This postulation has been termed the hyperfiltration theory and appears to explain the progressive nature of renal disease in several strains of laboratory rat.[236,237]

However, it is not known if hyperfiltration of remaining functional nephrons is a contributing factor in progressive renal disease in the dog or the cat. Several studies with dogs indicate that the adaptive changes that occur following a loss of renal tissue do not lead to the progressive glomerulosclerosis that has been seen in the rat.[229,238,239] Other factors that may contribute to the onset of progressive renal disease in dogs and cats include infection, administration of nephrotoxic agents, and decreased blood flow to the kidney.[234] The presence of multiple factors are responsible for the variable nature of renal disease in companion animals. Although chronic renal failure becomes progressive in some dogs, in others renal function remains stable for prolonged periods of time with no signs of progressive loss of nephron function.[234]

Role of Diet in the Progression of Chronic Kidney Disease

The development of glomerular hyperfiltration, hypertension, and hypertrophy in rats with reduced renal mass eventually leads to glomerularsclerosis and progressive renal failure.[232] Studies have shown that manipulations that limit the hyperfiltration and hypertension of surviving nephrons slow the progression of disease and help to preserve renal function in this species.[232] It is hypothesized that these factors alter the progression of disease because they slow the adaptive changes that occur in the surviving nephrons. Manipulations that have been shown to influence renal hemodynamics include changes in dietary protein, phosphorus, lipid, or energy levels.[240–242] The factor that has been studied most extensively in rats and other species is the restriction of dietary protein.

Feeding a high-protein diet results in increased renal blood flow and increased postprandial glomerular filtration rate in all species that have been studied, including the dog.[236,243] This effect is seen in both healthy animals and in animals with compromised kidney function. Studies in rats have shown that the restriction of dietary protein reduces these effects and also slows the progression of chronic renal disease in rats with experimentally reduced renal mass.[232,236] In other words, feeding a low-protein diet to rats that already have kidney disease causes a decrease in the hyperfiltration effect and slows the progressive loss of functioning tissue. Restricting dietary protein also slows the development of progressive disease in healthy Fischer 344 rats that are genetically predisposed to develop chronic renal disease as they age.[244,245]

However, this effect has not been observed in the dog. In contrast to rats, elevated protein levels have not been shown to cause a progression of renal disease in dogs with experimental or natural renal disease.[238,239,246,247] In one long-term study, diets con-

taining either 19%, 27% or 56% protein were fed to dogs with ¾ reduction in renal mass for a period of 4 years.[246] The dogs that were fed the high-protein diet had higher GFR and renal plasma flow rates than dogs that were fed the low-protein diet. However, significant morphological or functional deterioration in the remaining nephrons of the kidney were not observed in any dogs. The investigators were unable to establish a cause and effect relationship between protein feeding and the progression of renal disease in the dogs that were studied. Feeding the high-protein (56%) and the low-protein (19%) diets were associated with slight proteinuria, but the 27%-protein diet did not cause this effect. In contrast to the rats that were studied, none of the dogs in this study developed elevated BUN levels or clinical signs of chronic kidney disease in response to consuming moderate or high-protein diets.

In another study, three groups of dogs with induced renal failure were fed three diets varying in protein, fat, carbohydrate, and mineral content.[248] Over a 40-week period, dogs that were fed the high-protein, high-phosphorus diet (44.4% protein, 2.05% phosphorus) showed the highest mortality rate. However, mortality was associated with uremia caused by the increased protein, rather than uremia caused by the development of progressive nephron destruction. There was no evidence of a decline in GFR (an indication of progressive renal disease), in the dogs that were fed the high-protein diet. These results indicate that the increased mortality was caused by the extrarenal, clinical effects of feeding high amounts of protein to dogs with renal failure and not to an enhanced progression of renal disease caused by the diet.

Although the previous studies do not support the hypothesis that protein affects the progression of kidney disease in the dog, other studies have also failed to show that restricting dietary protein inhibits the initial development or progression of renal disease. Early studies with rats reported that feeding low-protein diets prolonged life and delayed the development of chronic renal disease.[236,249,250] However, subsequent studies have shown that the benefits that had been attributed to low protein were actually a result of the low intakes of these diets and the subsequent low energy consumption of the rats throughout life. The low energy intake significantly slowed growth (which continues throughout life in rats) and retarded the progression of chronic renal disease.[223,240,245] Unfortunately, the belief that feeding a low-protein diet prevents the development and the progression of renal disease had already been applied to several other species, including companion animals. However, this theory is currently without supportive scientific evidence in either dogs or cats.

In dogs, the moderate restriction of dietary protein is not effective in modifying glomerular hypertrophy after a loss of kidney function. When dogs with ¹⁵/₁₆ loss of kidney function were fed a moderately restricted diet containing 16% protein, the adaptive changes of hyperfiltration, capillary hypertension, and glomerular hypertrophy still occurred.[229] A second study of dogs with ⅞ loss of functional kidney tissue reported that renal lesions were indistinguishable between dogs that were fed a diet containing 15% protein and those that were fed a diet containing 31% protein over a fourteen-month period.[231] Severe restriction of protein may have resulted in a reduction in the adaptive changes, but there are inherent dangers in severe restriction of dietary protein for dogs

and cats. Protein deficiency results in impaired immunological response and resistance to infection, reduced hemoglobin production and anemia, growth retardation, decreased plasma protein levels, and muscle wasting.[251] In addition, cats will not tolerate reduced protein diets (see Section 2, pp. 107–109). Therefore the health problems associated with protein and amino acid deficiency may offset any suspected benefits of severe protein restriction.

Current evidence suggests that mechanisms that can alter progression of renal disease in the rat do not have the same effect in the dog. Dogs appear to be resistant to the glomerulosclerosis and loss of renal function that are associated with aging adaptive changes in nephrons, and protein-feeding in the rat. Studies indicate that, although high-protein feeding will exacerbate clinical signs by leading to azotemia in dogs with advanced renal failure, there is no evidence that dietary protein causes a progressive destruction of nephron functioning in remaining normal tissue. It is hypothesized that the absence of systemic hypertension in dogs with renal disease, and the fact that dogs do not normally develop the same type of renal disease as do rats that the differences between dogs and rats exist.[234,246] In addition, unlike the rat, the dog does not continue to grow throughout its life and typically consumes only one to two meals per day, compared with the nibbling regimen of the rat. In dogs, hyperfiltration following the consumption of a meal that contains protein lasts for a short period of time, as opposed to continuously throughout a 24-hour period in the rat.[223]

A distinction must be made between restricting protein with the proposed purpose of slowing or stopping progression of renal disease and restricting protein with the purpose of managing clinical signs. Although studies with rats indicate that protein restriction is beneficial in slowing the progression of chronic renal disease, research does not support this finding in dogs. Because it has been hypothesized that elderly pets experience losses of renal function as a normal process of aging, it has become popular to advocate feeding low-protein diets to older animals with the intent of slowing the rate of renal deterioration. However, no research has shown that there is an obligatory loss of kidney function with aging in dogs and cats. Elderly pets require adequate levels of high-quality protein to help to minimize losses of protein reserves and to satisfy their maintenance needs (see Section 5, pp. 255–256). Restricting protein when it is not necessary can lead to further loss of protein reserves, malnutrition, and clinical signs associated with protein or amino acid deficiency. In contrast, when chronic renal disease has been definitively diagnosed in a dog or cat through the appearance of clinical signs, diminished GFR, and changes in blood chemistry data, restriction of dietary protein may be beneficial and is recommended for the control of clinical signs. Protein restriction in the dietary management of existing renal disease is discussed in detail in the following section.

Another dietary factor that may be involved in the progression of renal disease in companion animals is the level of phosphorus in the diet. As chronic renal failure progresses, GFR declines and leads to a decreased ability to excrete phosphorus. In addition, declining kidney function leads to an inability to produce calcitriol (active vitamin D) and an inability to degrade parathyroid hormone (PTH). Together, these changes result in aberrations in phosphorus and calcium metabolism, and can ultimately result in hyperphosphatemia, bone demineralization (osteodystrophy), and the deposition of

calcium phosphate crystals in soft tissues. The deposition of calcium and phosphorus in renal tissue causes inflammation, scarring, and subsequent loss of nephrons.[252] It has been hypothesized that the restriction of dietary phosphorus will help to control renal secondary hyperparathyroidism, resulting in decreased mineralization and less damage to functioning nephrons.

Studies with rats have shown that phosphorus restriction is effective in minimizing or preventing proteinuria and in slowing the structural and functional changes that occur in the remaining healthy nephrons.[253] Similar studies with dogs have found that the dietary restriction of phosphorus can slow progression of clinical disease and prolong survival in azotemic dogs with induced chronic renal failure.[254] In addition, when diets containing 32% protein and varying levels of phosphorus were fed to dogs with induced renal failure, the dogs that were fed the low-phosphorus diets showed significantly higher GFR values compared with those that were fed the higher-phosphorus diets.[241] These data suggest a beneficial effect that is independent of the level of protein in the diet. However, the same study showed that over time, renal lesions developed that were not influenced by the level of phosphorus in the diet, indicating that other factors are involved in the progression of disease. There is also evidence that normal phosphorus intake in cats with induced renal disease causes increased mineralization of renal tissue and that dietary restriction can prevent these changes.[255] Current evidence suggests that dietary phosphorus may affect the progression of renal disease in dogs and cats, but progression of disease can still occur even with restricted dietary phosphorus.

DIETARY MANAGEMENT OF CHRONIC KIDNEY DISEASE

When chronic renal disease has been diagnosed in a dog or cat, dietary management can be implemented with the goals of minimizing the clinical, biochemical, and physiological consequences of the loss in kidney function. Alterations in the kidneys' ability to excrete waste products and to regulate metabolism of certain nutrients and hormones are the cause of the clinical signs that the animal experiences. Although dietary therapy does not "cure" chronic renal disease, it can minimize the clinical signs and contribute to the pet's health, well-being, and longevity. A major goal of dietary management is to minimize the accumulation of protein catabolites in the blood while still providing adequate protein for the pet's maintenance needs. In addition, adequate calories from nonprotein sources must be provided to prevent the use of either body tissues or dietary protein for energy. Other nutrients of concern include dietary phosphorus, sodium, potassium, and water-soluble vitamins (see the box on the following page).

Protein

The accumulation of the nitrogenous end products of protein and amino acid metabolism cause many of the clinical and metabolic signs of chronic renal failure. Urea is the most abundant of these metabolites and can be readily measured in the blood. Although urea is only a mild uremic toxin, its concentration parallels the levels of other, more

Goals of Dietary Management of Chronic Renal Disease

Provide adequate nonprotein calories.
Maintain nitrogen balance.
Minimize azotemia.
Normalize blood pH.
Normalize electrolyte balance.

potent nitrogenous toxins and can be used as an index to monitor the extent of disease and clinical signs. Together these components produce nausea, vomiting, osmotic diuresis, and a decreased life span of red blood cells.[225] Normalizing the levels of urea and other nitrogenous waste products in the blood through restriction of dietary protein contributes to a return of appetite, weight gain, and a lessening of other clinical signs.[226,251]

The generation of urea is directly proportional to the daily turnover of dietary and body protein. Protein that is ingested in excess of the animal's requirement will be metabolized for energy, producing urea and other end products that must then be excreted by the kidneys. Similarly, when inadequate calories are ingested or when an animal is in a catabolic state, body protein will be used for energy, also resulting in the synthesis of urea. A reduction in the excretory capacity of the kidneys results in an elevation of urea and other components in the blood as they are retained by the body. A primary goal of dietary therapy is to provide enough dietary protein to meet, but not exceed, the pet's daily requirement and to provide adequate nonprotein calories to prevent the breakdown of body tissue for energy. These changes will minimize the amount of urea and other nitrogenous end products that are produced. In most cases, this necessitates a restriction of dietary protein and a change in the type of protein that is included in the diet.

The decision to control protein intake is determined by the patient's clinical signs as well as the degree of impairment of renal function. Protein restriction is suggested only when the pet's BUN is greater than 80 mg/dl and when serum creatinine is greater than 2.5 mg per 100 milliliters (ml).[225,226] Although the normal range for fasting BUN is between 10 and 24 mg/dl, most dogs do not show clinical signs of renal disease until BUN exceeds 60 to 80 mg/dl.[226] Pets that have only slightly elevated BUN values (30 to 60 mg/dl) and are not showing clinical signs do not benefit from protein restriction.[256] GFR can be estimated by a measurement of creatinine clearance. If this test is conducted, a creatinine clearance of less than 15 ml/min/m^2 indicates a need to modify dietary protein. Elevated serum phosphorus is also a sign that protein should be limited in the diet.[225]

The goal of dietary protein restriction is to maintain the animal's BUN below a level of 60 mg/dl. In dogs and cats, as in other animals, a direct relationship exists between the BUN/serum creatinine and dietary protein ratio. The minimum protein requirement for dogs has been determined to be between 1.25 and 1.50 grams per kilogram (g/kg) of body weight per day of protein with high biological value.[257] Recommendations for

the level of protein to feed to uremic dogs have varied from 0.66 g/kg to 2.2 g/kg per day.[221,258,259] However, a study of dogs with induced renal disease found that feeding a diet containing 1.6 g/kg of protein or less caused signs of protein deficiency. Increasing the protein level to 2 g/kg still aided in the control of BUN levels and the clinical signs of renal disease but did not cause protein malnutrition.[259,260] The potential to induce protein deficiency necessitates conservative restriction of dietary protein in dogs with renal disease. Protein nutrition is particularly of concern because dogs with proteinuria may require more dietary protein than dogs without proteinuria. A level of dietary protein should be fed that will ameliorate clinical signs and control BUN levels but not compromise protein and amino acid nutrition.

In dogs with mild to moderate renal disease, a diet containing between 12% and 28% protein on a dry-matter basis is recommended, with the exact level dependent on the animal's clinical and biochemical response.[223,226] In cases of severe renal disease, when GFR has deteriorated to only 10% to 20% of normal, protein must be progressively restricted to approach a level that is close to the pet's minimum daily requirement. Depending on the degree of clinical signs and the energy level of the diet, a pet food containing between 5% and 15% protein should be fed in these cases, provided that the protein is of high biological value.[226] At this level of dysfunction, a balancing act occurs between providing a diet that will ameliorate clinical signs yet will provide adequate amounts of nutrients.

Protein restriction for cats with chronic renal failure must account for the cat's naturally higher protein requirement and for the cat's inability to adapt to low-protein diets (see Section 2, pp. 107–109). It is generally recommended that cats with uremia be fed the maximum level of protein that will control uremia and the associated clinical signs.[251] One method of accomplishing this is to determine the cat's current protein intake as a percentage of calories and to slowly decrease dietary protein until clinical signs are managed. For example, if a cat is currently eating a diet that contains 38% of protein calories, the proportion of protein in the diet should be reduced to 30% of metabolizable energy. Serum biochemistries and clinical signs are measured after 1 to 3 weeks, and, if necessary, the diet is adjusted further. This method allows precise control over the protein content of the cat's diet without the risk of unnecessarily restricting protein.

In all cases it is important to adjust the protein level of the diet to meet the needs of the individual animal. If protein restriction is adequate, a 50% or greater reduction in BUN should occur.[225] Improvement in clinical signs is generally seen within 3 to 4 weeks. Most dogs and cats will show a reduction in vomiting, improved appetite, weight gain, and improved physical activity. Consistent monitoring of BUN level and of clinical response to the diet should be used to indicate the need to either increase or decrease protein level. If progressive deterioration of renal function occurs, adjustments in the diet to maintain an acceptable BUN may be necessary. Chemistry profiles and complete blood counts should also be measured periodically to monitor the pet for anemia, acidemia, or electrolyte imbalances.

The type of protein that is included in the restricted protein diet is very important. Only protein sources that are highly digestible and that are of high biological value should be used. These sources include eggs, dairy products, and some lean muscle

meats. Poor-quality proteins and ingredients that are not highly digestible should be avoided. The therapeutic diet can be either a commercially prepared product or a home-made diet. Advantages of using a commercially prepared diet include convenience and the assurance of consistency in the formulation. However, preparing a homemade diet allows greater flexibility in the level of protein and other nutrients that are included, thus providing a diet that is specifically formulated to meet a pet's individual needs. Homemade diets may also be more palatable for some pets than commercially pre-pared products. Because of their tendency to develop anorexia, cats with renal disease should be fed diets that are highly palatable and acceptable. Decisions regarding the type of diet to use can be made based on the pet's response to treatment and the capa-bilities and preferences of the owner.

Energy

The diet that is fed to dogs and cats with renal disease should supply adequate calories from nonprotein sources. In general, the body's demand for energy is a higher priority than is its demand for protein. Therefore, if adequate carbohydrate or fat are not avail-able to supply energy, dietary protein or body protein will be metabolized. In pets with renal failure, this can further contribute to azotemia. To avoid this, the major proportion of energy in diets for these pets should be supplied as nonprotein calories. The inclusion of adequate levels of carbohydrate and fat will minimize the catabolism of protein for energy. Dietary fat has the added advantages of increasing the energy density of the diet and contributing to the diet's palatability and acceptability. Most pets who are uremic demonstrate a decrease in appetite or anorexia. Achieving adequate caloric intake in these animals is often a chief goal of dietary therapy. The fat in the prescribed diet makes the diet more palatable and may stimulate increased consumption in sick pets.

Phosphorus

The decrease in GFR that occurs during renal failure results in a decreased ability to excrete phosphorus from the body. This decreased ability leads to phosphorus reten-tion, hyperphosphatemia, and renal secondary hyperparathyroidism. These factors are believed to promote the formation of calcium phosphate crystals and the deposition of these crystals in the kidney and other soft tissues, which may lead to further loss of nephrons and progression of disease.[222,227] Additionally, the chronic elevation of parathyroid hormone (PTH) that is caused by retention of phosphorus results in exces-sive demineralization of bone and pathological changes that are associated with bone loss.

A goal of dietary therapy is to normalize serum phosphorus concentrations and pre-vent bone demineralization and deposition of calcium phosphate crystals in soft tissues. In moderate cases of renal disease, when serum phosphorus is slightly elevated, a decrease in the level of phosphorus in the diet may be sufficient to achieve normaliza-tion of serum phosphorus in some cases. Because dietary protein is a principal source of phosphorus, restriction of protein contributes to this dietary modification. However,

as disease progresses, dietary restriction is not adequate to control blood phosphorus levels and may not be sufficient to control the long-term effects of hyperparathyroidism and bone disease. Intestinal phosphate-binding agents must then be used in conjunction with reduced dietary phosphorus to normalize serum phosphorus concentration.[259] These agents are administered with the meal and limit the gastrointestinal absorption of phosphorus. The compounds that are most commonly used are aluminum hydroxide and aluminum carbonate.[226]

Blood phosphorus concentration should be monitored regularly and the diet and binding agents should be adjusted until normalization of serum phosphorus is achieved. Calcium supplementation and/or vitamin D supplementation should be avoided until serum phosphorus levels are under control. Providing additional calcium in the presence of hyperphosphatemia will contribute further to soft tissue mineralization. Once serum phosphorus concentration has been normalized, calcium and/or vitamin D can be supplemented to aid in the control of the renal hyperparathyroidism and bone disease. Calcium carbonate at a dosage of 100 mg/kg of body weight is recommended.[225]

Although some studies with dogs have shown that restriction of dietary phosphorus prevented or reversed renal secondary hyperparathyroidism, recent research indicates that dietary restriction alone does not cause a reduction in serum PTH levels in all dogs, even though it may normalize serum phosphorus levels.[256,261] Serum phosphorus levels do not appear to be a sensitive predictor of renal secondary hyperparathyroidism.[256] In other words, normalization of serum phosphorus may not always be effective in ameliorating the occurrence of renal secondary hyperparathyroidism and the resultant bone demineralization. These data are compatible with theories that factors other than intake and excretion of calcium and phosphorus are involved in the complications of renal disease. It has been hypothesized that chronically elevated PTH may be more affected by decreased levels of calcitriol than by elevated phosphorus. As kidney function declines, the ability to produce calcitriol is compromised. Subsequently, low calcitriol levels stimulate the release of PTH. It therefore appears that restriction of dietary phosphorus alone may not be sufficient to prevent hyperparathyroidism in some dogs with chronic renal failure. The use of phosphate-binding agents, calcium supplementation, and administration of calcitriol may be necessary to treat the hyperparathyroidism of renal disease in these animals.

Other Nutrients

Additional nutrients that are of concern in the diets of dogs and cats with renal disease include sodium, potassium, the water-soluble vitamins, and possibly bicarbonate. The major route of sodium excretion in dogs is through the urine.[262] In humans and other species, sodium retention and systemic hypertension is a common sequela of chronic renal disease. However, hypertension is not a common occurrence in dogs and cats.[263] In addition, dogs and cats with renal disease demonstrate limited renal responsiveness and decreased tolerance to sudden changes of sodium content in the diet.[225] Therefore dietary sodium should only be restricted in pets with renal disease that demonstrate systemic hypertension. In these cases, the level should be adjusted to meet the needs of

Practical Feeding Tips:
Summary of Dietary Management of Chronic Kidney Disease

Provide the highest dietary protein that will maintain a BUN of less than 60.
Provide a highly digestible protein source that is of high biological value.
Provide an adequate amount of nonprotein calories.
Restrict dietary phosphorus and regularly monitor serum phosphorus level.
Provide intestinal phosphate binding agents, if necessary.
Provide supplemental calcium and vitamin D, once serum phosphorus is normalized.
Monitor intake of sodium, sodium bicarbonate, potassium, and water-soluble vitamins closely. Adjust diet
  as necessary.

the individual animal, with the goal of controlling hypertension while still providing adequate sodium. Diets for pets with renal disease should also contain adequate levels of potassium to prevent the hypokalemia that occurs in some cases.[259] When polyuria is present, supplementation with water-soluble vitamins is advisable because of excessive losses of these vitamins in the urine.

Reduced renal mass is associated with an increase in the production of ammonia by the renal tubules. This results in a rise in renal tissue ammonia concentration that can cause local toxic and inflammatory effects and further contribute to renal damage.[259] In severe cases, systemic metabolic acidosis may occur as a result of compromised capacity to regulate acid-base balance. Supplementation with sodium bicarbonate or potassium citrate may ameliorate some of the damage as a result of increased ammonia production in the kidney and will aid in the treatment of metabolic acidosis. A dosage of five to ten grains of sodium bicarbonate, given orally every 10 to 12 hours is recommended[259] (see the box above).

CHAPTER 35

Feline Hepatic Lipidosis

F eline hepatic lipidosis is an acquired disorder caused by the excessive accumulation of triglycerides in the cells of the liver, ultimately interfering with the liver's ability to function.[264] The disorder is often referred to as idiopathic hepatic lipidosis (IHL) because the underlying cause is unknown in approximately 50% of cases.[265] In healthy animals, a dynamic relationship exists between the fatty acids that are located in adipose tissue, traveling in the blood, and stored in the liver. Circulating fatty acids are taken up by the liver, where they are either metabolized for energy or converted to triglycerides and secreted back into the circulation. If the supply of fatty acids to the liver exceeds the liver's capacity to oxidize or secrete them, lipidosis occurs.[266] Hepatic lipidosis may also occur as a result of impaired oxidation of fatty acids in hepatocytes or an inability of the liver to secrete the lipoproteins that carry triglycerides in the bloodstream. A recent study provided evidence that the origin of the excess hepatic triglycerides in cats with IHL is mobilized adipose tissue fatty acids.[267] Although it is possible that any one of these mechanisms is involved, the exact, underlying cause of hepatic lipidosis in cats is currently unknown.

IHL is fairly common and is usually is seen in middle-aged, obese cats. A recent study reported that females are twice as likely to be affected as males.[265] In the majority of cases, the cat has experienced a period of stress followed by partial or complete anorexia. It is believed that prolonged anorexia leads to the metabolic changes that cause severe hepatic fat accumulation and the clinical signs associated with liver disease. A recent study reported that when five obese cats were fasted for a period of 4 to 6 weeks, three of the cats remained healthy and two developed overt clinical and laboratory signs of IHL.[268]

Clinical signs of IHL include complete or partial anorexia with a duration of 7 days or longer, depression, jaundice, weight loss, and muscle wasting.[265,269,270] Vomiting and/or diarrhea are occasionally reported. Owners usually report that the cat suddenly stopped eating following a period of life-style change or stress. Laboratory findings show increased activities of liver enzymes, increased serum bilirubin and bile acid concentrations, and, in some cases, increased plasma blood urea nitrogen (BUN) and ammonia concentration.[269,271] A nonregenerative anemia characterized by irregularly shaped erythrocytes is typically seen.[265,271] Definitive diagnosis of IHL can be made using medical history, clinical signs, and results of a liver biopsy showing excessive lipid accumulation in the sampled hepatocytes. The prognosis for cats with IHL is often guarded because of the resistance of this disease to treatment. Hepatic lipidosis in cats is generally associated with a high mortality that can approach 100% in cases that are detected at a late stage.[269]

It has been hypothesized that deficiencies of arginine or carnitine, secondary to anorexia, are involved in the onset of IHL. The cat requires a dietary source of the amino acid arginine for the production of urea in the liver. When the cat stops eating, prolonged anorexia leads to a deficiency of arginine. Urea cycle activity is depressed and ammonia begins to accumulate in the blood. By-products of the disruption in the urea cycle also interfere with lipoprotein synthesis in the liver.[272] Decreased lipoprotein synthesis can lead to an accumulation of triglycerides. It has been theorized that obese cats may already have a fatty liver to start with, and this is further exacerbated by these changes. Supportive research has shown that the administration of small amounts of protein to obese cats during fasting helps to prevent the accumulation of hepatic lipds.[273]

Carnitine is a compound that is synthesized primarily in the liver and is necessary for the transport of long-chain fatty acids into cellular mitochondria for oxidation. Human subjects with carnitine deficiency show severe fat accumulation in the liver and other organs and develop signs of liver disease.[274] It has been hypothesized that a deficiency of carnitine may be the cause of IHL in cats. However, one study found that carnitine concentrations in the plasma, livers, and skeletal muscles of 11 cats with hepatic lipidosis were normal.[275,276] Only a small number of cats were included in the study, but these results do not support the theory that a deficiency of carnitine is an underlying cause of feline IHL.

Regardless of the metabolic cause of IHL, it is essential for the cat's recovery that an early diagnosis is made and that supportive fluid and nutritional therapy is started as soon as possible. In the majority of cases, force-feeding or tube feeding is necessary because afflicted cats will not eat voluntarily. Force-feeding is often not recommended because it can further stress the cat and does not provide an accurate measure of the pet's caloric intake. For these reasons, tube feeding with a nasogastric tube or gastrostomy is preferred by most veterinarians.[268,270] The use of a gastrostomy tube involves direct surgical entry into the cat's stomach. Although this procedure allows accurate and consistent delivery of nutrients and does not interfere with the cat's ability to swallow, complications associated with surgery may cause further medical problems in some cases.[276] However, most cats tolerate gastrostomy tubes better than pharyngostomy tubes.[271] A high-quality, balanced cat food should be used. A quantity of food that meets

the cat's daily requirements for energy should be administered. Four to six small meals per day should be provided. These meals will optimize digestion and absorption and allow the gastrointestinal tract to readjust to the delivery of food.[265] A gruel can be made by adding enough water to the food to reach a consistency that can be delivered through the tube.

The cat's owner must be willing to assist with the nursing care of the pet because cats with hepatic lipidosis may not eat well for several months. As the cat's appetite returns, the frequency of tube feedings should be slowly decreased until the cat is consuming adequate calories voluntarily. When vomiting can be controlled and long-term adequate protein and calorie intake is assured, treatment is usually successful. However, because many cats will refuse to eat voluntarily for a period of weeks to several months, management can be difficult for the pet owner and prognosis will be guarded until the cat begins to eat voluntarily. Supportive treatment involves minimizing any stress that the animal may experience and, in some cases, administering appetite stimulants.[264,277] Although some investigators advocate supplying supplemental carnitine during tube feeding, recent evidence indicates that this is probably unnecessary.[264,275] Throughout the treatment period, frequent monitoring of serum liver parameters can be used as an indicator of hepatic recovery.[268]

Because IHL is highly correlated with obesity, it is prudent to prevent weight regain following recovery. If the cat is still overweight, a program that allows a slow rate of weight loss is advised. Stress should be minimized to prevent the onset of subsequent episodes of anorexia. Because there is some evidence that prolonged fasting can lead to IHL in some cats, weight loss programs should be instituted with caution. Programs that severely restrict caloric intake should not be used (see Section 5, pp. 289–290).

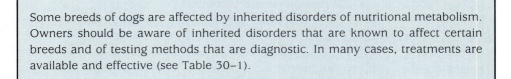

KEY POINTS

S E C T I O N   6

Some breeds of dogs are affected by inherited disorders of nutritional metabolism. Owners should be aware of inherited disorders that are known to affect certain breeds and of testing methods that are diagnostic. In many cases, treatments are available and effective (see Table 30–1).

Although inherited metabolic disorders are less well documented in cats than in dogs, feline lipoprotein lipase deficiency is well recognized. Feeding a low-fat diet often results in normalizing blood lipid levels and a regression of symptoms.

CAUTION: Treatment of primary hyperlipidemia in both the dog and cat entails feeding a diet restricted in fat and calories. Start with a diet containing between 8% and 12% fat on a dry-matter basis. Such a diet must be followed strictly for the remainder of the pet's lifetime. All snacks and table scraps must be eliminated. Dogs with hyperlipidemia may be susceptible to acute pancreatitis that could be brought on by a single, high-fat meal.

Dalmatians are the only breed of dog that excretes both urate and allantoin in their urine as end products of purine metabolism. They have higher levels of urate in their blood and urine than other breeds of dogs, as well as reduced renal tubular reabsorption of urate. Higher serum urate values in humans lead to a condition commonly known as "gout." The dalmatian excretes excess urate in the urine, leading to the development of urate urolithiasis or urinary tract "stones." Although approximately half of the dogs seen with urinary calculi are of the dalmatian breed, the overall incidence in the dalmatian breed has been estimated to be as low as 1%.

Diabetes is relatively uncommon in dogs and cats, but many cases of diabetes are related to obesity and are therefore controllable. Type I diabetes requires that the animal be given exogenous insulin replacement therapy. Type II diabetes, almost always associated with obesity, can usually be controlled through weight reduction and the administration of oral hypoglycemic agents. The careful control of Type II diabetes is critical in avoiding progression of the disease to Type I diabetes. High-quality pet food, consistency in feeding, and exercise are all important in controlling diabetes and bettering the health of your diabetic pet.

Tip: Pets with Type I diabetes should be fed several small meals instead of one large meal during the period of insulin activity. For example, if insulin is given early in the morning, the first meal should be provided immediately before the insulin injection. Once an appropriate feeding schedule and diet have been established, changes should not be made. Snacks should not be given, and feeding times should be consistent.

Owners should be aware of the common clinical signs of feline lower urinary tract disease (FLUTD). Complete obstruction is a medical emergency that can cause permanent kidney damage, bladder rupture, and death. FLUTD is likely to be a recurrent problem after the initial episode, and male cats are more prone to obstruction. Pay close attention to your cat's behavior and watch for signs of FLUTD.

Evidence indicates that a cat food that is energy dense and highly digestible will result in lower total dry-matter intake. This decrease leads to decreased fecal volume and fecal water, and increased urine volume. The urine will have a lower concentration of minerals, such as magnesium, that are a component of struvite. Increased urine volume also increases frequency of urination, leading to less time for struvite formation in the urinary tract.

CAUTION: When feeding a cat a diet formulated for the dissolution of feline struvite, the urine should be tested 4 to 8 hours after initial consumption to assure that the desirable pH of approximately 6.0 has been achieved. Such a diet should be continued for at least 1 month after complete dissolution of the struvite, and then a maintenance diet should be instituted. During maintenance, the urine's pH should be 6.6 or less to prevent recurrent formation of the struvite crystals. Owners should not select a diet based only on its ash or magnesium content; consider also the food's caloric density, digestibility, and urine-acidifying properties.

Some cutaneous disorders that respond to vitamin A therapy are not actually caused by a vitamin A deficiency. In these cases vitamin A therapy is required throughout the pet's life, but therapeutic dosages have not been found to be toxic. It is believed that there is a genetic basis for the disease in some breeds, the cocker spaniel in particular.

Interestingly, a pet can develop food hypersensitivity to a food it has been consuming on a regular basis for years without problems. In most cases, food hypersensitivity manifests as dermatological problems, usually intense pruritus, although gastrointestinal problems can also occur. The immunological mechanisms that cause food hypersensitivity are not completely understood.

By the time an animal shows clinical signs of renal failure the kidneys are functioning at only 15% to 30% of their original capacity. Increased water consumption and increased urination may be the first signs an owner notices. A tentative diagnosis can be inferred by medical history and clinical signs and confirmed by blood testing and urinalysis. Determination of an animal's glomerular filtration rate is the most accurate diagnostic test.

CAUTION: Feline idiopathic hepatic lipidosis is fairly common among middle-aged, obese cats. There is a female-to-male predominance of 2:1. It most often occurs after a period of partial or complete anorexia, usually brought on by stress. The mortality rate is very high for cats diagnosed at a late stage of the disease. Early diagnosis is critical and owners should take note of signs of developing anorexia.

Tip: Pay close attention to your pet's eating habits. A change may signal an illness, and if an owner is not observant, nutritional deficiencies may develop and affect the pet's ability to cope with illness. Like humans, pets often do not want to eat when they are ill. However, proper nutrition during illness is essential for recovery. Pets' energy requirements increase in response to stress induced by illness and the metabolic rate increases if fever is present. If the pet's appetite has decreased, owners should feed a well-balanced diet that is nutrient dense in order to assure that the nutritional needs are met even if the pet can only eat a small amount of food.

S E C T I O N   6

References

1. Batt RM, Horadagoda NU, Simpson KW: Role of the pancreas in the absorption and malabsorption of cobalamin (vitamin B_{12}) in dogs, *J Nutr* 121:S75–S76, 1991.
2. Fyfe JC, Jexyk PF, Giger U, and others: Inherited selective malabsorption of vitamin B_{12} in giant schnauzers, *J Am Anim Hosp Assoc* 25:533–539, 1989.
3. Thornburg LP, Polley D, Dimmitt R: The diagnosis and treatment of copper toxicosis in dogs, *Can Pract* 11:36–39, 1984.
4. Johnson GF: Inheritance of copper toxicosis in Bedlington terriers, *Am J Vet Res* 41:1865–1866, 1980.
5. Keen CR, Lonnerdal B, Fisher GL: Age-related variations in hepatic iron, copper, zinc and selenium concentrations in beagles, *Am J Vet Res* 42:1884–1887, 1981.
6. Thornburg LP, McAllister D, Ebinger WL, and others: Copper toxicosis in dogs. Part 1: copper-associated liver disease in Bedlington terriers. Part 2: The pathogenesis of copper-associated liver disease in dogs, *Can Pract* 12:33–38, 41–45, 1985.
7. Twedt DC, Sternlieb I, Gilbertson SR: Clinical, morphologic and chemical studies on copper toxicosis of Bedlington terriers, *J Am Vet Asso* 175:269–275, 1979.
8. Brewer GJ, Dick RD, Schall W, and others: Use of zinc acetate to treat copper toxicosis in dogs, *J Am Vet Med Assoc* 201:564–568, 1992.
9. Herrtage ME, Seymout CA, Jefferies AR: Inherited copper toxicosis in the Bedlington terrier: a report of two clinical cases, *J Sm Anim Pract* 28:1127–1140, 1987.
10. Twedt DC, Whitney EL: Management of hepatic copper toxicosis in dogs. In Kirk RW, editor: *Current veterinary therapy X*, Philadelphia, 1989, WB Saunders, pp 891–893.
11. Jezyk PF, Haskins ME, McKay-Smith WE, and others: Lethal acrodermatitis in bull terriers, *J Am Vet Med Assoc* 188:833–839, 1986.
12. Miller WH Jr: Nutritional considerations in small animal dermatology, *Vet Clin North Am Sm Anim Pract* 19:497–511, 1989.
13. Codner EC, Thatcher CD: The role of nutrition in the management of dermatoses, *Semin Vet Med Surg Small Anim* 5:167–177, 1990.
14. Kunkle GA: Zinc responsive dermatoses in dogs. In Kirk RW, editor: *Current veterinary therapy VII: small animal practice,* Philadelphia, 1980, WB Saunders, pp 472–476.
15. Fadok VA: Zinc responsive dermatosis in a Great Dane: a case report, *J Am Anim Hosp Assoc* 18:409–414, 1982.
16. Brown RG, Hoag GN, Smart ME, and others: Alaskan malamute chondrodysplasia. V. Decreased gut zinc absorption, *Growth* 42:1–6, 1978.
17. Anderson RK: A crusted skin disease resembling dry juvenile pyoderma: a case report, *J Am Anim Hosp Assoc* 13:701–703, 1977.
18. Watson TDG, Barrie J: Lipoprotein metabolism and hyperlipoproteinemia in the dog and cat: a review, *J Sm Anim Pract* 34:479–487, 1993.
19. Hubert B, Braun JP, de La Farge F, and others: Hypertriglyceridemia in two related dogs, *Comp Anim Pract* 1:33–35, 1987.
20. Whitney MS: Evaluation of hyperlipidemias in dogs and cats, *Semin Vet Med Surg Small Anim* 7:292–300, 1992.
21. Armstrong PJ, Ford RB: Hyperlipidemia. In Kirk RW, editor: *Current veterinary therapy X: small animal practice*, Philadelphia, 1989, WB Saunders, pp 1046–1050.
22. Johnson RK: Canine hyperlipidemia. In Ettinger SJ, editor: *Textbook of veterinary internal medicine*, vol 1, 3, Philadelphia, 1989, WB Saunders, pp 198–202.

23. Ford RB: Idiopathic hyperchylomicronemia in miniature schnauzers, *J Sm Anim Pract* 34:488–492, 1993.
24. Crispin SM: Ocular manifestations of hyperlipoproteinemia, *J Sm Anim Pract* 34:500–506, 1993.
25. Liu SK, Tilley LP, Tappe JP, and others: Clinical and pathological findings in dogs with atherosclerosis: 21 cases (1970–1983), *J Am Vet Med Assoc* 189:227–232, 1986.
26. Bodkin, K: Seizures associated with hyperlipoproteinemia in a miniature schnauzer, *Can Pract* 17:11–15, 1992.
27. DeBowes LJ: Lipid metabolism and hyperlipoproteinemia in dogs, *Comp Cont Ed Pract Vet* 9:727–736, 1987.
28. Connelly PW, Maguire GF, and Little JA: Apolipoprotein C-II St. Michael. familial apolipoprotein C-II deficiency associated with premature vascular disease, *J Clin Invest* 80:1597–1606, 1987.
29. Jones BR, Johnstone AC, Cahill JI, and others: Peripheral neuropathy in cats with inherited primary hyperchylomicronaemia, *Vet Rec* 119:268–272, 1986.
30. Watson TDG, Gaffrey D, Mooney CT, and others: Inherited hyperchylomicronaemia in the cat: lipoprotein lipase function and gene structure, *J Sm Anim Pract* 33:207–212, 1992.
31. Bauer JE, Verlander JW: Congenital lipoprotein lipase deficiency in hyperlipemic kitten siblings, *Vet Clin Pathol* 13:7–11, 1984.
32. Johnstone AC, Jones BR, Thompson JC, and others: The pathology of an inherited hyperlipoproteinaemia of cats, *J Comp Pathol* 102:125–137, 1990.
33. Peritz LN, Brunzell JD, Harvey-Clarke C, and others: Characterization of a lipoprotein lipase class III type defect in hypertriglyceridemic cats, *Clin Invest Med* 13:259–263, 1990.
34. Smerdon T: Hyperchylomicronaemia in a litter of Siamese kittens, *Bull Fel Advis Bur* Autumn, pp 51–53, 1990.
35. Jones BR: Inherited hyperchylomicronaemia in the cat, *J Sm Anim Pract* 34:493–499, 1993.
36. Barrie J, Nash AS, and Watson TDG: A method for the quantification of the canine plasma lipoproteins, *J Sm Anim Pract* 34:226–231, 1993.
37. Brunzell JD, Iverius PH, Scheibel MS, and others: *Primary lipoprotein lipase deficiency in lipoprotein deficiency syndromes*. In Angel A, Frolich J, editors: New York, 1986, Plenum Publishing, pp 227–239.
38. Grieshaber TL, McKeever PJ, Conroy, JD: Spontaneous cutaneous (eruptive) xanthomatosis in two cats, *J Am Anim Hosp Assoc* 27:509–512, 1991.
39. Harris WS: Omega-3 fatty acids: effects on lipid metabolism, *Curr Opin Lipidol* 1:5–11, 1990.
40. Logas D, Beale KM, Bauer JE: Potential clinical benefits of dietary supplementation with marine-life oil, *J Am Vet Med Assoc* 199:1631–1636, 1991.
41. Kuster G, Shorter RG, Dawson B: Uric acid metabolism in dalmatians and other dogs, *Arch Int Med* 129:492–496, 1972.
42. Duncan H, Curtiss AS: Observations on uric acid transport in man, the dalmatian and the non-dalmatian dog, *Henry Ford Hosp Med J* 19:105–114, 1971.
43. Sorenson JL, Ling GV: Metabolic and genetic aspects of urate urolithiasis in dalmatians, *J Am Vet Med Assoc* 203:857–862, 1993.
44. Briggs OM, Harley EH: Serum urate concentrations in the dalmatian coach hound, *J Comp Pathol* 95:301–304, 1985.
45. Duncan H, Wakim KG, Ward LE: The effects of intravenous administration of uric acid on its concentration in plasma and urine of dalmatian and non-dalmatian dogs, *J Lab Clin Med* 58:876–883, 1961.
46. Case LC, Lind GV, Ruby AL, and others: Urolithiasis in dalmatians: 275 cases (1981–1990), *J Am Vet Med Assoc* 203:96–100, 1993.
47. Giesecke D, Tiemeyer W: Defect of uric acid uptake in dalmatian dog liver, *Experentia* 40:1415–1416, 1984.

48. Trimble HC, Keeler CE: The inheritance of "high uric acid excretion" in dogs, *J Hered* 29:280–289, 1938.
49. Yu TF, Gutman AB, Berger L: Low uricase activity in the dalmatian dog simulated in mongrels given oxonic acid, *Am J Physiol* 220:973–979, 1971.
50. White EG: Symposium on urolithiasis in the dog. I. Introduction and incidence, *J Sm Anim Pract* 7:529–535, 1966.
51. Brown NO, Parks JL, Greene RW: Canine urolithiasis: respective analysis of 438 cases, *J Am Vet Med Assoc* 170:414–418, 1977.
52. Osborne CA, Clinton CW, Banman LK: Prevalence of canine uroliths, Minnesota Urolith center, Vet Clin *North Am Sm Anim Pract* 16:27–44, 1986.
53. White EG, Treacher RJ, Porter P: Urinary calculi in the god. I. Incidence and chemical composition, *J Comp Pathol* 71:201–216, 1961.
54. Porter P: Urinary calculi in the dog. I. Urate stones and purine metabolism, *J Comp Pathol* 73:119–135, 1963.
55. Fetner PJ, Uric acid dermatitis, *Dalmatian Quart* Spring, pp 11–13, 1991.
56. Lind GV, Ruby AL, Harrold DR: Xanthine-containing urinary calculi in dogs given allopurinol, *J Am Vet Med Assoc* 198:1935–1940, 1991.
57. Cornelius LM: Update on management of diabetes mellitus in dogs and cats, *Mod Vet Pract* 66:251–255, 1985.
58. Williams L: Canine diabetes mellitus, *Vet Tech* 9:168–170, 1988.
59. Stogdale L: Definition of diabetes mellitus, *Cornell Vet* 76:156–174, 1985.
60. Kirk CA, Feldman EC, Nelson RW: Diagnosis of naturally acquired type-I and type-II diabetes mellitus in cats, *Am J Vet Res* 54:463–467, 1993.
61. Intravartolo C: Diabetes in cats, *Vet Tech* 9:197–198, 1988.
62. Kirk CA, Feldman EC, Nelson RW: Spontaneous type I, type II and type III diabetes mellitus in the cat, *Proc Am Coll Vet Int Med* pp 1034, 1989.
63. Robertson KA, Feldman EC, Polonsky K: Spontaneous diabetes mellitus in 24 dogs: incidence of type I versus type II disease, *Proc Am Coll Vet Int Med* pp 1036, 1989.
64. Wolf AM: Management of geriatric diabetic cats, *Comp Cont Ed Pract Vet* 11:1088–1093, 1989.
65. Ford S, Nelson RW, Feldman EC: Intensive evaluation of glipizide therapy in the management of feline diabetes mellitus (DM), *Proc Am Coll Vet Int Med* pp 234–236, 1991.
66. Nelson RW, Feldman EC, Ford SL, and others: Effect of an orally administered sulfonylurea, glipizide, for treatment of diabetes mellitus in cats, *J Am Vet Med Assoc* 203:821–827, 1993.
67. Miller AB, Nelson RW, Kirk CA, and others: Effect of glipizide on serum insulin and glucose concentrations in healthy cats, *Res Vet Sci* 52:177–181, 1992.
68. Holste LC, Nelson RW, Feldman EC, and others: Effect of dry, soft moist, and canned dog foods on postprandial blood glucose and insulin concentrations in healthy dogs, *Am J Vet Res* 50:984–989, 1989.
69. Vinik A: Report of the American Diabetes Association's task force on nutrition, *Diabetes Care*, 11:127–128, 1988.
70. Anderson JW: Physiological and metabolic effects of dietary fiber, *Fed Proc* 44:2902–2906, 1985.
71. Crapo PA: Carbohydrate in the diabetic diet, *J Am Coll Nutr* 5:31–43, 1986.
72. Riccardi G, Rivellese A, Pacioni D, and others: Separate influence of dietary carbohydrate and fiber on the metabolic control of diabetes, *Diabetologia* 26:116–121, 1984.
73. Jenkins JA: Dietary fiber and carbohydrate metabolism. In Spiller GA, Kay RM, editors: *Medical aspects of dietary fiber*, New York, 1980, Plenum Press, pp 175–192.
74. Anderson JW: Dietary fiber and diabetes. In Vahouny GV, Kritchevsky D, editors: *Dietary fiber in health and disease*, New York, 1982, Plenum Press, pp 151–167.
75. O'Connor N, Tredger J, Morgan L: Viscosity differences between various guar gums, *Diabetologia* 20:612–615, 1981.

76. Holt S, Heading RC, Carter DC, and others: Effect of gel fiber on gastric emptying and absorption of glucose and paracetamol, *Lancet* 1:636–639, 1979.

77. Kay RM, Truswell AS: Effect of citrus pectin on blood lipids and fecal steroid excretion in man, *Am J Clin Nutr* 30:171–175, 1977.

78. Nelson RW, Ihle SL, Lewis LD, and others: Effects of dietary fiber supplementation on glycemic control in dogs with alloxan-induced diabetes mellitus, *Am J Vet Res* 52:2060–2066, 1991.

79. Blaxter AC, Cripps RJ, Gruffyd-Jones TJ: Dietary fibre and postprandial hyperglycemia in normal and diabetic dogs, *J Sm Anim Pract* 31:229–233, 1990.

80. Nelson RW: Dietary management of diabetes mellitus, *J Sm Anim Pract* 33:213–217, 1992.

81. Nelson RW: Nutritional management of diabetes mellitus, *Semin Vet Med Surg Sm Anim* 5:178–186, 1990.

82. Struthers BJ: Warning: feeding animals hydrophilic fiber sources in dry diets, *J Nutr* 116:47–49, 1986.

83. Toth B: Effect of metamucil on tumour formation by 1,2-dimethylhydrazine dihydrochloride in mice, *Food Chem Toxicol* 22:573–578, 1984.

84. Burrows CF, Kronfeld DL, Banta CA, and others: Effects of fiber on digestibility and transit time in dogs, *J Nutr* 112:1726–1732, 1982.

85. Reinhart GA, Moxley RA, Clemens ET: Dietary fibre source and its effects on colonic microstructure and histopathology of beagle dogs, Waltham Symposium on the Nutrition of Companion Animals. In Association with the 15th International Congress on Nutrition, Adelaide, Australia, Sept 23–25, 1993 (abstract).

86. Sunvold GD, Fahey GC Jr, Merchen NR, and others: Fermentability of selected fibrous substrates by dog faecal microflora as influenced by diet, Waltham Symposium on the Nutrition of Companion Animals. In Association with the 15th International Congress on Nutrition, Adelaide, Australia, Sept 23–25, 1993 (abstract).

87. Mattheeuws D, Rottiers R, Baeyens D, and others: Glucose tolerance and insulin response in obese dogs, *J Am Anim Hosp Assoc* 20:287–290, 1984.

88. Mattheeuws D, Rottiers R, Kaneko JJ, and others: Diabetes mellitus in dogs: relationship of obesity to glucose tolerance and insulin response, *Am J Vet Res* 45:98–103, 1984.

89. Nelson RW, Himsel CA, Feldman EC, and others: Glucose tolerance and insulin response in normal-weight and obese cats, *Am J Vet Res* 51:1357–1362, 1990.

90. Bar RS, Gordon P, Roth J, and others: Fluctuations in the affinity and concentration of insulin receptors on circulating monocytes of obese patients: effects of starvation, refeeding and dieting, *J Clin Invest* 58:1123–1135, 1976.

91. Lockwood DH, Hamilton CL, Livingston JN: The influence of obesity and diabetes in the monkey on insulin and glucagon binding to liver membranes, *Endocrinology* 104:76–81, 1979.

92. Olefsky JM, Ciaraldi TP, Kolterman OG: Mechanisms of insulin resistance in noninsulin-dependent (type II) diabetes, *Am J Med* 79:12–21, 1985.

93. Ferguson D, Hoenig M, Cornelius L: Diabetes mellitus in dogs and cats. In Lorenz MD, Cornelius LM, Ferguson DC, editors: *Small animal medical therapeutics*, Philadelphia, 1992, JP Lippincott, pp 85–96.

94. Norswothy G: The difficulties in regulating diabetic cats, *Vet Med* April, pp 342–348, 1993.

95. Osborne CA, Johnston GR, Polzin DJ, and others: Feline urologic syndrome: a heterogenous phenomenon?, *J Am Anim Hosp Assoc* 20:17–32, 1984.

96. Kruger JR, Osborne CA: The role of uropathogens in feline lower urinary tract disease, *Vet Clin North Am Sm Anim Pract* 23:101–123, 1993.

97. Osborne CA, Kruger JM, Johnston GR, and others: Feline lower urinary tract disorders. In Ettinger SJ, editor: *Textbook of veterinary internal medicine,* ed 2, vol 2, Philadelphia, 1989, WB Saunders, pp 2057–2082.

98. Markwell PJ: Feline lower urinary tract disease: a broader view, *Vet Tech* 14:585–589, 1993.

99. Kruger JM, Osborne CA, Goyal SM: Clinical evaluation of cats with lower urinary tract disease, *J Am Vet Med Assoc* 199:211–216, 1991.

100. Osborne CA: Feline lower urinary tract disease: state of the science, *Proceedings of the Kal Kan Symposium for the Treatment of Dog and Cat Diseases*, Kal Kan foods, Vernon, California, 1992, pp 89.

101. Lawler DF, Sjolin DW, Collins JE: Incidence rates of feline lower urinary tract disease in the United States, *Fel Pract* 15:13–16, 1985.

102. Fennel C: Some demographic characteristics of the domestic cat population in Great Britain with particular reference to feeding habits and the incidence of the feline urological syndrome, *J Sm Anim Pract* 16:775–783, 1975.

103. Carey D: Unpublished report, The Iams Company, Lewisburg, Ohio, 1994.

104. Willeberg P: Epidemiology of naturally occurring feline urologic syndrome, *Vet Clin North Am Sm Animal Pract* 14:455–470, 1984.

105. Bovee KC, Reif JS, Maguire TG, and others: Recurrence of feline urethral obstruction, *J Am Vet Med Assoc* 174:93–96, 1979.

106. Osborne CA: Feline uro-illogical syndrome, *Proc Am Anim Hosp Assoc* pp 85–87, 1982.

107. Gaskell CJ: Feline urological syndrome (FUS)—theory and practice, *J Sm Anim Pract* 31:519–522, 1990.

108. Jackson OF: The treatment and subsequent prevention of struvite uroliths in cats, *J Sm Anim Pract* 12:555–568, 1971.

109. Bohonowych RO, Parks JL, Greene RW: Features of cystic calculi in cats in a hospital population, *J Am Vet Med Assoc* 173:301–303, 1978.

110. Buffington CA: Acid questions: potential dangers associated with cat food acidification, *Pet Food Industry*, Sept/Oct, pp 4–8, 1993.

111. Osborne CA, Kruger JP, Lulich JP, and others: Feline matrix crystallin urethral plugs: a unifying hypothesis of causes, *J Sm Anim Pract* 33:172–177, 1992.

112. Buffington CA, Rogers QR, Morris JF: Effect of diet on struvite activity product in feline urine, *Am J Vet Res* 51:2025–2030, 1990.

113. Rich LJ, Kirk RW: The relationship of struvite crystals to urethral obstruction in cats, *J Am Vet Med Assoc* 154:153–157, 1969.

114. Gaskell CJ: Nutrition in diseases of the urinary tract in the dog and cat. In *Veterinary annual*, 25:383–390, 1985.

115. Barsanti JA, Finco DR, Shotts EB: Feline urologic syndrome: further investigation into etiology, *J Am Anim Hosp Assoc* 18:391–395, 1982.

116. Fabricant CG: Herpes-induced urolithiasis in specific-pathogen-free male cats, *Am J Vet Res* 38:1837–1842, 1977.

117. Martens JG, McConnell S, Swanson CL: The role of infectious agents in naturally occurring feline urologic syndrome, *Vet Clin North Am Sm Anim Pract* 14:503–511, 1984.

118. Kruger JM, Osborne CA: The role of viruses in feline lower urinary tract disease, *J Vet Int Med* 4:71–78, 1990.

119. Osborne CA, Polzin DJ, Kruger JM, and others: Relationship of nutritional factors to the cause, dissolution and prevention of feline uroliths and urethral plugs, *Vet Clin North Am Sm Anim Pract* 19:561–581, 1989.

120. Barsanti JA, Blue J, Edmunds J: Urinary tract infection due to indwelling bladder catheters in dogs and cats, *J Am Vet Med Assoc* 187:384–388, 1985.

121. Osborne CA, Johnston GR, Polzin DJ, and others: Redefinition of the feline urologic syndrome: feline lower urinary tract disease with heterogenous causes, *Vet Clin North Am Sm Anim Pract* 14:409–438, 1984.

122. Osborne CA, Clinton, CW, Brunkow HC, and others: Epidemiology of naturally occurring feline uroliths and urethral plugs, *Vet Clin North Am Sm Anim Pract* 14:481–491, 1984.

123. Willeberg P: A case-control study of some fundamental determinants in the epidemiology of the feline urological syndrome, *Nord Vet Med* 27:1–14, 1975.

124. Willeberg P, Priester WA: Feline urological syndrome: associations with some time, space and individual patient factors, *Am J Vet Res* 37:975–978, 1976.

125. Dorn CR, Sauerssig S, Schmidt DA: Factors affecting risk of urolithiasis-cystitis-urethritis in cats, *Am J Vet Res* 34:433–436, 1973.

126. Sauer LS, Hamar D, Lewis LD: Effect of diet composition on water intake and excretion by the cat, *Fel Pract* 15:16–21, 1985.

127. Bushman DH, Emerick RJ, Embry LB: Experimentally induced ovine phosphatic urolithiasis: relationships involving dietary calcium, phosphorus and magnesium, *J Nutr* 87:499–503, 1965.

128. Chow FHC, Brase JL, Hamar DW, and others: Effect of dietary supplements and methylene blue on uninary calculi, *J Urol* 104:315–319, 1970.

129. Rich LJ, Dysart I, Chow FHC, and others: Urethral obstruction in male cats: experimental production by addition of magnesium and phosphate to diet, *Fel Pract* 4:44–47, 1974.

130. Lewis LD, Chow HC, Taton GS, and others: Effect of various dietary mineral concentrations on the occurrence of feline urolithiasis, *J Am Vet Med Assoc* 172:559–563, 1978.

131. Lewis LD, Morris ML: Diet as a causative factor of feline urolithiasis, *Vet Clin North Am Sm Anim Pract* 14:513–527, 1984.

132. Kallfelz FA, Bressett JD, Wallace RJ: Urethral obstruction in random source and SPF male cats induced by high levels of dietary magnesium or magnesium and phosphorus, *Fel Pract* 10:25–35, 1980.

133. National Research Council: *Nutrient requirements of cats*, Washington, DC, 1986, National Academy of Sciences.

134. Association of American Feed Control Officials: Pet food regulations. In *AAFCO official publication*, Atlanta, 1994, pp 87–108, The Association.

135. Finco DR, Barsanti JA, Crowell WA: Characterization of magnesium-induced urinary disease in the cat and comparison with feline urologic syndrome, *Am J Vet Res* 46:391–400, 1985.

136. Ross LA: Feline urologic syndrome: understanding and diagnosing this enigmatic disease, *Vet Med* 85:1194–1203, 1990.

137. Buffington CA, Rogers QR, Morris JG, and others: Feline struvite urolithiasis: magnesium effect depends upon urinary pH, *Fel Pract* 15:29–33, 1985.

138. Cook NE: The importance of urinary pH in the prevention of feline urologic syndrome, *Pet Food Ind* 27:24–31, 1985.

139. Tarttelin MF: Feline struvite urolithiasis: factors affecting urine pH may be more important than magnesium levels in food, *Vet Rec* 121:227–230, 1987.

140. Taton GF, Hamar DW, Lewis LD: Evaluation of ammonium chloride as a urinary acidifier in the cat, *J Am Vet Med Assoc* 184:433–436, 1984.

141. Taton GF, Hamar DW, Lewis LD: Urinary acidification in the prevention and treatment of feline struvite urolithiasis, *J Am Vet Med Assoc* 184:437–443, 1984.

142. Chan JCM: Nutrition and acid-base metabolism, *Fed Proc* 40:2423–2428, 1981.

143. Klahr SD: Disorders of acid-base metabolism. In Chan JCM, Gill JR, editors: *Disorders of mineral, water, and acid-base metabolism*, New York, 1982, Wiley and Sons.

144. Kane E, Douglass GM: The effects of feeding a dry commercial cat food on the urine and blood acid-base balance of the cat, *Fel Pract* 16:9–13, 1986.

145. Holsworth J: Nutrition and nutritional disorders. In *Diseases of the cat: medicine and surgery*, vol 1, Philadelphia, 1987, WB Saunders, pp 37–38.

146. Harrington JT, Lemann J: The metabolic production and disposal of acid and alkali, *Med Clin North Am* 54:1543–1554, 1970.

147. Skoch ER, Chandler EA, Douglas GM, and others: Influence of diet or urine pH and the feline urological syndrome, *J Sm Anim Pract* 32:413–419, 1991.

148. Buffington CA: Feline struvite urolithiasis: effect of diet. In *Proceedings of the European Society of Veterinary Nephrology and Urology Annual Symposium*, Barcelona, Spain, 1988, Intercongress, pp 60–112.

149. Kurtz I, Maher T, Hutter HT: Effect of diet on plasma acid-base composition in normal humans, *Kidney Int* 24:670–680, 1983.

150. Ching SV, Fettman MJ, Hamar DW: The effect of chronic dietary acidification using ammonium chloride on acid-base and mineral metabolism in the adult cat, *J Nutr* 119:902–915, 1989.

151. Dibartola SP, Buffington CA, Chow DJ: Development of chronic renal disease in cats fed a commercial diet, *J Am Vet Med Assoc* 202:744–750, 1993.

152. Dow SW, Fettman MJ, LeCouteur RS, and others: Potassium depletion in cats: renal and dietary influences, *J Am Vet Med Assoc* 191:1569, 1987.

153. Fettman MJ: Feline kaliopenic polymyopathy/nephropathy syndrome, *Vet Clin North Am Sm Anim Pract* 19:415–419, 1989.

154. Schwille PO, Hermann U: Environmental factors in the pathophysiology of recurrent idiopathic calcium urolithiasis (RCU) with emphasis on nutrition, *Urol Res* 20:72–76, 1992.

155. Osborne CA, Sanna JJ, Unger LK: Mineral composition of 4500 uroliths from dogs, cats, horses, cattle, sheep, goats, and pigs, *Vet Med* 84:750–755, 1989.

156. Markwell PJ: Nutrition and aspects of feline lower urinary tract disease, *J Sm Anim Pract* 34:157–162, 1993.

157. Anderson RS: Water balance in the dog and cat, *J Sm Anim Prac* 23:588–598, 1982.

158. Thrall BE, Miller LG: Water turnover in cats fed dry rations, *Fel Pract* 6:10–17, 1976.

159. Seefeldt SL, Chapman TE: Body water content and turnover in cats fed dry and canned rations, *Am J Vet Res* 40:183–185, 1979.

160. Kane E, Rogers QR, Morris JG, and others: Feeding behavior of the cat fed laboratory and commercial diets, *Nutr Res* 1:499–507, 1981.

161. Hart BL: Feline behavior, *Fel Pract* 9:10–12, 1979.

162. Finco DR, Adams DD, Crowell, WA, and others: Food and water intake and urine composition in cats: influence of continuous versus periodic feeding, *Am J Vet Res* 47:1638–1642, 1986.

163. Finke MD, Litzenberger BA: Effect of food intake on urine pH in cats, *J Sm Anim Pract* 33:261–265, 1992.

164. Hamar DW, Chow FHC, Dysart MI, and others: Effect of sodium chloride in prevention of experimentally produced phosphate uroliths in male cats, *J Am Anim Hosp Assoc* 12:514–517, 1976.

165. Osborne CA, Polzin DJ: Prospective clinical evaluation of feline struvite urolith dissolution, *Proc Am Coll Vet Int Med* 1:4–11 to 4–16, 1986.

166. Lewis LD, Morris ML: Feline urologic syndrome: causes and clinical management, *Vet Med Sm Anim Clin* 79:323–327, 1984.

167. Senior DF, Sundstrom DA, and Wolfson BB: Testing the effects of ammonium chloride and di-methionine on the urinary pH of cats, *Vet Med* 81:88–93, 1986.

168. Lloyd WE, Sullivan DJ: Effects of orally administered ammonium chloride and methionine on feline urinary acidity, *Vet Med* 80:773–778, 1984.

169. Fau D, Smalley KA, Morris JE, and others: Effect of excess dietary methionine on weight gain and plasma amino acids in kittens, *J Nutr* 117:1838–1843, 1987.

170. Meade Y, Hoshino T, Inaba M, and others: Methionine-induced hemolytic anemia with methemoglobinemia and Heinz body formation in erythrocytes in cats, *Am J Vet Res* 48:289–293, 1987.

171. Osborne CA, Kruger JM, Polzin DJ, and others: Medical dissolution of feline struvite uroliths, *Minn Vet* 24:22–32, 1984.

172. Burger IH: Nutritional aspects of the feline urological syndrome (FUS), *J Sm Anim Pract* 28:447–452, 1987.

173. Kirk RW: Nutrition and the integument, *J Sm Anim Pract* 32:283–288, 1991.

174. Scott DW: Vitamin A-responsive dermatosis in the cocker spaniel, *J Am Anim Hosp Assoc* 22:125–129, 1986.

175. Ihrke PJ, Goldschmidt MH: Vitamin A-responsive dermatosis in the dog, *J Am Vet Med Assoc* 182:687–690, 1983.

176. Parker W, Yager-Johnson JA, Hardy MH: Vitamin A responsive seborrheic dermatosis in the dog: a case report, *J Am Anim Hosp Assoc* 19:548–554, 1983.

177. Cho DY, Frey RA, Guffy MM, and others: Hypervitaminosis A in the dog, *Am J Vet Res* 36:1597–1603, 1975.

178. Kamm JJ: Toxicology, carcinogenicity, and teratogenicity of some orally administered retinoids, *J Am Acad Derm* 6:652–660, 1982.

179. Fiqueriredo C: Vitamin E serum contents, erythrocyte and lymphocyte count, PCV, and hemoglobin determinations in normal dog, dogs with scabies, and dogs with demodicosis, Proceedings of the Annual American Academy of Veterinary Dermatology and American College of Veterinary Dermatology, pp 8, 1985.

180. Scott DW, Walton DK: Clinical evaluation of oral vitamin E for the treatment of primary canine acanthosis nigricans, *J Am Anim Hosp Assoc* 21:345–356, 1985.

181. National Research Council: *Nutrient requirements of dogs*, Washington, DC, 1985, National Academy of Sciences.

182. Ayres S, Mihan R: Is vitamin E involved in the autoimmune mechanism? *Cutis* 21:321–325, 1978.

183. Miller WH; Nonsteroidal anti-inflammatory agents in the management of canine and feline pruritus. In Kirk RW, editor: *Current veterinary therapy*, Philadelphia, 1989, WB Saunders, pp 566–569.

184. Lloyd DH: Essential fatty acids and skin disease, *J Sm Anim Pract* 30:207–212, 1989.

185. Codner EC, Thatcher CD: Nutritional management of skin diseases, *Comp Cont Ed Pract Vet* 15:411–424, 1993.

186. Muller GH, Kirk RW, Scott DW: *Small animal dermatology*, Philadelphia, 1989, WB Saunders, pp 796–806.

187. Miller WH, Griffin GE, Scott DW, and others: Clinical trial of DVM derm caps in the treatment of allergic disease in dog: a nonblinded study, *J Am Anim Hosp Assoc* 25:163–168, 1989.

188. Vaughn DM, Reinhart GA, Swaim SF, and others: Evaluation of dietary n-6 to n-3 fatty acid rations on leukotriene B synthesis in dog skin and neutrophils, *J Vet Int Med* 8:155, 1994.

189. Miller WH Jr, Scott DW, Wellington JR: Efficacy of DVM Derm Caps Liquid in the management of allergic and inflammatory dermatoses of the cat, *J Am Anim Hosp Assoc* 29:37–40, 1993.

190. Scott DW, Buerger RG: Nonsteroidal anti-inflammatory agents in the management of canine pruritus, *J Am Anim Hosp Assoc* 24:425–428, 1988.

191. Lloyd DH, Thomsett LR: Essential fatty acid supplementation in the treatment of canine atopy, *Vet Dermatol* 1:41–44, 1989.

192. Bond R, Lloyd DH: A double-blind comparison of olive oil and a combination of evening primrose oil and fish oil in the management of canine atopy, *Vet Rec* 131:558–560, 1992.

193. Campbell KL: Fatty acid supplementation and skin disease, *Vet Clin North Am Sm Anim Pract* 20:1475–1486, 1990.

194. Miller WH, Scott DW, Wellington JR: Investigation on the antipruritic effects of ascorbic acid given alone and in combination with a fatty acid supplement to dogs with allergic skin disease, *Can Pract* 17:11–13, 1992.

195. Harvey RG: Effect of varying proportions of evening primrose oil and fish oil on cats with crusting dermatosis (miliary dermatitis), *Vet Rec* 133:208–211, 1993.

196. Harvey RG: Management of feline miliary dermatitis by supplementing the diet with essential fatty acids, *Vet Rec* 128:326–329, 1991.

197. White PD: Essential fatty acids: use in management of canine atopy, *Comp Cont Ed Pract Vet* 15:451–457, 1993.

198. Scott DW, Miller WH: Nonsteroidal management of canine pruritus: chlorpheniramine and a fatty acid supplement (DVM Derm Caps) in combination, and the fatty acid supplement at twice the manufacturers' recommended dosage, *Cornell Vet* 80:381–387, 1991.

199. Paradis M, Scott DW: Further investigations on the use of nonsteroidal and steroidal anti-inflammatory agents in the management of canine pruritus, *J Am Anim Hosp Assoc* 27:44–48, 1991.

200. Paradis M, Lemay S, and Scott DW: The efficacy of clemastine (Tavist), a fatty acid-containing product (Derm Caps), and the combination of both products in the management of canine pruritus, *Vet Dermatol* 2:17–20, 1991.

201. Campbell KL: Effects of oral sunflower oil and olive oil on serum and cutaneous fatty acid concentrations in dogs, Proceedings of the Seventh Annual Meeting of American Association of Veterinary Dermatologists, 1991, ACVD, pp 13.

202. van den Broek AHM, Thoday KL: Skin disease in dogs associated with zinc deficiency: a report of five cases, *J Sm Anim Pract* 27:313–323, 1986.

203. Sousa CA, Stannard AA, Ihrke PJ: Dermatosis associated with feeding generic dog food: 13 cases (1981–1982), *J Am Vet Med Assoc* 192:676–680, 1988.

204. Robertson BT, Burns MJ: Zinc metabolism and zinc-deficiency syndrome in the dog, *Am J Vet Res* 24:997–1002, 1963.

205. Halliwell REW: Management of dietary hypersensitivity in the dog, *J Sm Anim Nutr* 33:156–160, 1992.

206. August JR: Dietary hypersensitivity in dogs: cutaneous manifestations, diagnosis and management, *Comp Cont Ed Pract Vet* 7:469–477, 1985.

207. White SD: Food hypersensitivity in 30 dogs, *J Am Vet Med Assoc* 188:695–698, 1986.

208. Doering GG: Food allergy: where does it fit as a cause of canine pruritus? *Pet Vet* May/June, pp 10–16, 1991.

209. Walton GS: Skin responses in the dog and cat due to ingested allergens: observations on one hundred confirmed cases, *Vet Rec* 81:709–713, 1967.

210. Scott DW: Immunologic skin disorders in the dog and cat, *Vet Clin North Am Sm Anim Pract* 8:641–664, 1978.

211. Baker E: Food Allergy, *Vet Clin North Am Sm Anim Pract* 4:79–89, 1974.

212. Reedy LM, Miller WH: Food hypersensitivity. In *Allergic skin diseases in dogs and cats*, Philadelphia, 1989, WB Saunders, pp 147–158.

213. Rosser EJ: Proceedings of the Annual Meeting of the American College of Veterinary Dermatology, San Francisco, pp 47, 1990.

214. Harvey RG: Food allergy and dietary intolerance in dogs: a report of 25 cases, *J Sm Anim Pract* 34:175–179, 1993.

215. Rosser EJ: Diagnosis of food allergy in dogs, *J Am Vet Med Assoc* 203:259–262, 1993.

216. Jeffers JG, Shanley KJ, Meyer EK: Diagnostic testing of dogs for food hypersensitivity, *J Am Vet Med Assoc* 198:245–250, 1991.

217. Hodgkins E: Food allergy in cats: considerations, diagnosis and management, *Pet Vet* Nov/Dec, pp 24–28, 1991.

218. Leib MS, August JR: Food hypersensitivity. In Ettinger SJ, editor: *Textbook of veterinary internal medicine*,ed 3, Philadelphia, 1989, WB Saunders, pp 194–197.

219. Johnson LW: Food allergy in a dog: diagnosis by dietary management, *Mod Vet Pract* 68:236–239, 1987.

220. Kunkle G, Horner S: Validity of skin testing for diagnosis of food allergy in dogs, *J Am Vet Med Assoc* 200:677–680, 1992.

221. Bovee KC: Diet and kidney failure. In *Kal Kan Symposium for the Treatment of Dog and Cat Disease*, Kal Kan Foods Inc, Vernon, California, pp 25–28, 1977.

222. Churchill J, Polzin D, Osborne C, and others: The influence of dietary protein intake on progression of chronic renal failure in dogs, *Semin Vet Med Surg Sm Anim* 7:244–250, 1992.

223. Kronfeld DS: Dietary management of chronic renal disease in dogs: a critical appraisal, *J Sm Anim Pract* 34:211–219, 1993.

224. Ross LA, Finco DR: Relationship of selected clinical renal function tests to glomerular filtration rate and renal blood flow in cats, *Am J Vet Res* 42:1023–1026, 1981.

225. Bovee KC: The uremic syndrome: patient evaluation and treatment, *Comp Cont Ed Pract Vet* 1:279–283, 1979.

226. Cowgill LD, Spangler WL: Renal insufficiency in geriatric dogs, *Vet Clin North Am Sm Anim Med* 11:727–749, 1981.

227. Finco DR, Coulter DB, Barsanti JA: Simple, accurate method for clinical estimation of glomerular filtration rate in the dog, *Am J Vet Res* 42:1874–1877, 1981.

228. Finco DR, Brown SC, Crowell WA, and others: Exogenous creatinine clearance as a measure of glomerular filtration rate in dogs with reduced renal mass, *Am J Vet Res* 52:1029–1032, 1991.

229. Brown SA, Finco DR, Crowell WA, and others: Dietary protein intake and the glomerular adaptations to partial nephrectomy in dogs, *J Nutr* 121:S125–S127, 1991.

230. Brown SA, Finco D, Crowell WA: Single-nephron adaptations to partial renal ablation in the dog, *Am J Physiol* 258:F495–F503, 1990.

231. White JV, Finco DR, Brown SA, and others: Effect of dietary protein on kidney function, morphology, and histopathology during compensatory renal growth in dogs, *Am J Vet Res* 52:1357–1365, 1990.

232. Hostetter TH, Olson JL, Rennke HG: Hyperfiltration in remnant nephrons: a potentially adverse response to renal ablation, *Am J Physiol* 241:F85–F92, 1981.

233. Olivetti GP, Anversa P, Rigamonti W, and others: Morphometry of the renal corpuscle during normal postnatal growth and compensatory hypertrophy, *J Cell Biol* 75:573–585, 1977.

234. Brown SA: Dietary protein restriction: some unanswered questions, *Semin Vet Med Surg Sm Anim* 7:237–243, 1992.

235. Anderson S, Brenner BM: The role of intraglomerular pressure in the initiation and progression of renal disease, *J Hypertens* 4(suppl 5):S236–S238, 1986.

236. Brenner BM, Meyer TW, Hostetter TH: Dietary protein intake and the progressive nature of renal disease: the role of hemodynamically mediated glomerular injury in the pathogenesis of progressive glomerular sclerosis in aging, renal ablation and intrinsic renal disease, *N Engl J Med* 307:652–659, 1982.

237. Shimamura T, Morrison AB: A progressive glomerulosclerosis occurring in partial five-sixths nephrectomized rats, *Am J Pathol* 79:95–106, 1975.

238. Finco DR, Crowell WA, Barsanti JA: Effects of three diets on dogs with induced chronic renal failure, *Am J Vet Res* 46:646–653, 1985.

239. Polzin DJ, Leininger JR, Osborne CA, and others: Development of renal lesions in dogs after 11/12 reduction in renal mass, *Lab Invest* 58:172–183, 1988.

240. Tapp DC, Kobayoshu S, Fernandes S: Protein restriction or calorie restriction? a critical assessment of the influence of selective calorie restriction on the progression of experimental renal disease, *Semin Nephrol* 9:343–353, 1989.

241. Finco DR, Brown SA, Crowell WA, and others: Effect of phosphorus/calcium-restricted and phosphorus/calcium-replete 32% diets in dogs with chronic renal failure, *Am J Vet Res* 53:157–163, 1992.

242. Keane WF, Kasiske BL, O'Donnell MP: Hyperlipidemia and the progression of renal disease, *Am J Clin Nutr* 47:157–160, 1987.

243. Bourgoignie JJ, Gavellas G, Martinex E, and others: Glomerular function and morphology after renal mass reduction in dogs, *Lab Clin Med* 109:380–388, 1987.

244. Maeda H, Gleiser CA, Masoro EJ, and others: Nutritional influences on aging of Fischer 344 rats. II. Pathology, *J Gerontol* 40:671–688, 1985.

245. Masoro EJ, Iwasaki K, Gleiser CA, and others: Dietary modulation of the progression of nephropathy in aging rats: an evaluation of the importance of protein, *Am J Clin Nutr* 49:1217–1227, 1989.

246. Bovee KC: Influence of dietary protein on renal function in dogs, *J Nutr* 121:S128–S139, 1991.

247. Robertson JL, Goldschmidt M, Kronfeld DS, and others: Long term renal responses to high dietary protein in dogs with 75% nephrectomy, *Kidney Int* 29:511–519, 1986.

248. Polzin DJ, Osborne CA, Hayden DW: Influence of reduced protein diets on morbidity, mortality, and renal function in dogs with induced chronic renal failure, *Am J Vet Res* 45:506–517, 1984.

249. Tucker SM, Mason RL, Beauchene RE: Influence of diet and feed restriction on kidney function of aging male rats, *J Gerontol* 31:264–270, 1976.

250. Berg BN, Simms HS: Nutrition and longevity in the rat. II. Longevity and onset of disease with different levels of food intake, *J Nutr* 71:255–263, 1960.

251. Osborne CA, Polzin DJ, Abdullahi S, and others: Role of diet in management of feline chronic polyuric renal failure: current status, *J Am Anim Hosp Assoc* 18:11–20, 1982.

252. Polzin DJ, Osborne CA, Lulich JP: Effects of dietary protein/phosphate restriction in normal dogs and dogs with chronic renal failure, *J Sm Anim Pract* 32:289–295, 1991.

253. Lau K: Phosphate excess and progressive renal failure: the precipitation-calcification hypothesis, *Kidney Int* 36:918–937, 1989.

254. Brown SA, Crowell WA, Barsanti JA: Beneficial effects of dietary mineral restriction in dogs with marked reduction of functional renal mass, *J Am Soc Nephrol* 1:1169–1179, 1991.

255. Ross LA, Finco DR, Crowell WA: Effect of dietary phosphorus restriction on the kidneys of cats with reduced renal mass, *Am J Vet Res* 43:1023–1026, 1982.

256. Hansen B, DiBartola SP, Chew DJ, and others: Clinical and metabolic findings in dogs with chronic renal failure fed two diets, *Am J Vet Res* 53:326–334, 1992.

257. National Research Council: *Nutrient requirements of dogs*, Washington, DC, 1974, National Academy of Sciences.

258. Polzin DJ, Osborne CA: Update—conservative medical management of chronic renal failure. In Kirk RW, editor: *Current veterinary therapy VI*, Philadelphia, 1956, WB Saunders, pp 1167.

259. Polzin DJ, Osborne CA: Current progress in slowing progression of canine and feline chronic renal failure, *Comp Anim Pract* 3:52–62, 1988.

260. Polzin DJ, Osborne CA, Stevens JB, and others: Influence of modified protein diets on the nutritional status of dogs with induced chronic renal failure, *Am J Vet Res* 44:1694–1702, 1983.

261. Kaplan MA, Canterbury JM, Bourgoignie JJ: Reversal of hyperparathyroidism in response to dietary phosphorus restriction in the uremic dog, *Kidney Int* 15:43–48, 1979.

262. Smith RC, Haschem T, Hamlin RL, and others: Water and electrolyte intake and output and quantity of feces in the healthy dog, *Vet Med Sm Anim Clin* 59:743–748, 1964.

263. Mitchell AR: Salt intake, animal health and hypertension: should sleeping dogs lie? In Burger IH, Rivers JPW, editors: *Nutrition of the dog and cat*, New York, 1989 Cambridge University Press, pp 275–292.

264. Hubbard BS, Vulgamott JC: Feline hepatic lipidosis, *Comp Cont Ed Pract Vet* 14:459–464, 1992.

265. Center SA: Feline hepatic lipidosis, *Vet Ann* 33:244–254, 1993.

266. Thornburg LP, Simpson S, Digilo K: Fatty liver syndrome in cats, *J Am Anim Hosp Assoc* 18:397–400, 1982.

267. Hall JA, Barstad LA, Voller BE, and others: Lipid composition of liver and adipose tissues from normal cats and cats with hepatic lipidosis, *J Vet Int Med* 6:127, 1992 (abstract).

268. Biourge V: Sequential findings in cats with hepatic lipidosis, *Fel Pract* 21:25–28, 1993.

269. Cornelius LM, Rogers K: Idiopathic hepatic lipidosis in cats, *Mod Vet Pract* 66:377–380, 1985.

270. Bauer JE, Schenck P: Nutritional management of hepatic disease, *Vet Clin North Am Sm Anim Pract* 19:513–527, 1989.

271. Evans KL, Cornelius LM: Dietary management of feline idiopathic hepatic lipidosis, *Fel Pract* 18:5–10, 1990.

272. Hardy PM: Diseases of the liver and their treatment. In Ettinger SJ, editor: *Textbook of veterinary internal medicine*, Philadelphia, 1989, WB Saunders, pp 1479–1527.

273. Biourge VC, Massat B, Groff JM, and others: Effects of protein, lipid, or carbohydrate supplementation on hepatic lipid accumulation during rapid weight loss in obese cats, *Am J Vet Res* 55:1405–1415, 1994.

274. Chapoy PR, Angelini C, Brown WJ: Systemic carnitine deficiency—a treatable inherited lipid storage disease presenting as Reye's syndrome, *N Engl J Med* 303:1389–1394, 1980.

275. Jacobs G, Cornelius L, Keene B, and others: Comparison of plasma, liver, and skeletal muscle carnitine concentrations in cats with idiopathic hepatic lipidosis and in healthy cats, *Am J Vet Res* 51:1349–1351, 1991.

276. Jacobs G, Cornelius L, Allen S, and others: Treatment of idiopathic hepatic lipidosis in cats: 11 cases (1986–1987), *J Am Vet Med Assoc* 195:635–638, 1989.

277. Wolf AM: Hepatic lipidosis, *Vet Med Rep* 1:67–70, 1988.

Glossary

acanthosis nigricans   diffuse hyperplasia of the spinous layer of the skin, with gray, brown, or black pigmentation.

accretion   growth by addition of material.

acrodermatitis   severe skin lesions.

adipocyte hyperplasia   an increase in the number of fat cells, occuring normally during certain developmental periods such as early growth and occasionally during puberty.

adipocyte   specialized cells that store large amounts of triglyceride.

alopecia   the absence of hair from the skin areas where it is normally present.

anabolism   any process by which organisms convert substances into other components of the organism's chemical architecture.

anorexia   lack or loss of the appetite for food.

ascites   effusion and accumulation of serous fluid in the abdominal cavity.

ataxia   failure of muscular coordination; irregularity of muscular action.

azotemia   an excess of urea or other nitrogenous compounds in the blood.

bone meal   the dried, ground, and sterilized product from undecomposed bones.

BUN   blood urea nitrogen.

by-product   secondary products in addition to the principle product; the parts that are left after the economically valuable pieces are harvested.

calculolytic   pertaining to the destruction or decomposition of a calculus.

calorie   the amount of heat energy that is necessary to raise the temperature of 1 gram of water from 14.5°C to 15.5°C. Because the calorie is such a small unit of measure, the kilocalorie (kcal), equal to 1000 calories, is most often used in the science of animal nutrition.

carnivorous   eating or subsisting on primarily animal material.

carpus   the joint between the paw and the forelimb (the wrist in humans).

cation   an ion carrying a positive charge owing to a deficiency of electrons; in an electrochemical cell, cations migrate toward the cathode.

cellulose   an unbranched, long-chain polysaccharide that is a component of dietary fiber. It forms the skeleton of most plant structures and plant cells.

chylomicron   a class of lipoproteins responsible for the transport of exogenous cholesterol and triglycerides from the small intestine to tissues after meals.

colostrum   the first product of the mammary gland following parturition.

coprophagy   the ingestion of dung or feces.

corn gluten meal   the dried residue from corn after the removal of the larger part of the starch and germ and the separation of the bran.

costochondral   pertaining to a rib and its cartilage.

creatinine   the end product of creatine metabolism, found in muscle and blood and excreted in the urine.

crystalluria   excretion of crystals in the urine in some cases, producing urinary tract irritation.

cyanosis   a bluish discoloration of the skin and mucous membranes as a result of excessive concentration of reduced hemoglobin in the blood.

cystitis   inflammation of the urinary bladder.

cystocentesis   perforation or tapping, as with an aspirator, trocar, or needle, to remove urinary bladder contents.

demodicosis   skin disease caused by the mange mite *Demodex canis* in dogs.

deoxyribonucleic acid (DNA)   a nucleic acid that constitutes the genetic material of all cellular organisms.

dietary thermogenesis   Also called the specific dynamic action of food, dietary thermogenesis refers to energy needed by the body to digest, absorb, and assimilate nutrients.

duodenum   the first or proximal portion of the small intestine extending from the pylorus to the jejunum.

dystocia   abnormal labor or birth.

eicosanoid   biologically active substances that are metabolites of 20-carbon fatty acids. Includes prostaglandins, leukotrienes, prosacyclins, and thromboxanes.

endogenous   developing or originating within the organism, or arising from causes within the organism.

energy density   the energy density of a pet food refers to the number of calories provided by the food in a given weight or volume. In the United States it is expressed as kilocalories of metabolizable energy per kilogram or pound of diet; in Europe, kilojoule per kilogram is used.

energy imbalance   occurs when an animal's daily energy consumption is either greater or less than its daily requirement, leading to changes in growth rate, body weight, and body composition.

enterohepatic   pertaining to the intestine (entero) and the liver (hepatic).

epiphysis   the expanded articular end of a long bone, developed from a secondary ossification center.

erythropoiesis   the production of erythrocytes (red blood cells).

essential nutrients   that cannot be synthesized by the body at a rate adequate to meet body needs and must be supplied in the diet.

estrus   the recurrent, restricted period of sexual receptivity in female mammals.

exogenous   developing or originating outside the organism.

extravasation   a discharge or escape, as of blood from a vessel into the tissues.

germ (as in wheat germ)   the plant embryo found in seeds and frequently separated from the bran (outer coat of a seed) and starch endosperm during milling.

glomerulosclerosis   fibrosis and scarring that result in senescence of the renal glomeruli.

gluconeogenesis   the formation of glucose from molecules that are not carbohydrates, as from amino acids, lactate, and the glycerol portion of fats.

gluten   the tough, thick, proteinaceous substance remaining when the flour or wheat or other grain is washed to remove the starch.

glycosuria   the excretion of an abnormal concentration of glucose in the urine.

grain   the seed from cereal plants (for example, wheat, rice, barley, and oats).

Heinz body   coccoid inclusion bodies resulting from oxidative injury to and precipitation of hemoglobin, seen in the presence of certain abnormal hemoglobins and erythrocytes with enzyme deficiencies.

hematocrit   the ratio of the total red cell volume to the total blood volume.

hemicellulose   a heterogenous group of branched-chain polysaccharides that, together with pectin, forms the matrix of plant cells within which cellulose fibers are enmeshed.

hemolytic anemia   anemia as a result of intravascular fragmentation of red blood cells.

hepatic lipidosis   an abnormal accumulation of fats and fat-like substances in the liver.

hepatomegaly   enlargement of the liver.

homeostasis   the maintenance of stability in the body's internal environment, achieved by a system of control mechanisms activated by negative feedback.

hydrolysis   the splitting of a compound into fragments by the addition of water. The hydroxyl group is incorporated in one fragment and the hydrogen atom in the other.

hydroxyapatite   an inorganic compound, that is found in the matrix of bone and the teeth, composed of calcium, phosphorous, hydrogen, and oxygen and gives rigidity to these structures.

hypercalcemia   increased calcium concentration in the blood.

hyperlipidemia   a general term for elevated concentrations of triglyceride and/or cholesterol in the plasma of fasted animals.

hyperphagia   ingestion of a greater than optimal quantity of food.

hyperplasia   increase in cell number.

hypertrophy   increase in cell size.

hypophosphatemia   decreased phosphorous concentration in the blood.

hypothalamus   gland located in the brain that exerts control over the function of a portion of the pituitary gland. Its nuclei comprise part of the mechanism that activates, controls, and integrates the peripheral autonomic mechanisms, which include a general regulation of water balance, body temperature, sleep, and food intake.

iatrogenic   any adverse condition occurring as the result of treatment, especially infections acquired during the course of treatment.

icterus   jaundice.

idiopathic   self-originated, or of unknown causation.

inappetence   lack of appetite.

indole   a compound that is produced by the decomposition of tryptophan in the intestine, being partly responsible for the peculiar odor of the feces.

jejunum   the portion of the small intestine that extends from the duodenum to the ileum.

keratin   a scleroprotein that is the principal constituent of epidermis, hair, nails, horny tissues, and the organic matrix of the enamel of teeth.

keratinization   the development of or conversion into the structural protein keratin.

kilojoule   the amount of mechanical energy that is required for a force of 1 newton to move a weight of 1 kilogram a distance of 1 meter. To convert kilocalories to kilojoule, the number of kilocalories is multiplied by 4.184.

lactic acid   an end product of glycolysis that provides energy anaerobically in skeletal muscle during heavy exercise. It can be oxidized aerobically in the heart for energy production or can be converted back to glucose (gluconeogenesis) in the liver.

leukotriene   one of a group of biologically active compounds formed from 20-carbon fatty acids that function as regulators of allergic and inflammatory reactions.

ligand   a molecule that binds to another molecule; commonly refers to a small molecule that binds specifically to a larger molecule.

lipemia retinalis   a milky appearance of the veins and arteries of the retina, occurring as a result of hyperlipidemia.

lipidosis   a term for several of the lysosomal storage diseases in which there is an abnormal accumulation of lipids in the reticuloendothelial cells. Also called lipid storage disease.

lipogenesis   the formation of fat; the transformation of nonfat food materials into body fat.

lipoid granuloma   a small, nodular, delimited aggregation of lipid cells; a **xanthoma**.

lumen   the cavity or channel within a tube or tubular organ (for example, the intestine).

meal   an ingredient that has been ground or otherwise reduced in particle size.

meat and bone meal   the same as meat meal, except that meat and bone meal can contain a great deal more bone (raising the ash content and lowering the protein quality).

meat by-products   the nonrendered, clean parts, other than meat, derived from slaughtered mammals. Include but are not limited to: lungs, spleen, kidneys, brain, liver, blood, bone, and stomach/intestine, without their contents.

meat meal   the rendered product from mammal tissues exclusive of blood, hair, hoof, horn, hide trimmings, manure, stomach and rumen contents, except in such amounts as may occur unavoidably in good processing practices.

metabolism   the sum of all the physical and chemical processes by which living, organized substance is produced and maintained (anabolism), and also the transformation by which energy is made available for the uses of the organism (catabolism).

metabolizable energy (ME)   the amount of energy that is ultimately available to the tissues of the body after losses in the feces and urine have been subtracted from the gross energy of food. It is the value that is most often used to express the energy content of pet food ingredients and commercial diets.

metaphysis   the wider part at the extremity of the shaft of a long bone, adjacent to the epiphyseal disk. During development it contains the growth zone and consists of spongy bone; in the adult it is continuous with the epiphysis.

methemoglobinemia   the presence of methemoglobin in the blood, resulting in cyanosis.

necrosis   cell/tissue death.

neoplasia   the progressive multiplication of cells under conditions that would not elicit, or would cause cessation of, multiplication of normal cells. May be malignant or benign.

nephrosclerosis   sclerosis (invasion of connective tissue at the expense of active tissue) of the kidney.

neuropathy(ies)   a general term denoting functional disturbances and/or pathological changes in the peripheral nervous system.

nonessential nutrients   nutrients that can be synthesized by the body at a level sufficient to meet body needs. These nutrients can be obtained either through de novo synthesis or from the diet.

omnivorous   subsisting on both plants and animals.

os penis   a heterotopic bone developed in the fibrous septum between the corpora cavernosa and above the urethra, forming the skeleton of the penis.

osmosis   the passage of pure solvent from a solution of lesser to one of greater solute concentration when the two solutions are separated by a membrane that selectively prevents the passage of solute molecules but is permeable to the solvent.

osteochondrosis   a disease of the growth or ossification centers of bones that begins as a degeneration or necrosis, followed by regeneration or recalcification.

parturition   the act or process of giving birth.

pearled barley   dehulled barley grain.

periosteum   a specialized connective tissue covering all bones of the body and possessing bone-forming potentialities.

peristalsis   the rhythmic movements produced by the functioning longitudinal and circular muscle fibers of the small intestine to propel food forward.

phylogeny   the evolutionary history of a group of organisms.

polydipsia   chronic excessive thirst.

polyphagia   excessive eating.

polyuria   the passage of a large volume of urine in a given period of time.

postprandial   occurring after a meal.

poultry meal   (also includes chicken meal if the origin is strictly chicken) the dry rendered product from a combination of clean flesh and skin with or without the accompanying bone derived from the parts of whole carcasses of poultry exclusive of feathers, heads, feet, and entrails.

poultry by-product meal   ground, rendered, clean parts of the carcasses of slaughtered poultry such as necks, feet, undeveloped eggs, and intestines, exclusive of feathers except in such amounts as might occur unavoidably in good processing practices.

poultry by-products   nonrendered, clean parts of carcasses of slaughtered poultry such as heads, feet, and viscera free from fecal content and foreign matter except in such trace amounts as might occur unavoidably in good processing practices.

prepuce   a covering fold of skin over the penis.

proprioception   perception/awareness of position provided by sensory nerve terminals that give information concerning movements and position of the body.

prostacyclin   a prostaglandin synthesized by endothelial cells lining the cardiovascular system. A physiological, antagonist of thromboxane.

prostaglandins   any of a group of components derived from unsaturated 20-carbon fatty acids, primarily arachidonic acid.

pruritus   descriptive of any of various conditions marked by itching.

purulent   consisting of or containing pus.

pylorus   the distal opening of the stomach surrounded by a strong band of circular muscle through which the stomach contents are emptied into the duodenum.

pyoderma   any purulent skin disease.

pyrexia   a fever or febrile condition; abnormal elevation of body temperature.

senescence   the process or condition of growing old, especially the condition resulting from the transitions and accumulations of the deleterious aging processes.

skatole   a crystalline amine with a strong characteristic odor, found in feces. It is produced by the decomposition of proteins in the intestine and directly from the amino acid tryptophan by decarboxylation.

stenosis   narrowing or stricture of a duct or canal.

struvite   a urinary calculus composed of magnesium ammonium phosphate.

subluxation   an incomplete or partial dislocation; in the case of canine hip dysplasia, the head of the femur partially dislodges from the cup (acetabulum) of the pelvic bone.

suppuration   the formation of pus.

taurine   a beta-amino acid that contains a sulfonic group rather than a carboxylic group and so cannot form a peptide bond. It is an essential amino acid for cats, but not for dogs.

theobromine   a methyxanthine contained in chocolate, it has physiological properties similar to those of caffeine.

thermogenesis   the production of heat by physiological processes.

thromboxane   an extremely potent inducer of platelet aggregation and platelet-release reactions, and also a vasoconstrictor. It is a physiological antagonist of prostacyclin.

urethritis   inflammation of the urethra.

urolithiasis   the disease condition associated with the presence of urinary calculi or stones.

villi   multitudinous, threadlike projections that cover the surface of the mucosa of the small intestine and serve as the sites of absorption (by active transport and diffusion) of fluids and nutrients.

vulva   the region of the external genital organs of the female.

xanthoma   a tumor composed of lipid-laden foam cells.

ESTIMATED METABOLIZABLE ENERGY REQUIREMENTS OF DOGS*

K = activity constant
K = 132 (inactive adult)
K = 160 (active adult)

BW = body weight in kilograms
K = 145 (moderately active adult)
K = 200 (performance)

WEIGHT (LBS)	WEIGHT (KG)	MBS	INACTIVE KCAL/DAY	MODERATE KCAL/DAY	ACTIVE KCAL/DAY	PERFORMANCE KCAL/DAY
2	0.91	0.94	123.83	136.03	150.10	187.63
4	1.8	1.49	197.03	216.43	238.82	298.53
6	2.7	1.96	258.53	283.99	313.37	391.71
8	3.6	2.37	313.49	344.36	379.99	474.98
10	4.5	2.76	364.04	399.89	441.26	551.58
12	5.5	3.12	411.34	451.85	498.60	623.24
14	6.4	3.46	456.10	501.01	552.84	691.05
16	7.3	3.78	498.78	547.90	604.58	755.73
18	8.2	4.09	539.74	592.89	654.23	817.79
20	9.1	4.39	579.22	636.26	702.08	877.6
25	11.4	5.10	672.62	738.86	815.30	1019.12
30	13.6	5.76	760.01	834.86	921.23	1151.54
35	15.9	6.38	842.71	925.70	1021.46	1276.83
40	18.2	6.98	921.58	1012.34	1117.06	1396.33
45	20.5	7.55	997.25	1095.46	1208.79	1510.98
50	22.7	8.11	1070.19	1175.59	1297.20	1621.50
55	25.0	8.64	1140.76	1253.11	1382.74	1728.42
60	27.3	9.16	1209.24	1328.33	1465.74	1832.18
65	29.5	9.67	1275.86	1401.51	1546.50	1933.12
70	31.8	10.16	1340.81	1472.86	1625.22	2031.53
75	34.1	10.64	1404.24	1542.54	1702.11	2127.64
80	36.4	11.11	1466.29	1610.70	1777.33	2221.66
85	38.6	11.57	1527.08	1677.47	1851.00	2313.76
90	40.9	12.02	1586.69	1742.96	1923.27	2404.08
95	43.2	12.46	1645.23	1807.26	1994.21	2492.77
100	45.5	12.90	1702.75	1880.44	2063.94	2579.92
105	47.7	13.33	1759.33	1932.60	2132.52	2665.65
110	50.0	13.75	1815.03	1993.78	2200.04	2750.05
115	52.3	14.17	1869.90	2054.06	2266.54	2833.18
120	54.5	14.58	1923.99	2113.47	2332.11	2915.13
125	56.8	14.98	1977.34	2172.07	2396.77	2995.96
130	59.1	15.38	2029.98	2229.91	2460.59	3075.73
135	61.4	15.77	2081.97	2287.01	2523.60	3154.50
140	63.6	16.16	2133.32	2343.42	2585.85	3232.31

*Based on metabolic body size (MBS): kcal required = $K(BW_{kg})^{0.67}$

STANDARD WEIGHTS FOR AKC DOG BREEDS (lb)

Group 1: Sporting

BREED	MALE	FEMALE
Brittany	35–40	30–40
Pointer	55–75	45–64
German shorthaired pointer	55–70	45–60
German wirehaired pointer	60–75	50–65
Chesapeake Bay retriever	65–80	55–70
Curly-coated retriever	65–70	65–70
Flat-coated retriever	50–65	45–60
Golden retriever	65–75	55–65
Labrador retriever	65–80	55–70
English setter	60–75	55–65
Gordon setter	55–80	45–70
Irish setter	~ 70	~ 60
American water spaniel	28–45	25–40
Clumber spaniel	70–85	55–70
Cocker spaniel	25–30	20–25
English cocker spaniel	28–34	26–32
English springer spaniel	49–54	40–45
Field spaniel	35–50	35–50
Irish water spaniel	55–65	45–58
Sussex spaniel	35–45	35–45
Welsh springer spaniel	35–45	30–40
Vizsla	45–55	40–50
Weimaraner	60–75	55–70
Wirehaired pointing griffon	55–65	50–60

Group 2: Hounds

BREED	MALE	FEMALE
Afghan hound	~ 60	~ 50
Basenji	~ 24	~ 22
Basset hound	65–75	50–65
Beagle, 13"	13–18	13–16
Beagle, 15"	17–22	15–20
Black and tan coonhound	70–85	55–70
Bloodhound	90–110	80–100
Borzoi	75–105	70–90
Dachshund, miniature	~ 10	~ 10
Dachshund, standard	16–22	16–22
American foxhound	65–75	55–65
English foxhound	65–75	50–70
Greyhound	65–70	60–65
Harrier	40–50	35–45
Ibizan hound	~ 50	~ 45
Irish wolfhound	~ 120	~ 105
Norwegian elkhound	~ 55	~ 48

BREED	MALE	FEMALE
Otter hound	75–115	65–100
Petit basset griffon vendeen	40–45	40–45
Pharaoh hound	55–70	50–65
Rhodesian ridgeback	~ 75	~ 65
Saluki	50–70	45–65
Scottish deerhound	85–110	75–95
Whippet	20–28	18–23

Group 3: Working

BREED	MALE	FEMALE
Akita	70–85	65–75
Alaskan malamute	85–95	75–85
Bernese mountain dog	75–90	65–80
Boxer	55–70	50–60
Bullmastiff	110–130	100–120
Doberman pinscher	65–80	55–70
Giant schnauzer	70–85	60–75
Great Dane	120–180	100–130
Great Pyrenees	100–125	85–115
Komondor	100–130	80–110
Kuvasz	100–115	70–90
Mastiff	75–190	160–180
Newfoundland	130–150	100–120
Portuguese water dog	42–60	35–50
Rottweiler	80–95	70–85
Saint Bernard	130–180	120–160
Samoyed	50–65	45–60
Siberian husky	45–60	35–50
Standard schnauzer	30–40	25–35

Group 4: Terrier

BREED	MALE	FEMALE
Airedale terrier	45–60	40–55
American Staffordshire terrier	45–55	40–50
Australian terrier	12–14	12–14
Bedlington terrier	17–23	17–23
Border terrier	13–15	11–14
Bull terrier	52–62	45–55
Cairn terrier	~ 14	~ 13
Dandie dinmont terrier	18–24	18–24
Fox terrier (smooth)	17–19	15–17
Fox terrier (wire)	17–19	15–17
Irish terrier	~ 27	~ 25
Kerry blue terrier	33–40	30–38
Lakeland terrier	~ 17	~ 17
Manchester terrier (standard)	12–22	12–22
Miniature bull terrier	15–20	15–20
Miniature schnauzer	16–18	12–16
Norfolk terrier	11–12	11–12

BREED	MALE	FEMALE
Norwich terrier	11–12	11–12
Scottish terrier	19–22	18–21
Sealyham terrier	23–24	21–23
Skye terrier	25–30	20–25
Soft-coated Wheaten terrier	35–40	30–35
Staffordshire bull terrier	28–38	24–34
Welsh terrier	18–22	16–18
West Highland white terrier	12–14	11–13

Group 5: Toy

BREED	MALE	FEMALE
Affenpinscher	7–8	7–8
Brussels griffon	10–12	8–10
Chihuahua	2–5.75	2–5.75
English toy spaniel	8–14	8–14
Italian greyhound	8–15	5–15
Japanese chin	4–20	4–20
Maltese	4–6	4–6
Manchester terrier	7–12	7–11
Miniature pinscher	10–12	9–11
Papillon	8–10	7–9
Pekingese	10–14	10–14
Pomeranian	4–7	3–5
Toy poodle	7–10	7–10
Pug	14–18	14–18
Shih Tzu	12–17	10–15
Silky terrier	8–10	8–10
Yorkshire terrier	4–6.75	3–6

Group 6: Nonsporting

BREED	MALE	FEMALE
Bichon frise	9–12	9–12
Boston terrier	15–24	15–24
Bulldog	45–55	40–50
Chinese Shar Pei	45–55	35–45
Chow chow	45–60	40–50
Dalmatian	50–65	45–55
Finnish spitz	25–35	25–30
French bulldog	20–28	20–28
Keeshond	40–50	40–50
Lhasa apso	13–15	13–15
Poodle, standard	50–60	45–55
Poodle, miniature	17–20	15–20
Schipperke	12–18	12–16
Tibetan spaniel	9–15	9–15
Tibetan terrier	18–30	18–30

Group 7: Herding

BREED	MALE	FEMALE
Australian cattle dog	35–45	35–45
Australian shepherd	45–65	45–65
Bearded collie	55–65	50–60
Belgian Malinois	60–70	43–55
Belgian sheepdog	60–70	43–55
Belgian Tervuren	60–70	43–55
Bouvier des Flanders	70–90	70–90
Briard	65–75	60–70
Collie	65–75	50–65
German shepherd dog	75–90	65–80
Old English sheepdog	60–70	60–70
Puli	29–33	29–33
Shetland sheepdog	16–22	14–18
Welsh corgi, Cardigan	30–38	25–34
Welsh corgi, Pembroke	27–30	25–28

AAFCO Nutrient Profiles: Dog Foods*

NUTRIENT	UNITS DMB†	GROWTH AND REPRODUCTION (MIN.)	ADULT MAINTENANCE (MIN.)	MAXIMUM
PROTEIN	%	22.0	18.0	
Arginine	%	0.62	0.51	
Histidine	%	0.22	0.18	
Isoleucine	%	0.45	0.37	
Leucine	%	0.72	0.59	
Lysine	%	0.77	0.63	
Methionine-cystine	%	0.53	0.43	
Phenylalanine-tyrosine	%	0.89	0.73	
Threonine	%	0.58	0.48	
Tryptophan	%	0.20	0.16	
Valine	%	0.48	0.39	
FAT	%	8.0	5.0	
Linoleic acid	%	1.0	1.0	
MINERALS				
Calcium	%	1.0	0.6	2.5
Phosphorus	%	0.8	0.5	1.6
Ca:P ratio		1.1	1:1	2:1
Potassium	%	0.6	0.6	
Sodium	%	0.3	0.06	
Chloride	%	0.45	0.09	
Magnesium	%	0.04	0.04	0.3
Iron	mg/kg	80	80	3000
Copper	mg/kg	7.3	7.3	250
Manganese	mg/kg	5.0	5.0	
Zinc	mg/kg	120	120	1000
Iodine	mg/kg	1.5	1.5	50
Selenium	mg/kg	0.11	0.11	2
VITAMINS				
Vitamin A	IU/kg	5000	5000	50,000
Vitamin D	IU/kg	500	500	5000
Vitamin E	IU/kg	50	50	1000
Thiamin	mg/kg	1.0	1.0	
Riboflavin	mg/kg	2.2	2.2	
Pantothenic acid	mg/kg	10	10	
Niacin	mg/kg	11.4	11.4	
Pyridoxine	mg/kg	1.0	1.0	
Folic acid	mg/kg	0.18	0.18	
Vitamin B_{12}	mg/kg	0.022	0.02	
Choline	mg/kg	1200	1200	

*Presumes an energy density of 3.5 kcal ME/g DM.
†DMB = dry-matter basis. Reproduced with permission from 1994 AAFCO Official Publication.

AAFCO NUTRIENT PROFILES: CAT FOODS †

NUTRIENT	UNITS DMB*	GROWTH AND REPRODUCTION (MIN.)	ADULT MAINTENANCE (MIN.)	MAXIMUM
PROTEIN	%	30.0	26.0	
Arginine	%	1.25	1.04	
Histidine	%	0.31	0.31	
Isoleucine	%	0.52	0.52	
Leucine	%	1.25	1.25	
Lysine	%	1.20	0.83	
Methionine-cystine	%	1.10	1.10	
Methionine	%	0.62	0.62	1.5
Phenylalanine-tyrosine	%	0.88	0.88	
Phenylalanine	%	0.42	0.42	
Taurine (extruded)	%	0.10	0.10	
Taurine (canned)	%	0.20	0.20	
Threonine	%	0.73	0.73	
Tryptophan	%	0.25	0.16	
Valine	%	0.62	0.62	
FAT‡	%	9.0	9.0	
Linoleic acid	%	0.5	0.5	
Arachidonic acid	%	0.02	0.02	

(Continued)

Reprinted with permission from the 1994 AAFCO Official Publication. Copyright 1994 by the Association of American Feed Control Officials.
*DMB = dry matter basis.
†Presumes an energy density of 4 kcal/g ME, based on the "modified Atwater" values of 3.5, 8.5 and 3.5 kcal/g for protein, fat and carbohydrate (nitrogen-free extract, NFE), respectively. Rations greater than 4.5 kcal/g should be corrected for energy density; rations less than 4.0 kcal/g should not be corrected for energy.
‡Although a true requirement for fat per se has not been established, the minimum level was based on recognition of fat as a source of essential fatty acids, as a carrier of fat-soluble vitamins, to enhance palatability, and to supply an adequate caloric density.
§If the mean urine pH of cats fed as libitum is not below 6.4, the risk of struvite urolithiasis increases as the magnesium content of the diet increases.
‖Because of very poor bioavailability, iron from carbonate or oxide sources that are added to the diet should not be considered as components in meeting the minimum nutrient level.
¶Add 10 IU of vitamin E above minimum level per gram of fish oil per kilogram of diet.
#Vitamin K does not need to be added unless diet contains greater than 25% fish on a dry matter basis.
**Because processing may destroy up to 90% of the thiamin in the diet, allowances in formulation should be made to ensure the minimum nutrient level is met after processing.
††Biotin does not need to be added unless diet contains antimicrobial or antivitamin compounds.
‡‡Methionine may substitute for choline as a methyl donor at a rate of 3.75 parts for 1 part choline by weight when methionine exceeds 0.62%.

NUTRIENT	UNITS DMB*	GROWTH AND REPRODUCTION (MIN.)	ADULT MAINTENANCE (MIN.)	MAXIMUM
MINERALS				
Calcium	%	1.0	0.6	
Phosphorus	%	0.8	0.5	
Potassium	%	0.6	0.6	
Sodium	%	0.2	0.2	
Chloride	%	0.3	0.3	
Magnesium§	%	0.08	0.04	
Iron‖	mg/kg	80	80	
Copper	mg/kg	5	5	
Iodine	mg/kg	0.35	0.35	
Zinc	mg/kg	75	75	2000
Manganese	mg/kg	7.5	7.5	
Selenium	mg/kg	0.1	0.1	
VITAMINS				
Vitamin A	IU/kg	9000	5000	750000
Vitamin D	IU/kg	750	500	10000
Vitamin E¶	IU/kg	30	30	
Vitamin K#	mg/kg	0.1	0.1	
Thiamin**	mg/kg	5.0	5.0	
Riboflavin	mg/kg	4.0	4.0	
Pyridoxine	mg/kg	4.0	4.0	
Niacin	mg/kg	60	60	
Pantothenic acid	mg/kg	5.0	5.0	
Folic acid	mg/kg	0.8	0.8	
Biotin‡	mg/kg	0.07	0.07	
Vitamin B_{12}	mg/kg	0.02	0.02	
Choline#	mg/kg	2400	2400	

NRC Required Minimum Concentrations of Available Nutrients in Dog Food Formulated for Growth

NUTRIENT	PER 1000 kcal ME	DRY BASIS (3.67 kcal ME/g)
PROTEIN*		
Indispensable amino acids		
Arginine	1.37 g	0.50%
Histidine	0.49 g	0.18%
Isoleucine	0.98 g	0.36%
Leucine	1.59 g	0.58%
Lysine	1.40 g	0.51%
Methionine-cystine	1.06 g	0.39%
Phenylalanine-tyrosine	1.95 g	0.72%
Threonine	1.27 g	0.47%
Tryptophan	0.41 g	0.15%
Valine	1.05 g	0.39%
Dispensable amino acids	17.07 g	6.26%
FAT	13.6 g	5.0%
Linoleic acid	2.7 g	1.0%
MINERALS		
Calcium	1.6 g	0.59%
Phosphorus	1.2 g	0.44%
Potassium	1.2 g	0.44%
Sodium	0.15 g	0.06%
Chloride	0.23 g	0.09%
Magnesium	0.11 g	0.04%
Iron	8.7 mg	31.9 mg/kg
Copper	0.8 mg	2.9 mg/kg
Manganese	1.4 mg	5.1 mg/kg
Zinc[†]	9.7 mg	35.6 mg/kg
Iodine	0.16 mg	0.59 mg/kg
Selenium	0.03 mg	0.11 mg/kg

(Continued)

Reproduced with permission from 1994 AAFCO Official Publication.
[*]Quantities sufficient to supply the minimum amounts of available indispensable and dispensable amino acids as specified below. Compounding practical foods from natural ingredients (protein digestibility ± 70%) may require quantities representing an increase of 40% or greater than the sum of the amino acids listed below, depending upon ingredients used and processing procedures.
[†]In commercial foods with natural ingredients resulting in elevated calcium and phytate content, borderline deficiencies were reported from feeding foods with less than 90 mg zinc per kg (Sanecki et al, American Journal of Veterinary Research, 43:1642, 1982).
[‡]A fivefold increase may be required for foods of high PUFA content.
[§]Dogs have a metabolic requirement, but a dietary requirement was not demonstrated when foods from natural ingredients were fed.
[||]Overages must be considered to cover losses in processing and storage.

NUTRIENT	PER 1000 kcal ME	DRY BASIS (3.67 Kkcal ME/g)
VITAMINS		
Vitamin A	1,011 IU	3,710 IU/kg
Vitamin D	110 IU	404 IU/kg
Vitamin E[‡]	6.1 IU	22 IU/kg
Vitamin K[§]	——	——
Thiamin[‖]	0.27 mg	1.0 mg/kg
Riboflavin	0.68 mg	2.5 mg/kg
Pantothenic acid	2.7 mg	9.9 mg/kg
Niacin	3 mg	11.0 mg/kg
Pyridoxine	0.3 mg	1.1 mg/kg
Folic acid	0.054 mg	0.2 mg/kg
Biotin[§]	——	——
Vitamin B_{12}	7 µg	26 µg/kg
Choline	340 mg	1.25 g/kg

NRC Minimum Requirements for Growing Kittens
(units per kg of diet, dry basis)*

NUTRIENT	UNIT	AMOUNT
FAT†		
Linoleic acid	g	5
Arachidonic acid	mg	200
PROTEIN‡ (N × 6.25)	g	240
Arginine	g	10
Histidine	g	3
Isoleucine	g	5
Leucine	g	12
Lysine	g	8
Methionine plus cystine (total sulfur amino acids)	g	7.5
Methionine	g	4
Phenylalanine plus tyrosine	g	8.5
Phenylalanine	g	4
Taurine	mg	400
Threonine	g	7
Tryptophan	g	1.5
Valine	g	6

(Continued)

Reproduced with permission from 1994 AAFCO Official Publication.

*Based on a diet with an ME concentration of 5 kcal/g dry matter fed to 10- to 20-week-old kittens. If dietary energy is greater or lesser, it is assumed that these requirements should be increased or decreased proportionately. Nutrient requirement levels have been selected based on the most appropriate optional response (that is, growth, nitrogen retention, metabolite concentration or excretion, lack of abnormal clinical signs, etc.) of kittens fed a purified diet. Some of these requirements are known adequate amounts rather than minimum requirements. Since diet processing (such as extruding or retorting) may destroy or impair the availability of some nutrients, and since some nutrients, especially the trace minerals, are less available from some natural feedstuffs than from purified diets, increased amounts of these nutrients should be included to ensure that the minimum requirements are met. The minimum requirements presented in this table assume availabilities similar to those present in purified diets.

†No requirement for fat is known apart from the need for essential fatty acids and as a carrier of fat-soluble vitamins. Some fat normally enhances the palatability of the diet.

‡Assuming that all the minimum essential amino acid requirements are met.

§The minimum potassium requirement increases with protein intake.

‖This minimum should be adequate for a moderate to low-fat diet. It may be expected to increase three- to fourfold with a high PUFA diet, especially when fish oil is present.

¶These vitamins may not be required in the diet unless antimicrobial agents or antivitamin compounds are present in the diet.

#Choline is not essential in the diet but if this quantity of choline is not present, the methionine requirement would be increased to provide the same quantity of methyl groups.

**A dietary requirement for myo-inositol has not been demonstrated for the cat. However, almost all published studies in which purified diets have been used have included myo-inositol at 150 to 200 mg/kg diet and no studies have tested a myo-inositol-free diet.

NOTE: The minimum requirements of all the nutrients are not known for the adult cat at maintenance. It is known that these levels of nutrients are adequate and that protein and methionine can be reduced to 140 and 3 g/kg diet, respectively. It is likely that the minimum requirements of all the other nutrients are also lower for maintenance than for the growing kitten. The minimum requirements of all the nutrients are not known for reproduction for the adult male or female cat. It is known that with the following modifications the nutrient allowances as recommended in the 1978 NRC report are adequate for gestation and lactation (in units/kg purified diet, note these recommendations are based on 4 kcal/g dry diet): arachidonate, 200 mg; zinc, 40 mg; vitamin A, 5500 IU; and taurine 500. It is probably that the minimum requirements for growing kittens in this table would satisfy all requirements for reproduction if the following were modified as shown: vitamin A, 6000 IU/kg diet, and taurine, 500 mg/kg diet.

NUTRIENT	UNIT	AMOUNT
MINERALS		
Calcium	g	8
Phosphorus	g	6
Magnesium	mg	400
Potassium[§]	g	4
Sodium	mg	500
Chloride	g	1.9
Iron	mg	80
Copper	mg	5
Iodine	µg	350
Zinc	mg	50
Manganese	mg	5
Selenium	µg	100
VITAMINS		
Vitamin A (retinol)	mg	1 (3333 IU)
Vitamin D (cholecalciferol)	µg	12.5 (500 IU)
Vitamin E[‖] (α-tocopherol)	mg	30 (30 IU)
Vitamin K[¶] (phylloquinone)	µg	100
Thiamin	mg	5
Riboflavin	mg	4
Vitamin B_6 (pyridoxine)	mg	4
Niacin	mg	40
Pantothenic acid	mg	5
Folacin (folic acid[¶])	µg	800
Biotin[¶]	µg	70
Vitamin B_{12} (cyanocobalamin)	µg	20
Choline[#]		2.4
Myo-inositol[**]	g	——

General Guidelines for Feeding Ill Animals

One of the most common side effects of illness in companion animals is lack of appetite. Cats are especially likely to develop anorexia when they are ill. The introduction of a new, thereapeutic diet can also contribute to a pet's unwillingness to eat. This problem can be further exacerbated when the pet's energy needs increase in response to illness or injury. The body's energy requirement increases in response to the stress that is induced during illness and to the increased metabolic rate that accompanies a rise in body temperature if the animal develops a fever. If left untreated, a decrease in food intake may contribute further to illness. Therefore one of the chief concerns when working with sick pets is to ensure that they continue to consume adequate calories and adequate levels of their required nutrients. Several feeding management guidelines can be used to help achieve this goal.

In all cases, the diet that is provided should be well balanced and, if applicable, formulated to treat the specific disorder that is present. The diet should also be highly digestible. If the volume of food that is consumed has decreased, it is important that the diet is nutrient dense and that nutrients are highly available to ensure that needs can be met even when a relatively small quantity of food is consumed.

The palatability and acceptability of the diet can be enhanced in several ways. If a dry diet is being fed, adding water to increase its moisture content or adding a small amount of animal fat will often increase its attractiveness. In addition, feeding the food at approximately body temperature often increases acceptability, but feeding food at either very warm or very cold temperatures decreases acceptability.

Any change in diet should be made very slowly by mixing the new diet in with the old in 25% increments. This gradual addition will prevent digestive tract upsets and facilitates acceptance of the new food. The pet should be offered several small meals throughout the day. Any food that has not been eaten should be removed after 20 minutes, and fresh food should be frequently offered. The amount that the pet eats should

Practical Feeding Tips: Guidelines for Feeding Ill Animals

Feed a well-balanced and (if applicable) specifically formulated diet.
Feed a highly digestible product.
Add water or a small amount of animal fat to increase palatability of dry food.
Warm food to body temperature.
If switching diets, mix the old diet with the new in 25% increments.
Feed small, frequent meals.
Closely monitor food intake and strictly adhere to the therapeutic diet.

be recorded at each meal, which allows the owner or veterinarian to closely monitor the animal's nutritional status throughout illness. Lastly, strict adherence to the therapeutic diet, if one is being used, should be encouraged once the pet has acclimated to the new diet. Strict compliance is necessary for the successful treatment of most diseases that involve nutritional management (see the accompanying box).

Index